EXTRATERRITORIALITIES IN OCCUPIED WORLDS

Before you start to read this book, take this moment to think about making a donation to punctum books, an independent non-profit press,

@ http://punctumbooks.com/checkout/

If you're reading the e-book, you can click on the image below to go directly to our donations site. Any amount, no matter the size, is appreciated and will help us to keep our ship of fools afloat. Contributions from dedicated readers will also help us to keep our commons open and to cultivate new work that can't find a welcoming port elsewhere. Our adventure is not possible without your support.

Vive la open-access.

Fig. 1. Maayan Amir & Ruti Sela, *Exterritory Project*, preview 2010.

EXTRATERRITORIALITIES IN OCCUPIED WORLDS. Copyright © 2016 by the authors and editors. This work carries a Creative Commons BY-NC-SA 4.0 International license, which means that you are free to copy and redistribute the material in any medium or format, and you may also remix, transform and build upon the material, as long as you clearly attribute the work to the authors (but not in a way that suggests the authors or punctum books endorses you and your work), you do not use this work for commercial gain in any form whatsoever, and that for any remixing and transformation, you distribute your rebuild under the same license.
http://creativecommons.org/licenses/by-nc-sa/4.0/

First published in 2016 by punctum books, Earth, Milky Way.
www.punctumbooks.com

ISBN-13: 978-0692629437
ISBN-10: 0692629432

Library of Congress Cataloging Data is available from the Library of Congress

Cover design: Eileen A. Joy & Vincent W.J. van Gerven Oei
Typographic design: Vincent W.J. van Gerven Oei

EXTRA TERRITORIALITIES IN OCCUPIED WORLDS

Edited by
Maayan Amir &
Ruti Sela

punctum books MMXVI

Contents

Maayan Amir & Ruti Sela
Introduction   13

EXTRATERRITORIAL ETHICS

Emmanuel Levinas
The Rights of Man and the Rights of the Other   31

Robert Bernasconi
Extra-Territoriality: Outside the State, Outside the Subject   41

Zygmunt Bauman
The World Inhospitable to Levinas   59

Steven Galt Crowell
Authentic Thinking and Phenomenological Method   89

EXTRATERRITORIAL GEOGRAPHIES

Giorgio Agamben
Beyond Human Rights   109

Anselm Franke, Eyal Weizman & Ines Weizman
"Islands": The Geography of Extraterritoriality   117

Stuart Elden
Outside Territory … 123

Angus Cameron
Where Has All The (Xeno)money Gone? … 137

Victoria Bernal
Extraterritoriality, Diaspora, and the Space of Cyberspace … 157

EXTRATERRITORIAL CRIMES

Mireille Hildebrandt
Extraterritorial Jurisdiction to Enforce in Cyberspace?:
Bodin, Schmitt, Grotius in Cyberspace … 173

Julien Seroussi
The Rise of Legal Cosmopolitism:
Denationalization & Territorialization of Law … 203

Cedric Ryngaert
Extraterritorial State Action in the Global Interest:
The Promise of Unilateralism … 215

Ed Morgan
Franz Kafka: Extraterritorial Criminal Law … 243

EXTRATERRITORIAL POETICS

Martin Jay
The Extraterritorial Life of Siegfried Kracauer … 275

Matthew Hart & Tania Lown-Hecht
The Extraterritorial Poetics of W.G. Sebald … 335

Homi K. Bhabha
The World and The Home … 361

Gerhard Richter
Homeless Images:
Kracauer's Extraterritoriality, Derrida's Monolingualism of the Other 377

Caryl Emerson
The Outer World and Inner Speech:
Bakhtin, Vygotsky, and the Internalization of Language 423

EXTRATERRITORIAL OBJECTS

Theodor W. Adorno
Valéry Proust Museum 447

Graham Harman
Subspatial and Subtemporal 459

✖

About the Contributors 475

Acknowledgements

This anthology collects previously published seminal writings alongside new essays written especially for the present volume. The work on the publication began when we initiated a series of public symposia on extraterritoriality in various global locations in the framework of the ongoing artistic platform *Exterritory Project*. These events opened an indispensable discursive platform for us on the concept of extraterritoriality and instigated some of the contributions now included in the book. The first symposium, held in Paris in May 2012, was organized in collaboration with the Kadist Art Foundation and the Evans Foundation. The second symposium took place in Jaffa in May 2012. The third event was hosted by Beit HaGefen Culture Center in Haifa in December 2013, while the fourth was organized in collaboration with the Stedelijk Museum in Amsterdam, which also hosted the event in March 2015. We would like to express our deep gratitude to the writers whose inspiring essays are republished here as well as to those who generously agreed to engage in this effort. It is with the great help of the contributors, the hosting institutions, and the project's various supporters that this volume was made possible; we are grateful for their encouraging willingness to take part and aid. Our special thanks go to Sandra Terdjman, then-Director of the Kadist Art Foundation and currently Co-Founder and Director of Council, for her keen involvement in organizing the first and third symposia and for her valuable and enduring faith in the project. We are also thankful for the dedicated help of Émilie Villez, current Kadist Director and Curator Léna Monnier of the Kadist Art Foundation as well as to Anne Davidian, Head of the Paris Office of the Evens Foundation. In addition, we thank Curator Jelle Bouwhuis and Assistant Curator Joram Kraaijeveld at the Stedelijk Museum;

Director and Curator Yeala Hazut and artist and Curator Farid Abu Shakra at Beit-HaGefen; Goethe-Institut Tel-Aviv, in particular Dr. Georg Blochmann; and Institut français de Tel-Aviv, in particular Olivier Tournaud. We owe a special debt of gratitude and appreciation to Tal Yahas, Dr. Anat Ben-David, Maya Feldman, Carolina Ben Shemesh, Dganit Turjeman, Renrad Gluzman, Shony Rivnay, Shlomo Gross and Alon Agmon, and to all those who supported the project over the years. In particular, we are forever indebted to the generosity of Vivian Ostrovsky and the Ostrovsky Family Fund. Finally, we wish to give our thanks to Rachel Katz for her assistance in the project.

Introduction

*Maayan Amir
& Ruti Sela*

The concept of extraterritoriality designates certain relationships between space, law, and representation. This collection of essays explores contemporary manifestations of extraterritoriality and the ways in which the concept has been put to use in various disciplines. Some of the essays were written especially for this volume, while others are brought together here for the first time. The inquiry into extraterritoriality found in these essays is not confined to the established boundaries of political, conceptual, and representational territories or fields of knowledge; rather, it is an invitation to navigate the margins of the legal–juridical and the political, but also the edges of forms of representation and poetics.

Within its accepted legal and political contexts, the concept of extraterritoriality has traditionally been applied to people and to spaces. In the first case, extraterritorial arrangements could either exclude or exempt an individual or a group of people from the territorial jurisdiction in which they were physically located; in the second, such arrangements could exempt or exclude a space from the territorial jurisdiction by which it was surrounded. The special status accorded to people and spaces had political, economic, and juridical implications, ranging from immunity and various privileges to extreme disadvantages. In both cases a person or a space physically included within a certain territory was removed from the usual system of laws and subjected to another. In other words, the extraterritorial person or space was held at what could be described as a legal distance. (In this respect, the concept of extraterritoriality presupposes the existence of several competing or overlapping legal systems, whether officially recognized or not.) It is this notion of being held at a legal distance around which the concept of extraterritoriality may be understood as revolving.

This publication is a part of *Exterritory Project*, an ongoing art project that wishes to encourage both the theoretical and practical exploration of ideas concerning extraterritoriality in an interdisciplinary context. The project aims not only to draw on existing definitions of extraterritoriality but seeks to reload it with new meanings, searching for ways in which the notion of extraterritoriality could produce a critique of discriminating power structures and re-articulate new practical, conceptual and poetical possibilities.

The project was initiated in 2009 when we decided to screen a video compilation of works by Middle-Eastern artists onto the sails of boats sailing in the extraterritorial waters of the Mediterranean as a response to the enduring Israeli–Palestinian conflict. We wished to create a neutral space to exhibit art that would be unrestricted by any single set of national constraints. Extraterritorial waters seemed to us a space that could offer the suspension of the neighboring states' regimes.

The naval limits of sovereign territories were originally demarcated in order to establish trade relations between nations. In the Western legal tradition as articulated in the early seventeenth century, the high seas were perceived as a space of "experiential unruliness."[1] The extent of a state's territorial waters was originally defined by the range covered by a cannon shot fired from the state's land territory out to sea. In ensuing centuries, the range of territorial waters became increasingly determined by the technological limits of a nation's ability to wage war and exercise its control.[2] For these reasons, we wanted to launch the project in extraterritorial waters at the point at which the sovereignty of the state is no longer effective, if only symbolically.

We commenced the project wishing to bring together artists and thinkers from conflict areas where such meetings are normally forbidden. We decided to initiate a meeting in the extraterritorial waters of the Mediterranean, openly inviting people from diverse disciplines to offer their interpretation of the concept of extraterritoriality and to project their artworks onto the sails of the participating boats. By using this unoccupied space and exploring different ideas of extraterritoriality, we wished to emphasize the need to create unstable sites that could depart from familiar ways of experiencing political

---

1   Mireille Hildebrandt, "Extraterritorial Jurisdiction to Enforce in Cyberspace?: Bodin, Schmitt, Grotius in Cyberspace," *this volume*, 188.
2   Cornelius van Bynkershoek, *A Treatise on The Law of War* (Clark, NJ: The Law Book Exchange, 2008). The establishment of cannon shot as a rule may be traced to the writings of several French and Dutch jurists from as early as the eighteenth century: see W.L. Walker, "Territorial Waters: The Cannon Shot Rule," *British Year Book of International Law*, no. 22 (1945): 210.

concepts. We sought to produce an image that would transgress the usual territorial conventions of art exhibitions, where national politics and market interests intersect. Under such conditions, works of art are exploited to promote national agendas and profits, and are, as such, often seemingly de-politicized. By exhibiting works of art in an extraterritorial space, we sought to challenge and recontextualize these conventions. During 2010, the project expanded into an ongoing collaborative art initiative that strove to provide a platform for producing and sharing knowledge, critical thinking, and various forms of artistic and cultural production. In particular, our goal was to explore the relationships between various forms of what may be termed extraterritoriality.

The idea that informs our exploration is that rather than being a single static form, extraterritoriality always involves a practice with its own logic of representation. Understanding extraterritoriality in such terms helps to explain its applicability in multiple and diverse types of discourse ranging from legal theory—where the concept designates both a legal status and a geographical jurisdiction—to sociology, political philosophy, literature, economy, architecture, and many others fields. Viewing extraterritoriality in this manner also helps explain why the concept has been applied to widely different, even conflicting phenomena. For these reasons, rather than trying to redefine what extraterritoriality is, we propose to adopt it as a vital prism from which to reflect on and decipher certain aspects and possibilities of contemporary political life.

This book is an attempt to bring together for the first time seminal theoretical writings pertaining to the notion of extraterritoriality. In doing so, we hope to promote the production of new knowledge by exploring these and related notions. This endeavor is part of the *Exterritory Project*'s effort to identify and rethink the unique features of extraterritoriality as a logic of representation and to contribute to its broader understanding.

Based as it is in the arts, this project builds on a view that extraterritoriality—the quality of being held at a legal distance—may characterize not only *people* and *spaces*, but any entity or thing that follows the same *logic of representation*, where "entities," or "things," may be physical objects, but also intangible entities such as visual images. Extraterritoriality regulates the function and circulation of people and things within space and across borders, sometimes by exclusion, sometimes by exemption. Under conditions of extraterritoriality, people and things are placed in a space that is beyond the reach of particular legal or political systems that would otherwise apply to them. This book presents several attempts to expand this understanding of extraterritoriality to a wider range of objects and spheres of activity.

As with all legal and political concepts, the concept of extraterritoriality has acquired different meanings in different historical contexts based on the myriad ways in which it has been put to use. Etymologically, the term "extraterritoriality" is derivative of the Latin *extra territorium*—"outside the territory." An examination of the different definitions of extraterritoriality, both historical and contemporary, not only reveals a complex dynamics between the term's various early meanings ("being outside of one's territory," "having no territory," etc.), but also shows how new extraterritorial phenomena helped redefine these terms over time, imbuing them with new meanings.

Since the establishment of the state system from the sixteenth century onward, the notion of extraterritoriality has emerged in various fields of knowledge, where it has been applied in different ways. Extraterritoriality is often dialectically defined in relation to and as a result of *territoriality*. That is, extraterritoriality is understood as a corollary of the post-Westphalian division of the globe into distinct sovereign territories. However, the relationship between the concept of extraterritoriality and that of sovereign territoriality is much more complex. A more careful look at the history of extraterritoriality shows that its origins were not simply derivative of territorial definitions; on the contrary, the notion of extraterritoriality and its applications have often been the product of attempts to evade territorially based laws (including those regulating the circulation of images). To understand the notion of extraterritoriality as it is currently deployed, we must therefore conceptualize it within a larger context. As the essays in this volume suggest, such a context must also include literature and the arts.

✖

This anthology is divided into five parts. In doing so, we do not mean to erect closed borders within the book or limit the reader's movement. Rather, we suggest this arrangement and the order of the essays within each section as a possible sequence, a recommended path for the reader to take. Moreover, to signify the fluidity and permeability of the book's division into sections, the essay that concludes each section of the book presages some of the themes of the following one. The present selection of essays also suggests various links to writings from similar intellectual genealogies. Focusing on perceptions of extraterritoriality presented in them, however, unravels the different readings of these genealogies and sometimes even reveals essential distinctions in their applications.

The book's first part, "Extraterritorial Ethics," comprises four interrelated essays, each offering a different interpretation of extraterritoriality. In the essay, "The Rights of Man and the Rights of the Other," philosopher Emmanuel Levinas develops a reinterpretation of the concept of the "rights of man." Departing from the term's original eighteenth-century meaning and surveying its subsequent development in Western thought, Levinas points to the risks and limitations of defending such rights within existing social, political, conceptual, and ideological frameworks. Stressing the need to defend these rights beyond rational calculation and the law in general, Levinas resorts to extraterritoriality as a vital space from which forms of dictatorship and totalitarianism, but also the inequalities found in the liberal state, can be fought. According to Levinas, any effort to protect human rights must rely on the understanding that these rights are located outside the state; "defense of the rights of man," he writes, "corresponds to a vocation *outside* the state [...] a kind of extraterritoriality, like that of prophecy in the face of the political power of the Old Testament."[3] Furthermore, extraterritoriality is an essential site from which "the I frees itself from its 'return to self,' from its auto-affirmation, from its egotism of a being persevering in its being, *to answer for the other*, precisely to defend the rights of the other man."[4] In this sense, according to Levinas, the rights of man and the rights of the other are inseparable.

In "Extraterritoriality: Outside the State, Outside the Subject" philosopher Robert Bernasconi explores Levinas's conception of extraterritoriality in the larger context of his oeuvre. According to Bernasconi, Levinas's aim was to account for the ethical threats to the "rights of man" posed by totalitarianism but also by liberalism. To this end, he addressed certain dilemmas and antinomies in political philosophy such as the tensions between solidarity and the liberal articulation of individual freedom, between individualism or communitarianism, between multiple types of freedoms, between the public and the private spheres as conceived in liberal and other ideologies, and so forth. Drawing on multiple sources, from Biblical prophetic and eschatological traditions to Moses Mendelssohn and Karl Marx, Levinas eventually

---

3 Emmanuel Levinas, "The Rights of Man and the Rights of the Other," *this volume*, 37.
4 Ibid.

turned to extraterritoriality as a dimension essential to the protection of the oppressed and for human freedom. According to Bernasconi, Levinas postulates a conception of moral freedom that transcends phenomenology as an ethics of asymmetry, at the center of which is one's self-imposed commitment to defend the Other. In this manner, the "rights of man" are located both outside of the state and outside the subject, neither in the realm of politics nor in that of ethics, but in the extraterritorial conjunction between the two.

In the next essay "The World Inhospitable to Levinas," sociologist Zygmunt Bauman criticizes Levinas's conception of morality in terms of a face-to-face encounter with the Other, arguing that Levinas's Other is no more than a mirror image of one's responsibility. Unlike Bernasconi, then, Bauman locates Levinasian ethics within phenomenology. In place of the Levinasian approach, he emphasizes the importance of morals established on reason. Instead of basing ethics solely on acquaintance with the "other as a face," he contends, we must also base it to some inevitable extent on the various social "masks" worn by "faceless" others.[5] In addition, Bauman warns against the hazards of categorical stereotyping when adopting a model of the Other, highlighting the dialectical constraints of any ethics based on the "moral party of two."[6] He argues that in contemporary times, when economy has gained independence from the state, it is not ethics but rather "the real powers which decide the shape of things [which] have acquired a genuine exterritoriality."[7] The extraterritorial nature of power serves an extraterritorial elite whose "liquid" resources are extraterritorial as well. This state of affairs exempts the elite from the obligation or the need to "engage with [the] consequences" affecting those who remain confined to locality and territoriality.[8] This process, Bauman argues, has made it more difficult to maintain a distinction "between the internal and global market, or more generally between the 'inside' and the 'outside' of the state [...] in any but the most narrow, 'territory and population' policing sense."[9]

In "Authentic Thinking and Phenomenological Method," philosopher Steven Galt Crowell discusses the notion of authentic thinking as introduced by the founder of phenomenology, Edmund Husserl, in his *Logical Investigations*. In particular, Crowell examines the claim that Husserl's concept of au-

---

5   Zygmunt Bauman, "The World Inhospitable to Levinas," *this volume*, 63.
6   Ibid.
7   Ibid., 74.
8   Ibid., 75.
9   Ibid., 77.

thentic thinking enabled the move to a philosophy of speculation, that is, to speculative and constructive phenomenological approaches which argue for a givenness beyond human intuition. Revisiting Husserl's claim that thinking itself is a form of intuition, Crowell suggests that the crucial distinction for Husserl is not between thought and intuition, but rather between intuition and signification. While for Husserl "every expression has signification, whether or not it has an intuitive fulfillment," some categorical formation of intuition might nevertheless remain merely "empty" or "symbolic."[10] Intuition, Crowell stresses, "continues to play its cognitively critical or normative role with respect to signification, but it does so precisely *as thinking*, thus not as something foreign to the space of reasons."[11] In later readings of Husserl, this understanding of perception presents a break in Husserl's phenomenology, allowing symbols to "have a life of their own."[12] According to Jean-Luc Marion, for example, this makes signification "a kind of givenness without intuition";[13] signification comes before intuition, of which it is the Other. Against this reading, Crowell claims that according to Husserl, "to say that signification can be 'valid' without a confirming intuition—that is, can be *empty*—is not yet to say that it is 'extraterritorial' with respect to intuition,"[14] for according to Husserl, signification is itself given intuitively. Crowell's essay thus presents yet another entry point into rethinking Levinasian extraterritorial ethics. By following the above logic of "authentic thinking," Crowell reaches a somewhat similar conclusion to Bauman's, claiming that Levinas's view of the Other as transcending intuition can be traced back to our experience.

Part two of the book consists of five essays exploring "Extraterritorial Geographies." The first essay, Giorgio Agamben's "Beyond Human Rights," proceeds from similar ethical concerns invoked by Levinas. But whereas Levinas uses extraterritoriality as a spatial metaphor in order to resolve the abstract philosophical problem of the Other, Agamben turns to extraterritoriality in order to grapple with the very concrete spatial problem of stateless refugees; even more concretely, he proposes that adopting notions of extraterritoriality may help resolve the Israeli–Palestinian conflict over Jerusalem. According to Agamben, the figure of the refugee marks the need to abandon cur-

10 Steven Galt Crowell, "Authentic Thinking and Phenomenological Method," *this volume*, 97.
11 Ibid., 93.
12 Ibid., 94.
13 Ibid., 97.
14 Ibid.

rent political concepts. The existing state of affairs, he claims, is a product of the nation-state system, which is based on the triad state–nation–territory. To solve the refugee problem, we must first re-examine and re-articulate the very concepts by which political subjects are represented. In his view, extraterritoriality (or "better yet, aterritoriality") could serve as a generalized "model of new international relations."[15] Accordingly, Jerusalem could be governed by a mutual condition of extraterritoriality, creating a multifaceted collective political space: "Instead of two national states separated by uncertain and threatening boundaries, it might be possible to imagine two political communities insisting on the same region and in a condition of exodus from each other—communities that would articulate each other via a series of reciprocal extraterritorialities in which the guiding concept would no longer be the *ius* (right) of the citizen but rather the *refugium* (refuge) of the singular."[16]

In "Islands: The Geography of Extraterritoriality," Anselm Franke, together with Eyal and Ines Weizman, maps diverse extraterritorial phenomena that often inhabit concrete spaces of legal and political voids. These in turn shape landscapes of islands of exclusions, topographies of free-floating legal lacunae, enclaves of "abused geographies," but also forms of utopia and the contours of attempts to create a better place.[17] Focusing on such "extraterritorial islands" as churches, tax-free ports, and city-states offering refuge from prosecution, they trace their architecture to pre-Westphalian Europe, before the advent of territorial sovereignty. Extraterritoriality, they write, "is rooted in the concept of sovereignty, although it is usually considered as its violation."[18] Surveying the ways in which extraterritorial islands served for colonial territorial expansion, they contend that "figures of extraterritoriality returned to haunt current political order"[19] and can be identified in contemporary extraterritorial military camps, in special enterprise zones, but also in zones of humanitarian intervention and refugee camps, to give just a few examples. Often operated by deterritorialized powers as a way to enhance the flow of people beyond the borders of the state, such extraterritorial islands mark the limits of the current spatio-political regime.

---

15 Giorgio Agamben, "Beyond Human Rights," *this volume*, 115.
16 Ibid.
17 See, e.g., Anselm Franke, Eyal Weizman, and Ines Weizman, "'Islands': The Geography of Extraterritoriality," *this volume*, 121.
18 Ibid.
19 Ibid., 119.

The question of what exists beyond the limits of political spaces is the point of departure for geographer Stuart Elden's "Outside Territory." Territory, Elden writes, is often defined in terms of what it encompasses, as a "bounded space" or "a bordered power container."[20] The concept requires a more complex definition, however, to account for the varied practices that shape its meanings across time and space, but also to capture its relationship with other geographical concepts and spatio-political orderings. Noting that in Latin *territorium* originally referred to the area surrounding a place and marking its outside, Elden proposes that we look at conceptions of "outside territory" in the Western literary canon, especially in the plays of William Shakespeare, written in the seventeenth century around the time modern sovereign territories were conceived. We can think of the Homeric story of Odysseus's adventures on his journey home, the "outside" as the domain of King Lear's madness, or as a lawless zone of rape and murder in *Titus Andronicus*; the idea of exile as punishment; the tension between common and private landownership—all these instances of being outside a political space echo the imaginary ways in which extraterritoriality has been represented.

Angus Cameron's "Where Has All the (Xeno)money Gone?" is an attempt to understand two recent financial crises in which trillions of dollars evaporated: the 2008 subprime mortgage crisis and the so-called Flash Crash of 2010. The answer Cameron proposes to his titular question is that we must rearticulate the question itself by historically and conceptually exploring the spatiality of money and its intrinsically extraterritorial nature. Money, he claims, is a legal rather than a material entity—the product of a vast system of laws. But whereas many view money as created purely on a national level by state apparatuses, it is in fact the product not only of national but also of international laws. By combining historical and sociological perspectives with insights drawn from literature and the arts, Cameron discusses the ways money has been used as an extraterritorial tool, both to consolidate territories and to circumvent the state's legal space. According to Cameron, we must reject misleading perceptions of money as territorially "fixed," as "connected unambiguously to a territory or territories."[21] Instead, he claims, we must understand money as transcending the territorial borders of sovereign states.

---

20 Stuart Elden, "Outside Territory," *this volume*, 123.
21 Ibid., 139.

Cameron's critique of the territorial view of money finds certain parallels in anthropologist Victoria Bernal's discussion of cyberspace in her essay "Extraterritoriality, Diaspora, and the Space of Cyberspace." Just as Cameron argues that money is not to be construed as primarily territorial, Bernal claims that cyberspace should not be cast in purely territorial terms. However, should it be conceived in purely extraterritorial terms, either: neither territoriality nor extraterritoriality, she contends, enable us to understand the full complexity of cyberspace. In her essay, Bernal examines the extraterritorial online participation in national politics by Eritrean diaspora against the oppressive Isaias Afewerki regime. Through an analysis of the complex spatiality of cyberspace, she explores how the diverse ways in which cyberspace is utilized reshapes the borders of citizenship and extraterritorial belonging. Resistance and criticism, Bernal claims, can be practiced from varied territorial locations through an extraterritorial network of diasporic communities. In this respect, cyberspace transcends the territorial–extraterritorial dichotomy, serving instead as a kind of "extra territory," a "national space that is outside the nation and free of government control."[22]

The spatiality of the Internet is elaborated from another point of view in the opening essay of the next section, "Extraterritorial Crimes," whose four essays present a juridical and conceptual discussion of the borders of law enforcement. In "Extraterritorial Jurisdiction to Enforce in Cyberspace?: Bodin, Schmitt, Grotius in Cyberspace," Mireille Hildebrandt confronts the legal challenges posed by cross-border cybercrimes vis-à-vis the borders of state jurisdictions and the current limits of territorial criminal law. In an "age of interconnected digital infrastructures," she claims, certain questions emerge regarding extraterritorial jurisdiction.[23] In this context, Hildebrandt explores the meanings of jurisdiction and territory in modern Western legal-philosophical thought. Pointing to the possibility of unbounded territorial jurisdiction, she explores the potentialities opened up by conceiving cyberspace in comparison with extraterritorial maritime space. In particular, she probes the affinities between cyberspace and maritime law, especially in relation to the law of war and global free trade. Among other questions, Hildebrandt examines whether the territorial understanding of cyberspace is productive or even possible given the inability of cartographic technology to encompass

---

22 Victoria Bernal, "Extraterritory, Diaspora, and the Space of Cyberspace," *this volume*, 161.
23 Hildebrandt, "Extraterritorial Jurisdiction to Enforce in Cyberspace?," 177.

the unique spatiality of extraterritoriality. Stressing the need to redefine the relations between spatiality and jurisdiction, Hildebrandt concludes that cyberspace must remain a *res communis* which "may not come under exclusive sovereign control"—a space accessible to the public, yet conducive to the enforcement of human rights.[24]

In "The Rise of Legal Cosmopolitism: Denationalization and Territorialization of Law," Julien Seroussi, member of the French International Crime Unit and former analyst at the International Criminal Court (ICC) at The Hague, underscores the challenges of prescribing and enforcing international criminal justice by exploring the tension between the universalization of criminal jurisdiction and the primacy of national sovereignty. Through this lens Seroussi reviews the historical development of international criminal law, locating its origins in both national criminal law and public international law. Particular attention is given to the ways in which the cataclysmic events of the twentieth century—the two World Wars and the Cold War—shaped the expanding application of international law, from transnational criminality to human rights violations.

More than just a historical survey, Seroussi's essay examines actual cases of conflict between territorial and extraterritorial jurisdiction handled by the International Criminal Court. The conflict between ICC rulings and diplomatic immunity is represented by the failure to arrest former Chilean dictator Augusto Pinochet and Sudanese president Omar El-Beshir despite issued warrants, while the limits of the ICC as an international investigative institution are discussed in reference to the trial of former Congolese militia leader Germain Katanga. Though Seroussi stresses the importance of denationalizing criminal law, he also argues that encouraging individual states to enforce international law on a local territorial basis is in many cases crucial to investigative reliability.

The failure of international institutions to "adequately tackle collective action problems"[25] motivates the following essay, "Extraterritorial State Action in the Global Interest: The Promise of Unilateralism," by international law scholar Cedric Ryngaert. Since international institutions often prove unable to cope with global challenges, the latter, Ryngaert suggests, may best be met by expanding state law extraterritorially, that is, by allowing states to

---

24 Ibid., 201.
25 Cedric Ryngaert, "Extraterritorial State Action in the Global Interest: The Promise of Unilateralism," *this volume*, 215.

apply and enforce certain laws beyond their own borders. Though Ryngaert acknowledges the risks involved in states abusing extraterritorial power to promote their interests and imperialist ambitions, he challenges the passive role of states as bystanders in favor of cosmopolitan responsibility. The essay critically probes the principle of sovereignty in modern international law and the decline of its discursive force in favor of a rhetoric of humanity. To establish his claims, Ryngaert revisits the concept of hegemony and examines the relationship between conceptions of territoriality and policies of non-intervention.

The last essay in this section, Ed Morgan's "Franz Kafka: Extraterritorial Criminal Law," discusses the hazards posed by various states' efforts to invoke extraterritorial jurisdiction in order to expand their power, with particular focus on the complex legal rhetoric involved in such efforts. Reflecting on the relationship between constitutionalism and internationalism, Morgan looks at criminal cases that involve Supreme Court decisions concerning the boundaries of a state's extraterritorial power. His focus is on Canada, which like other former British colonies was permitted to expand its sovereignty extraterritorially only when its constitution was severed from that of the United Kingdom in 1982. Morgan's analysis is combined with a legal examination of Franz Kafka's short story "In the Penal Colony." Comparing Kafka's surprising reversals of "law and crime, reason and violence" with the way Canada's Supreme Court justices deployed international arguments to promote constitutional goals, he concludes that "internationalism has become, in the Supreme Court's hand, a medium of inflicting punishment, while constitutionalism has become a medium of enduring it."[26]

The five essays of the book's next section, "Extraterritorial Poetics," explore the possibility of extraterritoriality as both an aesthetic and an ideological medium. In Martin Jay's seminal essay "The Extraterritorial Life of Siegfried Kracauer," the pioneering works of the Frankfurt School film theorist are reviewed within the broad context of his personal and intellectual biography. Having fled Germany with the rise of the Nazi Party, Kracauer spent the rest of his life in exile, writing in a non-native language. Focusing on Kracauer's anti-psychological and anti-subjectivist analyses of Weimar cinema, Jay portrays him as leading an extraterritorial existence, not only geographically but also intellectually. Through the spatial metaphor of extraterritorial-

---

26 Ed Morgan, "Franz Kafka: Extraterritorial Criminal Law," *this volume*, 272.

ity, Jay also probes the temporal obscurities of Kracauer's life and thought: adamant not to disclose his age, Kracauer viewed "chronology [...] itself [as] an arbitrary code imposed by men."[27] In his view, thinkers must occupy an extraterritorial position in order to achieve self-transcendence—to bracket the self in order to achieve "openness to the material." Extraterritoriality, for Jay, is thus a prism through which to understand Kracauer's conception of time as the simultaneous co-existence of diverse temporalities.

In their exploration of literary works by W.G. Sebald, Matthew Hart, and Tania Lown-Hecht build on some of Jay's ideas to establish a unique perception of extraterritoriality as a form of poetics. Contesting the reductive application of the term as interchangeable with a "state of multilingual plenitude and postnational migrancy,"[28] the two identify extraterritoriality both as a recurring theme in Sebald's works and as a distinct mode of narration characterized by certain formal patterns. In the authors' view, it is Sebald's extraterritorial prism that makes possible his abrupt shifts in perspective—from long shots to extreme close-ups, from vivid memories to an evasive present and from individual experiences to collective engagement. Sebald's literary tactics are also informed, they claim, by the extraterritorial practice of exception—the creation of spaces in which law is suspended—making his extraterritorial poetics an effort to understand the paradoxes of state violence.

In the next essay, "The World and the Home," Homi K. Bhabha proposes the notion of the unhomely to capture the post-colonial experience and rearticulate the distinction between the public and the private spheres. In his view of the relationship of the world and the home, "the intimate recesses of the domestic space become sites for history's most intricate invasion."[29] "The unhomely," he states, "is the shock of recognition of the world-in-the-home, the home-in-the-world."[30] This insight also applies in his view to the evasive borders between the historical and the fictional. Reflecting on expressions of the "unhomely" in works by Henry James, Toni Morrison, Rabindranath Tagore, Nadine Gordimer, and others, Bhabha argues that the aesthetic process "introduces into our reading of social reality not another reified form of mediation—the art object—but another temporality in which to signify the 'event' of history."[31] According to him, the "unhomely" is "inherent in [the]

---

27 Martin Jay, "The Extraterritorial Life of Siegfried Kracauer," *this volume*, 325.
28 Matthew Hart & Tania Lown-Hecht, "The Extraterritorial Poetics of W.G. Sebald," *this volume*, 335.
29 Homi K. Bhabha, "The World and The Home," *this volume*, 361.
30 Ibid., 362.
31 Ibid., 361.

rite of 'extraterritorial' initiation" and connected to inhabiting the world, while at the same time representing its outside.[32]

The connection between homelessness, extraterritoriality, and forms of representation is also among the themes of "Homeless Images: Kracauer's Extraterritoriality, Derrida's Monolingualism of the Other" by Gerhard Richter. For Richter, philosophical thought and images are "means of dwelling within homelessness."[33] The image, he claims, turns "historical when it tells us of its own departure from history, capturing time most fully when it removes itself from time."[34] Precisely for this reason, however, images are incapable of fully representing the events they purportedly depict. In the book from which the essay is taken, *Thought-Images: Frankfurt School Writers' Reflections from Damaged Life*, Richter interprets the work of such theorists as Theodor W. Adorno, Walter Benjamin, Ernst Bloch, and Siegfried Kracauer in order to explore the literary genre of the *Denkbild*, defined as an "image of reflection [...] inseparable from the aesthetic dimension of conceptual thought" and existing in a form of "perpetual displacement."[35] In the essay included here, he compares Kracauer's concept of the "homeless image," especially in relation to extraterritoriality, with Derrida's notion of exteriority in relation to language and the Other. These themes are discussed in the context of linguistic exiles and the ties between language and cultural identity. Instead of aspiring to the essentialist "promised land of cultural identity," Richter concludes, we must seek "the realm of extraterritoriality [...] where selves can be recognized as the ones gathered and dispersed in language."[36] By doing so, he adds, we will also avoid the alienation inscribed in monolingualism.

The relationship between extraterritoriality and language or speech is further elaborated in Caryl Emerson's "Outer Word and Inner Speech: Bakhtin, Vygotsky, and the Internalization of Language." Emerson looks at the attempts of Russian philosopher and literary critic Mikhail Bakhtin and other members of the so-called Bakhtin Circle to synthesize two competing theories: Saussurean linguistic and semiotic theory on the one hand, Marxist theory of ideology on the other. For Marxists, the Saussurean approach was

---

32   Ibid.
33   Gerhard Richter, "Homeless Images: Kracauer's Extraterritoriality, Derrida's Monolingualism of the Other," *this volume*, 378.
34   Ibid., 377.
35   Gerhard Richter, *Thought-Images: Frankfurt School Writers Reflections from Damaged Life* (Stanford: Stanford University Press, 2007), 1, 18, 36.
36   Gerhard Richter, "Homeless Images," 421.

suspect for its opposition between the social and the individual. Saussurean linguistic investigation was completely absorbed in an "inner logic of the system of signs itself," excluding "the ideological meanings that give the signs their content."[37] To reconcile the two theories, the members of the Bakhtin Circle rearticulated the interplay between language and consciousness. Rather than viewing the sign and its effect as mental constructs, they relocated them in outer experience. This called for a reorientation of linguistic study, replacing individual psychology with the social phenomena of interrelation and interaction. In Bakhtin's view, Emerson argues, the psyche is constituted by a spatial model comprising the individual's communication with others, as well as by a parallel "inner speech" or internal relationship between the psyche and the outer world. According to Emerson, the crucial role ascribed by the Bakhtinian model to extraterritoriality is at the heart of the process that constitutes the psyche. For Bakhtin, the psyche, rather than an internal phenomenon, is a "boundary phenomenon," "a space to be filled with ideological signs."[38] Extraterritoriality is a special status that the psyche enjoys which enables it to move between an external horizontal relationship with other individuals and an internal vertical relationship with the outer world. "The psyche," Bakhtin thus argues, "enjoys extraterritorial status [...] [as] a social entity that penetrates inside the organism of the individual person," from social intercourse to outer speech, and from outer speech to inner speech.[39]

An understanding of extraterritoriality as the ability to move between spheres of representation, especially in relation to artworks, informs the opening essay of the book's final section, "Extraterritorial Objects." In "Valéry Proust Museum," Theodor W. Adorno begins his discussion with the nexus between the museum and the mausoleum: both, he writes, are home to "objects to which the observer no longer has a vital relationship and which are in the process of dying."[40] By juxtaposing poet Paul Valéry and novelist Marcel Proust's contrasting approaches to the museum, Adorno illustrates their different attitudes to art's role and articulates his own. Valéry describes the museum as the place in which "Dead visions are entombed."[41] For him, Adorno writes, "art is lost when it has relinquished its place in the imme-

---

37 Caryl Emerson, "The Outer World and Inner Speech: Bakhtin, Vygotsky, and the Internalization of Language," *this volume*, 425.
38 Ibid., 428.
39 Ibid.
40 Theodor W. Adorno, "Valéry Proust Museum," *this volume*, 447.
41 Ibid., 449.

diacy of life."⁴² His "ultimate question" is "that of the possible use of the work of art."⁴³ For Proust, by contrast, "it is only the death of the work of art in the museum which brings it to life."⁴⁴ The work's afterlife, or second life, is therefore located in the spectator of consciousness. For Adorno, Proust's attitude is somewhat extraterritorial. Criticizing Proust for overestimating "the act of freedom in art," Adorno himself locates the artwork in the "force field" between the subject and the object.⁴⁵ The notion of extraterritoriality is again implicit in his approach when he concludes that "[t]he natural-history collections of the spirit have actually transformed works of art into hieroglyphics of history and brought them a new content while the old one shriveled up."⁴⁶ In the book's final essay, "Subspatial and Subtemporal," philosopher Graham Harman interprets the concept of extraterritoriality from the perspective of an object-oriented philosophy that conceptualizes the relationship between time, space and objects. Harman develops a fourfold model of objects based on the distinction between sensual and real objects and qualities (whereby real objects can have sensual qualities, and so forth). Spatial and temporal qualities are in his view sensual qualities; they are "the accidental chaff that shift atop the surface of any object, whirling like a kaleidoscope without changing the underlying object."⁴⁷ At the same time, space and time (like other sensual qualities) are the vehicles through which real objects can "announce their presence" to us; they are therefore "the sole emissaries of change in the world."⁴⁸ Real objects, in themselves, "are not localizable in any given place because they punch holes in every place they touch."⁴⁹ To have a sense of space, we must therefore find ways to mark the absence of real objects within it. According to this model, the extraterritorial qualities of space and time are crucial to understanding the reality of objects; extraterritoriality is therefore, according to Harman, none other than the principle of reality.

42   Ibid., 452.
43   Ibid.
44   Ibid., 454.
45   Ibid., 456.
46   Ibid., 457.
47   Graham Harman, "Subspatial and Subtemporal," *this volume*, 462.
48   Ibid., 465, 468.
49   Ibid., 473.

EXTRATERRITORIAL ETHICS

1. THE
ORIGINAL RIGHT

The Rights of Man and the Rights of the Other

Emmanuel Levinas

The rights claimed under the title rights of man, in the rigorous and almost technical sense which that expression has taken on since the eighteenth century—the right to respect for the human dignity of the individual, the rights to life, liberty, and equality before the law for all men—are based on an original sense of the right, or the sense of an original right. And this is the case, independently of the chronology of the causes, the psychological and social processes and the contingent variations of the rise of these rights to the light of thought. For today's way of thinking, these rights are more legitimate than any legislation, more than just any justification. They are probably, however complex their application to legal phenomena may be, the measure of all law and, no doubt, of its ethics. The rights of man are, in any case, one of the law's latent principles, whose voice—sometimes loud, sometimes muffled by reality's necessities, sometimes interrupting and shattering them—can be heard throughout history, ever since the first stirrings of consciousness, ever since Mankind.

These rights are, in a sense, a priori: independent of any power that would be the original share of each human being in the blind distribution of nature's energy and society's influence, but also independent of the merits the human individual may have acquired by his or her efforts and even virtues. Prior to all entitlement: to all tradition, all jurisprudence, all granting of privileges, awards or titles, all consecration by a will abusively claiming the name of reason. Or is it perhaps the case that its a priori may signify an ineluctable authority, older and higher than the one already split into will and reason and that imposes itself by an alternance of violence and truth; the

---

Originally published as Emmanuel Levinas, "The Rights of Man and the Rights of the Other," trans. Michael B. Smith, in *From Outside the Subject* (London: Athlone Press, 1993), 116–25. Reprinted with permission of Bloomsbury Publishing Plc.

authority that is, perhaps—but before all theology—*in* the respect for the rights of man itself, God's original coming to the mind of man.

These rights of man, that do not need to be conferred, are thus irrevocable and inalienable. Rights that, independently of any *conferral*, express the alterity or absolute of every person, the suspension of all *reference*: a violent tearing loose from the determining order of nature and the social structure in which each of us is obviously involved; an alterity of the *unique* and the incomparable, due to belonging of each one to mankind, which, *ipso facto and paradoxically*, is annulled, precisely to leave each man *the only one* of his kind. A tearing loose and a suspension—or freedom—which is no mere abstraction. It marks the absolute identity of the person, that is, of the non-interchangeable, incomparable and unique. A uniqueness beyond the individuality of multiple individuals within their kind. A uniqueness not because of any distinctive sign that would serve as a specific or individuating difference. A unity prior to any distinctive sign, a uniqueness logically indiscernible from the first person. A uniqueness that is not forgotten, beneath all constraints of Being, History, and the logical forms that hold it in their grip. It remains concrete, precisely in the form of the various rights of man, claimed unconditionally, under the various necessities of the real, as various modes of freedom. Later, I shall discuss the phenomenology of these claims, the structure of the consciousness in which they take shape concretely.

The rights of man manifest the uniqueness or the absolute of the person, despite his or her subsumption under the category of the human species, or because of that subsumption. This is the paradox, or mystery, or novelty of the human in being, which I have just stressed. It seems to me to be suggested by a *remarkable talmudic apologue, which I quote*:

> Grandeur of the Holy-Blessed-Be-He: Behold man, who strikes coins with the same die and gets coins all alike: but behold the King of kings, the Holy-Blessed-Be-He, who strikes all men with the die of Adam and not one is the same as another. That is why each is obliged to say: The world was created for me![1]

The fact that the identity of species can include the absolutely dissimilar, a multiplicity of non-additive, unique beings—that the unity of Adam marks

---

1   *Babylonian Talmud, Tractate Sanhedrin*, 37a.

the individuals of incomparable uniqueness in which the common species disappears and in which the individuals cease being interchangeable like coins—that they affirm themselves to be, each one, the sole purpose of the world (or the sole one responsible for the real): surely this is the trace of God in man, or, more precisely, the point in reality at which the idea of God comes only to man. This is a possible meaning of that apologue, which is not the equivalent of some deduction of the rights of man on the basis of a prior Revelation, but means, on the contrary, the coming of the idea of God on the basis of the patency of the rights of man.

That the rights of man or respect for those rights *does not proceed* from the sternness or the grace of God, as the latter are expressed in theologies appealing to Revelation, that is, to "truths about God" already acquired elsewhere (an appeal that would still bear witness to the extra-ordinary aspect of those rights, recognized as super-natural, but also already to the jurisprudence and mediation of the religious authorities)—*that* has been, since the Renaissance, the trait that has characterized the consciousness of the rights of man.

2. THE BROAD NOTION OF THE RIGHTS OF MAN

The possibility of ensuring the actual enjoyment of these rights—of making the facts respond to the unconditional claim to human freedom and all the rights therein implied, despite the weight of physical and political necessity, and even despite the violence in which the person may experience the pure undergoing of the things of the world—this possibility is not immediately given. The conditions for the respect of these rights are only apparent once man has already assumed his first right, in becoming aware of the natural and social determinism that hampers the person, and once, consequently, he catches sight of the practical procedures, issuing from that *knowledge*, capable of freeing the person from these pressures and of subordinating them to the exercise of his rights.

The taking up of one's freedom from within knowledge is not an inevitable fact for the humanity of all eras and all lands. A taking up of freedom which is itself free! That is a revolutionary act in the most radical sense of the term. It is the mark of an era and a civilization, an event of the Western world! Science and the possibilities of technology are the first conditions for the factual implementation of the respect of rights of man. *Technical development thanks to the flourishing of theoretical knowledge* [savoir] *through which Eu-*

ropean humanity passed on its way toward its modernity is probably, in itself, the essential modality in which the idea of the rights of man, placed at the center of self-awareness, broadened in its conception and was inscribed or required as the basis of all human legislation; which legislation at least thought of itself as being the rights of man in their indispensable or hoped-for entirety. A rational discipline, born in Europe, could broaden out and be available to all humanity. Into a world that until then was felt to be doomed to an arbitrary play of forces that (natural or supposedly supernatural, individual and social) only counted in proportion to their power, in the obstinacy that Beings and institutions invest in persevering in their being and their traditions—there came the a priori of the rights of man understood as intellectual a priori, and becoming in fact the measure of all law. Since the Renaissance, the actual laws regulating society began to be judged in reference to so-called "natural" law, which, as we know, means the latter's belonging to the order of truths bearing intelligibility and evidence and deriving, one way or another, from a consciousness of the rights of man. Need I recall the works of such men as Hugo Grotius and Puffendorf, in the seventeenth century, who developed the idea of law based on considerations similar to those of mathematics? The mind was thought capable of working from its own foundation, from its "innate" ideas, to undertake and carry out the construction of the Realm of Law. A law that would be valid independently of all tradition, indifferent to the empirical data of accepted laws. To other thinkers, the legal givens themselves seemed to make possible the formulation of these fundamental rights by induction, after a fashion. Montesquieu reduced the diversity of positive laws to determined principles, and brought out the spirit of those laws and their systematic interdependence.

Henceforth there would be attached to the notion of the rights of man—inseparably, and in ever-increasing numbers—all the legal rules that are the necessary conditions for the actual exercise of those rights. Behind the rights to life and security, to the free disposal of one's goods and the equality of all men before the law, to freedom of thought and its expression, to education and participation in political power—there are all the other rights that extend these, or make them concretely possible: the right to health, happiness, work, rest, a place to live, freedom of movement, and so on. But also, beyond all that, the right to oppose exploitation by capital (the right to unionize) and even the right to social advancement; the right (utopian or Messianic) to the refinement of the human condition, the right to ideology as well as the right to fight for the full rights of man, and the right to ensure the necessary political conditions for that struggle. The modern conception of the rights of man surely extends that far! True, it is also necessary to ascertain the urgency, order and hierarchy of these various rights, and to enquire as to whether they may not compromise the fundamental rights, when all is required unreflectively. But that is not to recognize any limitation to the defense of these rights; it is not to oppose them, but to pose a new problem in connection with an unquestionable right, and, without pessimism to devote necessary reflection to it.

Thus the dynamic and ever-growing fullness of the rights of man appears inseparable from the very recognition of what are called the fundamental rights of man, from their requirement of transcendence, in a sense, of the inhuman that may be contained in pure nature, and of blind necessity in the social body. The uniqueness and irreducibility of human persons are respected and concretely affirmed by the diminishing of the violence to which they are exposed in the order, or disorder, of the determinism of the real.

But the development of science and technology which are supposed to make possible the actual respect for the enlarged rights of man may, in turn, bring with it inhuman requirements that make up a new determinism, threatening the free movements that it was to make possible. For example, in a totally industrialized society or in a totalitarian society—which are precisely the results of supposedly perfected social techniques—the rights of man are compromised by the very practices for which they supplied the motivation. Mechanization and enslavement! And this is the case even before adducing the banal theme of the necessary connection between technical advances, the development of destructive armaments, and the abusive manipulation of societies and souls. Whence a dialectic that could be too easily led toward the challenging or the condemning of technology, without any hope of a possibility of equilibrium, an eventual turning back of science and technology upon themselves. These are problems that cannot go undiscussed, for it is not only a new development of the rights of man in "civilized" countries that depends upon technical progress, but also respect for the elementary rights of man in the "third" and "fourth" worlds, threatened by disease and hunger.

3. THE RIGHTS OF THE OTHER MAN

But do not the rights of man (that is, individual freedom, the uniqueness of the person) also run the risk of being belied or infringed upon by the rights of the other man? What Kant calls "a kingdom of ends" is a plurality of free wills united by reason. But is the freedom of one not, for another's will, the latter's possible negation, and thus at least a limitation? Is it not a principle of possible war between multiple freedoms, or a conflict between reasonable wills that must be resolved by justice? A just legality, in agreement with universal laws, would in Kant's view be obtainable through the resolution of a plurality of opposing wills. And, indeed, through or with the rigor of justice being imposed upon the "incomparable uniqueness" of free persons, we witness the miraculous birth, a birth "out of suffering," of the objective spirit of truth. But that justice represents nonetheless a certain limitation of rights and free will.

Is it so certain that the entire will is *practical reason* in the Kantian sense? Does the will not contain an incoercible part that cannot be obligated by the formalism of universality? And we might even wonder whether, Kant notwithstanding, that incoercible spontaneity, which bears witness both to the multiplicity of humans and the uniqueness of persons, is not already pathology and sensibility and "ill will." There also remains the question of determining whether the limitation of rights by justice is not already a way of treating the person as an object by submitting him or her (the unique, the incomparable) to comparison, to thought, to being placed on the famous scales of justice, and thus to calculation. Whence the essential harshness of a law that offends, within the will, a dignity other than that which attaches to respect for universal laws. The dignity of goodness itself! The universality of the maxim of action according to which the will is assimilated to *practical reason* may not correspond to the totality of good will.

Thus limited by justice, does not the fundamental principle of the rights of man remain repressed, and does not the peace it inaugurates among men remain uncertain and ever precarious? A bad peace. Better, indeed, than a good war! But yet an abstract peace, seeking stability in the powers of the state, in politics, which ensures obedience to the law by force. Hence recourse of justice to politics, to its strategies and clever dealings: the rational order being attained at the price of necessities peculiar to the state, caught up in it. Necessities constituting a determinism as rigorous as that of nature indifferent to man, even though justice—the right of man's free will and its agreement with the free will of the other—may have, at the start, served as an end or pretext for the political necessities. An end soon unrecognized in the deviations imposed by the practicalities of the state, soon lost in the deployment of means brought to bear. And in the eventuality of a totalitarian state, man is repressed and a mockery made of the rights of man, and the promise of an ultimate return to the rights of man is postponed indefinitely.

This also means (and it is important that this be emphasized) that defense of the rights of man corresponds to a vocation *outside* the state, disposing, in a political society, of a kind of extraterritoriality, like that of prophecy in the face of the political powers of the Old Testament, a vigilance totally different from political intelligence, a lucidity not limited to yielding before the formalism of universality, but upholding justice itself in its limitations. The capacity to guarantee that extraterritoriality and that independence defines the liberal state and describes the modality according to which the conjunction of politics and ethics is intrinsically possible.

But, given these considerations, in defending the rights of man, the latter should no longer be considered exclusively from the point of view of a conception of freedom that would already be the potential negation of every other freedom and in which, among freedoms, the just arrangement could only come from reciprocal limitation. Concession and compromise! The justice that is not to be circumvented requires a different "authority" than that of the harmonious relations established between wills that are initially opposed and opposable. These harmonious relations must be agreed upon by free wills on the basis of a prior peace that is not purely and simply nonaggression, but has, so to speak, its own positivity. Its dis-interestment is suggested by the idea of goodness, a dis-interestment emerging from love, for which the *unique* and *absolutely other* can only mean their meaning in the loved one and in oneself. To limit oneself in the matter of justice, to the norm of pure measure, or moderation, between mutually exclusive terms, would be to revert to assimilating the relations between members of the human race to the relation between individuals of logical extension, signifying between one another nothing but negation, additions or indifference. In humanity, from one individual to another, there is established a *proximity* that does not take its meaning from the spatial metaphor of the extension of a concept. Immediately, one and the other is one *facing* the other. It is myself *for* the other. The essence of the reasonable being in man designates not only the advent in things of a psychism in the form of knowledge, in the form of *consciousness* rejecting contradiction, that would encompass the other things under concepts, disalienating them within the identity of the universal: it also designates the ability of the individual, who initially appears to exist relatively to the extension of a concept—the species man, to posit himself as *the only one of his kind*, and thus as absolutely different from all the others, but, in that difference, and without reconstituting the logical concept from which the *I* disengaged myself, to be non-in-different to the other. Non-indifference, or original sociality—goodness; peace, or the wish for peace, benediction; "shalom"² —the initial event of the meeting. Difference—a non-indifference in which the other—though absolutely other, "more other," so to speak, than are the individuals with respect to one another within the "same species" from which the *I* has freed itself—in which the other "regards" me, not in order to "perceive" me, but in "concerning me," in "mattering to me as someone for whom I am answerable." The other, who—*in this sense*—"regards" me, is the face.³

This is a goodness in peace, which is also the exercise of a freedom, and in which the *I* frees itself from its "return to self," from its auto-affirmation, from its egotism of a being persevering in its being, *to answer for the other*, precisely to defend the rights of the other man. Non-indifference and goodness of responsibility: these are not neutral, midway between love and hostility. They must be conceived on the basis of the meeting, in which the *wish for peace*—or goodness—is the first language.

Should not the fraternity that is in the motto of the republic be discerned in the prior non-indifference of one for the other, in that the original goodness in which freedom is embedded, and in which the justice of the rights of man takes on an immutable significance and stability, better than those guaranteed by the state? A freedom in fraternity, in which the responsibility of one-for-the-other is affirmed, and through which the rights of man manifest themselves *concretely* to consciousness as the rights of the other, for which I am answerable. Their original manifestation as rights of the other person and as duty for an *I*, as my fraternal duty—that is the phenomenology of the rights of man. But in their original *mise-en-scène*, there is also the affirmation, as a manifestation of freedom, of the rights of the obligated person, not only as the result of a simple transference and thanks to a generalization of the rights of man as they appear in others to the obligated person. One's duty

---

2   *Shalom*—peace and benediction—in Hebrew, which resonates, in Psalm 120:7, as a way for a man to refer to himself: "I peace ..."
3   [Translator's note: In French, "l'autre me regarde" means both "the other looks at me" and "the other *concerns* me." While both senses are "intended" in the passage, it is in the letter sense that the other is, for me, "visage" or face: and in this latter sense, normally considered the more "figurative," that Levinas makes primary.]

regarding the other who makes appeal to one's responsibility, is an investing of one's own freedom. In responsibility, which is, as such, irrecusable and non-transferable, I am instituted as non-interchangeable: I am chosen as unique and incomparable. My freedom and my rights, before manifesting themselves in my opposition to the freedom and rights of the other person, will manifest themselves precisely in the form of responsibility, in human fraternity. An inexhaustible responsibility: for with the other our accounts are never settled.

In his preface to *Beyond the Verse*, written in 1981, Emmanuel Levinas poses the following provocative question: "Can democracy and the 'rights of man' divorce themselves without danger from their prophetic and ethical depth?"[1] The question is clearly in-

EXTRATERRITORIALITY: OUTSIDE THE STATE, OUTSIDE THE SUBJECT

Robert Bernasconi

tended to threaten the comfortable consensus that has gathered around these icons of our time and, more specifically, to displace what have come to be known under the title the "rights of man" from the context of the European Enlightenment with which they are so often identified. Levinas performs this act of displacement in the first instance by relocating them within the tradition of the Jewish prophets. However, this effort ultimately leads him to a more radical displacement, one that amounts to a certain replacing of them, a relocating of them elsewhere altogether. What does that mean? What are its implications for the doctrine of the "rights of man"?

In "The Rights of Man and the Rights of the Other," an essay written about the same time as the preface to *Beyond the Verse*, Levinas answers the questions he poses there. He explains that the "rights of man" find their justification not within the political sphere alone, but outside the state from what he calls somewhat enigmatically "extraterritoriality." More specifically, he refers to "a kind of extraterritoriality, like that of prophecy in the face of the political powers of the Old Testament."[2] My aim in this essay is to throw

---

An earlier version of this essay was delivered as a lecture at the Hangzhou International Conference on Levinas at Zhejiang University, Hangzhou, China on September 11, 2006. I am grateful to the participants for their comments and to the organizers for their invitation. Originally published as Robert Bernasconi: "Extraterritoriality: Outside the Subject, Outside the State," in *Levinas Studies: An Annual Review*, vol. 3, ed. Jeffrey Bloechl (Pittsburgh: Duquesne University Press, 2008), 61–77. Reprinted with permission of Duquesne University Press.

1 Emmanuel Levinas, *Beyond the Verse: Talmudic Readings and Lectures*, trans. Gary D. Mole (Bloomington: Indiana University Press, 1994), xv. Originally published as *L'au-delà du verset* (Paris: Minuit, 1982), 12–13.
2 Id., "The Rights of Man and the Rights of the Other," *this volume*, 29–40. Originally published as *Hors sujet* (Cognac: Fata Morgana, 1987), 185.

some light on these enigmatic notions of an extraterritoriality and an outside the state, and in particular to pursue the question of what they reveal about Levinas's relation to liberalism. Within Western political thought, since the seventeenth century, to be outside the state is to be in the state of nature. Does Levinas's use of the phrases "outside the state" and "extraterritoriality" amount to an underwriting of the state of nature? Does he join with liberalism in locating the basis of the "rights of man" in the state of nature? Indeed, does Levinas's appeal to the "rights of man" align him with liberalism?

In the sentence that follows the reference to the defense of the "rights of man" to extraterritoriality, Levinas explicitly evokes liberalism and its contribution to the attempt to bring ethics and politics into relation: "The capacity to guarantee that extraterritoriality and that independence defines the liberal state and describes the modality according to which the conjunction of politics and ethics is intrinsically possible."[3] This is not Levinas's only endorsement of liberalism. In an interview from 1988, he suggests that democracy and liberalism provide the possibility for an ethical corrective of politics. The work of justice involves comparing what is incomparable, but this cannot be done with a good conscience. That is why one must always be trying to correct the severity of justice, not least by enacting new legislation. Levinas privileges liberalism in this regard. He writes: "That is perhaps the very excellence of democracy, whose fundamental liberalism corresponds to the ceaseless deep remorse of justice: legislation, always unfinished, always resumed, a legislation open to the better."[4] Levinas in this place seems to be inviting his readers to think of him as an adherent of liberalism and some scholars read him this way uncritically.[5]

However, what makes this apparent celebration of liberalism somewhat surprising and ultimately misleading is the fact that Levinas was, from the time of his earliest essays, and most notably in "Reflections on the Philosophy of Hitlerism" from 1934, outspoken in his critique of liberalism. He there acknowledges a certain debt of liberalism to the Judeo-Christian conception of freedom, but his focus is on the way that liberation by grace came in the

---

3   Ibid.
4   Emmanuel Levinas, *Entre nous: Thinking-of-the-Other*, trans. M. Smith and B. Harshov (New York: Columbia University Press, 1998), 229–30. Originally published as *Entre nous: Essais sur le penser-à-l'autre* (Paris: Grasset, 1991), 260. See also Francois Poirié, *Emmanuel Levinas. Qui êtes-vous?* (Lyon: La Manufacture, 1987), 98. Translated by Jill Robbins as *Is it Righteous to Be?* (Stanford: Stanford University Press, 2001), 52.
5   See, for example, Thaddée Ncayizigiye, *Réexamen éthique des droits de l'homme sous l'éclairage de la pensée d'Emmanuel Levinas* (Boston: Peter Lang, 1997), 485.

course of the Western tradition to be replaced in liberalism by autonomy.[6] This leads him to offer the following critique:

> Man in the liberal world does not choose his destiny under the weight of history. He does not know his possibilities as troubled forces churning within, that already orient him on a determined track. He sees them simply as logical possibilities offered to serene reason that chooses while eternally keeping its distance.[7]

Levinas here is not simply drawing a distinction between positive and negative freedom: it is not a matter of a freedom for giving way to freedom from. He believes that, prior to modernity and at least in the West, freedom meant, paradoxically to us, being committed to the point of being captivated, and it was only subsequently confined to the now more familiar idea of a capacity to make arbitrary choices. Freedom, hitherto located in the whole human being, was in liberalism concentrated in the realm of thought. Furthermore, Levinas judges that a high price was paid for that shift in focus. It was, on his analysis, this degenerate conception of freedom, which included liberation from one's body, that deprived Europe of the adequate intellectual resources to combat Hitlerism.[8] By denying the evident significance of the body, liberalism left biological determinism without a credible alternative. In this way, Levinas already in 1934 sets out to find a way beyond both Hitlerism and liberalism.

Immediately after the end of the Second World War, in a brief essay welcoming Sartre's *Anti-Semite and Jew*, Levinas renews his attack on liberalism. This text is significant here because in it we see Levinas putting in question the ideas of the "rights of man." Levinas complains that the Enlightenment was one-sided in its tendency to subordinate the world of concrete economic and social conditions to the inner realm in which thought is free. He employs an anecdote to illustrate the problem:

> In a memorandum that UNESCO recently circulated among philosophers, while preparing a report for the Unite Nations on the "rights of man," the emphasis is on the antinomy facing reason when it tries to specify hu-

---

6   Emmanuel Levinas, *Unforeseen History*, trans. Nidra Poller (Urbana: University of Illinois Press, 2004), 15. Originally published as *Les imprévus de l'histoire* (Cognac: Fata Morgana, 1987), 32.
7   Levinas, *Unforeseen History*, 16 [32].
8   Ibid., 19 [38–39].

man rights: personal freedom is inconceivable without economic liberation, while the organization of economic freedom isn't possible without an enslavement of the moral person—temporary but for an indeterminate duration.[9]

This antinomy has not only been the classic dilemma that all developing countries have faced in modernity when they are determining their order of priorities, it has also been the choice that since the late 1940s the two dominant ideologies imposed on those countries. But that is perhaps only another version of the problem that Levinas already identifies in "Reflections on the Philosophy of Hitlerism": *Either* one allows human thought to be overwhelmed by historical, social, and economic phenomena, *or* the concrete situation in which we find ourselves is reduced to mere thought and structures of knowledge.[10]

Levinas continues the same train of thought in "The I and the Totality." He explains that "The impasse of liberalism resides in the exteriority of my consciousness to myself," an exteriority that exhibits one's lack of identity with oneself.[11] One finds the law of one's actions, the meaning of one's existence, even one's own self-consciousness, not in the depths of one's heart or in introspection, but outside oneself.[12] It is outside oneself that one is asked to give an account of oneself.[13] This is the crucial first step in Levinas's attempt to overcome the opposition between individualism and communitarianism, the alternatives that, in one form or another, have shaped political philosophy since the advent of modernity. It starts from the insight in 1934 that there is no isolated self-identical individual and culminates in 1968 in the insight that the self as self is for the other to the point of substitution, but nevertheless still separate from the other.[14]

Levinas was not the only philosopher who was convinced of the ultimate inability of liberalism to combat the threat posed by totalitarianism. Hannah Arendt's questioning of the capacity of the "rights of man" to serve as

9   Emmanuel Levinas, "Existentialism and Anti-Semitism," *October* 87 (Winter 1999): 28. Levinas is referring to the "Memorandum and Questionnaire Circulated by UNESCO on the Theoretical Basis of the Rights of Man," reprinted in *Human Rights: Comments and Interpretations*, ed. UNESCO (London: Allan Wingate, 1969), 251–7.
10 Levinas, *Les imprévus de l'histoire*, 27–41.
11 Levinas, *Entre nous: Thinking-of-the-Other*, 23 [36].
12 Ibid.
13 Ibid., 30 [44].
14 I have chartered this itinerary in "No Exit: Levinas's Aporetic Account of Transcendence," *Research in Phenomenology* 35 (2005): 101–17.

a resource with which to combat the persecution of stateless refugees paralleled Levinas's own sense that liberalism and the much-vaunted values of the European Enlightenment were ill equipped to combat Hitlerism at its core. Arendt in *The Origins of Totalitarianism* in 1951 complained that the existence of stateless refugees had shown that the idea of the "rights of man" was worthless: the refugee was by definition stateless and as such without protection. Civil rights, the rights that belonged to citizens, proved to be the only rights worth having. Those who lacked citizenship were reduced to the status of mere human beings without anybody on whom they could rely.[15] In 1973, Levinas echoed Arendt's observation and associated it with his earlier suspicion of liberalism when, in "Antihumanism and Education," after recalling the inhumanity of men towards their fellow men in the twentieth century, he asked himself: "Is this the fragility of humanism in Western liberalism? Is it a basic inability to guarantee the privileges of humanity of which humanism had considered itself the repository?" Levinas answered his own question this way: "We, as Jews, were the first to feel it."[16]

So what led Levinas to be apparently more open to liberalism by the time of "The Rights of Man and the Rights of the Other"? One cannot be sure, but the historical record points to Levinas's study of the eighteenth century Jewish thinker, Moses Mendelssohn. This took place when Levinas responded to an invitation to write a preface to a French translation of Mendelssohn's masterpiece, *Jerusalem*. There are very few other references to Mendelssohn elsewhere in Levinas's writings, but this preface offers one of his few major discussions of an Enlightenment thinker. It is also his only prolonged discussion of any political thinker as such.[17] In his essay on Mendelssohn, Levinas does not step back from his critique of "the fragility of Europe's democratic institutions, which were unable to prevent two world wars, fascism and

---

15 Hannah Arendt, *The Origins of Totalitarianism* (New York: Harcourt Brace, 1973), 293. Arendt's ideas on this issue were given a renewed currency when they were recalled in the late 1980s and 1990s both by Julia Kristeva in *Etrangers à nous-mêmes* (Paris: Fayard, 1988), 220–29, translated by Leon S. Roudiez as *Strangers to Ourselves* (New York: Columbia University Press, 1991), 148–54; and by Giorgio Agamben in *Homo Sacer*, trans. Daniel Heller-Roazen (Stanford: Stanford University Press, 1998), 126–35.

16 Emmanuel Levinas, *Difficult Freedom: Essays on Judaism*, trans. Seàn Hand (Baltimore: Johns Hopkins University Press, 1990), 152. Originally published as *Difficile liberté: Essais sur le judaïsme*, 2nd ed. (Paris: A. Michel, 1976), 360–1.

17 It is surprising that more attention has not been paid to this essay. For an exception, see Ephraim Meir, *In Proximity: Emmanuel Levinas and the Eighteenth Century*, eds. Melvyn New, Robert Bernasconi, and Richard Cohen (Lubbock: Texas Tech University Press, 2001), 243–59. There are, of course, a few references to Thomas Hobbes, but no real engagement at any level of detail. See Cheryl L. Hughes, "The Primary of Ethics: Hobbes and Levinas," *Continental Philosophy Review* 31 (1998): 79–94.

Auschwitz,"[18] but he also acknowledges the historical impact of the idea of natural rights, particularly for Jews, whose emancipation preceded and survived the holocaust. This text is of more than marginal interest here because Levinas identifies Mendelssohn as a representative of liberalism.[19] Nevertheless, it is important to understand that Levinas recognizes this as a different kind of liberalism because of its radically different conceptions of freedom and of the relation between religion and the state.

Levinas makes clear that the holocaust and the advent of the new philosophical framework introduced by phenomenology have made much of Mendelssohn's philosophy unsustainable today. He celebrates the continuing relevance of Mendelssohn's "liberalist scruples,"[20] but at the same time insists that the conception of freedom Mendelssohn introduced requires "a philosophical elaboration more complex" than that which Mendelssohn could provide in the context of the Enlightenment. I shall show here that "The Rights of Man and the Rights of the Other" is an attempt to supply this "more complex" elaboration in the form of an implicit critique of the original framework on which Mendelssohn relied. What is at stake is indicated by Levinas when he explains that Mendelssohn's idea of freedom needs "a less abstract theology and an eschatology less unproblematically optimistic."[21] Levinas thereby announces that he plans to develop an idea of concrete freedom within the context of an eschatology divorced from teleology.[22] Such an eschatology owes little or nothing to the philosophy of history introduced by Kant and Hegel, but instead draws on Judaism. According to Levinas, the Jews of the nineteenth century already recognized in Mendelssohn's ideas of freedom and of the "rights of man" "something close to their own prophetic traditions."[23] However, it should be emphasized that Levinas, so far as I am aware, nowhere identifies a prophetic dimension in liberalism, except in relation to Mendelssohn. By contrast, he goes out of his way to emphasize a prophetic dimension to Marxism, which he characterizes as having the interrupting force of ethics.[24] This

---

18   Emmanuel Levinas, *In the Time of Nations*, trans. Michael B. Smith (Bloomington: Indiana University Press, 1994), 138. Originally published as *A l'heure des nations* (Paris: Editions de Minuit, 1988), 161.
19   Ibid., 139 [162].
20   Ibid., 138 [161].
21   Ibid., 144 [167–8].
22   See further Robert Bernasconi, "Different Styles of Eschatology," *Research in Phenomenology* 28 (1998): 3–19.
23   Levinas, *In the Time of Nations*, 138 [161].
24   Emmanuel Levinas, *Of God Who Comes to Mind*, trans. Bettina Bergo (Palo Alto: Stanford University Press, 1998), 4. Originally published as *De Dieu qui vient à l'idée* (Paris: J. Vrin, 1982), 19. See also

is, at least in part, because he appreciated its strong commitment to address the impact of the material dimension of poverty.

In order to emphasize the Judaic heritage he shares with Mendelssohn, Levinas, when introducing Mendelssohn's radical idea of freedom, recalls the title of his first collection of confessional writings, *Difficult Freedom*.[25] To be sure, in this book, Levinas is clearer about the philosophical problem posed by freedom than he is about the solution. When, in "A Religion for Adults," he asks how Judaism integrated the need for a virtually vertiginous freedom into a desire for transcendence, he is in fact identifying a dilemma that haunts his own thinking from beginning to end.[26] Nevertheless, elsewhere in the book, he brilliantly encapsulates his conception of freedom: "man's freedom is that of an emancipated man remembering his servitude and feeling solidarity for all enslaved peoples."[27] This sentence goes to the heart of Levinas's philosophy, a philosophy born not from the individual's experience of an arbitrary free choice,[28] but from the solidarity of the oppressed that emerges from suffering at the hands of others. In that context freedom emerges as moral freedom.[29]

Surprisingly, given the idiosyncrasies of most of Levinas's readings in the history of philosophy, his exposition of Mendelssohn relies on the best scholarship available to him. More specifically, he draws heavily on Alexander Altmann's essay, "The Quest for Liberty in Moses Mendelssohn's Political Philosophy."[30] What Altmann supplies, and what Levinas certainly would

ibid., 77 [126].
25   Id., *In the Time of Nations*, 144 [167].
26   Levinas, *Difficult Freedom*, 16 [32]
27   Ibid., 152 [201].
28   Ibid., 10 [24].
29   Ibid., 71 [98]. I have recently elaborated this idea, with its clear biblical resonances, in "Strangers and Slaves in the Land of Egypt: Levinas and the Politics of Otherness," in *Difficult Justice*, ed. Asher Horowitz and Gadd Horowitz (Toronto: University of Toronto Press, 2006), 246–61. To be sure, the question immediately arises as to the whether all share equally in this "memory of the totalitarianisms that still haunt today's humanity" (Levinas, *In the Time of Nations*, 138 [161]). The privilege Levinas accords to Judaism in his philosophical works arises from its memory of suffering. His thereby comes to rely on a memory philosophy that seems to be available only to those who share in the cultivation of this memory. This raises serious questions about his attempt to translate Hebraic wisdom into a Jewish philosophy to one that is truly universal. I have explored these questions elsewhere, but by no means exhausted them.
30   Levinas cites the essay in the Hebrew version which appeared in *Daat* 5 (1980), with an English summary (23–4). The full English text appeared in a supplement to the Lessing Yearbook: *Humanität und Dialog*, ed. E. Bahr, E.P. Harris, and L.G. Lyon (Detroit: Wayne State University Press, 1982), 37–65. On this topic, see also "Moses Mendelssohn über Naturrecht und Naturzustand," in *Ich handle mit Vernunft...*, ed. N. Hinske (Hamburg: Felix Meiner, 1981), 45–82. Altmann is the author of a 900-page biography of Mendelssohn: *Moses Mendelssohn* (University: University of Alabama Press, 1973).

not have been able to provide on his own, is an account of what is original in Mendelssohn's contribution to social contract theory. Mendelssohn radicalizes the sense in which the freedom of natural law cannot be limited by the social contract: the social contract is not a way to guarantee security, but a necessary step in the pursuit of freedom. There is not, as in Hobbes, an exchange where one sacrifices a measure of one's freedom the better to enjoy what freedom is left to one. Freedom is moral freedom, in the sense of the exercising of beneficence, which one can only do effectively as a citizen.[31] According to Mendelssohn, in the state of nature one is already looking for fulfillment in beneficence. That is why he can say that it is for the sake of promoting beneficence that one takes on citizenship through the social contract.[32] One enters society not to avoid a state war but to fulfill a preexisting obligation, an obligation from which no agreement, tacit or explicit, could release one. It is in that sense that Altmann attributes to Mendelssohn "a moral, even a metaphysical" quality to freedom in its inalienability, a point Levinas makes his own by referring to a "quasi-ontological impossibility of relinquishing one's freedom."[33]

Levinas repeatedly complains that the fact that the traditional conception of the "rights of man" is based on the right to a free will leads social contract theory to be faced with the problem of competing freedoms.[34] In other words, because social contract theory takes its starting point in the individual within the state of nature, the advent of society is understood as a necessary attempt to address the problem of constraining and limiting those competing freedoms in such a way that we are persuaded to believe that we have imposed these limitations on ourselves. This complaint mirrors Mendelssohn's critique of his predecessors in social contract theory, and, following Altmann, Levinas judges that when Mendelssohn presents freedom as a right and a duty at the same time it is in order to negotiate this problem.[35] To

---

31   One should not be misled by the fact that Mendelssohn insists that the social contract is not for the sake of peace, to establish a difference on that issue between him and Levinas who is constantly invoking peace. Both are arguing against a broadly Hobbesian approach. Levinas's way of saying this is to set out not from a state of war, but "on the basis of a prior peace" (Levinas, *Outside the Subject*, 123 [185]). Levinas was always clear that what he meant by peace was not security and the cessation of war. Peace for Levinas is eschatological in his sense of an interruption of history.
32   Levinas, *In the Time of Nations*, 138 [160–62]; *Humanität und Dialog*, 48.
33   Id., *In the Time of Nations*, 137 [160]; *Humanität und Dialog*, 44.
34   See also id., *Outside the Subject*, 121–2 [183]; Lionel Ponton, *Philosophie et droits de l'homme de Kant à Levinas* (Paris: J. Vrin, 1990), 194–5; and Emmanuel Levinas, *Alterity and Transcendence*, trans. Michael B. Smith (New York: Columbia University Press, 1999), 145–9, originally published as *Altérité et transcendence* (Paris: Fata Morgana, 1995), 151–5.
35   Levinas, *In the Time of Nations*, 137 [160]; *Humanität und Dialog*, 44.

be sure, it suggests another approach to the problem only to the extent that the obligations do not proceed from the rights, but the other way around. Indeed, according to Altmann, Mendelssohn believes that rights flow from obligations.[36] This idea reemerges transformed in Levinas's "The Rights of Man and the Rights of the Other" as the claim that the original manifestation of the "rights of man" is in the form of rights for the other and duty for an I.[37] Nevertheless, there is surely something spurious about the suggestion in Levinas and Altmann that appeals to obligations somehow resolves the problem when it simply relocates it. With Levinas one never leaves behind competing obligations. It is the source of bad conscience.

Levinas expresses a similar idea in another essay from 1981, "The Prohibition against Representation and 'the Rights of Man.'" He again summarizes his thoughts on rights in a way that suggests his proximity to Mendelssohn: "You shall not kill" is not simply a prohibition but means "You shall cause your neighbour to live." He adds: "Event of sociality prior to all association in the name of an abstract and common 'humanity.' *The right of man, absolutely and originally,* takes on meaning only in the other, as the right of the other man. A right with respect to which I am never released!"[38] This last phrase echoes Mendelssohn's recognition that leaving the state of nature by way of the social contract cannot release one from the obligations existing there. Unlike the traditional perspective on the "rights of man," which highlights the struggle between my rights and those of others, such that it seems that my rights can always be compromised by the rights of the other, Levinas highlights the fact that the other's rights represent obligations for me.

This is not just a typical Levinasian assertion of the asymmetry of ethics. It is a phenomenological point about how rights appear, as Levinas is careful to specify.[39] Rights do not become manifest when I make demands for myself. This is indistinguishable from egoism. As he said many years earlier, "My consciousness of my I reveals no right to me. My freedom shows itself to be arbitrary."[40] Rights appear as such only when one comes to the defense of others.[41] In other words, Levinas takes from the traditional idea of the "rights of man" its formal structure as a priori, but locates the concretization of such

36 *Humanität und Dialog,* 41.
37 Levinas, "The Rights of Man and the Rights of the Other," 38 [187].
38 Id., *Alterity and Transcendence,* 127 [127].
39 Id., "The Rights of Man and the Rights of the Other," 32 [177].
40 Id., *Difficult Freedom,* 17 [33].
41 Id., "The Rights of Man and the Rights of the Other," 32, 38 [177, 187].

rights elsewhere than where the tradition finds it. They are no longer to be understood as concretized originally in the right of a free will, but in the rights of the other.[42] Hence Levinas describes the transcendent dimension of the exercise of freedom in these terms: "the I frees itself from its 'return to self,' from its auto-affirmation, from its egotism of a being persevering in its being, *to answer for the other*, precisely to defend the rights of the other man."[43]

However, Levinas's theory passes beyond phenomenology. In locating originary right in the rights of others, he thereby locates it not only apart from the state but also beyond the subject. Rights are located "outside the subject," to employ the phrase he used as the title of the book in which he published "The Rights of Man and the Rights of the Other." It needs to be understood that when Levinas refers to an extraterritoriality beyond political society, he is not invoking anything like a state of nature, but distancing himself from any such framework. To be sure, he initially used the term "extraterritoriality" in *Totality and Infinity* in his discussion of the home or domicile: "Man has overcome the elements only by surmounting this interiority without issue by the domicile, which confers upon him an extraterritoriality."[44] This extraterritoriality is "produced in the gentleness or the warmth of intimacy" in a welcome that is itself "produced primordially in the gentleness of the feminine face."[45] In this way Levinas seeks to combat totalitarianism, which is defined in part by its denial of any outside the state. But as a number of critics have noticed, this account of extraterritoriality seems to be in danger of confining the feminine to the home, which would reproduce for women the same exclusion from which Mendelssohn suffered as a Jew. That is why it is so important when we read the paragraph on extraterritoriality from "The Rights of Man and the Rights of the Other" to understand that the term "extraterritoriality" is being used in a very different way. It can no longer be construed as simply referring to a private realm outside the state such as we find it in classical liberalism. Levinas's discussion of Mendelssohn is indispensable in this context because it offers some guidance as to how to differentiate his somewhat enigmatic language from that of the social contract tradition in all its variations.

---

42 Ibid., 38 [187].
43 Ibid., 38 [186].
44 Id., *Totality and Infinity*, trans. Alphonso Lingis (Pittsburgh: Duquesne University Press, 1969), 131. Originally published as *Totalité et infini: Essai sur l'extériorité* (The Hague: Martinus Nijhoff, 1961), 104.
45 Ibid., 150 [124].

Although many adherents of the social contract tradition see themselves as promoting freedom, it seems likely that when Levinas presents Mendelssohn as a philosopher who, writing from the experience of oppression, promotes natural law as "mankind's protection against oppression,"[46] he means to distinguish him from the others. Altmann provides the basis for this interpretation by relating Mendelssohn's account of freedom to his experience of being excluded from citizenship as a Jew. The question facing Mendelssohn as a Jew was whether a Christian society could legitimately constrain dissidents.[47] Mendelssohn was dissatisfied with the standard liberal solution whereby one submits to the state in the public realm but exercises freedom of conscience privately.[48] He rejected the radical separation of private and public that was reflected in conventional liberalism's sharp division between religion and the state. By emphasizing the function of religion, its right to admonish, instruct, fortify, and comfort, Mendelssohn brought church and state into contact.[49] However, neither church, nor state, had a right to subject one's principles and convictions to coercion.[50] Altmann claims that Mendelssohn was particularly concerned with the danger that some people might focus on exclusively cultivating religion in private at the expense of the affairs of this world, a concern which was also Levinas's, as is apparent from his refusal to find in mysticism the concretization of transcendence, insisting instead that transcendence is produced as ethics and fecundity. But Levinas also knew the danger in granting autonomy to the political. He thus attempted to locate the "rights of man" not as what politics must secure, or even as the very foundation of the political, but at the point of intersection of ethics and politics.[51]

What is of lasting significance in Levinas's question about whether the "rights of man" can be divorced from their prophetic and ethical depths is the way that it highlights the dangers that ensue once politics — however well-intentioned in terms of its goal — is separated from ethics, as, for exam-

---

46 Id., *In the Time of Nations*, 138 [161].
47 *Humanität und Dialog*, 47.
48 Altmann explores this further in another essay: "The Philosophical Roots of Moses Mendelssohn's Plea for Emancipation," *Essays in Intellectual Jewish History* (Hanover, NH: University Press of New England, 1981), 154–69.
49 Moses Mendelssohn, *Jerusalem oder über religiöse Macht und Judentum* (Berlin: Friedrich Maurer, 1783), 62. Translated by Allan Arkush as *Jerusalem or on Religious Power and Judaism* (Hanover, NH: University Press of New England, 1983), 59.
50 Ibid. 70 [85].
51 For the essential background, see Robert Bernasconi, "The Third Party," *Journal of the British Society for Phenomenology* 30 (1999): 76–87.

ple, when the expectation of some desired result distracts attention from the atrocities that occur along the way, allowing them to be dismissed as so much "collateral damage." Even though the relation of ethics to politics dominates the preface to *Totality and Infinity* from the opening sentences about war and morality, there is no final resolution of this problem within the confines of the book because Levinas never fully follows through on the reconception of ethics as an eschatology, understood as "a relation with being *beyond the totality* or beyond history."[52] This is perhaps because *Totality and Infinity* is directed primarily against totalitarianism, and so Levinas is content to look to the family as the concretization of that outside the state which nevertheless reserves a place for the state, even as it resists totalitarianism's claims to dominate everything. Hegelianism, which regards the family as merely "a step toward the anonymous universality of the State,"[53] is thereby resisted. But when, at the beginning of the 1980s, Levinas interrogates democracy and the "rights of man" a more nuanced approach is called for, one that transforms the meaning of "extraterritoriality." To be sure, as I shall now show, Levinas had already prepared for this transformation, but until then he had not seen the need to address directly how his own still embryonic account of the relation of ethics and politics necessitates a refiguring of the relation of the private and the public.

Levinas introduces the central paragraph of "The Rights of Man and the Rights of the Other" by recalling that the quest for justice submits the incomparable singular individual to comparison and calculation, so that the limitation of one person's rights to satisfy another's rights seems inevitable.[54] In this context Levinas immediately reiterates what had been for him, as it was for Arendt, one of the lessons of Auschwitz: one cannot rely on the state to secure one's rights. But that is not the last word. Just as justice needs to be always put in question from elsewhere so that conformity to its abstract rule does not become a new tyranny, so one cannot rely on the politicians for protection and implementation of the "rights of man." Hence the need for voices from outside, like those of the Old Testament prophets.

> This also means (and it is important that this be emphasized) that the defense of the rights of man corresponds to a vocation *outside* the state,

---

52 Levinas, *Totality and Infinity*, 22 [xii].
53 Ibid., 306 [283].
54 Id., "The Rights of Man and the Rights of the Other," 36 [184].

disposing, in a political society, of a kind of extraterritoriality, like that of prophecy in the face of the political powers of the Old Testament, a vigilance totally different from political intelligence, a lucidity not limited to yielding before the formalism of universality, but upholding justice itself in its limitations."[55]

Elsewhere Levinas offered an illustration of such a vigilance when he celebrated the visit of President Sadat of Egypt to Jerusalem.[56] This was a break from political prudence. Levinas continues in "The Rights of Man and the Rights of the Other":

The capacity to guarantee that extraterritoriality and their independence defines the liberal state and describes the modality according to which the conjunction of politics and ethics is intrinsically possible.[57]

The reference to the prophets in the previous sentence is decisive because it interrupts any expectation that reliance on the time-honored distinction between public and private, so beloved of classical liberalism, will be sufficient. Hence the focus is not on the separation of politics and ethics, but on their conjunction.

Classical liberalism, through its insistence on separating the public and the private, reduces ethics to a private morality. It is ethics in an entirely different sense that, according to Levinas, conjoins with politics in the form of an eschatological interruption of it, as when supplying justice with the bad conscience that arises from an awareness of the tears that the bureaucrat cannot see.[58] And yet Levinas seems to allow, and we saw it reiterated in the 1988 interview, that this conjunction of an eschatological ethics and a politics respectful of rights is most likely in liberalism, because liberalism does not allow politics to be everything. I propose that Levinas has in mind here a Mendelssohnian, prophetic liberalism, not the classical version. The shift in the meaning of "extraterritoriality" is an indication of this. In 1964

---

55 Ibid., 37 [185].
56 Id., *Beyond the Verse*, 188–95 [221–28].
57 Id., "The Rights of Man and the Rights of the Other," 37 [185].
58 Id., "Transcendence et Hauteur," in *Liberté et commandement* (Cognac: Fata Morgana, 1994), 80–1. Translated by Tina Chanter and Simon Critchley as "Transcendence and Height," in *Basic Philosophical Writings*, ed. Adriaan Peperzak, Simon Critchley, and Robert Bernasconi (Bloomington: Indiana University Press, 1996), 23.

"extraterritoriality" still suggests to Levinas a kind of irresponsibility, as "The Temptation of Temptation," a talmudic lecture, makes clear.[59] It is only in the 1980s that Levinas reserves the word to point to an intersection of ethics and politics that traditional liberalism cannot readily accommodate, but that Mendelssohnian liberalism makes possible.

This more profound meaning of "extraterritoriality" can perhaps best be approached through the idea of the trace and in a way that confirms how, notwithstanding the changes I have just documented in the use of that word, Levinas remains faithful to the fundamental trajectory of his thought. Already in 1953, in "Freedom and Command," and apparently quite independently of any impact of Mendelssohn, Levinas presents the command issued to me by the defenseless face as presenting a model of freedom that not only challenges the tyranny of the state, but predates it. Leaning heavily on the phenomenological idea that reflection draws on an unreflective fund of experience which forms a kind of "past that has never been present," Levinas locates the command of the face in such a past, thereby anticipating his notion of the trace.[60] The notion of extraterritoriality is, as it were, the equivalent of the trace, albeit in another idiom. Freedom in Levinas is not the experience of free choice but the "experience" of an exit from oneself.[61] However, this exit is not from the private realm into the public arena of the world, as in existentialism, but an exit that passes beyond being, albeit not in such a way that the material dimension of life can be ignored. Substitution, the one-for-the-other, is to pass outside the subject, while retaining a responsibility that is mine alone. This is the concrete meaning of transcendence for Levinas and he evokes it in the essay, "The Rights of Man and the Rights of the Other," when he writes of an exercise of freedom in which "the I frees itself from its 'return to self,' from its auto-affirmation, from its egotism of a being persevering in its being, *to answer for the other*, precisely to defend the rights of the other man."[62]

---

59 Id., *Nine Talmudic Readings*, trans. Annette Aronowicz (Bloomington: Indiana University Press, 1994), 36. Originally published as *Quatre lectures talmudiques* (Paris: Editions de Minuit, 1982), 78.
60 Id., *Collected Philosophical Papers*, trans. Alphonso Lingis (Pittsburgh, Duquesne University Press, 1998), 22; *Liberté et commandement* (Cognac: Fata Morgana, 1994), 46. On the trace, see Robert Bernasconi, "The Trace of Levinas in Derrida," *Derrida and Différance* (Evanston: Northwestern University Press, 1988), 13–29. Already in *Totality and Infinity* there is some suggestion of a connection between Levinas's first conception of extraterritoriality and his idea of the anterior posteriori, which is a forerunner of the trace (see *Totality and Infinity*, 170 [144]).
61 Levinas, *Difficult Freedom*, 10 [24].
62 Id., "The Rights of Man and the Rights of the Other," 38 [186].

What this all amounts to still remains highly abstract, so I will close by offering an account of an ancient right, the so-called right of necessity, which determined that if the poor in case of necessity took what they needed to survive from someone else's surplus, they were not committing theft but reasserting a common ownership that was ultimately inalienable. This idea was of long standing, widely articulated in twelfth-century Europe, and it survived intact in modern rights theory with Hugo Grotius.[63] I have argued elsewhere that it was in the chapter on property in John Locke's *Second Treatise of Government* that this right of necessity for the poor was supplanted by the right to amass private property without limit.[64] Whereas for Grotius the rights of the poor were inalienable, Locke tells us, albeit only in passing, that those rights were abandoned when we allegedly gave tacit agreement to the invention of money: That is to say, the poor were sacrificed to the interests of the unlimited accumulation of private property. In other words, the poor were sacrificed to the interests of the unlimited accumulation of private property. In other words, classical liberal social contract theory highlights the rights of property, thereby securing the home or domicile which guarantees the independence of the private realm, but at the same time ignores those who do not have a home: the homeless and, of course, refugees.

Even if mainstream political philosophy, with the striking exception of Hegel, largely forgot the rights of the poor and only a relatively few scholars have kept the memory of it alive, it resurfaces in Levinas. In "A Religion for Adults" from 1977,[65] he reports the conviction of the eleventh-century commentator Rachi that one must know that God created the earth in order to possess the Promised Land, because without that knowledge possession would be mere usurpation. Levinas adds: "No rights can therefore ensue from the simple fact that a person needs *espace vital*."[66] The consciousness of my ego (*moi*) reveals no right to me. This might sound like a reassertion of the Lockean theory in all its harshness: the spoils go to the industrious and rational, and not to all by virtue of their existence. However, it is, on the con-

---

63 On the background, see Scott G. Swanson, "The Medieval Foundations of John Locke's Theory of Natural Rights," *History of Political Thought* 18 (1997): 399–459. However, it should be clear that I am on the opposite side of the debate when it comes to the interpretation of Locke.
64 See Robert Bernasconi, "Locke and the Politics of Desire," *Acta Institutionis Philosophiae et Aestheticae* 7 (1989): 97–110; and, "On Giving What is Not Mine to Give: A Critique of John Locke's Displacement of the Rights of the Poor to Charity" in *Le don et la dette*, ed. Marco Olivetti (Milan: Cedam, 2004), 419–29.
65 Levinas, *Difficult Freedom*, 17 [33].
66 Ibid.

trary, in conformity with the phenomenological approach elaborated in "The Rights of Man and the Rights of the Other" where the focus falls on my experience of an obligation imposed on me by virtue of the rights of the other. I am confronted not by a specific set of obligations or duties that I might fulfill to establish my good con-science, but by an infinite responsibility. One hears a similar suspicion of the rights of property in *Entre nous*: "My 'being in the world' or my 'place in the sun,' my home — are they not a usurpation of places that belong to the other man who has already been oppressed or starved by me?"[67] In one of his Talmudic lectures Lévinas poses the problem even more dramatically. He writes: "The problem of a hungry world can be resolved only if the food of the owners and those who are provided for ceases to appear to them as their inalienable property, but is recognized as a gift they have received for which thanks must be given and to which others have a right."[68]

Levinas does not associate the privileging of property rights over the rights of the poor with a specific strand of individualism within the social contract tradition. Nor does Levinas draw attention to Mendelssohn's recognition that the notion of beneficence (*Wohltum*) calls for the benevolence (*Wohlwollen*) that was expressed in the right of necessity:

> If, therefore, a man possesses goods or owns certain means of attaining felicity, which he can spare, that is, which are not necessarily required for maintaining his existence but serve the *improvement of his existence*, he is obligated to employ a part of them for the benefit of his fellow man, that is, for *benevolence*. For the *improvement of one's existence* is inseparable from *benevolence*.[69]

This was in marked contrast with mainstream political philosophy, with the striking exception of Hegel, that used the right to private property as a way of denying the rights of the poor. Nevertheless, the rights of the poor resurface in Levinas.

Levinas was not a great political thinker in the way that Jean-Paul Sartre was, for example, but he pinpointed the deep-seated deficiencies in classical liberalism and saw the direction from which a new thinking of the

---

67   Id., *Entre nous*, 130 [149].
68   Id., *Nine Talmudic Readings*, trans. Annette Aronowicz (Bloomington: Indiana University Press, 1994), 133. Originally published as *Du sacré au saint* (Paris: Editions de Minuit, 1977), 77.
69   Mendelssohn, *Jerusalem or on Religious Power and Judaism*, 47 [33–34].

conjunction between ethics and politics might arise: from outside the state and outside the subject. Central to that new direction was the notion of extraterritoriality which points beyond the division of private and public, and thus threatens the classical version of the state of nature, which takes as its starting-point the isolated individual for whom others are a threat. "Extraterritoriality" is not the "outside all places" of more pious thoughts,[70] any more than it is the state of nature of liberal thought. It names the site of the conjunction of ethics and politics, where politics is called to go beyond its own procedure of comparing the incomparable in order to meet ethical obligations that come from elsewhere and face the complexity of difficult choices.

In the works published after *Totality and Infinity* Levinas accomplished a departure from possessive individualism without embracing the totalizing tendencies of communitarianism. This was achieved, not only by introducing an eschatological conception of peace in place of the Hobbesian state of war, but, more particularly, by construing the event of identity in a being for the other that undoes the conception of personal identity on which liberalism relies. In consequence, the "rights of man" could no longer be understood as a function of classical liberalism, even if it was in the context of liberalism that they were first articulated. To the extent that Levinas in the early 1980s is more open to liberalism, it is only a certain kind of Mendelssohnian liberalism in which he finds a rough anticipation of some ideas at which he had already arrived, particularly that of primordial duties that belong, according to Levinas, to an ethical subject, a subject not identical with itself, but responsible for the other. Mendelssohn's contribution to Levinas's philosophy, by contrast, helps him to locate himself in this the history of political thought attempting to pass beyond the opposition of liberalism and totalitarianism. It is my conviction that although Levinas's ideas of the "rights of man" are only presented by him in broad outline so that, particularly in the English-language discussion, they have not been given much prominence, they are a valuable resource for anyone committed to the struggle for social justice and particularly the struggle to transform a world that persistently turns its back on the victims of famine.

---

70   Id., *Beyond the Verse*, 82 [70].

The World Inhospitable to Levinas

Zygmunt Bauman

All great thinkers create powerful concepts and/or images of their own but as a rule design them together with a complete universe to accommodate them and infuse them with sense. For Emmanuel Levinas, the world he constructed was "the moral party of two," which was self-consciously a utopia in both of its inseparable senses (i.e., of no place and good place). The moral party of two was the primal scene of morality, the test-tube in which moral selves germinate and sprout. It was also the only stage on which such selves could play themselves, i.e., as moral beings, instead of playing scripted roles and reciting someone else's lines. The primal scene of morality is the realm of the face-to-face, of the tremendous encounter with the Other as a Face.

Morality, which in Levinas's terms referred to being for the Other, has a notoriously awesome potential for love and hatred, for self-sacrifice and domination, care and cruelty. Ambivalence is its prime mover. And yet the moral party of two is capable of sustaining the universe on its own. In this party, morality does not need codes or rules, reason or knowledge, argument or conviction. It would not understand them anyway; morality is "before" all that (one cannot even say that the moral impulse is "ineffable" or "mute" since ineffability and dumbness come after language). The moral impulse triggered by the Face precedes speech. It sets its standards as it goes. It does not know guilt or innocence. It is pure in the only true sense of purity, the purity of naivety. As Vladimir Jankélévitch has pointed out, one cannot be pure except under the condition of not having purity, that is to say of not possessing it knowingly.[1]

Originally published as Zygmunt Bauman: "The World Inhospitable to Levinas," *Philosophy Today* 43, no. 2 (1999): 151–67. Reprinted with the permission of the author.

1   Vladimir Jankélévitch, *Traité des vertus* (Paris: Mouton, 1968), 1024–7.

The "moral party of two," postulated by Levinas as the birth-home and the homeland of morality, is naive; it does not know (has not been told) that it is a party, let alone a moral one. Only when gazed upon from outside, does the moral party congeal into a "couple," a "pair," a "they out there." It is the outside gaze that "objectifies" the moral party and thus makes it into a unit, a thing that can be described as it is, "handled," compared with others "like it," assessed, evaluated, and ruled on. But from the point of view of me as a moral self there is no "we," no "couple," no supraindividual entity with its "needs" and "rights."

"Inside" the moral party there is just me, with my responsibility, with my care, with the command that commands me and me alone, and there is the Face, the catalyst and the midwife. My togetherness with the Other won't survive the disappearance or the opting out of myself or the Other. There would be nothing left to "survive" that disappearance.

"Togetherness" in the "moral party" is vulnerable, weak, fragile, and lives precariously with a shadow of death never far away and all this because neither I nor the Other is replaceable. It is precisely this non-replaceability that makes our togetherness moral. Because each of us is irreplaceable, it makes no sense to think of actions in terms of "interests." There is no way in which the actions of either of us could be classified as "egoistic" or "altruistic." Good can be seen only in its opposition to evil. How can one say inside a "society" in which no one is replaceable, that what is good for one partner may be bad for another? It is inside such a "moral society," the "moral party of two," that my responsibility cannot be fathomed and "fulfilled"; it feels unlimited and becomes a whole life responsibility. It is under this condition that the command needs no argument to gain authority, nor the support of a threat of sanctions. It feels like a command, and an unconditional command at that.

But all this changes with the appearance of the Third. Now, true society appears, and the naive, unruled, and unruly moral impulse, simultaneously the necessary and the sufficient condition of the "moral party," does not suffice anymore.

THE MORAL PARTY BROKEN INTO

In society, unlike in the universe of two, Levinas's postulate of putting ethics "before ontology" sounds odd. In the party of two, priority means "being before," not "being better." The pristine, naive togetherness of I and the Other is neither pristine nor naive. There are now a lot of questions that can be, and are asked about that togetherness. Love now has self-love to reckon with: *Für-sein* has the *Mitsein* as its sometime competitor and always as its judge. Responsibility desperately seeks it limits; it is flatly denied that the "command" is "unconditional." Baffled, the moral impulse pauses and awaits instructions.

Now I live in a world populated, as Agnes Heller wittily put it, by "All, Some, Many and their companions. Now there is Difference, Number, Knowledge, Now, Limit, Time, Space, Freedom, Justice and Injustice, and, certainly, Truth and Falsity."[2] These are the main characters in the play called Society, and all of them stay far beyond the reach of my moral (now, merely intuitive) wisdom, apparently immune to whatever I may do, powerful against my powerlessness, immortal against my morality. They are secure against my blunders, so that my blunders harm me only, not Them. They are the characters who act now: as Heller puts it, "Reason reasons, Imagination imagines, Will wills, and Language speaks (*die Sprache spricht*). This is how characters became actors in their own right. They come into existence and live independently of their creators."[3] And all this had been made possible, nay inescapable, by the entry of the Third, that is, due to the "moral party" outgrowing its "natural" size and turning into society.

The Third is also an Other, but not the Other we encountered at the "primal scene" staged by Levinas in which the moral play, not knowing itself to be a moral play, was scripted and directed by my responsibility alone. The "otherness" of the Third is of an entirely different order. The two "others" reside in different worlds. They are two planets each with its own orbit that does not cross with the orbit of the other, Other. Neither would survive the swapping of orbits. They do not converse with each other; when one speaks, the other one does not listen. If the other one did listen, she would not understand what she heard. Each one can feel at home only if the other one steps aside, or better still stays outside. The Other who is a Third can be met with only if we have already left the realm of Levinas's morality, and entered another world, the realm of Social Order, which is ruled by Justice. As Levinas put it, "this is the domain of the State, of justice, of politics. Justice differs from charity in that it allows the intervention of some form of equality and measure, a set of social rules established according to the judgment of the

---

2   Agnes Heller, *A Philosophy of History in Fragments* (Oxford: Blackwell, 1993), 85.
3   Ibid.

State, and thus also of politics. In the domain of justice, the relationship between me and the other must leave room for the third, i.e., a sovereign judge who decides between two equals."[4]

What makes the Third so unlike the Other that we met in the pristine moral encounter? In his assessment of the sociological meaning for the role of the third element, Georg Simmel brought the unique and seminal role of the Third down to the fact that in any triad, "the third element is at such a distance from the other two that there exist no properly sociological interactions which concern all three elements alike."[5] Mutual distance, when void of encounters, congeals into "objectivity" (disinterestedness or non-commitment). From the vantage point of the Third, what was a "moral party" becomes a group, an entity endowed with a life of its own, a totality which is "greater than the sum of its parts."[6] Thus the selves can be set and seen against the "totality" and their motives against the "interest of the whole." The selves turn into individuals who are comparable, measurable and can be judged by extra-personal, "statistically average" or "normative" standards. Under this condition, the Third is firmly placed in the position of the potential jury or umpire. Against the moral selves' hopelessly subjective and thus non-rational propulsions, the Third may now set the objective criteria of rational interests. The asymmetry of the moral relationship is all but gone. The social partners are now equal, and exchangeable, and replaceable. Actors have now to explain what they do, lay down and stand up to arguments that are made, justify themselves by reference to standards that are not of their own making. The site is cleared for norms, laws, ethical rules, and courts of justice.

And that site must be build upon, and urgently. Objectivity, that Trojan Horse of the Third, has delivered a mortal, or at least potentially terminal blow to the affection that moved the moral partners. "A third mediating element deprives conflicting claims of their affective qualities," says Simmel; but it also deprives affection of its authority as the life-guide. Reason, understood as the enemy of passion, must step in lest disorientation and chaos should rule. Reason is what we name the ex post-facto accounts of actions from which passion of the naive past has been drained. Reason is what we hope will tell us what to do when passions have been tamed or extinguished. We cannot live without reason once the survival of the "group" is something

4   Roger-Pol Droit, "Un entretien avec Emmanuel Levinas," *Le Monde* (June 2, 1992).
5   Georg Simmel, *The Sociology of Georg Simmel* (Glencoe: Free Press, 1950), 145.
6   Ibid.

else than the life of the Other that is sustained by my responsibility: once the unique Other has dissolved in the otherness of the Many. It is now a matter between my life and life of the many. Survival of the many and my own survival being two different Survivals, I might have become an "individual," but the Other has most certainly forfeited her individuality and is dissolved in a categorical stereotype. My being-for has been split into the potentially conflicting tasks of self-preservation and the preservation of the group.

When the Other dissolves in the many, the first thing to be washed out is the Face. The Other(s) is/are now faceless. They are persons (persona refers to mask, and masks, e.g., classes, stereotypes, that hide rather than reveal faces). It is the mask that determines who I am dealing with and what my responses ought to be. I have to learn the meaning of each kind of mask and memorize the responses each one calls for. But even then I cannot be totally secure. Masks may be taken on and off, they hide more than they disclose. The innocent confidence of moral drive has been replaced by the unquenchable anxiety of uncertainty. With the advent of the Third, fraud crawls in, more horrifying in its premonition than in its confirmed presence, more paralyzing still for being a non exorcizable specter. In society, one has to live with this anxiety. Whether I like it or not, I must trust the masks, not that I can trust them. Trust is the way of living with uncertainty, not a way to dispose of anxiety.

The "moral party of two" is a vast space for morality. It is large enough to accommodate the ethical self in its full flight. It scales the highest peaks of saintliness and reaches down to the underwater reefs of moral life, the traps that must be avoided by the self before (as much as and after) it takes responsibility for its responsibility. But that party is too cramped a space for the human-being-in-the-world. It has room for no more than two actors. It leaves out most of the things that fill the daily bustle of every human being: pursuit of survival and self-aggrandizement, rational consideration of ends and means, calculation of gains and losses, pleasure, or power in politics and economics. To be in the moral space, one needs to re-enter it. Re-entry can be accomplished only by taking time-off from daily business, by bracketing off time in order to come back to the moral party of two. But can we make a comeback? The party is so starkly different from the one described by Levinas "before ontology." I and the Other must derobe or be derobed of all social trappings, stripped of status, social distinctions, handicaps, positions, or roles. We must once more be neither rich nor poor, high or lowly, mighty or disempowered. We must be reduced to the bare essentiality of common humanity which, in Levinas's moral universe, was given to us at birth.[7]

MORALITY'S FIGHT FOR SURVIVAL

The moral self, as it is constituted inside Levinas's moral universe, cannot but feel uncomfortable the moment the moral party of two is gate-crashed by the Third. But it is not just the moral self that feels uncomfortable, so does its producer and director, Levinas himself. There is no better proof of his discomfort than the obsessive urgency, in later writings and interviews, to return to the "problem of the Third" and to the possibility of salvaging his description of the ethical relationship in the "presence of the Third party." There is a remarkable similarity between his attempts as he grew older to bring back into the picture (with zeal and success) what he struggled to exclude all his life, and Husserl's attempts to accommodate inter-subjectivity in the transcendental subjectivity that, all his life, he had tried to purify of all "intercontaminations" (never to anybody's, and least of all to his own, full satisfaction). The question was: is it necessary to cut the Gordian knot also in the case of Levinasian ethics? Can an ethic, which is born and grows old in the safe seclusion of a greenhouse-for-two, withstand the assault by a Third party? And more to the point, can the moral capacity, made to the measure of the responsibility for the Other as Face, be vigorous enough to carry an entirely different burden of responsibility for the "Other as such," i.e., the Other without a Face?

Already in 1954, in "Le Moi et la Totalité," Levinas signaled an essential discontinuity between the self's relation to the Other, out of respect for the Other's freedom and integrity, and the relation towards the concept of the human being. In that second domain, the domain of totality, the other is "a free being to whom I may do harm by violating his liberty."[8] "Totality," sadly concluded Levinas, "cannot constitute itself without injustice."[9] What is more, by itself the "totality" would not set me on the road to justice. Very much in the Husserlian spirit, Levinas suggested that "justice does not result from the normal play of injustices. It comes from the outside, 'through the door,' from

---

7   Ibid.
8   Id., "Le Moi et la Totalité," in *Entre nous: Essais sur le penser à l'autre* (Paris: Editions Grasset, 1991), 23–48.
9   Ibid., 38.

beyond the melee and appears as a principle external to history."[10] Justice comes in defiance of the "theories of justice which are forged in the course of social struggles, in which moral ideas express the needs of one society or one class"; it appeals to the "ideal of justice," which requires that all needs-all of them after all are but relative-be abandoned on "approaching the absolute."[11] Justice comes, therefore, not out of history, but as a judgment made on history: "Human is the world in which it is possible to judge history."[12]

Almost thirty years passed, and in "La souffrance inutile" (1982), old worries were restated more bluntly: "Interhumanity in the proper sense lies in one's non-indifference towards the others, one's responsibility for the others, but before the reciprocity of such responsibility is inscribed into the impersonal law."[13] For this reason, "the interhuman perspective may survive, but may be also lost in the political order of the City or in the Law which establishes mutual obligations of the citizens."[14] There are—so it now seems—two mutually independent, perhaps even unconnected orders: political and ethical.

> Political order—whether pre- or post-ethical—which inaugurates the social contract is neither the sufficient condition nor the necessary outcome of ethics. In the ethical position "I" is distinct from the citizen and from that individual who, in his natural selfishness, precedes all order yet from whom political philosophy, from Hobbes onward, tried to derive or derived the social and political order of the City.[15]

It is that time-honored philosophical strategy Levinas declared mistaken and therefore vain, but what is there to replace it, given the separation and, indeed, virtual absence of communication between the two orders?

In the same year an interview with Levinas appeared under the title "Philosophie, Justice et Amour."[16] Pressed by the questions put to him by R. Fornet and A. Gomez, Levinas seemed to moderate his position, allowing for certain mutual dependency between political and ethical orders. "Without the or-

10 Ibid., 41.
11 Ibid.
12 Ibid.
13 Id., "La souffrance inutile," in *Entre nous*, p. 111.
14 Ibid.
15 Ibid.,
16 Id., "Philosophie, Justice et Amour" in *Entre nous*, 113–32.

der of justice," he consented, "there would be no limit to my responsibility," and thus cohabitation with Others as generalized citizens would not be possible.[17] "But," he hastened to qualify, "only departing from my relation to the Face, from me in front of the Other, may one speak of the State's legitimacy or illegitimacy."[18] Ethics born of the moral party of two shall sit in judgment when it comes to decide the State's legitimacy. And then, in response to the straightforward question "do you think that such a (just) state is possible," came the equally straightforward answer: "Yes, an agreement between the ethics and the State is possible. The just State will be the work of just people and the saints, rather than of propaganda and preaching..."[19]

"De l'Unicité" appeared two years later.[20] Here, an attempt is made to treat the difference between the ethical and the formal or legal in a systematic way. The difference is traced to the loss of the uniqueness of the ethical Other, the Other's dissolution in the similarity of the Individual as citizen. Such dissolution is a foregone conclusion since the appearance of "the Third"—someone different from the one close to me (*mon prochain*), but at the same time close to the one close to me and moreover close to me in his own right, is an "also close." Now there are "they." They, those various others, do things to each other, may harm each other and make each other suffer. This is the hour of justice. The uniqueness of the Other won't help much now. One needs to appeal to a force one could do without before, i.e., to reason, that allows us first, to "compare the incomparable," and second, to "impose a measure upon the extravagance of the infinite generosity of the 'for the Other.'"[21] But note, this recourse to Reason feels necessary thanks precisely to the memory of that "uniqueness" of the Other which was experienced in the moral relationship; it is because each of the multiple others is unique in her challenge to my responsibility, in her claim on my "being for," that the new situation "postulates judgement and thus objectivity, objectivation, thematization, and synthesis. One needs arbitrating institutions and the political power that sustains them. Justice requires the foundation of the State. In this lies the necessity of the reduction of human uniqueness to the particularity of a human individual, to the condition of the citizen." That latter particularity waters down the splendor of ethically formed uniqueness; but without

17 Ibid., 115.
18 Ibid.
19 Ibid., 131.
20 Id., "De L'Unicité," in *Entre nous*, 195–204.
21 Ibid., 202.

that already-ethically-experienced uniqueness it would itself be inconceivable, it would never come to pass.[22]

Justice is in many ways disloyal to its ethical origins, unable to preserve its heritage in all its inner richness—but it won't be justice if it forgets its origins and tries to preserve its birthmark. "It cannot abandon that uniqueness to political history, which finds itself subjected to the determinism of power, reason of the State and the seduction of the totalitarian temptations."[23] It must measure itself over and over again by the standards of original uniqueness, however unattainable such standards may be among the multiplicity of citizens. Hence the indelible trait of all justice is its dissatisfaction with itself: "justice means constant revision of justice, expectation of a better justice."[24] Justice, one may say, must exist perpetually in a condition of noch nichtgeworden, setting itself standards higher than those already practiced.

The same paradox is pondered at length in the extensive conversations with François Poirie. In the presence of the Third, said Levinas, "we leave what I call the order of ethics, or the order of saintliness or the order of mercy, or the order of love, or the order of charity where the other human being concerns me regardless of the place he occupies in the multitude, and even regardless of our shared quality as individuals of the human species. He concerns me as one close to me, as the first to come. He is unique."[25] Beyond this order stretches the realm of choice, proportion, judgement and comparison. Comparison already entails the first act of violence: it is defiance of uniqueness. This violence cannot be avoided since among the multiplicity of others certain divisions (assignment to classes, to categories) are necessary because they are "justified divisions." Ethics demands, one may say, certain self-limitation; for the ethical demand to be fulfilled, certain sacred axioms of ethics must be sacrificed.

The liberal state, said Levinas—the state grounded on the principle of human rights—is the implementation, and conspicuous manifestation, of that contradiction. Its function is nothing less than to "limit the original mercy from which justice originated." But "the internal contradiction" of the liberal state finds its expression in perceiving "beyond and above all justice already incorporated in the regime, a justice more just..." "Justice in the lib-

22 Ibid.
23 Ibid.
24 Ibid., 203.
25 François Poirie, *Emmanuel Levinas: Qui êtes-vous?* (Lyon: Editions la Manufacture, 1987).

eral state is never definitive." "Justice is awakened by charity—such charity which is before justice but also after it." "Concern with human rights is not the function of the State. It is a non-state institution inside the State—an appeal to humanity which the State has not accomplished yet." Concern with human rights is an appeal to the "surplus of charity," one may say, to something larger than any letter of Law, than anything that the State has done so far. State-administered justice is born of charity gestated and groomed within the primary ethical situation. And yet justice may be administered only if it never stops being prompted by its original *spiritus movens*; if it knows of itself as of a never ending chase of a forever elusive goal—the re-creation among the individuals/citizens of that uniqueness which is the birthmark of the Other as Face; if it knows that it cannot "match the kindness which gave it birth and keeps it alive"—but if it knows as well that it cannot ever stop trying to do just that.[26]

Just what can one learn from Levinas's exploration of the "world of the Third," the "world of the multiplicity of others" the social world? One can learn, to start with, that this world of the social is, simultaneously, the legitimate offspring, and a distortion, of the moral world. The idea of justice is conceived at the moment of encounter between the experience of uniqueness (as given in the moral responsibility for the Other) and the experience of multiplicity of others (as given in social life). It cannot be conceived under any other circumstances, it needs both parents and to both of them it is genetically related, even if the genes, though being complementary, also contain contradictory genetic messages. Thus, paradoxically, morality is the school of justice even if the category of justice is alien to it and within the moral relationship redundant (justice comes into its own together with comparison, but there is nothing to compare when the Other is encountered as unique). The "primal scene" of ethics is thereby also the primal, ancestral scene of social justice.

One learns also that justice becomes necessary when the moral impulse, quite selfsufficient inside the moral party of two, is found to be a poor guide once it ventures beyond the boundaries of that party. The infinity of the moral responsibility, the unlimitedness (even the silence!) of moral demand simply cannot be sustained when "the Other" appears in the plural (one may say that there is an inverse ratio between the infinity of "being for" and the infin-

---

26   Emmanuel Levinas, "L'Autre, Utopie et Justice," in *Entre nous*, 235.

ity of the others). But it is that moral impulse which makes justice necessary: it resorts to justice in the name of self-preservation, though while doing so it risks being cut down, trimmed, maimed or watered down.

CAN ETHICS EARN ITS SALVATION?

In the *Dialogue sur le penser-à-l'autre*, the interviewer asked Levinas[27]:

> As far as I am an ethical subject, I am responsible for everything in everybody; my responsibility is infinite. Is not it so that such a situation is unlivable for me, and for the other, whom I risk to terrorize with my ethical voluntarism? Does not it follow that ethics is impotent in its will to do good?[28]

To which Levinas gave the following answer:

> I do not know whether such a situation is unlivable. Certainly, such a situation is not what one would call agreeable, pleasant to live with, but it is good. What is extremely important — and I can assert this without being myself a saint, and without pretending to be a saint — is to be able to say that a human truly deserving that name, in its European sense, derived from the Greeks and the Bible, is a human being who considers saintliness the ultimate value, an unassailable value.[29]

This value is not surrendered once the uncompromising ethical requirement of "being-for" is replaced by a somewhat diluted and less stressful code of justice. It remains what it was, the ultimate value, reserving to itself the right to invigilate, monitor, and censure all deals entered into, in the name of justice. Constant tension and never becalmed suspicion rule in the relationship between ethics and the just State. Ethics is not a derivative of the State; the ethical authority does not derive from the State powers to legislate and to enforce the Law. It precedes the State; it is the sole source of the State's legitimacy and the ultimate judge of that legitimacy. The State, one may say, is justifiable only as a vehicle or instrument of ethics.

---

27 Id., "Dialogue sur le penser-il'autre," in *Entre nous*, 220–27.
28 Ibid., 222.
29 Ibid.

This is much—but far too little to account for the complex social/political processes that mediate between individual moral impulses and the overall ethical effects of political actions. Levinas's view of the ethical origins of justice and the State itself as an instrument of justice (and, obliquely, of ethics itself) neither is nor pretends to be a sociological statement. It is in its intention and its final shape a phenomenological insight into the meaning of justice; or it can perhaps be interpreted as an "etiological myth," setting the case for the subordination of the State to ethical principles and its subjection to the ethical criteria of evaluation. It can hardly be seen, though, as an insight into the process through which ethical responsibility for the other comes (or does not come, as the case may be) to be implemented on a generalized scale through the works of the State and its institution. It goes a long way towards explaining concerns with the plight of the "generalized other"—the far away Other, the Other distant in space and time; but it says little about the ways and means through which that concern may bring practical effects, and even less about the reasons for such effects falling so saliently short of needs and expectations, or not being visible at all.

Levinas's writings offer rich inspiration for the analysis of the endemic aporia of moral responsibility. They offer nothing comparable, though, for the scrutiny of the aporetic nature of justice. They do not confront the possibility that, as with the case of assuming moral responsibility for the Other, the work of the institutions that Levinas wished to be dedicated to the promotion of justice can fall short of moral ideals or even have consequences detrimental to moral values. Neither did he allow for the possibility that such detrimental consequences may be more than just side-effects of mistakes and neglect, being rooted instead in the very way such institutions can—must—operate to remain viable.

Quite a few insights into the latter issue can be found in the work of Hans Jonas. Unlike Levinas, Jonas puts our present moral quandary in historical perspective, representing it as an event in time, rather than an extemporal, metaphysical predicament. According to Jonas, for the greater part of human history the gap between "micro" and "macro" ethics did not present a problem; the short reach of the moral drive was not fraught with terminal dangers for the simple reason that the consequences of human deeds (given the technologically determined scale of human action) were equally limited. In recent times, however, the magnitude of immediate and oblique consequences of human action has grown exponentially and the growth of theory has not been matched by a similar expansion of human moral capacity. What we can do now, may have profound and radical effects on distant lands and distant generations we can neither explore nor imagine. Yet the same development which put in the hands of human kind powers, tools, and weapons of unprecedented magnitude, requiring close normative regulation, "eroded the foundations from which norms could be derived; it has destroyed the very idea of norm as such."[30] Both departures are the work of science that brooks no limits to what humans can do, nor easily accepts that not all that could be done should be done. The ability to do something is, for science and for technology, science's executive arm and is all the reason needed for doing it. As Jonas points out, while new powers need new ethics, and need it badly, they simultaneously undermine the very possibility of satisfying that need by denying ethical considerations the right to interfere with, let alone to arrest, their own infinite, self-propelling growth.

This blind tendency must be reversed, Jonas demands. But how? By working out a new ethics, made to the measure of new human powers. This is a Kantian answer: what we need to pull ourselves out of our present quandary and stave off even greater catastrophes, in Jonas's view, are certain rules so apodeictically true that every sane person would accept them. We need, in other words, a sort of a categorical imperative mark two—like, for instance, "Act so that the effects of your action are compatible with the permanence of genuine human life."[31]

Working out a categorical imperative for our present predicament is not easy, though. First, negation of any of the candidates for the "imperative mark two" status, unlike the original, Kantian imperative, does not entail logical contradiction. Secondly, it is notoriously difficult, nay impossible, to know for sure which actions inspired by the progress of technoscience are, and which are not "compatible with the permanence of genuine human life"—at least not before the damage, often irreparable, has been done. Even in the unlikely case of the new categorical imperative having been awarded unchallenged normative authority, the vexing question of its application would still remain open: how to argue convincingly that a controversial development should be stopped, if its effects cannot be measured in advance with such a degree of precision, with that near algorithmic certainty, which

---

30 Hans Jonas, *The Imperative of Responsibility* (Chicago: University of Chicago Press, 1984), 22.
31 Ibid., 11.

scientific reason would be inclined to respect? If a truly algorithmic calculation of the looming dangers is not in the cards, Jonas suggests, we should settle for its second best substitute, a "heuristics of fear": to try our best to visualize the most awesome and the most durable among the consequences of given technological action.[32] Above all, we need to apply the "principle of uncertainty": "The prophecy of doom is to be given greater heed than the prophecy of bliss." We need, Jonas implies, a kind of "systematic pessimism ethics"[33] so that we may err, if at all, solely on the side of caution.[34]

Kant's trust in the grip of ethical law rested on the conviction that there are arguments of reason which every reasonable person, being a reasonable person, must accept; the passage from ethical law to moral action led through rational thought—and to smooth the passage one needed only to take care of the non-contradictory rationality of the law, counting for the rest on the endemic rational faculties of moral actors. In this respect, Jonas stays faithful to Kant-though he is the first to admit that nothing as uncontroversial as Kant's categorical imperative (that is, no principle which cannot be violated without violating simultaneously the logical law of contradiction) can be articulated in relation to the new challenge to human ethical faculties. For Jonas, as for Kant, the crux of the matter is the capacity of the legislative reason; and the promotion, as well as the eventual universality, of ethical conduct is ultimately a philosophical problem and the task of the philosophers. For Jonas, as for Kant, the fate of ethics is fully and truly in the hands of Reason and its spokesmen, the philosophers. In this scheme of things there is no room left for the possibility that reason may, in some other of its incarnations, militate against what is, in its name, promoted by ethical philosophers.

In other words, there is no room left for the logic of human interests, and the logic of social institutions—those organized interests whose function is, in practice if not by design, to do exactly the opposite to what Kantian ethical philosophy would expect them to do: namely, to make the bypassing of ethical restrictions feasible and ethical considerations irrelevant to the action. Neither is there room left for the otherwise trivial sociological observation that for the arguments to be accepted they need to accord with interests in addition (or instead of) being rationally flawless. There is no room either for another equally trivial phenomenon of "unanticipated consequences" of hu-

32 Ibid., 26, 202.
33 Ibid., 31.
34 Ibid.

man action—of deeds that bring results left out of account, or unthought-of at the time the action was undertaken. Nor is there room for the relatively simple guess that when interests are many and at odds with each other, any hope that a certain set of principles will eventually prevail and will be universally obeyed must seek support in a sober analysis of social and political forces capable of incurring that victory.

I suggest that a mixture of all those factors—overlooked or ignored and left out of account in Jonas's search for the new ethics—can be blamed for the curious paradox of our times, in which the growing awareness of the dangers ahead goes hand in hand with the growing impotence in preventing them or alleviating the gravity of their impact. In theory, we seem to know that if catastrophe is to be averted, the presently unruly forces must be kept in check and controlled by other factors than endemically disperse and diffuse, as well as short-sighted, interests. In practice, however, the consequences of human actions rebound with a blind, elemental force reminiscent more of earthquakes, floods, and tornadoes than of the model of rational and self-monitored behavior. As Daniele Sallenave has reminded us, Jean-Paul Sartre could aver a few decades ago that "there are no such things as natural disasters"; but today natural disasters have turned into the prototype and model of all the miseries that afflict the world, and one could as well reverse Sartre's statement and say that "there are no other than natural catastrophes."[35] Not just the dramatic changes in the degree of livability of our natural habitat (pollution of air and water, global warming, ozone holes, acid rains, salination, or dessication of the soil etc.), but also the thoroughly human aspects of global conditions (wars, demographic explosions, mass migrations and displacements, outbursts of ethnic hostilities, growing gaps between rich and poor, social exclusion of large categories of population) come unannounced, catch us unaware and seem utterly oblivious to the anguished cries for help and to the most frantic efforts to design, let alone to provide, the remedy.

ETHICS UNDER SIEGE

But a categorical imperative mark two and a heuristics of fear do not move us to follow Jonas's ethical strategy. A dearth of ethical knowledge and understanding cannot be blamed for what is happening. No one except luna-

---

35   Daniele Sallenave, "L'alibi de la compassion," *Le Monde Diplomatique* (July 1995): 32.

tic fringes would seriously argue that it is good and beneficial to pollute the atmosphere, to pierce the ozone layer, to wage wars, to overpopulate the land, to deprive people of their livelihood or to make them into homeless vagabonds. Yet all this happens despite its consensual, almost universal and vociferous condemnation. Some factors other than ethical ignorance, or philosophers' inability to agree on principles, must be at work if the grinding, systemic consistency of the global damage outmatches the cohesion of ethical indignation. One may sensibly surmise that those other factors are entrenched in aspects of social reality that are unaffected by ethical philosophy, or are unable to withstand or bypass its pressures; or better still, to render ethical demands inaudible or — if audible — ineffective.

Among such factors, the increasingly deregulated market forces, exempt from all effective political control and guided solely by the pressures of competitiveness must be awarded the pride of place. Thanks to technical advances aided and abetted by the progressive dismantling of political constraints, capital is now free to move whenever and wherever it desires. The potential promoters and guardians of social justice have been deprived of the economic muscle to enforce ethical principles. Political institutions stay local, while the real powers which decide the shape of things have acquired a genuine ex-territoriality. As Manual Castells puts it in his monumental three-volume study of The Information Age, power in the form of capital, and particularly financial capital, flows — while politics remains tied to the ground bearing all the constraints imposed by its local character.[36] Power has been, we may say, "emancipated from politics." But when this happens, the State in which Levinas invested his hopes for the promotion of morally inspired justice becomes wishful thinking. It is increasingly difficult to locate an agency capable of undertaking the task of implementing the new categorical imperative that Jonas sought. As a consequence, we may say that the problem of applying Levinas's ethics to the troubles of a contemporary world is first and foremost the question of an agency gap.

Mobility has become the most powerful and most coveted stratifying factor; it is the stuff out of which new, increasingly worldwide, social, political, economic, and cultural hierarchies are daily built and rebuilt. The mobility acquired by the owners and managers of capital is new, indeed unprecedented, in its radical unconditionality and its disconnection of power from

---

36　Manual Castells, *The Information Age* (Oxford: Blackwell, 1998).

obligation. Mobility disconnects employers from duties towards employees, towards the younger, weaker and yet unborn generations—towards the self-reproduction of the living conditions of all. In short, mobility provides freedom from the duty to contribute to daily life and the perpetuation of the community. There is a new asymmetry emerging between the exterritorial nature of power and the continuing territoriality of the "whole life" of a locality—which the now unanchored powers, able to move at short notice or without warning, are free to exploit and abandon. Shedding responsibility for consequences is the most coveted and cherished gain that the new mobility brings to free-floating, locally unbound capital. The costs of coping with consequences need not be counted in the calculation of the "effectiveness" of investment.

This new freedom of capital brings to mind the absentee landlords of yore, notorious for their resented neglect of the needs of the populations that fed them. Creaming off the "surplus product" from the land they owned was their sole interest. There is certainly some similarity here but the comparison does not do full justice to the kind of freedom from worry and responsibility which the mobile capital of the late twentieth century has acquired, that absentee landlords could not secure.

In contradistinction to the absentee landlords of early modern times, the late-modern capitalists and land-brokers (thanks to the new mobility of their by now liquid resources) do not encounter limits sufficiently real—solid, tough, resistant enough—to enforce compliance. The limits that can make themselves felt are those administratively imposed on the free movement of capital and money. Such limits are few and far between and the handful that remain are under tremendous pressure. The moment when those on the receiving side—targeted or accidental victims of the profit-making drive—try to flex their muscle and make their strength felt, the capital has little difficulty packing its tents and finding more hospitable environment. Capital has no need to engage with consequences, if avoidance will do.

Rather than homogenizing the human condition, the technological and political annulment of temporal/spatial distances tends to polarize it. The emancipation of certain human beings from territorial constraints renders community-generating meanings extraterritorial, and at the same time, denudes the territory of its meaning and its identity-endowing capacity, yet those left behind go on being confined to it. For some people capital provides unprecedented freedom, for others, it portends the impossibility to appropriate and domesticate the locality from which they have little chance of cutting themselves free in order to move elsewhere. If distances no longer mean very much, localities lose much of their meaning. Some people move out of a locality at will, while others watch helplessly as the ground washes out from under their feet.

Information floats independently from its carriers. Bodies shift and rearrange in physical space. For some people—for the mobile elite, the elite of mobility—that means literally, the "dephysicalization" or the new weightlessness of power. Elites travel in space and travel faster than ever before, but the spread and density of the power web they weave is not dependent on that travel. Thanks to the new "body-less-ness" of power, in its mainly financial form, the power-holders become truly extraterritorial even if, bodily, they happen to stay "in place." Their power is not "out of this world," not out of the physical world; they do build heavily guarded homes and offices. They are extraterritorial in the sense that they are free from intrusion, from unwelcome neighbors, cut off from what may be called a local community and inaccessible to whoever is, unlike them, confined to it.

And so another gap yawns—alongside that of the agency. This gap grows and widens between the meaning-making elites and all the rest. In the same way that today's power-holders remind us of pre-modern absentee landlords, so the learned, cultivated and culturally creative elites show striking similarity to the similarly extraterritorial, Latin-speaking and writing scholastic elites of medieval Europe. It seems that the modern nation-building episode was the sole exception to a much more permanent rule. The excruciatingly difficult task of reforging the mishmash of languages, cults, lores, customs, and ways of life into homogenic nations under homogenic rule, for a time brought the learned elites into direct engagement with "the people." (Both "intellectuals" and the "people," as well as the link between knowledge and power, are modern inventions!). With that episode by and large over at least in the affluent part of the globe, the home of the most influential section of the cultural elite there seems to be no need for continuing that engagement. Cyberspace, securely anchored in web sites on the Internet, is the contemporary equivalent of mediaeval Latin, i.e., the space that the learned elite of today inhabit. There is little the residents of that space could talk about with those still hopelessly mired in an all-too-real physical space. Nor could they gain anything from that dialogue. The word "people" is quickly falling out of fashion, except during electoral campaigns.

The new states, and longer-living ones in their present condition, are no longer expected to perform most of the functions once seen as the *raison d'être* of nation-state bureaucracies. The function that has most conspicuously dropped out, or was torn out, of the hands of the orthodox state, is the maintenance (as Cornelius Castoriadis put it in *La montée de l'insignifiance*) of a dynamic equilibrium between the rhythms of the growth of consumption and the elevation of productivity. This task led sovereign states at various times to impose intermittently import or export bans, custom barriers, or state-managed Keynes-style stimulation of internal demand.[37] The control of dynamic equilibrium is now beyond the means, and indeed beyond the ambitions, of almost all so-called sovereign (in the strictly order-policing sense) states. The very distinction between the internal and the global market, or more generally between the "inside" and the "outside" of the state, is exceedingly difficult to maintain in any but the most narrow, "territory-and-population policing" sense.

All three legs of the sovereignty tripod—economic, military and cultural—have been shattered. The state is no longer capable of balancing its books, guarding its territory or promoting its distinctive identities; contemporary states turn more and more into executors and plenipotentiaries of forces that they have no hope of controlling politically. In the incisive verdict of a radical Latin American political analyst (reported in *Le Monde Diplomatique*, August 1997), thanks to the new "porousness" of all allegedly "national" economies, and to the ephemeral, elusive, non-territorial dimensions of space in which they operate, global financial markets impose their laws and precepts on the planet. Globalization is nothing more than a totalitarian extension of their logic on all aspects of life. States have not enough resources or freedom of movement to withstand the pressure, for the simple reason that "a few minutes is enough for enterprises and the states themselves to collapse" (as witnessed quite recently, we may add, in the case of Mexico, Malaysia, or South Korea). In the cabaret of globalization, the state goes through a striptease and by the end of the performance it is left with the bare necessities: its powers of repression. With its material basis destroyed, its sovereignty and independence annulled, its political class effaced, the nation-state becomes a simple security service for mega-companies. The new masters of

---

37 Cornelius Castoriadis, *La montée de l'insignifiance* (Paris: Seuil, 1996).

the world have no need to govern directly. National governments are charged with the task of administering affairs on their behalf.

The "economy" is being progressively exempted from political control; indeed the prime meaning conveyed by the term "economy" is that of "the area of the non-political." The state is not allowed to touch what concerns economic life: any attempt in this direction is met with prompt and furious punitive action by the world markets: hence, the economic impotence of the state. According to the calculations of Rene Passet, purely speculative intercurrency financial transactions reach the total volume of 300 billion dollars a day. This is fifty times greater than the volume of all commercial exchanges and almost equal to the total of one 500 billion dollars for the reserves of all the "national banks" of the world.[38] "No state therefore," Passet comments, "can resist for more than a few days the speculative pressures of the 'market.'" The sole economic task the state is allowed, is to handle and secure an equilibrated budget by policing and keeping in check the local pressures for more vigorous state intervention in the running of businesses and for the defense of the population from the more sinister consequences of market anarchy. As Jean-Paul Fitoussi has recently pointed out:

> Such programs, though, cannot be implemented unless in one way or another economy is taken out from the field of politics. A ministry of finances remains certainly a necessary evil, but ideally one would dispose of the ministry of economic affairs (that is, of the governing of economy). In other words, the government should be deprived of its responsibility for macroeconomic policy.[39]

For their liberty of movement and for their unconstrained freedom to pursue their ends, global finance, trade and information industries depend on the political fragmentation, the *morcellement*, of the world scene. They all, one may say, have developed vested interests in weak states, that is, in states that are weak but nevertheless remain states. Deliberately or subconsciously, such interstate, supra-local institutions—as have been brought into being and are allowed to act with the consent of the global capital exert coordinated pressures on all member or dependent states to systematically destroy

---

38 René Passet, *Le Monde Diplomatique* (July 1997).
39 Jean-Paul Fitoussi, *Le Monde* (August 29, 1997).

everything which could stem or slow down the free movement of capital and limit market liberty. Throwing open the gates and abandoning any thought of autonomous economic policy is the preliminary condition of eligibility for financial assistance from world banks and monetary funds, a condition that gains meek compliance. Weak states are precisely what the New World Order, all too often looking suspiciously like a new world disorder, needs to sustain and reproduce itself. Weak, quasi states are easily reduced to the (useful) role of local police precincts, securing the modicum of order required for the conduct of business; it need not be feared that they will put the brakes on the global companies' freedom.

The separation of economy from politics, and the exemption of the first from regulatory intervention of the second resulting in the disempowerment of politics as an effective agency, augurs much more than just a shift in the distribution of social power. As Claus Offe points out, political agency as such, i.e., "the capacity to make collectively binding choices and to carry them out"[40] has become problematic "Instead of asking what is to be done, we might more fruitfully explore whether there is anybody capable of doing whatever needs to be done."[41] Since "borders have become penetrable" (highly selectively, to be sure), "sovereignties have become nominal, power anonymous, and its locus empty."[42] We have not yet reached the ultimate destination; the process goes on, and seemingly is unstoppable. "The dominant pattern might be described as 'releasing the brakes': deregulation, liberalization, flexibility, increasing fluidity, and facilitating the transactions on the financial real estate and labor markets, easing the tax burden, etc." The more consistently this pattern is applied, the less power remains in the hands of the agency that promotes it; and the less can an increasingly resourceless agency retreat from following the pattern, even if it wished or felt pressed to do so.

One of the seminal consequences of the new global freedom of movement is that it becomes increasingly difficult, perhaps altogether impossible, to re-forge social issues into effective collective action. Sections of societies traditionally charged with the task of re-forging increasingly look the other way; nothing in their own position and socially framed vocations prompts them to take up the role which dropped, or was torn, out of their hands. These two

---

40 Claus Offe, *Modernity and the State: East, West* (Cambridge: Polity Press, 1996), vii.
41 Ibid., viii.
42 Ibid. viii, ixff.

significant departures, taken together, make the present-day world ever less hospitable to Levinas's ethics, while the clarion calls of Hans Jonas bear uncanny resemblance to crying in the wilderness.

THE CASE OF THE NEW POOR

One phenomenon of the contemporary world provides a spectacular case of the overall trend: the fast-growing inequality of income and living conditions (the quality of health, education or housing, life prospects, range of life choices and longevity of life). In the increasingly affluent world, the ranks of the poor are steadily expanding, and in the last decades expanding at a steadily accelerating rate. Growing poverty is universally known and universally condemned; for an important majority, those better off, it is also a matter of shame; there is an urge not to stay idle but to do something to efface the stain on their conscience. Time and again, the miserable lot of the poor is brought dramatically into global awareness by widely publicized cases of famine and destitution, prompting spouts of massive charity. And yet the phenomenon grows instead of going away. Moral sensibility stops short of being reforged in the daily and effective concern with intersocietal, let alone global, justice.

The poor will always be with us (so the popular wisdom insists), but what it means to be poor depends on the kind of "us" the poor are "with." It was not the same to be poor in a society of half a century or more ago. That was a society that needed every single adult member to engage in productive labor. Our society, thanks to the enormous powers accumulated by centuries of labor, may well produce everything needed, and much more, without the participation of a large and growing section of its members. It is one thing to be poor in a society of producers and universal employment; it is quite different to be poor in a society of consumers, in which life projects are built around consumer choices rather than work, professional skills, or jobs. If "being poor" derived its meaning from the condition of being unemployed in an earlier time, today it draws its meaning primarily from the plight of being flawed consumers. This is a difference which truly makes a difference in the way living in poverty is experienced and in the chances and prospects to redeem its misery.

Societies have typically taken a characteristically ambivalent attitude toward the poor, reflected in an uneasy mixture of fear and revulsion on one hand, and pity and compassion on the other. Both ingredients in the social attitude were equally indispensable. The first allowed for the harsh treatment of the poor which the defense of order required; the second underlined the pitiful lot of those who fell below the standards, a lot that made all the hardships of following the norm for the norm-abiding part of the population, pale into insignificance. The latter circumstance awarded the poor a useful role in the promotion of obedience to noxious and stringent social norms of the time. Depending on its specific model of order and norm, each society constructs its poor in its own image, offering different explanations for their presence, finding a different use for the poor and deploying different strategies for tackling the problem of poverty.

Pre-modern Europe came closer than its modern successor to finding an important function for its poor. The poor, like everybody else and everything else in pre-modern Christian Europe, were Children of God—a legitimate and indispensable link in the "Divine Chain of Beings"; as part of God's creation they were, like the rest of the world before its modern desacralisation or "disenchantment," saturated with meaning and purpose. The poor suffered, but their misery made them blessed, since their suffering was repentance for original sin and a warrant of redemption. It was up to the more fortunate to bring succor and relief to the sufferers and so to practice charity and in the process gain their own share in salvation. The presence of the poor was therefore God's gift to everyone else: an occasion to practice self-sacrifice, to live a virtuous life, to repent from sin and to earn heavenly bliss. One can almost say that a society which sought the meaning of earthly life in life-after-death would need to invent another vehicle of personal salvation, were the poor not already at hand.

This was no longer the case in the "disenchanted" world of modernity, in which nothing that was had the right to be merely because of the accident of being there, and in which everything that was had to show a legitimate and reasonable proof of its right to be. Most importantly, the brave new world of modernity was one that set its own rules and took nothing for granted, subjecting everything extant to the incisive scrutiny of reason, recognizing no limits to its own authority and above all rejecting the "power of the dead over the living," the authority of tradition, inherited lore or custom. The projects of order and the norm now replaced the placidly accepted, preordained, Divine Chain of Beings. Unlike the vision it replaced, order and norm were human products; they were designs yet to be implemented by human action things to be yet made or built, not things found and meekly addressed. If inherited reality did not match the projected order, all the worse for reality.

And so the presence of the poor became a problem ("problem" is something which causes discomfort, is illegitimate or abnormal, and thus prompts the urge to "resolve" it—to cure or to remove it). The poor were a threat and an obstacle to order; they also defied the norm.

The poor were double jeopardy. Since their poverty was no more the verdict of Providence, there was no reason why they should humbly and gratefully accept their lot; they had reasons to complain and rebel against the more fortunate, who they blamed for their deprivation. On the other hand, the old Christian ethics of charity appeared now an intolerable burden, a drain on the nation's wealth. The duty to share one's good fortune with those who failed to curry fortune's favors was no longer a sensible investment in life-after-death; charity "did not stand to reason"—certainly not to the reason of the business of life here and now, on earth.

Soon a third threat was added to the other two: the poor who compliantly accepted their plight as Divine verdict and made no effort to extricate themselves from their misery, proved immune to blandishment to factory work and refused to sell their labor once the meager needs they grew accustomed to, and perceived as "natural," had been gratified. The early decades of industrial society were plagued by constant shortages of labor. The poor who were satisfied with their lot, or resigned to it, were a nightmare for industrial entrepreneurs: they were immune and unresponsive to the inducements of regular wages and saw no reason why they should go on bearing with the long hours of drudgery once they had enough bread to see them through the day. A vicious circle began: the poor objecting to their misery spelled rebellion or revolution; the poor reconciled to their misery curbed and hampered the progress of industrial enterprise. Forcing the poor into perpetual factory labor seemed the miraculous way to square the circle.

And so the poor of the industrial era were redefined as the reserve army of labor, employment, steady employment; employment which left no room for mischief, had become a norm—while poverty had been identified with unemployment, breaching of the norm, an anomaly. Under the circumstances, the obvious prescription for curing poverty and nipping it in the bud, was to induce the poor, or force them if need be, to accept the lot of factory labor. The most obvious means to achieve that effect was to deprive the poor of any other source of livelihood: accept the conditions on offer, however repulsive they might be and however deeply you might resent them, or forfeit all hope for a helping hand.

Strictly speaking, given that no alternative was available, preaching about ethical duty was superfluous. And yet the work ethic was viewed almost universally as useful, perhaps indispensable medicine for the triple ailment of poverty, the insufficient supply of labor, and the threat of revolution. Opting for the work ethic was made much easier, indeed it seemed obvious and natural because the middle classes were already converted to it and viewed their own life in its light.

If one follows politicians, economists and other spokesmen for the public mood, one can be excused for getting an impression that the poor of today have retained the function assigned to them in the early years of the new, modern and industrial era as a reserve army of labor. Just as it did in the heyday of industrial expansion, this assignment casts doubt and suspicion on the probity of those not in active service, and points the way to bringing them back into line. This impression is false, though. The philosophy which once tried to grasp and articulate emerging realities of the industrial age has outlived its purpose and lost touch with the new reality emerging at the end of the modern age. The work ethic, which casts the poor in the role of the "reserve army of labor" began its life as a revelation; it leads its posthumous life as a cover-up.

Grooming the poor of today into the laborers for tomorrow used to make economic and political sense: it lubricated the wheels of an industry-based economy and served well the task of "social integration," that is, of order maintenance and normative regulation. Neither of the two senses holds anymore in a postmodern, consumer, society. The present-day economy does not need a massive labor force. It has learned how to increase, not just profits, but the volume of its products while cutting down on labor and its costs. At the same time, the obedience to norm and "social discipline" in general are by and large secured through the allurements and seductions of the commodity market, rather than through state-managed coercion and the drill administered by the network of panoptical institutions. Economically and politically, the late-modern or postmodern society of consumers may thrive, without dragging the bulk of its members through the millstones of industrial labor. For all practical intents and purposes, the poor cease to be a reserve army of labor, and invocations to the work ethic sound increasingly nebulous and out of touch with the realities of the day.

Contemporary society engages its members primarily as consumers; only secondarily, and partly, does it engage them in the role of producers. To meet the norm, to be a fully-fledged member of society, one needs to respond promptly and efficiently to the temptations of the consumer market; one needs to contribute to the "supply-clearing demand" and in the case of economic trouble be part of the "consumer-led recovery." The poor do not fit in: they lack a decent income, credit cards and the prospect of a better time. Accordingly, the norm which is broken by the poor, which makes them "abnormal," is the norm of consumer competence or aptitude, not that of employment. First and foremost, the poor of today are "non-consumers," not "unemployed"; they are defined in the first place through being flawed consumers since the most crucial of the social duties which they do not fulfill is that of the active and effective buyers of goods and services that the market offers. In a book-balancing consumer society, the poor are unequivocally a liability, and by no stretch of the imagination can they be recorded on the side of present or future assets.

And so for the first time in recorded history, the poor are now purely and simply a worry and a nuisance. They have no merits that relieve, let alone balance, their vices. They have nothing to offer in exchange for the "taxpayer's" outlay of resources. They are a bad investment, unlikely ever to repay, let alone bring profit. They are a black hole, sucking in whatever comes near and spitting back nothing—except, perhaps, trouble. Decent and normal members of society—true consumers—want nothing from them and expect nothing. The poor are totally useless. No one who truly counts, speaks, and is heard, needs them. For them, it is zero tolerance. Society would be much better off if the poor just burnt their tents and left. The world would be that much more pleasant without them. The poor are not needed. They are unwanted. And because they are unwanted, they can be, without much regret or compunction, forsaken.

Not surprisingly, the Welfare State is in retreat virtually everywhere. The few countries where its provisions are yet intact or are being dismantled slowly or half-heartedly, are alternatively reproached or ridiculed for their imprudence and obsoleteness by the chorus of current economic authorities. They are warned by economic sages and world banking institutions against the impending "overheating of the economy" and other freshly invented horrors. The sole choice brandished in front of governments by current economic wisdom depicts a choice between fast rising unemployment, as in Europe, and the even faster fall of lower class income, as in the USA.

The poor of today are not only banished from the streets and other public places used by normal people. They are out of sight and out of heart: physical isolation is reinforced with mental separation, resulting in the banishment of the useless, "iniquitous" poor from the universe of moral empathy, the community of human beings, and the world of ethical duty. This is accomplished by rewriting their story, using the language of depravity to replace the language of deprivation. The poor supply the "usual suspects," rounded up when the public hue-and-cry detects a fault in the habitual order. The poor are portrayed as lax, sinful, and devoid of moral standards. The media cheerfully cooperate with the police in presenting to the sensation—greedy public lurid pictures of the crime, drug, and sexual promiscuity infested "criminal elements" who find their shelter in the darkness of mean streets. And so the point is made that the question of poverty is, first and foremost, perhaps solely, the question of law and order—an issue of law breaking. Once it stops being an ethical problem, poverty tends to be criminalized.

All this is bad news for the prospects of moral sensitivity and responsibility for the Other who needs help. This is not the whole story, though, since, as Norberto Bobbio alerts us, "even if we console ourselves by saying that in this part of the world we have created affluence for two-thirds, we cannot close our eyes to the fact that in the majority of countries two-thirds, or even four-fifths or nine-tenths, are experiencing the opposite."[43] And yet most of us, most of the time, do close our eyes.

As Ryszard Kapuscinski, one of the most formidable chroniclers of contemporary living, has recently explained, that effect is achieved by three interconnected expedients consistently applied by the media which preside over the charity fairs during which the plight of the poor is recalled, only to vanish back into oblivion shortly afterwards.[44]

First, the news of a successive famine or another wave of uprooting and enforced homelessness in some far away countries come as a rule coupled with the reminder that the same distant lands where the people "as seen on TV" die of famine and disease are the birthplace of "Asian tigers." It does not matter, that all the "tigers" together embrace no more than a tiny per cent

---

43 Norberto Bobbio, *Destra e Sinistra* (Rome: Donizelli, 1994).
44 Ryszard Kapuscinski, *Lapidarium III* (Warsaw: Czytelnik, 1997).

of the population of Asia alone. They are assumed to demonstrate what was to be proved—that the sorry plight of the hungry and the homeless is their sui generis choice-alternatives are available, but not taken, because they lack industry or resolve. The underlying message is that the poor themselves bear responsibility for their fate. They could, as the "tigers" did, choose a life of work and thrift instead—but apparently decided not to, due to inferior intelligence or the lack of virtue.

Second, the news is so scripted and edited that it reduces the problem of poverty and deprivation to the question of hunger alone. This stratagem achieves two effects in one go: the real scale of poverty is played down (800 million people are permanently undernourished, but something like four billion—two thirds of the world population—live in poverty), and the task ahead is limited to finding food for the hungry. But, as Kapuscinski points out, such a presentation of the problem of poverty (as exemplified by one of *The Economist*'s recent issues analyzing world poverty under the heading "How to Feed the World") "terribly degrades, virtually denies full humanity to people whom we want, allegedly, to help." What the equation "poverty = hunger" conceals, are many other and complex aspects of poverty—"horrible living and housing conditions, illness, illiteracy, aggression, falling apart families, weakening of social bonds, lack of future, and non-productiveness"—afflictions that cannot be cured with high-protein biscuits and powdered milk. Kapuscinski remembers wandering through African townships and villages and meeting children "who begged me not of bread, water, chocolate or toys, but a ballpoint pen, since they went to school and had nothing to write their lessons with."

Let us add that all associations of the horrid pictures of famine presented by the media with the plight of the poor accused of violating the principles of the work ethic, are carefully avoided. People are shown together with their hunger but however the viewers strain their eyes, they would not see a single work tool, plot of arable land or head of cattle in the picture. As if there was no connection between the emptiness of the work ethic's promises in a world that needs no more labor, and the plight of people offered as an outlet for pent-up moral impulses. The work ethic emerges from this exercise unscathed—ready to be used again as a whip to chase the poor nearer home away from the shelter they seek in vain in the Welfare State.

Third, the spectacles of disasters, as presented by the media, support and reinforce the ordinary, daily moral withdrawal in another way, apart from unloading the accumulated supplies of moral sentiments. Their long-term effect is that "the developed part of the world surrounds itself with a sanitary belt of uncommitment; it erects a global Berlin Wall. All information coming from 'out there' are pictures of war, murders, drugs, looting, contagious diseases, refugees and hunger; that is, of something threatening," revolting and repulsive. Only rarely, and in a half-voice with no connection to scenes of civil wars and massacres, do we hear of the murderous weapons used, and even less often are we reminded of what we know but prefer not to be told about: that all those weapons used to make far-away homelands into killing fields have been supplied by our arms factories, jealous of their order-books and proud of their competitiveness, which is the lifeblood of our own cherished prosperity. A synthetic image of the self-inflicted brutality sediments in public consciousness: an image of "mean streets," "no go areas" writ large, a magnified rendition of a gangland, an alien, subhuman world beyond ethics and beyond salvation. The message is chat attempts to save that world from the worst consequences of its own brutality may bring only momentary effects which in the long run are bound to fail; all the lifelines thrown eventually become nooses for the poor to hang themselves.

Next, the best tried, most trusty tool of "adiaphorisation": the exemption of conduct from ethical significance and evaluation, comes into its own: the sober, rational calculation of costs and effects. Money spent on this kind of people is money wasted. Wasting money is one thing that, as everybody will readily agree, we cannot afford. The victims of famine are not ethical subjects. Our own stance toward them is not a moral issue. Morality is for carnivals only, the spectacular, instantaneous, short-lived, explosive condensations of pity and compassion. When it comes to our, the affluents' collective responsibility for the continuing misery of the world's poor, economic calculation takes over, and the rules of free trade, competitiveness and productivity replace ethical precepts. When economy speaks, ethics better keep silent.

Unless, of course, it is the work ethic. This is the sole variant which the economic rule tolerates: an ethics which (contrary to Levinas's image of ethics and the idea of justice as whips for the sinners and watchdogs for the rulers) is not an adversary of the economy bent on profitability and competitiveness, but its necessary support and supplement. For the affluent part of the world and the affluent sections of well-off societies, the work ethic is a one-sided affair. It spells out the duties of those who struggle with the task of survival; it says nothing about the duties of those who rose above mere survival and went on to more elevated, loftier concerns. In particular, it denies the dependency of the first upon the second, and so releases the second from responsibility for the first.

Today, the work ethic is instrumental in bringing the idea of "dependency" (which, in the last account, is nothing but the flip side of our moral responsibility) into disrepute. "Dependency" is, increasingly, a dirty word and so also, by proxy is the idea of ethical responsibility. The Welfare State is accused of cultivating dependency, of raising it to the level of a self-perpetuating culture and this is a crowning argument for dismantling it. Moral responsibility is the first victim of this holy war against dependency. But the dependency of the Other (it needs to be repeated over and over again) is but a mirror image of my responsibility, the starting point of any moral relationship and the founding assumption of all moral action. To denigrate the dependency of the poor and describe it as sin, the work ethic, in its present rendition, brings relief mostly to the moral scruples of the affluent.

1. INTRODUCTION

AUTHENTIC THINKING AND PHENOMENOLOGICAL METHOD

Steven Galt Crowell

At no time since its "breakthrough" in Edmund Husserl's *Logische Untersuchungen* (1900–1) has phenomenology been absent from the world's philosophical stage, but today there are remarkable signs of the continuing vitality of this philosophical approach. It thus seems appropriate to ask just what it is that makes phenomenology a distinctive way of philosophizing. And with its centenary year recently behind us, it is also appropriate that this question be posed to the *Logical Investigations*, a work that Robert Sokolowski has described as "literally a new beginning" since what Husserl started here "cannot be considered as continuing a tradition that had taken shape before him."[1] Just what was the breakthrough that occurred in the *Logical Investigations*, and what claim does it have on us today? These questions matter not only because they are important for Husserl scholarship, but because they are much disputed now, and upon their answer depend our expectations of what phenomenological philosophy can accomplish, and what, if anything, lies beyond its scope. For if there is renewed interest in phenomenology today, this has brought with it—or is it the consequence of?—a tendency to inflate the very concept of phenomenology. Today the borders between phenomenological philosophy, metaphysical speculation, and neo-Kantian construction show signs of collapsing. One reason for this is clear enough: the ascetic, anti-metaphysical "positivism" of Husserl's early writing belongs to a cultural and philosophical milieu that is no longer our own, and if its residue cannot be excised from the phenomenological program, that program will be felt by some to be too restrictive. Yet

---

Originally published as Steven Galt Crowell: "Authentic Thinking and Phenomenological Method." in *Husserl's Logical Investigations in the New Century: Western and Chinese Perspectives* (Dordrecht: Springer, 2007), 119–33. Reprinted with the permission of Springer Netherlands.

1 Robert Sokolowski, *Introduction to Phenomenology* (Cambridge: Cambridge University, 2000), 211.

Dominique Janicaud seems to speak well when he says that "[p]henomenology is not all philosophy. It has nothing to win [...] by an overestimation of its possibilities."[2] Must a renewal of phenomenology involve its overestimation?

The overestimation to which Janicaud refers frequently justifies itself by rejecting a principle of phenomenological method that the *Logical Investigations* deemed essential—the principle of intuitive givenness or *Evidenz*. If, following Martin Heidegger, we identify three elements of the "breakthrough" to phenomenology made in the *Logical Investigations*—intentionality, categorical intuition, and the apriori[3]—it is the theory of categorial intuition that forms the basis of the breakthrough, since the concept of intuition that gets worked out there made it possible for Husserl to give a distinctly *phenomenological* sense to the Brentanian notion of intentionality and the Kantian notion of the apriori. Only by insisting on the epistemological primacy of intuition in just the way he did was Husserl able to develop a non-psychological approach to intentionality and a non-constructivist concept of the apriori. And yet it is just this commitment to intuition that has seemed too restrictive to many phenomenologists. On the one hand, there are thinkers like Jean-Luc Marion and Emmanuel Levinas who abandon the principle in favor of what might be called "speculation"—invoking "revelation" as a kind of givenness not reducible to intuition. On the other hand, there are thinkers like Eugen Fink who abandon the principle in favor of construction—arguing that intuition provides only the *starting point* for a phenomenology that can construct "Ideas" of what cannot be given with *Evidenz*. The question to be posed to any such proposal is whether phenomenology can transcend intuition while still remaining phenomenology. The present essay will begin to address this question, first by clarifying what Husserl's concept of intuition actually entails and then by showing that while both speculative and constructive phenomenology fail as phenomenology, at least some aspects of their agendas can be fulfilled without abandoning the principle of intuitive givenness.

---

2   Dominique Janicaud, "The Theological Turn of French Phenomenology," in *Phenomenology and the Theological Turn*, ed. and trans. Bernard Prusak (New York: Fordham University, 2000), 34. Originally published as *Le tournant théologique de la phénoménologie*, (Paris: Editions de l'éclat, 1991), 21.
3   Martin Heidegger, *Prolegomena zur Geschichte des Zeitbegriffs*, ed. Petra Jaeger, *Gesamtausgabe* 20 (Frankfurt a. M.: Klostermann, 1979), 34. Translated by Theodore Kisiel as *History of the Concept of Time: Prolegomena* (Bloomington: Indiana University Press, 1985), 27.

2. INTUITION AND AUTHENTIC THINKING

The heart of the matter is found in the chapter of the *Logical Investigations* entitled "The Apriori Laws of Authentic and Inauthentic Thinking," in which Husserl, writing in the heyday of neo-Kantianism, claims that his theory of categorial intuition has defined "the much used, but little clarified, relation between *thinking* and *intuiting*."[4] At first it seems odd to identify a philosophical breakthrough with a theory of *intuition*, since philosophy's strength is usually taken to lie in thinking, the *logos*, the power that reason exercises over intuition. Certainly, philosophers such as Hermann Cohen and Heinrich Rickert would follow Kant's dictum that intuitions alone are "blind," a night in which all cows are black, a mythical "given"—to use Wilfred Sellars's term—that has no authority in the "space of reasons." To hold thought accountable to intuition is to ask the sun to reflect the moon. And yet Husserl's breakthrough to phenomenology lies precisely in his recognition that both neo-Kantianism and its empiricist opponent operate with an unclarified view of thought and intuition—specifically, a view that holds them to be distinct *kinds*, distinct "faculties." For Husserl the genuine contrast is not between thought and intuition, but between *signification* and intuition[5]—that is, between empty or "merely symbolic" intentions and intentions that are *fulfilled* in the way appropriate to them—and this allows him to determine the concept of thinking in a wholly new way. This he does in the chapter on authentic thinking, whose bold thesis is that thinking is *itself* a kind of intuiting, *categorial* intuiting. As Husserl puts it, "authentic *acts of thinking* [...] lie in [...] the *intuitions* of states of affairs, and all intuitions which function as possible parts of such states of affairs."[6] To assess the implications of this for phenomenological method, let us look more closely at the concept of intuition that facilitates Husserl's move beyond the Kantian dichotomy.

The apriori laws of authentic thinking occupy the role in Husserl's *Logical Investigations* that transcendental logic occupies in Kant's *Critique of Pure Reason*: they express the conditions which "no knowledge can contradict [...]

---

4 Edmund Husserl, *Logical Investigations*, trans. J. N. Findlay (London: Routledge, 1970), II:832. Originally published as *Logische Untersuchungen*, Zweiter Band, Zweiter Teil, ed. Ursula Panzer Husserliana XIX/2 (The Hague: Nijhoff, 1984), 730.
5 Husserl, Logical Investigations, 833 [732].
6 Ibid., 825 [722].

without at once losing all content, that is, all relation to any object."[7] In Husserl's terms, a "pure" logic deals with the apriori laws of "meaning," that is, "all possible matters and all possible categorial forms." But since, as he argues, the "realm of meaning is much wider than the realm of intuition," not every such categorial formation can attain "reality."[8] The laws of authentic thinking, then, are the "laws [...] of categorial *intuitions*"—that is, of those categorial forms to which "a unitary correlate of fulfillment can correspond."[9] Like Kant's transcendental logic, Husserl's laws of authentic thinking are a "logic of truth," delimiting those categorial combinations that are possible *cognitions*. Unlike Kant, however, Husserl neither sets out a restricted set of categories nor determines possible cognitions in terms of a presupposed faculty of sensuous intuition. Thus, where Kant can claim an apriori content for his transcendental logic, Husserl's laws of authentic thinking have no such content. Rather, he admits that "what categorial formations are in fact permitted by given materials of perception or imagination" cannot be determined by the laws in advance.[10] At best one can say that *given* the reality of a certain categorial formation, certain other ones are logically possible and impossible. But why do Husserl's laws not reduce to mere empiricism, then? What is it in Husserl's theory that serves the critical function that, in Kant's theory, is served by the apriori intuitions of space and time?

Husserl's answer turns on rejecting Kant's dualism between thinking and intuiting altogether: authentic thinking is defined not as a thinking *accompanied* by confirming intuition, but as *that very* intuition itself. Husserl notes that though acts of "categorial union and formation" are not "necessarily" given by the material upon which they are founded—since what is given in straightforward fashion allows for multiple categorial articulations—this "freedom [...] still has its law-governed limits." These limits are exposed precisely in the attempt to "carry out [*vollziehen*]" the categorial acts in question. This *Vollzug* is what gives "reality" to the categorial act; it is categorial "intuition." But it is also nothing other than (authentic) *thinking* itself. As Husserl puts it, we "can no doubt 'think' any relation between any set of terms [...]

---

7   Immanuel Kant, *Critique of Pure Reason,* trans. Norman Kemp Smith (London: Macmillan, 1968), 100. Originally published as *Kritik der reinen Vernunft,* in *Kant's gesammelte Schriften 3,* ed. Königlich Preußische Akademie der Wissenschaften (Berlin: de Gruyter, 1904/11), A63/B87.
8   Husserl, *Logical Investigations,* 824 [721].
9   Ibid.
10 Ibid., 823 [719]. This is why there can be nothing in Husserl that corresponds to the chapter of Kant's *Critique of Pure Reason* entitled "The Analytic of Principles."

think them, that is, in the sense of merely *meaning* them. But we cannot really carry out "foundings" on every foundation: we cannot *see* sensuous stuff in any categorial form we like."[11] Husserl thus replaces Kant's dualism with a three-fold distinction. There is, first, a concept of thinking that is equivalent to mere signification, according to which we can combine any term with any other, subject only to syntactic rules of meaning. Thus I can say (or "think" in this sense): "The camera is part of the lens." This, however, is not properly called "thinking" at all, since it is the mere *indication* of a categorial act. Thus, second, there is thinking in the pregnant sense, namely the attempt to *carry out* a categorial "founding" on some given "foundation." Such thinking is not mere signification but a concrete attempt to grasp some given material (in this case the perceived camera) in light of some specific categorial form (here, part—whole). This leads, thirdly, to a concept of *authentic* thinking, which, as categorial *intuition*, is the *successful* carrying out of the categorial act—as when I succeed in "seeing" that "the lens is part of the camera." That this is not a grammatical truth should be obvious; just as it should be obvious that I cannot authentically think that the musical note, middle C, is purple—that is, I cannot carry out a categorial synthesis of identification on this material.

It is the notion of categorial intuition as carrying out (*Vollzug*), then, that allows Husserl to get beyond Kant's dilemma: Kant failed to extend "the concepts of perception and intuition over the categorial realm" because he failed to grasp "the deep difference between intuition and signification"[12]—that is, between authentic *thinking* and signification. Instead, he worked with a concept of thinking that was *equivalent* to signification, and thus could not see how categorial acts could of themselves be intuitive. For this reason Kant had no choice but to treat sensuous intuition as normative for cognition, with the psychologistic consequences Husserl seizes upon. For Husserl, in contrast, intuition continues to play its cognitively critical or normative role with respect to signification, but it does so precisely *as thinking*, thus not as something foreign to the space of reasons. There is no gap between thinking and intuiting and hence no anxiety that thinking, restricted to what can be intuited, might fall short of truth.

The implications of Husserl's move here are quite far-reaching. For it is not merely that intuition insures that thinking can attain at least some truth.

---

11 Ibid., 821 [771].
12 Ibid., 833 [732].

Rather, the very idea of a *truth-functional* discourse is tied to the laws of authentic thinking. As Husserl puts it, "categorial intuitions [...] *impart* to statements [...] the logical values of truth and falsehood." In the absence of possible categorial intuition, one cannot assign to a statement *any* relation to truth, since it is on the "laws" of authentic thinking that "the normative regulation of purely signitive, or admixedly signitive, thought depends."[13] Hence, to suppose that there could be a kind of thinking that would both escape the restrictions of intuitive givenness *and* remain truth-functional—a supposition made both by speculative and constructivist phenomenologists—is to suppose that symbols have a life of their own.

And yet proponents of a post-intuitionistic phenomenology might well object that categorial intuition is called "intuition" only by equivocation; thus that authentic thinking and the norm of truth is not tied to "intuition" in any interesting sense of the word. In what sense, then, is it true that for Husserl all that is "given" is "intuitively given"? Husserl introduces the notion of categorial intuition by contrasting it with sense intuition, arguing that "in the mere form of a judgment"—for instance, "S is P"—"only certain antecedently specifiable parts [...] can have something which corresponds to them in intuition"—namely "S," "P"—"while to other parts"—namely "is"—"*nothing intuitive* possibly can correspond."[14] One might then suppose that Husserl limits intuition in the strict sense to the *sensuously* given, while leading phenomenology beyond that to the categorial—and so beyond intuition. One might also point out that Husserl says only that the "state of affairs" constituted in the categorial act expressed in the "is" must be "given to us [...] by way of an act which gives it, an *analogue* of common sensuous intuition"[15]—which, precisely as an analogue, need not really *be* an intuition. Thus, even when Husserl states explicitly that the "essential homogeneity of the function of fulfillment [...] obliges us to give the name 'perception' to each fulfilling act of confirmatory self-presentation, to each fulfilling act whatever the name of an 'intuition,' and to its intentional correlate the name of 'object,'"[16] one might insist that this, being a mere analogy, should carry no weight in defining phenomenological method.

---

13 Ibid., 823 [720].
14 Ibid., 778 [663].
15 Ibid., 784 [670].
16 Ibid., 785 [671].

Husserl has already anticipated this objection, however. Even before he speaks of an "analogy" between sensuous and categorial fulfillments, he maintains a more nuanced view about the way in which terms like "intuition" and "perception" operate, noting that "*Perception* and *object* are concepts that cohere most intimately together, which *mutually assign sense to one another*, and which widen or narrow this sense conjointly."[17] Thus while Husserl's introduction of categorial intuition "made use of a certain mutually delimited, natural, but also very narrow concept of perception (or of object)"—namely, that of sense perception—this does not mean that some literal meaning of intuition has been analogized to other kinds of fulfillments in a perhaps illegitimate way. Rather, Husserl simply takes seriously an obvious feature of our everyday talk: "I *see* what you mean," "I finally got *insight* into the matter," "I *perceive* a discrepancy between your statement and your behavior." In such cases of what Donn Welton has called "natural meaning," there "is not a clean difference between literal and metaphorical meaning."[18] The relevant difference between sense perception and other perception/object correlations is not between literal intuitive givenness and merely analogically intuitive givenness, but between "straightforward" or direct, and categorially structured, perception.[19] Thus there can be no talk of an object without a corresponding notion of perception or intuition; an in principle imperceptible object is not thinkable, since to be an object at all is to be perceptible in some modality or other, whether directly or synthetically.

If this is so, then to tie phenomenological method to intuition is not to tie it to a restricted domain of objects—the intuitively given ones, as opposed to the "unapparent"—but to open it responsibly, as authentic thinking, to anything that can be an object of thought at all. Here, however, a more serious objection arises, one that will force us to consider some views that hold phenomenology's intuitionism to be *phenomenologically* unsupportable. For it may be that the notions of perception and object mutually define one another, but phenomenological investigation itself uncovers phenomena—for instance, the *alter ego*, temporality, and the world—that cannot be taken to be *objects* at all. And if they do not have the structure of an object, there may be no reason to think that they are intuitively given or perceived. If phenomenology uncovers such phenomena, then it has already *transcended* its own

---

17 Ibid., 781 [666].
18 Donn Welton, *The Other Husserl* (Bloomington, IN.: Indiana University, 2000), 386.
19 Husserl, *Logical Investigations*, 791 [679].

supposed intuitionism.[20] On this objection, authentic thinking (categorial intuition) is not necessary for phenomenology, and this would explain why Husserl drops both the notion of categorial intuition and authentic thinking after the *Logical Investigations*.[21] To answer this objection, it is necessary to show that the structure of authentic thinking is indeed at work in uncovering these horizonal phenomena. This task will be approached in two steps. First, some of the arguments put forth by those who propose to abandon Husserl's principle of intuition in favor of speculation will be criticized (Section 3). Then a proper and an improper sense of phenomenological "construction" will be distinguished so as to show that the former retains precisely the structure of categorial intuition or authentic thinking (Section 4).

3. SPECULATIVE PHENOMENOLOGY?

Calling into question the centrality of intuition for phenomenological method has brought phenomenology into contact with a strain of thought to which, at the time of the *Logical Investigations*, Husserl was manifestly hostile: speculation. This is evident in the work of those whom Dominique Janicaud associates with a "theological turn" in French phenomenology—for instance, in the writings of Jean-Luc Marion. Now Marion's thought, which develops Heidegger's late suggestion of a "phenomenology of the unapparent" into a post-metaphysical approach to God without Being, is a fecund provocation that is not to be dismissed in a sentence. However, as Janicaud remarks, "we are not forced to take or leave any *œuvre* as a whole," but have the "right, and even the duty," to question and test its individual steps.[22] Thus we shall restrict ourselves to a critical examination of that point in the *Logical Investigations* where Marion claims to find already a break with the principle

---

20 In Edmund Husserl, *Ideas Pertaining to a Pure Phenomenology and to a Phenomenological Philosophy*, First Book, trans. F. Kersten (The Hague: Nijhoff, 1983), 10, originally published as *Ideen zu einer reinen Phänomenologie und phänomenologischen Philosophie*, Erstes Buch, *Jahrbuch für Philosophie und phänomenologische Forschung*, vol. 1 (1913), 11, Husserl offers another definition of "object" as "any subject of possible true predications," and on that definition, of course, all horizonal phenomena would count as objects. Whether this means that they must therefore be intuitable—as is implied by the *Logical Investigations*' conception of the correlation of object and perception—or whether Husserl would be willing to abandon the correlation thesis under pressure from this "logical" concept of object is an interesting question that cannot be explored here.
21 Husserl, *Logical Investigations*, 662–3 [535]: "It does not affect what I have said to add that, after twenty years of further work, I should not write at many points as I then wrote, and that I do not approve of much that I then wrote, e.g., the doctrine of categorial representation."
22 Janicaud, "The Theological Turn of French Phenomenology," 51 [40].

of intuition that, he believes, leads from a "reduction to the intuitively given" to a reduction of intuition itself.[23]

Marion begins by asking whether "the characteristic of givenness [is] equivalent to the characteristic of presence through intuition"[24] and concludes by asserting the "unconditional primacy of the givenness of the phenomenon," of which "intuitive givenness" is only a particular "illustration."[25] What authorizes this split between givenness and intuition, such that phenomenology is defined essentially in terms of the former and only incidentally in terms of the latter? Is there any authorization in Husserl's text for thinking givenness without intuition?

It does not appear so. Marion's whole argument turns on the claim that signification is a kind of givenness without intuition, and this argument seems to be based on an equivocation. To establish what he calls the "intuitive extraterratoriality of signification,"[26] Marion follows Derrida in noting that for Husserl signification is supposedly "valid without the confirmation of an intuition,"[27] that there is a kind of "autonomy of signification" with respect to intuition. But what exactly is meant by "valid" here? Certainly, Husserl claims that signification operates without *fulfilling* intuition—that is, that there can be empty intentions—but in what sense can we speak of "autonomy" from intuition? It is not as though the act of signification, empty though it may be, eluded intuition and presence in some absolute sense, since phenomenological reflection is able to grasp such acts *in* their intuitive presence. To say that signification can be "valid" without a confirming intuition—that is, can be *empty*—is not yet to say that it is "extraterritorial" with respect to intuition. Nevertheless, Marion takes Husserl's remark about the "deep difference between intuition and signification" to mean that "signification [...] is defined as the other of intuition" and therefore is somehow "*before* intuition."[28] Just here, however, we find a crucial equivocation.

First, it is true that signification is defined as the "other" of intuition in the sense that terms can be combined without fulfilling intuition—indeed, without any *possible* fulfillment. But in contrast to Husserl, who ties significa-

23 Jean-Luc Marion, *Reduction and Givenness*, trans. Thomas A. Carlson (Evanston, IL: Northwestern University Press, 1998), 30. Originally published as *Réduction et donation: recherches sur Husserl, Heidegger et la phenomenologie française* (Paris: PUF, 1989), 49.
24 Marion, *Reduction and Givenness*, 6 [14].
25 Ibid., 32 [53].
26 Ibid., 22 [38].
27 Ibid., 20 [35].
28 Ibid., 23 [39].

tion back to authentic thinking or intuitively fulfilled categorial acts, Marion understands "purely symbolic" thought—for instance, in mathematics—as a "capacity to think significations that remain irreducible to any intuition."[29] This is, to say the least, an astounding position to attribute to Husserl, who from first to last sought to show how purely symbolic thinking—especially the "technology" of mathematical symbolism—was *not* irreducible to intuition. Leaving this point aside, however, Marion's argument for the independence of signification from intuition is based, secondly, on the following equivocation. Claiming, correctly, that for Husserl "every expression [...] has a signification, whether or not it has an intuitive fulfillment," Marion concludes that Husserl rejects the view that "signification becomes 'true' only by finding its foundation in intuition."[30] But here we must note that if by "true" is meant "valid" (*Gelten*, holding), this conclusion does not follow. We saw clearly how for Husserl it is the possibility of intuitive fulfillment, authentic thinking, that "imparts" to signification a relation to truth or falsity.[31] On the other hand, if by "true" is meant only that a *Bedeutung* is present even in the absence of fulfilling intuition, it is only by equivocation that one could claim, as Marion does, that signification is "given evidently" in a mode that is *itself* non-intuitive, a "mode of presence [that is] deployed *sui generis* when signification, by itself and itself alone, presents itself."[32] For though the signifying act be empty of fulfilling intuition, its correlate, the *Bedeutung*, is no more something whose presence would escape the functional concept of intuition Husserl outlines[33] than is categoriality itself. Signification is itself given intuitively if it is given at all: it is given intuitively to that phenomenological reflection that thematizes signification itself "in person" rather than merely signifying (talking about) it. There is nothing to suggest that this "in person" is somehow autonomous from intuition in Husserl's functional sense, and therefore nothing in the phenomenon of signification, as Husserl presents it, that would challenge the correlation between intuition and givenness.

On this slender basis, however, Marion feels entitled to argue that when Husserl invokes the fundamental "correlation between the appearing and

---

29 Ibid., 24 [40].
30 Ibid., 26 [43].
31 Though there is no room to make the argument here, consideration of the role played by the "telos of truth" in Husserl's genetic phenomenology would show that were there no "relation to fulfilling intuition" there would be no signification at all.
32 Marion, *Reduction and Givenness*, 28 [47].
33 Husserl, *Logical Investigations*, 785 [671].

that which appears as such" in the *Crisis*, this constitutes a "belated recognition" that "appearing" was never properly tied to intuition but rather counts "*first* as the givenness of what thus appears." Givenness is then taken to be independent of intuition since it is "the appearing"—and not intuition—that "gives that which appears."[34] But if nothing in the *Logical Investigations* allows us to argue that givenness ("appearing") can be separated from intuition—that is, if there *is* no *leibhafte Gegebenheit* that would not be intuitive presence[35]—then the claim that what matters to phenomenology is givenness, and that phenomenological method can extend itself to supposedly non-intuitive givens without becoming groundless speculation, has no basis.

Without claiming to do justice to the depth of Emmanuel Levinas's phenomenology of radical alterity, it is possible to locate in it, too, a point at which authentic phenomenological thinking moves "with aplomb"—that is, with mere *affirmation*—into speculation.[36] Levinas's thought proceeds, with a double movement, first from an ontological phenomenology that remains intuitive to an ethical phenomenology that challenges the primacy of intuition in the experience of the "face" of the Other; and then, secondly, to an affirmation of the infinity and even divinity of this face. While Levinas's first move seems phenomenologically justified, similar phenomenological authorization is lacking for his second move. When Levinas writes that "[i]t is our relations with men [...] that give to theological concepts the sole signification they admit of,"[37] he utters the precise point at which phenomenology, bounded by the intuitive givenness of our "relations with men," wanders forth into speculation, that is, into a theological stance that is neither necessarily nor sufficiently motivated by phenomenology. And it may well be that if the apriori laws of authentic thinking circumscribe the field of what *can* have the "logical values of truth and falsehood," statements of the sort Levinas (and Marion) propound may not be assessable in terms of truth or falsity—though they may respond to other normative principles.

But what makes Levinas's first move—in which the principle of intuition is already challenged in the name of the experience of the "face" of the Other—phenomenologically compelling? If this is not already an instance

---

34 Marion, *Reduction and Givenness*, 32 [52].
35 Ibid., 34 [56].
36 On this "aplomb," see Janicaud, "The Theological Turn of French Phenomenology," 25 [14].
37 Emmanuel Levinas, *Totality and Infinity*, trans. Alphonso Lingis (Pittsburgh: Duquesne University, 1969), 79. Originally published as *Totalité et Infini: Essai sur l'extériorité* (The Hague: Martinus Nijhoff, 1961), 51;

of speculation it must be possible to reconstruct Levinas's insight in such a way that the principle of intuition, or authentic thinking, is preserved. This can be achieved by distinguishing between an improper and a proper concept of phenomenological "construction," a task to which the final section of the present essay is devoted.

4. PHENOMENOLOGICAL CONSTRUCTIONS, PROPER AND IMPROPER

In stating why his investigation "owes everything to the phenomenological method," Levinas identifies the very spot at which the motive for a constructive phenomenology becomes apparent. Reflecting on intentional acts, phenomenology discovered them "to be implanted in horizons unsuspected by [these acts]," horizons that "endow them with a meaning." "What does it matter," Levinas continues, "if in the Husserlian phenomenology taken literally these unsuspected horizons are in their turn interpreted as thoughts aiming at objects! What counts is the idea of the overflowing of objectifying thought by a forgotten experience from which it lives."[38] The question is whether, in order to get at these "unsuspected horizons," phenomenology must give up its principle of intuitive givenness. Can horizonality be thought authentically in the sense of the *Logical Investigations*?

One answer is provided by the "constructive phenomenology" that Eugen Fink proposed in his *Sixth Cartesian Meditation*.[39] Starting with the intuitive givenness of the "living present," a regressive phenomenology unfolds all the horizonal intentional implications that "become accessible through the phenomenological reduction."[40] These unfoldings remain intuitively given (in a sense to be explored below), but at a certain point regressive analysis encounters "horizons" that refer "to something that precisely by its transcendental mode of being is *in principle* deprived of givenness."[41] For this reason, Fink argues, "the theorizing directed to them"—namely, constructive phenomenology—"is not an 'intuitive having-given,' is not 'intuitive.'" For instance, regressive analysis moves back along the temporally sedimented

---

38 Levinas, *Totality and Infinity*, 28 [16–17].
39 Eugen Fink, *Sixth Cartesian Meditation*, trans. Ronald Bruzina (Bloomington, IN: Indiana University, 1995). Originally published as *VI. Cartesianische Meditation. Teil I: Die Idee einer transzendentalen Methodenlehre*, ed. Hans Ebeling, Jann Holl, and Guy van Kerckhoven, Husserliana Dokumente II,1 (Dordrecht: Kluwer, 1988).
40 Ibid., 57 [63].
41 Ibid., 56 [62].

constitutions of a single ego, uncovering the horizons that give meaning to its current intentionalities. With the phenomena of "birth and death," however, it reaches a "limit" or horizon that, though it contributes "sense," cannot be "exhibited in an immediate way in the being-context of ongoing world constitution." Thus, if we are "to gain any understanding at all," writes Fink, "we have to '*construct.*'"[42]

Fink's constructive phenomenology is thus motivated largely—if not exclusively[43]—by questions of wholeness or totalities that, precisely as totalities, elude the grasp of intuitive reflection. However, there lurks in this concern for totality what Kant calls a "transcendental illusion," and if this is so, then the rationale for a non-intuitive constructive phenomenology is not compelling.[44] Recalling that for Husserl it is not possible to carry out a given categorial synthesis on just *any* material whatsoever, it is evident that precisely the sort of material Fink focuses on—world, temporal stream, history, as horizons of the transcendental field itself—cannot be authentically thought in the category of part–whole. Just as they are not properly objects, neither can they be totalized; in the attempt to do so one encounters antinomies. It is thus extremely problematic to say, as Robert Sokolowski does, that phenomenology takes "a view that is appropriate to the whole" and to argue that "mind and being are moments to each other," since it is not clear that the category of part–whole applies to notions like "mind" and "world" at all.[45]

Interestingly, Donn Welton raises this objection against Husserl himself as he tries to show how Husserl's thinking about the world-horizon was held captive to a "Cartesian way" of posing phenomenological problems. In response, Welton argues for a version of constructive phenomenology that, unlike Fink's, does not relinquish the principle of intuition but proposes only to recognize the "mediating role of argument in establishing transcendental structures."[46] A look at what Welton means by the "mediating role of argument" can help us both to appreciate the continuing relevance of Husserl's concept of authentic thinking and to distinguish between what can respon-

---

42 Ibid., 62 [70].
43 Ibid., [63] 70–1.
44 For further discussion of Fink's position, see my *Husserl, Heidegger, and the Space of Meaning: Paths Toward Transcendental Phenomenology* (Evanston, IL: Northwestern University Press, 2001), chap. 13: "Gnostic Phenomenology: Eugen Fink and the Critique of Transcendental Reason." This essay may also be found in *The New Yearbook for Phenomenology and Phenomenological Philosophy* I (2001), 257–77.
45 Sokolowski, *Introduction to Phenomenology*, 209 and 25.
46 Welton, *The Other Husserl*, 289.

sibly be said to belong to those horizons to which Levinas referred and what remains groundless speculation.

According to Welton, phenomenological constructions are needed to get at horizonal phenomena such as the lifeworld. Do such constructions transcend the principle of intuition? Welton sometimes suggests as much, saying that "the horizon is not itself an appearance but is always 'pregiven,'" and that "the world does not appear."[47] But such statements are directed only against a very restricted notion of intuition—namely, Husserl's "Cartesian strategy of directly intuiting consciousness,"[48] according to which "appearances" are *objects* for *epistemic* intentionality. To treat the world as "appearing" in this sense is to treat it exclusively as an object for consciousness and thus to miss its horizonal character. On Welton's view, because Husserl linked his "notion of intuition" to a "Cartesian notion of evidence" with its claim to transparency, adequacy, and immediacy, he had no choice but to treat the world as an object *for* consciousness.[49] But once the restrictions of the Cartesian notion of evidence are abandoned, nothing stands in the way of recognizing that the world-horizon *appears* as the "correlate of experience or intuition." One must simply avoid characterizing it in categorial terms that inappropriately "totalize" it.[50] What then is the specific relation between construction and intuition in the phenomenological method that grasps the world-horizon as such?

Welton argues that Husserl turns to construction when he recognizes the impossibility of defining the transcendental field through "directly intuiting" consciousness. Given the temporal structure of consciousness, the demand for adequate intuitive evidence seems to reduce phenomenology to the "sterile 'I am.'"[51] At the very least phenomenology must incorporate recollection and so become, "in a minimal sense, *historical reflection*."[52] It might seem, then, that phenomenology must renounce the principle of basing its claims solely upon intuitive evidence, thereby placing its trust in empty significations. But here Welton invokes the "mediating role" of "transcendental arguments" in uncovering elements of the horizon that condition intentionality, the experience of meaningful objects.[53] And although he does not note

47 Ibid., 332.
48 Ibid., 270.
49 Ibid., 338, 287.
50 Ibid., 344–45.
51 Ibid., 280.
52 Ibid., 281–283.
53 Ibid., 294.

the connection, Welton's account of transcendental arguments retrieves precisely Husserl's doctrine of authentic thinking.

First, there is something quite elusive about this idea of a transcendental "argument." As Welton admits, it is not really an *argument* in the sense of a deduction.[54] Further, if he correctly describes Husserl's genetic or constructive practice as a "methodologically induced reflective analysis that opens up the transcendental as a field to *direct intuition* and then uses *eidetic variation* to regressively discover different sets of transcendental conditions,"[55] it seems that transcendental arguments require little beyond the staples of phenomenological method. Apparently, the mediating role of argument functions in the process of eidetic variation itself. Just what kind of thinking, then, is in play in such arguments?

Welton borrows a central feature of his account from Charles Taylor, who suggests that transcendental arguments lay out a "chain of indispensability claims" that "articulate a certain insight we have into our experience."[56] Taylor, for instance, finds such an argument at work in Merleau-Ponty, who shows that given the phenomenologically discernible features of our sense perception, a "field of this structure can only be experienced by an embodied agent;" hence, our sense of ourselves as embodied agents "is not a contingent fact we might discover empirically" but is "*constitutive* of our experience."[57] This differs from a Kantian transcendental deduction because, in working back to the transcendental condition (embodied subjectivity), I do not work back to something that, though itself incapable of being experienced (like the "unity of apperception"), is posited as necessary for the experience I *do* have. Rather, I recover something that in a certain sense I have always already known. This condition has the character of a horizon: although my embodiment is not an intentional *object*, it is horizonally experienced, pregiven, and thus intuited along with my direct perception of objects. And only because it can be recovered, made intuitively explicit, as *having been* experienced, does it count as a phenomenologically established feature of transcendental subjectivity. By contrast, the claim that a "body made up of carbon molecules" is indispensable to such perceptual intentionality would *not* count as a phenomenologically warranted claim. Although it is perhaps *true*,

54 Ibid.
55 Ibid., 287.
56 Ibid., 294–5.
57 Charles Taylor, "Transcendental Arguments," in Philosophical Arguments (Cambridge, Mass.: Harvard University, 1995), 24–25.

it is not something that can be established by a transcendental "argument" or phenomenological construction in the relevant sense.

What makes the difference here? It is precisely the demand that transcendental arguments must articulate an insight that we have into our experience—that is, that the conditions be tied to intuitive evidence of the actual features of my experience. In this sense, the notion of a "condition" is relative to the level at which one starts (just as "material" for categorial formation is relative: it can already be categorially formed). For instance, if one starts with a phenomenology of perceptual experience, embodied agency may emerge as the implicit horizonal condition. But one could also begin with our sense of ourselves as embodied agents and find that *its* condition is a certain implicit character of world or time. The crucial point is that at every step the indispensability claim must be cashed in on the basis of "an insight I have into my own experience." The argument just brings to light what is intuited—or given—precisely there. Thus a constructive phenomenology does not move from the intuited (part) to the unintuitable (whole), as Fink suggested, but from the explicitly intuited to its implicitly intuited horizonal condition. And though such a move can be put in the *form* of an argument, it is clear that eidetic variation does all the work.[58]

But if this is what constructive phenomenology amounts to, then it is not a break with Husserl's doctrine of authentic thinking so much as its essential elaboration. For authentic thinking is just the actual carrying out of those categorial syntheses that are allowed on the basis of a certain material. The fact that in this case the material is the transcendental–phenomenological field itself does not mean that such thinking has changed its stripes. Actually carrying out these categorial elaborations just *is* the intuiting of the structures that condition this field—not a construction of, or inference to, what does not appear. In this respect, constructive phenomenology is no different than any other phenomenology. All authentic thinking is beholden to its material, whether it is directed as a particular state of affairs or at one that is mediated by transcendental "arguments," that is, by eidetic variations that yield insight into necessary conditions. Indeed, only authentic thinking in the sense of categorial intuition can show that the categories appropriate to objects (e.g., part–whole) are not necessarily appropriate to horizons—pre-

---

58 For one thing, the argument is circular. For another, if one relies on such arguments alone, one can generate naturalistic, non-phenomenological conditions, such as the "necessity" of carbon molecules.

cisely by trying *and failing* to carry out such categorial syntheses on that material. At no point, then, does constructive phenomenology provide a rationale for abandoning the field of intuitive, first-person evidence.

The importance of this may be illustrated, in conclusion, by returning to Levinas's claim that one of the horizons of object-intentionality is the face of the Other. The whole of *Totality and Infinity* can be read as a transcendental argument designed to show that not only do the way things show up in our practical and theoretical dealings with them depend on intersubjectivity, as Husserl already knew, but that this very intersubjectivity is phenomenologically constituted by a response to an ethical claim (the face of the Other as the phenomenon of obligation). If this is truly a *phenomenological* result, it should be possible to show that this indispensability claim articulates an insight we have into our own experience. This I do by actually carrying out the thought of its conditioning; that is, by showing, through eidetic variation, that the sort of intersubjective world I inhabit is unthinkable without my always already having acknowledged the Other's ethical claim on me. Thus, if Levinas asserts that the face of the Other is not an "appearance," that it "transcends intuition," and so on,[59] this can be understood to mean that it is not an intentional *object*. But in thinking it authentically—in carrying out the categorial syntheses that link it, as condition, with what it conditions—I *do* in fact intuit the face, in Husserl's sense. By contrast, the further claim that this face (ethical obligation) is a "trace of the Divine" as the "absolutely unapparent" or "infinite," cannot be accepted as phenomenological. It is speculative (mere signification). Even a world bereft of God is thinkable only in terms of a face that makes an ethical claim on me, and just here lies the difference. I can eidetically vary divinity out of the face in a way that I cannot vary its ethical claim—just as I can vary carbon molecules out of embodiment in a way that I cannot vary its agency. This does not mean that Levinas's theological turn makes no sense, any more than it means that the chemistry of carbon molecules makes no sense. But if phenomenology understands itself, it will be no more at home with the one than with the other. Its contribution lies in tethering philosophy to authentic thinking, thereby allowing it to serve a deeply important critical role. And nothing in either chemistry or theology provides a convincing rationale for it to abandon that role.

---

59   See, e.g., Levinas, *Totality and Infinity*, 50–1 [21–2].

EXTRATERRITORIAL GEOGRAPHIES

BEYOND HUMAN RIGHTS

Giorgio Agamben

In 1943, Hannah Arendt published an article titled "We Refugees" in a small English-language Jewish publication, the *Menorah Journal*. At the end of this brief but significant piece of writing, after having polemically sketched the portrait of Mr. Cohn, the assimilated Jew who, after having been 150 percent German, 150 percent Viennese, 150 percent French, must bitterly realize in the end that "on ne parvient pas deux fois," she turns the condition of countryless refugee—a condition which she herself was living—upside down in order to present it as the paradigm of a new historical consciousness. The refugees who have lost all rights and who, however, no longer want to be assimilated at all costs in a new national identity, but want instead to contemplate lucidly their condition, receive in exchange for assured unpopularity a priceless advantage. "History is no longer a closed book to them and politics is no longer the privilege of Gentiles. They know that the outlawing of the Jewish people of Europe has been followed closely by the outlawing of most European nations. Refugees driven from country to country represent the vanguard of their peoples."[1]

One ought to reflect on the meaning of this analysis, which after fifty years has lost none of its relevance. In is not only the case that the problem presents itself inside and outside of Europe with just as much urgency as then. It is also the case that, given the by now unstoppable decline of the nation-state and the general corrosion of traditional political-juridical categories, the refugee is perhaps the only thinkable figure for the people of our time and the only category in which one may see today—at least until the

---

Originally published as Giorgio Agamben, "Beyond Human Rights," in *Means Without End: Notes on Politics*, trans. Vincenzo Binetti and Cesare Casarino (Minneapolis: University of Minnesota Press, 2000), 15–28. Reprinted with the permission of University of Minnesota Press.

1 Hannah Arendt, "We refugees," *Menorah Journal* 31, no. 1 (1943): 69–77.

process of dissolution of the nation-state and of its sovereignty has achieved full completion—the forms and limits of a coming political community. It is even possible that, if we want to be equal to the absolutely new tasks ahead, we will have to abandon decidedly, without reservation, the fundamental concepts through which we have so far represented the subjects of the political (Man, the Citizen and its rights, but also the sovereign people, the worker, and so forth) and build our political philosophy anew starting from the one end only figure of the refugee.

✖

The first appearance of the refugees as a mass phenomenon took place at the end of World War 1, when the fall of the Russian, Austro-Hungarian, and Ottoman empires, along with the new order created by the peace treaties, upset profoundly the demographic and territorial constitution of Central Eastern Europe. In a short period, 1.5 million White Russians, seven hundred thousand Armenians, five hundred thousand Bulgarians, a million Greeks, and hundreds of thousands of Germans, Hungarians, and Romanians left their countries. To these moving masses, one needs to add the explosive situation determined by the fact that about thirty percent of the population in the new states created by the peace treaties on the model of the nation-state (Yugoslavia and Czechoslovakia, for example), was constituted by minorities that had to be safeguarded by a series of international treaties—the so-called Minority Treaties—which very often were not enforced. A few years later, the racial laws in Germany and the civil war in Spain dispersed throughout Europe a new and important contingent of refugees.

We are used to distinguishing between refugees and stateless people, but the distinction was not then as simple as it may seem at first glance, nor is it even today. From the beginning, many refugees, who were not technically stateless, preferred to become such rather than return to their country. (This was the case with the Polish and Romanian Jews who were in France or Germany at the end of the war, and today it is the case with those who are politically persecuted or for whom returning to their countries would mean putting their own survival at risk.) On the other hand, Russian, Armenian, and Hungarian refugees were promptly denationalized by the new Turkish and Soviet governments. It is important to note how, starting with World War 1, many European states began to pass laws allowing the denaturalization and denationalization of their own citizens: France was first, in 1915, with regard to the naturalized citizens of "enemy origin"; in 1922, Belgium followed this example by revoking the naturalization of those citizens who had committed "antinational" acts during the war; in 1926, the Italian Fascist regime passed an analogous law with regard to citizens who had shown themselves "undeserving of Italian citizenship"; in 1933, it was Austria's turn; and so on, until in 1935 the Nuremberg Laws divided German citizens into citizens with full rights and citizens without political rights, Such laws—and the mass statelessness resulting from them—mark a decisive turn in the life of the modern nation-state as well as its definitive emancipation from naive notions of the citizen and the people.

This is not the place to retrace the history of the various international organizations through which single states, the League of Nations, and later, the United Nations have tried to face the refugee problem, from the Nansen Bureau for the Russian and American refugees (1921) to the High Commission for Refugees from Germany (1936) to the Intergovernmental Committee for Refugees (1938) to the UN's International Refugee Organization (1946) to the present Office of the High Commissioner for Refugees (1951), whose activity, according to its statute, does not have a political character but rather only a "social and humanitarian" one. What is essential is that each and every time refugees no longer represent individual cases but rather a mass phenomenon (as was the case between the two world wars and is now once again), these organizations as well as the single states—all the solemn evocations of the inalienable rights of human beings notwithstanding—have proved to be absolutely incapable not only of solving the problem but also of facing it in an adequate manner. The whole question, therefore, was handed over to humanitarian organizations and to the police.

The reasons for such impotence lie not only in the selfishness and blindness of bureaucratic apparatuses, but also in the very ambiguity of the fundamental notions regulating the inscription of the *native* (that is, of life) in the juridical order of the nation-state. Hannah Arendt titled the chapter of her book *Imperialism* that concerns the refugee problem "The Decline of the

Nation-State and the End of the Rights of Man."[2] One should try to take seriously this formulation, which indissolubly links the fate of the Rights of Man with the fate of the modern nation-state in such a way that the waning of the latter necessarily implies obsolescence of the former. Here the paradox is that precisely the figure that should have embodied human rights more than any other—namely, the refugee—marked instead the radical crisis of the concept. The conception of human rights based on the supposed existence of a human being as such, Arendt tells us, proves to be untenable as soon as those who profess it find themselves confronted for the first time with people who have really lost every quality and every specific relation except for the pure fact of being human.[3] In the system of the nation-state, so-called sacred and inalienable human rights are revealed to be without any protection precisely when it is no longer possible to conceive of them as rights of the citizens of state. This is implicit, after all, in the ambiguity of the very title of the 1789 *Déclaration des droits de l'homme et du citoyen*, in which it is unclear whether the two terms are to name two distinct realities or whether they are to form, instead, a hendiadys in which the first term is actually always already contained in the second.

That there is no autonomous space in the political order of the nation-state for something like the pure human in itself is evident at the very least from the fact that, even in the best of cases, the status of refugee has always been considered a temporary condition that ought to lead either to naturalization or to repatriation. A stable statue for the human itself is inconceivable in the law of the nation-state.

✖

It is time to cease to look at all the declarations of rights from 1789 to the present day as proclamations of eternal metajuridical values aimed at binding the legislator to the respect of such values; it is time, rather, to understand them according to their real function in the modern state. Human rights, in fact, represent first of all the originary figure for the inscription of natural naked life in the political-juridical order of the nation-state. Naked life (the human being), which in antiquity belonged to God and in the classical world

---

2   Hannah Arendt, *Imperialism*, Part 2 of *The Origins of Totalitarianism* (New York: Harcourt, Brace, 1951), 266–98.
3   Ibid., 290–5.

was clearly distinct (as *zoè*) from political life (*bios*), comes to the forefront in the management of the state and becomes, so to speak, its earthly foundation. Nation-state means a state that makes nativity or birth [*nascita*] (that is, naked human life) the foundation of its own sovereignty. This is the meaning (and it is not even a hidden one) of the first three articles of the 1789 *Déclaration*: it is only because this declaration inscribed (in articles 1 and 2) the native element in the heart of any political organization that it can firmly bind (in article 3) the principle of sovereignty to the nation (in conformity with its etymon, *native* [*nario*] originally meant simply "birth" [*nascita*]). The fiction that is implicit here is that *birth* [*nascita*] comes in to being immediately as *nation*, so that there may not be any difference between the two moments. Rights, in other words, are attributed to the human being only to the degree to which he or she is the immediately vanishing presupposition (and, in fact, the presupposition that must never come to light as such) of the citizen.

✖

If the refugee represents such a disquieting element in the order of the nation-state, this is so primarily because, by breaking the identity between the human and the citizen and between nativity and nationality, it brings the originary fiction of the sovereignty to crisis. Single exceptions to such a principle, of course, have always existed. What is new in our time is that growing sections of humankind are no longer representable inside the nation-state—and this novelty threatens the very foundations of the latter. Inasmuch as the refugee, an apparently marginal figure, unhinges the old trinity of state–nation–territory, it deserves instead to be regarded as the central figure of our political history. We should not forget that the first camps were built in Europe as spaces for controlling refugees, and that the succession of internment camps–concentration camps–extermination camps represent a perfectly real filiation. One of the few rules the Nazis constantly obeyed throughout the course of the "final solution" was that Jews and Gypsies could be sent to extermination camps only after being fully denationalized (that is, after they have been stripped of even that second-class citizenship to which they had been relegated after the Nuremberg Laws). When their rights are no longer the rights of citizen, that is when human beings are truly *sacred*, in the sense that this term use to have in the Roman law of the archaic period: doomed to death.

✖

The concept of refugee must be resolutely separated from the concept of the "human rights," and the right of asylum (which in any case is by now in the process of being drastically restricted in the legislation of the European states) must no longer be considered as the conceptual category in which to inscribe the phenomenon of refugees. (One needs only to look at Agnes Heller's recent *Theses on the Right of Asylum* to realize that this cannot but lead today to awkward confusions.) The refugee should be considered for what it is, namely, nothing less than a limit-concept that at once brings a radical crisis to the principles of the nation-state and clears the way for a renewal of catagories that can no longer be delayed.

Meanwhile, in fact, the phenomenon of so-called illegal immigration into the countries of the European Union has reached (and shall increasingly reach in coming years, given the estimated twenty million immigrants from Central European countries) characteristics and proportions such that this reversal of perspective is fully justified. What industrialized countries face today is a permanently resident mass of noncitizens who do not want to be and cannot be either naturalized or repatriated. These noncitizens often have nationalities of origin, but, inasmuch as they prefer not to benefit from their own states' protection, they find themselves, as refugees, in a condition of de facto statelessness. Tomas Hammar has created the neologism of "denizens" for these noncitizen residents, a neologism that has the merit of showing how the concept of "citizen" is no longer adequate for describing the social-political reality of modern states.[4]

On the other hand, the citizens of advanced industrial states (in the United States as well as Europe) demonstrate, through an increasing desertion of the codified instances of political participation, an evident propensity to turn into denizens, into noncitizens permanent residents, so that citizens and denizens at least in certain social strata are entering an area of potential indistinction. In a parallel way, xenophobic reactions and defensive mobilizations are on the rise, in conformity of the well-known principle according to which substantial assimilation in the presence of formal differences exaeerbates haterd and intolerance.

---

4   Tomas Hammar, *Democracy and the Nation State: Aliens, Denizens, and Citizens in a World of International Migration* (Brookfield: Gower, 1990).

Before extermination camps are reopened in Europe (something that is already starting to happen), it is necessary that the nation-states find the courage to question the very principle of the inscription of nativity as well as the trinity of state–nation–territory that is founded on that principle. It is not easy to indicate right now the ways in which all this may concretely happen. One of the options taken into consideration for solving the problem of Jerusalem is that it become—simultaneously and without any territorial partition—the capital of two different states. The paradoxical condition of reciprocal extraterritoriality (or, better yet, aterritoriality) that would thus be implied could be generalised as a model of new international relations. Instead of two national states separated by uncertain and threatening boundaries, it might be possible to imagine two political communities insisting on the same region and in a condition of exodus from each other—communities that would articulate each other via a series of reciprocal extraterritorialities in which the guiding concept would no longer be the *ius* (right) of the citizen but rather the *refugium* (refuge) of the singular. In an analogous way, we could conceive of Europe not as an impossible "Europe of the nations," whose catastrophe one can already foresee in the short run, but rather as an aterritorial or extraterritorial space in which all the (citizen and noncitizen) residents of the European states would be in a position of exodus or refuge; the status of European would then mean the being-in-exodus of the citizen (a condition that obviously could also be one of immobility). European space would thus mark an irreducible difference between birth [*nascita*] and nation in which old concept of people (which, as is well known, is always a minority) could again find a political meaning, thus decidedly opposing itself to the concept of nation (which has so far unduly usurped it).

This space would coincide neither with any of the homogeneous national territories nor with their *topographical* sum, but would rather act on them by articulating and perforating them *topologically* as in the Klein bottle or in the Mobius strip, where exterior and interior in-determine each other. In this new space, European cities would rediscover their ancient vocation of cities of the world by entering into a relation of reciprocal extraterritoriality.

As I write this essay, 425 Palestinians expelled by the state of Israel find themselves in a sort of no-man's-land. These men certainly constitute, according to Hannah Arendt's suggestion, "the vanguard of their people." But that is so not necessarily or not merely in the sense that they might form the originary nucleus of a future national state, or in the sense that they might solve the Palestinian question in a way just as insufficient as the way in which Israel has solved the Jewish question. Rather, the no-man's-land in which they are refugees has already started from this very moment to act back onto the territory of the state of Israel by perforating it and altering it in such a way that the image of that snowy mountain has become more internal to it than any other region of Eretz Israel. Only in a world in which the spaces of states have been thus perforated and topologically deformed and in which the citizen has been able to recognize the refugee that he or she is, only in such a world is the political survival of humankind today thinkable.

We were told that geopolitics is the great play of power across a solid continuous Euclidian surface. Cut apart by linear borders, the state system—a territorially based juridical formation—appeared to dominate all forms of sovereignty over individuals and action. Later we began to imagine all solid national spaces were melting into a single smooth ocean of ever-present connectivity. We assumed borders were replaced with bureaucracies, issues with concepts, and that regulation was replaced with boundless flow.

"ISLANDS": THE GEOGRAPHY OF EXTRATERRITORIALITY

*Anselm Franke,
Eyal Weizman &
Ines Weizman*

But various fault lines have now steered against this order. Just as along Norwegian coasts—fjords, islands, and lakes break the coherent continuity of both water and land—political surface has now splintered into discontinuous territorial fragments set apart and fortified by makeshift barriers, temporary boundaries, or invisible security apparatuses. Instead of its edges clearly demarcated by continuous lines, political spaces have now grown to resemble a territorial patchwork of introvert enclaves located side by side, each within the other, simultaneously and in unprecedented proximities.

These shreds are ISLANDS—externally alienated and internally homogenized extraterritorial enclaves, spaces of political void or strategic implants—lying outside the jurisdiction that physically surrounds them. ISLANDS are the territorialized nodes of a deterritorialized power—one distributed through military, political or financial networks. It is although, and perhaps because the new world-order, governed by super-national and

---

This text was first published as the introduction to a special issue of Archis titled ISLANDS, edited by Anselm Franke, Ines Geisler (now Weizman), and Eyal Weizman and published in December 2003. It has been edited and extended for a catalogue titled ISLANDS+GETTOS, published in the frame of an exhibition project by Heidelberger Kunstverein, Germany, 2008: Anselm Franke & Eyal Weizman & Ines Weizman: "Islands: The Geography of Extraterritoriality," *ARCHIS* 6 (2007): 18–54, and was presented at an Exterritory Project Symposium, May 8, 2012, Jaffa, Israel.

non-localized institutions, is non-territorial, that it increasingly relies on the physical infrastructure that only real space can provide.

ISLANDS are reminiscent of the complex political architecture that dominated Europe before the 1648 Treaty of Westphalia, characterized by a multiplicity of overlapping quasi-sovereign powers, a dispersed control over the use of coercion and organized violence and the whole presence of fortifications in an evolving landscape of permanent conflict. Then, ISLANDS as city-states provided an exclusive citizenship; ISLANDS as places of refuge provided sanctuary from persecution; ISLANDS as tax-free ports provided financial havens. But within this political landscape of feudalism, the Catholic church provided perhaps the clearest example of power operating a deterritorialized political system; its physical manifestations—churches, palaces and monasteries, much like the present-day Vatican—were placed (mostly) beyond the reach of the political order within whose territory they rested.

ISLANDS were later exported to the margins of European geography, thus extending its frontiers. Europe's encounters with realms "outside" of the global colonial order also produced extraterritorial ISLANDS of jurisdiction in China, Japan, the Ottoman Empire, Morocco, Persia, Siam, and Abyssinia.

In the nineteenth century, capitulations or "un-equal treaties" were the principal expression of the subaltern status of non-European powers. Under the capitulation system, merchants, military personal, missionaries and new settlers enjoyed liberty of trade religion along with immunity from local jurisdiction and taxation. Beyond the reach of the laws in the countries in which they chose to reside, they generally lived in enclaves that were subject to the legal and social norms represented by the leaders of the expatriate communities—consuls or, in the case of Constantinople, ambassadors—and according to the laws of their nation states. The system ended only in the 1960s when the Master of Pembroke College, Oxford, ceased to exercise jurisdiction over Commonwealth citizens in the Persian Gulf Emirates.[1]

These places were seen as "outposts of civilization," in a sea of as-yet "unordered barbarity" and their spatial layout expressed a geography of segregation and exclusion, as well as response to the Western politics of hygiene. The Eng-

---

[1] Capitulations began with the concessions granted by the Ottoman Empire to Venice in the sixteenth century. The demise of the system began with the first demand for liberation. Japan freed itself of this extraterritorial jurisdiction in the 1980s, Turkey in 1923, Egypt in 1936, and China in gradual process that stretched from 1924 to 1946.

lish extraterritorial zones that spread across the colonial world were revealingly described by Jane Austen as "a retention of an England outside itself."

Figures of extraterritoriality returned to haunt current political order. They become the nodes of a deterritorialized system that operates across geopolitical networks. They are the physical infrastructure for the distribution of finance and strategic power. This return to dormant colonial practices is what critical geographer Derek Gregory has called the "colonial present"—a world that is looking forward but moving backwards, culturally (seemingly) post-colonial but politically regressing into a new form of colonialism. This colonial present is simultaneously marked by increased deterritorialization and trans-border connectivity for the global rich and increased territorialized segregation and exclusion for the global poor. Instead of the illusionary promise of a smooth and networked "flat world," we have found ourselves negotiating the fragments of a fenced-up apartheid planet.

The historical ISLANDS of extraterritorial refuge and sovereignty have evolved into today's zones of humanitarian intervention—set in responses to states of emergency or extreme humanitarian crisis. The ancient military outposts into present days military camps (in the Green Zone in Baghdad American mobile phones operate on American dialing codes) —deployed for the defense of foreign investments, natural resources, international transport or on behalf of nationals abroad; or "Special Enterprise Zones"—set as manufacturing enclaves for the financial exploitation of advancing nations by advanced ones.

Humanitarian zones, temporarily set up around sites of "natural" or "man-made" catastrophes (although the difference is not always clear), frequently evolve into cordoned-off, improvised ISLANDS where normal sovereignty is suspended. Ad hoc tent cities mushroom and even diurnal rhythms are confused in the never-ending day of 24-hour floodlit humanitarian activity. Humanitarian spaces become small universes operating by their own rules. The French doctor and activist, Rony Brauman, former president of Doctors Without Borders, famously and more or less felicitously coined the metaphor of the "humanitarian bubble":

> Trucks, four-wheel drive vehicles, walkie-talkies, satellite phones, and computers create an artificial environment, whose perverse effect is to put the terms in a quasi-virtual world where time and space are measured in different units from those the country where they find themselves. So

they find themselves, almost without knowing it, in a bubble, a "non-place," a humanitarian mission which could be everywhere and which is nowhere.

In international law, the term extraterritoriality refers to those instances where a state extends its jurisdiction or effective control over zones, individuals or activities beyond its borders. The concept may apply to military movements of foreign soil as well as to embassies or diplomats in the form of diplomatic immunity. Extraterritoriality is therefore rooted in the concept of sovereignty, although it is usually considered as its violation.

There are other very different circumstances too, in which the term extraterritoriality applies, namely when a state fails to exercise its sovereignty over all its territory, in which case fissures and lacunae appear within its formerly coherent geographical order, giving shape to territorial units that are beyond the reach of state power. Extraterritoriality violates thus juridical territoriality in a way that sets a clear challenge to the sovereign power of the state in which it exists, and indeed to the Westphalian state system in general.

There exist, as well, spaces of another type of interiority, shadowing the more visible economical and political network. These are "lawless" zones in various states of "anarchy, poverty, decay and crime." The refugee camp, the favela and the protected corridors in Afghanistan or Central America are for the drug traffickers and arms dealers what Tax Havens and international banking are to the financial market. Here they are shadow ISLANDS of disorder floating within the smooth sea of ordered international flows. Partly retreating, partly forced into isolation, shadow ISLANDS are governed by warlords, private entrepreneurs, clan chiefs, armies for hire, or youth gangs, and are in a state of low intensity, permanent conflict. Indeed of the 70 recognized political conflicts across the world today, only six manifest themselves as war between two or more sovereign state actors, while at least half are carried out besides any juridical framework of any legitimate power. These shadow conflicts most often only come into light when they disturb the official flow of goods, capital and resources. At the frontiers, when shadow ISLANDS meet the space of flow, counter warlords of various types emerge — private security companies and other such mercenaries of various types operating "Anywhere, Anytime" — offering their form of violence to the service of the middle classes as a ready-made product on the market.

Pirates, the natural inhabitants of ISLANDS, learn how to abuse the advantage of their geography—the political voids and legal loopholes help constitute an alternative, faster, deadlier, more efficient systems of flow. Piracy was indeed for trans-oceanic trade what terrorism is for economic globalization. The extraterritorial nature of terrorism (and the narcotics trade) prompted the creation of a legal system aspiring to an equal extraterritorial nature. This form of legal extraterritoriality applies to individuals or activities, such as those of US citizens, regardless of their location outside the territory of their state. Extraterritorial extension of modern American criminal law means in some cases that the US national is legally considered as an embodiment of the State abroad.

United Nations trust territories in the Pacific, the Panama canal, Bosnia Herzegovina, tax havens in the Caribbean, Palestinian refugee camps, no fly zones, international courts, Guantánamo Bay in Cuba, gated communities in Orange County and in China, warships cruising the high seas, or settlements perched on occupied land, may all be extraterritorial spaces designating an exceptional juridical state while being alienated from their surrounding order.

ISLANDS are sites of internally regimented order. Utopia has ever been imagined as an ISLAND artificially cut off from the land—a place of exile for the perfection of society. In fact, every effort made since for the realization of Utopia began with the establishment of an extraterritorial space surrounded by the "social matter" it aimed to leave behind.

ISLANDS are fragments of a "left-over" geography, an enclaved type of space set for the colonization of internal frontiers from which "there is no longer an outside." Their diversity of conditions exemplify the inconsistent behavior and self-destructive impulses of the present political order.

Outside Territory

Stuart Elden

What would it mean to be outside territory? I'm going to discuss this question in three registers: conceptually; historically; politically. The first two will be brief; the third literary.

BEING OUTSIDE TERRITORY CONCEPTUALLY

Territory, for me, is actually quite a specific concept. If territory extends from a room, a building, a group of them, to a campus, an urban area, a city, a region, a nation-state, and so on, it seems to me that the term becomes so general that it becomes not especially helpful. If we extend a human notion of "territory" to understand animals, as ethologists did in the late 19th and early 20th centuries, this may yield some fruitful insights. But it does not seem, to me, to be especially helpful then to take that notion of animal behavior, a notion of *territoriality*, of hunting and mating areas, to understand humans. Thus, for me, territoriality is a consequent notion to that of territory; not the means to understand it. Territoriality is one of a number of strategies that produce territory, but conceptually it succeeds it. Territoriality is that which produces territory. The latter term still needs conceptual unpacking. It does not seem especially helpful to understand territory simply as the outcome of territoriality.

Nor are standard definitions of territory as a "bounded space" or the state as a "bordered power container" especially helpful. This might open up the kinds of questions we need to ask—What do we mean by boundary? What kind of space? What relations of power?—but only as a spur to further questions. Conceiving of territory as the bringing together of a range of different political phenomena—economic, strategic, legal, and technical—is not an attempt to offer a better single definition of territory, which can be con-

This text was first presented in an Exterritory Project Symposium in collaboration with Kadist Art Foundation and with the support of Evans Foundation, May 2, 2012, Le Comptoir Général, Paris, France.

trasted with other ones. Rather it is an attempt to raise the kinds of questions we would need to ask to understand how territory has been understood and practiced in a range of different times and places.[1]

Territory is then, a historically and geographically limited notion, one that needs to be understood and comprehended in its specificity. This means that there is a role for other concepts such as area, region, place, space, domain—these, it seems to me, open up ways of understanding geographies that are, in an important, conceptual sense, outside territory.

In my book *The Birth of Territory*, I try to account for the emergence of this concept of "territory."[2] There is no time today to sketch the aspects of the history of the concept of territory in Western political thought. Nonetheless, on my terms, and contrary to many accounts, territory is not that central or even general a category of geography; not all problems should be seen through a territorial lens; and while it is certainly of fundamental importance in the modern period, territory historically is not the key concept of political theory and its relation to place. Rather we should recognize the emergence of a concept out of a complicated and multi-layer set of chronologies, fragments and aporias.

BEING OUTSIDE TERRITORY HISTORICALLY

Following this, if territory has a history, and emerged at a particular conjuncture, then it follows that before this there were political-spatial orderings that were not territory. We can therefore think of examples of configurations of the relation between power and place that were not territorial, that is what is outside territory historically.

One thing that is worth noting is that, initially, "territory" *was* the outside. *Territorium*—an extremely rare word in classical Latin—was the area surrounding a place, perhaps a town or a colony. The suffix *-orium* means area around; a notion we maintain in words like sanatorium, auditorium, and crematorium. The territory was the area around a settlement, the surrounding agricultural lands. This is the way it is used in Cicero, in Varro—who claims it is the area trodden on most—and in Seneca. (Of the other uses of the term in classical Latin, Pliny the Elder uses it in the neutral sense of an area.) In the

---

[1] Stuart Elden, "Land, Terrain, Territory," *Progress in Human Geography* 34, no. 6: 799–817.
[2] Id., *The Birth of Territory* (Chicago: University of Chicago Press, 2013).

later Roman Empire, Ammianus Marcellinus makes the point that while they avoided the towns, the Germanic tribes frequented their territories. So, there is a story to be told about how territory moved from being the thing that was outside, outside the city walls and external to the *urbs*, to becoming the thing within which the city was located, within which the law was exercised.

There are political spaces, then, that were other than territory. This could be polities such as the Greek *polis*, which had surrounding lands, *khora*, but was not inside them in a complete way; the Roman *urbs* or the empire, which while divided into *territoria* did not see the areas outside as such; the medieval church or kingdom. Did the native Americans or African tribes have their own *territory*, in the specific sense, before Europeans reordered the spaces of their lands? Or did they have a different way of experiencing, ordering and understanding that was transformed into territories and through "territory"? Each of those different configurations would need to be understood through the words, concepts and practices that would have made sense to those who lived in, fought over, worked in and wrote about them. Equally there are areas that are outside territory in the spaces between such designated and designed sites.

BEING OUTSIDE TERRITORY POLITICALLY

This is what I meant by being outside territory politically, which I am going to explore through some literary examples.

If the first text of the Western tradition, the *Iliad* is about struggle over a city and its lands, or what we might today call territory, Homer's *Odyssey*, where Odysseus journeys home after the Trojan wars, is about what it means to be outside it. In Sophocles' tragedy *Oedipus at Colonnus*, one of Oedipus's most plaintive pleas in exile is when he asks "will they even shroud my body in Theban soil?"[3] In the play about one of his daughters, and the fate of his sons, *Antigone*, the whole story is around the question of burial and site, and the dislocation of familial and political relations.[4]

In the Anglo-Saxon poem *Beowulf* there are isolated human settlements such as the village of Heorot where the mead hall stands. But outside, espe-

---

3   Sophocles, *Oedipus at Colonnus*, in *The Theban Plays*, trans. Robert Fagles (London: Penguin, 1984), l. 406.
4   For a reading of Antigone in this regard, see Stuart Elden, "The Place of the *Polis*: Political Blindness in Judith Butler's *Antigone's Claim*," *Theory and Event* 8 (2005).

cially after dark, there are spaces of great danger, what we might today call the wild. Grendel, for instance, is described as a *mearcstapa*, a march-stepper or border-walker; a figure who prowls the margins, the edges, the limits, the liminal.[5] The *mere*—the pool of deep water—where his mother dwells is similarly beyond the reach of ordinary man, though not the hero Beowulf himself. Similarly dangerous places, outside territory or dominant ordering of political space, puncture the Norse myths of the *Edda*.[6]

So it is with Shakespeare. Perhaps the most famous of such places is the heath in *King Lear*, where Lear in his madness, Kent in his exile, Edgar in his disguise as Poor Tom, and Gloucester in his blindness all end up.[7] All are outside, outsiders in some way, all are outside territory, the political space that was divided by the King between his daughters in the famous opening scene: "Since now we shall divest us both of Rule, / Interest of territory, cares of state."[8]

Such a sense runs through a number of Shakespeare's plays. Exile is a recurrent theme. Take, for example, *As You Like It*, where the deposed Duke ends up in the Forest of Arden, a kind of site that is a place outside of enclosure. But the play is ambiguous because the new society is, at the end, replaced by the return of the old, and the exiles, with the exception of Jacques, return to the place they left.[9] Enclosure was, of course, a key issue at Shakespeare's own time, explored perhaps most interestingly in Edward Bond's play *Bingo: Scenes of Money and Death*.[10] In that play, Shakespeare himself is a landowner,

---

5 *Beowulf: A Student Edition*, ed. George Jack (Oxford: Oxford University Press, 1994), l. 103. At ll. 1348–52, both Grendel and his mother are described this way, as those who trod "the path of exile." On these themes, see Manish Sharma, "Metalepsis and Monstrosity: The Boundaries of Narrative Structure in Beowulf," *Studies in Philology* 102, no. 3 (2005): 247–75, 265–6; and S.L. Higley, "Aldor on Ofre, or the Reluctant Hart: A Study of Liminality in Beowulf," *Neuphilologische Mitteilungen* 87 (1986): 342–53. For a fuller discussion, see Stuart Elden, "Place Symbolism and Land Politics in Beowulf," *Cultural Geographies* 16, no. 4 (2009): 447–63.

6 Snorri Sturlson, *The Prose Edda*, trans. Jesse L. Byock (London: Penguin, 2005); *The Poetic Edda*, trans. Carolyne Larrington (Oxford: Oxford University Press, 1996).

7 On this see Henry S. Turner, "*King Lear* Without: The Heath," *Renaissance Drama* Vol. 28 (1997): 161–83.

8 William Shakespeare, *King Lear*, Act I, scene i. For a discussion of the complexities of this scene and the play as a whole, see Stuart Elden, "The Geopolitics of *King Lear*: Territory, Land, Earth," *Law and Literature* 25, no.2 (2013): 147–65. For Shakespeare's plays I have used the most up-to-date version of the Arden Shakespeare.

9 See Richard Wilson, "'Like the Old Robin Hood': *As You Like It* and the Enclosure Riots," *Shakespeare Quarterly* 43, no 1. (1992): 1–19; and more textually, Andrew Barnaby, "The Political Consciousness of Shakespeare's *As You Like It*," *Studies in English Literature: 1500–1900* 36, no. 2 (1996): 373–95. On the complications, see A. Stuart Daley, "The Dispraise of the Country in 'As You Like It,'" *Shakespeare Quarterly* 36, no. 3 (1985): 300–14.

10 Edward Bond, *Plays Three: Bingo, The Fool, The Woman, Stone* (London: Methuen, 1987). For a contemporary updating of Shakespeare to land struggles, see Martin Orkin, *Shakespeare Against Apartheid* (Craighall: Ad. Donker, 1987). A recent excellent study is Alvaro Sevilla-Buitrago, "Ter-

trying to work out if he should accept William Combe's offer of protection for his own lands at the expense of local farmers.[11] Bond himself writes of Shakespeare that while he "created Lear, who is the most radical of all social critics."[12] "His behaviour as a property-owner made him closer to Goneril than Lear. He supported and benefitted from the Goneril-society—with its prisons, workhouses, whipping, starvation, mutilation, pulpit-hysteria and all the rest of it."[13]

Another play where the forest plays an important role is *Titus Andronicus*. Much of the initial action takes place in the forest, a wild site, which relates to the homeland of the Goths Tamora and her sons, in contrast to the urban Rome. It is in the forest, this outside to the city, that Titus's daughter Lavinia is raped, muted and mutilated; that her lover (and brother to the Emperor) Bassianus is murdered; and that Titus's sons Martius and Quintus are framed for his death. It is here that we discover than Aaron the Moor is lover to Tamora, now married to the Emperor Saturninus. I won't go into the details of all the deaths in the play, one of Shakespeare's most shocking, but at the end Tamora's body is thrown outside the city to be devoured by wild beasts; and Aaron is buried chest-deep within it to starve and thirst to death.

Coriolanus works with the figure of exile in a related way. Despite his military prowess on behalf of the city, when he stands for political office he so outrages the people that the tribunes end up expelling him. Sicinius declares:

And in the power of us the tribunes, we,
Ev'n from this instant, banish him our city,
In peril of precipitation
From off the rock Tarpeian, never more
To enter our Rome gates.[14]

Yet Coriolanus's response is forthright and characterizes his attitude to the city—"I banish you!"

---

ritory and the Governmentalisation of Social Reproduction: Parliamentary Enclosure and Spatial Rationalities in the Transition from Feudalism to Capitalism," *Journal of Historical Geography* 38, no. 3 (2012): 209–358.
11 Bond bases his account on the papers in E.K. Chambers, *William Shakespeare: A Study of Facts and Problems*, vol. 2 (Oxford: Clarendon Press, 1930).
12 Bond, "Bingo: Introduction," Plays Three, 4.
13 Ibid., 6.
14 *Coriolanus*, III, iii, 99–105.

> You common cry of curs, whose breath I hate
> As reek o'th'rotten fens, whose loves I prize
> As the dead carcasses of unburied men
> That do corrupt my air: I banish you!
> And here remain with your uncertainty!
> ... Despising
> For you the city, thus I turn my back.
> There is a world elsewhere![15]

When he does leave, it is to the Volscian city of Antium. In the compressed dramatic action of the play, his journey is short and his arrival, disguised, follows quickly after. But the recent film version directed by and starring Ralph Fiennes, captures this effectively in showing a lengthy journey whose passage of time is tracked by the transformation in Fiennes's appearance. Shaven head and face become ever lengthening hair and a thick beard. By the time he arrives in Antium, the transformation is such that stage devices such as a hooded cloak are unnecessary. But the geographical complications are shown in this version. The play is set by Shakespeare in early Republican Rome, not long after the uprising against and expulsion of the Tarquin kings. The play is written in early 17th century England. The film is set in a near contemporary pseudo-Balkans. It was shot in Serbia and Montenegro. The film, making effective use of newsreel and TV, shows that the Volscians are in close proximity to the "place calling itself Rome." The initial war footage, of the siege of the Volscian city of Corioli which gives Coriolanus his name, talks of a "border dispute." That implied a more proximate location, or at least, a contested front between the sides that appeared largely absent when he is making his way to Antium. The means used to mark the transition at other points in the film, where a motorway is punctuated by road blocks, with a kind of no-man's-land between them, was more effective. But if this is so, and the two neighbors share a narrow, effectively modern border, a boundary, where does Coriolanus go when he moves into exile? Why does it take him so long to move between these places?

And yet, in republican Rome, it is indeed the case that there would have been areas outside of Rome that were not yet part of its neighbors. Places that were not yet spaces; lands that were not yet cultivated, not yet territory. In

15   Ibid., 117–35.

the early seventeenth century, Shakespeare could effectively play this spatial politics. Exile was still a potential punishment, and features importantly in his history plays. The transportation of convicts to the new world or slavery were merely modern examples of an age-old practice. In the later 17th century John Locke would discuss the "Indian who knows no Inclosure, and is still a Tenant in common" and yet still laid claim to private property and thus a nascent form of civil society;[16] Locke declaring that "in the beginning, all the World was America."[17] Not all places within Shakespeare's England were yet enclosed, much less if Scotland and Ireland were included.

But in the late 20th and early 21st century, and especially in the Balkan setting which is otherwise so effective in Fiennes's adaptation, the idea of a place *outside* territory is harder to grasp. Where is Coriolanus as he moves through that sequence of locations, sleeping rough and his hair growing ever longer? He could be in isolated locations. He is undoubtedly making his way through war-ravaged landscapes, contested places in the present or recent past. But given the modes of modern warfare and territorial settlements, he is either still within the "place calling itself Rome," or behind enemy lines. It's hard to conceive of a no-man's-land of such extent that the time could have passed in such a way. He is effectively either in one territory or another. It's hard to imagine him outside of territory, but for early Rome, or even in Shakespeare's England, it's not so difficult.

Richard II is another play where banishment is a crucial element. The King wants to prevent bloodshed on the land between the feuding noblemen Bolingbroke and Mowbray: "For that our kingdom's earth should not be soiled / What that dear blood which it hath fostered."[18] As as result he stops their duel and banishes them. The punishment is for life for Mowbray; shorter for Bolingbroke.

> Therefore, we banish you our territories.
> You cousin Hereford, upon pain of life,
> Till twice five summers have enriched our fields,
> Shall not regreet our fair dominions,
> But tread the stranger paths of banishment.[19]

16 John Locke, *Two Treatises of Government*, ed. Peter Laslett (Cambridge: Cambridge University Press, 1988 [1960]), V, 26.
17 Ibid., V, 49.
18 Shakespeare, *Richard II*, I, iii, 125–6.
19 Ibid., I, iii, 139–143.

He wants to make sure they do not plot against the land. But Bolingbroke's father, John of Gaunt, makes the powerful and famous speech where he both praises the land and deplores what it has become:

> This royal throne of kings, this sceptred isle,
> This earth of majesty, this seat of Mars,
> This other Eden, demi-paradise,
> This fortress built by Nature for herself
> Against infection and the hand of war, [...]
> This blessed plot, this earth, this realm, this England, [...]
> Is now leased out—I die pronouncing it—
> Like to a tenement or pelting farm.
> England, bound in with the triumphant sea,
> Whose rocky shore beats back the envious siege
> Of wat"ry Neptune, is now bound in with shame,
> With inky blots and rotten parchment bonds.
> That England that was wont to conquer others
> Hath made a shameful conquest of itself.[20]

This is a play suffused with the language of soil, land, earth, and ground. The King is condemned for selling rights and farming the realm. He is condemned as "Landlord of England... not king."[21] He has also, crucially, dispossessed the exiled Bolingbroke of the lands and title he inherits from Gaunt. He thus creates a legitimate grievance in Bolingbroke, who returns to England at the head of an army. He does this while Richard is abroad seeking to pacify the Irish rebellion. This is part of the reason Richard needed the funds he raised by such illegitimate means, suggesting "We are enforced to farm our royal realm."[22]

While Bolingbroke claims to only be after his own title and lands, he ends up with Richard's crown and kingdom as well. The King complains that "Our lands, our lives and all are Bolingbroke's."[23] And then, in one of their final exchanges, Bolingbroke states "My gracious lord, I come but for mine own," to which King Richard replies "Your own is yours, and I am yours and all."[24]

20   Ibid., II, I, 31–66.
21   Ibid., II, I, 113.
22   Ibid., I, iv, 42.
23   Ibid., III, ii, 251.
24   Ibid., III, iii, 196–7.

Returning to one of the opening images, Carlisle says that if Bolingbroke is crowned King "The blood of English shall manure the ground."[25] And then, in two of the final lines of the play, King Henry IV, the former Bolingbroke, looks for redemption through geography; through the voluntary exile of pilgrimage: "I'll make a voyage to the Holy Land / To wash this blood off from my guilty hand."[26]

The Tempest is another play in which the question of inside and outside, possession and dispossession of territory or land, take a crucial role. Four key figures are important here: Prospero and Caliban, naturally, but also Antonio, the usurper, and Gonzalo, the advisor.

Prospero is the rightful Duke of Milan, but has been dispossessed of his lands. He is banished but becomes the colonizer of the island; removing it from Caliban. Of his own dispossession, Prospero is eloquent:

> To have no screen between this part he played
> And him he played it for, he needs with be
> Absolute Milan. Me, poor man, my library
> Was dukedom large enough. Of temporal royalties
> He thinks me now incapable; confederates,
> So dry he was for sway, wi'th' King of Naples
> To give him annual tribute, do him homage,
> Subject his coronet to his crown, and bend
> The dukedom yet unbowed (alas poor Milan)
> To most ignoble stooping.[27]

This needs a little explanation. Antonio wanted no distinction between his own role and the position he aspired to, occupied by Prospero. He needed to be absolute ruler of Milan. Prospero suggests he — "poor man" — had otherworldly concerns. (We hear later how Antonio had paid off Prospero: "Knowing I loved my books, he furnished me / From mine own library with volumes that / I prize above my dukedom."[28]) "Temporal royalties' are secular, as opposed to spiritual, powers; incapable means that he is both unable to exercise them but also unable to pass them on: the standard lineage has been broken.

---

25 Ibid., III, iv, 138.
26 Ibid., v, vi, 49–50.
27 Shakespeare, *The Tempest*, I, ii, 107–116.
28 Ibid., I, ii, 166–8.

So thirsty for power, Antonio has entered into an alliance with the King of Naples, to whom he pays allegiance, and has bound his rule (the coronet) to the larger kingdom (the crown). A previously proud and superior Milan now bows to Naples.

Caliban is the son of the "foul witch Sycorax,"[29] and Prospero recounts to the spirit Ariel how "the blue-eyed hag was hither brought with child / And here was left by th" sailors."[30] While Prospero thus acknowledges that Caliban was born on the island, and before he, Prospero, arrived, he does everything he can to diminish his birth-right. After Sycorax died, Prospero contends that "Then was this island / (Save for the son that she did litter here, / A freckled whelp, hag-born) not honoured with / A human shape."[31] Ariel responds in a more humanizing way: "Yes, Caliban, her son,"[32] but Prospero seeks to deny the humanity. While he too uses the word "son," he uses the verb "litter," more commonly used of animal births than human; "freckled whelp" suggests a canine pup; "hag-born" again demeans the mother. He even denies that Caliban shares the shape of humans. Shortly after, Prospero calls Caliban "Thou poisonous slave, got by the devil himself / Upon thy wicked dam [mother]."[33]

Caliban is thus the dispossessed, and directly claims this of Prospero. "This island's mine by Sycorax, my mother, / Which thou tak'st from me."[34] He notes that at first Prospero treated him with kindness, and that he responded by love and showing him "all the qualities o'th'isle: / The fresh springs, brine pits, barren places and fertile."[35] Now, Caliban alone is "all the subjects that you [Prospero] have, / Which first was mine own king; and here you sty me / In this hard rock, whiles though do keep from me / The rest o'th' island."[36] Initially he was his own master, a king, ruler of and able to roam over the whole island, but now he is imprisoned within a specific site, a slave, the only subject of a new master, reduced to an animal—sty again implies a bestial dwelling. Prospero responds that he is only imprisoned because of what he has done, which we learn is an attempted rape of Prospero's daughter Miranda. Caliban dreams of colonizing the island for himself, wishing

---

29 Ibid., I, ii, 258.
30 Ibid., I, ii, 269–70.
31 Ibid., I, ii, 281–284.
32 Ibid., I, ii, 284.
33 Ibid., I, ii, 320–1. Slave, service, and servant are frequently used of both Caliban and Ariel.
34 Ibid., I, ii, 332–3.
35 Ibid., I, ii, 338–9.
36 Ibid., I, ii, 343–5.

this had been done, with the idea of how he would have "people else / This isle with Calibans."[37] Shakespeare uses the phrase "violate / The honour of my child."[38] Rape, of course, while today having primarily a sexual sense, comes from the Latin word *rapere* meaning to seize, to abduct, to capture.[39] The rape of Caliban's island through Prospero's actions is paralleled by Caliban's attempted rape of Prospero's daughter.

Caliban continually stresses his dispossession: "As I told thee before, I am subject to a tyrant, / A sorcerer, that by his cunning hath / Cheated me of the island."[40] "I say, by sorcery he got this isle. / From me he got it."[41] And he uses these to try to persuade the butler Stephano and the jester Trinculo of his right to the island, and to get them to help him re-seize it. Caliban's initial welcome of Prospero is paralleled by that he shows to Stephano and Trinculo: "I'll show thee every fertile inch o'th' island, / And I will kiss thy foot. I prithee, be my god. / ... I''ll swear myself thy subject."[42] For Vaughan and Vaughan, Caliban is "in tune with nature and lord of the island until overthrown by Prospero and later corrupted by Stephano and Trinculo."[43] It is the latter that may perhaps be most important in the long run, but the former is the spur to his immediate grievance.

Antonio has seized the territory of Naples from Prospero, but then is lost at sea. His old counsellor Gonzalo speaks for them all when he declares:

> Now would I give a thousand furlongs of sea for an acre of barren ground—long heath, brown furze, anything. The wills above be done, but I would fain die a dry death.[44]

We thus have a triumvirate with relations to territory: the one who is outside territory who creates it anew, truly a place he can be master of the domain; the one who is dispossessed and enslaved but dreams of a biological colonization of his own; and the one who dispossessed but then himself loses all. All

---

37 Ibid., I, ii, 351–2.
38 Ibid., I, ii, 347–8.
39 *Stuprum*—defilement, dishonor, disgrace—is the more common Latin word for "rape" in the modern, sexual sense.
40 Ibid., III, ii, 40–2.
41 Ibid., III, ii, 50–1.
42 Ibid., II, ii, 145–49.
43 Alden T. Vaughan and Virginia Mason Vaughan, *Shakespeare's Caliban: A Cultural History* (Cambridge: Cambridge University Press, 1991).
44 Shakespeare, *The Tempest*, I, i, 65–68.

three figures have colonizing tendencies; all three have moments when they are set outside of territory.

There is an unusual interlude in the play when Iris and Ceres appear in Prospero's masque. Their speeches are profoundly geographical. What Prospero's masque accomplishes is the idea of agri-culture, of improving the land more than those who merely lived in it, of—in the language of a modern colonial project—making the desert bloom.[45]

Later Gonzalo wishes he had "plantation of this isle," with its clear colonial connotation of the plantations first in Ireland and then in the new world; though Antonio and Sebastian (brother to the King) respond with more agricultural ideas: "He'd sow't with nettle-seed./Or docks, or mallows."[46] But Gonzalo has loftier ideals:

> I'th' commonwealth I would by contraries
> Execute all things, for no kind of traffic
> Would I admit; no name of magistrate;
> Letters should not be known; riches, poverty
> And use of service, none; contract, succession,
> Bourn, bound of land, tilth, vineyard—none;
> No use of metal, corn, or wine, or oil;
> No occupation, all men idle, all;
> And women, too, but innocent and pure;
> No sovereignty—[...]
> All things in common should produce
> Without sweat or endeavour; treason, felony,
> Sword, pike, knife, gun, or need of any engine
> Would I not have; but nature should bring forth
> Of its own kind all foison, all abundance,
> To feed my innocent people. [...]
> I would with such perfection govern, sir.[47]

Despite Antonio and Sebastian's interruptions, and often modern editor's accusations of hyperbole, Gonzalo is actually outlining a near-utopian

---

45 In *The Tempest*, II, I, 37, Adrian says this place "seems to be desert," which while he most obviously means deserted, relates the idea of a place that is un- and under-inhabited.
46 Ibid., II, i, 144–45.
47 Ibid, II, i, 148–65.

commonwealth. There are many aspects to be noted. The commonwealth or body politic will not be ruled by the market or commerce ("traffic"); no bureaucracy or written records ("letters"); no discrepancy of wealth or indentured servitude; no inheritance; no "bourn" (a boundary or limit) or "bound of land"—again, a critique of enclosure—and no agricultural working of the soil; no occupation—a multi-faceted term that means a literal sense of seized presence, and employment, but also marital cohabitation; no sovereignty; but instead shared property, an absence of ills, producing abundance and happiness. But if this is a commonwealth without internal divisions, it is still hard to imagine it without boundaries on the outside, to imagine it entirely outside territory.

CONCLUSION

Shakespeare was writing at a time when the modern conception of sovereign territory was emerging and so he helps us understand its variant aspects, tensions, ambiguities and limits. In his own England the dominant form of political power was absolutism, conducted in a space that was, by his time, relatively ordered and bordered. But its recent past—explored in the history plays such as, notably, *Richard II*—was anything but. The earlier setting of *King Lear* shows a place that is historically distant and spatially disrupted. In that it is more similar to the Europe in which he set most of his tragedies, and comedies. This was a space that was contested and fractured, both politically and spatially. We see that, especially, in *Coriolanus*. And in *The Tempest* he explores what this might mean when Europe came into contact with its outside. Shakespeare helps us to understand what it means to be outside territory, conceptually, historically, and politically.

It is not particularly worrying if you and I, ladies and gentlemen, do not know exactly what money is. But it is absolutely terrifying if even the specialists and those who are responsible for money don't know, don't really know what money is.
— J.P. von Bethmann, 1984[1]

WHERE HAS ALL THE (XENO)MONEY GONE?

Angus Cameron

INTRODUCTION: TWO DISAPPEARANCES, ONE RETURN

The graph climbs steadily, business as usual, shares trading normally almost up to the moment of collapse. Things start to dip a little as media reports proliferate, but nothing catastrophic. Then, suddenly on September 15, 2008, the graph drops like a stone—the point at which the global economy goes into free fall. This was the moment US Bank Lehman Brothers collapsed and became the first major casualty of the "credit-crunch." Lehman did not cause the ensuing crisis single-handedly (though they certainly did their bit), but their demise has nevertheless come to symbolize the collective insanity and ineptitude that gripped the financial markets and institutions at the time. In the days following the Lehman collapse we all learned more about "sub-prime markets," "toxic debt" and "market correction" than we'd ever wanted, and that US$ trillions had been "wiped" from the value of the global economy. That's the disappearance everyone knows about.

The lesser known disappearance happened 17 months later. To be precise it happened at 2.45pm, EST, May 6, 2010. In fact the "Crash of 2.45" as it became known (more commonly the "Flash-Crash') unfolded over a slightly longer period of time—about half an hour all in—2.45 representing the bottom of a dizzying 995.55 point fall in the Dow Jones Industrial Average.

This text was first presented in an Exterritory Project Symposium in collaboration with Kadist Art Foundation and with the support of Evans Foundation, May 2, 2012, Le Comptoir Général, Paris, France.

1   Joseph Beuys et al., *What is Money?: A Discussion* (Forest Row: Clairview Press, 2010).

Shortly before 2.45 someone had the wherewithal to pull the plug on the machines that, in the space of a few hectic minutes, had traded away much of America's (and by extension the world's) accumulated and future wealth. Once again, $US trillions were "wiped" off the value of the major US stocks. This time, however, and much to everyone's relief (and surprise), shortly after 2.45 the machines started behaving themselves and within half an hour or so most of the value of the markets had been restored. A few people got very rich, some got burned, some of the sillier trades had to be cancelled, but by and large things went back to "normal." In the case of the Flash Crash, this is to say, the "wiped" US$ trillions came back.

In 2008, once the scale of the disaster became apparent, the question, "Where has all the money gone?" was routinely asked. Given the way that the "losses" were reported in the media, this seemed eminently logical. If, as everyone claimed, the markets were worth x trillion one day, hour or minute, and $x-n$ trillion the next, what did this mean in practice? The response to this question — technically correct, but unsatisfactory — was that the lost "money" had never actually existed. Rather, what was being described as a "loss" was the difference between the nominal values of stocks, assets, securities, cash and the rest before and after market "corrections." If, however, the "losses" reported in 2008 were simply "corrections," was this also true of all that reported value "regained" in the minutes after 2.45 on May 6, 2010? The restoration of market value once the machines had calmed down was certainly treated as real enough at the time. If the money lost in 2008 never actually existed, surely the money regained in 2010 was similarly illusory? This, of course, begs the further and much more important question: "What is money, anyway?" And this question, again routinely asked in 2008, was not really answered at all, even by (perhaps *especially* by) Bethman's "specialists and those who are responsible for money."

In practice the "what" and the "where" of money are, at any given time, intimately connected, if never simple. If the questions provoked by the "disappearances" of 2008 and 2010 were not answered satisfactorily this is because the nature of this interconnection is both ambiguous and counterintuitive. This is partly because of the peculiarity of money as a "substance." Money's effectiveness, as has been observed many times before, is a function of its *mobility* — the velocity with which it circulates and the spaces within and across which it is able to move. These spaces include, of course, the ones we imagine when we read media reports about the economy which roughly equate to the ones we see when we consult a world-map—areas of flat color enclosed by neat black lines. These are supposed to be the "national economies" of, say, France, Greece, Australia, Russia, Somalia, and the other 190 or so (depending on what and who you count) "sovereign" states. But the spatiality of money cannot be reduced to the "formal" spaces of sovereignty. Not only can money's mobility not be explained fully through conventional spaces of economy, its complexity also creates "other" spaces—spaces without magnitude and without territory, but which arguably represent the true domain of contemporary money. Money, this is to say, is intrinsically *extraterritorial*—it is always *beyond* territory however much we might kid ourselves that "we" have pinned it down.[2] And this begs the question not only of where it might go during and after financial crises, but what it is and where it might have started from in the first place.

MOBILE MONEY: VENEZUELAN TAXIS, GHOST COINS AND THE STATE

One of the counter-intuitive aspects of money stems from the "truths" about it we, as economically active citizens of states, have had drummed into us throughout our lives: that it is both *fixed* and *legible*. Fixed, because we give it a name that connects it unambiguously to a territory or territories—Pound, Dollar, Euro, Rouble, Dinar, Rupee, Real, Yen, etc. *National* and/or inter-*national* currencies, but all connected in our minds with known places and spaces. Legible, because whenever money is discussed, these are the terms used to establish a common frame of reference and, therefore, exchange. That common frame always involves some level of allusion to, or simply assumption of, money's territoriality even if in practice we might be a bit hazy about what actually means. Defining money in this way is, however, always problematic.

Although, as suggested above, the currencies we use in daily life all have some form of territorial referent, the money they represent (and here it is important to note that currency is not money, but a representation of it[3]) moves very freely. Should we, as happily cash-rich individuals, for example, wish to move a sterling-denominated bank account or even a suitcase of sterling

[2] In the terms of this project money is also fundamentally "exterritorial"—without territory altogether rather than simply being outside territories, which is the literal meaning of extraterritorial. Exterritorial is rarely used in English and so I will stick to extraterritorial for the purposes of this paper.
[3] Georg Simmel, *The Philosophy of Money* (London: Routledge, 1991); Geoffrey Ingham, *The Nature of Money* (Cambridge: Polity Press, 2004).

notes into Euros there is little or no restriction on that movement. This is because both the £ and the € are freely exchangeable with each other and with most other major national and international currencies. Whilst most of us now simply take this for granted this was not always the case. Until relatively recently many states imposed tight controls on the scale of exchanges with other currencies in an attempt to protect their reserves of "hard currency" and thus their balance of payments with international trading partners. Although this has now become a distant memory for most people in the so-called "advanced" economies, such attempts to restrict monetary mobility persist.

Travelers from the wealthier "advanced" economies of the world traveling to Venezuela, for example, encounter the difficulties of "currency controls" even before they arrive, and from an unexpected source. Booking a taxi from the airport to Caracas involves not just arranging a time and destination, but also a brief but important lesson in Venezuela's complex monetary system. The local taxi firm "Taxi to Caracas" devotes an entire section of its website to helping its prospective clients negotiate the anachronism of state-controlled money. The site helpfully includes a brief account of Venezuela's recent monetary history, including the devaluation of 2008 in which the *Bolivar Fuerte* was adopted resulting in the confusing circulation of three differently denominated local currencies. More importantly, it provides user-friendly advice in faultless English on how to circumvent the poor official exchange rates through the local black-market in foreign currencies:

> The black market gives far higher rates of exchange than the official, government regulated ones. If you do not use the black market rate, Venezuela is a very expensive country to visit. The only way a tourist will usually encounter the black market is in the form of a man approaching you (at the airport for example), quietly saying "dollars, euros." Changing money this way has a huge amount of risk (you could be given old bills/notes or simply be led away and robbed), however it is the only way to get the best value for your currency and consequently the best value for your visit to Venezuela.[4]

4   "Venezuela's Currency Control System," *Taxi to Caracas*. http://www.taxitocaracas.com/cambio-dinero.html (accessed July 13, 2012).

The emphasis on the risks of black market transaction may not be entirely unrelated to the firm's invitation to help with "useful tips" on currency exchange further down the page. Indeed, it is possible that this firm is offering more than transport. However, what is important here is what this says about Venezuela's "national" money. The attempt by the government to control the flows of currency in and out of Venezuelan currency space—in an effort to protect the *Bolivar Fuerte* from the ravages of the international monetary system—is clearly simply stimulating alternative routes. The controls will slow down the flows of currency to some extent, but the evident freedom with which the black market operates suggests not by very much.

Venezuela's attempts to control currency flows at a time when most states have long-abandoned such restrictions highlights a peculiarity of modern "state" money. Venezuela's attempts to control its currency does not have a significant effect on the global economy, but others, particularly China, can inhibit the circulation of major capital flows, hence the pressure China has been under from many capital-starved "advanced" economies to float, even partially, the Renminbi on international markets.[5] It is often assumed that the historical transition from monies based on and often made from *specie* (precious metals such as gold and silver) to paper banknotes and electronic currencies, signals increasing mobility. In practice, however, the creation of "national" currencies guaranteed by law rather than backed by metal (though the two systems have often run concurrently and not without confusion) was an attempt to curb money's tendency to move freely. Prior to the introduction of fully paper monetary systems (starting at the very end of the 18th century, but taking over a century to fully develop[6]) and also before any form of functional currency control, specie money was, paradoxically, highly mobile. In Europe, for example, during the seventeenth century many hundreds of different currencies were in circulation at the same time. Their mobility arose not from where they were issued or by whom, but by the capacity of the network of money-changers (precursors to modern banks) to translate between coinages on the basis of the weight of metal they contained. Thus, for example, London merchant Gerard de Malynes's *Lex Mercatoria* first published in

---

5 Sebastian Mallaby and Olin Wethington, "The Future of the Yuan: China's Struggle to Internationalize Its Currency," *Foreign Affairs* (Jan/Feb 2012): 135–46.
6 Glyn Davies, *A History of Money From Ancient Times to the Present Day* (Cardiff: University of Wales Press, 2002); Eric Helleiner, *The Making of National Money: Territorial Currencies in Historical Perspective* (Ithaca: Cornell University Press, 2003).

1622 as a guide to "international"[7] trade, lists hundreds of different coins with their corresponding weights, fineness, and, therefore, relative values.[8,9] Most of these would have circulated within relatively small geographical areas, but some, such as the *solidus* (or *bezant*)—the so-called "dollar of the Middle Ages"—were used for long-distance trade over centuries.[10]

The gradual process of "standardizing" money began with institutions such as the Bank of Amsterdam (f. 1609) which, at the centre of one of the world's predominant trading ports at the time, had to process many different coinages. To make transactions within the port simpler and cheaper, the Bank took in any coinage or bullion as deposits and recoined and reissued the whole lot as the standard *guilder*.[11] This standardization of coinage greatly increased the efficiency and profitability of Dutch trade and over time became the model used by "national" banks as they emerged at the end of the seventeenth century (e.g., Bank of Sweden, f. 1668; Bank of England, f. 1694).

Although the standardization of coinages happens everywhere eventually, it is not in itself a simple process whereby money becomes steadily and more legibly materialized. This is because even long before the advent of paper and electronic monies, functional money need never have any material embodiment. Writing about the major "currencies" of the European middle ages, for example, Carlo Cipolla notes the strange existence of spectral coinages:

> [H]ere the mystery begins, during the greatest part of the Middle Ages and the first centuries of the modern period, with the exception of a few short periods, nobody ever saw many of these "moneys" about which everybody talked. For instance, nobody for centuries saw a real pound, for the simple, but paradoxical, reason that the pound during the greatest part of

---

[7] As this was prior to what we would now call either inter-national or even "global" trade, this term is a little misleading. De Malynes and his colleagues and competitors could trade with anyone, anywhere and in any currency they liked, the only restrictions being the geographic reach of shipping and the difficulties of translating monetary and commodity values. The *Lex Mercatoria* was intended to ease the latter of these.

[8] Gerard de Malynes, *Lex Mercatoria: Or, the Ancient Law-Merchant Divided into Three Parts of Traffick* (London: 1685).

[9] A transcription of the names of all the coins cited in Malynes' treatise can be found here: http://xenotopia.wordpress.com/2010/10/21/the-poetry-of-money/ (accessed Jan 13, 2016).

[10] Robert Sabatino Lopez, "The Dollar of the Middle Ages," *The Journal of Economic History* 11, no. 3 (1951): 209–34.

[11] Jan de Vries, *The Economy of Europe in an Age of Crisis, 1600–1750* (Cambridge: Cambridge University Press, 1976), 229.

its life did not materialize into a real, visible, and touchable coin. It was a ghost money.[12]

Ghost, "imaginary," "bank," "political" moneys, and "money of account" were all categories used to describe the phenomenon of monetary units in use in daily calculations of prices (particularly by banks and merchants, but also the wider population when needed), and treated as coins, but which were seldom, if ever, actually coined. Although used largely for the convenience of accounting (it is much more practical to tally large sums in "ghost" pounds than in "real" silver shillings), in the context of Europe's burgeoning banking and finance markets these imaginary monies became every bit as "real" as their metal counterparts and were, of course, the distant forerunners of the "fiat" money of the modern state.[13]

The imperative to limit the territorial mobility of money coincides with the efforts of the state to define its boundaries (social, cultural, political, legal, as well as economic) and to define a "national" population—the "imagined community" of the nation state.[14,15] The standardization of money in the form of national currency is part of the efforts by emergent states particularly in the nineteenth century to create what Mary Poovey described as a "social body"[16]—the state as a single, integrated, quasi-organic, corporeal whole. In Britain, for example, which because of its industrial power largely defined what a "normal" state would look like,[17] shift from specie-based to wholly paper money—starting with the "Suspension Act" of 1797—led to the introduction of, among other things the income tax (1799), disciplinary "Poor Laws" (1820s onwards), the reining in of the autonomous power of "Municipal Corporations" (1835), banking "reform" (i.e., consolidation and agglomeration, 1844 onwards) and much else that forced the "nation" together and disciplined the way it used money. As Pierre Bourdieu noted with respect to the significance of taxation to the creation of a "disciplined" and

12 Carlo M. Cipolla, *Money, Prices, and Civilization in the Mediterranean World, Fifth to Seventeenth Century* (New Haven: Princeton University Press, 1956), 38.
13 Luigi Einaudi, "The Theory of Imaginary Money from Charlemagne to the French Revolution," in *Enterprise and Secular Change: Readings in Economic History*, ed. Lane and Riemersma (Homewood: Richard D. Irwin, 1953), 229–61.
14 Benedict Anderson, *Imagined Communities: Reflections on the Rise of Nationalism* (London: Verso, 1991).
15 Angus Cameron and Ronen Palan, *The Imagined Economies of Globalization* (London: Sage, 2004).
16 Mary Poovey, *Making a Social Body: British Cultural Formation 1830–1864* (Chicago, University of Chicago Press, 1995).
17 Cf. Jürgen Habermas, *The Structural Transformation of the Public Sphere* (Cambridge: Polity, 1992).

monetized national community such legislation and tendencies towards territorialization were mutually reinforcing:

> The institution of the tax (over and against the resistance of the taxpayers) stands in a relation of *circular causality* with the development of the armed forces necessary for the expansion and defense of the territory under control, and thus for the levying of tributes as well as for imposing via constraint the payment of that tax. The institution of the tax was the result of a veritable *internal war* waged by the agents of the state against the resistance of the subjects, who discover themselves as such mainly if not exclusively by discovering themselves as taxable, as tax payers.[18]

Money in the form of national currencies and tax systems was used to consolidate "territory" and to link it, for a time at least, with a "national population," but this does not mean that money itself is necessarily territorialized. This is why despite the restrictions, foreign travelers, black market traders, and, on occasions, taxi firms can circumvent the strong nation-state simply by creating a temporary extraterritorial monetary space between themselves. This also explains why, as the routes by which money can circumvent the conventional legal space of the state proliferate (whether through helpful taxi firms or, more likely, the Internet), we are increasingly discovering ourselves as nations of "tax-avoiders."[19]

SOMETHING FOR NOTHING — PLACELESS MONEY

That we no longer have "ghost" or "imaginary" money as formal accounting categories, is not because money has all somehow become real, but because since all money is now effectively fictive such categories are redundant. Contemporary state money — so-called *fiat money* — is fundamentally a creature of law.[20] There is nothing new, of course, about the legalization of

---

18   Pierre Bourdieu, *Rethinking the State: Genesis and Structure of the Bureaucratic Field*, trans. Loïc J.D. Wacquant and Samar Farage, *Sociological Theory* 12, no. 1 (1994): 1–18, at 6 (emphasis in the original).
19   At the time of writing (July 2012), for example, the issue of tax avoidance is gaining extensive news coverage in the UK and continental Europe. In the UK many wealthy "celebrities" are being exposed as "tax-dodgers" by pressure groups such as UKuncut, whilst in Europe, the ongoing crises of the Greek, Italian, and Spanish economies in particular are in part being attributed to endemic tax avoidance among both corporations and the general population.
20   F.A. Mann, *The Legal Aspect of Money: With Special Reference to Comparative Private and Public International Law* (Oxford: Oxford University Press, 1992); Ingham, *The Nature of Money*.

money—not least because at least since the beginnings of the centralized monarchic states of the early European Middle Ages, the issuance and regulation of money has been a function of "sovereignty"—hence the many coinages named in relation to "sovereign" entities: *sovereigns* themselves most obviously, but also *riyals, crowns, nobles, ducats, krone*, etc.

Until the introduction of first paper and then fiat monies, the value of money was, at least in theory, fundamentally guaranteed by the substance from which it was made—gold, silver, and copper/bronze. As has been noted many times, however, even during periods when specie coinages were paramount, metal alone was never enough to define or maintain value.[21] This is partly because of the perennial problem of "debasement"—monarchs manipulating the metal content of coinages to artificially, and always temporarily, increase their apparent wealth—but also because the relationship between "tale" (what a coin is supposed to be worth and/or the number stamped on it) and "weight" (what its metal content is actually worth according to the money-changers' scales and the vagaries of the market) was never stable.[22] Values fluctuated both in relation to other coinages of the same metal and to the many thousands of fractional currencies of different metals that circulated alongside larger value coins.[23] It is for this reason that economic historian Luigi Einaudi described the experience of the modern analyst looking at medieval money as being "to wander for a while in a dark forest."[24] If the standardization of money during the period of the "strong" nation state (roughly 1870s to 1950s) was supposed to make this dark forest easier to navigate, by thinning out both the trees and the undergrowth, more recent events have caused it to grow back more strongly than ever.

To return briefly to the first of our "disappearances" above, for example, the precise nature of money with respect to some of Lehman's later transactions is at best ambiguous. The Valukas Report,[25] commissioned by the SEC to explain the collapse of Lehman, closely examined the bank's use of a particular accounting technique called "Repo 105." This monetary sleight

---

21 John Maynard Keynes, "What is Money" [Review of A Mitchell Innes's Article], *The Economic Journal* 24, no. 95 (1914): 419–21.
22 Davies, *A History of Money*.
23 Richard H. Timberlake, "The Significance of Unaccounted Currencies," *The Journal of Economic History* 41, no. 4 (1981): 853–66; Thomas J. Sargent and François R. Velde, *The Big Problem of Small Change* (Princeton University Press, 2002).
24 Einaudi, "The Theory of Imaginary Money," 235.
25 Anton R. Valukas, *Lehman Brothers Holdings Inc. Chapter 11 Proceedings Examiner Report* (Chicago: Jenner & Block, 2010). http://www.jenner.com/lehman/ (accessed December 7, 2012).

of hand involved Lehman making a "loan" to the financial markets, but, by undertaking to repay 105% of the value, the loan was defined as a sale. The sum in question—around US$ 20 million worth of outstanding debt in Lehman's case—was thus removed from the books until the "sale" was completed. According to the Valukas Report: "Lehman's Global Financial Controller confirmed that 'the only purpose or motive for [Repo 105] transactions was reduction in the balance sheet' and that 'there was *no substance* to the transactions.'"[26]

Although not clarified in the report, "substance" here refers primarily to the transaction because no "real" asset was transferred. Essentially Repo 105 and related processes use legal and accounting loopholes to *redefine* one asset in terms of another in order to conceal it and/or to make it more "tax efficient." However strange and sometimes fraudulent such activities may seem, they are routine aspects of the management of the byzantine financial structures of contemporary corporations. The various activities that allow wealth to be concealed in the world's many tax-havens or protected by the many varieties of "tax-shelter" currently marketed by the world's accountancy industry, all involve the manipulation of the legal meaning and/or location of money.[27] Such activities are only possible because the money in which such transactions are denominated is itself without substance. Since money is already a legal fiction, this is to say, it is not very surprising that enterprising lawyers and accountants find ways of rewriting that fiction to their own advantage.

These substanceless transactions on the part of Lehman, for all the damage they ultimately caused, were relatively minor examples of the abstract nature of contemporary money, particularly those rarified creatures of the global financial markets that circulate on a very large scale—Eurocurrencies, Eurobonds and derivatives of all kinds. Such monies—for all that they continue to be *reported* in familiar currency terms—are in practice of a very different "substance" to the money embodied in the notes and coins used for ordinary daily circulation. As Jean-Joseph Goux noted some years ago even with respect to small-scale transactions, the means of payment—cash, check, or charge—has a determinant effect on the meaning of money and

---

26 Ibid. (emphasis in the original).
27 Angus Cameron and Ronen Palan, *The Imagined Economies of Globalization* (London: Sage, 2004); Angus Cameron and Peter North, "Money and Liberation: The Micropolitics of Alternative Currency Movements.," *Economic Geography* 84, no. 3 (2008): 373–4.

our personal relationship to it.[28] This is even more the case with transactions that take place in the distanciated currencies of high finance and the obscure mathematical markets through which they continuously flow. It is partly because of this that no adequate or final explanation has yet been found either for what caused the flash-crash or, more worryingly, perhaps, what the "loss" and "return" of so much ostensible "value" actually means.[29]

Because of their social as well as economic significance, various attempts have been made to make sense of these monies over recent years, particularly in terms of their location. Brian Rotman famously described the "placeless" monies of the Eurodollar markets that emerged in the late 1950s, for example, as "xenomoney" (literally "strange money"):

> For "Euro" and "dollars" one should write "xeno" and "money" respectively. The Eurodollar has long since shed its attachment to Europe. It is in fact, no longer geographically located, but circulates within an electronic global market which, though still called the Eurodollar market, is now the international capital market.[30]

Rotman is correct to emphasize the separation of "euro" currencies from the territorial space of Europe (they are so named because they originated in the 1950s as US$ traded in European interbank markets[31]), but this does not mean that they have no geographical location. The "space" of Eurocurrency trades may no longer equate to the territories of the currencies they adopt, but that does not remove it altogether as though the domains printed on the map exhaust the possibilities of space.[32] A rather different way of visualizing this space comes more recently from Italian economists Amato and Fantacci, in trying to explain the nature of finance after the crisis of 2008:

---

28 Jean-Joseph Goux, "Cash, Check, or Charge?," in *The New Economic Criticism: Studies at the Intersection of Literature and Economics*, eds. M. Woodmansee and Osteen (London: Routledge, 1999), 114–28.
29 Various explanations have been put forward blaming, variously, anomalous trades, algorithmic and high volume trading systems, worries about the Greek economy (a riot against fiscal austerity took place in Athens just before 2.45pm), an extra o added to a purchase order by mistake by a "fat-finger" on a keyboard, etc. The SEC report into the Flash Crash did not reach a definitive explanation, but recommended the installation of circuit breakers to trading system to at least prevent the fall being so great if, or perhaps when, such an event recurs.
30 Brian Rotman, *Signifying Nothing: The Semiotics of Zero* (Stanford: Stanford University Press, 1987), 90.
31 Gary Burn, "The State, the City and the Euromarkets," *Review of International Political Economy* 6, no. 2 (1999): 225–61.
32 Angus Cameron, "Splendid Isolation: 'Philosopher's Islands' and the Reimagination of Space," *Geoforum* 43 (2012): 741–9.

It was precisely in virtue of the totally free space reserved for capital movements on the eurodollar market that it was possible to prevent them from generating pressure on balances of payments and hence on national currencies, at least as long as that space remained separate from the national monetary and financial systems. On this condition—which, however, remained implicit and problematic—the eurodollar market can be considered an autonomous monetary area with its own currency.[33]

In contrast to Rotman's non-geographical space, Amato and Fantacci are suggesting that the Eurodollar markets effectively have their own mode of quasi-territoriality—an "*autonomous* monetary *area* with its *own currency*." Whilst this may make the Euromarkets seem more legible as monetary spaces, it does not really capture their spatial peculiarity. Eurocurrencies, for all they are traded completely independently of their "home" currency domain, nevertheless trade on the existence of that home: even as they undermine its "fiscal sovereignty." Similarly, Eurocurrency markets are not defined positively in terms of an "area" they create, but negatively in terms of the territorial currency area that they do *not* inhabit. This means that they are defined as the very *antithesis* of territorial money.

Whatever the strengths and limitations of these attempts to explain current monetary realities, it is important to note that both start from the assumption that money is *normally* territorialized. Hence, although they do it differently, both accounts find a way to express the relationship of the "new" money of the Eurodollar markets using the language of "normal" spatiality. However, as suggested above, the "strong" territorialization of money practiced by the nation state and its national currency has in fact been a relatively short exception (less than a century) in a much longer history of monies with little or no necessary connection to territory.

Although this comes as a surprise to many commentators for whom all money is necessarily territorial, the intrinsically exterritorial nature of money is a function of its more general and fundamental lack of substance. This aspect of money was explored throughout the 1970s by performance artist Joseph Beuys who staged many events that sought both to highlight and investigate the paradoxical "nothingness" of money. These involved, for example, "defacing" banknotes with slogans such as "Kunst = Kapital" (art

---

33   Massimo Amato and Luca Fantacci, *The End of Finance* (Cambridge: Polity, 2011), 104.

equals capital) and signing them. Such an act both destroyed the face value of the note as money, but at the same time massively increased its value as an object by turning it, with a few strokes of a pen, into an artwork. Beuys was commenting as much on the dubious and still controversial relationships between art, money and systems of value as he was on the nature of money itself, though many of his "lectures" dwelt almost exclusively on the latter.[34] This aspect of his work culminated in a public panel discussion held in 1984 in Ulm that brought together Beuys himself with a group of bankers and economists to address the question, "What is Money?" The difficulty of defining money in substantive terms was posed directly by development economist Rainer Willert in his opening remarks to the meeting:

> "What is Money?" "Nothing": that's the only possible answer. But it works. Money works because in our heads, yes, we don't think of it as nothing. And because entire networks of institutions—here I'll mention only banks and the pricing system—emerged from this same falsehood and established themselves on its basis, making it their business to hide this nothingness from view. So money works. And its most important work is to secure its future: in other words to make sure we go on desiring it in [the] future too.[35]

The "nothingness" of money is, paradoxically, crucial to its capacity to carry and store value in advanced economies. In place of the relatively inflexible (though arguably more stable) currencies of the period of the gold standard (which finally died with the unpegging of the US$ in 1971), contemporary money derives its value from a highly complex mix of legal decree, global market interactions, banking policies and practices and the definition of what "counts" as money at all. Only a money evacuated of any and all substance (including a fixed territorial location) can function in such a complex system. It is because money is essentially nothing that also means that it is potentially everything—money is a "meta-commodity" that is universally applicable. Beuys own interest in money stemmed precisely from this transcendent universality, something he felt had been undermined by contemporary monetary practices (such as the style of high-risk banking practiced by the likes of Leh-

---

34 For a recent exploration of these same issues, see Maria Lind and Olav Velthuis, eds., *Art and Its Commercial Markets* (Berlin: Sternberg Press, 2012).
35 Ibid., 11.

man), but which nevertheless had an emancipatory potential. Just as Beuys's ethos as an artist was based on the idea of universal participation, so he envisioned a de-institutionalised money that would serve mankind.[36]

This potentiality of money was noted a long time ago by Jorge Luis Borges in his short story "The Zahir" in which the main protagonist considers the power of a "substanceless" coin:

> [...] I reflected that there is nothing less material than money, since any coin whatsoever (let us say a coin worth twenty centavos) is, strictly speaking, a repertory of possible futures. Money is abstract, I repeated; money is the future tense. It can be an evening in the suburbs, or music by Brahms; it can be maps, or chess, or coffee; it can be the words of Epictetus teaching us to despise gold; it is a Proteus more versatile than the one on the Isle of Pharos. It is unforeseeable time, Bergsonian time, not the rigid time of Islam or the Porch. The determinists deny that there is such a thing in the world as a single possible act, *id est* an act that could or could not happen; a coin symbolizes man's free will.[37]

The "substance" of money is, therefore deeply ambiguous. The mobility of contemporary money is both a product of its successive abstraction from national currencies (i.e., from attempts to regulate in through territorial legal/political systems) and the source of its power and value. Although the velocity at which huge volumes of electronic "money" can now circulate is partly a function of its lack of material substance, the significance of velocity to its function has long been recognized. Hence Georg Simmel in his *Philosophy of Money* noted — after paper money was the norm, though before fully-fledged "national" currencies had been fully realized: "The functional value of money exceeds its value as a substance the more extensive and diversified are the services it performs and the more rapidly it circulates."[38] In other words, the functionality of money stands in inverse proportion to its physical "reality."

---

36 Cf. Keith Hart, *Money in an Unequal World* (New York: Texere Publishing, 2001); Peter North, *Money and Liberation: The Micropolitics of Alternative Currency Movement* (Minneapolis: University of Minnesota Press, 2007).
37 Jorge Luis Borges, *The Aleph and Other Stories* (Harmondsworth: Penguin Classics, 2004 [1949]).
38 Simmel, *The Philosophy of Money*, 143.

MONEY IN BETWEEN OR MONEY'S MORBIDITY?

If money has more functional "substance" the less real it is, however, this begs a question about the nature of its mobility. If there is no substance — as Lehman's financial controller happily admits — what moves? The immediate answer is, of course, nothing. If money is, as Willert suggests above,[39] fundamentally nothing, then the answer to "Where has all the money gone?" is easy (if troubling): it has gone nowhere.

Although this may sound peculiar, historically money has not necessarily been a mobile thing in its own right, but a special sort of boundary zone through which other things, commodities of various kinds, are able to move. Money, this is to say, is fundamentally a means of intermediation — translating the worth of disparate objects, services and entities through a common framework of value. As such, money is the means by which mobility is achieved for commodities, rather than being a mobile commodity itself. This mediating boundary function of money and markets is of great antiquity, long predating the creation of the stuff we now call money. For example, idea of a money/market space was attributed by the ancient Greeks to Hermes — messenger of the Gods (and thus, just like money, able to move between states of being), but also in his own right God of both theft and the market place. In his analysis of *Hermes the Thief*, Norman O. Brown describes the connection between the divine trickster and the spatialization of trade:

> The most primitive form of trade, "silent" trade, has features which we have already noticed in the cult of Hermes. In "silent" trade the parties to the exchange never meet: the seller leaves the goods in some well-known place; the buyer takes the goods and leaves the price. The exchange generally takes place at one of those points which are sacred to Hermes — a boundary point such as a mountaintop, a river bank, a conspicuous stone or a road junction.[40]

Money and the "sacred" space of the market here perform no other function than intermediation — a neutral, exterritorial space (with divine protection) — through which trade could be managed without conflict. This exter-

---

39 Cf. Rotman, *Signifying Nothing*.
40 Norman Oliver Brown, *Hermes the Thief: The Evolution of a Myth* (Madison, WI: University of Wisconsin Press, 1947), 39.

nalized and externalizing feature of money and trade continued for centuries until the market place and the institutions of money were gradually brought inside the city walls of medieval Europe and then progressively interpolated into the territories of the state.[41]

At its most fundamental, money however defined and whatever it happens to be made of retains this intermediating function and for that it needs no substance. However, over many centuries we have given money concrete form as currency and, in doing so, allowed it to become not just the conduit for commodity value, but a commodity in its own right. This produces the paradoxical-sounding situation whereby money as currency is traded through the intermediating space of money—territorial money mediated by extraterritorial money.

The question, "Where has the money gone?" therefore appears not as "wrong," but as anachronistic: it assumes that money has one set of essences—solidity, durability, physicality and, above all, territoriality, when in practice all of these have largely dissipated. Contemporary money retains a vestige of these attributes because to function as a commodity, it must maintain a connection—even if only negatively—to a territorial currency and, more importantly perhaps, to the various institutions, laws, debts, assets and the other paraphernalia of contemporary societies through which its value is established. The abstraction of currency into the quasi-spatiality of the Euromarkets has allowed some articulations of "currency" (the currencies used by the markets rather than the ones embodied in the notes and coins in your pocket) to become very close to money in the "pure" sense, but without ever losing its capacity for that internal differentiation (a consequence of borders, interest rates, banking reserve requirements, taxation, etc.) that allows it to generate profits. Why trade in the messy and unpredictable corporeality of a "real" commodity, when—assuming you can trade enough of them, fast enough—the marginal fluctuations between the commodity monies of the forex markets will generate vast revenues. And because the substance and spatiality of currency is already fictional, the new fictions generated by the hedge funds, the futures markets, the accountants and the lawyers cannot be excluded from the mix of commodity monies in circulation. As the "treasury function" of the world's bigger companies has gradually overtaken their

---

41 Cf. Henri Lefebvre, *The Production of Space* (Oxford: Blackwell, 1991); Charles Tilly, *Coercion, Capital and European Cities: AD 990–1992* (Oxford: Blackwell, 1992).

manufacturing and trading functions as a source of profit, so "money" in all its strange and abstracted forms, has more and more come to dominate economic global activity.

Although the scale of this shift in the nature and importance of money has grown at a geometric rate in recent decades (particularly since the vast influx of petrodollars into the forex markets in the 1970s), the uneasy relationship between money as intermediary and money as commodity is not new. John Maynard Keynes recognized the dangers inherent in it long before it grew beyond our collective control. Dreaming of a future when we would *not* value money as something to own and horde, he argued:

> We shall be able to afford to dare to assess the money motive at its true value. The love of money as a possession—as distinguished from the love of money as a means to the enjoyments and realities of life—will be recognized for what it is, a somewhat disgusting morbidity, one of those semi-criminal, semi-pathological propensities which one hands over with a shudder to the specialist in mental disease.[42]

Commodity money, territorialized money, Keynes was already suggesting in the 1930s, is a sign of collective insanity. The curious disappearances of 2008 and 2010, and our manifest inability to comprehend them, despite their concerning that substance that we use every day of our lives—money—might seem to confirm the madness at the heart of our economies.

CONCLUSION: CHANGING THE MENTAL MAP

For all his condemnation of what territorial money had become, Keynes did not suggest that it should or could simply be abolished. Rather he envisaged a gradual change over the course of a century or so, after which the contradictions in and unsustainability of modern money would render it obsolete. Whether his prognosis will prove accurate remains to be seen, but it is certainly possible that the crises witnessed since 2008 not just in the functioning of money but in its very meaning, signal what Amato and Fantacci suggest might be the "end of finance."[43]

---

42   John Maynard Keynes, *Essays in Persuasion* (London: Macmillan, 1931), 369.
43   Amato & Fantacci, *The End of Finance*.

At the very least our "terrifying" collective inability to understand the true nature of money—"you and I, ladies and gentlemen, *and* the specialists"—should cause us to start to re-examine it. With respect to its location, international political economist Benjamin Cohen concluded his analysis of *The Geography of Money* in the following terms:

> If public policy is to remain at all effective [...] we must update our mental maps of money to close the widening gap between image and fact—between the conventional myth of One Nation/One Money and the reality of a deterritorialized galactic structure of currency. Westphalia's territorial trap must be avoided. We all need to learn to think anew about the spatial organization of monetary relations.[44]

More recently, the "Occupy Wall Street" protesters began to issue new mental "maps" of money, using money itself. To highlight inequalities in the US economy, they overstamped dollar bills with graphic representations of the huge disparities of income and wealth in the US.[45]

This may not look like a map, mental or otherwise, but that is only because we assume that all money is the same—a dollar is a dollar. But in addition to pointing out how unequal the distribution of dollars of all kinds is, the "Occupy George" bill also subtly alludes to the fact that the dollars represented to the left—those controlled by the four hundred richest Ameri-

---

44 Benjamin J. Cohen, *The Geography of Money* (Ithaca: Cornell University Press, 1998), 168.
45 There are various different versions, all available to download from: http://www.occupygeorge.com/ (accessed July 13, 2012).

cans—have a fundamentally different *location* to those on the right. Where money *is*, where money *goes* and, ultimately, *what* money is, are, therefore, a matter of *scale*. Those to the left of the Occupy George Bill are able to access the extraterritorial world of the so-called HNWIs and Ultra-HNWIs.[46] Most of those to the right have no choice but to live within the confines of territorial money—the relatively immobile domain of state controlled money: of cash.

Clearly, and despite the efforts of Occupy George, our mental maps are not yet up to date with the emergent geographies of money. The anomalous, partial explanations of the crises of 2008 and 2010—both of which are, of course ongoing—further underline the disconnect Cohen observes between the "image" and the "fact" of money. That we cannot yet with any degree of certainty answer the question, "Where has all the money gone?," suggests that we need not just an "updating" of our mental maps, but some fundamental changes in the way extraterritorial money is created, managed, regulated, and distributed.

---

[46] "High-Net Worth Individuals" and "Ultra- High-Net Worth Individuals." There are various definitions for these people, but the most commonly used is that HNWIs have at least US$1 million in disposable income available to them (i.e., not fixed assets such as real estate). Ultra-HNWIs have at least US$20 million.

Extraterritoriality, Diaspora, and the Space of Cyberspace

Victoria Bernal

The relationship of the Internet to territory is complex, contradictory, and changing. Exploring the diverse and shifting ways that Eritreans in diaspora have used websites to participate in national politics from outside the country sheds light on the dynamics of digital extraterritoriality and its significance for politics. At first cyberspace may be appear to be simply an extraterritorial space, where websites are constructed as spaces with no territorial location. A contributor to a recent volume on digital anthropology notes that, "few aspects of digital media, cyberspace or the network society are as commonly perceived as fundamental as its disembodying aspects, its placelessness and subordination of physical proximity to network connectivity."[1] At the same time it can be said that, "[a] cardinal rule of the geography is that social life takes place in 'constructed' spaces."[2] If we understand cyberspace as a constructed space, its significant feature is not its extraterritoriality but rather that the space of cyberspace is ambiguous and elastic, allowing it to support diverse constructions, alternative imaginaries, and multiple forms of territoriality and extraterritoriality.

Eritrea is located in the Horn of Africa bordered by Ethiopia, Sudan, Djibouti, and the Red Sea. First colonized by Italy, Eritrea was later annexed by Ethiopia in 1962. Three decades of war fought on Eritrean soil followed.[3] The Eritrean People's Liberation Front won independence in 1991 and Eritrea has been governed since then by ex-guerilla fighter Isaias Afewerki and his ruling party, the People's Front for Democracy and Justice. The original Eritrean

---

[1] Lane DeNicola, "Geomedia: The Reassertion of Space within Digital Culture," in *Digital Anthropology*, ed. H. Horst & D. Miller (London and New York: Berg, 2012), 81.
[2] Ronan Palan, "Offshore and the Institutional Environment of Globalization," in *Political Space: Frontiers of Change and Governance in a Globalizing World*, ed. Y.H. Ferguson and R.J.B. Jones (Albany: SUNY Press, 2002), 212.
[3] Lionel Cliffe and Basil Davidson, *The Long Struggle of Eritrea for Independence* (Trenton: Red Sea Press, 1998).

diaspora was a product of the war with Ethiopia that drove Eritreans to flee their homes or stranded them abroad as was the case for Eritrean students studying overseas who could not safely return. Hundreds of thousands of Eritreans were forced to make new lives for themselves in other lands under various circumstances. The Isaias regime entered into a new conflict with Ethiopia from 1998 to 2000 over the border between the two nations. From 2001 on, its policies and practices became increasingly repressive. This has created a new diaspora, particularly among young people who have been fleeing the country in thousands every month.[4]

Diaspora, much like cyberspace, allows new imaginaries of the meaning of territorial locations and borders and makes possible new spatializations of relationships. Diaspora can be understood as a form of extraterritoriality. Diasporas possess no territory; they exist, not through occupying space, but by transcending it. Migrants, refugees, diasporas, and similar populations live in ambiguous and simultaneous relationships with multiple territorial locations and communities. They are at once connected to and disconnected from the places where they live and work on a daily basis (where they may consider themselves temporary and/or be treated like outsiders), and also from the territory they no longer inhabit (the places they left behind but to which they still belong or feel attached). The concept of diaspora and related notions of displaced people capture the disconnect between such populations and territory, giving them an extraterritorial identity. Moreover, the extraterritorial aspect of diasporic identity is not simply the fact of living outside a homeland. Diasporic belonging is extraterritorial in the way that it bridges and creates continuity out of the discontinuous spaces occupied by members of dispersed populations. Diasporas, thus, are not simply located outside of the nations they left; through their presence and their absence they remap citizenship and sovereignty across and within national territories.

The Internet also makes possible new forms of connection and disconnection involving mediated absences and presences. The next section of this paper considers how the metaphor of space has been used in relation to the Internet in ways that lead us to conceptualize it as extraterritorial. Then I consider how we might complicate our conceptualization of the Internet as extraterritorial. I do so through an analysis of Eritrean diaspora websites that reveal more complex possibilities of the relationship of digital media to ter-

4   Gaim Kibreab, *Eritrea: A Dream Deferred* (Rochester: James Currey, 2009).

ritory and to extraterritoriality. This suggests that the Internet is best viewed not simply as extraterritorial, but as enabling the re-envisioning of territorial relations. In particular, the Internet can be used to remake our sense of place in a number of ways that are significant for nations, states, and sovereignty. The Internet is more than simply a cheap, convenient mode of communication. Cyberspace does more than simply shrink distances, it serves diasporas as a space that is ambiguously located, easily accessed, and in some sense equidistant from all locations on the globe. It is at once neither here nor there (neither inside the nation nor outside it), and yet it is also both here and there simultaneously. Cyberspace thus disrupts the homeland/diaspora dichotomy. The political impact of new media, moreover, appears to be much greater outside of established democracies, in autocratic systems where information and public debate are state-controlled or highly centralized.

EXTRATERRITORIALITY AND CONCEPTIONS OF THE INTERNET

The connectivity of the Internet is both a deterritorializing force and a reterritorializing force. Through the Internet people communicate across political and geographic borders in ways that can make location seem invisible or irrelevant. Digital connectivity can upend our sense of geography by shrinking distances and bridging physical gaps thereby bringing faraway places close. A sense of "co-presence" is created online.[5] The Internet also allows for the production of virtual spaces. We "visit" websites, we take "virtual tours." We "go" online and "go to" or "visit" websites, we speak of web "sites" rather than "sights" even though we are looking at visual data on a screen. We speak of "cybersquatting" and "lurking." Spatiality may be a distinctive feature of cyberspace as a medium. We do not experience or conceptualize our engagement with other media whether print, radio, or film in quite these ways.

Our notion of cyberspace as space and websites as places is a cultural construction. Schulte writes of this development:

> As Internet use gained popularity, two initially separate practices, "computing" and "the Internet," began to merge. This terminological melding signaled a conceptual collapse, as computing was increasingly imagined

---

5 Jeffrey Juris, "Reflections on #Occupy Everywhere: Social Media, Public Space, and Emerging Logics of Aggregation," *American Ethnologist* 39, no. 2 (2012): 259–79.

as networking and the computer apparatus was imagined primarily as a gateway to the Internet. As the Internet lost its body, in a sense, it became easier to imagine the Internet as a deterritorialized space or experience rather than a product of hardware.[6]

This process was neither natural nor inevitable, as Schulte points out:

> Internet hardware and software development, institutions of government finance, state regulation, and corporate prerogatives actively re-imagined the Internet as a space to explore or inhabit or as a state of being rather than a product of digital code and programs contained within computer infrastructures and networking wires.[7]

Cloud computing is a growing development in digital media that is represented by a new extraterritorial metaphor. People talk about "the cloud" as if cyberspace exists above our heads, even though we know that servers, computers, and users are all situated in specific locations on the ground. Data you store "in the cloud" may not be located on your device, but it is stored in a terrestrial location somewhere.

While cyberspace is imagined as an extraterritorial place, the focus of much Internet scholarship on the virtual, on online communities, and on the distinctiveness of digital media has tended to obscure the interpenetration of online and off-line worlds. As Christensen, Jansson, and Christiansen note, the Internet too often has been seen "as a territory in its own right" and thus detached from context.[8] Yet, as they argue, "It is precisely these processes of co-construction, the interplay between structural forces and the social and cultural affordances of online media, that call for a critical re-examination of how territories are (re)produced and legitimized."[9] Diasporas similarly trouble assumptions about the meaning of territory and its relation to social formations and political orders.

---

6   Stephanie Ricker Schulte, *Cached: Decoding the Internet in Global Popular Culture* (New York and London: New York University Press, 2013), 3.
7   Ibid., 10.
8   M. Christensen, A. Jansson, and C. Christiansen, "Introduction: Globalization, Mediated Practice and Social Space, Assessing the Means and Metaphysics of Online Territories," in *Online Territories* (2011); xi.
9   Ibid., 3.

DIASPORA, TERRITORY, AND CYBERSPACE

Diaspora involves territorial connections and disjunctures that engender acts of imagination and affect that are linked to territory, yet not bound by it. Eritreans in diaspora were early adopters of digital media as a means of connecting to Eritrean politics.[10] The speed of communications on the Internet is significant for politics because it makes distant places seem as close and accessible as near ones and, moreover, eliminates the delays normally associated with distance. This technologically constructed proximity achieved through Internet communications makes it possible for members of the diaspora to respond immediately to current events, national crises, and scandals in Eritrea. In this way they can actually participate in unfolding events, framing issues, shaping opinions, and mobilizing action.

Eritreans in diaspora created public space for themselves online through the establishment of several key websites that have proven long-lasting. These websites (most notably *Dehai*, *Awate*, and *Asmarino*[11]) form an online public sphere that constitutes Eritrean space in cyberspace. This Eritrean space online was not established purely for the diaspora or primarily as an online community *sui generis* but was intended to connect Eritreans in diaspora to Eritrea and serve Eritreans wherever they might be located.

Through the websites they established, Eritreans in diaspora created Eritrean space online. Eritrean online space is not simply extraterritorial, but serially and simultaneously engaged in multiple and shifting relationships to Eritrea itself. Sometimes websites serve as national space that extends the nation beyond its borders and sometimes websites serve as national space that is outside the nation and independent from it. In this latter sense websites may serve not as extraterritory in the sense of a non-terrestrial space, but rather more as extra territory, Eritrean national space that is outside the nation and, therefore, free of government control. Websites may serve as extraterritorial when the aspect of virtual space is foregrounded, offering a space that has no particular location but is everywhere and accessible from anywhere. The ambiguity of location on the Internet thus makes possible different forms of territorialization, deterritorialization, reterritorialization and, extraterritoriality.

10 Victoria Bernal, "Eritrea On-line: Diaspora, Cyberspace, and the Public Sphere," *American Ethnologist* 32, no. 4 (2005): 660–75.
11 Respectively, http://www.dehai.org, http://www.awate.com, http://www.asmarino.com.

We can complicate the notion of the Internet as extraterritorial by considering the ways that cyberspace can be used not only to deterritorialize, but also to reterritorialize. Eritreans in diaspora, for example, sometimes treat websites as national space where they in effect relocate themselves within the nation of Eritrea, even writing their posts in ways that sound as if they are inside the country, as for instance, when writing things like "if we are to develop this country," meaning Eritrea, when the writer is actually posting from Germany, where they live. Cyberspatiality blurs the distinction between Eritreans inside Eritrea and Eritreans outside it. Since Eritreans in diaspora have more access to the Internet and are responsible for creating and maintaining the popular Eritrean websites, as well as for producing most of the posts, this blurring of spatial distinctions works as a kind of illusion that bridges the diaspora's separation from Eritrea, concealing their distance from Eritrea and their dispersal from one another. In this sense, the websites they created reterritorialize the diaspora, locating them in Eritrea. Sometimes, cyberspace and diaspora are not so much outside of Eritrea as they are extensions of Eritrea.

I consider cyberspace as a space where the Eritrean diaspora is located. As Daniel Miller has argued, "Instead of regarding SNS [social networking sites] as simply a means to communicate between two given localities, it is also possible to start thinking about SNS as places in which people in some sense actually live."[12] Georgiou found that among the Greek Cypriot diaspora, "For those active participants of online Greek Cypriot fora, an online territoriality of community emerges against a grounded territoriality that excludes them from participating in what happens at the actual place (Cyprus as a nation-state and as a grounded territory."[13] Through their websites Eritreans can be inside and outside Eritrea at the same time.

Dehai was the first computer-mediated network of Eritreans and is now the longest-running Eritrean website. It has been part of Eritrean politics since 1992, the year before Eritrea was officially recognized as a nation. *Dehai* was established by a group of Eritreans in diaspora in the US and by design it was devoted to Eritrean politics and nation-building. *Dehai* built upon a non-technological worldwide web of Eritrean nationalist associations that had been organized in many countries by the Eritrean People's Liberation Front

---

12   Daniel Miller, "Social Networking Sites," in *Digital Anthropology*, 155–56.
13   Myria Georgiou, "Diaspora, Mediated Communication and Space: A Transnational Framework to Study Identity," in *Online Territories* (2011): 208.

throughout the 1970s and '80s, and on other social networks and kinship relations that sustained a transnational Eritrean community of interlinked and overlapping networks.[14] *Dehai* remained the gathering place for Eritreans around the world through the 1990s. Since connectivity within Eritrea was largely limited to government offices throughout that time, the Internet, furthermore, offered a special conduit from Eritreans in diaspora to the state. Through *Dehai* Eritreans used the Internet to expand the boundaries of the nation so that it encompassed the diaspora and the virtual national space of a website. *Dehai* could be seen as an extension of national territory rather than existing outside it. The catch-phrase underneath *Dehai* on the website's home page is "Eritrea online" suggesting that the site is meant to be experienced as Eritrea or to be understood as representing the nation. The extraterritoriality or placelessness of cyberspace is thus turned to the opposite purpose of creating Eritrean national territory.

The space of cyberspace is elastic; it can connect the diaspora and the homeland online in ways that blur the distinction between Eritreans living in Eritrea and those settled abroad. In that sense, it reterritorializes the diaspora and reshuffles territory-related distinctions. A recent post referring to an event where a speaker critical of the government was challenged by audience members proclaimed: "Here are Eritrea's volunteer sons & daughters right in the heart of North America fighting tooth and nail once again against all odds, so that our precious nation & people remain fiercely independent forever & ever." The author went on to say "it is my strong belief that the good bad and the ugly we have gone through pre & post independence has brought us all, the people and the leadership more closer than ever before with strong & resolute determination never seen before to stay the course of absolute unity indefinitely."[15] Here is a vision of the nation that transcends place, binding "the people and the leadership" in "absolute unity."

This is not to say location has no place online. In fact, *Dehai* posters often mention their city or country of residence or include it in their signature line. Posters generally use their real names and *Dehai* includes their email addresses from which their country can be determined since email addresses outside the US have a country suffix—itself an interesting expression of territoriality online. Yet the cyberspatial public sphere appears borderless since

---

14 Victoria Bernal, "Eritrea Goes Global: Reflections on Nationalism in a Transnational Era," *Cultural Anthropology* 19, no. 1 (2004): 3–25.
15 *Dehai* post, January 17, 2015.

people access it from diverse countries, and analyses, comments, and debates from anywhere appear seamlessly in conversation. Furthermore, while posters' identities and even locations may be known, readers are anonymous and their locations unknown. This, along with the belief that Eritrea's leaders not only read posts, but might themselves post under pseudonyms all have contributed to a sense of accessing Eritrea itself through the Internet. A recent post exemplifies the pro-government stance of many *Dehai* posters while blurring the boundaries between diaspora and homeland and between the people and the state in its call to defend Eritrea:

> Still the evil mission of the Human Rights Group is in action. Therefore, it is up to us Eritreans all over the world to stop it. Yes we can stop it for we are armed by the same if not more powerful weapon to fight back. We have ERI-TV [the state television] as the vanguard and then add all the following patriotic websites to give them hell. They are: www.shabait.com, www.shaebia.org, www.dehai.org.[16]

The list of patriotic websites puts *Dehai* right after the official websites of the government and the ruling party and then goes on to include a number of other websites, while not including politically critical websites like *Asmarino* or *Awate*.

Sometimes what the Internet offers might best be understood not as extraterritorial, but as extra territory. In analyzing Eritrean experience I have likened diaspora and websites to a kind of "offshore" that is important for the loosened grip that national sovereignty can exercise over it.[17] Successful rival Eritrean websites, *Asmarino* and *Awate*, being paramount among them, began to compete with *Dehai* in the aftermath of the devastating border war that Eritrea and Ethiopia waged between from 1998 to 2000. To say that *Dehai*, *Asmarino*, and *Awate* serve as Eritrean territory does not mean that no others ever go there, but rather, that when they do, they are entering Eritrean space. The Eritrean character of the websites is their defining feature as evidenced by the Eritrean identities of their web managers and content producers, the focus of their content on Eritrean national politics, and even the names of the websites. *Dehai* is a Tigrinya word that means both "voice" and "news," *Awate*

---

16 *Dehai* post, January 24, 2015.
17 Victoria Bernal, "Nation as Network: Diaspora, Cyberspace, and Citizenship (Chicago: University of Chicago Press, 2014).

is the name of a nationalist hero, and *Asmarino* is a term for someone from Asmara, Eritrea's capital.

Like *Dehai*, *Asmarino*, and *Awate* were founded by Eritreans living in the US; but from the start they differed from *Dehai*. *Dehai* used the Internet to extend Eritrean national territory and sovereignty to the diaspora and to cyberspace, supporting President Isaias Afewerki and the ruling party, the People's Front for Democracy and Justice. Through *Dehai* Eritreans in diaspora participate in Eritrean nationalism and nation-building. *Asmarino* and *Awate*, in contrast, used cyberspace more like an offshore territory from which Eritreans could develop alternative and independent perspectives from those of the state, and challenge the legitimacy of the Isaias regime. While still constituting Eritrean territory online, these websites used cyberspace to create Eritrean space that is not dominated by the government. *Asmarino*'s tag line is "Independent." These websites have responded to growing repression and the lack of independent media within Eritrea since 2001 when the government closed down the free press and imprisoned journalists along with high officials who had who had publicly expressed criticism of President Isaias Afewerki. *Awate* and *Asmarino* attracted posters and readers by attempting to transcend the self-censorship and policing that often inhibited dissent and critical debate on *Dehai*. A recent example from *Dehai* employs the common theme of accusing critics of being traitors allied with Eritrea's enemies, particularly Ethiopia.

> [S]ince the 1950s, Eritrea has had her fair share of elements who betrayed Eritrea. The ugliest and the most disgraceful of these elements were the one[s] who wanted us to be "Ethiopians"? Where are these elements these days? Where else. Just like their predecessors, they are counting their days in this life with no country and people to belong to. Just like the rest, one after another they will evaporate into thin air in "NO MAN'S LAND."[18]

It is significant that the disastrous fate envisioned for these critics is non-existence represented as a kind of extraterritory— "no-man's-land." It is not a question, then, of living in diaspora rather than in the homeland, but rather of social death symbolized by being cut off from meaningful, inhabited territory.

18   *Dehai* post, January 24, 2015.

The Internet has expanded the spaces available to people to express their views, engage in debate and discussion, petition, protest, and organize. *Awate*'s motto, "Inform. Inspire. Embolden. Reconcile" conveys in the word "embolden" the need for Eritreans to overcome fear of expressing themselves. This is all the more significant for Eritreans because within the country no opposition is allowed, the media are controlled by government, and dissenters are harshly punished. The significance of Eritrean space in cyberspace is heightened by the fact that people can experience freedoms of expression and critical debate not possible on Eritrean soil. As Sassen points out,

> Electronic space is, perhaps ironically, a far more concrete space for social struggles than that of the national political system. It becomes a place where nonformal political actors can be part of the political scene in a way that is much more difficult in national institutional channels.[19]

The diaspora websites, particularly *Asmarino* and *Awate*, have come to be used as an offshore platform for civil society where Eritreans engage in national politics outside the authority of the state. In these online spaces, politically independent perspectives and subjectivities can be developed collectively as posters construct alternative histories and reframe and revise national narratives, engaging in activities not possible on Eritrean soil.

The use of websites as a space for Eritrean civil society and expression is thus particularly important since government repression makes it impossible for these to take place in Eritrea. A recent post on *Asmarino* calls for donations to support the website "so that it will continue to keep the lights on for a new generation of Eritreans to be reporters, editors, poets, writers, commentators, designers, artists, painters, etc. Most importantly, to continue to be the voice of the voiceless Eritreans at home and elsewhere."[20] A post on *Awate* urging Eritreans to testify about human rights abuses to the United Nations Commission of Inquiry on Eritrea notes the difficulty of speaking against the regime. It also presents a vision of the nation that foregrounds mutual obligations among countrywomen and men rather than ties to land or loyalty to a government:

---

19 Saskia Sassen. "Electronic Markets and Activist Networks: The Weight of Social Logics," in *Digital Formations: IT and New Architectures in the Global Realm*, ed. Robert Latham and Saskia Sassen (Princeton: Princeton University Press, 2005), 82.
20 *Asmarino* post, January 9, 2015.

It takes courage to give testimony on behalf of oneself or on behalf of those whose rights were violated by PFDJ [Eritrea's ruling party]. And yes, there may be certain deterrents that discourage one from speaking out; the sense of shame or betrayal are examples of familiar cultural offenses. Nevertheless, the courage to speak out, in this case, is just as much a quest for justice on behalf of an entire nation as it is on behalf of oneself and other victims. To stand up for your rights and for those of your countrywomen and men, is to stand up for the future welfare of the nation that thousands have bled, died and sacrificed for...[21]

In the beginning Eritreans used the Internet in ways that extended the nation-state beyond its territorial borders and blurred the boundaries between the homeland and the diaspora. On *Dehai* the distinction between the people and the state was also left ambiguous and undefined in posters' focus on the deterritorialized nation. These effects are created when diaspora posters write as if they are located in Eritrea, and when posts discuss Eritrea as if the citizens, the diaspora, and the state were a single entity. While these practices continue in some posts on any of the websites up to now, *Awate* and *Asmarino* generally operate as spaces that are distinct and separate from the nation-state and the ruling party. As an offshore civil society, then, websites like these allow Eritreans inside and outside of Eritrea to challenge the government from cyberspace. The online public sphere operates as an offshore platform outside state authority, offering important counterpoints to the state's authority and to the national media it controls.

As emerges from this discussion, there are interesting parallels and synergies between diasporas as extraterritorial populations in relation to their homeland, and cyberspace as used by Eritreans and other diasporas as an extraterritorial space that does not reflect their territorial location, but rather their affective ties or emotional location. Although Eritreans in diaspora have settled abroad and made new lives for themselves as citizens of other countries, their sense of who they are is not defined by their legal status or place of residence, but rooted in Eritrea's turbulent past, uncertain present, and possible future in which all Eritreans have a stake.

The dynamic online territory of Eritrean websites reconfigures territorial relations. Through *Asmarino* and *Awate* Eritreans in diaspora have used cy-

---

21   *Awate* post, October 17, 2014.

berspace to de-center the nation, shifting its primary locus from the state's center of power in Asmara, to Eritreans wherever they may be located. This was particularly striking in the virtual national war memorial established online by the Eritrean diaspora website *Awate*. The Martyrs Album as it was called, commemorated Eritrean lives lost in the 1998–2000 border war.[22] The texts of the memorial written by the web managers of *Awate* constructed the Eritrean nation as rooted in Eritrean people themselves, in contrast to official narratives that locate Eritrea in national territory and the sovereign state that controls it under the leadership of President Isaias Afewerki. Eritrean websites reveal the creative strategies of the less powerful to construct new spaces and strategies of political participation and to expand the boundaries of what can be publicly expressed.

CONCLUSION

Cyberspace can be an extraterritorial space in the sense of "an autonomous sphere at a removal from the confines of any one national territory."[23] Yet, in profound ways it remains tethered to the earth and to the geo-political configurations of power and relations of sovereignty. The Internet's freedom from constraints has often been overestimated by scholars and others. Perhaps the vision of openness and equality associated with the Internet represents merely a hypothetical potential that we can seek to approach but can never reach. In practice, identities, power differentials, and authority are reproduced online as well as contested. Censorship and self-censorship of various kinds define what is and is not expressed on Eritrean websites, for example. Self-appointed citizens monitor and seek to police online spaces and, Eritreans believe that in some cases they are recruited by the state to serve this purpose. All of the three websites are expressly democratic in their mission statements and ideals and their claims to being uncensored are credible. Nonetheless there is a paradox in that the Internet appears to be unbounded and totally open, and was likened by some scholars to a new frontier, while in practice, it is structured and limited by the ways people use it. The Eritrean online public sphere is not boundless and completely free of constraints. Even though websites are not administered or regulated by the state, or even

22 Victoria Bernal, "Diaspora, Digital Media, and Death Counts: Eritreans and the Politics of Memorialisation," *African Studies* 72 (Nov. 2013): 246–64.
23 *Extraterritory Project* (June 16, 2013). http://exterritory-project.org (accessed Jan. 25, 2016).

censored by web managers, posters impose political norms on themselves and on others that construct the boundaries of what is expressed and what is suppressed. There are ongoing tensions arising from existing political and cultural structures that do not vanish simply because a group has access to the Internet. Though many have theorized the democratizing potential of the fact that in principle anyone can post any view online, in practice people are often intimidated to post unpopular or dissident perspectives and those who do are met with harsh responses that serve to silence others.

In the wake of Snowden's revelations about NSA data collection, it is becoming ever more clear that the often invisible architecture of the Internet, the servers and cables that constitute its infrastructure, as well as the locations of developers, designers, web managers, and posters are territorial and that their locations make a political difference in jurisdictions, regulations, and rights. As Castells reminds us, "The Internet Age has been hailed as the end of geography. In fact, the Internet has a geography of its own, a geography made of networks and nodes that process information flows generated and managed from places."[24]

Nonetheless as the Eritrean experience shows, the Internet remains a powerful tool for reconfiguring territorial relations and unsettling distinctions between categories of experience. It has altered the landscapes of citizenship and sovereignty and given rise to new political spaces. Eritreans have developed new political practices and discourses to negotiate the deterritorialized relations between citizens and the state. Eritreans in diaspora are experimenting online in ways that suggest new forms of citizenship, democracy, and the public sphere emerging out of the new technologies and the heightened mobility of our times. Diasporas and other mobile populations are altering nations' centers of gravity through the powerful transnational fields they sustain, in part, through the Internet. Eritreans' engagement with the Internet shows we cannot define its quality of extraterritoriality or its relation to territory in narrow or fixed terms. We need to explore the various and shifting permutations of cyberspatial and territorial relations that are always both grounded and virtual.

The affordances of digital media are increasingly woven into the fabric of people's lives, and today cyberspace is perhaps no more magical than elec-

---

24 Manuel Castells, *The Internet Galaxy: Reflections on the Internet, Business, and Society* (Oxford: Oxford University Press, 2002), 207.

tricity. Yet the Internet remains an inspiration, stimulating imaginaries of an unbound world where borders are crossed with ease and intimacies transcend distance, where collaboration and community persist on the basis of mutual interest rather than on repression, and where new spaces of creativity and connection continue to be sited.

EXTRATERRITORIAL CRIMES

1. INTRO-
DUCTION

Extraterritorial Jurisdiction to Enforce in Cyberspace?: Bodin, Schmitt, Grotius in Cyberspace

Mireille Hildebrandt

What is at stake if our justice authorities decide to hack a computer system that is physically located on a server outside the territory of the state they represent, for instance because a webbot was operated from that location,[1] causing serious harm to a variety of computing systems in our own jurisdiction—harm that renders the perpetrator criminally liable under our own criminal law? How would we respond to Ukrainian, Chinese, Iranian, British, or Argentinian justice authorities that hack a computer system that is located within our own jurisdiction? Does it make a difference whether the hack by law enforcement authorities targets a dissident whose right to free speech is denied or a network disseminating child pornography? Should we evaluate such groping for extraordinary jurisdiction in terms of just versus unjust causes (a *bellum iustum privatum*?) or is this about the Westphalian interplay of internal and external sovereignty? Might the attempt to extend or initiate extraterritorial jurisdiction-to-enforce be understood as an *occupatio*, grounded in what Schmitt coined "a-legality,"[2] or should we follow

---

Originally published as Mireille Hildebrandt, "Extraterritorial Jurisdiction to Enforce in Cyberspace? Bodin, Schmitt, Grotius in Cyberspace," *University of Toronto Law Journal* 63, no. 2 (2013): 196–224. Reprinted with the permission of University of Toronto Press. This text was presented at an Exterritory Project Symposium in collaboration with Stedelijk Museum, March 15, 2015, Stedelijk Museum, Amsterdam, Netherlands. This chapter was published in the *University of Toronto Law Journal* 63, no. 2, (Spring 2013): 196–224.

1 A bot is "an automated software program that can execute certain commands when it receives a specific input (like a ro-'bot')," see http://www.techterms.com/definition/bot. On the web it is used to search or crawl the web to retrieve information. In the case of cybercrime "[a] zombie (also known as a bot) is a computer that a remote attacker has accessed and set up to forward transmissions (including spam and viruses) to other computers on the Internet. The purpose is usually either financial gain or malice. Attackers typically exploit multiple computers to create a botnet, also known as a zombie army." See http://searchmidmarketsecurity.techtarget.com/definition/zombie.

2 E.g., (based on Carl Schmitt) Hans Lindahl, "A-Legality: Postnationalism and the Question of Legal Boundaries," *Modern Law Review* 73 (2010): 30; Markus D. Dubber, "Common Civility: The Culture of Alegality in International Criminal Law," *Leiden Journal of International Law* 24 (2011): 923.

Grotius's *Mare Liberum* and consider cyberspace to be a common good that requires us to reinvent natural law theory?

In the following I start out with a brief introduction on the move "from computer crime to cybercrime," explaining how it connects to the notions of cyberspace and cybernetics (Section 2). Next I discuss "sovereignty and the *makings* of territorial jurisdiction," fleshing out the territorial spatiality of modern jurisdiction by tracing the history of mutually exclusive jurisdictions, generated by the technologies of cartography, tracking down the connection between terror and Bodin's absolute sovereignty,[3] and finally inquiring into the notion of occupation as central to territorial sovereign jurisdiction (Section 3). Next I investigate the powers of "extraterritorial jurisdiction in the light of Grotius's *Mare Liberum*," interpreting the freedom of the seas as an "economic theology"[4] and as a solution based on natural law theory (Section 4). Finally, I discuss the idea of a "cyberspace *liberum*," beginning with the question of the experiental unregulability of cyberspace, following up with an account of various attempts to gain control over parts of cyberspace—for instance by means of so-called indirect extraterritorial effect. I conclude with a question. Studying the implications of the use of extraterritorial search and seizures in cyberspace confronts us with the issue of spatiality. Cyberspaces demand a reconceptualization of jurisdiction in terms of novel spatialities. This means a critical stance toward cyberspace as a mere utopia and a rejection of cyberspace as a mere *isotopia* that can be framed on the regulation of territorial sovereignty and the freedom of the sea. The question is whether we can sustain cyberspace-as-a-passage and a global commons even though cyberspace is a *heteropia*,[5] crossing over into the landscape of territorial jurisdiction while also evading its mutually exclusive boundaries. It would be grotesque to pretend that I can do more in this article than spell out the pertinence of this question (Section 5).

---

3 Jean Bodin, *Bodin: On Sovereignty*, ed. Julian H Franklin (Cambridge University Press, 1992 [1576]).
4 Giorgio Agamben, *The Kingdom and the Glory: For a Theological Genealogy of Economy and Government*, trans. Lorenzo Chiesa & Matteo Mandarini (Stanford: Stanford University Press, 2011).
5 On these terms, building on Foucault, see Julie E. Cohen, "Cyberspace as/and Space," *Columbia Law Review* 107 (2007): 213.

2 FROM COMPUTER CRIME TO CYBERCRIME

In the "old" days one could speak of "computer crime," conveniently discriminating between criminal offenses *against* computers (hacking), offenses *with* computers (a distributed denial of service attack DDOS), or offenses *whereby computers played an incidental role* (for instance, storing the evidence).[6] The exponential growth of the Internet, the world wide web, search engines, online gaming and social networking sites and a host of applications for mobile devices have resulted in the integration of offline and online life worlds, creating a continuity of cyberspaces that interconnect, transform and redirect spaces, events and time lines. This has not only changed our sense of place and duration, it has also altered the unity of time, place and action that informed the notion of *actus reus* in the criminal law. Physical actions behind a computer screen can easily trigger devastating consequences in other time zones, on other continents, stretching the scope of what qualifies as an action. Understanding an action in terms of its effects, even if they occur at a distance from the original physical motion, is not a new thing. People can act through various types of instruments and even use other people to commit fraud, murder or criminal damage. In fact, this has led to the effects doctrine in the case of transnational crime: if criminal harm has been caused in the territory of a state, that state can punish the perpetrator even if she was outside the territory whence committing the crime. For a long time, however, the default has been that the criminal law applies only to those within the territory of the state; extraterritorial jurisdiction has been the exception. This is even more clearly the case for jurisdiction to enforce. In the famous *Lotus* case the Permanent Court of International Justice decided that extraterritorial jurisdiction to prescribe is allowed in the case of an effect within the territory or to a national of the state, whereas extraterritorial jurisdiction to enforce is in principle not allowed, unless the other state agrees (by treaty or in the course of judicial or police cooperation).[7] This prohibition is challenged by the emergent transnational cyberspace to the extent that the investigation of crimes committed with or against computing systems cannot restrict

---

6 Patricia L Bellia, "Chasing Bits Across Borders," *University of Chicago Legal Forum* 35 (2001): 37–8, n 11.
7 *SS Lotus (France v Turkey Case)* (1927) PCIJ (Ser A) No 10.

itself to "local" computing systems. The gradual shift towards cloud computing amplifies this challenge.[8]

Meanwhile, the distinction between crimes with or against *computers* seems to miss the point, since the most salient factor in cybercrime is not a stand-alone computer but a networked computing system that is interconnected with other computing systems, RFID-tagged commodities,[9] human implants, smart mobile devices, and smart homes. Attacks against these systems proliferate, vulnerabilities abound, malware is refined, reinvented, copied, and commodified and the number, the effects and the gravity of cybercrime offenses increase by the minute. The combination of simultaneity, speed and automation of machine-to-machine communication in cyberspace produces the famous "network effect" that constitutes potentially critical threats to identity management systems (IDMs), personal data, trade secrets and public infrastructure.[10] One of the major software security companies, Symantec, reported more than 403 million unique variants of malware over 2011; worldwide around 1.1 million identities were exposed per data breach, amounting to a total of 232.4 million breaches. Vulnerabilities in mobile computers (smartphones) increased by 42% in 2011, while in toto 4,989 new vulnerabilities were detected. Rustock, the largest botnet of 2010 had well over 1 million bots under its control, it was shut down in 2011 causing spam rates to plummet (from 88.5% of all email in 2010 to 75,1% in 2011). In 2010, in an underground economy advertisement 10.000 bots were promoted for $15 (often used for DDOS attacks), whereas the price range for a stolen credit card number was between $0.07 and $100.[11] Most, if not all of the attacks summed up, can be made from outside the territory of the targeted state and even if an

---

[8] In that respect the jurisdictional vacuum of cyberspace may add up to that of the high seas, cf. Steven R. Swanson, "Google Sets Sail: Ocean-Based Server Farms and International Law," *Connecticut Law Review* 43 (2009): 709.

[9] "RFID tags are intelligent bar codes that can talk to a networked system to track every product that you put in your shopping cart. [...] RFID tags, a technology once limited to tracking cattle, are tracking consumer products worldwide. Many manufacturers use the tags to track the location of each product they make from the time it's made until it's pulled off the shelf and tossed in a shopping cart. Outside the realm of retail merchandise, RFID tags are tracking vehicles, airline passengers, Alzheimer's patients and pets." http://electronics.howstuffworks.com/gadgets/high-tech-gadgets/rfid.htm.

[10] E.g., on the "network effect" for cybersecurity issues, Konstantin Beznosov and Olga Beznosova, "On the Imbalance of the Security Problem Space and Its Expected Consequences," *Information Management & Computer Security* 15 (2007): 429. On network effects and its relevance for law, see e.g., Katherine J. Strandburg et al, "Law and the Science of Networks: An Overview and an Application to the "Patent Explosion,"" *Berkeley Tech Law Journal* 21 (2006): 1294.

[11] Symantec Enterprise Security, *Internet Security Threat Report* 16 "Trends for 2012" (2011); Symantec Enterprise Security, *Internet Security Threat Report* 17 "2011 Trends" (2012); http://www.symantec.com/threatreport/.

attack is initiated within the same state there is a high probability that computing systems outside that state will be somehow involved, for instance but not only in the case of cloud computing. Instead of speaking of "computer" crime it makes sense to use the term "*cyber*crime," highlighting the fact that many of the relevant crimes take place in the realm of interconnected computing systems and are somehow related to both cyberspace and cybernetics.[12] To understand the challenges to extraterritorial jurisdiction in the age of interconnected digital infrastructures, we need to at least briefly explore the notions of cyberspace and cybernetics.

2.1 Cyberspace

The term cyperspace was coined by science fiction author William Gibson in 1984, in his novel *Neuromancer*. He describes it as:

> [a] consensual hallucination experienced daily by billions of legitimate operators, in every nation , by children being taught mathematical concepts. [...] A graphical representation of data abstracted from the banks of every computer in the human system. Unthinkable complexity. Lines of light ranged in the non-space of the mind, clusters and constellations of data.[13]

We should note that Gibson coined the term before anything like what we now call cyberspace existed. In fact, the Internet, the interconnection between different computing systems on the basis of the TCP/IP protocol, was still under construction when he published his novel. The world wide web originated even later, in the early 1990s, on the basis of the http and html protocols that enable hyperlinking, thus creating what is often called a "virtual space" in which humans and machines from anywhere can communicate, exchange information and present themselves anytime anywhere to anyone. The unprecedented collapse of geographical and temporal distance that was

---

12 In principle, the present chapter restricts itself to criminal jurisdiction to enforce, though we must admit that the distinction between crime and war will require hard work in cyberspace. On espionage and foreign intelligence see e.g., David E. Sanger, "Obama Ordered Wave of Cyberattacks Against Iran" *The New York Times* (June 1, 2012), http://www.nytimes.com/2012/06/01/world/middleeast/obama-ordered-wave-of-cyberattacks-against-iran.html (accessed Feb. 2, 2016). On cyberterrorism Kelly Gable, "Cyber-Apocalypse Now: Securing the Internet Against Cyberterrorism and Using Universal Jurisdiction as a Deterrent" (2009), *SSRN Working Paper Series*, http://papers.ssrn.com/sol3/papers.cfm?abstract_id=1452803.
13 William Gibson, *Neuromancer* (New York: Ace, 1984), 51.

generated by the Internet and Web created the euphoria of cyber-utopianism and cyber-exceptionalism. The idea was that cyberspace allowed for a new type of direct democracy, outside the reach of territorial governments or commercial enterprise. In 1996 John Perry Barlow published his "cyberspace manifesto,"[14] claiming that cyberspace was inherently unregulable—that its technological foundations resisted territorial boundaries, thus disabling law enforcement based on a physical monopoly of violence. In the wake of such optimism Castells announced the demise of the nation state, still based on mutually exclusive jurisdictions, suggesting that territorial states are like dinosaurs in the evolving network society.[15] Legal scholarship developed along similar lines: also in 1996 Johnson and Post wrote their famous "Law and Borders—The Rise of Law in Cyberspace," arguing that Cyberspace is a distinct, separate space where geographical borders and territorial jurisdiction make no sense. They explain that cyberspace is not a physical space and therefor does not fall under the powers of sovereigns whose control is limited to whoever and whatever stays within their territory; they continue to point out that in cyberspace the assumption that the effects of any particular behavior is restricted by physical proximity does not hold. They suggest that such proximity informed the legitimacy of territorial government, notably because these physical constraints allow governments to give *notice* of a change in the law. They proclaim:

> Because events on the Net occur everywhere but nowhere in particular, are engaged in by online personae who are both "real" (possessing reputations, able to perform services, and deploy intellectual assets) and "intangible" (not necessarily or traceably tied to any particular person in the physical sense), and concern "things" (messages, database, standing relationships) that are not necessarily separated from one another by any physical boundaries, no physical jurisdiction has a more compelling claim than any other to subject these events exclusively to its laws.[16]

---

14 John Perry Barlow, *A Declaration of the Independence of Cyberspace* (Davos, Switzerland, 1996), https://projects.eff.org/~barlow/Declaration-Final.html (accessed Feb. 2, 2016).
15 Manuel Castells, *The Rise of the Network Society* (Oxford: Blackwell Publishers Ltd, 1996); Jan Van Dijk, *The Network Society: Social Aspects of New Media*, 2nd ed. (London: Sage, 2006).
16 David R. Johnson and David B. Post, "Law and Borders: The Rise of Law in Cyberspace," *Stanford Law Review* (1996): 1367.

In "Cyberspace as/and space" Julie Cohen traced the various positions on what she calls the "cyberspace metaphor."[17] She discusses Johnson and Post's cyber-exceptionalism, various types of traditionalism that view cyberspace as just another communications network, postmodernist cultural studies that claim to uncover undesirable political and ideological implications, and finally she considers the cognitive theory that proclaims the inevitability of place- and space-based metaphors as dictated by our cognitive make-up. Cohen, however, rejects the easy dichotomies between cyber- and physical space that inform much of the debate. She notes that:

> To say that humans reason spatially is not to say that we are place-bound, or property-bound, but simply to say that we are embodied, situated beings, who comprehend even disembodied communications through the filter of embodied, situated experience.[18]

Her point is that understanding cyberspace as either a separate space (often a utopia) or a regular part of physical space (an isotopia) are two easy ways out of a far more complex challenge. Referring to Foucault's term "hetertopia" she denotes cyberspaces as real spaces in which ordinary rules of behaviour may be suspended or transformed as compared to ordinary spaces, thus highlighting the relation between cyber- and ordinary spaces as well as "the embodied spatiality of cyberspace users, who are situated in both spaces at once."[19] She concludes that utopian theories of cyberspace as an entirely separated space fail not because of their unregulability but because of the untenable presumption of experiental separateness. Thereby she goes one radical step further than Lessig and Reidenberg, who demonstrated that the unregulability of cyberspace was "neither a permanent nor a technologically necessary feature."[20] In opting for a heterotopian conception of cyberspace Cohen acknowledges both the "malleability of cyberspace" and the fact that such malleability can be made to serve the economic and political goals of businesses as well as governments.[21] In foregrounding the embodied spatial-

---

17 Cohen, "Cyberspace as/and Space," 210.
18 Ibid., 213.
19 Ibid., 214–5, referring to Michel Foucault, "Of Other Spaces," *Diacritics* 16 (1986): 22; Kevin Hetherington, *The Badlands of Modernity: Heteropia and Social Ordering* (London: Routledge, 1997), 20–38.
20 Ibid., 217, referring to Lawrences Lessig, *Code and Other Laws of Cyberspace* (New York: Basic, 1999); Joel R. Reidenberg, "Lex Informatica: The Formulations of Information Policy Rules through Technology," *Texas Law Review* 76 (1998): 553.
21 Ibid., 222.

ity of cyberspace users she can moreover come to terms with the fact that cyberspace is not a unitary phenomenon but a rich variety of entanglements between virtual and physical spaces that are real to the extent that they generate real consequences. Cybercrime, from this point of view, is a unitary concept for a diversity of criminal offenses that play out on the nexus of the Internet, the Web and a plethora of applications that generate real consequences for legal subjects across a multiplicity of national jurisdictions. Geography and territory seem to loose their hold on the effects of malicious attacks due to the unprecedented possibilities for the invisible remote control of computing systems.

2.2 Cybernetics

This explains the relevance of the notion of "cybernetics," which derives from the same Greek root as governing, both meaning "to steer, rule, guide."[22] Cybernetics refers to the study of *control at a distance*, coined as such by Norbert Wiener in 1948.[23] It concerns the use of technologies to affect the behaviors of remote systems and is closely related with the development of artificial intelligence. It is important to observe that cyberspaces—situated at the nexus of online and offline life-worlds—are built on a computational layer that produces sophisticated artificial intelligence for business enterprises and governmental agencies. In both cases algorithms are used to mine so-called "big data" to predict consumer or criminal behaviors, aiming to pre-empt human intention on the basis of profiling technologies such as machine learning, artificial neural networks and the more.[24] Cyberspace is not merely a "place" where registration is becoming paramount, pervasive and highly profitable. Increasingly it is becoming a space rooted in a layer of automated decision-making systems. These computational layers enable and inform all kinds of remote control, which are not only used to create added

---

22 *Online Etymology Dictionary*, sub verbo "cybernetics," http://www.etymonline.com/index.php?term=cybernetics.
23 Norbert Wiener, *Cybernetics: Or the Control and Communication in the Animal and the Machine*, 2nd ed. (Cambridge, MA: MIT Press, 1965). For an interesting overview of cybernetics and artificial intelligence, see N. Katherine Hayles, *How We Became Posthuman: Virtual Bodies in Cybernetics, Literature, and Informatics* (Chicago: University of Chicago Press, 1999).
24 Andrew McStay, *The Mood of Information: A Critique of Online Behavioural Advertising* (New York: Continuum, 2011), 3. McStay indicates how proactive computing allows for the pre-empt of users" intention by always remaining one step ahead of them on the bases of machine learning techniques. For a critiques of such predictive analytics in the sphere of the criminal law see Bernard E. Harcourt, *Against Prediction: Profiling, Policing, and Punishing in an Actuarial Age* (Chicago: University of Chicago Press, 2007).

value for the industry or to uncover criminal networks; they also underpin malicious attacks against both individual netizens and private and public organizations. The increasing usage of tracking technologies to enable data analytics produces a host of novel vulnerabilities that enable misuse, abuse and attacks against individuals, systems, and infrastructure. The fact that the Internet facilitates remote control across national borders at low costs basically means that the fundamental assumptions of territorial criminal jurisdiction will increasingly fail to accurately describe what is at stake. This presents an intriguing challenge to the territorial basis of internal and external sovereignty as we know it.

3. SOVEREIGNTY AND THE *MAKINGS* OF TERRITORIAL JURISDICTION

At this point I want to remind us that the interplay of internal and external sovereignty that defines the modern state is not only constitutive for the power to enact, to enforce and to speak the law within a specific territory. It is also a condition of possibility for the protection of human rights and for the internal division of sovereignty that defines the Rule of Law. Such protection depends on the monopoly of violence within a specific jurisdiction, that enables to enforce the law as determined by the courts. Though Montesquieu is rightly applauded for having argued for the internal division of sovereignty,[25] it is imperative that we acknowledge that without such sovereignty there is nothing to divide. Without some form of sovereignty as we know it, there is no actor that can be addressed as the subject of negative and positive obligations that constitute human rights law. If territory loses its defining role in constituting jurisdiction we cannot take for granted that such historical artifacts as human rights and the Rule of Law will be sustainable. We should admit that even the enforcement of international human rights law depends on national courts and national enforcement.[26] To come to terms with the consequences of a post-territorial spatiality we need to inquire into the specific "makings" of jurisdiction in the era of territory. To this end I will investi-

---

25 See for an unconventional but convincing interpretation of his maxim on the judge as "bouche de la loi," K. M. Schoenfeld, "Rex, Lex et Judex: Montesquieu and *La bouche de la loi* Revisted," *European Constitutional Law Review* 4 (2008): 274.
26 This is why the study of International Relations cannot assume the balance of power that inheres in the Rule of Law, often taking refuge in a social scientific — often coined "realist" — understanding of international law. A refreshing alternative can be found in Claude Lefort, *Writing: The Political Test*, trans. David Ames Curtis (Duke University Press Books, 2000).

gate the rise of territorial jurisdiction and its relation to modern cartography, followed by an analysis of terror, territory and occupation as the foundations of modern sovereignty.

3.1 The Territorial Spatiality of Modern Jurisdiction

"Jurisdiction" is a term first encountered in the early fourteenth century, initially referring to the administration of justice and soon meaning "extent or range of administrative power." The term "territory" first appeared in the early fifteenth century, then meaning "land under the jurisdiction of a town, state, etc."[27] Thus "jurisdiction" is the older term and "territory" was initially defined in terms of jurisdiction. This suggests that jurisdiction need not be based on territorial rule and that the concepts of sovereignty and of territory, defining characteristics of jurisdiction, emerged simultaneously in modern history. In "Law's Territory (A History of Jurisdiction)," Richard Ford develops two theses on the history and scope of territorial jurisdiction.[28] One thesis is that territorial jurisdictions, "the rigidly mapped territories within which formally defined legal powers are exercised by formally organized governmental institutions,"[29] are a recent invention, even though we tend to take them for granted and have problems imagining jurisdiction that is not defined by territory. The second thesis is that territorial jurisdiction is an affordance of modern cartography,[30] in the sense that it could not have developed without the modern, scientific demarcation of distinct territories that depends on cartography as its enabling technology.[31] This observation is of great import for our investigation, because, if correct it raises the question of whether cyberspace will overrule the specific production of space that is inherent in cartographic mappings and its affordances in terms of territorial jurisdiction. Ford highlights four prototypical characteristics of modern, ter-

27 *Online Etymology Dictionary, sub verbo* "jurisdiction," and *sub verbo* "territory."
28 Richard T. Ford, "A History of Jurisdiction," *Michigan Law Review* 97 (1999): 843.
29 Ibid.
30 On the role of cartography in the formation of the modern state, see also: Michael Biggs, "Putting the State on the Map: Cartography, Territory, and European State Formation," *Comparative Studies in Society and History* 41 (1999): 374; Mark Neocleous, "Off the Map On Violence and Cartography," *European Journal of Social Theory* 6 (2003): 409.
31 The concept of an affordance was coined by psychologist Gibson. See James G. Greeno, "Gibson's Affordances," *Psychological Review* 101 (1994): 338: "The term affordance refers to whatever it is about the environment that contributes to the kind of interaction that occurs." It thus indicates what a specific technology makes possible for a specific organism or type of person, entailing a non-deterministic and relational understanding of both technology and the human subject. This implies that technologies have normative implications, see Mireille Hildebrandt, "Legal and Technological Normativity: More (and Less) Than Twin Sisters," *Techné* 12, no. 3 (2008): 169.

ritorial jurisdiction: first, he confirms that if jurisdiction is territorially defined, this means that authority is to be exercised primarily by area, instead of status or family, second, he notes that territorial jurisdiction is definitely bounded, while these boundaries are not ambiguous or contested (except in times of crisis or transition), third, he notes that territory is abstractly and homogeneously conceived, meaning that jurisdiction refers to an abstract space in the sense that the authority does not depend on the concrete characteristics of the territory it concerns. Ford points out that such abstract and homogeneous mapping implies authority over an empty space, defined by latitude and longitude, not by its contingent contents. As a result such mapping "*eliminates the need for the specific enumeration and classification*" of whatever resides in the territory, at least for the constitution of authority.[32] A related implication is that actual social relations and distribution of resources are invisible from the perspective of the abstract map; the abstraction of modern jurisdiction presents social and political relationships as impersonal. One could sum this up as the proposition that modern jurisdictional space is conceptually empty: it "reduces space to an empty vessel for government power."[33] His fourth point is that cartographic mapping produces a "'gapless' map of contiguous political territories,"[34] thus grounding the Westphalian system of mutually exclusive territorial jurisdictions. Ford goes on to explain that territorial jurisdictions are inherently synthetic (artificial) to the extent that they do not depend on an organically grown *Gemeinschaft*; they stipulate whoever falls within the scope of their jurisdiction irrespective of social status or family relationship. Thereby the individual becomes the primary agent, instead of the religious, ethnic or other group she may belong to. This allows governments to base their rule on a strange combination of artificial administrative units and an appeal to the loyalties of a "thicker" community, which is not given requires construction work. In short, Ford's history of modern jurisdiction demonstrates that: "The abstract space created by mod-

---

32 Ford, "A History of Jurisdiction," 854.
33 Ibid., 854. The notion of mutually exclusive territorial jurisdictions as the enabling metaphor for the Westphalian system describes a way of looking at jurisdiction. It creates the institutional fact of internal and external sovereignty. Compare Friedrich Kratochwil, *Of Maps, Law, and Politics: An Inquiry into the Changing Meaning of Territoriality*, Danish Institute for International Studies Working Paper (2011). Kratochwil notes the fuzzy reality and the many counterveiling claims made against the unitary and monopolistic tendencies of the Westphalian system, already from its inception.
34 Ford, "A History of Jurisdiction," 854.

ern cartography, what we will call territorial jurisdiction, was the midwife of the administrative state."³⁵

3.2 Terror and Modern Sovereignty

In *The Ethos of Pluralization*, Connolly discusses the notion of territory in a way that seems remarkably relevant for our purpose. The following passage is worth quoting at length:

> *Territory*, the *Oxford English Dictionary* says, is presumed by most moderns to derive from terra. Terra means land, earth, soil, nourishment, sustenance; it conveys the sense of a sustaining medium that fades off into indefiniteness. People, you might say, feel the claim the land they belong to makes upon them. This experience of belonging to a place, as long as it does not exclude other identifications, and as long as it incorporates the disruptive experiences of earthquakes, tornadoes, floods, and firestorms into the experience itself (this essay is being written during a year in California), can play a positive role in the cultivation of care and critical responsiveness. But the form of the word *territory*, the OED says, suggests something different from the sustenance of *terra*. *Territory* derives from *terrere*, meaning to frighten, to terrorize, to exclude. And *territorium* is "a place from which people are warned." *Territorium* seems to repress the sustaining relation to land that it presupposes. Perhaps a modern territory, then, is land organized and bounded by technical juridical, and military means. Perhaps the experience of land as sustenance is both presupposed and repressed by the modern organization of territory. To occupy territory, then, is both to receive sustenance and to exercise violence. To become territorialized is to be occupied by a particular identity.³⁶

We could summarize Connolly as proposing that "territory is sustaining land occupied and bounded by violence."³⁷ I would like to suggest that this links territorial jurisdiction to the monopoly of violence, and claim that the territorial monopoly of violence is the foundation of the modern state. It provides a "gapless" map of mutually exclusive sovereign entities that defines

---

35 Ibid., 870.
36 William E. Connolly, "Introduction," *The Ethos of Pluralization* (Minneapolis: University of Minnesota Press, 1995), xxii; citing *Online Etymological Dictionary, sub verbo* "territory" [emphasis in the original].
37 Ibid., xxii.

and determines their internal and external sovereignty since the peace of Westphalen. This "gapless" map also underlies Bodin's triple definition of absolute power that still informs our understanding of sovereignty, even when we confront its limits.[38] The impact of Bodin's *On Sovereignty* (1576) warrants a brief discussion here, linking notions of territory with those of occupation and a-legality.

As Goyard-Fabre has argued, Bodin should not be understood as an advocate of corrupt absolutism.[39] His main concern was the protection of the *res publica*, which he thought could only be safeguarded if the sovereign cannot be corrupted by other powers within his realm. The sovereign should not be seen as the most powerful person, but as the highest office, tasked with the safety and the well being of his subjects. Bodin articulated three constitutive conditions for such sovereignty: the *puissance publique de commandement*, the *continuité de la puissance publique*, and the *puissance absolue*. The first marks the transition from "suzerainty"—feudal lordship based on a complex asymmetrical reciprocity—to sovereignty. The public power to command implies a unilateral public competence to enact laws that bind the subjects; the validity of the law does not depend on the consent of those to whom it applies. This entails a transition from jurisdiction that is mainly based on adjudication to one firmly grounded in legislation.[40] The second marks the transition from rule by man to rule by law, from the military or economic power of a *person* to the institutional authority of an abstract sovereign. The continuity of the public power is thereby constituted, generating a type of legal certainty that transcends the arbitrary power of the king as a person. This conforms the position taken by Kantorowicz in his *The King's Two Bodies* that explain sovereignty as an abstract institution that is capable of surviving the death of whoever happens to fulfil the role of the king.[41] The fact that sovereign power does not depend on the person of the king, nor on the contingent consent of his subjects is seen here as a protection against arbitrary rule and as a particular type of legal certainty that is not available in the negotiations that nourish feudal suzereignty. Finally, the third condition marks the transi-

---

38 Bodin, *Bodin: On Sovereignty*, Book 1, Ch. 10 ("On the True Marks").
39 Simone Goyard-Fabre, *Jean Bodin et le droit de la République* (Paris: PUF, 1989).
40 On the shift from adjudication to legislation as the core of jurisdiction, see Harold Berman, *Law and Revolution: The Formation of the Western Legal Tradition* (Cambridge, MA: Harvard University Press, 1983), e.g., at 404–5.
41 Ernst H. Kantorowicz, *The King's Two Bodies: A Study in Mediaeval Political Theology* (Princeton: Princeton University Press, 1957).

tion from a system of interdependent lords and overlords that requires permanent military and economic struggle, to a centralized hierarchical distribution of authority that guarantees the independence of the sovereign from his subjects and towards his fellow sovereigns. Absolute power defines the independence of the sovereign, but for Bodin it did not imply that the sovereign can rule according to "le bon plaisir du prince." He is still bound by "les lois divines et naturelles; les lois fondamentales du royaume et le respect du droit de propriété."[42] This entails that the sovereign has absolute power but is still bound by laws; for Bodin this tension within his concept of sovereignty was not a problem. The king had to give an account of his actions to God, which was a much more powerful constraint than the contingent opinion of his subjects.

It seems that the role of territory in jurisdiction emerged from the simultaneous appearance of a particular technology — and the birth of the abstract sovereign state, based on an effective territorial monopoly of violence. As recounted above, Connolly proposes that "territory is sustaining land occupied and bounded by violence."[43] To the extent that jurisdiction is territorial the making of jurisdiction would be a matter of occupation: the taking of land is part of establishing sovereign jurisdiction. Occupation in this particular case must be understood as the process of terrorizing both the inhabitants (internal sovereignty) and the rulers of other lands (external sovereignty). "Terrorizing" then has the double meaning of ruling by means of the threat of terror and protecting those within the territory against threats of terror by their fellows (criminal law) or by the rulers of other lands (law of war). Terror refers then to the monopolies of violence that prevail within mutually exclusive territories.

3.3 Occupation and Modern Sovereignty

In his *Political Theology* Carl Schmitt argues that "sovereign is he who decides on the exception."[44] He finds that "the precondition as well as the content of jurisdictional competence in such a case [of extreme emergency, MH] must necessarily be unlimited."[45] Schmitt refers to Bodin's understanding of sovereignty as indivisible, thus — according to Schmitt — finally settling the

---

42 Goyard-Fabre, *Jean Bodin*, 162–3.
43 Connolly, *The Ethos of Pluralization*, xxii.
44 Carl Schmitt, *Political Theology: Four Chapters on the Concept of Sovereignty* (Chicago: University of Chicago Press, 2005).
45 Ibid., 7.

question of power in the state. This relates to Bodin's answer to the question of whether the sovereign is bound by natural or divine laws in a case of emergency.[46] Bodin finds that in cases of urgent necessity the sovereign must take the law in his own hands instead of becoming dependent upon whatever other powers within the state think. In the end, sovereignty resides in the authority to suspend valid law. Such authority is deemed even *more fundamental than* and *preconditional* for the authority to command new laws. The decision on the exception is in fact an *occupatio* that reduces the territory to a *res nullius* that is "taken" by the sovereign on the basis of his factual dominion. Schmitt explains the emergence of a new political order at the end of the middle ages, created by the constitution of the territorial state:

> First, it created clear internal jurisdictions by placing feudal, territorial, estate, and church rights under the centralized legislation, administration, and judiciary of a territorial ruler. Second it ended the European civil war of churches and religious parties, and thereby neutralized creedal conflicts within the state through a centralized political unity. [...] Third, on the basis of the internal political unity the state vis-à-vis other political unities, it constituted within and of itself a closed area with fixed borders, allowing a specific type of foreign relations with other similarly organized territorial orders.[47]

This new territorial legal order derives from the initial a-legal occupation that precedes the institution of legality. In his discussion of *nomos* (Greek for law) Schmitt reminds the reader of its first meaning, that he claims to be "to take" or "to appropriate," whereas the second would be "to divide or distribute": "the division and distribution, i.e., the *suum cuique*, presuppose the appropriation of what is to be distributed, i.e., and *occupatio* or *appropriatio primaeva*."[48] To give, to enact the law, the competence to make jurisdiction must first be occupied, conquered and according to Schmitt even Kant admitted that acquisition of land precedes the rule by law.[49] By implication such occupation must be a-legal, since it precedes as well as constitutes a legal order.[50]

---

46   Ibid., 8, referring to Bodin, *Bodin: On Sovereignty*, Book 1, Ch. 10 ("On the True Marks").
47   Schmitt, *The Nomos of the Earth in the International Law of the Jus Publicum Europaeum* (New York: Telos Press, 2006), 128–9.
48   Ibid., 326, n 6.
49   Ibid., 328.
50   On a-legality see Lindahl, "A-Legality"; Dubber, "Common Civility."

4. EXTRATERRITORIAL JURISCTION IN THE LIGHT OF GROTIUS'S *MARE LIBERUM*

At some point during his discussions on the primacy of *occupatio*, Schmitt arrives at "the distinction between the surfaces of firm land and free sea, which was important for the distinction between land war and sea war. Each had its own concepts of enemy, war, and plunder."[51] This refers to the different jurisdiction that applies to the "free sea" as compared to that of the "occupied territories." Schmitt explains that the legal regime that rules the *mare liberum* has major consequences for the relationships between territorial states that meet outside their territories on the high seas; the abstract cartographic order that determines sovereignty in the spatial order of firm land is absent at sea. Noting Julie Cohen's depiction of cyberspace as/and space, it may be of interest to look more closely into the non-territorial jurisdiction of the high sea. Julie Cohen proposed that "[t]o understand cyberspace's spatiality, one must disentangle the concept of experienced spatiality from abstract, conceptual models of 'space,' and also from the related but distinct concepts of place and property."[52] In this section I will tease out the manner in which the humanist legal scholar Grotius disentangled the spatiality of the high seas from the concepts of place and property. He advocated that the sea, as a *res communis*, is distinct from both private and public property. Basically he claimed that the sea may be a *res nullius*, but not one that—due to its experiental unruliness—lends itself to any kind of occupation. Grotius depicted the high seas as a passage instead of a place and a common good instead of a private or public property.

In his *Mare Liberum* (1608) Grotius contested the monopolist claims of Spain and Portugal on parts of the high seas,[53] which they aimed to appropriate as part of their trade route to South and South-East Asia. Grotius, who was asked to defend free trade on the high seas in order to safeguard the interests of the Dutch Republic, argued that the high seas cannot be appropriated. While land was occupied, divided and distributed, the sea remained open to all. Whereas lands turned into territory, the sea remained outside the grasp of territorial sovereignty. It was considered as part of a different spatiality, not portioned into mutually exclusive jurisdictions but left to the rights and

---

51 Schmitt, *The Nomos of the Earth*, 184.
52 Cohen, "Cyberspace as/and Space," 227.
53 Hugo Grotius, *The Freedom of the Seas*, ed. & trans. Ralph Van Deman Magoffin (New York: Carnegie Endowment for International Peace, Oxford University Press, 1960 [1688]).

obligations of Grotius's natural law, the same natural law that obligated people before they concluded the social contract that constituted their territorial sovereign.[54] Remaining outside the realm of sovereignty his law of the sea must also be distinguished from his other radical invention: the laws of war that constitute the rules for a *ius ad bellum* (the rules for determining what makes for a just cause) and the *ius in bello* (the rules for the conduct of warring states irrespective of whether their cause is just or not).

4.1 Mare Liberum as an Economic Theology

In the introductory note to the English translation of *Mare Liberum* Brown Scott refers to "the famous Latin tractate of Grotius" as "proclaiming, explaining, and in no small measure *making* the 'freedom of the seas.'"[55] This highlights the constructive as well as performative nature of jurisdiction at sea. According to Johannes Thumfart, Grotius uses the text to put forward his "normative ideals of global free trade, including those of equality, reciprocity and private responsibility," thus for instance influencing the founding father of the invisible hand of political economy, Adam Smith.[56] Thumfart detects a theological undercurrent in Grotius's treatise, which he shares with and took from the Spanish Dominican Francisco de Vitoria who defended free trade as an implication of the Christian mission. Thumfart suggests that both assume "a historico-teleological tendency inherent in global free trade, such that the purpose of free trade is to unite the world in peace."[57] He finds that this eschatological understanding of global free trade fits what Agamben has called an "economic theology" and, *mutatis mutandis*, Schmitt's "political theology."[58] It entails that theological notions such as salvation are transformed so as to survive in the secular era, while still producing a series of expectations and legitimizations that derive from their discarded theological roots. In the case of the freedom of the seas this eschatological notion of salvation by means of global free trade provided the legitimacy for the Dutch trading company, the Vereenigde Oost-Indische Compagnie, "to secure its trading expeditions

---

54 Natural law is an essentially contested concept that might mean anything to anyone. For a view on Grotius's engagement with natural law see Jon Miller, "Hugo Grotius," in *The Stanford Encyclopedia of Philosophy*, ed. Edward N. Zalta. http://plato.stanford.edu/archives/fall2011/entries/grotius/ (accessed Feb. 2, 2016).
55 James Brown Scott, "Introductory Note," in Grotius, *The Freedom of the Seas*, v.
56 Johannes Thumfart, "On Grotius's *Mare Liberum* and Vitoria's *De Indis*, Following Agamben and Schmitt," *Grotiana* 30 (2009): 68.
57 Ibid., 69.
58 Agamben, *The Kingdom and the Glory*; Schmitt, *Political Theology*.

by military means, which also included preemptive strikes."[59] We may notice that, in the struggle for a free Internet, various stakeholders come up with very similar arguments, based on the idea that a free Internet will automatically bring salvation for oppressed people outside the West.[60] We will return to this point later. For now, it seems interesting to trace Grotius's argument for the freedom of the sea, since it legitimizes what he coined a *bellum iustum privatum*, paraphrasing what the VOC had coined "coophandel met force" (trade supported by the force of arms).[61] If cyberspace, like the high seas, is structured as a spatiality different from that of the territorial state, some of Grotius's arguments may be relevant for the extraterritorial jurisdiction to enforce in cyberspace.

4.2 Mare Liberum *as Natural Law Theory*

Apart from "making" the freedom of the seas, Grotius was one of the founding fathers of natural law theory, opening his tractate with a dedication that posits a fundamental difference between things that are to be enjoyed in common with all men and things that belong distinctly and exclusively to one individual. This difference is based on the nature of things as created by God and inscribed in the minds of men, ruling out that this could be a matter of convention or opinion. In the first chapter, Grotius claims that:

> [E]very nation is free to travel to every other nation, and to trade with it. [...] So by the decree of divine justice it was brought about that one people should supply the needs of another, in order, as Pliny the Roman writer says, that in this way, whatever has been produced anywhere should seem to have been destined for all.[62]

From this Grotius concludes that trading routes—especially those over seas—should be free for all to use. In the fifth chapter Grotius argues that sovereign nations cannot gain property or sovereignty over parts of the high

---

59   Thumfart, "On Grotius's *Mare Liberum*," 70.
60   Compare Evgeny Morozov, *The Net Delusion: The Dark Side of Internet Freedom* (New York: PublicAffairs, 2011); Jack Goldsmith and Tim Wu, *Who Controls the Internet?: Illusions of a Borderless World* (New York: Oxford University Press, 2008); Milton Mueller, "The New Cyber-Conservatism: Goldsmith/Wu and the Premature Triumphalism of the Territorial Nation-State: A Review of Goldsmith and Wu's "Who Controls the Internet? Illusions of a Borderless World," *Internet Governance Project* (2006). http://internetgovernance.org/pdf/MM-goldsmithWu.pdf (accessed Feb. 2, 2016).
61   Thumfart, "On Grotius's *Mare Liberum*," 76.
62   Grotius, *The Freedom of the Seas*, 7, Ch. 8.

sea by means of occupation. He explains that the sea is often framed as having the legal status of a *res nullius*, a *res communis*, or a *res publica*. His point is, however, that the high seas fall within the scope of natural law and he claims that nature of itself knows no exclusive rights such as sovereignty or private property. The emergence of private property originates in an act of occupation, mostly of things formerly held in common. On the one hand, this act of occupation was initiated by individuals, resulting in private property; on the other hand, states began to occupy certain territories that resulted in public property. He concludes that all property has arisen from occupation and that non-rivalrous goods cannot and should not be occupied, since nature has clearly meant to exclude exclusive rights to such goods.[63] He refers to sun, air and, waves as incapable of becoming private property and calls them public gifts. This means that the seas are "common" to all men, first because they cannot be occupied and second because they have been marked out for common use. He continues to argue that whatever cannot become individual private property also cannot become the public property of a state, since this would exclude parts of what he calls the human race from enjoying the common use of these goods. It seems that Grotius hidden assumption is that the experiental spatiality of land—though originally used as a common good—lends itself to occupation, division and distribution as private or public property, whereas the experiental spatiality of the outer sea does not lend itself to such compartmentalization. This claim was countered in 1652 by John Selden in his *Mare Clausum*,[64] who advocated the British claims to jurisdiction over the high seas surrounding the isles. Let's note that Grotius views the spatiality of the outer sea as a passage, a route to conduct trade and to travel between different nations. He argues that "even over land which had been converted into private property either by states or individuals, unarmed and innocent passage is not justly to be denied to persons of any country, exactly as the right to drink from a river is not to be denied."[65] Grotius thus claims that even territorialized lands retain the spatiality of a passage. The difference with the high

---

63 Ibid., 27. Grotius often mingles "is" and "ought," one of analytical philosophy's mortal sins. If the sea cannot be appropriated, it makes no sense to discuss whether it should be so. If it should not be appropriated we assume that it can be so. There is logic in this, but perhaps reality is more fuzzy and more complex. In some ways you probably could not occupy the seas at that point in time, in other ways you could (the Spanish and the Portuguese did, in their way). In that sense "can" and "should" are interdependent when "making" an institutional fact like jurisdiction.
64 John Selden and Marchamont Nedham, *Of the Dominion, Or, Ownership of the Sea*, reprint of the first edition in English. (New Jersey: The Lawbook Exchange, 2004).
65 Grotius, *The Freedom of the Seas*, 43–4.

seas seems to be that its spatiality is exhausted by the metaphor of the passage, as—according to Grotius—they are not conducive to occupation and distribution. His freedom of the sea is grounded in the sea as an in-between, a connection, a passage from one nation to another, the precondition for the global free trade that will achieve global peace and well-being according to economic theology of the laws of nature. The fact that Grotius's vision won out over Selden's attempted refutation was not obvious; it is a prime example of the "making" of a special type of jurisdiction that seems to defy the logic of occupation. Attempts to achieve some form of command over the commons of the high seas are not uncommon,[66] and the distributed jurisdiction over the high seas that was consolidated in the 1982 United Nations Convention on the Law of the Sea (UNCLOS) cannot be taken for granted.[67]

What does this imply for extraterritorial jurisdiction to enforce? For a start, let's acknowledge that Grotius admits of no monopoly of violence on the high seas; the freedom of the seas signifies the absence of sovereign claims that exclude other nations. This implies that natural law applies; there is no social contract that stipulates the establishment of a human-made jurisdiction. For Grotius natural law rules in three types of situations: first, it rules the interactions of people that have not established a state on the basis of a social contract; second, it rules the interactions between states in times of war and peace; third, it rules the interactions of both state and private actors on the high seas. Grotius's natural law starts from the notion of individual rights, that derive from the need for self-preservation and the need for society. Before the social contract is concluded these individual rights pertain to individual persons, after the social contract these rights are also attributed to sovereign states, while the subjects of the state will lose some of their rights and will be attributed rights on the basis of sovereign legislation. *Mare Liberum* argues that at sea both sovereign states and private parties under the flag of a sovereign state have the natural right to defend themselves and the duty to respect the communal character of the sea as a route for free trade. Pirates can be caught and punished by all parties since they "beset and infest

---

66 Craig H. Allen, "Command of the Commons Boasts: An Invitation to Lawfare?," in *Global Legal Challenges: Command of the Commons, Strategic Communications and Natural Disasters*, ed. Michael D. Carsten (Newport, RI: Naval War College Press, 2007), 21.

67 See *Convention on the Law of the Sea*, December 10, 1982, 1833 UNTS 3, pt VII, arts 86–120 (entered into force November 16, 1994). For an interesting attempt to compose a clone of the *Convention* regarding the legal regime of cyberspace, see Raymond K. Joe, "Cyberspace and the Seas: Lessons to Be Learned," *Master Thesis*, MIT (Cambridge, MA: 1998), http://dspace.mit.edu/bitstream/handle/1721.1/47725/42662346.pdf?sequence=1.

our trade routes";[68] nations can agree to bring pirates under a specific jurisdiction when caught in this or that part of the sea, but such agreements have no binding force on those not party to the agreement.[69] If a party attempts to monopolize a trade route by prohibiting passage, natural law allows others to take up arms:

> If many writers, Augustine himself among them, believed it was right to take up arms because innocent passage was refused across foreign territory, how much more justly will arms be taken up against those from whom the demand is made of the common and innocent use of the sea, which by the law of nature is common to all?[70]

In fact he suggests that whoever hinders free trade by obstructing the use of roads or the export of merchandise must be prevented from doing so "*via facti* even without waiting for any public authority."[71] This natural right against whatever hinders free trade constitutes a cause for a just war, even if it is a private party that retaliates. In that case Grotius speaks of a *bellum iustum privatum*—a private just war.

In what sense could cyberspace be equivalent with Grotius's high seas? It may be interesting to compare the relationship between territorial sovereignty and the freedom of the sea, with the relationship between territorial jurisdiction and the often claimed unregulability of the Internet. Taking it from there, we can investigate how the notion of extraterritoriality depends on a particular spatial mapping that may not apply in the case of either Grotius's sea or our own cyberspace.

5. CYBERSPACE LIBERUM?

Julie Cohen suggested that "[t]o understand cyberspace's spatiality, one must disentangle the concept of experienced spatiality from abstract, conceptual

---

68 Grotius, *The Freedom of the Seas*, 10. See UNCLS, art. 100: "All States shall cooperate to the fullest possible extent in the repression of piracy on the high seas or in any other place outside the jurisdiction of any State." For the definition of piracy see art. 101 UNCLS.
69 Ibid., 35. The UNCLS stipulates in art. 92(1) that ships "shall sail under the flag of one State only," and subject to minor exceptions "shall be subject to its exclusive jurisdiction on the high seas." Art. 97(3) stipulates exclusive penal jurisdiction to enforce for the flag State.
70 Ibid., 74. Note that the rhetorical strategy of quoting the Ancients was a canonical method to convince one's audience in Grotius's time.
71 Ibid., 75.

models of "space," and also from the related but distinct concepts of place and property." Grotius, who lived on the verge of a new area, in which abstract spatiality was the new kid on the block in the arts, politics and the law, reinvented the abstractions of natural law theory and developed a law of nations that matched an abstract spatial understanding of the surface of the earth.[72] The exception he argued for jurisdiction at sea partly rests on the experiental unregulability of the high seas at that point in time. For another part the natural law that he proposes depends on an abstract conception of individual actors with individual rights; Grotius was indeed one of the first authors to develop the abstract notion of subjective rights that do not depend on privilege and exist as legal rights beyond moral entitlement.[73]

5.1 Experiental Unregulatity of Cyberspace?
In the first decade of its existence, cyberspace seems to have evoked an experiental unregulability similar to Grotius's high seas. Even the eschatological undertones detected in Grotius's expectations of world peace based on free trade returned with the birth of cyberspace. In the preface to their *Who Controls the Internet?*, Goldsmith and Wu cite the following passage:

> The new technologies will bring "every individual [...] into immediate and effortless communication with every other," "practically obliterate" political geography, and make free trade universal. Thanks to technological advance, "there [are] no longer any foreigners, "and we can look forward to "the gradual adoption of a common language."[74]

These words were, however, inspired by the telegraph, one century before the emergence of cyberspace. They resonate with numerous writings on the challenges posed to the rule of nation states in the last decade of the 20th century, reiterating the eschatological expectations unmasked by Schmitt's notion of a political theology and Agamben's economic theology. Some would say

---

72 Earlier natural law theory developed within the realm of scholasticism, notably in Aquinas's *Summa Theologiae*. At that point natural law theory was still a branch of moral philosophy that determined the validity of positive law. With Grotius natural law theory begins the process of disentanglement from theology.
73 William A. Edmundson, *An Introduction to Rights* (Cambridge: Cambridge University Press, 2004), 17–22.
74 Goldsmith & Wu, *Who Controls the Internet?*, vii, quoting Julian Hawthorne, "June 1993," *The Cosmopolitan* (Feb. 1893): 456–7, recounted and quoted in Carolyn Marvin, *When Old Technologies Were New: Thinking About Electric Communications in the Late Nineteenth Century* (New York: Oxford University Press, 1988), 201–2.

that eschatological expectations must be hardwired into our cognitive make-up. Though the idea of a political theology referred to the notion of territorial sovereignty as a road to salvation for a divided humanity, cyber-utopism seeks salvation in an undivided global cyberspace under the banner of Internet Freedom. Goldsmith and Wu summarize the dreams of cyber-utopism as those of "self-governing cyber-communities that would escape geography forever."[75] But, in their history of the (partial) territorialization of cyberspace they argue that even if geography no longer rules, national states still manage to pulls the strings—or, rather, the wires. This has required hard work, by legislators and especially courts, in order to come to terms with the unprecedented extraterritorial effects of action in cyberspace. They describe the Yahoo case,[76] in which a French court decided that the US First Amendment does not have force of law in French jurisdiction. The case concerned the sale of Nazi paraphernalia on an Internet auction site that could be accessed in France, where the sale of Nazi relics is a criminal offense. Yahoo claimed that it could only comply with French law if it blocked access to the site for all its users—which would practically enforce French law in the US. Once it became clear that it is technically possible to discriminate between users based on their geo-location, the court ordered the US-based provider Yahoo to block access to certain Web sites for French users. Reidenberg has described this decision under the heading of "the democratisation of the Internet," arguing that it demonstrates respect for local, i.e., national, democratic constituencies.[77] This may be a relevant argument for territorial demarcations in the case of democracies, but as Goldsmith and Wu discuss at some length, such demarcations are also used by non-democratic states like China, to prevent their subjects from gaining unrestricted access to the global public sphere. Mueller goes even further, raising the difficult question of the relationship between human rights and democracy:

> They [Goldsmith and Wu] criticize the global extension of the First Amendment and its implied universalism. But why *not* extend it globally? If you believe that individuals have rights that are over and above those of states, how does the fact that a (possibly temporary) majority happened to

---

75 Goldschmidt & Wu, *Who Controls the Internet?*, vii.
76 Trib gr inst Paris, Ordonnance de refere du 20 nov. 2000, online: http://www.juriscom.net/txt/jurisfr/cti/tgiparis20001120.htm. Unofficial English translation at http://www.lapres.net/yahen11.html (accessed Feb. 2, 2016).
77 Joel R. Reidenberg, "Yahoo and Democracy on the Internet," *Jurimetrics* 42 (2001/2002): 261.

seize political control in one territory for a few years alter the basis of the claim? And if you believe that it is illegitimate to apply the First Amendment stand globally, why is it legitimate to apply Goldsmith and Wu's amoral utilitarian standard? Some standard has to be applied.[78]

Mueller agrees that the cyber-utopism of early adapters of the Internet is not only naïve but dangerous, because it turns a blind eye to the sophisticated methods used by nation states to regain—remote—control over whatever affects their jurisdiction. However, he warns against what he calls *the new cyber-conservatism* that assumes that cyberspace does not pose critical threats to the system of nation states. Apart from this contestable assumption such cyber-conservatism often involves a normative position, claiming that only the combination of internal and external sovereignty of nation states can provide adequate solutions for the governance of cyberspace. Goldsmith and Wu justify this normative position by means of mainstream utilitarian arguments,[79] even though they recognize the fact that oppressive governments can use the Internet to achieve an unparalleled granular control over their subjects. Mueller warns, however, that cyberspace does pose unique challenges, and at the same time generates novel opportunities to counter some of the drawbacks of the rule of mutually exclusive territorial monopolies of force.[80] He finds that intellectual property, cyber-security, content regulation, and the control of critical Internet resources (domain names and IP addresses that are the condition of possibility of any cyberspace) require transnational governance at a level and in a manner that cannot be provided by any nation state in itself for itself.

5.2 Regaining Control: Indirect Extraterritorial Effect?

In 2001, before the US ratified the Cybercrime Convention (in 2007), Goldsmith wrote a paper on the legitimacy of remote cross-border searches.[81] He describes one of the first known cases of remote cross-border searches and seizures in the context of cyberspace. After tracing the source of malicious hackings into computing systems of banks, Internet service providers (ISPs)

---

78   Mueller, "The New Cyber-Conservatism."
79   E.g., Goldsmith & Wu, *Who Controls the Internet?*, 153.
80   Milton L. Mueller, *Networks and States: The Global Politics of Internet Governance* (Cambridge, MA: MIT Press, 2010).
81   Jack Goldsmith, "The Internet and the Legitimacy of Remote Cross-Border Searches," *The University of Chicago Legal Forum* (2001): 103.

and other US firms to data servers in Russia, the FBI tried to gain Russian assistance in monitoring and redressing the criminal activities. When the Russian authorities turned out to have other priorities the FBI "decided to act unilaterally."[82] They obtained a search warrant in the US, figured out the hackers" usernames and passwords via a keystroke "sniffer" and thus gained access to the servers in Russia, downloading the information necessary to charge them and to prevent further attacks. Goldsmith recalls that the "normal" way to proceed in the case of extraterritorial jurisdiction to enforce is judicial or police cooperation, but he explains:

> The problem is that such cooperation is often difficult. Sometimes the source-country government lacks legal authority to seize and freeze computer information within its borders. Sometimes it lacks the technological capacity. Sometimes the enforcement machinery in the source country will simply take too long, because evidence of the crime can quickly be destroyed or anonymized. And sometimes, as in the opening example, the source country government simply fails to cooperate.[83]

He notes that "for these and other reasons, officials in the target country might take matters into their own hands."[84] Goldsmith then refers to international law, observing that many authors would find this a violation of the territorial sovereignty of the source-country.[85] His essay, however, is meant to argue that remote searches are indeed restricted by international principles of enforcement jurisdiction, but that such restrictions cannot be deduced from norms of territorialism. He adds that, though he does not see jurisdictional grounds to prohibit unilateral extraterritorial searches, there may be other grounds to restrict or prohibit these searches, notably potential violations of privacy or free speech rights. The main reason why Goldsmith contends that under certain conditions states are free to engage in remote searches is necessity. He observes that the Cybercrime Convention prohibits unilateral exterritorial enforcement, but considers that the "Convention will have little in-

---

82   Ibid., 103.
83   Ibid., 104.
84   Ibid.
85   Ibid. He refers to the Restatement (Third) of Foreign Relations Law of the United States, § 432, comment b (1987). Note that he does not refer to international law, but to the US restatement of its position on obligations under international law.

fluence on crimes committed from safe-haven nations that do not ratify it."[86] Necessity will require officials to take the law in their own hands, and—for Goldsmith—this evokes another necessity: the need to reinterpret the prohibition on extraterritorial jurisdiction. In short, Goldsmith proposes that remote searches do not violate this prohibition because the officials doing the search do not leave the territory of the US. The argument—which returns in *Who Controls the Internet?*—is that states will find ways to achieve *indirect* extraterritorial effect; they will use local infrastructure, local ISPs and local divisions of foreign companies to target the source of the harm they wish to redress. Just like cyberspace destroys the unity of time, place and action of the *actus reus* of a cybercriminal, it does the same for the enforcement action of national authorities; the scope of the extraterritorial effect of territorial action is transformed by cyberspace. Goldsmith actually links this effect to cross-border surveillance on the high seas and international air space and concludes that "[n]orms of 'territorial sovereignty' have never precluded such offshore espionage."[87] Goldsmith's argument oscillates between pragmatic arguments entailing that because judicial cooperation does not always work unilateral action is needed and a curious understanding of international law entailing that states can always act in their own best interest. To the extent that this violates international law, he asserts that the law will simply have to be changed: "There is little doubt that if such searches prove necessary to redress cross-border internet attacks, international law will adapt to permit them in some circumstances."[88]

There is no doubt that, for Goldsmith, the sovereign is he who decides on the exception. Norms are nice, but in case of necessity we are better off with decisions.[89] He acknowledges potential abuse—for instance, if officials resort to cross-border searches even if alternative means of investigation are available—and warns against the threat of reciprocity and retaliation, for instance if Russia decides to engage in cross-border enforcement in cyberspace on the territory of the US. But ultimately the claim stands that unilateral

---

86 Ibid., 106; at 106 n 14 he refers to art. 19, 20, 23(a) and 32 of the *Convention on Cybercrime*, November 23, 2001, ETS No 185 that restrict cross-border searches to publicly available data or consent in the case of private data.
87 Ibid., 114. It is not clear what is the relevance of this observation, since espionage is not the same as extraterritorial enforcement of the criminal law.
88 Ibid., 116.
89 On Schmitt's view of legal order in terms of legal norms and a-legal decisions, see Mireille Hildebrandt, "The Indeterminacy of an Emergency: Challenges to Criminal Jurisdiction in Constitutional Democracy," *Criminal Law and Philosophy* 4 (2010): 161.

actions are inevitable and require adjustment of international law. Interestingly, after his paper was published the US ratified the Cybercrime Convention, which forbids these searches without express permission of the source country. What does this mean for the competence of US officials to engage in unilateral cross-border search? Are they bound by their agreement to the Convention, or is there space for an a-legal decision in the case of necessity? In their book on the control over the Internet, Goldsmith and Wu advocate that territorial sovereignty will hold in cyberspace, whereas Goldsmith's earlier position suggests that territorial sovereignty will be redefined to allow extraterritorial enforcement jurisdiction in cyberspace. It seems that Schmittian decisionism will rule cyberspace when things get nasty, leaving international law and respect for the internal sovereignty of other states for times of relative peace.

6. CONCLUSIONS: NOVEL SPATIALITIES, CYBERSPACE AS PASSAGE AND COMMON GOOD?

Let us now return to Grotius's *Mare Liberum*. I briefly recall the four dimensions of territorial jurisdiction, distinguished above: territorial demarcation overrules personal status, it creates abstract boundaries that define an empty space, capable—I might add—of a simple way of producing an inside and an outside, that produces a gapless map of contiguous jurisdictional territories. The high seas escaped this totalitarian scheme due to their value as a common good, their status as a passage and the vigilance of different players who resisted occupation. Cyberspace can be territorialized, but only by redefining territory in a way that defies the original connection of the notion of territory to the land, to the earth. As discussed above, this connection portrays territorial jurisdiction as exclusive and gapless; there is no outside that is not an inside and a subject or an object cannot be inside two different territories. The novel connection to territory, however, would have to be inclusive and overlapping; as soon as there is an inside there are numerous ways to extend the inside—for instance by means of what Goldsmith calls indirect extraterritorial effect.

This marks the difference between cyberspace and Grotius's high seas: the high seas—unlike cyberspaces—were not everywhere nor anywhere.[90] This difference implies that the metaphor of *Mare Liberum* has its limits,

---

90 Thanks to Markus Dubber for pointing this out during the workshop in Toronto, June 2012.

because—other than cyberspace—it depends on the territoriality of the land it surrounds. This is precisely why cyberspaces require novel negotiations between jurisdiction and spatiality. The boundaries of the high seas were determined by those of the land; there was no overlap. The boundaries of territory in the era of cyberspace are, however, liquid.[91] Cyberspace does not stop where ordinary space begins. This means that territorialisation of cyberspaces easily generates cross-border communication, commerce and crime, situating the same action seamlessly in different territories (both online and offline). On the side of cybersecurity this will trigger universal extraterritorial jurisdiction to enforce. As we have seen above, as long as the official conducting a remote extraterritorial search is physically located in the territory of the investigating state some will define the action as an intraterritorial search with indirect extraterritorial effects. It may be the case that the legal requirement that the other state must agree to such a search is contingent upon a previous spatiality, on artificial demarcations that have run out of steam.

A redefinition of the scope of territorial jurisdiction that justifies indirect extraterritorial effects will nevertheless run into problems. It builds on an a-legal *occupatio* because it claims and seizes access to computing systems located in the realm of another state that may decide to exercise its monopoly on violence. Retaliation and reciprocity may turn cyberspace into a platform for cyberwar; to the extent that our critical infrastructure is increasingly rooted in cyberspace such a-legality is not something to look forward to. The recent history of the malware program "Olympic Games" is a primary example of such a-legal occupation. The program, developed by the National Security Agency of the US and Israel's secret services with the aim to disturb the nuclear plant at Natanz (Iran), sets an example that will be—and undoubtedly has been—followed.[92]

We thus have to face the question of whether cyberspace *liberum* grounds a-legal *occupatio* or requires "grounding" in a novel version of natural law

---

91 Cf. Julie JCH Ryan, Daniel Ryan, and Eneken Tikk, "Cybersecurity Regulation: Using Analogies to Develop Frameworks for Regulation," in *International Cyber Security Legal & Policy Proceedings* (Tallinn: CCD COE, 2010). They distinguish between the natural commons (notably the sea, air, the Antarctic, outer space, and cyberspace).
92 See Symantec Enterprise Security, *Internet Security Threat Report* 16 & 17. Note that the example does not refer to criminal jurisdiction to enforce but to something more like cyberwar. Obviously the distinction may not hold in cyberspace, unless we find a way to construct an effective legal demarcation that re-invents the distinction between internal sovereignty (criminal law) and external sovereignty (war) for the era of cyberspace.

that attributes subjective natural rights based on a distributed control over cyberspace infrastructure.[93] Part of Grotius's scheme may work, namely where we view cyberspace — in analogy to the high seas — as a passage that affords international trade, communication at a distance, the proliferation of information and of the techniques to transform information into knowledge. This would entail that we see cyberspace as a global commons. But, even if we manage to escape the temptations of an "economic theology" that takes the benefits of cyberspace as a global commons for granted, we still need to find ways to ensure that cyberspace "as a passage, a conduit" is instituted and maintained as a *res communis* that cannot be appropriated, may not come under exclusive sovereign control and requires a vigilant international community to safeguard the distributed control that is needed to prevent violent, exclusionary monopolies.[94]

This seems to be the challenging alternative to accepting that the power will be with those who take control, thus imposing their sovereignty in cyberspace to the extent that others let them.[95] However, to face this challenge we still need to figure out what it means to take care of a common good that cannot be separated from the territorial landscape it pervades. Cyberspace is "everyware."[96] If we want to save ourselves from an a-legal cyberspace we need to build a new — heterotopian — spatiality, taking into account the novel mappings that cyberspace affords. We must remember that sovereign jurisdiction entails unilateral enforcement of the criminal law, but — so far — is also the precondition of the unilateral enforcement of human rights such as the fair trial, privacy, and non-discrimination. The challenge will be to sustain a measure of safety, freedom, and respect for human rights in cyberspace, based on a legality that cannot, however, be grounded in the monopolistic spatiality of territorial sovereignty.

---

93 Though the idea of "natural rights" seems to defy the idea of attribution this is precisely the point of natural law: it attributes rights it claims to be inherent in the nature of human beings. This rhetorical strategy is based on the performative nature of the construction of reality and some relate it to the so-called endowment effect of our cognitive make-up, cf. Edmundson, *An Introduction to Rights*, 13.

94 On potential threats to the distributed control over the root structure of cyberspace (the Internet) see one of the founding fathers of the Internet, Vinton Cerf, "Keep the Internet Open," *The New York Times* (May 24, 2012), http://www.nytimes.com/2012/05/25/opinion/keep-the-internet-open.html. Also Mueller, *Networks and States*.

95 Cf. Allen, "Command of the Commons Boasts."

96 Adam Greenfield, *Everyware: The Dawning Age of Ubiquitous Computing* (Berkeley: New Riders, 2006).

THE RISE OF LEGAL COSMOPOLITISM: DENATIONALIZATION & TERRITORIALIZATION OF LAW

Julien Seroussi

International criminal justice deals with a limited number of core crimes, which have a deep impact on the international community: genocide, crimes against humanity, and war crimes. All of these crimes are usually described as ordinary crimes committed in extraordinary circumstances, which lawyers call contextual elements. If one takes the Rome Statute of the International Criminal Court (ICC), a murder can amount to a crime against humanity if it's committed as part of a widespread or systematic attack directed against a civilian population with knowledge of the attack pursuant of an organizational policy to commit such an attack.

The international criminal justice system had tremendously developed itself since the end of the Cold War. Schematically speaking, it rests on three different concentric circles:

— The smaller circle comprises national judges, each of whom investigates international crimes in his own country where they occurred, just like he would do with ordinary crimes. Inside this limited territory, the so-called "national judge" can use very important coercive police powers to search for evidence.

— The middle circle comprises extraterritorial judges who can claim extraterritorial jurisdiction by prosecuting crimes committed abroad between strangers. These foreign national judges can resort to police force to investigate inside their own country, but they depend on the cooperation of other States to collect evidence abroad.

— The largest circle comprises the eighteen "international judges" of the ICC, which territorial jurisdiction expands as increasing numbers of States ratify the Rome Statute signed in 1998, although an investigation

This text was first presented in an Exterritory Project Symposium, December 12, 2013, Beit HaGefen, Haifa, Israel.

can also be triggered by the Security Council on any situation in the world. Despite the fact that the Prosecutor of the ICC has its own team of investigators, fact-finding mainly depends on international cooperation, since there is no international police force.

Looking at this three-legged system, it is striking to notice how the coercive powers of the different judicial bodies that compound the international criminal justice system diminish as their jurisdiction widens.

In this essay, I would like to show that the balanced, multi-layered international criminal justice system is the result of two seemingly opposite processes of universalization of the jurisdiction to prescribe and territorialization of the jurisdiction to enforce, which are both essential to the fight against impunity.

I. DENATIONALIZATION OF LAW

International criminal law emerged at the crossroads of national criminal law and public international law. On the one side, national criminal lawyers created the International Criminal Law Association (ICLA) in 1889 to address the existence of conflicting independent national law order. On the other, international law professors created the International Law Institute (ILI) in 1873 in an effort to build an international public law independent from international private law. The career of Henri Donnedieu de Vabres illustrates the rising of this new combined legal discipline, which is both criminal and international, all along the 20th century. He started his career as a national criminal law professor, worked on the coordination of States for the control of immigration and ended his professional life as the French international judge at the Nuremberg Trial.

At the start, the notion of universal jurisdiction was a topic of academic discussion which referred to an attempt to encourage the cross application of national criminal law, that is the possibility for a national judge to implement the law of a foreign State, even if the crime cannot be found in its own criminal code. Henri Donnedieu de Vabres will defend this idea in his famous book, the first textbook ever written on international criminal law, entitled *Les principes modernes du droit pénal international* (*Modern Principles of Interna-*

tional Criminal Law), published in 1926.[1] He requests the duty of every state to take an active part in the repression of a foreign national order: "universal jurisdiction is the negation of the rights of asylum just like extradition.".Even if this reform has never been implemented, this first move towards the denationalization of law is very important intellectual step because it weakens the identification of the law with the State.

As the dramatic event of the beginning of the twentieth century unfolded, the definition of universal jurisdiction changed. Until the First World War, international crises had been regulated by the "bons offices" of good-willing high-profiled leaders. Lawyers were only asked to translate the will of the State they represented into judicial babble. However, the deepening of the international crisis in post-war Europe requested the professionalization of mediation embodied by the creation of the League of Nations and the permanent international Court of Justice. With the rise of these institutions, diplomats started taking an interest in the academic discussion about universal jurisdiction.

Within these new legal and political dynamics, the definition of universal jurisdiction stopped referring to the cross-application of national law to point to the possibility for a national judge to prosecute on its own territory crimes directly defined by the international community. This new approach to universal jurisdiction surfaced with the development of transnational criminality which breached the direct interest of different countries at the same time: the international community agreed on a legal definition of money counterfeiting in 1929, state representatives held an international meeting on terrorism in 1934 to fight the multiplication of political assassination all over Europe and so forth with war crimes committed during international armed conflicts, human trafficking or plane hijacking. From the 1930s onward, an individual could now be held accountable directly to the international community for a limited number of crimes and brought to justice in any signing State Party to these different treaties under the *aut dedere aut judicare* principle, a Latin formula meaning, "either you prosecute or you extradite."[2]

---

1   Henri Donnedieu de Vabres, *Les principes modernes du droit pénal international* (Paris: Panthéon-Assas, 2005).
2   Marc Henzelin, "Universal Jurisdiction," in *Encyclopedia of Genocide and Crimes Against Humanity*, ed. D. Shelton, vol. 3 (Farrington Hills, Michigan: Macmillan Reference USA, 2004), 1116–23.

After the Second World War, the scope of universal jurisdiction was slowly expanded form transnational criminality to human rights violations, which can occur inside the border of one given country. However, there is quite a big historical gap between the codification of international human rights law and the prosecution of human rights violations through universal jurisdiction just like transnational crimes. If the convention for the repression of genocide signed in 1948 was a step forward, the delegates rejected the *aut dedere aut judicare* principle, fearing that international private litigation targeting the internal affairs of one country would be politically driven.[3] Although they agreed on the fact that genocide could be prosecuted by an international judge, they were not taking much of a risk since the ICC did not exist back then, and was not likely to be created anytime soon in a world stage divided between two ideological antagonistic systems known as capitalism and communism.

However, the initial rejection of universal jurisdiction for human rights violations should not only be blamed of political cynicism. Most country delegates felt strongly that investigations abroad would be very complicated to conduct, an issue that is still pervasive nowadays, even if it is partially addressed by the development of a web of NGOs, which monitor most conflicts all around the world with very professional commitment. As a matter of fact, the legal breakthrough was stirred by the dedication of a famous NGO, Amnesty International, during the negotiation of the convention against torture was ratified in 1984. Amnesty International's senior legal advisor, Sir Nigel Rodely, recalled that the Swedish proposal to enshrine the *aut dedere aut judicare* principle into the torture convention was first discussed inside an Amnesty International caucus and that other countries accepted it only after a strong lobbying by the same organization.[4] By attending the conference and reporting on the debate, NGOs prevent State delegates from developing too many interest-driven arguments and automatically raise the debate towards more universal norms. As a matter of fact, the successful efforts of Amnesty International are a good example on how potential shaming before the public eye is able to change the structure of a legal agreement.

---

3   Matthew Lippman, "The Drafting of the 1948 Convention on the Prevention and Punishment of the Crime of Genocide," *Boston University International Law Journal* (1984): 1–64.
4   Rodley Nagel, "NGO and the Prevention and Repression of Torture," in *International Human Rights Law and Non-Governmental Organizations*, ed. G. Cohen-Jonathan and Jean-François Flauss (2005), 103–17.

This denationalization of law is very important for the protection of human rights. No one is now able to hide behind its national laws to avoid being held accountable for the most serious crimes. However, this process of denationalization of law should not be mistaken for the process of deterritorialization of law, which has been largely rejected by the States.

2. TERRITORIALIZATION OF ENFORCEMENT

Since the degree of control of the State over the judicial process is directly measurable by the level of independence it is willing to give the Prosecutor, the scope of the ICC's jurisdiction has been under important scrutiny at the Rome Statute. In this controversy, there were two radical opposite sides. On the one hand, the NGOs' Coalition for the International Criminal Court asserted that the legal incrimination developed in the Rome statute had already reached the level of international customary law long before the start of the negotiations. According to them, the future ICC Prosecutor should therefore be entitled with the right to investigate crimes committed worldwide and prior to the establishment of the Court. In other words, they supported a deterritorialized universal jurisdiction based solely on the nature of the crimes. On the other side, most state delegates reminded that the ICC Prosecutor's jurisdiction should not extend to countries which are not members of the Rome Statute by stressing that an international treaty cannot bind third parties which have not signed it. According to them, States should have the exclusive power to trigger the jurisdiction of the Prosecutor over a specific situation happening either in their own country or in another country if they can claim a legal interest.

Under the intensive scrutiny and mobilization of NGOs, the negotiation between the countries' delegation led to a compromise: member states are able to refer a situation occurring on their territory, the Prosecutor is able to trigger an investigation at his own initiative to investigate crimes committed on the territory of any state party, and the Security Council can ask the Prosecutor to open an investigation of a situation in any country in the world. Thus, the Prosecutor of the ICC has been granted territorial jurisdiction over an area solely composed of all the State parties and the deterritorialized universal jurisdiction has been strictly subdued to a Security Council decision. Even if it carries us away from the question of territoriality, it is important to add that the Prosecutor's territorial corset is strengthened by a judicial review. In exchange for the right of the Prosecutor to launch an investigation on his own, the States decided that a Preliminary Chamber should be created to monitor the prosecutor's action on very carefully chosen legal grounds. In several steps of the proceedings, the Prosecutor has to obtain the judges' green light to move forward in his investigation, to issue an arrest warrant and to go to trial.

To understand how the ICC deals with territorial challenges, we can take a look at the great difficulties encountered in the arrest of Omar El-Beshir, the current President of Sudan, who is wanted for crimes against humanity and genocide.[5] To grasp different aspects of this hard case, we have to recall a few facts. The situation in Sudan was referred to the ICC by the Security Council in 2005 and was followed by an arrest warrant in 2009 issued by the Preliminary Chamber. As of today, Beshir has visited several countries in the world without being arrested: Qatar, Egypt, Chad, Malawi, Kenya, and Nigeria. All these different failures to arrest cannot be set on the same level, but they all pertain interesting questions of territoriality.

Since the situation in Darfour has been referred to the Court by the Security Council, one could argue that every State has the duty to arrest President Beshir. Although this option could be considered a logical consequence of the United Nations referral, the international community has not accepted the logic of deterritorialization of law entailed by this mechanism. The Security Council has never taken any steps to request that all countries be obligated to execute arrest warrants targeting crimes committed in a situation it has itself referred to the ICC. Without any pressure from the Security Council, it is not surprising that non-members of the ICC like Egypt or Qatar have not arrested the Sudanese President. If the lack of adherence of non-member States to the Rome Statute thrives on the United Security Council's inaction, the refusal of member States to arrest El-Beshir is based on a vigorous legal advocacy by the African Union. The African regional organization rests on the argument of Article 98 of the Rome Statute which states that the Court may not proceed with a request for surrender or assistance that would require the requested State to act inconsistently with its obligations under customary international law with respect to the State or diplomatic immunity. Without going into the legal debate, one must acknowledge a conflict between Article 27 of

---

[5] Gwen P. Barnes, "The International Criminal Court's Ineffective Enforcement Mechanisms: The Indictment of President Omar Al Bashir," *Fordham International Law Journal* 34, no. 6 (2011): 1584–619.

the International Criminal Court which rebuts immunity for international crimes and the case-law of the International Court of Justice which forbids national authorities to arrest a foreign sitting head of State since the Yerodia judgement issued in 2002. After examining this legal conflict, the ICC has decided that regarding arrest warrants, Article 27 should prevail over article 98.[6] Far from abating, the conflict has now became a political problem for States, which are both party to the African Union and the Rome Statute, and has yet radicalized to another extent with the indictment of the President of Kenya for his alleged responsibility in the 2007 post-election violence.

All these examples mean to show that the ICC has to face huge territorial issues. Although this could be described as a weakness of the international justice system, one must keep in mind that member States have given birth to the ICC precisely because the Statute respects the core elements of sovereignty, and especially, territoriality. To my mind, the problem lies more in the fact that the Security Council does not take any action to oppose the advocacy of the African Union against a decision of the ICC. Since the signature of the Rome Statute in 1998, many activists have nevertheless tried to overcome the territorial limits of the International Criminal Court by promoting the deterritorialized universal jurisdiction of national judges. The case law shows however that they faced the same obstacle of territorialization they had encountered in the debates around the creation of the ICC.[7]

If you look at the Spanish arrest warrant sent to Britain for the arrest of Pinochet who was undergoing medical treatment in the UK, you will notice that it is based on the murder of a Spanish citizen under Pinochet's rule. On the 16th of October 1998, the Judge of the Audiencia Nacional had based its decision on passive jurisdiction, which allows a Court to prosecute crimes committed against one of its nationals, precisely because they distrusted universal jurisdiction, which was not sustained by any previous case-law. However, the human rights activist described in the media this arrest warrant as the first attempt to implement deterritorialized universal jurisdiction in order to push the agenda that had been rejected at the Rome Conference a few months earlier in July 1998. This media coverage was efficient enough to change the course of the proceedings. In its decision on the arrest warrant

---

6   Dire Tladi, "The ICC Decisions on Chad and Malawi: On Cooperation, Immunities and Article 98," *Journal of International Criminal Justice* 11, no. 1 (2013): 199–221.

7   Julien Seroussi, "The Cause of Universal Jurisdiction: The Rise and Fall of an International Mobilization," in *Lawyers and the Construction of Transnational Justice*, ed. Yves Dezalay and Bryant Garth (London: Routledge, 2012), 48–61.

review, filed on the November 5, 1998, the High Court of Spain decided to live with the newly raised expectations of international public opinion by moving to universal jurisdiction. According to this decision, Spain was now seeking from England the extradition of Pinochet for crimes committed against Chileans in their home country since his 1973 coup d'état. Moreover, the British House of Lords followed the same path by deciding on the November 25, 1998, to lift Pinochet's immunity in order to proceed with his extradition to Spain. As we all know, this decision did not prevail in the end and Pinochet was able to go back to Chile on health grounds, but the activist had a case-law stating that prosecutions was not limited in time or space when it comes to grave breaches of human rights and they were willing to try to strengthen it with new cases.

From the Pinochet case onward, multiple attempts have been carried to foster the deterritorialized universal jurisdiction of national judges, but lawmakers have curbed the NGO's enthusiasm by imposing important territorial constraints. The most eloquent example is the case against Hissene Habre, the former dictator of Chad, who settled in Senegal after he was ousted form power by his successor. Although Belgium has managed to compel Senegal to judge Habre under the *aut dedere aut judicare* principle, after winning an arbitration of the International Court of Justice in 2012, the Belgian law, which allowed the judges to have jurisdiction over crimes committed abroad with no territorial link whatsoever, was cancelled in 2003. In other words, the Habre proceedings are only a surviving case of a former law which had been stripped from the Belgian criminal code already a decade ago. After a worldwide debate over the limits of universal jurisdiction, most counties consider now that only the presence of the accused on their territory is able to set off the judicial process. As far I know, only Spain still supports deterritorialized universal jurisdiction, but it has not had the opportunity to go beyond preliminary investigations. Also, it seems that the prime minister of Spain is contemplating amendments to its Universal Jurisdiction law after arrest warrants against top Chinese politicians for alleged crimes committed in Tibet recently infuriated Beijing.

Fearing the loosening of the fight against impunity, many activists were disappointed by the territorial limits imposed on jurisdiction to enforce, but others think that it grants national judges with the necessary legitimacy to prosecute crimes committed in another country. The presence of the accused on the territory gives a very objective triggering mechanism that shields the judges from the very frequent accusation of neo-colonization that international criminal justice has to regularly face. Also, it enables the government to justify itself in front of its own public opinion, which does not always understand why so many resources should be spent on crimes which did not cause a tort to any citizen of the country.

3. EMPOWERING THE TERRITORIAL STATE

The relationship between the International Criminal Court and the States is encapsulated by the principle of complementarity, regulated by Article 17 of the Rome Statute, which states that it is first and foremost the duty of national courts to prosecute the perpetrators of the most serious international crimes. If the purpose of this principle is to give clear primacy to the territorial States over the ICC, the international judges monitor the States to verify whether they are taking active investigative steps. In the words of Article 17, the judges have to check if the State is able and willing to prosecute crimes falling in the Court's jurisdiction. Until the examination of the Libyan Senoussi case, every time a State had requested to judge the suspect by itself, the judges of the ICC ruled that the government was not giving sufficiently specified evidence that it was conducting serious investigations into the crimes. While the judges are setting a minimal international standard of fair trial against which most states have stumbled on, the ICC Prosecutor is genuinely trying to foster national action by providing direct assistance and advice to countries, among the different situations on which he is carrying out a preliminary investigation. For example, the Prosecutor of the ICC is advising the Colombia government on different aspects of the "Legal Framework for Peace" and the "Military Reform Act" to ensure that this new piece of legislation will enable the national judges to prosecute international crimes that he might otherwise have to investigate himself.[8]

Notwithstanding legal arguments regarding complementarity, the fact that the international judges have to rule over crimes committed in foreign countries creates a number of challenges, which also explain the effort to foster the natural judge. Firstly, the International Criminal Court has to face translation issues. For example, the English lawyer of Germain Katanga was

---

8   Office of the Prosecutor, "Report on Preliminary Examination," 2013, http://www.icc-cpi.int/en_menus/icc/structure%20of%20the%20court/office%20of%20the%20prosecutor/comm%20and%20ref/reports/Pages/default.aspx.

listening to witness through an English interpreter who translated what the French interpreter was himself translating from Congolese Swahili. Obviously, the risk of losing some key contents increases with the numbers of interpreters. In the Katanga case, one witness testified for several days about airlifts between one city and the line of combat by using the Swahili word *mbegu* to talk about the freight. For a while, the interpreter translated this Swahili word as "seed" before one Swahili speaker in the Courtroom said that this word is a metaphor to say "ammunition."[9] With this new translation, the whole interpretation of the testimony radically changed from exculpatory to incriminating. Therefore, the manifestation of the truth in a case before the International Criminal Court stems from the permeation of the language of the witness, the interpreters choices of translation and the lawyer's strategy. Although the ideal of justice would require to stay as close as possible to what the witness has come to say, every translator knows that switching languages is not a neutral operation and every lawyer is willing to use these discrepancies to his benefit.

Needless to say, the problem of language is not only a question on transparency but introduces us to the sensitive issue of understanding someone else's culture in order to understand the meaning of what he says when he testifies. In the Germain Katanga and Mathieu Ngudjolo case, the prosecutor discarded the local specificities of the armed groups led by the accused to focus on what most resembles a Western chain of command. If you read the transcript of the trial, you will notice that the soldiers paid a lot of respect to sorcerers who were dispatched in every single camp. As the Prosecutor had dismissed all these allusions to the *feticheurs* as non-essential, he denied himself evidence that could have helped him in his case, particularly in the demonstration of the automatic compliance of soldiers. If he had taken witchcraft seriously, he might have been able to use the fact that the leaders also exerted control over their troopers through the distribution of fetish, which is as essential as weapons for local militiamen.[10] This relative inability to engage in thick description of the mobilization is not a question of opposition between the Western world and the African world since the prosecution teams put together people from different national backgrounds. It is related

9   International Criminal Court, transcript of Mathieu Ngudjolo Chui and Germain Katanga at the International Criminal Court, T-302, August 31, 2011, http://www.icc-cpi.int/iccdocs/doc/do c1235418.pdf, 1–6.
10 Trial Chamber II, "Judgement Pursuant to Article 74 of the Statute," December 18, 2012, http:// www.icc-cpi.int/iccdocs/doc/doc1579080.pdf, para. 122.

to the fact that the understanding of judicial categories is still too dependent on Nazi and Communist ideologically driven political experience.

Beyond the question of truth, investigations conducted abroad raise the more pervasive question of trust. If the course of a trial moves away from historical truth, it will never impede the proceedings, but the trial will not be able to proceed at all if judges cannot rest on reliable evidence. In the case against Germain Katanga and Mathieu Ngudjolo, the Court had to face the important issue of assessing the age of witnesses who said they were child-soldiers during the Congolese wars. According to the Rome Statute, a combatant qualifies as child-soldier if he (or she) is under fifteen years old. Yet what everyone expected to be a very simple identification process became quite complicated. For each witness, passports, school reports, demobilization cards and oral testimony bare different birthdates which brought us by turns under or over the fifteen years old threshold. The disarray became very significant when one realizes that the question is not whether the witness was telling the truth or not, but that one simply did not have the right reliability test to assess it.[11] In the end, the prosecutor himself gave up the factual allegations stating that several of his witnesses were in fact under fifteen years old when they participated in the attack. Trust is conveyed through various signs that differ from one country to another, some are very explicit, such as signatures and stamps on documentary evidence, and others are very evanescent, such as a way of looking or the tone of a voice of a witness. One has to know a society from the inside as much as possible to assess the credibility of any piece of evidence.

Complementarity regulates the relationship between the international judges and the national judges of its member States. There is no equivalent mechanism to organize the relationship between the extraterritorial judge and other state national judges. Obviously, one can expect an extraterritorial judge to accept the extradition of a suspect to his home country if it can guarantee a fair trial to him. Nevertheless, it is hard to tell on what basis one country can assess the proper functioning of the judicial system of another. Once the question of death penalty has been set aside, a national judge does not have the legitimacy of the ICC to assert that a foreign State requesting a suspect through a fair extradition process is either unable or unwilling to

---

11 Office of the Prosecutor, "Mémoire Final," Mathieu Ngudjolo Chui and Germain Katanga at the International Criminal Court, July 3, 2012, http://www.icc-cpi.int/iccdocs/doc/doc1436782.pdf (in French), para. 780–790.

judge. Similarly, there is no legal grounds enabling an extraterritorial judge to prosecute a suspect that acquitted by its own national courts after an over-indulgent trial. According to me, it would be interesting if the question of conflicting jurisdiction between the national and the extraterritorial judges could be submitted to the Appeal Chamber of the International Court which could render a decision on the basis of Article 17 of the Rome Statute.

✖

Denationalization of law is an important cornerstone in the fight against impunity as it forbids anybody to hide behind its national legislation to commit heinous crimes. However, when you consider enforcement, territorialization of law is an important pillar of the international justice system as the closer the judge is to the case the better he can understand it. It is true that the territorial restrictions imposed on universal jurisdiction explain that some suspects can slip through the net. However, the primacy given to territorialization guarantees better the ability to find compelling evidence against those who do get arrested.

EXTRATERRITORIAL STATE ACTION IN THE GLOBAL INTEREST: THE PROMISE OF UNILATERALISM

Cedric Ryngaert

Advocates of "global justice" or "cosmopolitanism" propound that ethical duties are universal, and apply regardless of nationality, citizenship, race etc. In pure cosmopolitanism, individuals owe ethical duties towards other individuals who are worse off, wherever on earth they may be. Individual agency is not particularly practical, however. Therefore, global justice advocates have proposed to mediate individuals' ethical duties via institutions, in particular international (governmental) organizations.[1] In this institutional view, international organizations ought to be oriented towards furthering cosmopolitan ideals and tackling collective action problems, such as protecting human rights and the environment, guaranteeing collective security, and ensuring distributive justice, in particular alleviating world poverty.[2] Some such institutions, such as the United Nations, have been duly created. But because of design faults, political unwillingness, or resource limits, they have not been able to deliver on the promises they initially held: human rights are still trampled on, corruption remains rampant, and global warming continues unabated.

International institutions' failure to adequately tackle collective action problems invites the question of whether instead, "bystander" states should not assume their cosmopolitan responsibility, apart from catering to the

---

This contribution draws on the author's inaugural address accepting the Chair of Public International Law at Utrecht University, March 30, 2015, "Unilateral Jurisdiction and Global Values" (published with Eleven 2015), and has been sumbitted for publication in a law review. The research which resulted in this publication has been funded by the European Research Council under the Starting Grant Scheme (Proposal 336230—UNIJURIS) and the Dutch Organization for Scientific Research under the VIDI Scheme.

1 E.g., Michael J. Green, "Institutional Responsibility for Global Problems," *Philosophical Topics* 30, no. 2 (Fall 2002): 79, 85–6.
2 Simon Caney, *Justice Beyond Borders: A Global Political Theory* (New York and Oxford: Oxford University Press, 2005), 159. See on poverty in particular Thomas Pogge, *World Poverty and Human Rights: Cosmopolitan Responsibilities and Reforms*, 2nd ed. (Cambridge: Polity Press, 2008).

needs of their own citizens. Contemporary political theorist Simon Caney, in any event, is of the view that individual states do have global responsibilities: while they are free to pursue their own ends and to discharge their "contractual" duties towards their own citizens, they should do so "within the context of a fair overall framework," i.e, "a set of parameters defined by a theory of justice."[3] These words echo international lawyer Emmer de Vattel's statements in his classic treatise *Le droit des gens* (*The Law of Nations*, 1770): while a nation is under an obligation to preserve itself and its members,[4] it also has duties for the preservation of others, and to contribute to the perfection of other nations.[5] In this contribution, I examine an aspect of this state cosmopolitanism, namely the question whether states can *unilaterally extend their jurisdiction* to address global ills. Put differently, I inquire how a state can apply *its own laws* to address globally undesirable situations that arise (largely) *extraterritorially*, i.e., outside their territorial borders. Well-known instances of such unilateral jurisdiction are the US Department of Justice's indictment of corrupt FIFA officials, Spanish Investigating Judge Garzon's attempts to have former Chilean dictator Augusto Pinochet extradited to Spain to stand trial for international crimes, and the European Union's move to subject foreign air carriers to the EU's own stringent climate change legislation to the extent that they frequent EU airports.

Such an inquiry requires that we confront the centrality of the principle of sovereignty in modern international law, while keeping our eyes open for more global justice-friendly semantic understandings which the principle may have taken on (Section 1). Such an inquiry also invites us to ascertain the existence of common values or interests which states acting unilaterally/extraterritorially supposedly vindicate on behalf of an alleged "international community" (Section 2). The legitimacy of such action obviously suffers if the state only promotes its own idiosyncratic values. But even where values are more or less universally shared, the question remains whether individual states rather than international institutions should be entrusted with cosmopolitan jurisdictional powers. Can benevolent hegemons be trusted, or does trusteeship risk degenerating into imperialist imposition (Section 3)?

---

3 Ibid., 139–40.
4 Emer de Vattel, *Le droit des gens* (Paris: Guillaumin, 1863), Book I, Ch. II, para. 16–18.
5 Ibid., Book II, Ch. I, para. 1–6. Justifying the latter duties toward others, he approvingly cites the Roman orator Cicero, who said in *De Officiis* that "[N]othing is more agreeable to nature, more capable of affording true satisfaction, than, in imitation of Hercules, to undertake even the most arduous and painful labours for the benefit and preservation of all nations."

While acknowledging the risk of self-serving behavior, this contribution is inclined to support benevolent unilateralism, as the alternative—no action—may be worse. It argues that the justification of such unilateralism should be sought in the substantive values it furthers rather than in tired "anti-commons" legal formalisms (Section 4).

1. COSMOPOLITAN STATE JURISDICTION: FROM TERRITORIAL SOVEREIGNTY TO CORRECTIVE JUSTICE

Advocates of the unilateral cosmopolitanism posit that states *can*, and perhaps *should* assume responsibility for, and on behalf of all members of a perceived international community *irrespective of artificially created national borders*. Its adherents should not fail to realize that this—laudable—position is in apparent tension with a principle on which the entire temple of contemporary international law has been built: the principle of *territorial sovereignty*. The pedigree of this principle can be traced from the Peace of Westphalia of 1648, a series of treaties which ended the Thirty Years' War and introduced the concept of co-existing states with full internal and external sovereignty, until the present times.[6] Territorial sovereignty implies that final political authority and jurisdiction is exclusively vested in a territorially delimited political community, and that no other authority has a legal say (*juris dicere*) over this community.[7] The role of international law is simply to ensure that this sovereignty is not trampled on, and that the territorial state-based system survives. In practice, state sovereignty has at times been violated when one state reasoned that respect for another state's sovereignty was not in its interest—which may lead one to question indeed whether sovereignty is not just organized hypocrisy. But it remains an enduring "cognitive script" that guides the actions of participants in international relations,[8] and requires them to at least pay lip-service to the principles of non-intervention and territoriality.

6   See for a historical account: Derek Croxton, *Westphalia: The Last Christian Peace* (New York: Palgrave Macmillan, 2013); and for a discussion of the influence of the Peace until the 20th century: Leo Gross, "The Peace of Westphalia, 1648–1948," *American Journal of International Law* 42 (1948): 20.
7   See also Stephen D. Krasner, *Sovereignty: Organized Hypocrisy* (Princeton: Princeton University Press, 1999), 11.
8   Ibid., 69 (arguing that sovereignty—while being organized hypocrisy in his opinion—has proved remarkably "durable in the sense that it has affected the talk and conception of rulers since at least the end of the 18th century, despite substantial changes in the international environment").

The law of jurisdiction, with which we are concerned here, is closely related to the principle of territorial sovereignty, and may even be co-extensive with it. It contains rules of the road that limit the reach of a state's prescriptive, adjudicatory and enforcement jurisdiction to the state's territorial boundaries, with some limited exceptions to protect and punish its own nationals (personality principle), its political independence (protective principle), and certain enemies of mankind (universality principle). The basic rule of territoriality, and the limited extraterritorial exceptions to it, are geared towards *protecting the sovereignty and self-interest* of states.[9] Jurisdictional rules may also be inspired by a utilitarian rationale based on efficiency and procedural economy,[10] and, as such, prevent courts and prosecutors from wasting scarce state resources to address problems that are another state's concern. The presumption against extraterritoriality as it is applied in the US—a canon of statutory construction pursuant to which the US Congress is presumed not to legislate extraterritoriality—appears to be largely based on this rationale.[11]

Such understandings of jurisdiction—which consider *states*, with *territorial* boundaries, as the primary units of analysis—are not particularly amenable to cosmopolitan action. For cosmopolitans indeed, *individuals*, making up an *international community* with common values, are the focus of attention.[12] Nevertheless, in recent international law scholarship and prac-

---

9   This applies both in a positive and a negative sense: states are allowed to unilaterally project their power, but when so doing, they should not unduly interfere in other states' affairs. Theoretically, reciprocity ensures that states will by and large respect the requirement of non-interference, although in reality, as a result of disparities of power, strong states have an incentive to extend their jurisdiction to the detriment of other states' sovereignty, without being hampered by a concern over adverse foreign reactions (notably the US, European states and the EU have been at the vanguard of exercising "extraterritorial" jurisdiction).

10 Adeno Addis, "Community and Jurisdictional Authority," in *Beyond Territoriality: Transnational Legal Authority in an Age of Globalization*, ed. Gunther Handl, Joachim Zekoll, Peter Zumbansen, (Boston and Leiden: Martinus Nijhoff, 2012), 16–17, appears to consider this efficiency-based rationale to be the main informant of the norms of jurisdiction, stating that "jurisdictional norms emerge for the purpose of maximizing aggregate social welfare."

11 Cedric Ryngaert, *Jurisdiction in International Law*, 2nd ed. (New York: Oxford University Press, 2015), 69–70.

12 Cosmopolitans do not necessarily deny the existence, or use of states, but for them, states only have instrumental value, insofar as they contribute to the primary cosmopolitan ideal of realizing the worth of every human being. See Roland Pierik and Wouter Werner, "Introduction," in *Cosmopolitanism in Context: Perspectives from International Law and Political Theory* (Cambridge and New York: Cambridge University Press, 2010), 4–5. Note that non-cosmopolitan moral philosophers, however, may well ascribe moral value to (territorially delimited) states. See e.g., Mervyn Frost, *Ethics in International Relations* (Cambridge: Cambridge University Press, 1996), 155 ("sovereign states and the system of sovereign states are necessary to the flourishing of individuals"). A similarly "Hegelian" view is even embraced by John Rawls, whose theory on—national—justice cosmopolitans have applied to international relations. In one of his last works, *The Law of Peoples* (Cambridge, MA: Harvard University Press: 1999), Rawls adheres to a society of states approach to

tice, sovereignty has lost some of its discursive power, and considerations of humanity have instead risen to prominence.[13] This humanity-centeredness has also found its way to the law of jurisdiction, part of which has become based on the rationale of *corrective justice*, i.e., on the cosmopolitan notion that states owe ethically-based duties towards citizens of other nations.[14] This ethical imperative has *already* grounded legal principles that allow, and — under certain circumstances — even *require* states to exercise so-called "universal jurisdiction" over a number of treaty- and customary law-based international crimes, such as war crimes and torture,[15] in the absence of any territorial or personal link of the crime or the presumed offender with the asserting state.[16]

The incorporation of the obligatory dimension of this imperative — jurisdiction as a duty of states rather than just a discretionary choice that is *restricted* by international law — has been hailed as a shift in jurisdictional thinking. It points to a reconceptualization of the regulation of jurisdiction, in Mills" words, "a not merely a "ceiling," defining the maximum limits of state power, but also [...] as a "floor," reflecting minimum requirements for the exercise of regulatory power by states in order to satisfy their international obligations."[17]

One could envisage that this notion of jurisdiction as corrective, cosmopolitan justice may also inform and justify jurisdictional assertions beyond

---

international morality, considering peoples organized in states as the primary units of analysis. This is reminiscent of the work of Frost and Hedley Bull, the main representative of the so-called English school in international relations, who similarly regarded the state-based system as the best system to realize justice. See Hedley Bull, *The Anarchical Society: a Study of Order in World Politics* (New York: Columbia University Press, 1977) 287–8. Pierik and Werner have incisively observed that Rawls's approach is very much in keeping with the Westphalian structure of current international law: it gives pride of place to state sovereignty, self-determination, and the principle of non-intervention (ibid., 8).

13 See Theodor Meron, *The Humanization of International Law* (Boston and Leiden: Martinus Nijhoff, 2006); Ruti G. Teitel, *Humanity's Law* (New York: Oxford University Press, 2011).
14 Addis, "Community and Jurisdictional Authority," 17.
15 See, e.g., Article 7(1) of the UN *Torture Convention*.
16 States may however require the presumed offender's posterior territorial presence for jurisdiction to be triggered. Also the operation *aut dedere aut judicare* clause that features in a number of international conventions is based on the presence of the offender within the territorial jurisdiction of the state, as States Parties to such conventions only have the choice to extradite or prosecute the presumed offender when the latter is present in their territory in the first place. See e.g., Article 5(2) UN *Torture Convention* (1984) ("Each State Party shall [...] take such measures as may be necessary to establish its jurisdiction over such offences in cases where the alleged offender is present in any territory under its jurisdiction and it does not extradite him [...]").
17 Alex Mills, "Rethinking Jurisdiction in International Law," *British Yearbook of International Law* 84 (2014): 187, 209–12 (also stating at p. 212 that "the fact that (particularly positive) jurisdictional obligations have been recognized with growing frequency and scope supports the thesis of a broader shift in international law").

the sphere of international criminal law. To bring about a more just world, in keeping with the tenets of institutional cosmopolitanism set out above, states may wish to regulate corporations' overseas business practices that adversely affect human rights or the environment, or violate global anti-corruption standards; they may fine foreign-flagged vessels docking in their ports, even in relation to activities on the high seas (e.g., illegal or unsustainable fisheries, or pollution of the marine environment); they may restrict or prohibit the importation of goods of which the foreign production process runs afoul of human rights standards or contributes to global warming; they may use remote technology to address global Internet criminality; or they may extend their data protection laws to data processed abroad.[18] When states—or regional organizations such as the European Union—thus flex their muscles, they exercise unilateral jurisdiction to protect some notion of "global values" or "the common interest." In so doing, they compensate for the lack of international progress on governance challenges regarding global public goods, values, and interests. As is known, such progress requires the participation of all, or at least a substantial number of members of the international community.[19]

Admittedly, unilateral action may appear to be only a second-best option compared to consent-based, and supposedly more legitimate multilateral action. However, as Voltaire famously noted in his memoirs, *le mieux est l'ennemi du bien* ("the perfect is the enemy of the good"). Therefore, one could posit that states may exercise unilateral action to further the global interest, at least strategically, to up the ante until adequate multilateral action is taken. In that sense, unilateralism could be considered as temporary mechanism of pressure.

Empowering individual states to further the global interest in fact sits well with our current pluralistic and pluri-centric world, where different centers of power take experimental bottom-up global action, thereby providing best practices and inspiration for others to follow. The sociologist Saskia

---

[18] These are, as it happens, the PhD topics of seven of my PhD researchers on two five-year projects funded by the European Research Council and the Dutch Organization for Scientific Research (2013–2018).

[19] Nico Krisch, "The Decay of Consent: International Law in an Age of Global Public Goods," *American Journal of International Law* 108, no. 1 (2014): 1. This may not apply to single-best effort global public goods, for the realization of which no aggregate effort is required, e.g., geo-engineering techniques in which only one state, or a small group of states invests, but that may deliver benefits for the entire international community.

Sassen's work on global cities comes to mind here.[20] Moreover, some cosmopolitans themselves, wary of a Leviathan-like supreme world government responsible for dispensing global justice,[21] have admitted that "there is a case for different institutions operating at different levels," which has the advantage of preventing the centralization of coercive power.[22] They may have in mind, in the first place, different international organizations addressing different policy issues, and keeping each other in check. But there is no reason to exclude individual states from this pantheon. In fact, Kant saw *separate states* rather than international organizations as the cosmopolitan duty-bearers in *Perpetual Peace*.[23] Also Rawls defended the society of states in his approach to justice in *The Law of Peoples* (although then he famously went on to doubt the possibility of global justice and solidarity within a society of states that do not all share a liberal justice outlook).[24] And Bartelson, one of the leading contemporary sovereignty theorists, foregrounded the role of states as *media* and instruments of global justice in *Sovereignty as Symbolic Form*:

> [T]he universalistic visions invoked to justify the projection of [...] governmental strategies into the global realm today operate under the assumption that the international system of states is the only available medium for realizing such visions in the near future."[25]

---

20 Saskia Sassen, *The Global City: New York, London, Tokyo* (Princeton: Princeton University Press, 2013). This work chronicles how New York, London, and Tokyo became command centers for the global economy and in the process underwent a series of massive and parallel changes. What distinguishes Sassen's theoretical framework is the emphasis on the formation of cross-border dynamics through which these cities and the growing number of other global cities begin to form strategic transnational networks.
21 See already Immanuel Kant, *Perpetual Peace: A Philosophical Sketch* (1795), reprinted in *Kant: Political Writings*, ed. Hans Reiss (Cambridge University Press, 1991), 102 (submitting that "laws progressively lose their impact as the government increases its range, and a soulless despotism, after crushing the germs of goodness, will finally lapse into anarchy").
22 Caney, *Justice Beyond Borders*, 163.
23 Robert Howse and Ruti Teitel, "Does Humanity-Law Require (or Imply) a Progressive Theory of History? (and Other Questions for Martti Koskenniemi)," *Temple International and Comparative Law Journal* 27, no. 2 (2013): 377, 383 (writing that "according to Kant, we need the state as well as an order of cosmopolitan right where individuals can claim, as humans, to be treated in a certain way regardless of territorial boundaries," citing Kant's emphasis on the republican federation in Perpetual Peace); Thomas Pogge, "Cosmopolitanism and Sovereignty," *Ethics* 103 (Oct. 1992): 48–75.
24 Rawls, *The Law of Peoples*.
25 Jens Bartelson, *Sovereignty as Symbolic Form* (London and New York: Routledge, 2014), 78.

Ultimately, as the state remains a—or even *the*—central actor in international law-making and -implementation, one has to make do with states as the primary cosmopolitan actors.[26]

Practically speaking, when acting in a cosmopolitan manner, states recast global problems in local terms in order to take advantage of local political or social resources,[27] e.g., by locally suing foreign corporations participating in a global antitrust conspiracy, by prosecuting corporations engaging in foreign corrupt practices or foreign human rights violations, or by prosecuting individuals who committed atrocities abroad. These states do not act on their own account, but as agents of the international community.

2. STATES VINDICATING COMMON INTERESTS: A VAINGLORIOUS QUEST FOR AN OBJECTIVE "INTERNATIONAL COMMUNITY"

When a state desires to tackle global problems through the exercise of unilateral jurisdiction, from a justice perspective they may obviously want to ensure that others view these problems as global too, lest such jurisdiction be seen as illegitimate, self-serving, and intruding on other states' justified policy choices. It can be posited that the justification of a unilateral/extraterritorial measure hinges on the international community's recognition of the object of regulation (e.g., a stable climate, human rights, sustainable fisheries, a corruption-free world...), and thus on *internationally shared values*. When the international community has recognized an object as in need of protection, the assumption is that states may be justified in protecting this good unilaterally,[28] as they are, *arguendo*, just vicariously enforcing community

---

26 Roland Pierik and Wouter Werner, "Can Cosmopolitanism Survive Institutionalization?," in *Cosmopolitanism in Context: Perspectives from International Law and Political Theory* (Cambridge and New York: Cambridge University Press, 2010), 283 (noting also that "international treaties that embrace cosmopolitanism endow States with the primary task of guarding the interests of individuals and global society as a whole").

27 Hannah L. Buxbaum, "National Jurisdiction and Global Business Networks," *Indiana Journal of Global Legal Studies* 17 (2010): 165, 167.

28 Cf. Appellate Body Report, United States—Import Prohibition of Certain Shrimp and Shrimp Products, WT/DS58/AB/R (12 October 1998), para. 31 (observing that extraterritorial trade measures could in principle be justified when the measure concerns a shared resource, of which the value of its protection is as such recognized by the international community: "[g]iven the recent acknowledgement by the international community of the importance of concerted bilateral or multilateral action to protect living natural resources, and recalling the explicit recognition by WTO Members of the objective of sustainable development in the preamble of the WTO Agreement, we believe it is too late in the day to suppose that Article XX(g) of the GATT 1994 may be read as referring only to the conservation of exhaustible mineral or other non-living natural resources. Moreover, two adopted GATT 1947 panel reports previously found fish to be an "exhaustible natural resource" within the meaning of Article XX(g). We hold that, in line with the principle of ef-

values. The international dimension encourages[29] and "multilateralizes" unilateral action, and nuances its interventionist character. Unilateralism and multilateralism should therefore not necessarily be seen as opposites: contextualized unilateralism may in fact resemble multilateralism, where the unilaterally acting actor enforces multilaterally shared norms and values.[30]

The persuasiveness of this thesis is obviously a function of the actual existence of such shared norms, and of an international community of which the state purportedly is a guardian. It is an understatement in this respect that this notion of "international community" — an "imagined community" of principle that transcends borders and of which the members do not know each other[31] — is a particularly elusive one. Still, the notion is widely used in progressive international legal scholarship, where it denotes a community premised on common international interests that prevail over individual state interests. In international law, the best-known contemporary proponent of the international community and its interests is arguably former International Court of Justice judge Bruno Simma, who defined international community interests as a "consensus according to which respect for certain fundamental values is not to be left to the free disposition of States, individually or inter se, but is recognized and sanctioned by international law as a matter of concern to all States."[32] This definition, which harks back to

---

fectiveness in treaty interpretation, measures to conserve exhaustible natural resources, whether living or non-living, may fall within Article XX(g)" (footnotes omitted). See also Friedl Weiss, "Extra-Territoriality in the Context of WTO Law," in *Beyond Territoriality: Transnational Legal Authority in an Age of Globalization*, ed. Gunther Handl, Joachim Zekoll, Peter Zumbansen, (Boston and Leiden: Martinus Nijhoff, 2012), 481 (observing in respect of Article XX(g) GATT that trade-restrictive environmental measures adopted pursuant to multilateral environmental agreements easier to justify than fully unilateral measures).

29   Cf. Daniel Bodansky, "What's in a Concept? Global Public Goods, International Law, and Legitimacy," *European Journal of International Law* 23 (2012): 651, 660 (citing the transformative effect of a characterizing an obligation as an international one: "The existence of an international obligation [...] gives domestic actors both within and outside government a 'hook' for their arguments").

30   Pierik and Werner, "Can Cosmopolitanism Survive Institutionalization?," 286, relying on Jack M. Balkin, "Nested Oppositions," *Yale Law Journal* 99 (1990): 1669 (drawing attention to the specific context in which conceptual opposites receive their meaning, and arguing that "in certain contexts concepts may appear to be radically opposed, while in others they may look quite similar").

31   Benedict Anderson, *Imagined Communities: Reflections on the Origin and Spread of Nationalism* (London and New York: Verso Books, 2006); Addis, "Community and Jurisdictional Authority," 20. It is pointed out that the very fact the its members do not know each other has been used to discredit the notion of international community. See Pierik and Werner, "Introduction," 9–10 (citing the critique of cosmopolitanism that "humanity as a whole too large and abstract to evoke genuine passions of unity, loyalty and obligation").

32   Bruno Simma, "From Bilateralism to Community Interest in International Law," in *Recueil des Cours (Collected Courses of the Hague Academy of International Law)* (The Hague: Martinus Nijhoff Publishers, 1997), 217, 233 (also expressly including environmental protection as a community interest). See against consensualism also ICJ, *Accordance with international law of the unilateral declaration of independence in respect of Kosovo* (Advisory Opinion), Declaration of Judge Simma (speaking

such ethically-inspired international lawyers as Suarez, Grotius, Vattel, and Lauterpacht, who assumed the existence of an "international society" with a "general interest," brackets the principle of state consent and signals that the notion of international community has natural law roots.[33]

The problems with natural law are well-known: universal morality is arguably subjective, and enables powerful states to articulate a particularist view of it, while downplaying the potential conflict between conceptions of natural law held by different actors.[34] Grotius himself, for that matter, opened his *Mare Liberum* (1609) with a vehement critique of the great maritime nations of the era, Spain and Portugal—whose hold on the oceans had

> out against "anachronistic, extremely consensualist vision of international law, expressed in the Lotus judgment"). Also other ICJ judges have not shied away from referring to the "international community," including in their judicial opinions. Former ICJ Judge Mohammed Bedjaoui famously declared in the *Nuclear Weapons* advisory opinion that "[t]he resolutely positivist, voluntarist approach of international law [...] has been replaced by an objective conception of international law, a law more readily seen as the reflection of a collective juridical conscience and a response to the social necessities of States organised as a community." See ICJ, *Legality of Threat or Use of Nuclear Weapons* (Advisory Opinion), Declaration of Judge Bedjaoui, ICJ Reports 1996, 1345 (para. 13). Current ICJ Judge Cançado Trindade even has the habit of appending lengthy individual, and often dissenting opinions to ICJ judgments, in which he criticizes the majority for taking the interests of the international community, humanity, or justice insufficiently into account (see, e.g., ICJ, *Croatia v. Serbia*, 2015, diss op Cancado Trindade, para. 2: "I thus present with the utmost care the foundations of my own entirely dissenting position [...] guided above all by the ultimate goal of precisely the *realization of justice*"). In fact, many international lawyers have embarked on a reformist project to give the interests of the international community a more prominent place in the current legal system. Martti Koskenniemi, "International Law in a Post-Realist Era," 1 ("our discipline has implied a program for reforming the present international structures, perhaps to reflect better the 'interests of the world community'"). Note that a journal is also named after it: *International Community Law Review*.
>
> 33 See for probably the earliest legal articulation: See also F. Suarez, *Tractatus de Legibus ac Deo Legislatore* (1612), Book II, ch. 19, § 5 ("Mankind, though divided into numerous nations and states, constitutes a political and moral unity bound up by charity and compassion; wherefore, though every republic or monarchy seems to be autonomous and self-sufficing, yet none of them is, but each of them needs the support and brotherhood of others, both in a material and a moral sense. Therefore they also need some common law organizing their conduct in this kind of society"). See also Hersch Lauterpacht, *International Law: Being the Collected Papers of Hersch Lauterpacht. The law of Peace. International Law in General*, ed. E. Lauterpacht, vol. 2 (New York: Cambridge University Press, 1975), 88 (opining that the "relation of the state to the international community was not based on self-sacrifice nor blind acceptance of the overriding superiority of the general interest of the international society, but enlightened self-interest which admits the advisability in given circumstances, of the sacrifice of an immediate sectional interest for the sake of the general interest"). Note that Lauterpacht did not explicitly state that there is an international community that could be dissociated from the consent of states; rather he urged states to consensually abandon narrow state interests for the sake of the general interest.
>
> 34 Zygmunt Bauman, *Postmodern Ethics* (Oxford: Wiley-Blackwell, 1993), 42 (arguing that "there is more than one conception of universal morality, and that which of them prevails is relative to the strength of the powers that claim and hold the right to articulate it"); Immanuel Wallerstein, *European Universalism: the Rhetoric of Power* (New York: The New Press, 2006) 45 ("there are multiple versions of natural law that are quite regularly at direct odds with each other"); Koskenniemi, "International Law in a Post-Realist Era," 8–9 ("Even if we agreed on the need to understand the international in terms of interests, we would have difficulty in identifying the subjects whose interests count. Is it States, or perhaps 'peoples.' human beings or the global 'community'").

to be broken to advance the maritime interests of the Dutch United Provinces—on the ground that they mistook their particularist justice conceptions for universal justice.[35] Invoking humanity or objective justice may in fact just be a front for furthering one's own subjective preferences and interests.[36] Or as Proudhon and Schmitt have famously pointed out: "whoever invokes humanity, wants to cheat."[37] Thus, the question is whether global values can really exist in a non-egalitarian world, dominated by Western power in particular,[38] and characterized by very divergent value conceptions.

Cosmopolitan political theorists would counter this critique by positing that certain values are truly internationally shared: since there is a common human nature, there is often no principled disagreement regarding basic moral norms, which can be said to converge globally.[39] Communities may sometimes cherish other ideals, but this may be so because they face different scenarios and challenges,[40] or because they may be misled by self-interested rulers.[41] Even where some divergence is noticeable, cosmopolitan philosophers would argue that this can be accommodated within a culturally sensitive universalist framework that affirms a pluralism of values.[42]

---

35   Hugo Grotius, *Mare Liberum*, translated by Ralph van Deman Magoffin as *The Freedom of the Seas: A Dissertation by Hugo Grotius* (New York: Oxford University Press, 1916), 1 ("The delusion is as old as it is detestable with which many men, especially those who by their wealth and power exercise the greatest influence, persuade themselves, or as I rather believe, try to persuade themselves, that justice and injustice are distinguished the one from the other not by their own nature, but in some fashion merely by the opinion and the custom of mankind. Those men therefore think that both the laws and the semblance of equity were devised for the sole purpose of repressing the dissensions and rebellions of those persons born in a subordinate position, affirming meanwhile that they themselves, being placed in a high position, ought to dispense all justice in accordance with their own good pleasure, and that their pleasure ought to be bounded only by their own view of what is expedient. This opinion, absurd and unnatural as it clearly is, has gained considerable currency; but this should by no means occasion surprise, inasmuch as there has to be taken into consideration not only the common frailty of the human race by which we pursue not only vices and their purveyors, but also the arts of flatterers, to whom power is always exposed").
36   E.g., Bartelson, *Sovereignty as Symbolic Form*, 71 (pointing to the danger of universal thinking that "whatever is subsumed under the category of the global and its cognates will always necessarily reflect particularistic interests and identities, and will thus also represent imperial or hegemonic aspirations in disguise"); Ulrich Beck, "War is Peace: On Post-National War," *Security Dialogue* 36 (2005): 5, 15 (arguing that in so-called "humanitarian" military interventions, State interests may play a larger role than humanitarian concerns).
37   Carl Schmitt, *The Concept of the Political* (Chicago: University of Chicago Press, 2007), 54.
38   Wallerstein, *European Universalism*, 28 (noting that "we are far from yet knowing what [global universal] values are," which requires "a structure that is far more egalitarian than any we have constructed up to now"), observing at 51 that Europeans have considered their universalist claim as a scientific "assertion of objective rules governing all phenomena at all moments of time."
39   Caney, *Justice Beyond Borders* 45–6.
40   Ibid.
41   Ibid., 49 (pointing out that some disagreement arises from error, selfishness, and indoctrination, and that "values can be justified to all persons when those persons' reasoning is not distorted by self-interest, factual mistakes, complacency, and so on").
42   Ibid., 47 (citing Isaiah Berlin).

International lawyers steeped in the modern "positivist" tradition, however, have intuitive reservations about an instinctive reliance on a common human nature. In order to escape the risk of subjective determinations, they would demand evidence of officially sanctioned commonalities ("state practice") before they dare speak about "global values" or an "international community." When espousing this positivist mindset, an analysis of relevant state practice yields the conclusion that, indeed, some version of an international community, although a relatively thin one at that, could be witnessed, as states have entering into particular treaties affirming community interests that go beyond states' (joint) immediate interests: a substantial number of treaties and customary norms protect interests that are considered as common to humanity, such as human rights and the environment. These treaties and norms do not maximize states' interests, but limit their scope of action to the benefit of their true addressees: a global community consisting of individuals, the environment, and the global commons. The international community character of the pertinent treaties is reinforced by the fact that states parties to the relevant treaty may have been given the power to invoke the responsibility of the violating state on behalf of the international community, or at least of the collective state parties to that treaty.[43] This non-injured state's "cosmopolitan" right to unilaterally invoke another state's responsibility in respect of violations of obligations owed to the international community, is laid down as a secondary rule of international law in the International Law Commission's Articles on the Responsibility of States for Internationally Wrongful Acts (2001).[44] These articles codify the *erga omnes* obligations pioneered by the ICJ in the *Barcelona Traction* case (Belgium v. Spain, 1970), in which the Court held—developing an idea enunciated by Kant in his *Perpetual Peace*[45]—that "the obligations of a State towards the international

---

[43] Individuals and the environment do not often have the power or capacity to directly call to account state violators of obligations laid down in the treaty, although some human rights treaties, such as the European Convention on Human Rights, provide for standing of individuals before a supranational court.

[44] Article 48(1)(b) of the Articles. This article provides that any State other than an injured State is entitled to invoke the responsibility of another State, among other scenarios, "if the obligation breached is owed to the international community as a whole." The Articles also make reference to the "international community" in Article 25(1) regarding necessity as a circumstance precluding wrongfulness: "Necessity may not be invoked by a State as a ground for precluding the wrongfulness of an act not in conformity with an international obligation of that State unless the act: (a) is the only way for the State to safeguard an essential interest against a grave and imminent peril; and (b) does not seriously impair an essential interest of the State or States towards which the obligation exists, or of *the international community as a whole.*" (emphasis added).

[45] Kant, *Perpetual Peace*, 107–8 ("The peoples of the earth have [...] entered in varying degrees into a universal community, and it has developed to the point where a violation of rights in one part of

community as a whole" are "by their nature" "the concern of all States," and that, "[i]n view of the importance of the rights involved, all States can be held to have a legal interest in their protection; they are obligations *erga omnes*."[46]

This recognition of norms in which the "international community" and its constituent parts — states — have an interest, is surely a watershed in international law: it is an acknowledgment that international law is not just concerned with the interests of states but also those of individuals and the international community at large.[47] The doctrine of *erga omnes* enables states not injured by violations of international law (e.g., international human rights law) to act in a cosmopolitan fashion, and represent the international community through the mechanism of invocation of state responsibility. Regardless, the international community established by such obligations is necessarily a partial one. Given the abiding relevance of the principle of state consent to be bound by international legal norms, states are under no obligation to enter into treaties, or to accept the validity of a customary norm of the general international law in the common interest. Thus, legally speaking, the positivistic international community is a limited, consent-based one. As long as states do not formally sign up to legal commitments, they are not bound, and fellow states, posing as guardians of the international community cannot invoke their responsibility, since legally such an international community does simply not exist beyond the treaty or customary law regime.

This state of affairs may lead to serious collective action problems, where (major) states fail to join the protective legal regime, and global values accordingly do not enter the legal realm. Moreover, even the partial international community — or rather communi*ties* — established by law, are hardly beyond reproach when it comes to addressing collective action problems, for a variety of reasons. First, states joining treaty regimes protecting community interests often only pay lip-service to these interests; they may join out of reputational concerns rather than out of conviction.[48] Secondly, the *erga omnes* character of the community obligations in practice rarely has the consequence that bystander states invoke the responsibility of the violating

---

the world is felt everywhere").
46 ICJ, *Barcelona Traction (Belgium v. Spain)* (Second Phase), ICJ Rep 1970 3, para. 33.
47 Alex Mills, "Rethinking Jurisdiction in International Law," *British Yearbook of International Law* 84 (2014): 187, 213 (although not using the term *erga omnes* in this respect).
48 Andrew T. Guzman, "Chapter 3: Reputation," in *How International Law Works: A Rational Choice Theory* (New York: Oxford University Press, 2008).

state, for obvious political reasons.[49] Thirdly, invocation of responsibility, when it occurs, rarely has far-reaching consequences, as it is just a speech act naming and shaming an alleged violator.[50] It does not come with any enforcement powers, except retorsions, unfriendly but lawful measures that states can take anyway, even in the absence of a prior breach.[51] And fourthly, while the characterization of an obligation as *erga omnes* may foster the legitimacy of the exercise of unilateral jurisdiction over a violation of an obligation, it does not automatically confer a legal right on states parties to exercise extraterritorial jurisdiction over the violation, unless the treaty contains an explicit clause conferring extraterritorial/universal jurisdiction on the states parties (some treaties indeed feature such a clause).

A contradiction may thus be discerned: although *erga omnes* treaties appear to offer a high level of protection to community values, and give more states the right to address a breach, in practice fewer take the initiative—or, as Pauwelyn has observed, "the *actual* protection of international entitlements is [...] inversely related to how strongly international law *aims* or *pretends* to be protecting the entitlement."[52] This is not to say that the norms enshrined in these treaties are not enforced. Sometimes international courts have been established to bring states or individuals to account, such as the European Court of Human Rights, which offers direct standing to individual

---

49 Joost Pauwelyn, *Optimal Protection of International Law* (New York: Cambridge University Press, 2008), 190–1 (arguing that no one is willing to invoke the responsibility of others if they are not directly harmed, and that the ensuing collective action problem—no one protects the good—is the "result of the nature of the subject-matter"). See for a rare example of a state invoking another State's responsibility for violating *erga omnes* obligations, even before the International Court of Justice: ICJ, *Questions Concerning the Obligation to Prosecute or Extradite (Belgium v. Senegal)*, Judgment of July 20, 2012 (Belgium invoking the international responsibility of Senegal for failing to comply with the duty to either prosecute or extradite a presumed torturer present on Senegal's territory).

50 Where a bystander State invokes another State's responsibility before an international court, however, the chances that change is brought about, are much higher, as non-compliance within binding decision has reputational repercussions for the State proved wrong by the decision. See on the role of reputation in inducing compliance with international law: Guzman, *How International Law Works*. For example, after the ICJ rendered its judgment in Belgium v. Senegal (ICJ, *Questions Concerning the Obligation to Prosecute or Extradite (Belgium v. Senegal)*, Judgment of 20 July 2012), and found that Senegal had violated its obligations under the UN Torture Convention, Senegal established Extraordinary Chambers within its criminal justice system, so as to bring the presumed torturer to justice. See Statute of the Extraordinary African Chambers within the courts of Senegal created to prosecute international crimes committed in Chad between June 7, 1982 and December 1, 1990 (Unofficial translation by Human Rights Watch), available at http://www.hrw.org/news/2013/09/02/statute-extraordinary-african-chambers (accessed March 17, 2015).

51 Non-affected States cannot take countermeasures, only "lawful" measures. See International Law Commission, Draft Articles on Responsibility of States for Internationally Wrongful Acts, 2001, Article 54. Contra: Christian Tams, *Enforcing Obligations Erga Omnes in International Law* (New York: Cambridge University Press, 2005), 250.

52 Pauwelyn, *Optimal Protection of International Law*, 194–5.

plaintiffs, or the International Criminal Court, which has an independent prosecutor who can start investigations. And obviously, reputational concerns and fear of sanctions may exert a pull towards compliance. But it remains that the international community obligations confirmed in such treaties are under-enforced.

Accordingly, the formal international community conception based on *erga omnes* obligations fails in its mission to protect international community interests and to address collective action problems—even those which the *erga omnes* regime was precisely supposed to address. It overestimates the potential of the invocation of state responsibility as a remedial mechanism and does not as such give states a mandate to exercise unilateral jurisdiction to protect the said obligations. And it is held hostage by the "anti-commons" principle of consent, which allows states *not* to subscribe to a globally desirable collective regime. In other words, we are confronted with the inherent limits of a purely positivist approach to international community interests: such an approach may fail to ground the exercise of states' unilateral jurisdiction in the common interest.

Faced with these limits, and in particular with the collective action problems relating to international community interests that have not (yet) risen to the level of international obligations, recent scholarship, borrowing from institutional economics, has cast the international community in non-legal *global public goods* (GPG) terms. GPGs could be defined as goods that are "non-rival" and "non-excludable," meaning that no-one can be excluded from their benefits and that consumption by one person does not diminish consumption by another. The provision of such goods in not self-evident, as prisoners' dilemmas may prevent necessary multilateral action from being taken. Where individual states take action, other states may tend to free-ride, i.e., fail to take action but hope to profit from other states' investment in providing GPGs. The potential for free-riding behavior may ultimately discourage individual state action. However, if such action could bring free-riders within the state's jurisdictional ambit through extraterritorial jurisdiction, GPGs could yet be provided, even without multilateral intervention. Accordingly, the GPG approach holds particular promise for legitimating unilateral action in the common interest, as the relevant question is not whether states have enshrined this interest in international law but rather whether it is *expedient* for such action to be taken so as to avert a perceived threat posed to the GPG. In GPG-inspired unilateralism discourse, the end—GPG protection—may justify the means—nonconsensual action. State consent becomes less material, and unilateral action is hailed as a mechanism to compensate for multilateral regulatory failures,[53] and the lack of third-party enforcement in international law.[54]

GPGs have been defined rather broadly. Not only do they include common resources or goods that belong to "the common concern of mankind," such as the global climate, the ozone layer, the prevention of pollution, fish stocks, and biodiversity,[55] they may also cover such "values" as human rights, peace, and accountability for international crimes.[56] This may render them indistinguishable from "global problems," i.e., problems that concern the world at large, and "cannot be separated into different sub-problems that can be solved individually."[57] In this respect, Ralph Michaels has usefully categorized global problems as "global by nature" (e.g., climate change and other collective action problems that need to be solved by aggregate efforts of the international community), "global by design" (e.g., the globally accessible Internet), and "global by definition," even if these problems occur within one territory (e.g., crimes against humanity, which are directed at humanity at large, and thus at what it means to be an international community).[58] All these problems may arguably be amenable to the exercise of extraterritorial jurisdiction in the common interest.

53　Krisch, "The Decay of Consent," 2 (stating that unilateral action appears "more useful for problem solving and the effective exercise of power than formal institutions and the increasingly firm and demanding processes of multilateral treaty making"). Ibid., 4 ("consent-based structure presents a structural bias against effective action on global public goods, especially given the large number of foreign states today"); see also, but critically Jack L. Goldsmith and Eric A. Posner, *The Limits of International Law* (New York: Oxford University Press, 2005), 87.

54　It is conspicuous that Pauwelyn, after concluding that third-party enforcement does not work, suggests as alternatives robust community enforcement, direct standing for private parties, international procedure against individual criminals, and domestic courts, but not unilateral action (Pauwelyn, *Optimal Protection of International Law*, 196–7).

55　UN General Assembly, Protection of global climate for present and future generations of mankind, UN Doc A/RES/43/53 (1988), para. 1 ("Recognizes that climate change is a common concern of mankind, since climate is an essential condition which sustains life on earth"); Frank Biermann, "'Common Concern of Humankind': The Emergence of a New Concept of International Environmental Law," *Archiv des Völkerrechts* 34 (1996): 426, 449; Thomas Cottier, "The Emerging Principle of Common Concern: A Brief Outline," Working Paper No 2012/20, NCCR Trade Regulation (2012). Compare with the "common heritage of mankind," a term used to denote in particular areas beyond national jurisdiction, such the deep seabed and the celestial bodies. See, e.g., Treaty on Principles Governing the Activities of States in the Exploration and Use of Outer Space, Including the Moon and Other Celestial Bodies, January 27, 1967, 18 U.S.T. 2410, 610 U.N.T.S. 205.

56　See with respect to peace Goldsmith and Posner, *The Limits of International Law*, 87.

57　Ralf Michaels, "Global Problems in Domestic Courts," in *The Law of the Future and the Future of Law*, ed. Sam Muller et al. (Oslo: Torkel Opsahl 2011), 167.

58　Ibid., 171 (stating that a crime against humanity "is by definition de-territorialized, simply because humanity transcends all territoriality," and terming it a "world event").

However collective action failures are precisely characterized, what unites these characterizations is that they consider state consent and inaction, and ultimately sovereignty, as threats to the realization and protection of GPGs, global interests, or global values.[59] It is believed that unilateral action may remedy these failures where one state (or group of states such as the EU) extends its jurisdiction to include within its ambit foreign-based persons subject to an unduly permissive regulatory regime in their home or territorial state. Such unilateral action could be based on a (territorial or personal) nexus with the asserting state (e.g., a foreign corrupt person wired the proceeds of his activities to a bank account located in the state), or on no nexus at all, but simply on the underlying global value or interest to be protected (e.g., a *génocidaire* is brought to trial in a state without the latter having any territorial or personal connection with the crime or the criminal).

Approaches based on GPGs or global problems attempt to bypass the subjectivity of natural law approaches to the common interest by casting global remedial action in terms of efficiency, welfare-enhancement, urgency, or even plain human or planetary survival. However, also these approaches cannot entirely escape the legitimacy problems coming with "subjective" unilateral action. Even where an objective, quasi-scientific consensus exists on the good to be protected, unilateral action can cause distributional effects that lack international legitimacy in the absence of multilateral consent. States exercising unilateral jurisdiction could thus single-handedly decide on a global distribution of resources, with major resource allocation shifts being brought about as a result of the choice for a specific jurisdictional trigger. For instance, a broadly defined territoriality principle which brings foreign economic operators within the ambit of the asserting state may shift important resources from these operators and their home states to the asserting state.[60] The danger is real here that individual states will in reality be self-serving, by bringing about inward shifts of international resources under cover of defending the global interest. Having calculated the efforts required to ad-

---

59 Also Martti Koskenniemi, "What Use for Sovereignty Today?," *Asian Journal of International Law* 1 (2011), 61 (writing that international lawyers have criticized sovereignty from a *functional* perspective on the ground that it fails to deal with global threats).
60 See, e.g., Joanne Scott, "The New EU 'Extraterritoriality,'" *Common Market Law Review* 51 (2014): 1343, with respect to the territorial extension of EU law (arguing that "the EU's choice of trigger bears deeply upon the distribution of the burden of complying with EU law and upon how easy this burden is to evade," and "also impacts significantly upon how great a contribution a measure may make to the attainment of its stated objectives as well as upon the distribution of the benefits that flow from EU law").

dress a global public good challenge, e.g., reducing greenhouse gas emissions, individual states may well impose disproportionate burdens on *foreign* operators and states, e.g., via market access requirements or criminal prosecution. Moreover, different global public goods and values may be in tension with each other.[61] For example, justice considerations, which are arguably served by prosecuting human rights offenders, even in the courts of bystander states, may be in tension with the imperative to create peace and reconciliation, which is arguably served by deferring or foregoing prosecution of high-ranking perpetrators with a vocal constituency. Climate change mitigation for its part, which militates in favor of important emissions reductions, even if unilaterally imposed via market access requirements, may be in tension with the right to social and economic development, which precisely militates against such reductions. Balancing conflicting public goods and values, as well as deciding on issues of burden-sharing, are inherent to global public goods or global problems-inspired unilateralism. They are essentially moral choices which states make in—what they believe is—the global interest.

3. THE COSMOPOLITAN STATE AS A BENEVOLENT HEGEMON

Where global problems have not been addressed by treaties or multilateral institutions, or where treaties or customary law have not conferred remedial jurisdiction on states to act in the global interest, pure positivism will equal defeatism. Those who believe in humanity's progress, however, do not consider such defeatism as a viable option in light of contemporary global justice and governance challenges. They have, as an alternative, explored the relaxation of the principle of state consent to the exercise of cosmopolitan jurisdiction. In so doing, they have in essence replaced positivism with naturalism as a legitimating doctrine. When advocating natural law, however rationally its contents may have been constructed, one should be keenly aware of the charges of subjectivism that have been leveled at it. These charges pertain particularly to the danger of unilateral hegemonic imposition of the values and norms of the powerful on the weak, with the former's life choices supplanting the latter's.

---

61 Bodansky, "What's in a Concept?," 651, 656 (submitting that "different actors will have different preferences about which norm to choose," and that every choice will accordingly have distributive consequences).

But is cosmopolitan unilateralism's goal of "serving humanity" really a thinly disguised attempt at realizing imperialist or hegemonic ambitions, i.e., at dominating a weaker group?[62] To answer this question, let us first reflect on what hegemony actually means. In our times, thanks to Marxist writers such as Gramsci and Laclau, it surely has acquired an imperialist connotation of one society exercising power over a subordinate society, with the former forcing the latter to adapt to its own wishes and its own benefit.[63] Etymologically speaking, however, the Greek word *hegemon* simply means "leadership" or "rule."[64] No one will gainsay that, in order to address global collective action problems, some leadership is needed. Such first movers may first want to push the envelope at the multilateral level, by convincing other *agora* participants of the need for international action. Yet when these efforts fail to bear fruit as a result of myopic anti-cosmopolitan sentiment harbored by those participants, unilateral action may be appropriate. Such action need not be hegemonic in the domination sense of the word, i.e., interfering on an arbitrary basis with the range of options available to another agent.[65] Indeed, cosmopolitan action is not aimed at subordinating foreign peoples. Instead, it has emancipatory and empowering potential, in that it is protective of the human rights of the world's downtrodden or of a neglected natural environment.[66]

---

62 Unilateralism indeed generally remains a suspect word, conjuring up images of subjectivism at best and colonialism at worst. See, e.g., Jürgen Habermas, "Interpreting the Fall of a Monument," *German Law Journal* 4 (2003): 701, 706 ("justification through international law can, and should be replaced by the unilateral, world-ordering politics of a self-appointed hegemon."); Pierik and Werner, "Introduction," 9–10, citing the concern that cosmopolitanism may risk "becoming part and parcel of imperialistic policies," and referring in this respect to Costas Douzinas, *Human Rights and Empire: The Political Philosophy of Cosmopolitanism* (New York: Routledge, 2007). Note that the terms "imperialism" and "hegemony" have also been used in the context of extraterritorial jurisdiction, especially as exercised by the US. See Jeffrey Lena and Ugo Mattei, "U.S. Jurisdiction over Conflict Arising Outside of the United States: Some Hegemonic Implications," Hastings International and Comparative Law Review 24 (2001): 381, 382 ("[T]he expansionist thrust of the jurisdiction of U.S. courts [...] may be viewed as a sort of legal imperialism").
63 Ernesto Laclau and Chantal Mouffe, *Hegemony and Socialist Strategy: Towards a Radical Democratic Politics* (New York and London: Verso, 1985).
64 In ancient Greek times "hegemony" was notably used to denote one city-state's exercise of leadership over a league of city-states. Sparta, for instance, was the hegemon of the Peloponnesian League (6th–4th century BCE), Athens was the hegemon of the Delian League (5th century BCE), and Macedonia was the hegemon of the League of Corinth (4th century BCE). See, e.g., *Encyclopaedia Britannica*, http://www.britannica.com/ (accessed March 19, 2015).
65 Bartelson, *Sovereignty as Symbolic Form*, 101.
66 Howse and Teitel, "Does Humanity-Law Require (or Imply) a Progressive Theory of History?," 377, 384–5 (admitting that one may perhaps discern kinds of hegemonic power structures underlying or supporting "law among liberal nations," but arguing that this need to be fatal to hopefulness concerning the direction of the cosmopolitan project, citing the empowering potential of cosmopolitanism is the most important point). Ibid., 385 (submitting that worrying on behalf of the non-West may in itself be "a form of neo-colonial condescension").

To counter the critique of sovereigntists—who would consider cosmopolitan action as intervening in other states' internal affairs—such action could even be said to *strengthen* and *restore* rather than undermine *sovereignty*. One may object that such a strategy necessarily embraces a truncated view of sovereignty that isolates desirable, individual autonomy-enhancing aspects of sovereignty (democracy, human rights, accountability, the ability to deliver public goods) from undesirable aspects (militarization, quest for great power status, beggar-thy-neighbor economic policies),[67] and in so doing reduce the very analytical purchase of the concept of sovereignty. At the same time, however, one can only concur with Bartelson's observation that sovereignty has no meaning apart from its actual function.[68] Sovereignty is no more than a social construct. In the contemporary era, epistemic forces have embedded it in a larger international governance project that requires state authority to be exercised "responsibly." While the international community may leave a margin of appreciation to states as to the implementation of responsible authority, the core contours of the concept are defined at the international rather than national level.

Because of capacity advantages, it is obviously more likely that powerful states will take the lead to exercise cosmopolitan jurisdiction. This need not disqualify them, however, as powerful states are not necessarily intent on just furthering their own interests. Powerful states could well be enlightened and, as benevolent hegemons, use their stronger enforcement capacities to protect international community interests. In fact, precisely because they have more power and capacity, in accordance with the principle of common but differentiated responsibilities, it may be *incumbent* on them to do more than others to further the global interest, and thus to behave in—what may just in appearance be—a hegemonic fashion.[69] Thus, the notion of "power" should not be reified, or negatively stereotyped as militating against cosmo-

---

67 Bartelson, *Sovereignty as Symbolic Form*, 80 (submitting that "recent strategies for interfering in the domestic affairs of states are justified on grounds that such interference is necessary to strengthen their sovereignty" and that the concept of sovereignty is disaggregated and unbundled "so that its unnecessary or destructive aspects can be eliminated, before the health and useful aspects can be glued back together and imposed on the target state").

68 Ibid., 10 (drawing on the linguistic turn in philosophy and social sciences and stating that "sovereignty is what we make of it through our linguistic practices, given the contextual constraints at hand").

69 Cf. Karinne Coombes, "Universal Jurisdiction: A Means to End Impunity or a Threat to Friendly International Relations," *The George Washington International Law Review* 43, no. 3 (2011): 419, 457 ("there is the danger that universal jurisdiction may be perceived as hegemonistic jurisdiction exercised mainly by some Western powers against persons from developing nations") (emphasis added).

politan action. Rather, as Howse and Teitel have observed, it may be a shifting reality, becoming intertwined with "humanity-law."[70]

The view that state power should be used to further the international, rather than just the national interest is not new. It was a wildly popular idea in dominant progressive internationalist circles in the US in the early 20th century, that came to be championed by the US President himself, Woodrow Wilson (in office from 1913 through 1921). Triggered by the cataclysm of the First World War, Wilson held in his 1914 4th of July address that a great nation such as the US should use its influence and power not for aggrandizement and material benefit only, but to improve the world ("it is patriotic to concert measures for one another").[71] For Wilson, confronted with similar global governance challenges more than 100 years ago, this task was not just a matter of political morality, but of plain historical necessity:[72] the very survival of mankind arguably depended on the US taking the lead. This Wilsonian view informed the multilateral establishment of the League of Nations, and later the United Nations, but also the taking of US unilateral action to spread global values such as democracy and human rights.[73]

I am the first one to admit that such action has sometimes been heavy-handed and that "humanity" has been used a pretext for naked power interventions. But as far as the exercise of cosmopolitan jurisdiction is concerned, I do not hesitate to submit that, in various respects, the US has done a great service to humanity by extending its laws to address such global ills as corruption (Foreign Corrupt Practices Act), racketeering (Racketeer Influenced and Corrupt Organized Act), antitrust conspiracies (Sherman Act), and human rights violations (Alien Tort Statute)—even if the presumption against extraterritoriality has sometimes militated against a wide reach of US legislation. Also the European Union and European states have been serving humanity by projecting their environmental legislation abroad (notably to counter global warming), and by prosecuting the vilest international criminals.

---

70 Howse and Teitel, "Does Humanity-Law Require (or Imply) a Progressive Theory of History?," 377, 396 (citing "the endlessly dynamic relation of law to social reality").
71 Woodrow Wilson, *4th of July address*, July 4, 1914, PWW 30:251.
72 Frank Ninkovich, *The Wilsonian Century* (Chicago: University of Chicago Press, 1999), 68–9.
73 Before Wilson took office, the US also acted unilaterally, notably in its Latin American backyard under the Monroe doctrine. As Ninkevich has pointed out, however, such interventions were justified by anxiety about European intervention, or by economic rhetoric, whereas the interventions authorized by the Wilson were justified on the ground that they spread law, order, and democracy (Ninkevich, *The Wilsonian Century*, 51–2).

Critics may go on to object that oftentimes the powerful are not very likely to exercise extraterritorial jurisdiction in the global interest *without some national interest being present*, and that this national interest rationale is bound to engender justified international suspicion. In the field of business and environmental regulation, for instance, states will typically exercise unilateral jurisdiction when (also) the integrity of domestic regulation is undermined, and domestic actors' rights and interests are affected by foreign activity, e.g., where foreign cartels are preying on domestic markets, or foreign companies import substandard products.[74] This focus on safeguarding the business opportunities of domestic operators tends to create an impression of self-centeredness, arbitrariness,[75] exclusivity to the detriment of less powerful actors,[76] domination,[77] or outright legal imperialism.[78] One should realize, however, that such action is not meant simply to advance, in some sort of zero-sum game, one state's national interest to the detriment of another state's national interest. Rather, it levels a playing field that has become unhinged as a result of globally undesirable lax foreign regulation that puts domestic operators, who had *already* become subject to stricter regulation, at a competitive disadvantage. For instance, in the environmental field, the EU, in response to market distortions and citizen pressure, has provided for such a high level of environmental protection,[79] also with respect to global environmental goods such as a stable climate, that EU-based businesses have lost economic opportunities, which can only be restored by either scaling back regulation, or by "extraterritorializing" regulation, i.e., subjecting foreign op-

---

74 Tonya L. Putnam, "Courts Without Borders: Domestic Sources of US Extraterritoriality in the Regulatory Sphere," *International Organization* 63, no. 3 (Summer 2009): 459, 468; Jonathan Turley, "When in Rome: Multinational Misconduct and the Presumption Against Extraterritoriality," *Northwestern University Law Review* 84 (1990): 598.

75 Anthony J. Colangelo, "A Unified Approach to Extraterritoriality," *Virginia Law Review* 97 (2011): 1019, 1107 ("Unlike international law, other nations may not have consented to, say, unilateral projections of U.S. securities or antitrust laws within their territories, and absent a U.S. nexus, the choice of U.S. law appears arbitrary.")

76 Krisch, "The Decay of Consent," 31 ("nonconsensualism [...] creates more exclusive decision-making structures that reduce the number of decision-makers"); Ibid., 39 (nonconsensualism "does away only with the consent of the less powerful, and it can easily become a tool of hierarchy and control").

77 Jeffrey A. Meyer, "Dual Illegality and Geoambiguous Law: A New Rule for Extraterritorial Application of U.S. Law," *Minnesota Law Review* 95 (2010): 110–11 ("A superpower [the US] no longer bent on conquering more territory stands to benefit when it instead can unilaterally project its law and corresponding enforcement resources to regulate what people do in other countries").

78 Kal Raustiala, *Does the Constitution Follow the Flag? The Evolution of Extraterritoriality in American Law* (New York: Oxford University Press, 2009), 224 (submitting that extraterritorial jurisdiction "enabl[es] the United States to unilaterally manipulate legal difference so as to better serve its interests" while "enhancing American power and interests on the world stage").

79 Thanks to Natalie Dobson for pointing this out to me.

erators to EU law in the global interest. Surely, the latter option is preferable from an international community vantage point.

"Hegemonic" actors such as the US or the EU may thus have been *first movers* as far as globally desirable regulation is concerned, subjecting their domestic operators to strict rules regarding e.g., accountability for human rights violations, corruption, antitrust conspiracies, securities fraud, or climate change. They subsequently wish to cast the regulatory net wider, so as to allow their domestic operators to remain in business, and *at the same time* to more efficiently tackle global problems which may be exacerbated by businesses moving offshore to evade strict regulation. In this second stage, states "extraterritorialize" their laws, but in a manner that is less unilateral than may meet the eye.[80] Ultimately, they may just be enforcing shared values of, or challenges facing the international community, which, moreover, are often recognized by various binding or non-binding international instruments.[81]

4. REINTERPRETING STATE CONSENT: BEYOND FORMALISM

It will have become clear by now that the cosmopolitan action addressed in this contribution cannot be captured by orthodox legal positivism that puts a high premium on explicit state consent. However, neither is such action entirely subjective, pie-in-the-sky, or natural law based. True, where legal and political instruments do not confer extraterritorial jurisdictional authority on states to enforce the values enshrined in them, the exercise of such authority may transcend the explicit consent of states and thus undermine the main

---

80 Hannah L. Buxbaum, "Transnational Regulatory Litigation," *Virginia Journal of International Law* 46 (2006): 251, 255, 268, 298 (arguing that in "transnational regulatory litigation" cases, the US domestic regulatory law that is applied extraterritorially, e.g., regarding antitrust, securities, and corruption, "reflects an internationally shared norm"). But see opinion Justice Breyer in the *Hoffmann-LaRoche* case, *F Hoffmann-LaRoche Ltd v. Empagran SA*, 542 US 155, 169 ("where foreign injury is independent of domestic effects, Congress might have hoped that America's antitrust laws [...] would commend themselves to other nations as well [...] if America's antitrust policies could not win their own way in the international marketplace for such ideas, Congress, we must assume, would not have tried to impose them, in an act of legal imperialism, through legislative fiat").

81 See e.g., UN Convention against Corruption (New York 2004), UN General Assembly resolution 58/4 of October 31, 2003; OECD Convention on Combating Bribery of Foreign Public Officials in International Business Transactions (Paris 1997); Kyoto Protocol to the un Framework Convention on Climate Change (1997); Convention on the Prevention and Punishment of the Crime of Genocide, UN General Assembly Resolution 260 (III) A (1948); Rome Statute of the International Criminal Court (1998). See as regards cooperation in the field of antitrust law: the International Competition Network, which counts 104 competition agencies from 92 jurisdictions (www.internationalcompetitionnetwork.org). For cooperative networks in the field of securities/capital markets regulation: International Organization of Securities Commissions (IOSCO), the Financial Stability Board (FSB), the Council of Securities Regulators of the Americas (COSRA), and the Financial Action Task Force (FATF).

tenet of positivism. But as this authority is not made out of thin air, but finds its normative basis in international instruments and broadly defined international norms and policies, it can still be traced back to the consent of states. Most assertions of extraterritorial jurisdiction indeed enforce values which the community of states have deemed worthy of protection: international crimes and human rights violations are proscribed by treaties and customary international law, anti-corruption conventions have been widely ratified, and global environmental goods (e.g., a stable climate, biodiversity) have been recognized by a host of legal and political instruments. State consent may possibly not extend to all procedural issues of enforcement, but the relevant issue is that it pertains to certain *substantive values*. So as to strengthen the impact of such values, and eventually the rule of law, states may surely place their legal enforcement machinery at the international community's disposal.

This view ties in well with recent anti-formalistic legal scholarship that emphasizes extra-positivist sources of international law authority, namely those based on substantive authority and effectiveness. Nijman and Nollkaemper put it as follows:

> Part of the answer [as to who or what validates non-positive law sources of international law] is found in the fact that deformalization is a parallel development to the emergence of common values. International law does not (only) find its authority in binding rules and principles, i.e., in conformity with the positivist model, but is in a way more substantive since it is grounded on international norms as keepers of universal common *values* rather than as binding rules of positive international law. In this role, (binding or non-binding) international norms have authority because of the values they represent [...].[82]

This reasoning allows us to justify unilateralism on the basis of a legalized form of Kantian, deontological ethics,[83] as an international norm arguably provides the requisite substantive authority for unilateral action. From a constructivist international relations perspective, such unilateralism may, theoretically at least, be likely to gain acceptance by states, as the existence

---

[82] Janne Elisabeth Nijman and André Nollkaemper, "Beyond the Divide," in *New Perspectives on the Divide between International and National Law*, ed. Nijman and Nollkaemper (Oxford University Press, 2007), 353.

[83] Immanuel Kant, *Groundwork of the Metaphysic of Morals* (Harper and Row Publishers, 1964).

of the international norm may serve a socializing function and influence the perception of legitimate behavior.[84]

I admit that it may happen that no international norm can be discerned, namely where prisoners' dilemmas have made any agreement on substantive norms well-nigh impossible. Assume, for instance, that an international agreement on tackling climate change fails to materialize, even if all scientific evidence shows that collective action should be taken to avert a catastrophe. If states take unilateral remedial action, such action may not be justified on the basis of codified internationally shared values, let alone on the basis of classic international law, as there is simply no substantive norm to be enforced. Such action could yet be legitimate, however, insofar as proof is adduced that the consequences of such action may be globally beneficial. This view approaches legitimacy not from a deontological, rule-based perspective (codified shared values), but rather from a *consequentialist* or *utilitarian* ethical angle, which takes into account an action's potential to enhance global welfare.[85] It is submitted that, given the challenges which humanity faces in terms of supplying global public goods and providing global justice, value-based *consequentialism* may in certain circumstances have to prevail over formal rules.[86] Such a position finds its conceptual roots in Max Weber's "ethics of responsibility,"[87] and in the legal *processes* emphasized by the New Haven policy-approach to international law.[88]

---

84   Jeffrey L. Dunoff and Mark A. Pollack, "International Law and International Relations: Introducing an Interdisciplinary Dialogue," in *Interdisciplinary Perspectives on International Law and International Relations: The State of the Art*, ed. Dunoff and Pollack (Cambridge University Press, 2013), 8–12. See for an exposition of the relationship between constructivism and international law in the same volume: Jutta Brunnée and Stephen J. Toope, "Constructivism in International Law," 119–45.

85   See notably the works of the 19th century British philosophers Jeremy Bentham and John Stuart Mill, e.g., Jeremy Bentham, *Introduction to Principles of Morals and Legislation* (printed for publication 1780, published 1789) and John Stuart Mill, *The Principles of Political Economy: With Some of Their Applications to Social Philosophy* (1848).

86   Contra Koskenniemi, "What Use for Sovereignty Today?," 65 (denouncing the anti-formalist nature of contemporary global law, which in his view does no longer protect formal sovereignty, but replaces it by "global systems of management" that renders everything "negotiable, revisable in view of attaining the right outcome").

87   Max Weber, "Politik als Beruf (1918/19)," in *Gesammelte politische Schriften*, 3rd ed. (Tübingen: J.C.B. Mohr, 1971), 550 ("You should resist evil with force, otherwise you are responsible for its getting out of hand.")

88   See for the seminal work of the New Haven School, emphasizing processes over formal rules: Myres S. McDougal and Harold D. Lasswell, "The Identification and Appraisal of Diverse Systems of Public Order," in *Studies in World Public Order* 3, ed. M.S. McDougal et al. (The Hague: Martinus Nijhoff, 1960). Contra: Martti Koskenniemi, *The Gentle Civilizer of Nations* (Cambridge: Cambridge University Press, 2001), 485 (decrying this instrumentalism that replaces formal law by a wider standard policy guideline and the "values of liberal democracy").

Admittedly, this position abandons explicit state consent in the strict positivist sense of the word. However, consequentialist action may find its legitimation in states' *constructive consent*, inferred from Rawls's method of the "veil of ignorance." Rawls's moral theory puts agents in an "original position" where "no one knows his place in society, his class position or social status; nor does he know his fortune in the distribution of natural assets and abilities, his intelligence and strength, and the like."[89] Personal tastes, self-interest, and power differentials disappear in this constellation, and genuine moral choices will be made. Just like individuals, ignorant of what position they will hold upon entering society, will not normally choose a slave-owning society (where they could well end up on the receiving end), ignorant states are unlikely to want to enter a society characterized by environmental disaster, international crimes, rampant corruption, and corporate abuses. One can instead presume that they would a priori give their *consent* to an international society that is based on some minimum rules of conduct. From this perspective, the empirical reality that states, for self-interested reasons, do not give their *actual* consent to the protection of a global value, nor of states' right to extraterritorially protect the value, is not decisive. Key is that in the original position, states, for reasons of rational morality, would have given their consent if their vision had not been clouded by particularist considerations.

Consent is, like sovereignty, an enduring cognitive script that may require some reinterpretation in light of current governance challenges. The reinterpretation that I have propounded here, based on the urgency of the challenges and the method of the veil of ignorance, allows international law to progressively develop beyond its rudimentary state. In the Grotian tradition, as also espoused by Hersch Lauterpacht, reason, ethics, and the law of nature may demand that international legal action be taken beyond the express will of states.[90] For our research object, this means that asserted hold-outs" resort to "reasons of state" so as to block the taking of necessary multilateral action in the common interest should not be rewarded. In order to respond to such multilateral blockage, the development of international law should arguably

---

89 John Rawls, *A Theory of Justice* (Cambridge, MA: Harvard University Press, 1999), 118.
90 Hersch Lauterpacht, "The Grotian Tradition in International Law," *British Yearbook of International Law* 23 (1946): 1, 21–22, relying on Grotius's *De Jure Belli ac Pacis* ("The significance of the law of nature in the treatise is that it is the ever-present source for supplementing the voluntary law of nations, for judging its adequacy in the light of ethics and reason, and for making the reader aware of the fact that the will of states cannot be the exclusive or even, in the last resort, the decisive source of the law of nations.")

be geared toward relaxing the principles of non-intervention and territorial jurisdiction, so that unilateral action could more easily be taken.

5. CONCLUDING OBSERVATIONS

In this contribution I have supported the exercise of unilateral, extraterritorial jurisdiction by states in the common interest, on the ground that cosmopolitan consequentialism requires us to take substance rather than formality seriously. Therefore, classic international law notions such as "consent" and "sovereignty" are in need of reinterpretation so that they can facilitate and not inhibit the realization of global values and global public goods.

I am cognizant of the dangers of domination and abuse that go with an authorization to act unilaterally. But at the end of the day, allowing action in the common interest may surely be preferable to prohibiting altogether. States and regional organizations acting unilaterally in the common interest, as benevolent hegemons, may thus have to be applauded rather than criticized. Practice shows that such applause may be forthcoming indeed. For instance, when in 2015 US prosecutors indicted FIFA officials under US racketeering laws for accepting foreign bribes, international opinion was largely supportive of, and grateful to the US for cleaning up international football.[91] That being said, to counter the abuse of unilateralism, techniques that mitigate the impact of extraterritorial action on the addressees—foreign states, individuals, and operators—may have to be explored. This exploration is beyond the scope of this article, but it is tentatively suggested that, in light of democratic theory, foreign addressees' participation in the domestic design of such action may go quite some way to limit self-serving behavior,[92] and eventually reinforce the legitimacy of cosmopolitan extraterritoriality.

---

[91] Anon., "The World's Lawyer: America's Legal Reach," *The Economist*, June 6, 2015; John Gapper, "America is the Best Referee to Discipline FIFA," *Financial Times*, May 27, 2015.
[92] Eyal Benvenisti, "Sovereigns as Trustees of Humanity: On the Accountability of States to Foreign Stakeholders," *American Journal of International Law* 107 (2013): 295.

Franz Kafka was born in the Jewish ghetto of Prague in 1883 and died in a sanatorium near Vienna in 1924. His education was that of the upwardly mobile middle class, complete with German rather than Czech language schooling and a bar mitzvah conducted in the style of the secularized German-speaking reform Jews, before he settled into professional life as an insurance underwriter. His literary work portrays the bureaucratic weight of his native city struggling with modernity, lost cultural identity, generational conflict, and a world in which everyone is a silent worker at an overburdened desk.

FRANZ KAFKA: EXTRATERRITORIAL CRIMINAL LAW

Ed Morgan

1. WHEN THE COLONY GOES PENAL

It is common wisdom for international lawyers to consider the emergence of a political entity from colonial or dominion status to independence and sovereignty to connote full participation in the international legal system,[1] with all the rights and obligations that thereby attach.[2] Thus, for example, while English colonies prior to independence could exercise substantial self-government they did not possess international legal personality[3] and could not exploit or regulate their resources and territory without some act of

---

Originally published as Ed Morgan, "Franz Kafka: Extraterritorial Criminal Law," in *The Aesthetics of International Law* (Toronto: University of Toronto Press, 2007), 73–95. © University of Toronto Press 2007. Reprinted with permission of University of Toronto Press.

1   *Island of Palmas Case* [Netherlands v. United States], R.I.A.A. 2, 829 (P.CI.J. 1928) ("Sovereignty in the relations between States signifies independence). See also "European Community Guidelines on the Recognition of New States in Eastern Europe and the Soviet Union," *British Yearbook of International Law* 62 (1991): 559.
2   E.g., Statute of the International Court of Justice, Appendix to Charter of the United Nations, art. 34 (1) ("Only states may be parties in cases before the Court"); Vienna Convention on the Law of Treaties, 1155 U.N.T.S. 331, 8 I.L.M. 679 (1969), art. 1 ("The present convention applies to treaties between States").
3   *Madzimbamuto v. Lardner-Burke*, [1969] 1 A.C. 645 (P.C.) (Southern Rhodesia colony lacks external sovereignty). See generally J. Fawcett, *The British Commonwealth in International Law* (London: London Institute of World Affairs, 1963), 144 et seq.

delegation from the imperial government.[4] Likewise, provinces and states, as federal sub-units, typically lack the competence to legislate extraterritorially[5] or to exhibit other external badges of sovereignty.[6]

For Canada, the 1982 patriation of the constitution from the United Kingdom[7] and the accompanying achievement of permanent constitutional independence,[8] spoke not only to a new political stature but to a conformance of the nation with the requirements of international law.[9] For lawyers in particular, the changes had normative as well as formal significance, the amended constitution containing for the first time entrenched protections for individual rights broadly reflective of human rights standards.[10] Thus, the *Charter of Rights* era began with enormous promise for the convergence of international norms with the country's new constitutionalism. Indeed, the first several years of jurisprudence under the new constitution saw the Supreme Court of Canada reject the common law's unlimited police powers in favor of a "purposive" reading of search and seizure rights in Fourth Amendment terms.[11] The Court also curtailed the historically unrestricted power of immigration officials by incorporating Canada's international obligations under various United Nations refugee conventions.[12] Several decades down the constitutional law road, however, lawyers and courts have more often

---

4   *North Atlantic Fisheries Arbitration*, 11 R.I.A.A. 167 (Perm. Ct. Arb. 1910) (Great Britain responsible for territorial seas around Newfoundland colony).
5   *Interprovincial Cooperatives v. The Queen*, [1976] 1 S.C.R. 477 (no extraprovincial legislative competence for Canadian provinces); *Bob-Lo Excursion Co. v. Michigan*, 333 U.S. 29 (1948) (no extraterritorial enforcement for U.S. states).
6   On extraterritorial legislative authority as a badge of international personality see *B.C. Electric Railway v. R.*, [1046] A.C. 527 (Canadian federal government can impose income tax, if it wishes, on the entire world).
7   Canada Act, 1982, s. 2 ("No Act of the Parliament of the United Kingdom passed after the Constitution Act, 1982 comes into force shall extend to Canada as part of its law"). On the permanence of such a "patriating" enactment, see *Ndlwana v. Hofnzeyr*, [1937] AD. 229, 237 ("Freedom, once conferred, cannot be revoked").
8   For the full legal history of Canadian independence from the United Kingdom, see Peter W. Hogg, "Patriation of the Canadian Constitution," *Queen's Law Journal* 8 (1983): 123 and "Supremacy of the Charter," *Canadian Bar Review* 61 (1983): 69.
9   On the international law requirement that a sovereign be constitutionally uninhibited in its exercise of power see *Austro-German Customs Union Case* (Advisory Opinion), [1931] P.C.I.J. Ser. A /B, No. 41 (Austrian sovereignty depends on maintaining complete independence).
10 On the process of rights entrenchment, see Hogg, *Constitutional Law of Canada* (Toronto: Carswell, 2000), s. 33.2 ("Protection of Civil Liberties"), and Peter Russell, "The Political Purposes of the Canadian Charter of Rights and Freedoms." *Canadian Bar Review* 61 (1983): 30. The *Charter of Rights* portion of the amended constitution is Part I of the Constitution Act, 1982, being Schedule B to the Canada Act, 1982 (U.K.), 1982, c. 11, s. 15.
11 *Hunter v. Southam, Inc.*, [1984] 2 S.C.R. 145.
12 *Re Singh and Minister of Employment and Immigration*, [1985] 1 S.C.R. 177.

invoked the earlier "purposive" approach to rights interpretation to narrow rather than to expand the scope of constitutional rights.[13]

It is my ambition in this chapter to trace the ebb of constitutionalism against the flow of internationalism, focusing on those areas in which they have most starkly intersected. To that end, I undertake an assessment of two phenomena that sit at the confluence of criminal process and international norms: extradition in the face of domestic constitutional defenses, and domestic criminal prosecution in the face of foreign violations of constitutional rights. The chapter focuses on Canada as the place where the confluence of factors — emerging constitutional stature and increasing international engagement — is most stark. The goal of the exercise is to discern the force of an increasingly internationalist set of arguments on a simultaneously emerging constitutionalism, all in an effort to explain how these two thematic teammates have been transformed into apparent competitors.

This chapter also explores the most salient themes of Franz Kafka's famous story of violence and punishment, "In the Penal Colony."[14] On its most superficial level, Kafka's story presents a direct confrontation between criminal punishment, personified by the officer who administers with mathematical precision the penal outpost's renowned execution apparatus,[15] and constitutional rights, personified by the explorer who brings the outside world's critique to the cruel and unusual practice of the colony.[16] On a slightly more abstract reading, the officer's demonstrative lecture and impassioned justification of his execution machine, which forms the central portion of the story, parodies the logic of justice and the violence of punishment. Perhaps most importantly, Kafka's story narrates a contest between the parochial officer and the international explorer, the archaic colony of the officer's Old Com-

---

13 See, e.g., Hogg, *Constitutional Law of Canada*, para. 33.7(d) ("The effect of a purposive approach is normally going to be to narrow the scope of the right"), citing *Law Society of Upper Canada v. Skapinker*, [1984] 1 S.C.R. 357 (mobility rights do not guarantee a right to work); and *Andrews v. Law Society of British Colombia*, [1989] 1 S.C.R. 143 (equality rights only protect against discrimination on enumerated or analogous grounds). See also *Baker v. Minister of Citizenship and Immigration*, [1999] 2 S.C.R. 817 (Immigration Act need not be interpreted consistently with international convention, but international law has some persuasive power in interpreting domestic statute).
14 Franz Kafka, "In the Penal Colony," in *The Penal Colony: Stories and Short Pieces*, trans. Willa and Edwin Muir (New York: Schocken Books, 1948). The extended analogy with Kafka's story of pain and violence is suggested for any number of reasons, not the least of which is that, as Robert Cover observed, "legal interpretation takes place in a field of pain and death." Robert Cover, "Violence and the Word," *Yale Law Journal* (1986): 1601.
15 Kafka, *In the Penal Colony*, 192 ("the officer made the last adjustment with great zeal, whether because he was a devoted admirer of the aparatus or because of other reasons the work could be entrusted to no one else").
16 Ibid., 191 ("The explorer did not much care about the apparatus...").

mandant and the progressive metropole of the explorer's New Commandant; these identities of old/local and new/international correspond to competing portraits of an idealized past and a theatrical present nature of the law.

The operating theory presented here is that when constitutionalism meets internationalism, pivotal role reversals take place. These reversals generally parallel developments taking place in international law itself. Thus, for example, in international law there has been a movement back and forth on the nature of the fundamental normative debate. At times it is a contest between normative insularity and normative universality;[17] at other times it is a contest between isolationism and cooperation among states.[18] Domestically, there has been a parallel movement transforming international law's status from the soft, naturalist support for entrenched constitutional reform,[19] to that of the hard-bitten, positivist counterweight to constitutional activism.[20] These role reversals take on ideological qualities within legal debate. Thus, arguments styled as progressively internationalist have played the regressive constitutional law role, while those styled as parochially domestic have played the role of expanded, universal constitutionalism.

Like the doctrinal positions revealed in the case law, the world of Franz Kafka is notoriously propelled by metamorphosis; indeed, his characters' days begin with pivotal change: human to insect,[21] freedom to captivity.[22] The reversals not only come as a surprise, but are themselves reversible: a performing artist stages his transformation to inanimate object of art, only to be replaced by a caged spectacle brimming with animal life.[23] In the field of

---

17 This debate is most graphically illustrated by the pair of 1943 Supreme Court of Canada judgments: *Reference re Foreign Legations*, [1943] S.C.R. 208 (foreign sovereigns insulated from Canadian taxation by virtue of international law) and *Reference re Members of the Military or Naval Forces of the United States*, [1943] S.C.R. 487 (Canadian criminal law embodies universal norms, and, applies to armed forces of foreign sovereign).

18 This dichotomy is most succinctly set out in *Government of the Democratic Republic of the Congo v. Venne*, [1971] S.C.R. 997 (per Laskin, J., dissenting) ("Neither the independence nor the dignity of States, nor international comity require vindication through a doctrine of absolute immunity").

19 This approach, which characterizes the early Canadian Charter cases, was historically evident as far back as Lord Mansfield. See *Heathfield v. Chilton* (1767), 4 Burrow 2015 ("The law of nations will be carried as far in England, as anywhere").

20 It is this movement that is described in Sections 2.1 and 2.2, below.

21 Kafka, "Metamorphosis," in *The Penal Colony*, 67 ("As Gregor Samsa awoke one morning from uneasy dreams he found himself transformed in his bed into a gigantic insect").

22 Kafka, *The Trial*, trans. W. and E. Muir (New York: Schocken Books, 1968), 1 ("Someone must have been telling lies about Joseph K., for without having done anything wrong he was arrested one fine morning").

23 Kafka, "A Hunger Artist," in *The Penal Colony*, 255 ("'Well, clear this out now!' said the overseer, and they buried the hunger artist, straw and all. Into the cage they put a panther"). For a discussion of the relationship between "In the Penal Colony" and its portrayal of punishment, and "A Hunger Artist" and its portrayal of the self-punishment, see Margot Norris, "Sadism and Masochism in "In

law—a field with which Kafka was much concerned[24] but viewed as difficult to access[25]—subject and object, judge and judged, pleasure and pain, reason and passion, justice and injustice, are all theatrically reversed. Thus, for example, the interchangeable acts of violence and judgment are accomplished in the penal colony by means of the execution apparatus, which literally perforates the convict with the description of his offense, turning him into a living (dying) text of the law. It is this ultimate metamorphosis, whereby the law's subject matter becomes nothing more than its own dramatic script that sheds understanding on an otherwise inscrutable process in which surprising role reversals are the norm.[26] To achieve this understanding of the issues at hand one must therefore engage in one final reversal, looking through a lawyer's eyes at Kafka's story and its analytic insights, and through Kafka's eyes at the law's development and its storyline.

2. INTERNATIONALISM AND CONSTITUTIONALISM

When it comes to criminal law in the Anglo-Canadian courts, the trend towards internationalism can perhaps best be summed up by Kafka's guiding rule: "Guilt is never to be doubted."[27] In areas as diverse as robbery,[28] drug trafficking,[29] and securities fraud,[30] the courts have been unhesitant in their desire to expand the geographic bounds of prosecutions. In this line of cases national jurisdictions become, in Justice La Forest's words, their "brothers' keepers"[31] to the misfortune of those globetrotting defendants collectively portrayed as "an unholy alliance organized in modern trappings."[32] The real test, however, is not so much in the issue of jurisdiction itself, but in the field of cross-border process rights. It is here that the expanding international rub-

---

the Penal Colony" and "A Hunger Artist"" in *Reading Kafka: Prague, Politics and the Fin de Siècle*, ed. Mark Anderson (New York: Schocken Books, 1989), 170–86.

24 Michael Muller, "Kafka, Casanova and The Trial," in *Reading Kafka*, 189 ("This author who repeatedly thematizes the most diverse punishments—letting 'judgments' be passed, visiting 'penal colonies,' and populating his poetic world with judges, lawyers, and executioners - held in his hands the authentic account of a punishment that had been carried out").
25 See, e.g., Kafka, "Before the Law," in *The Penal Colony*, 148 ("Before the law stands a doorkeeper").
26 Kafka, "In the Penal Colony," 202 ("Of course the script can't be a simple one [...] So there have to be lots and lots of flourishes around the actual script; the script itself runs round the body only in a narrow girdle; the rest of the body is reserved for the embellishments").
27 Ibid., 198.
28 *Ecrement v. Cusson and Connolly* (1919), 33 C.C.C. 135 (Que. S.C.).
29 *Director of Public Prosecutions v. Doot*, [1973] A.C. 807.
30 *Libman v. The Queen*, [1985] 2 S.C.R. 178.
31 Ibid.
32 *Shulman v. The King* (1946), 2 C.R. 153, 156.

ber meets the travelling constitutional road. It is therefore to the *Charter of Rights*, and to its encounter with international crime and with international law, that this chapter turns.

2.1 Extradition: Growth of the International

From a constitutional law point of view, Canada's international stature can be traced to a succession of enactments importing a progressive increase in sovereign capacity. Thus, while the provinces can be seen in pre-Confederation case law as engaging in international relations pertaining to matters of extradition and cross-border crime,[33] they did so under the sovereign shelter of the British government's treaty-making powers.[34] With the confirmation of dominion status under the *Statute of Westminster*,[35] the international powers denied those maintaining colonial status[36] were affirmed for Canada, allowing the country a youthful, exuberant measure of extraterritorial regulation and offshore claims.[37]

The next stage in constitutional maturity, patriation from the imperial parent,[38] was, like a sovereign's coming of age, accompanied by a measure of previously unattained self-discipline in the form of the Charter's restrictions on state action.[39] And while the constitutional innovation did not eliminate the trappings of sovereignty,[40] it did impose limits on government authority that had previously only been bolstered by international law.[41] The country's new rights oriented constitutionalism, therefore, engaged the country's in-

---

33 E.g., *Re Burley* (1865), 60 B.F.S.P. 1241, 1261 (U.C.C.A.).
34 *Attorney General for Canada v. Attorney General for Ontario* ("The Labour Conventions Case"), [1937] A.C. 326 (P.C.) ("While the ship of state now sails on larger ventures and into foreign waters [...]"). See also Constitution Act; 1867, s. 132 ("All powers necessary or proper for performing the obligations of Canada, or of any Province thereof, as part of the British Empire, towards foreign countries, arising under treaties between the Empire and such foreign countries").
35 1933 (U.K.), 22 Geo. V, c. 4.
36 For discussion of the territorially restricted criminal law powers of a British colony, see *MacLeod v. Attorney General for New South Wales*, [1891] A.C. 455 (P.C.) ("All crime is local"); as it pertained to British North America, see Re Bigamy (1897), 27 S.C.R. 461.
37 *Reference Re Newfoundland Continental Shelf*, [1984] 1 S.C.R. 86 (offshore regulation); *Reference Re Ownership of the Bed of the Strait of Georgia*, [1984] 1 S.C.R. 388 (offshore ownership).
38 Part I of the Constitution Act, 1982, being Schedule B to the Canada Act; 1982 (U.K.), 1982, c. 11, s. 15. For the discussion of the partiation process, see *Reference re Resolution to Amend the Constitution* (the "Patriation Reference"), [1981] 1 S.C.R. 753.
39 *Regina v. Big M Drug Mart Ltd.*, [1985] 1 S.C.R. 295 (interpretation of rights must be "a generous rather than a legalistic one aimed at fulfilling the purpose of the guarantee and securing for individuals the full benefit of the Charter's protection").
40 *Law Society of Upper Canada v. Skapinker*, [1984] 1 S.C.R. 357 (constitutional mobility rights do not extend to cross-border mobility).
41 *Operation Dismantle Inc. v. The Queen* (1985), 18 D.L.R. (4th) 481, 491 (S.C.C.) ("I have no doubt that the executive branch of the Canadian Government is duty bound to act in accordance with the dictates of the Charter").

ternational stature at precisely the point of tension between muscle power and mind control, creating a hormonally charged contest between those who would subdue others and those who would themselves be subdued.

The applicant in *Schmidt v. The Queen*[42] raised a challenge that, for apparently the first time, pitted an extradition request against the constitutional guarantee against double jeopardy in the criminal process.[43] The case arose as a result of the desire of the United States for the return of the fugitive from her place of refuge in Kirkland Lake, Ontario, for the purposes of conducting a second trial on a charge that was virtually identical to one on which she had already been acquitted.[44] While there was some debate in the case over the precise definitions of the respective federal and state offenses for which extradition was sought,[45] it was equally clear that the two charges arose from the identical incident, put in issue the identical allegations, and, had both been pursued in Canada, would in all probability, have led to a defense of *autrefois acquit*.[46]

Schmidt was accused in the United States of having abducted a two-year-old girl from a sidewalk in Cleveland, Ohio, taking her to New York, and raising her as her own daughter for several years, all in the mistaken belief that the girl was the illegitimate child of her own son who had abandoned her as an infant.[47] At her trial on US federal kidnapping charges Schmidt admitted the factual allegations but was acquitted by a jury based on her defense of mistake of fact. Then, while a parallel state charge of "child stealing" was still pending, Schmidt escaped to Canada, where she was arrested a month later. Extradition proceedings were commenced almost immediately under the relevant statute and treaty provisions.[48]

On appeal to the Supreme Court of Canada, it was understood that if extradited to face the State of Ohio prosecution, Schmidt would be unable to

---

42 (1987), 33 C.C.C. (3d) 193 (S.C.C.).
43 *Canadian Charter of Rights and Freedoms*, s. 11 ("Any person charged with an offence has the right (h) if finally acquitted of the offence, not to be tried for it again and, if finally found guilty and punished for the offence, not to be tried or punished for it again").
44 The fugitive's first trial had been for the US federal offense of "kidnapping" under the United States Code, § 18. The second charge, for which extradition was sought, was for the state offense of "child stealing" under the Revised Code of Ohio, s. 2905.04.
45 *Schmidt*, 202 ("The two charges have some similarities but they also have important differences").
46 The lower court hearing the *habeas corpus* application at first instance reasoned that the fact that a defense can be raised in Canada is not in itself a valid reason for refusing extradition. *Schmidt v. The Queen* (1983), 4 C.C.C. (3d) 409 (Ont. Gen. Div.).
47 The background facts are recounted in the judgment of Justice La Forest in *Schmidt* at 202–3.
48 Extradition Act, R.S.C. 1970, c. E-21; Extradition Treaty Between Canada and the United States of America, Canada Treaty Series 1976, No. 3.

raise a plea of double jeopardy under the American constitution, notwithstanding her acquittal on a substantially similar federal charge. While the US courts have found repetitive prosecutions at the state level to constitute harassment and a denial of the Fourteenth Amendment's guarantee of due process,[49] the Fifth Amendment's double jeopardy clause itself applies only to federal prosecutions and therefore does not protect against subsequent exposure to state proceedings. Accordingly, the appeal went forward on the assumption that a constitutional defense in Canada, if permitted, would be her one and only opportunity to raise an issue that the English courts have placed at the core of the common law's notions of procedural justice.[50]

The first problem encountered by the Supreme Court, therefor, was to identify which side of the United States–Canada border the constitutional right claimed by Schmidt could credibly call home. Since the Court had determined several years previously that the Charter does not apply to the actions of foreign government,[51] it was necessary as a first step in the constitutional logic to characterize the site of the asserted breach. This, however, was easier said then done. It was not difficult to find a site for the double jeopardy: rather, the facts offered an embarrassment of riches. While the doctrine made it imperative to determine the location of the governmental wrong, there was no one perspective on this location question that truly objective observer could say identified the place of the right.

By a way of illustration, for Justice Wilson in her separate opinion in *Schmidt*, recognizing Canadian Charter rights in the Canadian extradition hearing, and applying the Charter to the discretionary powers of the Canadian executive branch, came as naturally as any other constitutional ruling. In her words, "the effect is right here in Canada, in the Canadian proceedings, although it will, of course, have repercussions abroad. But there is nothing wrong in this."[52] The issue for Justice Wilson, in other words, was not so much weather the Canadian constitutional ruling would give the *Charter of Rights* extraterritorial effect, but rather whether the extradition treaty on which the proceedings were founded could legally trump the constitutional restrains imposed on the very government that entered the treaty in the first

---

49 *Bartkus v. Illinois*, 359 U.S. 121 (1959).
50 See *Atkinson v. United States of America*, [1971] A.C. 197 (UK extradition court has jurisdiction to entertain plea of *autrefois acquit*).
51 *Spencer v. The Queen*, [1985] 2 S.C.R. 278.
52 *Schmidt*, 199 (Wilson, J. differed from the majority on the constitutional issue, but concurred in the result based on separate grounds).

place. Of paramount importance was not cooperation of the Canadian authorities with their American counterparts in the bringing the fugitive to justice, but the cooperation of the Canadian courts with their own governing and supreme constitutional norms. "If the participation of a Canadian court or the Canadian government is required in order to facilitate extradition so that the suspected criminals may be brought to justice in other countries," wrote Justice Wilson, "we must face up to the question whether such persons have the benefit of the Charter or not *in the Canadian proceedings*."[53] Geography, it would seem, depends very much on point of view.

By contrast, for Justice La Forest and the Supreme Court majority, the starting point of the analysis was that "a fugitive at an extradition hearing [is] not being charged with an offense, certainly not by the Government of Canada."[54] Mimicking the style adopted by Justice Wilson, the non-application of the Canadian constitutional rights was portrayed by Justice La Forest as simply a natural consequences of the foreign site of the substantive proceedings to come. Thus, comparing his own ruling favorably with its American cognate, he stated matter-of-factly that, like section 11(h) of the Charter, the Fifth Amendment right "not to be twice put in jeopardy," has been held to be available only in the United States.[55] The opening words of section 11 of the Charter—"any person charged with an offence"—in other words, the textual source of all of Canada's constitutionalized criminal procedure rights, were interpreted as being applicable only to those charges under a Canadian-defined substantive offense. Again, location of the right is entirely contingent on the initial perspective that the viewer brings to bear. Under the circumstances, what the Court found could only accurately be called a *double* jeopardy.

Justice La Forest's primary point, however, was that extradition, like all transnational legal process, requires respect for the foreign system even when measured against applicable domestic constitutional norms. Thus, he reasoned, "the judicial process in a foreign country must not be subjected to finicky evaluations against the rules governing the legal process in this country"[56]—the demands of the Charter's section 11 apparently being the finickiest of all. According to Justice La Forest and the *Schmidt* majority, such

---

53   Ibid., 200 (emphasis in the original).
54   Ibid., 212 (Dickson, C.J.C. and Beetz, McIntyre, and LeDain, JJ. concurred with Justice La Forest).
55   Ibid., citing Re Ryan, 360 F. Supp. 270 (E.D.N.Y. 1973).
56   *Schmidt*, 214.

minor nuances as "the presumption of innocence or, generally, [the] procedural or evidentiary safeguards [of the Charter]"[57] should not stand in the way of the Court's accommodation of a foreign system whose workings may not exhibit the finer points of technical detail that we have come to expect at home. "Any other approach," reasoned Justice La Forest, "would seriously impair the effective functioning of a salutary system for preventing criminals from evading the demands of justice in one country by escaping to another."[58]

Having reduced constitutional protections to technicalities for which there is no room in an environment of comity, effectively closing the country's constitutional principles to the outside world, Justice La Forest then proceeded to characterize his own approach as one of liberal openness. Taking his lesson from nineteenth-century English legal history, and the near evisceration of the extradition process through narrow judicial interpretation,[59] Justice La Forest contrasted what he viewed as the contemporary trend towards opening up a legal process to the rest of the family of nations. Far from his historically narrow views espoused by extradition courts, contemporary tendencies were portrayed as giving the underlying treaties "a fair and liberal interpretation."[60] Likewise, far from the avoidance of international duty implied by the nineteenth-century tendency to strictly "enforce the rights of the fugitives brought before the extradition courts, the contemporary approach is accomplished "with a view to fulfilling Canada's obligations."[61] Ultimately, the *Schmidt* majority articulated the perceived need for "reducing the technicalities of criminal law to a minimum"[62] as if the procedural rights of the accused were an obstacle to the progressive liberalism of contemporary treaty interpretation, and advocated "trusting the courts in the foreign country to give the fugitive a fair trial [...] including the dictates of due process generally,"[63] as if international cooperation in prosecutions replaces expansive constitutional rights in order to protect those very rights. Taking comfort in what were characterized as a parallel set of US constitutional

---

57 Ibid.
58 Ibid., 215.
59 Ibid., citing Sir Edward Clarke, *A Treatise Upon the Law of Extradition*, 4th ed. (London: Stevens & Haynes, 1903), c. V.
60 *Schmidt*, 215.
61 Ibid.
62 Ibid.
63 Ibid., 216.

rulings,[64] Justice La Forest interpreted the Charter's procedural protections away into nothing in the name of progressive liberalism in international law.

The theme of internationalism in the criminal process was repeated, with a slight doctrinal twist, in what has become the Supreme Court of Canada's leading extradition case, *U.S.A. v. Cotroni*.[65] Writing again for the majority and again taking on Justice Wilson in dissent, Justice La Forest this time championed the force of extradition treaties over the right of Canadians, under section 6(1) of the Charter, to remain in the country at their own will. And what is more, he did so, he indicated, out of a fundamental respect for constitutional values themselves. Thus, he opined, "extradition serves to promote a number of values that are central to a free and democratic society [...] having in mind that crime should not go unpunished,"[66] the idea apparently being that while criminal prosecutions are the stuff of constitutional jurisprudence, criminal defenses are not.

The facts of *Cotroni* started out promising enough for the defense, but ultimately clinched the victory for the requesting state. As recounted by Justice La Forest, Cotroni himself was a Canadian citizen, all of whose alleged criminal conduct took place in the confines of his Montreal home.[67] As made clear in the parliamentary committee debates in which section 6(1) of the Charter was considered,[68] and as can be discerned by comparison to other human rights instruments that provide for a more circumscribed right of mobility,[69] and as articulated in the relatively limited prior case law,[70] the right to remain as an subset of mobility rights generally rests on "the intimate relationship between a citizen and his country."[71] Indeed, it was this national bond that was stressed by Justice Wilson in her dissent; not only had the fugitive never voluntarily left his country of citizenship, but the very accusations at

---

64 See *Galling v. Fraser, 177* E Supp. 856 (2d Cir. 1960) (extradition to Italy granted despite contention that fugitive's conviction in absentia contrary to due process); and *Neely v. Henkel (No. 1)*, 180 U.S. 109,122 (1901) (constitutional provisions relating to writ of habeas corpus, bills of attainder, *ex post facto* laws, trial by jury for crimes, and guarantee of life, liberty, and property "have no relation to crimes committed without the jurisdiction of the United States against the laws of a foreign country").
65 (1989), 48 C.C.C. (3d) 193.
66 Ibid., 213-14, quoting Re Federal Republic of German and Rauca (1983), 4 C.C.C. (3d) 385,406 (Ont. C.A.).
67 For a description of the background facts, see *Cotroni*, 209.
68 See *Debates of the House of Commons*, January 1981,41-118.
69 See European Convention on Human Rights, 4th Protocol, art. 3(1); International Covenant On Civil and Political Rights, art. 12; Canadian Bill of Rights, R.S.C. 1970, Appendix III, s. 2(a).
70 *Law Society of Upper Canada v. Skapinker*.
71 *Cotroni*, 212.

issue in the extradition hearing represented an exercise in extraterritorial law enforcement by the United States.[72]

On the other hand, the second sentence of Justice La Forest's recitation of the facts seemed to go a long way towards ending the controversy over the asserted right to remain in Canada. Stressing the fact that Cotroni's extradition was sought by the United States "on a charge in that country of conspiracy to possess and distribute heroin,"[73] Justice La Forest placed the fugitive in a category of near statelessness. Since the early 1970s, with the House of Lords' specific assertion that "crime is an international problem—perhaps not least crimes connected with the illicit drug traffic,"[74] narcotics offenses have taken on a character that overrides most domestic legal concerns. While in the ordinary course criminal law might be a facet of legal process that is jurisdictionally restricted to the society in which the alleged offense occurred,[75] and, indeed, is grounded in the local community vindicating itself through prosecution of the crime,[76] drug trafficking has detached itself from any such local roots to become a universal legal problem. Cases that fall into this category transcend any one society much as the search for truth itself does. The "interests of society," reasoned Justice La Forest, are found in cases such as *Cotroni* insofar as they aspire to nothing more and nothing less than "to discover the truth in respect of the charges brought against the accused."[77]

For Justice Wilson in dissent, constitutionalism was the driving force, and the international aspects of the case rode behind. Accordingly, in the central passage of her dissenting reasons she first concluded that "[the citizen under s. 6(1) of the Charter] may come and go as he pleases. He may elect to remain."[78] Only after reaching that point did she allow herself to survey the international human rights law terrain, and when she did so she found it more restrictively expressed than section 6(1),[79] confirming her view that the Charter's guarantee of mobility rights was sufficiently expansive to preclude

72 Ibid., 197.
73 Ibid., 209.
74 *D.P.P. v. Doot* at 834 (per Lord Salmon).
75 See, e.g., *Board of Trade v. Owen*, [1957] A.C. 602 (conspiracy in England to commit offense abroad is not subject to English prosecutorial jurisdiction).
76 *Treacy v. Director of Public Prosecutions*, [1971] A.C. 537 (jurors drawn from country in which alleged offense occurred).
77 *Cotroni*, 217.
78 Ibid., 199.
79 Ibid., 200, citing European Convention on Human Rights, Protocol 4, art. 3(1): "No one shall be expelled, by means either of an individual or of a collective measure, from the territory of the State of which he is a national."

extradition. As in *Schmidt*, Justice Wilson focused on the national site of the constitutional right; here, however, there was an added measure tying the fugitive to his country. "I believe," she declared, "that the locus of the wrongdoing is very relevant [...] [to] a Canadian citizen's right to remain in Canada."[80] Extradition treaties, in her view, might attach to Cotroni going abroad, but they could not attach to him staying at home.

For Justice La Forest, the object of the *Cotroni* exercise appears to have been to send the citizen packing, but to do so in a kinder, gentler way than one might otherwise expect. He therefore paid considerable homage to prior Supreme Court pronouncements that Charter rights are to be subjected to "a generous rather than a legalistic" interpretation,[81] and advocating interpretive flexibility[82] in order to overcome any perceived formulaic rigidity of Charter tests such as that set out in *Regina v. Oakes*.[83] This interpretive approach, in turn, had an ideological gloss that took as its starting point the view expounded upon by Justice La Forest in *Schmidt*: international cooperation in law enforcement, of which extradition is the prime example, is the modern antidote to the historic problem of legal parochialism. In this rendition of international law, quite ironically, Charter protections are a retrograde force, "confin[ing] [Canadian society] to parochial and nationalistic concepts of community,"[84] in the face of "an emerging world community from which not only benefits but responsibilities flow."[85] Quoting approvingly from those modern international law scholars most closely associated with this view, Justice La Forest indicated that "this attitude of lack of faith and actual distrust,"[86] so typical of constitutional rights,[87] "is not in keeping with the spirit behind extradition treaties."[88]

The final irony of the *Cotroni* judgment is that its espousal of international progressivism as a bulwark against the perceived regressivism of

---

80 *Cotroni*, 203.
81 Ibid., citing the previous decision of La Forest, j. in *Jones v. The Queen*, [1986] 2 S.C.R. 284.
82 *Cotroni*, 218, citing R. v. Edwards Books & Art Ltd., [1986] 2 S.C.R. 713.
83 [1986] 1 S.C.R. 103.
84 *Cotroni*, 216.
85 Ibid.
86 Ibid., 223, quoting J.G. Castel and Sharon A. Williams, "The Extradition of Canadian Citizens and Sections 1 and 6(1) of the Canadian Charter of Rights and Freedoms," *Canadian Yearbook of International Law* 25 (1987): 268–9.
87 Whether intentionally or coincidentally, this formulation of the attitude underlying constitutional rights reflects a view expressed by constitutional theorists who come at constitutional law from the opposite ideological point of view from those expressed in Justice La Forest's judgment or in the Castel and Williams piece from which he quotes. See John Hart Ely, *Democracy and Distrust* (Cambridge, MA: Harvard University Press, 1984).
88 *Cotroni*, 223, quoting Castel & Williams, "Extradition," 268–9.

constitutional rights is itself premised on a view of the traditional place of extradition in the legal lexicon. "For well over 100 years," Justice La Forest noted, "extradition has been a part of the fabric of our law."[89] This placing of the extradition issue, along with the Charter itself, in historical context had its own interesting spin.[90] In effect, Justice La Forest succeeded in anchoring the unanchorable, and he did so by supporting change on tradition, erecting the imagined future on the discernible past. In one intricate set of reasons, Canada managed to look simultaneously forward and backward, ostensibly freeing itself from its nationalist past while realizing its time-honored internationalist traditions.

Perhaps the most difficult issue to confront the Supreme Court in post-Charter extradition law has been the prospect of Canada, a country that has eschewed the death penalty,[91] sending a fugitive through the extradition process to a potential execution in a foreign country. The full international jurisprudence on the death penalty is discussed in chapter 7 of *The Aesthetics of International Law*.[92] For the present chapter, however, it is relevant to note that during the La Forest era the extradition question was raised in two companion cases. The Court addressed arguments that sending an individual to Pennsylvania's electric chair (*Kindler v. Minister of Justice*)[93] or California's gas chamber (*Reference re Ng Extradition*)[94] would be contrary to the Charter's section 12 prohibition against cruel and unusual punishment and/or its section 7 guarantee of fundamental justice.[95] Writing this time for a narrow majority, Justice La Forest found his own prior reasoning in *Schmidt* and *Cotroni* to be dispositive of the constitutional challenges. While the specific constitutional right might be different for each fugitive, Justice La Forest compared the various cases by musing that "it would be strange if Canada could expel lesser criminals but be obliged by the Charter to grant sanctuary to individu-

---

89 Cotroni, 219.
90 Ibid., quoting *Rauca*, 404: "the Charter was not enacted in a vacuum and the rights set out therein must be interpreted rationally having regard to the then existing laws and, in the instant case, to the position which Canada occupies in the world and the effective history of the multitude of extradition treaties it has had with other nations."
91 The House of Commons, by a majority, supported the abolition of the death penalty in free votes held in 1976 and 1987. Prior to enactment of the Charter, the death penalty was upheld by the Supreme Court under the statutory Canadian Bill of Rights, S.C. 1960, c. 44 in cases of murder of a police officer or prison guard, *R. v. Miller*, [1977] 2 S.C.R. 680.
92 [Ed Morgan, "Vladimir Nabokov: Extradition to the Death Penalty," in *The Aesthetics of International Law* (Toronto: University of Toronto Press, 2007), 104–115 — Ed.]
93 (1991), 67 C.C.C. (3d) 1 (S.C.C.).
94 (1991), 67 C.C.C. (3d) 61 (S.C.C.).
95 For the Supreme Court's later assessment of the question of extradition to the death penalty, see *Burns and Rafay v. The Queen*, [2001] 1 S.C.R. 283.

als who were wanted for crimes so serious as to call for the death penalty in their country of origin."[96]

Justice La Forest's first move in the *Kindler* judgment was to dissociate Canadian public sentiment from the discretion of the minister of justice in acceding to a foreign country's extradition request. Since Charter case law has in any case downplayed the importance of statistical data as a measure of community approval or disapproval of various punitive practices,[97] he had little trouble shifting the focus from societal values to comity among nations. He therefore quickly pointed out that, "unlike the internal situation, the Minister's decision in the present case [...] takes place in a global setting where the vast majority of the nations of the world retain the death penalty."[98] Justice La Forest then went on to survey the field of international conventions on the subject, finding that while there is universal condemnation of certain horrific practices (e.g., genocide, slavery, torture),[99] other penal traditions (e.g., the death penalty), abhorrent perhaps to the Canadian majority, are nevertheless tolerated in all but the most sensitive human rights settings.[100] International public opinion was therefore allowed to replace domestic public opinion as a measure of the punishment and the right.

One of the footings on which Justice La Forest's majority judgment propped the extraditions of Kindler and Ng was the relationship of Canada not so much with the rest of the international community, but with the ever-present (to the Canadian psyche) United States. Specifically, he took note of the "long, relatively open border and similar cultures"[101] of the two countries, and the consequent "temptation of an accused to escape to Canada."[102] On the other hand, the judgment stressed the fundamental dissimilarities between the perceived law-abiding society to the north, where "the interests of protecting the security of Canadians"[103] is paramount, and the society to the

---

96 *Kindler*, 11.
97 See *R. u, Smith*, [1987] 1 S.C.R. 1045 and R. v. Lyons, [1987] 2 S.C.R. 309.
98 *Kindler*, 11.
99 Ibid., citing the International Covenant On Political and Civil Rights, 1976, 999 U.N.T.S. 172, arts. 6,7.
100 *Kindler*, 11, citing the Convention for the Protection of Human Rights and Fundamental Freedoms Concerning the Abolition of the Death Penalty, European Protocol No. 6,1985, Fur. T.S. No. 114. Article 6 of the Canada - United States Extradition Treaty, Can. T.S. 1976, No. 3, which gives each treaty the option of requesting assurances from the other regarding the death penalty was cited by La Forest, J. as additional proof that Canada itself has not accepted the abolition of the death penalty as a mandatory international norm.
101 Kindler, 13.
102 Ibid.
103 Ibid.

south where, "since 1976, approximately 300,000 homicides have occurred [...] [and where] Canada [is seen] as a 'safe haven' for murder suspects."[104] In the context of these similarities and dissimilarities between the two societies, Justice La Forest reminded himself that "the party requesting extradition in this case is the United States—a country with a criminal justice system that is, in many ways, similar to our own, and which provides substantial protections to the criminal defendant."[105]

It does not seem ungenerous to read the majority judgment as posing a choice between *their* homicidal constitutionalism and our protective internationalism; and, of course, if that were the choice, who could choose otherwise? What seemed galling to Justice La Forest was that Americans have themselves rejected (at least in Pennsylvania and California, among other states) the very constitutional norm which the US fugitives advocate here. In the end, the normative contest is almost petulant in tone: if the foreign sovereign, so similar in character to our own, will not restrain its state power in the name of constitutional supremacy, why should we?

More importantly for international law, Justice La Forest identified the treaty commitment to extraditing fugitives from other nations' justice systems as being an obligation that arises from, and is not a limit on, national sovereignty. Thus, while one might be tempted to view this international call to duty—the "global setting," to use Justice La Forest's term—as a curtailment of otherwise applicable Canadian constitutional norms, it turned out that Canada was being asked to exercise nothing more than "the supreme power in every State [...] to expel or deport from the State, at pleasure, even a friendly alien."[106] While the distinctions between the deportation and extradition processes were acknowledged, extradition was seen to be the less problematic of the two, "with its built-in protections geared to the criminal process."[107] The implication of this latter line of reasoning is that while the Charter, as a constitutional enactment, may represent the supreme law of Canadian sovereignty, its subordination, to the extradition process is equally a

---

104 Ibid.
105 Ibid. Justice La Forest's acceptance of the US criminal justice protections harks back to his own previous judgment in *U.S.A. v. Allard*, [1987] 1 S.C.R. 564 (Charter section 7 defense to extradition request requires showing that fugitive "would face a situation that is simply unacceptable").
106 *Kindler*, 11–12, citing *Attorney General for Canada v. Cain*, [1906] A.C. 542, 546 (PC.).
107 *Kindler*, 12. The deportation process has survived constitutional challenges on similar grounds. See *Shepherd v. Minister of Employment and Immigration* (1989), 52 C.C.C. (3d) 386 (Ont. C.A.). For a discussion of the constitutionality of deportation in respect of Kindler himself see *MacDonald v. Kindler*, [1987] F.C. 34 (Fed. C.A.).

manifestation of sovereign authority in the international sense. The ability to expel, deport, or extradite, is portrayed as a natural adjunct to sovereignty itself, much as the ability to control prosecutorial authoritarianism is otherwise presented as a natural adjunct to constitutional supremacy. State power is therefore restrained by constitutional rights, which are in turn restrained by the exercise of an apparently inalienable state power. In Justice La Forest's portrait of internationalism, no one, not even the constitutional law competition, is the loser.

2.2 Foreign Evidence Gathering: The Constitutionalists Arrest

If the post-Charter extradition cases display a reversal of roles from the primacy of constitutional rights to the submergence of those rights to the country's international obligations, cases of foreign interrogations and surveillance in aid of Canadian prosecutions pose the problem in precisely the reverse form. Instead of positioning the Supreme Court of Canada on the inside looking out, the constitutional issues arise from the outside looking in. Accordingly, with the reversed roles yet again reversed and constitutional arguments again assuming an international dimension,[108] one might expect that the former allies will again walk in tandem.[109] Like a syntactical double negative, we should be back to where we always expected to be. Nevertheless, having adopted the dramatic technique of the surprise reversal, the Supreme Court seems reluctant to let it go.

The first in the sequence of cases dealing with the plight of an accused arrested and interrogated by foreign police came at the end of the Supreme Court's sequence of extradition cases; the latter group of cases also commenced at the end of Justice La Forest's judicial career. In many respects, Justice La Forest's majority judgment in *Regina v. Harrer*[110] was his final summation on the internationalist theme. Taking as a starting point the notion that Charter rights pertain to the time of arrest or detention rather than to the time of the trial at which the evidence is admitted,[111] Justice La Forest led

---

108 This international dimension to constitutional law has been made most explicit by U.S. courts examining the scope of Fourth and Fifth Amendment rights in cases of foreign arrests and surveillance. See *United States v. Verdugo-Urquidez*, 856 F. 2d 1214, 1234 (9th Cir. 1988), rev'd, 494 U.S. 259 (1990) ("[Fourth Amendment term] People of the United States [includes] American citizens at home and abroad") (Wallace, J., dissenting).
109 See, e.g., *United States v. Barona*, 56 F. 3d 1087, 1090–1 (9th Cir. 1995) ("When determining the validity of a foreign wiretap [...] our analysis, then, is guided only the applicable principles of constitutional law").
110 (1995), 101 C.C.C. (3d) 193 (S.C.C.).
111 See *Regina v. Shafie* (1989), 47 C.C.C. (3d) 27 (Ont. C.A.).

the majority of the Court on a journey to see how far into the international arena — how far towards a foreign arrest and interrogation — the Canadian constitution could travel. As it turned out, the Charter did not travel well at all, and was yanked back home by special *Dolphin Delivery*[112] almost as soon as it threatened to take flight.

The accused in *Harrer* was the Canadian girlfriend of a prison escapee who had fled custody in Vancouver, where he was being held pending his extradition to the United States on drug charges.[113] During the course of investigating the drug offenses, the US marshal's office traced Harrer to her boyfriend's mother's house in Cleveland, where she was at first suspected of having established a residence contrary to US immigration laws. In conjunction with immigration authorities, the US marshals arrested their Canadian suspect, recited to her the *Miranda*[114] warning and then interrogated her about her immigration status; at some point, as recounted by the court, the interrogators' questions turned away from immigration matters and towards Harrer's involvement as a possible accessory to the Vancouver prison escape.[115] As it happens, the US marshals and their immigration colleagues, following the more limited *Miranda* requirements, did not repeat the warning when the investigation turned to the subject of a second crime, as would be required of Canadian police in a similar situation.[116]

Justice La Forest commenced his analysis by asserting that nothing he would say in the *Harrer* judgment would run counter to the Supreme Court's rulings in the extradition cases. Thus he reminded us that he would not wish "to give credence to the view that the ambit of the charter is automatically limited to Canadian territory,"[117] but, within a page of that statement, he concluded that "the Charter simply has no direct application to the interrogations in the United States."[118] Accordingly, although Justice La Forest acknowledged that the admissibility of Harrer's statements made during her stay in American custody might do violence to the principles of fundamental justice,[119] he equally conceded that "the application of the Charter could

---

112 *R.W.D.S.U., Local 580 v. Dolphin Delivery Ltd.*, [1984] 2 S.C.R. 573 (Charter applicable only to state action, not private action).
113 The background facts are set out in the Supreme Court judgment, *Herrer* at 197–9, and in the Court of Appeal judgment, *R. v. Herrer* (1987), 37 C.C.C. (3d) 1.
114 *Miranda v. Arizona*, 384 U.S. 436 (1966).
115 *Herrer*, 198.
116 See *Regina v. Black*, [1989] 2 S.C.R. 138; *Regina v. Evans*, [1991] 1 S.C.R. 869.
117 *Herrer*, 199.
118 Ibid., 200.
119 Ibid., 201.

only be triggered when the Canadian police began proceedings against the accused on her return to Canada"[120] effectively putting fundamental justice a long way off.

Turning his attention to the question of international relations, Justice La Forest analyzed the problem of illegally obtained evidence by postulating that, whatever else we might want to do as a nation, Canada cannot impose its own procedural requirements on other states operating within their own territories. Such an insistence, he reasoned, would "frustrate the necessary cooperation between the police and prosecutorial authorities among the various states of the world."[121] Accordingly, the case of foreign arrest and interrogation became the flip side of the extradition coin. Indeed, not only was Justice La Forest reluctant to impose domestic constitutional rules on foreign state parties, he borrowed his reasoning from the United States itself, as that country is similarly reluctant to extend its procedural constitutionalism abroad.[122] Ironically, therefore, there is no reciprocal trade in fundamental norms. While *our* constitutional requirements are barred from export, *their* constitutional rulings are imported at will.

In a final rebuke of expanded constitutional law, Justice La Forest engaged in some speculation about the alleged unfairness in the obtaining of evidence without a second warning by the interrogating officials. One must not jump to a hasty conclusion on this front, he admonished, as unfairness does not necessarily flow from the finding of a constitutional infirmity; indeed, since all such judgments were said to be subjective in nature, objective unfairness could not be presumed "simply because [the methods employed] would in this country violate a *Charter* guarantee."[123] Under the circumstances, the Charter was portrayed as an annoyance, imposing the small-minded rules of the constitutional Lilliput on Gulliver's large-scale world of international affairs. "I agree," stated Justice La Forest, "that one should not be overly fastidious or adopt a chauvinistic attitude in assessing practices followed in other countries." The Supreme Court therefore parried the contemporary cry of "taking rights seriously" by warning its constituents, at the very least, not to take them neurotically.

---

120 Ibid.
121 Ibid., 202.
122 Ibid., 203, citing *United States v. Toscamino*, 559 F. 2d 267, 276 (2d Cir. 1974) (evidence obtained abroad admissible unless obtained in a way that "shocks the conscience").
123 *Harrer*, 201.

The next case in the sequence, *Regina v. Terry*,[124] featured Justice McLachlin taking up the internationalist mantle laid down by Justice La Forest. The appellant, who had intervened in the *Harrer* case,[125] found little success in raising a constitutional issue that was, if anything, seen as even narrower than the argument advanced by Harrer. Having been arrested in California and given the usual *Miranda* warning prior to being interrogated later that day, Terry complained that the Charter requirement that he be advised of his right to counsel forthwith upon arrest had been overlooked by the California police. The problem with the appellant's argument, however, was not so much with the argument itself, but with the way the Court misread it. While Terry's challenge sought to exclude the foreign evidence from the Canadian criminal proceedings, Justice McLachlin analyzed it as if it sought to apply Canadian Charter rights in foreign courts.

Justice McLachlan's first move was to reaffirm—indeed, to cast as self-evident—the principle of territoriality that had emerged from a number of recent Supreme Court of Canada judgments. A quick review of those cases, however, reveals that territoriality was not, in fact, a feature of any of them, at least not in the way that Justice McLachlin used the term. Thus, for example, while the Court was said to have limited the Charter to refugees inside the country in *Singh*,[126] the very point of that ruling was to extend process rights to foreign claimants who had previously been excluded from Canadian process altogether; while the Court was said to have confirmed state sovereignty over all persons and property within its territory in *Finta*,[127] the essence of that ruling was that the federal Criminal Code had already incorporated international law into the domestic realm; and while the Court was said to have affirmed that the primary basis of criminal jurisdiction is territorial in *Libman*,[128] that case upheld the extraterritorial reach of criminal law wherever any factual link to Canada can be discerned.

As a final measure, Justice McLachlin reminded her readers that what was at stake in *Terry* was not even substantive criminal law itself, but rather its enforcement, and that the general proposition that criminal law applies only within the territory of the state is "particularly true of the legal procedures

---

124 (1996), 106 C.C.C. (3d) 508 (S.C.C.).
125 See *Harrer*, 197; *Terry*, 511.
126 [1985] 1 S.C.R. 177.
127 [1994] 1 S.C.R. 701.
128 [1985] 2 S.C.R. 178.

enacted to enforce it."[129] But, of course, to identify the foreign enforcement rule was to enforce a misreading of Terry's issue. The question in the appeal was one of Charter rights in the context of an arrest and interrogation, leading to issues of admissibility of evidence and the constitutional exclusionary rule. Law enforcement, in the sense of the term raised by the case, had little visible connection with the conflicts of law doctrine about the enforcement of criminal judgments cited by Justice McLachlin. The territorially protective position was driven, in the Court's reasoning, by a defective engine that was at least partially imported from another field of law.

The central themes of internationalism played out in the case in ways that seem to accomplish the impossible, in that they are both antagonistic and coordinated. Perhaps not surprisingly, given previous judgments in the extradition field, the Court embraced the primacy of international cooperation, citing the proliferation of bilateral mutual assistance treaties negotiated by the federal government under statutory authority.[130] Even under such conventions, however, the sovereignty of Canadian law was seen to begin and end with the sending of a request for assistance to a foreign state,[131] and international cooperation and territorial insularity were seen to be on the same side of the law enforcement coin.[132] Thus, while cooperation among states might characterize their interrelationship, self-containment within the states' respective territories was the *modus operandi* of that cooperation. The progressivism of contemporary international cooperation was thereby placed firmly on an early-nineteenth-century footing, the source of this forward-looking doctrine being identified as Chief Justice Marshall's renowned statement that "a state is only competent to enforce its laws within its own territorial boundaries."[133]

---

129 *Terry*, 515, citing D.P. O'Connell, *International Law*, 2nd ed. (London: Steven & Sons, 1970), vol. 2.
130 Mutual Legal Assistance in Criminal Matters Act, R.S.C. 1985, c. 30 (4th Supp.); and Treaty Between the Government of Canada and the Government of the United States on Mutual Legal Assistance, 1990, Can. T.S. No. 19.
131 *Regina v. Filinov* (1993), 82 C.C.C. (3d) 516, 520 (Ont. Gen. Div.) ("[t]he sovereignty authority of Canada ends with the sending of the request").
132 *Terry*, 516, citing S.A. Williams and J.-G. Castel, *Canadian Criminal Law: International and Transnational Aspects* (Toronto: Butterworths, 1981).
133 *The Schooner Exchange*, 11 U.S. (7 Cranch) 116, 136 (1812). It is difficult to overlook the irony of the Supreme Court of Canada's anti-constitutional, pro-convention invocation of Chief Justice Marshall, who is not only the author of *Marbury v. Madison*, 5 U.S. 137 (1803) and the father of constitutional review, but was the champion of popular sovereignty over the compact theory of constitutional law. On the relationship of this U.S. constitutional history to international legal thought, see E. Morgan, "Internalization of Customary International Law: An Historic Perspective," *Yale Journal International Law* 12 (1987): 63.

For the appellants in *Terry* and *Harrer*, the rights to counsel and against self-incrimination were located by the Court in surprising places—more specifically, in places other than their respective places of arrest and interrogation. Likewise, the national obligation of cooperation with other states, much to the surprise of the appellants, was located by the Court not only in international police work and law enforcement, but in the trial courtroom. Constitutional rights were prohibited from traveling with their holders, lest they interfere with the interstate compact of which international law is made.

Since constitutional rights could not cross the interstate divide, the only question that remained was what the Court would do in the event that the government actually sent for a rights violation abroad. The issue finally arose nearly two years after the *Terry* appeal, in the wake of the government's investigation of the international banking activities of a Canadian citizen. *Schreiber v. Canada (Attorney General)*,[134] came on the heels of a Canadian request for information from the relevant Swiss banking authorities, and arose by way of a stated case posed by the Canadian owner of the subject account.[135] In considering whether the letter of request mechanism, bereft of judicial authorization, amounted to a warrantless search contrary to section 8 of the Charter, the Supreme Court was again forced to ponder the location of the impugned process, this time from the perspective of the outward bound letter rather than, as in *Harrer* and *Terry*, the inward bound accused.

In a short majority judgment by Justice L'Heureux-Dubé, the now familiar refrain of international law enforcement was the dominant tune. "The reality of international criminal investigation and procedure," asserted Justice L'Heureux-Dubé, "is that it necessitates cooperation between states."[136] The "reality," however, was clearly in the eyes of the beholder; Justice L'Heureux-Dubé viewed the realistic aspect of the interstate request to have been sent to Switzerland, while Justice Iacobucd, in dissent, perceived the realistic location of the appellant's rights to have remained at home in Canada. None of this reasoning resolved the controversy at hand, but all of it went some way

---

134 (1998), 124 C.C.C. (3d) 129 (S.C.C.).
135 The question was stated before the Federal Court, Trial Division, as follows: "Was the Canadian standard for the issuance of a search warrant required to be satisfied before the Minister of Justice and Attorney General of Canada submitted the Letter of Request asking Swiss authorities to search for and seize the Plaintiff's banking documents and records?" (1996), 108 C.C.C. (3d) 208.
136 *Schreiber*, 145.

towards proving Nabokov's renowned observation that "reality" is "one of the few words which mean nothing without quotes."[137]

The other debate in the case was over the expectations of a Canadian in respect of the privacy of his or her financial affairs, which expectation was said by both the majority[138] and the dissent[139] to define the scope of the section 8 Charter right. This view was voiced most stridently by Chief Justice Lamer in his separate concurrence, where the question of whether the government action violated the governing constitutional noun was said to turn on whether the respondent had the requisite reasonable expectation of privacy in *his* Swiss banking interests.[140] Just asking the question, of course, invites a cynical response, since Canadians could hardly be expected to do their everyday banking in Switzerland if they did *not* expect a degree of privacy that surpassed that of financial institutions in their own country.

The more perplexing point, however, and one which Justice Iacobucci in dissent equally failed to address, is why expectations should form such a central part of constitutional analysis at all. Chief Justice Lamer recounted a number of instances in which the scope of section 8 has been found to conform with the individuals' expectations under the circumstances of the case—thus, the section 8 guarantee does not extend to the apartment of an accused's friend,[141] nor does it extend to a car where the accused is a passenger rather than the owner.[142] On the other hand, it is apparent that expectations and the case law move hand in hand; indeed, one would be hard put to identify whether the judiciary is the chicken and the public's expectations are the egg, or whether it is the other way around. In any event, the expectations technique effectively converted the issue of curbs on state power into a question of individual desert—an assessment of state of mind[143]—that would be beyond the "reasonable expectations" of most constitutionalists in the field.

---

137 Vladimir Nabokov, "On a Book Entitled Lolita," in *Lolita* (London: Corgi, 1961 [1956]), 314.
138 *Schreiber*, 144 (per Lamer, C.J.C., concurring) ("Therefore, it cannot be said that his reasonable expectation of privacy was violated").
139 Ibid., 154 (per Iacobucci, J., dissenting) ("s. 8 will apply to protect the respondent's privacy interests if the respondent is able to establish that he had a reasonable expectation of privacy with respect to his Swiss bank accounts").
140 Ibid., 140 ("It is clear that the Charter in general applies to such letters of request. The question to be decided in order to see if government actions comply with s. 8 is whether the respondent had a reasonable expectation of privacy in his banking records in Switzerland").
141 *Regina v. Edwards*, [1996] S.C.R. 128.
142 *Regina v. Belnavis*, [1997] 3 S.C.R. 341.
143 Compare, e.g., *Thomson Newspapers Ltd. v. Canada (Director of Investigation, Research, Restrictive Trade Practices Commission)*, [1990] 1 S.C.R. 425, 506 ("privacy [...] may vary significantly depending upon the activity that brings him or her into contact with the state"); *Regina v. McKinlay Transport*

By depositing the crux of Schreiber's Charter complaint alongside his money in Zurich, the Court managed to overcome the warrantless search in the most constitutionally feasible of ways. Although the international mantra of cooperation was carried forward, the more traditional international law impulse towards comity was equally expressed. According to Justice L'Heureux-Dubé, the Court "is much more reluctant to measure the laws of foreign states against guarantees contained in the Canadian Constitution."[144] Since the search was carried out *there*, and a request was merely made *here*, deference and a call to judicial passivity in the international realm were the order of the day. Far from an aggressive internationalism, the portrait drawn by Justice L'Heureux-Dubé was an accommodating one, giving play to constitutional guarantees even as they were swept like so many prisoners' remains into the penal colony's burial pit.

3. THE LAW AND ITS SUBJECTS

For Kafka, the characters' switching of roles is a fundamental thematic technique. The central drama of "In the Penal Colony" finds the officer, the personification of the law,[145] mounting the execution machine in place of the convict who is set free.[146] The Old Commandant of the colony, whose time has passed, stands in the shoes of the New Commandant, who is himself a prisoner of the elaborate, unending administrative designs of the Old.[147] The explorer, who sits passively through the officer's lecture about the machine while pondering the fate of the person in its grip, comes to take an active interest in and restrict his interest to the machine's mechanical functions once human blood starts to flow.[148] Even the machine, whose flawless operations had delivered human beings to their ultimate redemption and burial,

---

Ltd., [1990] 1 S.C.R. 627 (privacy rights vary with "context"). See also *Regina v. Plant*, [1993] 3 S.C.R. 281 (contextual factors in privacy interest).

144 *Schreiber* at 144.

145 Kafka, "In the Penal Colony," 198 ("This is how the matter stands. I have been appointed judge in this penal colony. Despite my youth").

146 Ibid., 221 ("The condemned man especially seemed struck with the notion that some great change was impending. What had happened to him was now going to happen to the officer").

147 Ibid., 193 ("We who were his friends knew even before he died that the organization of the colony was so perfect that his successor, even with a thousand new schemes in his head, would find it impossible to alter anything").

148 Ibid., 223-4 ("The explorer, on the other hand, felt greatly troubled; the machine was obviously going to pieces; its silent working was a delusion; he had a feeling that he must now stand by the officer, since the officer was no longer able to look after himself").

in a final dramatic switch delivers nothing of value to its human cargo[149] and lurches itself into the pit.[150]

The goal of the penal colony is to enforce, quite literally, the letter of the law, turning the law's human subjects into the letters of which the law is composed. While the method is scientific in the extreme[151] and its description as precise as it is graphic,[152] the project is only truly instructive in its abject failure. The law is presented, and, indeed, presents itself, as mysterious and rationally unknowable,[153] surpassing even Nietzsche's skeptical assessment that "it is today impossible to say with certainty why there is punishment."[154] Yet the law's promises—enlightenment for both individual[155] and society[156]—are all seen to be false.[157] In the idealized past, as recounted by the officer, the law's human subjects changed roles with the law itself, becoming a perfectly scripted text.[158] In the more sordid present, as demonstratively enacted by the officer, it is the lawmaker rather than the law itself that replaces the law's subject, creating a defective text in which the lawmaker becomes the lawbreaker.[159] The past precedent is mythologized to an extent that no rational person—least of all the explorer, with his humanistic response to the gruesome procedure—could take seriously, while the present content of the law is utterly inscrutable.[160]

Ironically, for a piece that centres on an impenetrable version of the law, most of Kafka's story is taken up by a detailed lecture by the officer on the

---

149 Ibid., 225 ("It [the face of the corpse] was as it had been in life [...]").
150 Ibid., 224 ("The Harrow tried to move back to its old position, but as if it had itself noticed that it had not yet got rid of its burden it struck after all where it was, over the pit").
151 Ibid., 202 ("It's no calligraphy for school children. It needs to be studied closely").
152 Ibid., 203 ("When it finishes the first draft of the inscription on the man's back, the layer of cotton wool begins to roll and slowly turns the body over, to give the Harrow fresh space for writing. Meanwhile the raw part that has been written on lies on the cotton wool, which is specially prepared to staunch the bleeding and so makes all ready for a new deepening of the script").
153 Ibid., 197 ("Many questions were troubling the explorer "Does he know his sentence?" "No," said the officer, eager to go on with his exposition [...] "There would be no point in telling him. He'll learn it on his body.").
154 Friedrich Nietzsche, *On the Genealogy of Morals*, trans. Walter Kaufmann (New York: Vintage Books, 1969), 80 ("All concepts in which an entire process is semi-otically concentrated elude definition; only that which has no history is definable"). For a discussion of the parallels between Kafka and Nietzsche on the position of suffering and punishment see Patrick Bridgwater, *Kafka and Nietzsche* (Bonn: Bouvier, 1974), 41–6.
155 Kafka, "In the Penal Colony," 204 ("Enlightenment comes to the most dull-witted").
156 Ibid., 209 ("They all knew: Now Justice is being done").
157 Ibid., 225 ("No sign was visible of the promised redemption").
158 Ibid., 197 ("'Whatever commandment the prisoner has disobeyed is written upon his body by the Harrow. This prisoner, for instance'—the officer indicated the man—'will have written on his body: HONOR THY SUPERIORS!').
159 Ibid., 224 ("For this was no exquisite torture such as the officer desired, this was plain murder").
160 Ibid., 219 ("The explorer made no remark, yet it was clear that he still could not decipher it").

workings of the penal system and its implementation via the execution machine. The officer's discourse, with its mathematical precision and scientific vocabulary, is so obsessive as to be a parody of professionalism,[161] and, ultimately, of reason itself, defending at great length a tortuous death to no rational end. Law and violence thereby trade places along with their protagonists; as explained by the officer, the law requires punishment to give it its only meaning, and the punishment requires the law to rationalize its violence. In becoming interchangeable with its opposite, the "reason" employed by the officer in the name of the law becomes the very medium for the attack on the law.

As the officer expounds with scientific or pseudo-scientific detail on the workings of the machine, elaborating on a romantic view of the past as a precedent for today's enforcement of the law itself, becoming perfectly stripped text.[162] In the more sordid present, as demonstratively enacted by the officer, it is the law maker rather then the law itself that replaces the law's subject, creating a defective text in which the law maker becomes the lawbreaker.[163] it becomes apparent that what is being presented is neither reason nor justice, but theatrics. For the officer, and Kafka, it is the very formality of the occasion, and the aesthetics rather than the flawed logic of the process, that gives the inflicting of punishment its meaning. The officer's demonstration is utterly divorced from the fate, or culpability, of the convict, who cannot even comprehend the explanation.[164] From the very opening line of the story, the officer's exposition is meant not to convince the explorer but to share with him the pleasures—indeed, the art form—of the machine. The farcical quality of the lecture and demonstration upstages the macabre aspects of the narrative, so that the story is to stories of violence much as mimicry is to authenticity.[165] Kafka's message is not to advocate a ghastly punishment void

---

161 Ibid., 193–4 ("All the more did he admire the officer, who in spite of his tight-fitting full-dress uniform coat, amply befrogged and weighed down by epaulettes, was pursuing his subject with such enthusiasm and, besides talking, was still tightening a screw here and there with a spanner").
162 Ibid., 196–7 ("'I am certainly the best person to explain our procedure, since I have here'—he patted his breast pocket—'the relevant drawings made by our former Commandant.' Then he inspected his hands critically; they did not seem clean enough to him for touching the drawings...").
163 Ibid., 194 ("The officer was speaking French, and certainly neither the soldier nor the prisoner understood a word of French").
164 Ibid., 191 ("'It's a remarkable piece of apparatus,' said the officer to the explorer and surveyed with a certain air of admiration the apparatus which was after all quite familiar to him.").
165 In this, Kafka has much in common with the writings of de Sade, which stress the fantasy of violence over violence itself. See Roland Barthes, *Sade/Fourier/Loyola*, trans. Richard Miller (New York: Hill and Wang, 1976), 181 ("Throughout his life, the Marquis de Sade's passion was not erotic [eroticism is very different from passion]; it was theatrical").

of meaningful purpose, but rather to accentuate the dramatic techniques entailed in arriving at such a position. One is never meant to feel the convict's or the officer's pain; rather, by undermining realism and rationality through the devices of fantasy and parody, Kafka enables the reader to appreciate the aesthetics of its infliction.[166]

Since the law's rationale is a mock rationale, and the tyrannical officer of the law is a mock tyrant, the subject of the law is nothing more than a mockery of itself. Not only can characters change places seemingly at will, but the apparent values of the story—law and crime, reason and violence, justice and torture, domination and submission, mathematical precision and aesthetics—all are equally prone to dramatic reversals revealing a parody of themselves. What the officer says is never important in its own right; indeed, it is ridiculous. The important thing is that in the dramatic finale, the upright, uniformed officer lies naked on the bed of the machine,[167] as a part of his theatrical demonstration, or his "reasons" for "justice." He is his own subject matter.

4. INTERNATIONALISM COMES OF AGE

Viewing Canada, as the Supreme Court does, as having come of post-Charter age by overcoming the parochial tendencies of domestic constitutionalism and proving itself a full adherent to international obligations, fills one with a sense of historical irony. After all, the enactment of the Charter and its entrenched guarantees is itself viewed as a process of national maturation, the 1982 patriation of the constitution being a form of worldly rights of passage. Moreover, the question of national stature was not exactly a novel, or even a contemporary one. The courts had determined that the nation had achieved its independent status in the international arena fifty years prior to the Charter, in a criminal law context that proved precisely the opposite point from that of the post-Charter international law cases—that is, one that demonstrated Canada's constitutional sovereignty in the face of, rather than in obedience to, international obligations.

---

166 Ibid. ("What happens in a story by de Sade is strictly fantastic").
167 Ibid., 220 ("In spite of the obvious haste with which he was discarding first his uniform jacket and then all his clothing, he handled each garment with loving care").

In *Croft v. Dunphy*,[168] a constitutional question was posed as to the federal government's jurisdiction under the Customs Act[169] to seize a cargo of rum eleven miles off the Nova Scotia shore. Whereas international law recognized a territorial sea jurisdiction of only three miles from the coast, Parliament had legislated itself a twelve-mile regulatory authority over the high seas. It was in this expanded enforcement zone that Canadian customs officials boarded the appellant's ship and seized his dutiable goods. In response to the appellant's challenge, the Privy Council found that Canada had by the 1930s been granted "plenary powers of legislation, as large, and of the same nature, as those of [the Imperial] Parliament itself,"[170] thereby confirming the constitutional sovereignty of Canada not by reference to its ability to comply with international law, but by reference to its capacity to breach it.[171] The legislation was upheld as a result of the federal Parliament's plenary ability to do as it pleased, regardless of the restraints imposed by international law.[172]

In another unexpected reversal, therefore, Canada's ability to violate international restrictions and Canada's ability to adhere to international obligations have become the two sides of the identical constitutional law coin. In this, the relationship between pre-Charter and post-Charter Canada is much like that between the Old Commandant's and the New Commandant's penal colony.[173] The new constitutional regime imports norms from the outside world — the explorer's ostensible human rights sensitivities[174] — only to find the law inflicting violence on itself with the machinery of state designed by the *ancien régime*. Since compliance with international law and breach of international law, like the officer and the convict, can be reversed with constitutional ease, the legal system's normative transformation becomes just one more adjustment in the elaborate penal apparatus. *Plus ça change…*

---

168 [1932] 59 C.C.C. 141 (RC.).
169 The then current version of the statute was the Customs Act, R.S.C. 1927, c. 42, At issue were ss. 131 and 207.
170 *Croft v. Dunphy*, 144.
171 For a discussion of the place of the Privy Council's decision in the history of Anglo-Canadian extraterritorial criminal jurisdiction, see E. Morgan, "Criminal Process, International Law and Extraterritorial Crime," *University of Toronto Law Journal* 38 (1988): 245.
172 On this point, see also *British Columbia Electric Railway Co. v. The King*, [1946] 4 D.L.R. 82 (P.C.) (Canadian Parliament's unrestricted capacity to impose income tax on residents of foreign countries).
173 The Commandant is personified as the entire socio-legal order. Kafka, "In the Penal Colony," 196 ("Did he combine everything in himself, then? Was he soldier, judge, mechanic, chemist and draughtsman?").
174 Ibid., 198 ("'But he must have had some chance of defending himself,' said the explorer, and rose from his seat").

The interchangeable nature of old and new likewise corresponds with the local and international influences on the penal quality of the colony's norms. Thus, the normative world of the Old Commandant is an isolated one, much as the old world of sovereigns is a jurisdictionally insular one in which the substantive offense must occur within the country in order for judicial authority to attach.[175] On the other hand, the normative world of the New Commandant, who imported the explorer, is an imperialistic one, much as modern pronouncements of criminal jurisdiction tie the penal outpost into the international scene as a protector of what is right.[176] The two approaches survive in the same story only insofar as they happen to coincide,[177] failing which one buries the other in obscurity.[178]

When, true to the Kafka form, the local and the international trade places, the Old Commandant's officer destroys the execution machine with a self-inflicted universal message,[179] while the New Commandant's explorer observes with indifference as the colony engages in one final torture.[180] In much the same way, when the normative insularity of sovereign jurisdiction gives way to international rules of cooperation,[181] the expanded constitutionalism of universal rights shrinks to become the parochial enforcement of domestic procedures.[182] Thus, in coming of age as a legal system, the humanitarian or constitutionalist impulse of the Supreme Court is submerged and domesticated by the authoritarian or internationalist impulse; moreover, the

---

175 *Board of Trade v. Owen*, [1957] A.C. 602 (conspiracy to commit offense abroad is not subject to English prosecution); R. a. *Brixton Prison Governor, ex parte Rush*, [1969] 1 All ER, 316 (C.A.) (multi-jurisdictional fraudulent scheme not subject to English criminal jurisdiction).
176 *Treacy v. Director of Public Prosecutions*, [1971] A.C. 537, 562 ("Indeed, where the prohibited acts are of a kind calculated to cause harm to private individuals it would savour of chauvinism rather than comity to treat them as excusable merely on the ground that the victim was not in the United Kingdom itself but in some other state").
177 International law and constitutional jurisdiction coexisted, because they perfectly coincided, in nineteenth-century common law. See, e.g., *Regina v. Keyn* (1876), 2 Ex.. D. 63 (Cr. Cas. Res.) (County Court jurisdiction up to high water mark, admiralty jurisdiction beyond high water mark to extent of territorial sea, parliamentary jurisdiction beyond British territory interacting with family of nations).
178 Kafka, "In the Penal Colony," 226 ("They pushed one of the tables aside and under it there was really a gravestone [...] There was an inscription on it in very small letters, the explorer had to kneel down to read it [...] 'Here rests the old Commandant. His adherents, who now must be nameless, have dug this grave [...].'").
179 Ibid., 218–19 (Now the officer began to spell it, letter by letter, and then read out the words, "BE JUST!").
180 Ibid., 220–1 ("The explorer bit his lips and said nothing. He knew very well what was going to happen, but he had no right to obstruct the officer in anything").
181 See Section 2.1, and the discussion of the Supreme. Court's extradition cases from *Schmidt* to *Kindler*.
182 See Section 2.2 of this chapter, and the discussion of the Supreme Court's cases dealing with constitutional rights and foreign evidence gathering, from *Herrer* to *Schreiber*.

dominant impulse replaces the old, regressive one by putting on a new, progressive face. In this way, the new universalist constitution becomes a passé form of parochial technicality, while the old local Crown authority becomes a modernist form of international cooperation. The role reversals engineered by the Court are as complete as those Kafka would stage.

Internationalism has become, in the Supreme Court's hands, a medium for inflicting punishment, while constitutionalism has become a medium for enduring it. It is little wonder, therefore, that they chafe where they join issue. While the Court has attempted to cauterize the wounds through the devices of mutual cooperation and international duties, the fact remains that one can either operate the execution machine or be operated upon. As in Kafka's story, the officer as prosecutor and the convict as rights holder may both be scripted as the law, and indeed they may be perfectly interchangeable, but they cannot together be made whole. In the age of Canadian constitutionalism, international law has matured to an Oedipal degree,[183] dominating and punishing the very constitution that gave it its stature.

---

183 For a discussion of Kafka's writings about the law and legal authorities from the perspective of his own difficult relationship with his father see Gerhard Neumann, "'The Judgment,' 'Letter to His Father,' and the Bourgeois Family," in *Reading Kafka*, 215–28.

EXTRATERRITORIAL POETICS

On February 8, 1889, Siegfried Kracauer was born in Frankfurt am Main, the son of a businessman, Adolf K. Kracauer and his wife, the former Rosette Oppenheim; he died seventy-seven years later in New York City on November 26, 1966. For any normal biography, this bracketing of a life between two chronological points is a natural and unexamined beginning. For a biography of Kracauer, however, it constitutes a betrayal of the strongest taboo of his later life, a taboo he expressed in a series of letters deliberately set aside in his well-organized *Nachlaß*[1] to give any future biographer pause. These letters, written in the 1960s when Kracauer was consumed by his final project on the philosophy of history, were filed under the heading of "extra-territoriality." In all of them, Kracauer vehemently opposed any effort to disclose his correct age, a campaign, as he surely must have known, which could only meet with temporary success.[2] His reason for waging it, despite the certainty of ultimate failure, transcended the petty vanity of those who refuse to age gracefully. As he wrote to his friend Theodor W. Adorno in 1963: "It is not as if there is something for me in appearing young or younger; it is simply the horror of losing chrono-

THE EXTRATERRITORIAL LIFE OF SIEGFRIED KRACAUER

Martin Jay

Originally published as Martin Jay, "The Extraterritorial Life of Siegfried Kracauer", *Salmagundi* 31–32 (Fall 1975–Winter 1976): 49–106. Reprinted with permission of the author.

1   Siegfried Kracauer's *Nachlaß* was deposited in 1973 in the Schiller National Museum in Marbach am Neckar. All letters quoted in the text can be found there, although I consulted the correspondence with Leo Löwenthal in Professor Löwenthal's own collection in Berkeley, California. I am deeply indebted to Dr. Werner Volcke and the staff of the Schiller National Museum for their courtesy and helpfulness during my stay in Marbach. I also must thank former friends of Kracauer for granting me illuminating interviews: Rudolf Arnheim, Bernard Karpel, Paul Oskar Kristeller, Leo Löwenthal, Hans Mayer, Sheldon Meyer, Henry Pachter, Meyer Schapiro, and the editor of his collected works, Karsten Witte. Leo Löwenthal, Karsten Witte, and my wife, Cathy Gallagher, who made helpful comments on the manuscript's first draft.

2   The only instance of "success" that I have found is in the article by Hans G. Helms, entitled "Der wunderliche Kracauer," *Neues Forum* (June/July, 1971): 27, where Kracauer's age in 1964 is said to be 70, when it was in fact 75.

logical anonymity through the fixating of a date and the unavoidable connotations of such a fixation."[3]

The "chronological anonymity" he so insistently guarded serves two functions. First, it helped to discourage efforts to place Kracauer in the context of any one period, such as those that would define him as a "Weimar intellectual" with all the resonances that label has acquired over the years. By avoiding such a placement, he hoped to thwart the compartmentalization of his own work that he had sought to resist in the work of those he studied. But secondly, and perhaps more significantly, on a psychological level, it served to ward off thoughts of the approaching death that would signify the closure of his work and give his life whatever final meaning it might have. When he finally did die, Adorno wrote in his obituary that Kracauer's utter refusal to confront death or aging had a heroic dimension to it, consonant with his longstanding concern for the redemption of the living.[4] To Kracauer, final meanings were anathema, whether in cultural phenomena or the record of a man's life. Wholeness and death were inextricably intertwined in his thinking, an association that energized much of his thought, and set him apart from the Weimar intellectuals who, in Peter Gay's phrase, "hungered for wholeness."[5]

Kracauer's concern for "chronological anonymity" grew out of a more general fascination with the condition that he chose to call, "extra-territoriality." Marginality, alienation, and outsiderness have been among the stock obsessions of intellectuals ever since the time of Rousseau. Few, however, focused as consistently on the manifestations of the malaise throughout their entire careers as did Kracauer. Fewer still found ways to fashion their own marginality into a positive good in quite the manner he did. As we shall see, Kracauer's life's work can be read as a series of seemingly disparate projects, almost all with the common goal of redeeming contingency from oblivion. In important, if not fully transparent ways, this effort paralleled Kracauer's personal struggle with the "extra-territorial" nature of his own life.

Kracauer's sense of marginality must have begun almost at birth. Physically, he was set apart from his peers by two characteristics. The first was a speech defect, a stammer which would preclude, among other things, a teaching career at any time in his life. The second was his physiognomy,

---

3 Kracauer to Adorno, November 8, 1963. The other correspondents with whom he discussed his "chronological anonymity" were Erika Lorenz, Michel Ciment, and Hans Kohn. Unless otherwise indicated, the letters were written in German and translated by me.
4 Theodor W. Adorno, "Siegfried Kracauer Tot," *Frankfurter Allgemeine Zeitung*, December 1, 1966, 2.
5 Peter Gay, *Weimar Culture: The Outsider as Insider* (New York: W.W. Norton, 1968), chapter 4.

whose peculiarity struck with all who knew him. To Adorno, who actually used the word "extra-territorial" in describing his face, he looked as if he were from the Far East.[6] Asja Lacis, the Latvian Marxist director who met him in the late 1920s, said he looked like an "African."[7] To Hans Mayer, the Marxist literary, he was "Japanese painted by an Expressionist."[8] And Rudolf Arnheim, the aesthetic theoretician, remembers him as having a squashed nose that made his face "almost grotesque, but somehow beautiful."[9]

Added to whatever stress may have been caused by these physical peculiarities was the trauma of his father's death when Kracauer was still a young child. He moved shortly thereafter to the house of his uncle, Isidor K. Kracauer, a distinguished historian of Frankfurt's Jewish community.[10] The atmosphere of the home was apparently religious, but the young Kracauer, like so many of his generation, sought assimilation rather than ethnic identification. Later, in the 1920s, he became friendly with the circle around the powerfully attractive Rabbi Nehemiah Nobel, which included Ernst Simon, Martin Buber, and Franz Rosenzweig. He even contributed a piece to the Rabbi's *Festchrift* in 1921,[11] but seems to have played no role in the creation of the Frankfurt *Lehrhaus*, which emerged from Nobel's circle. By 1926, however, what interest he may have had in the Jewish revival stimulated by the *Lehrhaus* group was clearly dead. In that year, he published a stinging criticism of the Buber-Rosenzweig translation of the Bible, which he damned as neo-*völkisch* in inspiration.[12] Thereafter, Jewish issues played no overt role in any of his writings, although certain residues can perhaps be said to have remained, if the religious element in his interest in redemption is stressed. Still, what his upbringing in a religious household whose tenets he rejected

---

6 Ibid.
7 Asja Lacis, *Revolutionär im Beruf; Berichte über proletarischer Theater, über Meyerhold, Brecht, Benjamin, und Piscator*, ed. Hildegard Brenner (Munich: Rogner & Bernhard, 1971), 62.
8 Conversation with Professor Mayer, Milwaukee, Wisconsin, November 30, 1973.
9 Conversation with Professor Arnheim, Cambridge, Massachusetts, December 21, 1973.
10 His most notable work was a two volume "Geschichte der Juden in Frankfurt a. M. (1150–1824)" published post-humously in 1925 and 1927 with the editorial help of his widow, Hedwig. He was supported by the Jewish Community of Frankfurt in this endeavor.
11 Siegfried Kracauer, "Gedanken über die Freudschaft," in *Gabe Herrn Rabbiner Dr. Nobel zum 50. Geburtstag* (Frankfurt, J. Kauffmann, 1921). This was the second part of an essay, whose first part appeared as "Über die Freundschaft," *Logos* 7, no. 2 (Tübingen: 1917/18). Both parts were published by Suhrkamp in 1972.
12 Siegfried Kracauer, "Die Bibel auf Deutsch," in *Frankfurter Zeitung* (henceforth FZ), April 27 and 28, 1926; reprinted in *Das Ornament der Masse* (Frankfurt a.M.: Suhrkamp, 1963). Buber and Rosenzweig answered the attack in the FZ on May 18, 1926; their essay is reprinted in *Die Schrift und ihre Verdeutschung* (Berlin: Schocken, 1936), 276ff. Kracauer also attacked Zionism in a 1922 article entitled, "Die Wartenden," reprinted in *Das Ornament der Masse*, 112.

meant was a strengthening of that marginality which characterized his life. After 1933, the myth of assimilation was exploded in a way that could only have reinforced his sense of outsiderness. Although Kracauer never directly dealt with the consequences of his Jewish background, there can be little doubt that it played a serious role in the development of his sensibility and intellectual concerns.

Kracauer's career pattern shows equal signs of deviation from the norm of intellectual maturation, if indeed such a norm can be said to exist. Before the First World War, he studied at the Klinger-Oberrealschule in Frankfurt and then at universities and technical colleges in Darmstadt, Berlin, and Munich. Although he prepared fields were in philosophy and sociology, his main interest was in architecture, which he hoped to make his career. In 1915, he earned a doctorate in engineering at the technical college of Berlin-Charlottenburg with a dissertation on the development of wrought iron decorations in Prussia from the seventeenth to the nineteenth centuries.[13] During the war, he seems to have avoided serious military service, if his semi-autobiographical novel, *Ginster*,[14] is any indication. Instead, he served as an apprentice architect in Hannover, Osnabruck, Frankfurt, and Munich.

Although architecture was only to be a temporary career, it left its mark on Kracauer's subsequent development. His heightened visual sensitivity, "the primacy of the optical" in Adorno's phrase,[15] led to a series of articles on urban space, both interior and exterior, in the 1920s.[16] It also, of course, underlies Kracauer's lifelong fascination with the film, for which he is best known in the English-speaking world. In addition, the constructive impulse nurtured by his architectural experience reappeared in the technique Kracauer called "construction in the material," which he developed in the Weimar period, as well as in the highly structured way he organized his books and articles.

But for reasons that are not entirely clear, architecture failed to engage his total personality and he gave it up in 1920. Encouraged by the eminent philosophers, Georg Simmel and Max Scheler, with whom he was person-

---

13 Siegfried Kracauer, *Die Entwicklung der Schmiedekunst in Berlin, Potsdam und einigen Stadten der Mark vom 17, Jahrhundert bis zum Beginn des 19. Jahrhunderts* (Worms: Wormser Verlag, 1915).
14 Siegfried Kracauer, *Ginster, Von ihm selbst geschrieben* (Berlin: S. Fischer, 1928); 2nd ed. *Ginster* (without final chapter), (Frankfurt a.M.: Fischer, 1963); 3rd ed. (with final chapter), (Frankfurt a.M.: Suhrkamp, 1973), published as vol. 7 of *Schriften* with his other novel, *Georg.*
15 Theodor W. Adorno, "Der wunderliche Realist", *Noten zur Literatur* III (Frankfurt a.M.: Suhrkamp, 1965), 87.
16 These have been collected as *Straßen in Berlin und anderswo* (Frankfurt a.M.: Suhrkamp, 1964).

ally acquainted, Kracauer turned to philosophical and sociological analysis as a new career. The first fruits of his shift were studies of Simmel, published only in part in 1920, and of sociology as a science, which appeared in 1922.[17] In both, the marks of Kracauer's interests in phenomenology as an antidote to neo-Kantianism were evident, but a phenomenology closer to Scheler's "material eidectics" than to Husserl's intuitionist search for essences beneath the flux of history. Central to Kracauer's vision of sociology was an anti-psychological, anti-subjectivist perspective. That is, he claimed that the attempt by the phenomenologists to counter psychologism in philosophy was appropriate to sociology as well. The reason for this parallel, Kracauer argued, could be found in the nature of his age. In characterizing it, Kracauer explicitly borrowed from Georg Lukács's recently published *Theory of the Novel*,[18] specifically, his distinction between meaningful, fulfilled periods of history and empty, barren ones. Like Lukács, Kracauer put his own era in the second category. A phenomenological sociology without psychological subjectivity was appropriate because the age was one in which meaning, community, and purpose were absent. The reality of the social world, he wrote, is a "bad infinity"[19] without material totality. The integrated personality so valued by generations of German philosophers was also an ideological illusion. Idealism, with its implicit assumptions of an immanently meaningful world, was thus a misleading metaphysics. The only alternative was a scientific sociology that would investigate the structural regularities of de-individualized social realms without worrying about the need to integrate the subject and object into a larger whole. Sociology, however, should not be expected to provide answers to the present cultural crisis, when the source was in society itself. Although Kracauer was soon to lose his enthusiasm for Scheler's materialist phenomenology, especially when Scheler began searching for eternal verities,[20] his underlying premise about the meaninglessness of the present period was a life-long conviction. Unlike Lukács, however, he never came to see a solution to the dilemma it presented.

---

17 Siegfried Kracauer, "Georg Simmel," *Logos* 9, no. 3, (1920); reprinted in *Das Ornament der Masse; Soziologie als Wissenschaft. Eine erkenntnistheoretische Untersuchung* (Dresden: Sibyllen-Verlag, 1922); reprinted in vol. 1 of *Schriften* (Frankfurt a.M.: Suhrkamp, 1971).
18 George Lukács, *Die Theorie des Romans* (Berlin: Luchterhand, 1920), cited on page 13 of *Soziologie als Wissenschaft* (1971 ed.). Kracauer reviewed this book twice, in *Die Weltbuhne* 17, no. 35 (Sept. 1, 1921) and *Neue Blatter für Kunst und Literatur* 4, no. 1 (October 4, 1921).
19 Lukács, *Die Theorie des Romans*, 29.
20 He attacked Scheler's turn to Catholicism in "Katholizismus und Relativismus," in *FZ*, November 19, 1921; reprinted in *Das Ornament der Masse*.

Although Kracauer was now seriously devoted to intellectual work, his speech defect and lack of advanced training in academic areas meant the impossibility of a university career. Following phenomenology's injunction to return to the *Lebenswelt* from the heights of philosophical speculation, and taking advantage of the increased prestige of journalism in the Weimar period, Kracauer took a position with the *Frankfurter Zeitung* in 1920. The *FZ*, founded in 1856 by Leopold Sonnemann, was one of the most prestigious of Germany's newspapers and a pillar of the democratic left-wing of bourgeois liberalism. Although its circulation after the war never exceeded 70,000, it retained a large measure of political and cultural influence among the middle-classes, especially the educated Jewish bourgeoisie from which Kracauer himself had come. It was, of course, not without its detractors. As a recent student of its history has written:

> In *Mein Kampf* Hitler devoted more space and invective to the *FZ* than to any other newspaper, considering it as the Gorgon of the *Judenpresse*, the sophisticated and highly effective organ of the Jewish world conspiracy, and an important contributor to Germany's defeat in the war.[21]

Although its liberal fervor began to slip by the late twenties, when its ownership changed hands, it continued to be a leading voice of middle-class opinion until the end of the Republic. Kracauer remained in its employ until 1933, when the Nazis decapitated "the Gorgon of the *Judenpresse*" with scarcely any resistance. He survived the purge of left-leaning staff after the change of owners, because he was not directly concerned with political reporting. Kracauer was assigned instead to its *feuilleton* section, where the emphasis was on cultural affairs.

Throughout the Weimar period, Kracauer and his colleague Benno Reifenberg[22] made the *feuilleton* page of the *FZ*, the most brilliant in the German-speaking world. Here, he carried out an extensive and penetrating critique

---

[21] Modris Eksteins, "The Frankfurter Zeitung: Mirror of Weimar Democracy," *Journal of Contemporary History* 4, no. 4 (1971): 5. Kracauer himself wrote an article on Leopold Sonnemann for the *Encyclopedia of the Social Sciences*, vol. 14 (London: Macmillan, 1934).

[22] Benno Reifenberg (1892–1970) was trained as an art historian. He joined the *FZ* in 1919 and became its *feuilleton* director in 1924. 1930–32, he was the head of its Paris bureau. After the war, he was a founder and leading writer for *Die Gegenwart*.

of everyday life, reminiscent of Simmel's, with the goal of stimulating his readers' critical faculties rather than merely diverting them. Among his more important substantive contributions was the systematic investigation of the cinema in social terms, which culminated in his widely read series "The Small Shopgirls Go to the Movies,"[23] written in 1927. Except for an isolated article by the Expressionist Kurt Pinthus in 1913,[24] Kracauer's pieces were the first in Germany to analyze the film from a social perspective. From a stylistic point of view, Kracauer's innovation was equally significant, reversing as it did one of the central weaknesses of the *feuilleton* as a genre. The *feuilleton* had its origins in the July Monarchy in Paris, when advertising had expanded the market for newspapers by lowering prices.[25] It served as a lure for new subscribers by printing gossip, intrigues, and serialized novels. By the turn of the century, especially in Vienna where it reached its greatest popularity under Theodor Herzl in the *Neue Freie Presse*, the *feuilleton* had become an occasion for the self-indulgence of personal impressions. As a recent historian has observed, "the subjective response of the reporter or critic to an experience, his feeling-tone, acquired clear primacy over the matter of his discourse. To render a state of feeling became the mode of formulating a judgement. Accordingly, in the *feuilleton* writer's style, the adjectives engulfed the nouns, the personal tint virtually obliterated the contours of the object of discourse."[26] This was the style, it might be noted in passing, that had aroused the ire of that scourge of Viennese decadence Karl Kraus, who denounced its narcissism and duplicity. Although there is no evidence of Kraus's scorn having had a direct effect on him, Kracauer filled the *feuilleton* page with pieces of a very different kind. Instead of drawing attention to his own quivering sensibility, he assumed a tone of ironic naiveté that allowed the material to speak for itself. Somewhat in the manner of the *Neue Sachlichkeit* (New Objectivity) style, which grew to prominence in Weimar's post-expressionist middle period, he maintained a cool, if clearly ironic, detachment towards his subject matter. From Simmel and the phenomenologists, he gained an attentiveness

---

23 "Die kleinen Ladenmachen gehen ins Kino," reprinted in *Das Ornament der Masse*. 1927.
24 Kurt Pinthus, "Quo Vaids—Kino?" cited in Karsten Witte's excellent *Nachwort* to Kracauer's *Kino* (Frankfurt a.M.: Suhrkamp, 1974), 266.
25 Walter Benjamin treated the early years of the *feuilleton* in Paris in his unfinished *Passagenarbeit*; see the selection in his *Charles Baudelaire: A Lyric Poet in the Era of High Capitalism*, trans. Harry Zohn (London: New Left Books, 1973), 27–34.
26 Carl Schorske, "Politics and the Psyche in fin-de-siècle Vienna; Schnitzler and Hofmannstahl," *American Historical Review* 116, no. 4 (July 1961): 935. For a more recent appraisal of the role of the *feuilleton* in Vienna, see Allen Janik and Stephen Toulmin, *Wittgenstein's Vienna* (New York: Simon and Schuster, 1973).

to the things themselves, which reinforced his architect's sensitivity to the visual world. But underlying his distance from the material he described was a subterranean fury at the irrationalities of Weimar life, which he saw embodied in such diverse phenomena, as the waiting room of an employment office or the reception given to the Tiller girls, those "ornaments of the masses" whose precision dancing reflected the disenchantment of the modern world.[27] Kracauer's attitude towards this trend was ambivalent; although he applauded its progressive, de-mythologizing side, he recognized the costs of social standardization and atomization. Moreover, as we shall see shortly, he identified many of its worst aspects with capitalism.

Throughout the twenties, Kracauer's reputation and influence steadily increased. For example, his advocacy in 1929 of the Soviet documentaries of Dziga Vertov and Esther Schub led to their popularity in Germany and ultimately in the USSR as well.[28] In retrospect, 1930 appears as the year of his greatest success. The *FZ* offered him directorship of the cultural section of its Berlin office, and anxious to be at the center of Weimar life, he accepted. In the same year, his study of the harried lower-middle classes, which had been serialized in the *FZ* the year before, was published in book form to generally favourable reviews.[29] *Die Angestellten: Aus dem neuesten Deutschland* dealt with more than 3,500,000 members of the recently enlarged white-collar sector of the working population, the group whose vulnerabilities the Nazis were to exploit with such fervor. Caught between the inexorable rationalization of industrial production, which rendered their positions precarious, and the fear of lowering their status through an identification with blue-collar proletarians, the *Angestellten* were fair game for political manipulation. Kracauer's most trenchant passages dealt with the weaknesses of *Angestelltenkultur*, which made this manipulation possible. Here, an earlier diatribe against the *Tat* circle's *völkisch* ideology gained new urgency because of the clear evidence of its widespread success. Protesting against vulgar Marxist assumption that the unemployed *Angestellten* would soon join their working-class brethren, Kracauer pointed out that lacking an ideological faith, they were spiritu-

---

27 Siegfried Kracauer, "Über Arbeitsnachweise," reprinted in *Straßen in Berlin und Anderswo*, and "Das Ornament der Masse," reprinted in the collection with the same title.
28 Lacis, *Revolutionär im Beruf*, 63. The crucial article was "Der Mann mit dem Kinoapparat," *FZ*, May 19, 1929, reprinted in *Kino*.
29 Siegfried Kracauer, *Die Angestellten: Aus dem neuesten Deutschland*, 1st and 2nd ed. (Frankfurt a.M.: Frankfurter Societäts-Druckerei, 1930); 3rd ed. (Bonn and Allensbach: Verlag für Demoskopie, 1959), with an introduction by Erich Peter Neumann; 4th ed. (Berlin: Suhrkamp, 1970); 5th ed. in vol. 1 of *Schriften*, and as separate book with review by Walter Benjamin appended.

ally, as well as often materially, homeless. The condition he had described in general terms in *Sociologie als Wissenschaft*, that Lukácsian "transcendental homelessness"[30] expressed in the modern novel, was now understood to be especially apparent in the lower-middle class, or new *Mittelstand*.

Apart from its substantive value, which helped inspire a widely read novel dealing with the same theme—Hans Fallada's *What Now, Little Man?*[31]— *Die Angestellten* broke new methodological ground. Based on the qualitative evaluation and reconstruction of a number of interviews with Berlin white-collar workers, the book pioneered a technique the Lynds were developing in America at approximately the same time in their study of *Middletown*,[32] a technique known as participant observation. Kracauer made no pretense of polling the average mentality of the people whose values he was investigating. "Reality," he argued "is construction,"[33] consisting of a mosaic of different observations. In a letter to Adorno, he spelled out the significance of his approach:

> I consider the work methodologically very important in so far as it constitutes a new form of presentation, one which does not juggle between the general theory and special practice. However, it presents its own special way of observation. It is, if you will, an example of materialist dialectics. Analogous cases are the analyses of situations by Marx and Lenin, which are excluded by Marxism as we know it today.[34]

Although difficult to emulate, Kracauer's method did produce a striking evocation of the *Angestellten* dilemma, which repays reading today, despite the large amount of subsequent work on the same subject.[35]

If 1930 saw Kracauer at the height of his public fame, it was also the year of perhaps his most important personal decision. On March 5th, at the age of 41, he ended his long bachelorhood and married Anna Elisbeth (Lili) Ehrenreich, then a librarian at the Institut für Sozialforschung in Frankfurt. Before his marriage, Kracauer's strongest personal attachment seems to have

---

30 One of the chapters in *Die Angestellten* is called as "Asyl fur Obdachlose," which echoes the phrase "transcendentale Obdachlosigkeit," a frequent refrain in *Die Theorie des Romans*.
31 Hans Fallada, *What Now, Little Man?*, trans. E. Sutton (London: Simon and Schuster, 1933).
32 R.S. and H.M. Lynd, *Middletown...Contemporary American Culture* (London: Harcourt Brace, 1929).
33 *Die Angestellten*, 216 in *Schriften* 1.
34 Kracauer to Adorno, May 25, 1930.
35 See the bibliography in Fritz Croner, *Soziologie der Angestellten* (Cologne: Kiepenheuer & Witsch, 1962).

been a platonically erotic bond with Adorno, fourteen years his junior.[36] Lili Kracauer was almost 37 at the time of her marriage, born a Catholic in Strasbourg when it was part of the Second German Reich. She studied art history and philology in Strasbourg and Leipzig before the war and was beginning to study music at the Leipzig conservatory when the post-war inflation forced her to take the Institut job. From all indications, it was an extraordinarily successful match with Lili Kracauer sharing her husband's intellectual interests and helping with his work until her death in 1971. To Kracauer, she was "the greatest happiness of my existence."[37] They remained inseparable for thirty-six years, except for the short period when Kracauer was interned in France in 1940.

And yet, despite the personal and professional success Kracauer enjoyed in 1930, he still remained very much the "extraterritorial" intellectual. As already noted, spiritual homelessness was a theme which ran throughout his writings in the Weimar period, mocking the myth of the "Golden Twenties." When attempts were made to transcend the meaninglessness of modern life—whether religious, in the case of Buber of Scheler, or political, in the case of the *völkisch Tat* circle[38] or Lukács—Kracauer treated them with scorn. Similarly, the then current *Wissenschaftskrise*, that collapse of historicism into relativism which Troeltsch and Weber had confronted but not resolved, was impervious to correction through solely mythological means. Kracauer reasoned:

> Not from science itself or with the help of philosophical speculation may the [...] crisis of science be resolved; its overcoming demands instead a real departure from the entire spiritual situation [...] Annihilation of relativistic thinking, blocking of vision against the infinite without bounds: that is all tied to a *complete change in the entire essence of reality*—and perhaps not only in it alone.[39]

---

36 Leo Löwenthal has remarked on this aspect of the Adorno–Kracauer friendship. In a letter to Adorno on December 10, 1962, Kracauer speaks of "reawaking the old Platonic eros" in connection with the writer Alexander Kluge. Before the war, Kracauer's closest friend was Otto Heinebach, who was the model for the character named Otto in *Ginster*. He died in the fighting (Letter from Lili Kracauer to Hans G. Helms, March 10, 1970).
37 Kracauer to Löwenthal, January 3, 1964.
38 "Aufruhr der Mittelschichten," in *FZ*, December 10 and 11, 1931; reprinted in *Das Ornament der Masse*.
39 "Die Wissenschaftskrise," in *FZ*, March 8 and 22, 1923; reprinted in *Das Ornament der Masse*, 208.

In fact, what gave Kracauer much of his success in the Weimar period was his willingness to face the dilemmas besetting Germany without illusions. Success did not signify an end to his "extra-territoriality" so much as his ability to speak for others with similar situations.

No better expression of Kracauer's continuing personal estrangement can be found than *Ginster*, the semi-autobiographical novel that he published without affixing his name in 1928. Although, it would be hazardous to draw overly precise parallels between Kracauer and his main character, it is clear that he exploited many of his own experiences and attitudes in writing the novel. Set in the vacuous world of the petit-bourgeoise, *Ginster* traces the attempts of one of its inhabitants to confront the idiocy of the First World War. Its hero, if the name is really applicable, is known simply by his nickname, Ginster, which means a type of shrub that grows by the side of railroad tracks. He is shown as a somewhat naive and passive victim of forces he cannot understand, although he musters the cunning to survive them. Trained, like his creator, as an architect, his uneventful and aimless life is interrupted by the war and the threat of conscription. He avoids the army for two years, but is finally drafted only to be released a few weeks later after starving himself into collapse. After he returns to civilian life, his existence resumes its meaningless ramble without Ginster having learned a great deal from his experience. His opposition to the war had been more visceral than ideological at the start and remains so at the end. No *Bildungsroman*, *Ginster* is written in a restrained, bittersweet, laconic style, that would place it as a product of the *Neue Sachlichkeit*, if not for the frequent flashes of surrealistic energy that indicate Kracauer's impatience with pure objectivity. Ginster reacts, but when he does so it is without any real introspective growth. Unlike Kracauer himself, he fails to transcend the world of the architect to become a writer with the power to give his life at least aesthetic order. An aura of melancholy pervades the novel, although its final chapter, which was unaccountably dropped from the 1963 re-edition, can be read in a somewhat optimistic way.[40]

Kracauer manages, however, to maintain a consistently critical tension in the work by juxtaposing Ginster's obviously underplayed reactions and the horrors of bourgeois life and the war which demand a more vigorous response. Included among his targets is his uncle, who had died in 1924. Kracauer gently, although pointedly, satirizes him as an archivist incapable of

---

40   Helms has stressed this in his essay on Kracauer.

connecting his fascination with the past to the problems of the present. In contrast to Ginster, his attitude towards the war is that of a superpatriot, who would "give up his entire Middle Ages for the occupied piece of land, and become the Fatherland in person."[41]

Although never achieving the notoriety of Erich Maria Remarque's *All Quiet on the Western Front*, *Ginster* ranks as one of Weimar's most effective fictional exposés of the insanity of the war and the society that spawned it. That Kracauer chose to publish it anonymously reveals much about the status of anti-war writing in the last years of the republic. Publicly lauded by Thomas Mann, Joseph Roth, Hermann Kesten, and Hermann Hesse, Kracauer was proudest of the private praise he received from Alban Berg, whose letter of December 12, 1928, he cherished throughout his life. To Berg, *Ginster* was "not only a literary masterpiece, but also, in the truest sense of the word, a human document [...]. Something appears that always seems to me as the ideal condition of a work of art, which I have found only in the most infrequent cases." Many years later, Adorno would concur with this judgment, calling the book Kracauer's "most meaningful achievement."[42]

With all the critical energies underlying Kracauer's work in the last half-decade of the Weimar period, it is not surprising that he was drawn into the orbit of the leftist opposition to the Republic. But here too, he remained an extraterritorial man, isolated from the dominant currents of radicalism. Judging from a biting satire of the post-war revolution in Osnabruck near the end of *Ginster*, Kracauer had not been caught up in the utopian climate of the early 1920s. And he consistently avoided any flirtation with the various parties of the left that survived those years. Nor did he regularly contribute to leftist publications, choosing instead to remain with the staunchly bourgeois *FZ*, even during its swing to the right. His attitude towards the Soviet experiment seems to have turned sour at an early point in its history. In short, he remained very much on the margins of Weimar's left-wing life. As an intellectual, he had no illusions about his qualifications as a potential proletarian. In the introduction to *Die Angestellten*, he wrote: "The intellectuals are either themselves employees, or they are free, and then the employees are uninteresting to them because of their routineness (*Alltäglichkeit*). The radical intellectuals also do not easily come behind the exotica of the everyday."[43] Kra-

---

41 Kracauer, *Ginster*, 2nd ed., 48.
42 Theodor W. Adorno, "Der wunderliche Realist," 98.
43 Kracauer, *Die Angestellten*, 212 in *Schriften* 1.

cauer's hope in that work was to awaken the consciousness of intellectuals to the condition of the white-collar workers. His target was the glib assumption of certain vulgar Marxists that this potentially dangerous stratum of society would join the working class. Just as he warned against the subsumption of the *Angestellten* under a simplified bipolar class rubric, Kracauer resisted the integration of the critical intellectual into any one movement or party.

This general stance was shared by the men who formed his closest friendships during the Weimar period: Theodor W. Adorno, Walter Benjamin, Ernst Bloch, and Leo Löwenthal. Like Kracauer they were all unaffiliated and experimental leftists who could have merited Benjamin's description of Kracauer's "consistent outsiderness."[44] All were fascinated by cultural questions more than economic ones and had little patience with the mechanistic economism of the Second International orthodoxy. Kracauer was less interested in high art than Adorno or Löwenthal, less drawn to religious questions than Banjamin or Bloch, but he shared with them a common vocabulary and general outlook. As friends, they avidly read each other's work, often reviewing them with an appreciative, if not always uncritical eye.[45] On certain occasions, one would complain about the appearance of his ideas in the writings of another,[46] and in fact, it is difficult to establish whose claim to originality in many cases.

Stylistically, they were also relatively similar, although Bloch's Expressionist prose was all his own. The similarity rested in their frequent reliance on short, aphoristic evocations to make a philosophically laden point. Benjamin's *Einbahnstrasse*, Bloch's *Spuren*, and Adorno's *Minima Moralia* all bear comparison with Kracauer's *feuilleton* pieces in the FZ.

---

44 Walter Benjamin, "Politisierung der Intelligenz," reprinted in *Die Angestellten*, 5th ed. not in *Schriften*, 118.

45 Among the reviews are the following: Kracauer review of Bloch's *Thomas Munzer als Theologe der Revolution* in FZ, August 2, 1922; Kracauer of Benjamin's *Ursprung des deutschen Trauerspiels* and *Einbahnstrasse* in FZ, July 15, 1928, reprinted in *Das Ornament der Masse*; Kracauer of Adorno's *Kierkegaard: Konstruktion des Aesthetischen*, written for FZ, but not printed because of the Nazi takeover; Bloch of Kracauer's *Die Angestellten* in *Neue Rundschau* 41, no. 12 (December, 1930) and in *Erbschaft dieser Zeit* (Frankfurt a.M.: Suhrkamp, 1962); Benjamin of Kracauer's *Die Angestellten* (see above footnote); Benjamin of Adorno's Kierkegaard in *Vossische Zeitung* (April 2, 1933; and Adorno of Kracauer's *Jacques Offenbach und das Paris seiner Zeit* in *Zeitschrift für Sozialforschung* 6, no. 3 (1937).

46 See, for example, Benjamin's complaint to Gershom Scholem that many of the ideas in Kracauer's critique of the Buber–Rosenzweig translation of the Bible were his. Letter to Scholem, March 29, 1926, in Walter Benjamin, *Briefe*, ed. Gershom Scholem and Theodor W. Adorno, 2 vols. (Frankfurt a.M.: Suhrkamp, 1966), p. 429. Many of the same ideas were later to play a prominent role in Adorno's attack on Heidegger in *Jargon of Authenticity*, trans. Kurt Tarnowski and Frederic Will (Evanston, IL: Northwestern University Press, 1973), as Adorno acknowledged in a letter to Kracauer (July 22, 1963).

Where they perhaps most strikingly differed was in their attitude towards the revolution in Marxist theory signalled by the appearance of Lukács's *History and Class Consciousness* and Karl Korsch's *Marxism and Philosophy* in 1923. Bloch and Adorno, although not entirely in agreement with the Hegelianized Marxism posited by those works, were far more favourable than Benjamin, Löwenthal, or Kracauer. Kracauer's interest in Simmel and Scheler had reinforced his strong distrust of the idealism so prevalent in the neo-Kantian prewar period. In fact, his general attitude towards metaphysical speculation was such that Benjamin could call him an "enemy of philosophy"[47] in 1923. If he did have a philosophical interest in the early 1920s, it was in the work of the master anti-Hegelian, Søren Kierkegaard, whose impact is clear on Kracauer's ambitious investigation of the detective novel, which has only recently been published.[48]

Although Kracauer had endorsed Lukács's diagnosis of the meaninglessness of the modern world in *Theory of the Novel*, he was far less willing to accept the solution implicit in Lukács conversion to Communism. An unpublished manuscript on "the Concept of Man in Marx," directed against Lukács, was lost during the emigration, but his argument has largely survived in a series of letters to Bloch during the mid-twenties. On May 27, 1926, he wrote:

> It seems to me that [Lukács] has attacked empty and worn out idealism, but instead of transcending it, has fallen into it again. His concept of totality, if despairing of its own formality, has more similarity to Lask than Marx. Instead of penetrating Marx with realities, he returns to the Spirit (*Geist*) and metaphysics of exhausted idealism and allows the materialist categories to fall on the way. [...] Rudas and Deborin [the Soviet philosophers who attacked Lukács], however disgustingly shallow they may be, unconsciously are correct against Lukács in many things. [...] He is philosophically—a reactionary; please think of his concept of personality.

After a return letter from Bloch, in which Lukács's materialist credentials were defended and the characterization of him as a reactionary was found wanting,[49] Kracauer replied on June 29:

---

47 Quoted in Adorno, "Der Wunderliche Realist," 86.
48 Siegfried Kracauer, *Der Detektiv-Roman: Ein philosphischer Traktat* in *Schriften* 1. For references to Kierkegaard, see 107–109.
49 Bloch to Kracauer, June 6, 1926. I am indebted to Karsten Witte for drawing my attention to the lost manuscript underlying the Lukács debate.

I spoke with [Korsch] in the Reichstag in January [1926] about Lukács. He approved of my arguments in general and explained that only out of very weighty tactical reasons did he intend to remain silent[...] . Through his reception of Hegel, Lukács covers the actual source of Marx's fundamental concepts in a fateful way. Marx comes, more decisively than Lukács presents and perhaps knows, from the French Enlightenment and, to be sure, from one branch of the Enlightenment that goes back to Locke and is represented by the names Helvetius and Holbach; that is, decisive categories of Marxism, such as the concept of "Man" or "Morality" can be understood only if one builds a tunnel under the massive mountain of Hegel to Marx and Helvetius. [...] Had Lukács seen clearer, it would have not been possible in the final chapter of his book, which dealt with organization, to introduce a bad concept of personality. [...] I would really like to know where, according to your conviction, Lukács' materialist intention can be placed. There is no room in the progress of this formal dialectic, which so smoothly leads to an empty totality. I can name many sentences in Marx which judge this dialectic. It means a regression behind Marx.

Although finishing with a positive appraisal of the brilliance of some of Lukács's passages on reification, Kracauer clearly rejected the basic burden of Lukács's argument. His distrust of totality, concern for the integrity of the individual personality, and adherence to the Enlightenment view of materialism informed all of his later work as well. In *Die Angestellten*, for example, he was to write of a "hunger for immediacy that without a doubt is the consequence of the undernourishment produced by German idealism."[50] Politically, his critique of *History and Class Consciousness*, especially of its advocacy of personal realization through submission to the will of the party led in one direction: "I am in the last analysis," he wrote Bloch, "an anarchist, to be sure sceptical enough to consider anarchism as it exists as a distorter of its intentions."[51] As Lili Kracauer would acknowledge after her husband's death, all forms of conformity, including solidarity with the working class movement and its parties, were anathema to him.[52]

What is, however, also significant in this correspondence is Kracauer's appeal to Marx, as he interpreted him, against Lukács. His self-image as a de-

50 Kracauer, *Die Angestellten*, 216.
51 Kracauer to Bloch, June 29, 1926.
52 Lili Kracauer to Hans G. Helms, June 19, 1970.

fender of Marxism during the late Weimar period is apparent in an exchange he had with Bloch in 1932, after he published a critical review of Brecht's film *Kuhle Wampe*.[53] Bloch was outraged by the review and its placement in the bourgeois *FZ*; he claimed Kracauer has a personal bias against Brecht (which was true, as several of his letters reveal)[54] and argued that he had abandoned his militancy of only a short time before. There were no classless intellectuals, Bloch warned. Kracauer responded with equal indignation, arguing that whatever his personal feelings towards Brecht, he had never allowed them to interfere with his critical judgment. As for writing for the *FZ*, he remarked that his reputation as an "enemy of the bourgeoisie" was known to all and that writing in a non-Marxist paper gave his words greater public impact. The accusation that he had repudiated his militancy was also nonsense: "I have advocated Marxism visibly enough and more than others and will continue to advocate it in a way that corresponds to my talents and energies and with growing influence on the general development."

This view of Kracauer as militant was also expressed in Benjamin's review of *Die Angestellten*,[55] which Kracauer always praised. The book, Benjamin argued, was a "signpost on the road to the politicization of the intellectuals [...]. This indirect influence is the only one that a revolutionary writer from the bourgeoisie can have today. Direct effectiveness can only come from praxis." Kracauer was a "rag-picker" in the "dawn of a revolutionary day." The characterization of rag-picker was one Kracauer always liked,[56] but unlike Benjamin, his faith in the dawning of a revolutionary day soon wavered. In more recent years, the nature of his radicalism has been debated by Adorno and Hans G. Helms, the former concerned about a growing conformity in his work, the latter anxious to maintain its radical impetus as long as possible.[57]

---

53 Bloch to Kracauer, April 29, 1931; Kracauer to Bloch, May 29, 1932. The review appeared in the *FZ* on April 5, 1932.
54 In a letter to Adorno, written on December 21, 1930, Kracauer wrote of a meeting with Brecht: "Once the conversation turned to theoretical matters, one had the feeling of talking with a school boy (*Obertertianer*). The craziest is that some people are taken in by this inverted Romanticism, whose brutality is possible only in a national socialist country. For Benjamin I have explanations, for others I don't." In a letter to Bloch on July 5, 1934, he made sarcastic remarks about Benjamin's trip to his "God" in Denmark (where Brecht was in exile) and said that Kafka would be astonished to learn that his work was so close to Brecht's and Communism (as Benjamin had asserted).
55 See fn. 44. Kracauer's appreciation is expressed in a letter to Erika Lorenz, October 22, 1961.
56 Ibid., 122. Benjamin did not choose the phrase "rag-picker" idly. It was a key concept in the understanding of nineteenth-century Paris and Baudelaire, who wrote a prose-poem about the figure. See Benjamin, *Charles Baudelaire*, 19–20 and 79–80.
57 See fns. 2 and 15. Helms demonstrates how the recent publication history of Kracauer's works, especially the first German translation of *From Caligari to Hitler* and the second edition of *Ginster*, helped mute his earlier radicalism.

Although Adorno's perception has been borne out by Kracauer's most recent work, Helms has successfully drawn attention to the extent of Kracauer's radicalism during the Weimar period. The correspondence with Bloch quoted above, which could not be examined when Helms wrote, confirms his case. So too does a remark Kracauer's friend and colleague on the FZ, the Austrian novelist Joseph Roth made to Stefan Zweig in 1930; Kracauer, he wrote, "is one of those Jehovah-Jews, Marxism is his bible; the eastern Jews have a name for these people: God's policemen."[58]

For all his Marxist rhetoric and intentions, however, it is clear that Kracauer was more a member of Weimar's celebrated "homeless left" than any established Marxist movement. *Die Angestellten* candidly admits that "the work is a diagnosis and as such consciously refuses to make suggestions for improvements."[59] Although Kracauer ends the text with the ringing words, "It does not depend on the institutions being changed, it depends on men changing the institutions,"[60] how this is to be accomplished is never determined. Thus, one might say that despite his increasing celebrity during the waning Weimar years, he remained very much an extraterritorial figure in political terms.

In yet another way, Kracauer remained an insecure and marginal intellectual. During the twenties, the lion's share of Kracauer's energies was spent in preparing his *feuilleton* columns, which were usually thrown out with the next day's trash. To a man of his philosophical and cultural ambitions, the ephemeral nature of his writings was a source of considerable chagrin, which he expressed in a letter to Adorno in 1930.[61] Other journalists such as Tucholsky and Ossietsky of the *Weltbühne* praised his work and tried to entice him into their circle, but he refused.[62] In later years, he would reject comparisons with them, just as he would bristle at the label of journalist.[63] But without a proper academic connection, Kracauer was never really accepted in the scholarly world either. In the twenties, several manuscripts, including his highly speculative study of the detective novel, went unpublished because

---

58 Joseph Roth, *Briefe*, 1911–39, ed. Hermann Kesten, (Cologne and Berlin: Kiepenheuer Witsch, 1970), 175.
59 Kracauer, *Die Angestellten*, 207.
60 Ibid., 304.
61 Kracauer to Adorno, July 22, 1930.
62 Letters from Tucholsky to Kracauer, March 4, 1927, and Ossietsky to Kracauer, July 7, 1929. Tucholsky, who lived in Paris, was very enthusiastic about Kracauer's descriptions of Parisian life. Ossietsky wrote positively about *Ginster*.
63 Kracauer to Erika Lorenz, March 31, 1962.

they fell between two stools. Philosophers were uninterested in his subject matter and readers of detective novels had no patience with his method.

Ultimately, however, Kracauer's fears were to prove unfounded as collections of his early work appeared in German.[64] And now thanks to the efforts of Siegfried Unseld of the Suhrkamp Verlag and Karsten Witte, who is preparing a major biography of Kracauer, his collected works are in the process of being published. Included in the seven volume series is Kracauer's second novel, *Georg*, written in 1934, but prevented from publication because of Kracauer's emigration from Germany. A social critique of the waning years of the Republic cantering around a newspaper editor, *Georg* was warmly praised by no less a figure than Thomas Mann while still in manuscript,[65] but attempts to place it with a Dutch publishing house were unsuccessful. Unlike some of his other manuscripts, however, it survived his sudden departure from Germany in March of 1933, after the burning of the Reichstag and shortly before some of Kracauer's own books were burned in the famous conflagration of May 10.

Kracauer was already in Paris when a letter came from the Frankfurter-Societats-Druckerei on August 25 informing him that his tenure with the *FZ* was at an end. The pretext was an article he had written for the left-wing *Das Neue Tage-buch*,[66] but it is clear that Kracauer had no place in the *FZ*'s future, which reached its nadir in 1939, when Max Amann presented it to Hitler as a birthday present. Still, Kracauer did not relish the exile that awaited him; in September, Benjamin reported to Brecht that he was still very depressed by the change.[67] From a position of power and prestige, he was reduced to freelance writing in a hostile environment. In his last work on history, when much of the pain had passed, Kracauer remarked on the condition of the emigré, who was like a palimpsest composed of different cultural superimpositions. Here, the ambivalence of his attitude towards extraterritoriality was clear:

> As he settles elsewhere, all those loyalties, expectations, and aspirations that comprise so large a part of his being are automatically cut off from their roots. His life history is disrupted, his "natural" self relegated to the

---

64 See fns. 12 and 16.
65 On December 8, 1934, Mann wrote to Kracauer that "the high literary qualities of your grand picture of society have not failed to make their impression on me." See Karsten Witte, *Nachwort* to *Schriften*, 7, 505.
66 The article, a review of an American film, was called "The Charlatan as President." It has been reprinted in *Kino*, 221–3.
67 Benjamin, *Briefe*, vol. 2, 62.

background of his mind [...] since the self he was continues to smolder beneath the person he is about to become, his identity is bound to be in a state of flux; and the odds are that he will never fully belong to the community to which he now in a way belongs. [...] Where then does he live? In the near-vacuum of extra-territoriality. The exile's true mode of existence is that of a stranger.[68]

In Paris, Kracauer supported himself by writing film criticism and book reviews for Swiss newspapers, such as the *Basler National-Zeitung* and the *Neue Zürcher Zeitung*, and for French journals like the *Revue du Cinéma*, *Mercure de France*, *La Vie Intellectuelle*, and *Figaro*. *Ginster* was translated into French by Clara Malraux, at that time the wife of the novelist. Although gaining him a reputation in Parisian intellectual circles, the translation brought in very little income. Most of his efforts were directed towards the publication of a book that would help him stay above water. His subject was a German Jew of an earlier era who had also lived in exile, albeit voluntarily, in Paris, Jacques Offenbach.

In 1937, *Jacques Offenbach and His Time* was published in German, French, and English editions.[69] Rather than the conventional life and works study, Kracauer attempted a "Social Biography" that paid as much attention to Second Empire Paris as to Offenbach himself. Continuing his interest in marginal cultural phenomena, he probed the world of the operetta and the related milieus of boulevard and journalistic society, where the deracinated modern man ruled supreme. The operetta, he argued, had "originated in an epoch in which social reality had been banished by the Emperor's orders";[70] its phantasmagorical quality mirrored the illusory nature of Napoleon's reign, where class conflict was only apparently overcome. But for all its escapist tendencies, it fulfilled a critical function during the Empire's most repressive period: "At a time when the bourgeoisie were politically stagnant and the Left was

---

68 Siegfried Kracauer, *History: The Last Things Before the Last* (New York: Markus Wiener, 1969), 83.
69 Siegfried Kracauer, *Jacques Offenbach und das Paris seiner Zeit* (Amsterdam: Allert de Lange, 1937); 2nd ed. as *Pariser Leben: Jacques Offenbach und seine Zeit* (Munich: List, 1962); *Jacques Offenbach ou le secret du Second Empire*, with a preface by Daniel Halevy, (Paris: Le promeneur, 1937); *Orpheus in Paris: Offenbach and the Paris of his Time*, trans. Gwenda David and Eric Mosbacher (New York: Columbia University Press, 1939). The English edition dropped Kracauer's foreword without explanation.
70 Kracauer, *Orpheus in Paris*, 289.

impotent, Offenbach's operettas had been the most definite form of revolutionary protest."[71]

Although a massively researched and fluidly written study, which successfully conveys the flavor of the period it examined, *Offenbach* was a less penetrating work than Walter Benjamin's *Passagenarbeit*, the unfinished project that dealt with much the same subject matter.[72] It lacked Benjamin's conceptual daring and breadth of vision and broke no new ground in probing the commodity form in bourgeois society, as had the *Passagenarbeit*. Although clearly indebted to Marx's *Eighteenth Brumaire*, *Offenbach* was no real landmark in Marxist cultural criticism, as Benjamin's work has come to be seen. Perhaps its greatest weakness, as Adorno predictably pointed out in a mixed review,[73] was its failure to deal directly with Offenbach's music, focusing instead on the libretti of Halévy and the general atmosphere surrounding the operetta world. Among Kracauer's major works, it is perhaps the least likely to justify our current interest in him.

Although the appearance of *Offenbach* lessened his financial burden somewhat, it was clear by 1938 that continued life in Paris was intolerable. With the growing threat of war and the lack of real opportunities to get a foothold in French society, emigration to America seemed the only solution. Although certain friends, such as Benjamin and Joseph Roth, remained in Paris, others, including Bloch, Adorno, and Löwenthal, were already in America or about to depart. The next three years were spent in a grim and frantic struggle to obtain the proper papers for the emigration. Reading his correspondence of those years is a painful experience, revealing as it does the desperation that Kracauer and doubtless many others felt in their desire to leave. In the light of his later disdain for filming historical dramas, it is a mark of his plight that on April 5, 1939, he wrote to the Hollywood producer Max Leammle to ask about the possibility of filming his *Offenbach*.

In 1939, some aid was given by the American Guild for German Cultural Freedom, but only for three months. Kracauer's best hope at that time was the Institut für Sozialforschung, which had resettled in New York in 1934. In 1937–8, he had worked on a commissioned study of "Totalitarian Propaganda: A Political Treatise" for the Institut's *Zeitschrift für Sozialforschung*, but Adorno's editorial emendations were of such magnitude that he withdrew

71 Ibid.
72 See fn. 25.
73 See fn. 45.

it in disgust. Nonetheless, Kracauer continued to hope that his friendships with Löwenthal and Adorno would lead to Institut support, even though he had never had very cordial relations with Max Horkheimer, the Institut's director. In the late thirties, however, the Institut suffered serious financial reversals that severely curtailed its ability to help other refugees. Still, Kracauer maintained his hopes even as he sailed for America and his disappointment was proportionately keen.[74]

Institut members, in particular Leo Löwenthal, were instrumental, however, in obtaining the necessary affidavits which allowed Kracauer to emigrate. Also helpful in this regard were Meyer Schapiro, the distinguished art historian, Iris Barry of the Museum of Modern Art's Film Library, and Varian Fry, who helped secure his release from the Centre de Rassemblement into which he had been put at the war's outbreak. In March of 1941, he left Paris for Lisbon and then on April 15, he and his wife set sail for New York on the Niassa; they arrived ten days later. His state of mind at this time can be seen in the letters he continued to send to Institut figures for help. To Adorno, he wrote that his time in Paris had been "eight years of an existence that doesn't deserve that name. I have grown older, also inside me. Now is the last station, the last chance that I don't dare misplay or else everything is lost."[75] To Friedrich Pollock, the Institut's Associate Director, he wrote of his anxiety, "anxiety at beginning with nothing that I can call my own and perhaps without a chance at the start."[76] Kracauer's situation was certainly not enviable, but at least, unlike Walter Benjamin and many others, he was alive to try to make a new start in America. At the age 52, Kracauer still had his most influential work ahead of him.

✖

Although disappointed by the Institut, Kracauer was fortunate to have found a sponsor with the Museum of Modern Art, where Alfred Barr and Iris Barry were making the serious study of film respectable. In subsequent years, grants from the Rockefeller, Guggenheim, Bollingen, and Mellon Foundations made his financial survival possible. Lili Kracauer continued to do research for her

---

74 Conversation with Henry Pachter, New York, September 4, 1973; Pachter was on the same ship as Kracauer.
75 Kracauer to Adorno, March 28, 1941.
76 Kracauer to Pollock, March 28, 1941.

husband, but also worked for the Central Location Index, which helped in the search for displaced persons in Europe. Their combined income, in addition to a compensatory stipend paid by the German government in the 1950s, prevented a repetition of the last years in Paris.

Kracauer's first project with the museum was a study of Nazi war propaganda. Bernard Karpel, the museum's film librarian, remembers him camped in the projection room watching films over and over again, smoking foul cigars, and bemoaning his diminished status.[77] The result was "Propaganda and the Nazi War Film," published in 1942.[78] Analysing both the form and content of the Nazi films, with a long and penetrating look at Leni Riefenstahl's *Triumph of the Will*, Kracauer came to a conclusion about the contrived nature of pseudo-documentaries that anticipated his later argument in *Theory of Film*: "Most films of fact affect audiences not so much through the organization of their material as through the material itself. [...] The two Nazi campaign films differ from them in that they not only excel in solid composition of their elements, but also exploit all propagandistic effects which may be produced by the very structure."[79] Kracauer was especially interested in the Nazis' perverse use of the montage techniques developed by the Russian directors of the 1920s to a fine art. Another argument foreshadowing his later position concerned the relative absence of anti-Jewish activities in the films he viewed, which suggested the Nazis feared a reaction produced by the direct presentation of their atrocities; "The image," he wrote, "seems to be the last refuge of violated human dignity."[80]

For the next five years, Kracauer was occupied with the first book that brought his name to prominence in the American film world, *From Caligari to Hitler; A Psychological History of the German Film*. In 1932, Kracauer had defined the task of the film critic in politically charged terms:

> The film in the capitalist economy is a commodity like other commodities. Apart from a few outsiders, they are produced not in the interest of art or the enlightenment of the masses, but for the sake of the profits they

---

77 Conversation with Bernard Karpel, New York, September 7, 1973.
78 Appended to Siegfried Kracauer, *From Caligari to Hitler* (Princeton: Princeton University Press, 1947).
79 Ibid., 289.
80 Ibid., 305.

promise to yield [...] They exercise extraordinarily important social functions that no film critic, who earns the name, can leave unobserved.[81]

"The film," he wrote six years earlier, "is the mirror of the existing society."[82] These presuppositions still underlay *From Caligari to Hitler*, despite its subtitle's stress on psychology; for Kracauer, the psychic states worth probing were "those deep layers of collective mentality which extend more or less below the dimension of consciousness."[83]

To uncover this subconscious dimension of the collective psyche, Kracauer qualitatively analyzed hundreds of German films, whose immanent development he tried to link to the changing fortunes of the Weimar Republic. Qualitative analysis of German cultural phenomena was in fact a popular occupation in the America of the 1940s, and Kracauer was in the company of other emigré scholars like Ernst Kris.[84] While paying some attention to technical development, such as the increasing use of studio interiors and new lighting techniques, Kracauer focused primarily on plots and significant motifs. His basic conclusion was that the cinema mirrored the shifts in the Republic's history with extraordinary fidelity. Among his most notable discussions was critique of the Expressionist classic, *The Cabinet of Dr. Caligari*, which revealed, for the first time, a reversal of its originally radical script by the director, Robert Wiene. No less significant was his devastating attack on Fritz Lang, then in Hollywood, in whose films Kracauer saw many of the marks of proto-fascism. Even *The Testament of Dr. Marbuse*, which Goebbels banned in 1933, "betrays the power of Nazi spirit over minds insufficiently equipped to counter its peculiar fascination."[85] The result, so a later defender of Lang claimed, was unfortunate: "No one has done more damage to Lang's reputation. [...] Kracauer gives the impression of carrying on a personal feud."[86]

---

81 Siegfried Kracauer, "Über die Aufgabe des Filmkritikers," in *FZ*, May 23, 1932; reprinted in *Kino*, 9.
82 "Die kleinen Ladenmadchen gehen ins Kino," in *Das Ornament der Masse*, 279.
83 *From Caligari to Hitler*, 6. This position marked his approach as early as "Die Kleinen Ladenmadchen gehen ins Kino," where he wrote: "the idiotic and unreal film fantasies are the day dreams of society..." (280, italics in original).
84 Ernst Kris, *German Radio Propaganda* (New York: Oxford University Press, 1944). Kracauer's social psychological approach to fascist behaviour also links him to the work done by his friends at the Institute for Social Research that led to Adorno's *The Authoritarian Personality* (New York: Harper & Brothers, 1950).
85 *From Caligari to Hitler*, 250.
86 Eric Rohde, *Tower of Babel: Speculations on the Cinema* (London: Weidenfeld & Nicholson, 1966), 86.

In general, Kracauer's verdict on the German cinema was strongly negative. As in his Offenbach study, he found a parallel between a mystifying cultural phenomenon and the general prevalence of false consciousness. Even the films of the middle years of the Republic, the "stabilized era" dominated by the *Neue Sachlichkeit*, came under fire. Following a critical reference to the *Neue Sachlichkeit* in *Die Angestellten*,[87] which demonstrated a certain uneasiness about his own "hunger for immediacy," Kracauer argued that "New Objectivity marks a state of paralysis. Cynicism, resignation, disillusionment; these tendencies point to a mentality disinclined to commit itself in any direction."[88] Even G.W. Pabst, whose fidelity to the photographic essence of film Kracauer found laudable, undercut the critical implications of his film through a weakness for melodrama and desire to remain a neutral observer. Here, in other words, was a realistic cinema with problematic political implications, implications which Kracauer was to minimize when he wrote his next major film book. *From Caligari to Hitler* bitterly condemned the German people as a whole with little effort spent on determining which film appealed to which audience: "Irretrievably sunk into retrogression, the bulk of the German people could not help submitting to Hitler. Since Germany thus carried out what had been anticipated by her cinema from its very beginning, conspicuous screen characters now came true in life itself."[89]

As might be expected, the book stirred an enormous critical storm.[90] Its obvious leftist political slant was denounced in a vicious anti-communist review by Seymour Stern, which appeared in several places. Kracauer's method, especially his reliance on "collective soul" was attacked by Franklin Fearing, Hans Sahl, and Eric Bentley, who called the book a "refugee's revenge" in *The New York Times Book Review*. Arthur Schlesinger, Jr. approved of

---

87 *Die Angestellten*, 287. For a Marxist discussion of Kracauer's critique of the *Neue Sachlichkeit*, see Helmut Lethen, *Die Neue Sachlichkeit* (Frankfurt a.M.: Suhrkamp, 1970), esp. 102–5. He attacks Kracauer for remaining a "free-floating intellectual" despite himself. Kracauer's distrust of groups is in fact clearly evident as early as his 1922 essay "Die Gruppe als Ideenträger," reprinted in *Das Ornament der Masse*.
88 Kracauer, *From Caligari to Hitler*, 165.
89 Ibid., 272.
90 Among the reviews were Seymour Stern in the *Los Angeles Daily News* (May 10, 1947) and *The New Leader* (June 28, 1947); Eric Bentley in *The New York Times Book Review* (May 18, 1947); Arthur Schlesinger, Jr. in *The Nation* (July 26, 1947); Richard Griffith in *New Movies* 22, no. 4 (Summer 1947); Franklin Fearing in *Hollywood Quarterly* 2, no. 4 (July 1947); David T. Bazelon in *Commentary* 4, no. 2 (August 1947); Iris Barry in *The New Republic* 116, no. 20 (May 19, 1947); Hans Sahl in *The Modern Review* (August, 1947); Herman G. Weinberg in *Sight and Sound* (Summer 1947); Karl W. Hinckle in *Etc., A Review of General Semantics* 5, no. 2 (Winter 1948); and L.M. Hanks, Jr. in *The Journal of Aesthetics and Art Criticism* 6, no. 2 (December 1947). Robert Warshow wrote a letter to *The New Leader* on August 9, 1947, defending Kracauer against Stern's attack.

Kracauer's conclusions, but argued "that the main trouble, of course, is that Dr. Kracauer knows in advance which dreams panned out." Others worried about the possibility of tracing a similar proto-fascist lineage in non-German cinema, a thought that continued to trouble Adorno as late as the 1960s, when he wrote that *King Kong* could be taken as an allegory of comparable regression in America.[91]

Kracauer was not, however, without his defenders. David T. Bazelon praised his method in *Commentary*; Iris Barry did the same from not a totally disinterested point of view in *The New Republic*, and Richard Griffith called it "the best book on the movies I have ever read" in *New Movies*. Robert Warshow was moved to answer Stern's Red-baiting attack in the *New Leader*'s letter columns and Herman Weinberg did the same in *Sight and Sound*, where he called it "perhaps the greatest book on the film ever written." The controversy has yet to be stilled as the different appreciations of the book in recent works by Peter Gay, I.C. Jarvie, Dieter Prokop, David Stewart Hull, and Michael Schroter illustrate.[92] And devotees of a non-social interpretation of the Weimar cinema still continue to draw sustenance from Lotte H. Eisner's *The Haunted Screen*,[93] originally written in French five years after *From Caligari to Hitler*.

With some distance between us and the book's publication, it seems safe to say that Kracauer's method, as flawed as it surely was, did uncover some remarkable tendencies in the cultural life of the Weimar years that make the collapse of the Republic more plausible. If disputable on certain films and occasionally doctrinaire in tone, *From Caligari to Hitler* nevertheless represents a milestone in the application of a sociological-psychological approach to a mass medium that can scarcely resist it. Although Kracauer's own later work contained certain implicit criticisms of the book, which will be examined shortly, it still deservedly commands the attention of students of both film and fascism.

---

91 Adorno, "Der Wunderliche Realist," 105.
92 Peter Gay's *Weimar Culture* follows Kracauer's judgments closely, but David Stewart Hull's *Film in the Third Reich: A Study of the German Cinema, 1933–1945* (Berkeley and Los Angeles: University of California Press, 1968), is far more critical, calling Kracauer's major thesis "preposterous" (3); I.C. Jarvie, *Towards a Sociology of the Cinema* (London: Routledge, 1970), and Dieter Prokop, *Materialen zur Theorie des Films, Aesthetik, Sociologie, Politik* (Munich: Hanser, 1971) are equally hostile. For a detailed and wide-ranging defense of Kracauer, see Michael Schröter, *Über Siegfried Kracauers Film theorie: Zugleich ein Beitrag zur Angewandte Psychoanalysis* (unpub. Diplomarbeit, Free University of Berlin, 1972).
93 Lotte H. Eisner, *The Haunted Screen: Expressionism in the German Cinema and the Influence of Max Reinhardt*, trans. R. Greaves (Berkeley and Los Angeles: University of California Press, 1969).

Thirteen years passed before Kracauer's next major analysis of the film. In that period, he continued to write film criticism and book reviews, now for American journals like *Harper's*, *Theater Arts*, and *Partisan Review*. He also helped support the efforts of others connected to the film in his new capacity as consultant to the Guggenheim Foundation. Project proposals by Arthur Knight, Robert Warshow, Shirley Clarke, Parker Tyler, Hans Richter, Gregory Markopolous, and others all received Kracauer's endorsement.

But financial considerations compelled Kracauer to direct his energies in less interesting areas. In 1950, Leo Löwenthal, then director of research at the Voice of America, offered his old friend a post as research analyst. Two years later, Kracauer began an association with Columbia University's Bureau of Applied Social Research, founded by Paul Lazarsfeld and headed at the time by Charles Y. Glock. The fruit of these two connections was an empirical study of the thinking of recent refugees from Eastern Europe, prepared in collaboration with Paul L. Berkman. Based on more than 300 interviews conducted in 1951–2 with exiles from Hungary, Poland, and Czechoslovakia, *Satellite Mentality* was published in 1956 under the auspices of the Bureau.[94] When first entering the Bureau, a stronghold of quantitative methods, Kracauer had published a paper defending the virtues of qualitative techniques.[95] *Satellite Mentality* was based on such a methodology, but it lacked the imaginative "construction in the material" that gave *Die Angestellten* its unique power. The conclusions reached by the authors, occasionally couched in Cold War rhetoric, were not very startling, and in later years, Kracauer would regard the book somewhat as an embarrassment.[96]

During the 1950s, the Kracauers had the opportunity to make several trips to Europe for the first time since their departure in 1941. Old friends like Adorno and Bloch had already returned; others like Benno Reifenberg, who helped found and edit the postwar periodical *Die Gegenwart*, were involved in re-establishing the continuities of German culture severed by the Nazis. Although Kracauer was encouraged to join them, like the majority of emigrés to America, he chose to remain in his adopted land where life,

---

94 Kracauer and Paul L. Berkman, *Satellite Mentality: Political Attitudes and Propaganda Susceptibilities of Non-Communists in Hungary, Poland, and Czechoslovakia* (New York: F.A. Praeger, 1956).
95 "The Challenge of Qualitative Content Analysis," *The Public Opinion Quarterly* 16, no. 4 (Winter 1952–53).
96 Kracauer to Erika Lorenz, October 22, 1961.

however "extra-territorial," was preferable to starting anew in Germany. Unlike Adorno, whose disparagement of the undialectical qualities of English is well-known, Kracauer took to his new language with total acceptance. His repudiation of Adorno's position was in fact a sore point between them.[97] In the early forties, he insisted on writing only in English and engaged friends like Bernard Karpel of the Museum of Modern Art to help him. When the editorial corrections of his works in the new language were minor, he was overjoyed, but he must have been equally chagrined when Pauline Kael belittled his English in a long critique of *Theory of Film* in 1962.[98]

If the Kracauers ever considered returning to Germany, their trips quickly disabused them of the notion. The Europeans, he wrote Löwenthal after a three month stay in 1956, "have lost the power of assimilating the new. Somehow it is suffocating over there."[99] "We would die if we had to live again in Germany for good," he wrote two years later; it is a country "frightening in its prosperity, politeness, sham depth and, complete formlessness."[100] And again in 1960: Germany "is no country but a place lying somewhere in a vacuum."[101] Kracauer enjoyed seeing old friends like the publisher, Peter Suhrkamp, the Blochs, the Adornos, and the Malraux's, and welcomed meeting new ones like the philosopher Karl Heinz Haag; but now over sixty, he was clearly loathe to break once again with a relatively comfortable environment.

The environment became more comfortable still when the Bollingen and Chapelbrook Foundations and later the American Philosophical Society awarded him the grants to work on his long planned second book on the cinema. Once again, the Museum of Modern Art put its film library and viewing room at his disposal; additional assistance came from Henri Langlois' Cinémathèque Française in Paris and the British Film Institute in London. In 1960, *Theory of Film: The Redemption of Physical Reality* was published by Oxford University Press.

The book represented the culmination of Kracauer's lifelong fascination with film, which began, so he recalled in his preface, as a child when

---

97 Kracauer to Leo Löwenthal, October 26, 1955; Adorno, "Der Wunderliche Realist," 100. For an implicit endorsement of Kracauer's position, see George Steiner's essay on Nabokov significantly entitled "Extraterritorial," in *Extraterritorial: Papers on Literature and the Language Revolution* (London: Macmillan, 1972).
98 Pauline Kael, "Is There a Cure for Film Criticism? Or, Some Unhappy Thoughts on Siegfried Kracauer's *Theory of Film*; The Redemption of Physical Reality," reprinted in *I Lost It at the Movies* (Boston: MW Books, 1965), 260.
99 Kracauer to Leo Löwenthal, October 20, 1956. (Original in English.)
100 Kracauer to Leo Löwenthal, August 16, 1958. (Original in English.)
101 Kracauer to Leo Löwenthal, October 29, 1960.

he devoted his first critical effort to "Film as the Discoverer of the Marvels of Everyday Life." Issues treated in the book—the primacy of photography, the non-filmic nature of historical or artistic subject matter, the virtues of the documentary, to mention a few—had all been treated in earlier essays.[102] His stress on the "redemptive" power of film, which meant its ability to make us attend to realities that were usually ignored, echoed his earlier concern for the neglected regions of cultural life: detective novels, the operetta, urban landscapes, troops of dancing girls, popular biographies, and the like. His reliance on what he called a "material" rather than formal aesthetic continued his quasi-phenomenological concern for the *Lebenswelt*, which had informed his work as early as *Soziologie als Wissenschaft*. And the motif of extraterritoriality strongly underlay his interpretation of the filmmaker's vision.

But what had disappeared in the years between *Caligari* and *Theory of Film* was Kracauer's earlier stress on the specifically social content of the reality film redeemed. In his 1927 essay on photography, Kracauer had discussed *inter alia* the function of illustrated newspapers as enemies of true consciousness through their meaningless juxtaposition of unrelated phenomena. In the same article, he developed the relationships between photography, the domination of nature, and capitalism that would be taken up by Benjamin and Adorno in later years. In his series on "The Small Shopgirls Go to the Movies," he probed the function of the film in the cultural desert of petit-bourgeois life. In his 1928 discussion of abstract films, he chastised Expressionism in the cinema for becoming "Kunstgewerbe"[103] (art commodities), not for being non-filmic. "The film," as we have already noted he said, "is the mirror of the existing society," not of physical reality per se. In fact, his entire critique of formalism, whether in sociological theory or daily life, was tied to a more basic attack on capitalist reification.[104] All of this was absent from *Theory of Film*. As Adorno and other radical critics were to complain,[105]

---

102 "Die Photographie," in *FZ*, October 28, 1927, reprinted in *Das Ornament der Masse*; "Der Historische Film," *National-Zeitung Basel*, May 9, 1940, reprinted in *Kino*; "Abstrakter Film," in *FZ*, March 13, 1928, reprinted in *Kino*.
103 "Abstrakter Film," 47. Still, it would be erroneous to deny that Kracauer also criticised *The Cabinet of Doctor Caligari* for what Paul Rotha called its "studio constructivism," that is, a violation of film's inherently realistic character. (*From Caligari to Hitler*, 76).
104 See, for example, his remarks on the relationship between the capitalist production process, the rationalization of the world, and the Tiller Girls precision dancing act in *Das Ornament der Masse*, 53–5.
105 Adorno to Kracauer, February 5, 1965; Kracauer responded on March 3, 1965, arguing that film did have an imminent development apart from its social function. For a vigorous defense of the essential unity of the two books, see Michael Schröter's Diplomarbeit.

redemption seemed to imply affirmation as well. Kracauer protested vehemently against this charge, but it was clear that the critical impetus of his previous work had been blunted. Although it would be mistaken to say it had disappeared entirely, the crucial absence of any analyses of capitalism meant an undeniable shift had occurred.

Within the world of film criticism as such, however, the issues *Theory of Film* provoked were very different.[106] The major impulse behind most serious film theory during the early years of the medium had been a desire to elevate movies into films, that is, to lift them from entertainment into an art form. Theoreticians like Rudolf Arnheim, who drew upon Gestaltist psychology for his argument, Paul Rotha, Vachel Lindsay, and even the Marxist Béla Balázs were all anxious to stress the disparity between the event photographed and the artistic end product that was the film.[107] Directors like Georges Méliès and Abel Gance in France and Pudovkin and Eisenstein in the Soviet Union were equally interested in exploiting the artistic potential of film, although of course the Russians had an ultimately political purpose. Techniques, especially the creative use of editing known as montage and the expressive employment of camera angles to produce dramatic images, were given primary attention by these critics and directors. When sound was introduced, Arnheim and some of the others bemoaned its injurious effect on the artfulness of film; true cinematic language was visual, not verbal.

In opposition to this position, which gained sufficient prominence to be called the "orthodoxy" by one recent observer,[108] two voices were raised, those of André Bazin,[109] the major theoretician of the *Cahiers du Cinéma* in the 1940s and 1950s, and Siegfried Kracauer. Although neither ever acknowledged the existence of the other, it is clear with hindsight that they were fighting a common battle. Whereas the artistic theorists had chosen Méliès as their model, Bazin and Kracauer picked the Lumière brothers, whose documentary realism and rejection of illusory effects prefigured a very different cinematic tradition. What the Lumières had called, in a frequently quoted

---

106 My discussion of the history of film criticism relies in large measure on V.F. Perkins, *Film as Film: Understanding and Judging Movies* (London: Penguin Books, 1972) and Andrew Tudor, *Theories of Film* (London: Seeker and Warburg, 1974).
107 Rudolf Arnheim, *Film as Art* (Berkeley and Los Angeles: University of California Press, 1957); Paul Rotha, *The Film Till Now* (New York: 1950); Vachel Lindsay, *The Art of the Moving Picture* (New York: Liveright, 1970); and Béla Balázs, *Theory of the Film* (London: Denis Dobson, 1952).
108 Perkins, *Film as Film*, 11.
109 André Bazin, *Qu'est-ce que le cinéma?*, 4 vols. (Paris: Les Editions du Cerf, 1958, 1959, 1961, and 1962); English trans, of vols. I and II as *What is Cinema?* (Berkeley and Los Angeles: University of California Press, 1967 and 1971).

phrase, "the ripple of the leaves," only the film could capture and preserve. Both Bazin and Kracauer agreed on the priority of *what* was photographed over *how* it was photographed and spliced together. "Photography and the camera," Bazin wrote in a phrase that Kracauer could have seconded, "are discoveries that satisfy, once and for all and in its very essence, our obsession with realism."[110] The artistic theoreticians' stress on montage and the expressive image were no more than misplaced fetishes. The great film comedians like Chaplin and Keaton, whose unimaginative use of the camera had earned them bad marks from the "orthodox" establishment, were now admitted to the company of successful filmmakers. Conversely, previous heroes like Eisenstein suffered, rightly or wrongly,[111] a fall from grace because of their excessive formalism.

Although Bazin was not as extreme in his insistence on non-artistic realism as Kracauer—compare, for example, their attitudes towards mixed cinema[112]—together they helped reorient the critical discussion about cinema in a radical way. The wave of Italian neo-realist films in the forties and fifties seemed a confirmation of their position. In more recent years, the rise of *cinéma vérité* provided yet another blow to the artistic orthodoxy of the medium's infancy. What perhaps served most to aid their cause was the very success of the orthodox campaign; by the time of the realistic counter-reformation, movies had indeed become films, and it was no longer necessary to defend their artistic credentials.

Kracauer's version of the anti-orthodox position is, of course, what concerns us here. Most commentators have found it to be more vulnerable than Bazin's, partly because Kracauer lacked the Frenchman's remarkable feel for individual films, partly because *Theory of Film* was far more doctrinaire than anything that Bazin wrote. According to Rudolf Arnheim,[113] Kracauer was a dogged conversationalist, who would worry an idea until all of its implications had been exposed; the argument in *Theory of Film* shows the effects of this character trait. Its basic premise is that there exists in film, as in all media, an essential characteristic that sets it apart from all others. This characteristic, which is derived from a phenomenological probe into its nature, is more than a descriptive term; it has normative value as well and can be used

---

110 Bazin, *What is Cinema?*, vol. 1, 12.
111 Tudor argues that Eisenstein should not be seen as the high priest of formalism, although this has frequently been the case.
112 Kracauer, *Theory of Film*, 215–231; Bazin, *What is Cinema?*, vol. 1, 76–124.
113 See fn. 9.

to separate "cinematic" from "non-cinematic" films. According to Kracauer, what makes a film conform to this norm is its fidelity to the photograph, which captures its subject matter, its "raw material," in a realistic way. The opposite genre is painting, where a "formative" tendency holds sway and the artist's subjective intervention is paramount. Without banishing the filmmaker's creative side entirely, Kracauer clearly believed that in the mix between realistic and formative tendencies, the former must be dominant. On a continuum between documentaries and cartoons, the truly "cinematic" is at the documentary end. But, to be fair to his position, a balance must be struck which admits both impulses, even if one is more heavily weighted than the other.

In using the term "realism," however, Kracauer was anxious to avoid sounding like a positivist with a belief in the pristinely mimetic character of the photographic image. The photograph, he acknowledged at one point in his argument, is not a mirror:

> Photographs do not just copy nature but metamorphose it by transferring three-dimensional phenomena to the plane, severing their ties with the surroundings, and substituting black, gray, and white for the given color schemes. Yet if anything defies the idea of a mirror, it is not so much these unavoidable transformations—which may be discounted because in spite of them photographs still preserve the character of compulsory reproductions—as the way in which we take cognizance of visible reality.[114]

What is striking in this paragraph is the ease with which he dismisses the "unavoidable transformations" that had been at the heart of the artistic theoreticians' argument. The fact that photographs are "compulsory reproductions" is enough to justify his insistence that the objects of perception are preserved, indeed "redeemed" by the camera. Later in his argument, Kracauer goes so far as to forget his admission that photographs are not mimetic reproductions of the physical world: "Now of all the existing media the cinema alone holds up a mirror to nature. Hence our dependence on it for the reflection of happenings which would petrify us were we to encounter them in

---

114 Kracauer, *Theory of Film*, 15.

real life."¹¹⁵ Unfortunately, he failed to draw the obvious distinction between realism and naturalism, which might have helped him out of this dilemma.

But what is equally important in this paragraph is Kracauer's shift at its end away from the object of perception to the subject, to "the way in which we take cognizance of visible reality." To Kracauer, the subjective vision necessarily entailed by photography is an alienated one. The selectivity exercised by the photographer is relatively passive in comparison with that of the painter; it is more empathetic than spontaneous. Significantly, Kracauer identifies this vision with a melancholic, elegiac reaction to the world:

> Now, melancholy as an inner disposition not only makes elegiac objects seem attractive but carries still another, more important implication: it favors self-estrangement, which on its part entails identification with all kinds of objects. The dejected individual is likely to lose himself in the incidental configurations of his environment, absorbing them with a disinterested intensity no longer determined by his previous preferences. His is a kind of receptivity which resembles Proust's photographer cast in the role of a stranger.¹¹⁶

Here we have all the elements of the *Neue Sachlichkeit*, disillusioned estrangement and unflinching objectivity, reproduced in an aesthetic of film. But, whereas in his earlier comments on the *Neue Sachlichkeit* Kracauer had shown some critical distance from its implications, here he succumbs to them entirely. The motif of extraterritoriality, which we have seen so evident in his life and much of his work, is transformed into a prescriptive norm by which the "cinematic" nature of films is to be judged.

Having postulated this normative realism, Kracauer then proceeded to spell out the "affinities" photography has for certain types of reality, which also draw upon his earlier attitudes. These affinities are for "unstaged reality," "the fortuitous," "endlessness," "the indeterminate" and "the flow of life."¹¹⁷ All of these are clearly related to his lifelong concern for the flux of the *Lebenswelt*, which resists formalized categorization. The film "redeems" these aspects of reality, which it alone can capture and preserve. In the present age, this power of redemption is extremely important. In his epilogue, Kracauer

---

115 Ibid., 305.
116 Ibid., 17.
117 Ibid., 60–74.

stressed two characteristics of the age as crucial: "the declining hold of common beliefs on the mind and the steadily increasing prestige of science."[118] The former confronts us with a normative void; ideology (understood in the non-Marxist sense of a unifying belief system) is on the wane. The latter interferes with our capacity to experience the physical world directly without the filter of formal abstractions.

Films cannot help us by restoring the lost sense of community and meaning for "the cooling process is irreversible."[119] This is in fact the major reason, so Kracauer argued, that prevents films from being seen as works of art: "Art in film is reactionary because it symbolizes wholeness and thus pretends to the continued existence of beliefs which 'cover' physical reality in both senses of the word."[120] Tragedy is especially inappropriate to the cinema because it presupposes an ordered cosmos, which the film relentlessly denies.[121]

If film is worthless in helping us recapture our sense of a meaningful universe, it is nonetheless useful in overcoming the other tendency of the modern world, scientific over-abstractness. Films help reawaken our openness to the concrete by making us confront unpleasant realities. As a "materialistically" minded medium, it proceeds from "below" to "above."[122] (Here, one hears a dim echo of his argument in the letter to Bloch in 1926 whereby Lukács had badly underestimated the influence of the Enlightenment materialists on Marx.) But anything beyond this "redemption of physical reality" was beyond the power of the film:

> Béla Balázs's thesis that the cinema comes into its own only if it serves revolutionary ends is an untenable one as are the kindred views of those schools of thought, neorealistic and otherwise, which postulate an intimate relationship between the medium and socialism or collectivism.[123]

Implicitly, this debunking of Balázs also contains a criticism of Walter Benjamin's celebrated essay "The Work of Art in the Era of Mechanical

---

118 Ibid., 286.
119 Ibid., 295.
120 Ibid., 301. For a similar argument, see the 1926 essay "Kult der Zerstreuung," reprinted in *Das Ornament der Masse*, 315–16.
121 Ibid., 265–270.
122 Ibid., 309.
123 Ibid., 309. Schröter makes the interesting point that the implications of Kracauer's film theory are anarchistic (44). This jibes with Kracauer's self-description in his letter to Bloch of June 29, 1926, which Schröter could not have seen.

Reproduction,"[124] which followed Brecht in seeing a revolutionary potential in the mass distraction of the cinema. Although it may appear as if Kracauer was attributing to the film something akin to Brecht's celebrated *Verfremdungseffekt*, it is clear that he had no confidence in the cognitive and ultimately political benefits of this estrangement. Kracauer may have still been a "rag-pick," but the "revolutionary day" had clearly failed to dawn.

Theory of Film created even more of a critical furor than *From Caligari to Hitler*. Positive voices were not absent, among them Herbert Read's, and surprisingly, Rudolf Arnheim's.[125] A friend of Kracauer's since the 1940s who had helped him choose the subtitle of the book,[126] Arnheim generously acknowledged the place of both his and Kracauer's approaches in understanding the cinema. *Theory of Film*, he wrote, "is probably the most intelligent book ever written on film;"[127] although needing "correction and clarification," "the core of his thesis is surely valid and important."[128] Arnheim endorsed Kracauer's stress on the realistic tendency in the cinema, a remarkable reversal of his own *Film as Art*, but unlike Kracauer, he connected it to a cultural decline rather than a return to our senses: "a concern with unshaped matter is a melancholy surrender rather than the recovery of man's grip on reality. Perhaps, then, we are witnessing the last twitches of an exhausted civilization, whose rarefied concepts no longer reach the world of the senses."[129]

Most of the critical reception of *Theory of Film* was, however, essentially hostile. The least charitable of his accusers was Pauline Kael, who wrote a lengthy and vitriolic attack in *Sight and Sound* in 1962.[130] Miss Kael's derogatory and sexist ire was aroused by the very attempt to theorize about film in the grand manner:

> What do movies [N.B. not "films"] have to do with the "redemption" of "physical reality"? Our physical reality—what we experience around us—is what we can't redeem: if it's good, marvelous; if it isn't, we can weep or booze, or try to change it. Redemption, like sublimation, is a dear

124 Walter Benjamin, *Illuminations: Essays and Reflections*, ed. with intro. by Hannah Arendt, trans. Harry Zohn (New York: Schocken Books, 1968).
125 Herbert Read in *British Journal of Aesthetics* 2, no. 2 (April, 1962); Rudolf Arnheim, in *Journal of Aesthetics and Art Criticism* 21 (1963); republished as "Melancholy Unshaped" in *Toward a Psychology of Art* (Berkeley and Los Angeles: University of California Press, 1972).
126 See fn. 9.
127 Arnheim, "Melancholy Unshaped," 180.
128 Ibid., 186.
129 Ibid., 191.
130 See fn. 97.

sweet thought. And Kracauer's theory of film is a theory imposed on motion pictures.[131]

In elaborating her attack, she scored her most telling points in demonstrating the lengths to which Kracauer went to include cinematic phenomenon he liked, such as Fred Astaire's dance routines, under the rubric of realism. She was somewhat less persuasive when hearing a German accent and noting a speculative mind, she compared Kracauer to Hegel, the philosopher he spent much of his adult life opposing.[132] Equally questionable was her call for movies to be "judged by the same kind of standards that are used in other arts,"[133] as if there was such a thing as "art" with one set of standards for all its subdivisions.

Other critical appraisals by Tyler, Linden, Engels, Jarvie, Perkins, and Tudor,[134] to mention the most prominent, were less bilious than Miss Kael's, but scarcely less disparaging. As a whole, the points they made, embellished by some of my own, are as follows:

1. The search for the essence of a medium (which Miss Kael called "the great lunatic tradition"[135]) is itself a highly questionable endeavor. There is no "nature" of film with prescriptive value by which good films can be separated from bad. Nor are there immanent laws of the cinema that can be abstracted from the social context in which films are made.
2. Film is particularly difficult to see in essentialist terms because the assumption that photography is its primary source is erroneous. One might equally stress the opposition between the static photograph and the dynamic motion picture. In a technical sense, such nineteenth-century phenomena as the magic lantern and other optical toys simulating motion are equally important. In a substantive sense, the traditions of the theatre and the novel cannot be discounted. In short, Méliès as well as the Lumière brothers must be given his due.
3. The distinction Kracauer makes between reality and "camera reality," the latter taking into account the distortions that cannot be overcome,

---

131 Ibid., 244.
132 Ibid., 245–246.
133 Ibid., 259.
134 Parker Tyler, *Sex Psyche Etcetera in the Film* (New York: Penguin, 1969); George W. Linden, *Reflections on the Screen* (Belmont, CA: Wadsworth, 1970); Gunther Engels, "In der Zwangsjacke der Theorie," in *Saarbrücken Zeitung* (January 30/31, 1965): for Perkins and Tudor, see. fn. 105.
135 Kael, "Is There a Cure for Film Criticism?" 245.

is poorly developed and inconsistently used. Although anxious to avoid a positivist copy-theory of reality, he frequently sounds as if he believes films "mirrored" the material world. At times, Kracauer calls films cinematic solely because of the techniques used, a stress on movement, for example, rather than because of their content. He sometimes justifies illusions that are convincing to the audience because of their fidelity to "camera reality," but in what way do they then redeem the physical world? Once technique is admitted as a criterion of realism, then the emphasis is once again shifted away from the object photographed to the subjective photographer and Kracauer is back on "orthodox" grounds.

4. In establishing his prescriptive aesthetic, Kracauer has posited norms that are far too exclusive. Not only do they rule out cartoons, fantasies (such as those of Cocteau, one of Kracauer's *bêtes noires*), filmed operas and plays, almost all avant-garde films including expressionist classics like *Caligari*, history films, and movies made from novels, but they also deny a priori the significance of the most widely admired directors of the post-neo-realist 1960s; Fellini, Antonioni, Resnais, Buñuel, Godard, and Bergman.[136] Any theory of film that lacks the room for these types of movies is intrinsically inadequate.

5. Finally, the more general cultural tasks Kracauer sets the cinema are grounded in questionable assumptions. Is it true that all normative systems have been shipwrecked, or is Kracauer merely succumbing to the myth of the 1950s: the end of ideology? Moreover, even if one were to grant Kracauer's assumption about the impoverishment of our perceptual apparatus caused by scientific abstraction, can one then say that films really return us to the sensuous, non-reified flow of "life?"[137] In fact, doesn't the very mediation of the film suggest an experience that is still passive and estranged? That melancholic alienation Kracauer sees as the essence of the camera eye is a poor candidate for the means to bring us back to our senses. Is there, in fact, any evidence that film-watching really

---

136 In *Theory of Film*, Kracauer does talk about some of Fellini's earlier films, especially *The Nights of Cabiria* and *La Strada*, but he sees them in the context of neo-realism. He also speaks highly of Buñuel, but it is the post-surrealist Buñuel of *Land Without Bread* and *Los Olvidados*. Bergman is mentioned only in passing, but Kracauer tries to save him for his thesis by saying that the "down-to-earth attitude" of certain characters in *The Seventh Seal* "in a measure acclimatize(s) the film to the medium" (308). Resnais, Godard, and Antonioni had not yet made enough of a mark to be considered in the book. But we do know from his later correspondence that he considered Resnais's *Last Year at Marienbad* a pretentious bore. (Kracauer to Michel Ciment, May 23, 1965).

137 Kracauer, *Theory of Film*, 169–170.

leads to renewed participation in "life," rather than compensating for its absence? Indeed, the very notion of "life," which Kracauer once criticized in Simmel,[138] but now accepts wholeheartedly, is highly suspect. To identify the real solely with process and flux is itself a Romantic assumption of dubious merit, as even Arnheim in his favourable review noted.[139] Finally, the desire to redeem physical reality suggests a kind of indiscriminate yea-saying that fails to separate what needs to be saved from what doesn't. The implications of this are apparent in Kracauer's reaction to films that force us to see the monstrosities of the world:

> The mirror reflections of horror are an end in themselves. As such they beckon the spectator to take them in and thus incorporate into his memory the real face of things too dreadful to be held in reality. In experiencing the rows of calves' heads or the litter of tortured human bodies in the films made of the Nazi concentration camps, we redeem horror from its invisibility behind the veils of panic and imagination. And this experience is liberating in as much as it removes a most powerful taboo.[140]

What Kracauer fails to consider here is the extent to which films numb us to horror through overexposure. The increasing tolerance for and even delight in graphic horror has been one of the most unsettling tendencies of the last decade. Removing taboos, especially if it entails the loss of our capacity for panic (or at least disgust) and imagination, may not always be liberating after all.

With the rough treatment that it received at the hands of most commentators, *Theory of Film* marked the end rather than the beginning of an era in film criticism. It helped lay to rest the old debate over the artfulness of film, but in turn, its failures made the extreme realist position clearly untenable. Attempts to judge films as "cinematic" or not according to a prescriptive aesthetic soon seemed highly dubious. Instead, film criticism turned to the so-called "auteur theory," which emerged from the pages of the *Cahiers du Cinéma* and was propagated in America by Andrew Sarris,[141] or it focused on the more modest task of investigating the nature of specific genres within

---

138 Kracauer, "Die Wartenden," in *FZ*, March 12, 1922; reprinted in *Das Ornament der Masse*, 108–9.
139 Arnheim, "Melancholy Unshaped," 183.
140 Kracauer, *Theory of Film*, 306.
141 Andrew Sarris, "Notes on the Auteur Theory in 1962," in *Film Culture* 27 (1962–63). Pauline Kael also ridiculed Sarris in "Circles and Squares; Joyes and Sarris" in *I Lost It at the Movies*.

the larger corpus of films. Most recently, a structuralist method has been applied to the language of film by Christian Metz in France and Peter Wollen in Britain.[142] *Theory of Film* remains a monument in the history of thinking about movies, but it also serves as a warning against building other monuments of its kind.

✶

In the 1960s, Kracauer's career took a relatively new turn. These last several years before his death appear to be among the happiest of his life. Within the academic world, he finally received a measure of the recognition that had eluded him previously; he became an associate member of the Seminar on Interpretation at Columbia University and was invited on several occasions to Germany for colloquia on poetry and hermeneutics at Cologne and Lindau. His early *FZ* writings were rediscovered by an appreciative German audience, which began to see his relationship to the more celebrated trio of Bloch, Benjamin, and Adorno. *Ginster* was republished in 1963 with its author's name affixed; the critical acclaim was almost universal. There was talk of a Kracauer renaissance[143] as some of his English works were translated into German for the first time. In Frankfurt, a student of Adorno's named Erika Lorenz prepared a *Diplomarbeit* on his career, which would have been expanded into a doctoral dissertation if not for her return to East Germany for personal reasons.[144] Although Kracauer was not completely won over by her interpretation—he objected to her attempt to assimilate him to the Frankfurt School's Critical Theory and to her calling him a journalist—he glowed in the recognition that such a project signified.

In 1964, Adorno himself wrote a piece on Kracauer for his 75th birthday, entitled "The Whimsical Realist."[145] Although he was initially flattered, Kracauer's opinion changed drastically when he read between the lines to see a number of implied criticisms. In a series of heated letters, he defended himself and struck back at Adorno. Although it would be impossible here to

---

142 Christian Metz, *Language et Cinéma* (Paris: Editions Albatros, 1971); Peter Wollen, *Signs and Meaning in the Cinema* (Bloomington, IN: Indiana University Press, 1972).
143 Helmut Günther, review of *Ginster* in *Welt und Wort* 3 (1964).
144 Erika Lorenz, *Siegfried Kracauer als Soziologe* (Frankfurt a.M.: Diplomarbeit, Johnann Wolfgang Goethe Universität, 1962). Adorno informed Kracauer of her decision to leave West Germany in a letter of January 10, 1964.
145 See fn. 15.

detail the issues between them, which I hope to do elsewhere at a later date, suffice it to say that their friendship of over forty years was severely strained by Adorno's "tribute."

Kracauer's increased concern for his place in history was matched by a new fascination with the philosophy of history itself. After a long period of wandering, he returned, at least intellectually, to his boyhood home with his uncle Isidor. From the completion of *Theory of Film* until his death, he worked with almost total absorption in an area he had never really explored with any rigor before. Although he was losing valuable time in preparing the German translation of the film book, Kracauer completed the lion's share of his manuscript by the time of his relatively sudden death from pneumonia in November, 1966. His architect's habit of constructing the manuscript in meticulous fashion before writing the final draft made its posthumous publication possible. In 1969, *History: The Last Things Before the Last* was brought out by Oxford University Press, but not without serious difficulties in the interim.

Sheldon Meyer of OUP had wanted Lili Kracauer to edit and organize her husband's manuscript, but lacking the self-confidence, she refused. Instead, a former acquaintance of Kracauer's, a German living in New York named Reinhard Koehne, was hired to put the book in order. The decision proved an unhappy one as Koehne and Lili Kracauer quickly developed a mutual distrust; her fidelity to the letter of Kracauer's drafts was not shared by Koehne, who finally withdrew in anger. A lawsuit followed, but was ultimately dropped, and the book was eventually published without any mention of Koehne's name. A very generous foreword was provided by Paul Oskar Kristeller, the distinguished historian of Renaissance philosophy with whom Kracauer had become close during his final years.

If *History* was ill-starred in its preparation, its fate after publication was scarcely more fortunate. The pre-publication review by the Virginia Kirkus Service was unsympathetic, and despite a very positive reaction by Georg Iggers in the *American Historical Review*, the book sank with scarcely a ripple.[146] By the early 1970s, it was remaindered and taken out of circulation. Kracauer was widely known in the film world, but he was neither a professional philosopher nor a historian and thus lacked a real constituency in those fields.

---

146 The unsigned *Kirkus* review of February 15, 1969, called the book "passé and muddled," ill-informed on contemporary writings in the philosophy of history, and in need of "a dose of analytic rigor." Iggers's review was in the *American Historical Review* 75, no. 3 (February, 1970); he called the book "a real gem," although he took issue with its interpretation of Marc Bloch.

The private expressions of enthusiasm by such celebrated historians as J.J. Hexter and Werner Kaegi were of little help.[147] Kracauer had had extraordinarily high expectations for what he considered his master work, but these were to be disappointed, at least in the short run.

And yet, in many ways, *History* is one of Kracauer's most compelling and original works, which deserves to be "redeemed," if one may borrow his own word, from an unmerited oblivion. In concluding this appreciation of Kracauer's career, it would be useful to linger a while with his final book, not merely because it has been denied the critical examination it deserves, but also because it ties together many of the themes of his previous work. Without an understanding of the perspective expressed in *History*, Kracauer's varied interests and conflicting approaches make little coherent sense. With that understanding, they begin to knit together.

In the book itself, he makes some astute observations about Proust's *Remembrance of Things Past*, which raise crucial questions about Kracauer himself. Discussing Proust's attempt to reconcile the antinomy between objective, chronological time and subjective, recapturable time, he remarks:

> The story of his (or Marcel's) fragmentized life must have reached its terminus before it can reveal itself to him as a unified process. And the reconciliation he effects between the antithetic propositions at stake—his denial of the flow of time and his (belated) endorsement of it—hinge on his retreat into a dimension of art. But nothing of the sort applies to history. Neither has history an end or is it amenable to aesthetic redemption.[148]

Before Proust, Dilthey had also argued that meaning was only perceivable at the end of a life, when its constituent moments could be seen as parts in a completed whole:

> One would have to wait for the end of a life and, in the hour of death, survey the whole to ascertain the relation between the whole and its parts.

---

147 J.H. Hexter to Sheldon Meyer, April 26, 1967; Werner Kaegi's praise was quoted in a letter from Lili Kracauer to Sheldon Meyer, December 11, 1969. Other letters favorable to Kracauer's essay on "Time and History" came from Karl Löwith (January 20, 1964), H.I. Marrou (April 20, 1964), Arnold Hauser (February 2, 1964), and Erwin Panofsky (March 16, 1964).

148 Kracauer, *History*, 163. Proust's work also played a crucial role in *Theory of Film*; Micheal Schröter has a number of illuminating observations on its significance (pp. 59f).

One would have to wait for the end of history to have all the material necessary to determine its meaning.[149]

But unlike Proust, Dilthey did not believe that an artificial, premature end could be achieved through an aesthetic recapitulation of a life still in progress, even though one might withdraw into a cork-lined room to prevent the future from having any meaning. Kracauer clearly shared Dilthey's qualms about this solution, as he did his argument about full meaning coming at the end of history, an end that would never come. Whereas, it seems to me he was somewhat ambivalent was in his attitude towards the closure of an individual life signified by death. That desperate insistence on chronological anonymity we have noted before can be read not merely in a psychological sense; it also suggests a desire to thwart the attribution of final meaning to his life which would follow its end. Kracauer was both driven by the need to order his life retrospectively, which was perhaps responsible for his early semi-autobiographical novels, and repelled by the thought that this meant the exhaustion of its open-ended potential. This ambivalence clearly paralleled his attitude towards extraterritoriality, which we have noted earlier.

The question then that must be asked is whether or not his death does give us an insight into the whole meaning of his life. In other words, do we now have a vantage point like the spire of Proust's Combray Church from which the landscape before us (or more correctly, behind us) becomes coherent? Failing this, can we say that *History: The Last Things Before the Last* provides a substitute reconciliation, very much like Marcel's "retreat into the dimensions of art," which was the only redemption Kracauer himself could achieve?

To answer the first part of the question, there is little in Kracauer's biography to suggest that the extraterritoriality that marked it from an early age was ever really overcome. Although Adorno worried that his friend had decided to seek "happiness"[150] after emigrating to America, thus becoming a conformist of sorts, Lili Kracauer's word that her husband had resisted conformity to the end must be given at least equal weight.[151] Despite his continuing marginality, however, there is little to indicate that Kracauer fashioned his life in such a way that made non-conformity itself a positive lifestyle.

---

149 Wilhelm Dilthey, *Pattern and Meaning in History: Thoughts on History and Society*, ed. with introduction by H.P. Rickman (New York: Harper & Row, 1961), 106.
150 Adorno, "Der Wunderliche Realist," 100. This accusation infuriated Kracauer.
151 Lili Kracauer to Hans G. Helms, June 19, 1970.

There is no hint of a Rimbaud or Jarry here, seeking to make his life into an artistic whole through the acting out of an alternative vision. Nor is there any suggestion of a Lukács or T.S. Eliot, finding wholeness in obedience to an external authority. Kracauer remained an outsider to the end, sceptical of all belief systems, false reconciliations, and communitarian solutions to alienation. As the economist Adolph Lowe, who spoke at his funeral, remarked: "I remember him wearing the mask he liked best: as Sancho Panza trotting on his ass behind the frantic visionaries in his *bunte Nuchternheit* [gay, many-colored sobriety], as his friend Ernst Bloch so well defined him."[152] In short, aside from whatever personal vision may have been granted him "in the hour of death," it is impossible for the historian to say that Kracauer's life achieved any really unified meaning at its end. Indeed, as Kracauer himself recognized in his discussion of Proust, personal histories cannot be set apart from the larger context of historical change, which admits of no real redemption.

What, then, of *History: The Last Things Before the Last*? Does it function the way Marcel's novel did to render his life a whole through a surrogate aesthetic (or in this case, intellectual) reconciliation? Does it succeed where earlier fictional attempts like *Ginster* and *Georg* were only partially successful largely because of their prematurity? The answer, it seems to me, is a guarded yes, even though Kracauer's substantive argument throughout is directed against reconciliation. At first glance, the book seems an improbable candidate for this task. Less than a month before his death, in his last letter to Leo Löwenthal, he wrote: "I am not yet out of the tunnel, but in the distance there is already something like a dim light."[153] His final illness prevented him from reaching the light in its full brightness, but even if he had lived to complete the book, its final form would not have suggested wholeness. As he planned it, *History* was to appear as a series of relatively autonomous mediations on aspects of history and historical craftsmanship.[154] It is not a sustained and rigorously developed argument, and indeed, many of its conclusions are directed against reconciliation. And yet, paradoxically, it does have certain unifying themes and more importantly from our point of view, it resurrects

---

152 Adolph Lowe, "Thoughts on Siegfried Kracauer," delivered at his funeral in New York, November 27, 1966, now in the *Nachlaß*.
153 Kracauer to Leo Löwenthal, October 29, 1966.
154 The chapters are as follows: "Nature," "The Historical Approach," "Present Interest," "The Historian's Journey," "The Structure of the Historical Universe," "Ahasuerus, or the Riddle of Time," "General History and the Aesthetic Approach," and "The Anteroom."

all of the major concerns of his previous work, casting them in a new and revealing light.

Shortly after starting the work, Kracauer wrote to Löwenthal that he had suddenly realized that the new book "is a direct continuation of my theory of film: the historian has traits of the photographer, and historical reality resembles camera-reality. The similarities are really startling: I had done on this route complete unconsciously."[155] He then asked Erika Lorenz to compile a list of his early essays in which history played a role. She wrote back that she had found six: "Die Wissenschaftskrise," "Der verbotene Blick," "Die Reise und die Tanz," "Das Ornament der Masse," "Zu den Schriften Walter Benjamins," and perhaps most importantly, "Die Photographie," the first time in which Kracauer explored the link between history and photography.[156] In his introduction to *History*, which he completed in February, 1962, he spelled out the connections revealed when he saw the link between the film book and his current interest, *Theory of Film*:

> Now appears to me in its true light: as another attempt of mine to bring out the significance of areas whose claim to be acknowledged in their own right has not yet been recognized. I say "another attempt" because this was what I had tried to do throughout my life—in *Die Angestellten*, perhaps in *Ginster*, and certainly in the *Offenbach*. So at long last all my main efforts, so incoherent on the surface, fall into line—they have all been served and continue to serve, a single purpose: the rehabilitation of objectives and modes of being which still lack a name and hence are overlooked or misjudged. Perhaps this is less true of history than photography; yet history too marks a bent of the mind and defines a region of reality which despite all that has been written about them are still largely *terra incognita*.[157]

The analogy between history and photography turned out to be a central prop of his argument, and not merely because of their shared redemptive role, to which I will return shortly. They resemble each other in a number

---

155 Kracauer to Leo Löwenthal, February 16, 1961.
156 All of these are collected in *Das Ornament der Masse*, with the exception of "Der Verbotene Blick," which appeared in the *FZ*, April 9, 1925 and is reprinted in *Strassen in Berlin und anderswo* (Letter From Erika Lorenz to Kracauer, Febrauary 2, 1962).
157 Kracauer, *History*, 4.

of ways. Both are "a means of alienation,"[158] which for reasons he never fully developed is a healthy condition to foster in the modern world. Both investigate and reveal the realities of the *Lebenswelt* in all its contingent, indeterminate open-endedness. Both are produced by a balance between "realistic" and "formative" tendencies, with an emphasis on the former. Both underwent a period when simple mimesis was assumed to be its special genius (the positivist historicism associated with Ranke's *wie es eigentlich gewesen* and the early years of nineteenth-century danguerrotypy). Although this period was marked by naiveté, both are still more heavily weighted on the realistic side, which separates history from historical fiction as it does film from painting. Both use close-ups and establishing shots, which in the historians' vocabulary are known as micro-history and macro-history. Finally, both are "anteroom areas," which elude over-systematization, ultimate answers, and the holistic shaping of art.

In drawing these parallels, Kracauer exhibited a far lighter touch than in *Theory of Film*. Whereas in the earlier book, overly artistic films were banished as "uncinematic," historical writing that fell on the formative side of the scale was now admitted as legitimate. In dealing with the structure of the historical universe, Kracauer arrived at a conclusion that had eluded him in his analysis of the film universe: that its structure was "non-homogeneous." Although suspicious of overly ambitious attempts to discern secular or cyclical patterns in history, he granted validity to macro-historical efforts on the scale of Burckhardt's study of the Renaissance, where the interpretive genius of the historian was allowed almost free rein. Arguing against advocates of what has been called "historical pointillism" such as Sir Lewis Namier and Tolstoy, he rejected the notion that the ultimate subject matter of history is the smallest possible detail, everything else being an inductive generalization from these fundamental "facts." Instead, he invoked two "laws" that govern historical understanding: the "law of perspective," which posits that

> [i]n the micro dimension a more or less dense fabric of given data canalizes the historian's imagination, his interpretative designs. As the distance from the data increases, they become scattered, thin out. The evidence thus loses its binding power, inviting less committed subjectivity to take over[159]

158 Ibid., 5.
159 Ibid., 123.

and the "law of levels," which parallels the cinematic distinction between close-ups and establishing shots, and means that

> contexts established at each level are valid for that level but do not apply to findings at other levels; which is to say that there is no way of deriving the regularities of macro-history, as Toynbee does, from the facts and interpretations provided by micro-history.[160]

In stressing the non-homogeneous structure of the historical universe, Kracauer was reinterpreting in historical terms what sociologists as far back as Comte and Durkheim had been advocating: social facts were in some sense generic and thus irreducible to psychological facts. Although not denying the traffic between the various levels, he was stern in warning against the belief in an effortless passage from one to another. In holding that no one level was primary, he contested the views of both psychohistorians and social historians who claim their level is the bedrock of historical analysis. Yet, still very much a champion of the realistic rather than formative tendency, he was anxious to warn against the dangers of an overly abstract and general history. An opponent of unrestrained methodological individualism, he nonetheless warned against the dangers of holism as well. The broadened intelligibility of macro-history did not, in fact, mean greater significance for its findings. In history, abstraction ought not to be equated with superior insight. Indeed, "one of the underlying assumptions of the present study" was that "the traditional identification of the extreme abstractions—say, the idea of the 'good' or that of 'justice'—as the most inclusive and essential statements about the nature of things does not apply to history."[161] Yet, it is equally mistaken to expect the accumulated data of micro-historical research eventually to translate into a full and adequate understanding of the past as a whole. Indeed, "the belief in the progress of historiography is largely in the nature of an illusion."[162]

Why then continue to do the monographic research that Carlyle, Nietzsche, Huizinga, Marc Bloch, and so many others have condemned as "dry-as-dust" pedantry? The answer Kracauer gave was taken almost directly from Benjamin:

160 Ibid., 134.
161 Ibid., 131.
162 Ibid., 138.

> There is only one single argument in its support which I believe to be conclusive. It is a theological argument, though. According to it, the "complete assemblage of the smallest facts" is required for the reason that nothing shall go lost. It is as if the fact-oriented accounts breathed pity with the dead. This vindicates the figure of the *collector*.[163]

Here, the redemption Kracauer sought in so many secular ways was finally allowed an explicitly religious moment.

The non-homogeneity of the historical universe had still further implications, which Kracauer explored in other chapters in the book. In his discussion of the relationship between history and nature and their corresponding methodologies, he admitted the Marxian point that "society is a second nature,"[164] which implies that scientific methods may well be applicable to history. But he also argued that there is an irreducibly contingent element in history which defies schematization. Thus, narrative description is equally as valid as social history with its stress on morphological regularities. Similarly, Dilthey's celebrated notion of *Verstehen* still had a place in the historian's methodological arsenal, but it was only one of several approaches that depended on the historical level that was being investigated.

The argument for the present-mindedness of the historian's vision, most notably advanced by Croce and Collingwood, also foundered in the face of the non-homogeneity of the historical universe. Kracauer contended that the historian cannot himself be understood as so embedded in his own period that all of his perceptions of the past are filtered through his current situation. The reason is simply that there is no present "period" to determine the historian's vantage point:

> If the historian's "historical and social environment" is not a fairly self-contained whole but a fragile compound of frequently inconsistent endeavours in flux, the assumption that it moulds his mind makes little sense. It does make sense only in the contexts of a philosophy which, like Croce's, hypostatizes a period spirit, claims our dependence on it, and thus determines the mind's place in the historical process from above

---

163 Ibid., 136.
164 Ibid., 25.

and without. Seen from within, the relations between the mind and its environment are indeterminate.[165]

The best counterexample is the maverick historian who defies his *Zeitgeist*; Kracauer defines him in now familiar terms:

> Vico is an outstanding instance of chronological extra-territoriality; and it would be extremely difficult to derive Burckhardt's complex and ambivalent physiognomy as a historian from the conditions under which he lived and worked. Like great artists or thinkers, great historians are biological freaks: they father the time that has fathered them.[166]

Instead of present-mindedness, Kracauer called for an effort of self-transcendence not unlike Proust's ability to succumb to involuntary memory. The historian must "bracket" himself—note the phenomenological term—and prepare his mind through a kind of surrender, an "active passivity,"[167] which allows the material to reveal itself to him. Although the morphological patterns of history have to be more aggressively pursued, narrative accounts must arise from an expectant openness to the material.

Yet another implication of the heterogeneity of the historical universe was the inadequacy of induction as the sole method of historical inquiry. Following Benjamin's discussion in his *Ursprung des deutschen Trauerspiels*,[168] Kracauer distinguished between generalizations and what he called "ideas." The latter are "genuine universals" arising out of a leap from the cumulative data of empirical research. They transcend the simple distinction between right and wrong because of their extraordinary power to illuminate the historical landscape:

> They are nodal points—points at which the concrete and abstract really meet and become one. Whenever this happens, the flow of indeterminate historical events is suddenly arrested and all that is then exposed to view

---

165 Ibid., 67.
166 Ibid., 68.
167 Ibid., 92.
168 Walter Benjamin, *Ursprung des deutschen Trauerspiels* in *Schriften*, 1 (Frankfurt a.M.: Suhrkamp, 1955). In a review of Kurt Breysig's *Vom geschichtlichen Werden*, vol. 2, *Die Macht des Gedankens in der Geschichte*, which is contained in the Kracauer *Nachlaß* under the category "Old German Manuscripts." Kracauer made a similar critique of induction as the sole mode of historical knowledge. Although no date is affixed, the review appears to be from the Weimar period.

is seen in the light of an image or conception which takes it out of the transient flow to relate it to one or other of the momentous problems and questions that are forever staring at us.[169]

Burckhardt's image of the Renaissance, Marx's distinction between substructure and superstructure, Weber's Protestant Ethic are examples of "ideas," which later historians have been able to refute in particular cases, but not really lay to rest. Beyond these "ideas" there is a realm—that "last" region referred to in Kracauer's title—that historians dare not enter. Here, Kracauer conflated the truths of metaphysics (last in an ontological sense) with the end of history (last in a chronological sense). Because the end of history was unthinkable, it was wrong to expect the historian to posses the vantage point from which metaphysical truth was attainable. Not even universal history, if it can be said to exist, could encompass that ultimate region.

As in film, an overly harmonious rendering of the material is an aesthetic distortion of the open-ended nature of history. Robert Merton's reading of Sterne's *Tristram Shandy*[170] captured the impossibility of the task; like Tristram Shandy, the historian has too much to relate before he can get to the end of his tale. If he tries to short-circuit the process by arbitrarily calling a halt, he makes the mistake Proust made by withdrawing into his cork-lined room. The result may be artistically successful, but it carries inevitable violence to the past as it opens into the future.

Of all the implications of the non-homogeneity of the historical universe, one stands out as central: the nature of historical time. Kracauer, the architect trained more in spatial than temporal terms, had become increasingly preoccupied by the mysteries of time, as we have seen with his insistence on his own chronological anonymity. The first section of *History* to be published, appearing in German, Italian, and English while Kracauer was still alive,[171] was entitled "Time and History." With minor emendations, it appeared in the book as "Ahaseurus, or the Riddle of Time."

---

169 Kracauer, *History*, 101.
170 Robert K. Merton, *On the Shoulders of Giants: A Shandean Postscript* (New York: The Free Press, 1965). Kracauer communicated his admiration to Merton in a letter, which Merton deeply appreciated. (Letter from Merton to Lili Kracauer, June 28, 1968).
171 In German in *Zeugnisse: Theodor W. Adorno zum sechzigsten Geburtstag*, ed. Hermann Schweppenhäuser and Rolf Tiedemann (Frankfurt a.M.: Suhrkamp, 1963); in English in *History and Theory*, Beiheft 6 (Middletown, CT: Wesleyan University Press, 1966); in Italian in *Tempo Presente* (1965).

Although he did not work out all the implications of his title, Kracauer did devote one very interesting paragraph to Ahaseurus, the Wandering Jew. After remarking that only this legendary figure might know at firsthand the continuity of history, he described the cost of this knowledge:

> How unspeakably terrible he must look! To be sure, his face cannot have suffered from aging, but I imagine it to be many faces, each reflecting one of the periods which he traversed and all of them combining into new patterns, as he restlessly, and vainly, tries on his wanderings to reconstruct out of the times that shaped him the one time he is doomed to incarnate.[172]

The pain distorting the Wandering Jew's face is thus a result of his trying to integrate the different experiences of his life into one coherent pattern. What is also implicit in the story, although Kracauer neglected to develop it, is the fact that Ahaseurus is condemned to eternal life because of his rejection of Jesus. In other words, he is denied the redemption that only death can make possible. He cannot step out of history to touch the eternal. His life will never have any meaning because it will lack an end. To Kracauer, he is thus an ambivalent figure, eternally extraterritorial, and yet possessed of an immortality that most men would envy.

Whatever the implications of his title, which might also be developed in an autobiographical direction, the content of the chapter is crucial for an understanding of Kracauer's position. Among other things, it demonstrates how far Kracauer himself had wandered from the assumptions of German historicism, which were still dominant during his youth. Historicism, either in its Rankean or Hegelian guises, had posited a continuous, developmental flow of chronological time in only one irreversible direction. Homogeneous chronicity was the solvent in which all historical events were immersed. This notion of time was similar to the spatialized, quantitatively ordered temporarily of the natural sciences, at least to the extent that both jettisoned the transcendental intervention into time preserved in the Judaeo-Christian tradition. Even the dialectical process of Hegelian time presupposed a homogeneous, unidirectional medium in which the Absolute manifested itself,

---

172 Kracauer, *History*, 157.

although dialectics meant that progress came through contradictions rather than the smooth working out of an evolutionary scheme.

In Germany, this view of time (or rather, the several views which shared a common belief in the homogeneity of the temporal process) had a strong hold on historical thinking well into the twentieth century, despite the crisis in values which befell historicism. Elsewhere, however, especially in modernist aesthetic circles, simultaneity and mythic recurrence were resurrected as legitimate alternatives. Nietzsche and Bergson were, of course, the prophets of the new sense of time, although they were not in perfect agreement on its characteristics.

Within the artistic realm, the most sustained exploration of non-historicist time was carried out by Proust in his *Remembrance of Things Past*, although other writers like Thomas Mann, Virginia Woolf, and James Joyce were also concerned with similar questions. Aesthetic realism, best exemplified by the nineteenth-century novel, was on the defensive, but historical writing, which retained many of the characteristics of the novel (narrative form, omniscient narrator, stress on the public world, etc.), continued to rely on traditional notions of time.

Kracauer saw three implications following from this state of affairs. First, dates within a chronological sequence were value-laden; that is, simultaneous occurrences were implicitly assumed to relate to each other in certain ways, usually parallel, where successive events were more often understood as relating to each other in casual ways. Second, large-scale units were often traced over a period of time as if they constituted discrete entities with lives of their own (the classic example being the historicist belief in the state as the true "individual" of history, which implied the neglect of internal social contradictions). And third, the formal property of an inexorable flow was often invested with substantive characteristics, as in Hegel's construction of the world process as the realization of rationality, or the less ambitious, but equally questionable notion of history as progress. All of these assumptions were undermined by a different, more subtle understanding of historical time.

Significantly, in making his case for this alternative view of temporality, Kracauer drew upon the work of art historians like Erwin Panofsky, George Kubler, and Henri Focillon,[173] with the figure of Burckhardt, the isolated anti-

---

173 Erwin Panofsky, *Renaissance and Renascences in Western Art* (Stockholm: Almqvist & Wiksell, 1960); George Kubler, *The Shape of Time: Remarks on the History of Things* (New Haven and London: Yale University Press, 1962); Henri Focillon, *The Life of Forms in Art* (New York: Zone Books, 1963). Dur-

historicist in nineteenth-century German historiography, looming in the background. Of perhaps equal importance was his reading of Proust, which benefitted from Hans Robert Jauss's interpretation of *The Remembrance*.[174] Even more interesting in the context of recent intellectual debates, he found another ally among the anthropologists in the person of Claude Lévi-Strauss. In December, 1963, Kracauer sent him a copy of "Time and History," adding the comment that he had just read *La pensée sauvage*:

> [A]nd to my most pleasant surprise discovered that in the wonderful section against Sartre you tackle the issue of historical time in terms similar to mine. To the best of my knowledge, no philosopher or historian has ever discussed the antinomy at the core of chronological time this way. [...] I have well taken note of your hints regarding the problem of the relationships between histories at different levels of generality: I shall discuss this problem in my forthcoming book. One more remark: it will take people a long time to understand your thought in all its consequences.[175]

Lévi-Strauss read the article and wrote back that he "was of course impressed with the many points of contact between your thinking and my own."[176]

What Kracauer liked in Lévi-Strauss's attack on Sartre was his insistence that chronology was itself an arbitrary code that men imposed on the world, rather than an intrinsic part of its essential nature. But in the final version of his chapter on this problem, he moved slightly away from the complete denigration of unilinear flow in the structuralist attack on historicism. As he wrote to the French historian Henri I. Marrou in the spring of 1964:

> [M]y agreement with [Lévi-Strauss] and Kubler is only partial. Actually, I am going beyond them and coming closer to your own position with its emphasis on the uniform flow of time. As against Kubler–Focillon–Lévi-Strauss, I too affirm the validity of such a flow; but it is true, I also uphold the notion of (Kubler's) "shaped times," assigning to them the same

ing the writing of History, Kracauer corresponded on several occasions with Panofsky and Kubler, who had been Focillon's students.

174 Hans Robert Jauss, *Zeit und Erinnerung in Marcel Proust's "A la recherche du temps perdu,"* (Heidelberg: Carl Winter Universitätsverlag, 1955). See also Jauss's *Literaturgeschichte als Provokation* (Frankfurt a.M.: Suhrkamp, 1970), 195–6, for positive remarks on Kracauer.
175 Kracauer to Lévi-Strauss, December 18, 1963 (original in English).
176 Lévi-Strauss to Kracauer, December 23, 1963 (original in English).

reality character as to that continuous, linear flow, which results in my basic assumptions of the antinomy at the core of Time. Indeed, even as an individual I believe we live in a veritable cataract of times. [...] Since you also speak of the "polyphonic structure" of time, the difference, if any, between our approaches may lie only in the fact that you seem to emphasize more than I do the share of homogeneous chronological time in the historical process, whereas I also stress the significance of the various existing peculiar time sequences and therefore hesitate to identify history as a process.[177]

In the final version of the chapter, the phrases "antinomy at the core of time" and "cataract of times" reappear, as does Kracauer's criticism of the Kubler–Focillon–Lévi-Strauss's dismissal of all homogeneous time. Walter Benjamin, who dealt with the same issue in his "Theses on the Philosophy of History,"[178] up braided for the same failing:

Benjamin on his part indulges in an undialectical approach; he drives home the nonentity of chronological time without manifesting the slightest concern over the other side of the picture. That there are two sides to it has rarely been recognized.[179]

Proust comes off a bit better, for even while blurring chronology, he was "at pains to keep it intact."[180] But, as we have already noted, Kracauer saw Proust's attempt to reconcile chronological and shaped, subjective time through an aesthetic, a posteriori synthesis as illegitimate. The antinomy between chronological flow and the multitude of shaped times which cut across it is insoluble, or if it can be solved, then only at the very last moment of Time itself. Short of this utopian apocalypse, the temporal visions of the historicists and the modernists are eternally at war.

In his final chapter, entitled "The Anteroom," Kracauer drew certain highly speculative conclusions from his investigation, many of which in

---

[177] Kracauer to Marrou, May 18, 1966; (original in English). Kracauer was indebted to Marrou's *De la connaissance historique* (Paris: Editions du Seuil, 1962) and to several of his articles on historical method.
[178] Bejamin, "Theses on the Philosophy of History," in *Illuminations*.
[179] Kracauer, *History*, 155.
[180] Ibid., 162. Kracauer's point is repeated in Roger Shattuck's recent Modern Masters Series study, *Proust* (London: 1974), 119.

fact were implicit in his earlier work.[181] As we have previously mentioned, he used the metaphor of the anteroom to characterize both and photography history, neither dealing with the "last things" of human concern. Just as there is an insoluble antinomy between and chronological shaped time, so one exists between the anteroom and what for want of a better term we may call the inner sanctum into which it may lead. The particular, contingent truths of history, which relate to the *Lebenswelt*, are different in kind from the universal truths sought by philosophy. Attempts to historicize philosophy in a radical way, whether in Hegelian, Diltheyan, or Heideggerean terms, fail to observe the boundary between the two spheres. Such immanentist absolutizations of the historical, which culminate in Hans-Georg Gadamer and the so-called hermeneutics movement[182] lead to a theodicy in which history becomes a success story. But the alternative of situating philosophical truths completely outside of history as transcendental and eternal verities is equally erroneous. Both the immanentists and the transcendentalists fail to meet the challenge of relativism raised by historical consciousness because of their outmoded views of time. Because of the antinomous character of time,

> [t]here are "pockets" and voids amidst these temporal currents, vaguely reminiscent of interference phenomena. This leads me to speak, in a provisional way, of the "limited" relativity of certain ideas emerging from such pockets. [...] Philosophical truths have a double aspect. Neither can the timeless be stripped of the vestiges of temporality, nor does the temporal wholly engulf the timeless. Rather, we are forced to assume that the two aspects of truths exist side by side, relating to each other in ways which I believe to be theoretically undefinable. Something like an analogy may be found in the "complementarity principle" of the quantum physicists.[183]

This insight, Kracauer believed, was best exemplified in the work of Burckhardt, who sought absolutes, but was sensitive to their ambiguities amidst the flux of historical change.

In getting us past the anteroom, however, Kracauer was no real help. The "side" he was concerned with in his "side-by-side" principle was clearly that

---

181 The essay in which many of these ideas are most clearly adumbrated is "Die Wartenden," in *FZ*, March 12, 1922; reprinted in *Das Ornament der Masse*.
182 Hans-George Gadamer, *Wahrheit und Methode* (Tübingen: Akademie Verlag, 1960).
183 Kracauer, *History*, 199–200.

of the *Lebenswelt*, for it was the anteroom "in which we breathe, move and live."[184] In trying to redeem this contingent and ephemeral world, the historian approaches the state Kafka attributed to Sancho Panza as that of a "free man" who dwells in a "utopia of the in-between—a terra incognita in the hollows between the lands we know."[185] To Kracauer, the best model for this type of intellectual stance was Erasmus, who followed the "middle way" as the "direct road to Utopia—the way of the humane."[186]

As an epilogue to *History*, Kracauer's editors appended a quotation from Kierkegaard that Kafka had cited and Kracauer had especially liked. In essence, it praises the simple man who defies the conventions of the world to remain true to his personal vision. The quotation is prefaced by an injunction that Kracauer himself had followed throughout his long and uneven career: "Focus on the 'genuine' hidden in the interstices between dogmatized beliefs of the world, thus establishing tradition of lost causes; giving names to the hitherto unnamed."[187]

The book's epilogue is a just epilogue to Kracauer's own life's work. *History*, despite its stress on non-homogeneity and fragmentation, or more correctly through its justification for that stress, gives a meaning to the checkered corpus of Kracauer's writings. In Sartrean terms, it "totalizes" the disparate elements of his work by revealing their inherent relatedness, without, however, reducing them to a single common denominator. It does this not merely by spelling out the implicit vision behind them, but also by placing certain of his books in a juxtaposition that turns their individual weaknesses into a composite strength. Thus *From Caligari to Hitler* and *Jacques Offenbach and his Time*, if looked at solely on their own terms, can be faulted for ignoring what Kracauer called the non-homogeneous structure of the historical universe. That is, both of them assume a somewhat simplistic and unmediated correspondence between social and cultural phenomena. The "shaped time" of the cinema and operetta are not differentiated to any real extent from the "shaped time" of Weimar and Second Empire society. Within the works, this is surely a shortcoming, as many critics were quick to notice. But set side by side with *Theory of Film*, where the immanent development of film is traced with scarcely any reference to social developments, *From Cali-*

184 Ibid., 195.
185 Ibid., 217.
186 Ibid., 14.
187 Ibid., 219.

gari to Hitler seems less one-dimensional. Although no comparable book was written by Kracauer dealing with Offenbach's music in a solely musical context, the argument of *History* suggests that he would have recognized its validity alongside of his "Gesellschaftsbiographie." Similarly, *History* puts into greater balance his concern for flux and process in forming inter alia *Theory of Film* (criticized by commentators like Parker Tyler for its overly Heraclitean bias)[188] with his somewhat more muted desire for stable values and order, which is apparent in his constant lament over the emptiness of modern life. It also allows us to view his earlier difficulties defining realism in *Theory of Film* with some understanding, for his several usages correspond to a reality which is itself multidimensional.

History also helps make sense of his strangely ambivalent attitude towards Marxism, which has continued to be a source of debate among his interpreters. Like so many of his contemporaries, Kracauer underwent a clear movement to the right during his exile in America. By the 1960s, so Kristeller remembers,[189] he was strongly hostile to the New Left and all it represented. In 1932, he could write that he was an advocate of Marxism and would continue to be one, but in *History*, Marxism came in for a large share of criticism. His basic complaint was that Marx, like Hegel before him, had succumbed to the magic of linear chronology. (Ironically, this charge was levelled at the same time that Louis Althusser in France was discovering a sensitivity to shaped times in the later Marx.)[190] To Kracauer, the humanist, even existentialist Marx championed by Sartre and others was far less important than the naturalist Marx who tried to apply scientific method to history and failed.

And yet, despite his clear shift to a kind of disillusioned liberalism, many of these same attitudes can be seen even during the Weimar period. In distrusting the idealistic Marxism of Lukács's *History and Class Consciousness*, Kracauer expressed his doubts about the Hegelian legacy in Marx's own writings, although he preferred to minimize it. In the 1960s, he still disapproved of Hegelianizing Marx, but now he admitted that both thinkers shared a fallacious view of time. What went along with this disapproval was a caution

---

188 Tyler, *Sex Psyche Etcetera in the Film*, 122.
189 Conversation with Professor Kristeller, New York, September 5, 1973.
190 Louis Althusser, *For Marx*, trans. Ben Brewster (London: Allen Lane, 1969), 134–137. Althusser's discussion is not specifically on Marx here, but on the dialectical notion of time in a play by Bertalozzi. In *Reading Capital*, written with Etienne Balibar, trans. Ben Brewster (New York: Verso, 1970), Althusser specifically deals with the concept of non-homogenous time in Marx himself (pp. 99f).

about the role of praxis in reshaping the world; the elegiac lethargy of *Ginster* went hand in hand with a view of Marx as a naturalist. It was not surprising that he would take Lévi-Strauss's side in his dispute with Sartre.

History is also illuminating in this regard because it helps us situate him more precisely in the context of his friendships with Benjamin, Bloch, and Adorno. As we have seen, Benjamin's distinction between "ideas" and generalities, his justification for the "collector," and his critique of unilinear time are all cited with approval by Kracauer, although the last is criticized for ignoring the place of chronological time as one stream in the cataract. But what is absent is Benjamin's guarded optimism about achieving fulfilled, utopian time (what Benjamin called *Jetztzeit*).[191] The side of Benjamin that had responded positively to Brecht was completely closed to Kracauer, who endorsed Gershom Scholem's appraisal of the pathological character of that relationship.[192] In a letter to Rolf Tiedemann, who had just written a study of Benjamin, Kracauer wrote that he shared certain of Benjamin's ideas about history:

> That nothing should be lost, that history must be shattered in order to find its actual content in details, and so forth. Other thoughts—such as his emphasis on surrealism—I considered bizarre. And I have always regretted that he hadn't seen the dialectic between the reality, in which we live, and the messianic end reality (which only plays a negative role for me).[193]

This negative attitude towards a utopian future also colored Kracauer's intellectual relationship to Bloch. Personally, the two men were on the best of terms in the years before Kracauer's death. The earlier friction over Kracauer's late Weimar politics had long since been forgotten. In fact, a still older dispute between them, which broke out in 1922, when Kracauer criticized Bloch's *Thomas Münzer als Theologe der Revolution* and Bloch answered in his *Durch die Wüste*, was also patched over, so much so that Bloch removed his rebuttal from the new edition of the book in 1964.[194] When Bloch's *Tübinger Einleitung in die Philosophie I* had appeared in the previous year, Kracauer had

---

191 Benjamin, *Theses on the Philosophy of History*, 263.
192 Gershom Scholem, "Walter Benjamin," in *The Leo Baeck Institute Yearbook* (New York: Oxford University Press, 1965). On May 23, 1965, Kracauer wrote to Scholem that he shared his view on Benjamin's Marxism, adding "I once had a very heated argument with him in Berlin over Benjamin's slavish masochistic attitude (*Haltung*) towards Brecht."
193 Kracauer to Tiedemann, February 21, 1966. To Löwenthal, he had complained years before of Benjamin's tendency towards "messianic dogmatism." (Letter of January 6, 1957.)
194 Siegfried Kracauer, *Durch die Wüste* (Frankfurt a.M.: Suhrkamp, 1964).

approvingly written: "You are to my knowledge the only one who presents the problem of time. And what you say about it strongly touches my own ideas on the antinomy at the center of the chronological concept of time."[195] Further evidence of their mutual affection appeared in Kracauer's contribution to a volume of tributes to Bloch in 1965.[196] In his essay, which took the form of a letter to Bloch, Kracauer stressed the side of Bloch's utopianism that was most amenable to him: its conservative, redemptive dimension. Bloch's love of narrative, which Benjamin had also shared, meant an awareness of continuities, even amidst the most radical changes. Bloch was thus superior to conceptual utopians who want to impose a rational form on the future, which severs it completely from the past. Bloch also possessed a laudable sensitivity to the concrete, material realities of the sensuous world; "you preserve something of the magic of things," Kracauer wrote, "which you disenchant."[197]

And yet, behind the expression of solidarity was a clear acknowledgment of the distance between them. Kracauer identified himself with Sancho Panza, who was short of breath trying to keep up with Bloch's Quixotic race towards utopia. Significantly, he appended the section on Erasmus later published in his introduction to *History* as a "gift" to Bloch. Erasmus's utopia, that of the middle way, the way of the humane, was not, however, Bloch's, which called for a far more radical transformation of man and society. Without any actual filiation, Kracauer's reading of Erasmus came close to that of an old enemy, Stefan Zweig, whose *Triumph und Tragik des Erasmus von Rotterdam* (1934)[198] also praised Erasmus's anti-extremism and moderation. In 1937, Georg Lukács had taken Zweig to task in *The Historical Novel* for advocating Erasmian non-revolutionary, pseudo-humanism.[199]

Erasmus's position was suspect, Lukács argued, because it was grounded in an elitist condemnation of the masses as irrational. Although Bloch had his own quarrels with Lukács, it seems likely that the champion of Thomas Münzer would have shared some of his qualms about the adequacy of Erasmian utopianism.

195 Kracauer to Bloch, June 17, 1963.
196 Siegfried Kracauer, "Zwei Deutungen in Zwei Sprachen," in *Ernst Bloch zu Ehren; Beiträge zu seinem Werk*, ed. Siegfried Unseld (Frankfurt a.M.: Fischer, 1965).
197 Ibid., 146.
198 Stefan Zweig, *Triumph und Tragik des Erasmus von Rotterdam* (Frankfurt a.M.: Fischer, 1934). Kracauer's distaste for Zweig's type of biography was expressed in his 1930 piece "Die Biographie als Neubürgerliche Kunstform," reprinted in *Das Ornament des Masse*.
199 Georg Lukács, *The Historical Novel*, trans. Hannah and Stanley Mitchell (Boston: Beacon Press, 1963), 266–69. For a discussion of the Zweig–Lukács dispute, see Albert William Levi, *Humanism and Politics* (Bloomington, IN: Indiana University Press, 1969).

If Kracauer's disillusionment about Marxist utopianism distanced him from Benjamin and Bloch, the opposite complaint was partly responsible for his growing estrangement from Adorno in the last years of his life. Although I hope to give a detailed account of the complicated course of their friendship elsewhere, certain points can be derived from a reading of *History* alone, which should be made here. In his anteroom chapter, Kracauer devoted half a paragraph to Adorno's recently published *Negative Dialektik*,[200] which advocated a radically anti-ontological position without any first principles or fixed points of reference. To Kracauer, this was an "unfettered dialectic" with unfortunate consequences:

> His rejection of any ontological stipulation in favor of an infinite dialectics which penetrates all concrete things and entities seems inseparable from a certain arbitrariness, an absence of content and direction in these series of material evaluations. The concept of Utopia is then necessarily used by him in a purely formal way, as a borderline concept which at the end invariably emerges like a *deus ex machina*. But Utopian thought makes sense only if it assumes the form of a vision or intuition with a definite content of a sort. Therefore the radical immanence of the dialectical process will not do; some ontological fixations are needed to imbue it with significance and direction.[201]

In other words, whereas Kracauer faulted Bloch and Benjamin for their hopes of realizing utopia in history, he attacked Adorno for eliminating ontology and utopia entirely. In his own thinking, history and ontology exist side by side, but still separately. Their coexistence, like that of the general and the particular, can only be defined by what he called "tact"[202] in each specific case.

Although raising an interesting objection to Adorno's negative dialectics, which has left many readers suspended in a conceptual whirl, Kracauer's alternative failed to answer a number of questions. Although chastising Adorno for lacking a utopia "that assumes the form of a vision or intuition with a definite content of a sort," he never really offered one himself. Without any of that belief in dealienation or the reconciliation of man and nature that animated Marxist Humanism, Kracauer fell back on a vague and general en-

---

200 Theodor W. Adorno, *Negative Dialectics*, trans. E.B. Ashton (New York: Bloomsbury, 1973).
201 Kracauer, *History*, 201.
202 Ibid., 200 and 206.

dorsement of Erasmian tolerance and flexibility. This may well be a posture worthy of emulation, but it is scarcely a utopian vision. Similarly, his advocacy of "tact" as a means to regulate the relationship between history and ontology, the general and the particular, is not very instructive. Kracauer assumed

> that speculations on the total nature of the universe are called for, or indeed indispensable, as gambles in Kafka's sense. They meaningfully enter the scene on (unpredictable) occasions and then presumably fulfil a vital function.[203]

But what the occasions were, which speculations are superior to others, and what functions they fulfilled, Kracauer could not say. There is, in short, a phenomenon here which might be called "metaphysical fellow-travelling": a belief in ontology and utopia without any specific content, a recognition of the legitimacy of ultimate thoughts without the daring to think them out loud, a belief that relativism can be overcome by the "pockets" of the absolute that exist in the interstices of chronological time, without speculating on the contents of the pockets.

Kracauer was surely right to point to the antinomies of time and the non-homogeneity of the historical universe. His efforts throughout his career to reawaken our sensitivity to the phenomenal *Lebenswelt* often lost amidst a welter of conceptual generalizations were equally laudable. His sober defiance of ideological panaceas, although uncomfortably close to the end-of-ideology fantasy of the 1950s, also merits respect. But despite these achievements, what leaves the observer of Kracauer's career uneasy is his tendency to freeze the posture of extraterritoriality and chronological anonymity, which he had made a personal virtue, into a universal condition incapable of change. What Arnheim called the "melancholy surrender"[204] in Kracauer's championing of cinematic realism was a leitmotif of his entire career, despite the utopian intentions of *History*. Adorno certainly exaggerated when he wrote that "in the treasure of motives in his thought one would have looked in vain for outrage against reification,"[205] but there was a grain of truth in the charge. Ginsterism may be a sensible reaction to certain circumstances, but it need not be made a model for all times. Nor is the mask

---
203 Ibid., 200.
204 Arnheim, "Melancholy Unshaped," 191.
205 Adorno, "Der Wunderliche Realist," 107.

of Sancho Panza the only one man can use if they are to avoid the follies of Don Quixote. In short, Kracauer's "side-by-side" principle may accurately represent the best hope in an era without integral meaning and real human community, but who is to say that his era is the last we shall experience in human history?

THE EXTRATERRITORIAL POETICS OF W.G. SEBALD

Matthew Hart & Tania Lown-Hecht

The word extraterritoriality is as multivalent as the space it describes. It is a legal coinage signifying personal immunity from local laws, the borderless space of the free seas, and a state's power to extend jurisdiction across borders; recently, it has also become a key concept in philosophical debates about what Giorgio Agamben calls the "state of exception as a paradigm of government."[1] More broadly, extraterritoriality has begun to figure as the object of cultural meditations on the relation between subjection and autonomy, stasis and movement, and exile and belonging—a discourse that has implications for intellectuals in many fields but has so far been most prominent in architectural studies.[2] Yet with few exceptions, literary critics have not engaged with it—and when they have, extraterritoriality has generally been mistaken as synonymous with a state of multilingual plenitude and postnational migrancy.

This essay explores how extraterritoriality figures within the prose writings of the late W.G. Sebald (1944–2001). Sebald's use of the Latinate German

---

Originally published as Matthew Hart and Tania Lown-Hecht. "The Extraterritorial Poetics of W.G. Sebald," *Modern Fiction Studies* 58, no. 2 (2012): 214–38. © 2012 Purdue Research Foundation. Reprinted with permission of Johns Hopkins University Press.

1   Giorgio Agamben, *State of Exception*, trans. Kevin Attell (Chicago: University Chicago Press, 2003), 1. For legal definitions see "Extraterritoriality," *West's Encyclopedia of American Law* (St. Paul, MN: West Group, 1998). For Agamben, the state of exception is epitomized in concentration camps, which create an "extraterritorial threshold in which the human body is separated from its normal political status and abandoned, in a state of exception" (Giorgio Agamben, *Homo Sacer: Sovereign Power and Bare Life*, trans. Daniel Heller-Roazen [Stanford: Stanford University Press, 1998], 159).

2   See, for example, Keller Easterling, *Enduring Innocence: Global Architecture and its Political Masquerades* (Cambridge, MA: MIT Press, 2005); Anselm Franke and Eyal Weizman, "Islands: The Geography of Extraterritoriality," *Volume* 6 (2003), http://volumeproject.org/islands-the-geography-of-extraterritoriality/ (accessec Jan. 18, 2016); Anselm Franke, Rafi Segal, and Eyal Weizman (eds), *Territories: Islands, Camps, and Other States of Utopia* (Berlin: Institute for Contemporary Art, 2003); Saree Makdisi, "The Architecture of Erasure." *Critical Inquiry* 36 (2010): 519–59; Adi Ophir, Michal Givoni, and Sari Hanafi (eds), *The Power of Inclusive Exclusion Anatomy of Israeli Rule in the Occupied Palestinian Territories* (Cambridge, MA: MIT Press, 2009); Eyal Weizman, "On Extraterritoriality" (Nov. 10, 2005), http://www.publicspace.org/en/text-library/eng/b011-on-extraterritoriality (accessed Jan. 18, 2016).

compound *extraterritorial* might at first seem unworthy of comment, given his acknowledged appetite for obscure stories and histories. The significance of the word lies, then, in the way Sebald reaches for it at moments that are emblematic of his most characteristic themes. It occurs in *The Emigrants (Die Ausgewanderten)* when Max Ferber, a German-Jewish refugee, calls the country of his birth "a curiously extraterritorial place, inhabited by people whose faces are both lovely and dreadful."[3] It returns in *Austerlitz* in a description of the Nazi camp at Theresienstadt.[4] And in *Rings of Saturn (Die Ringe des Saturn)*, it describes the site of a disused military base, which appears like "our own civilization after its extinction in some future catastrophe."[5] Mark Anderson has even adopted extraterritorial as the keyword for the ethical dilemma at the heart of Sebald's writing, asking: "How does one signal solidarity with the victims of Nazi genocide without denying one's own German origins?"[6] The answer: "To live for thirty years in extraterritorial limbo."[7] Although we do not claim that extraterritoriality is the Sebaldian Rosetta Stone, without which any interpretation of his work is incoherent, the centrality of extraterritorial themes to Sebald's oeuvre implies that his work can be read through this lens even when the word itself is not invoked. In fleshing out an aspect of his writing that several critics have noticed but none have explored at length, we feel justified in referring to Sebald's extraterritorial poetics.[8]

---

3   W.G. Sebald, *Die Ausgewanderten: vier lange Erzählungen* (Frankfurt am Main: Eichborn Verlag, 1992), 181. We quote from the English translations of Sebald's work, then referring to the German for emphasis or clarification. Although Sebald did not translate his own prose, he vetted and revised the English translations with an eye to his Anglophone audience (Mark McCulloh, "Introduction: Two Languages, Two Audiences: The Tandem Literary Œuvres of W.G. Sebald," in *W.G. Sebald: History, Memory, Trauma*, ed. Scott Denham and Mark McCulloh [Berlin: de Gruyter, 2006], 7–18). We therefore treat Sebald's English editions as neither autonomous from German, nor subordinate to it. McCulloh concludes that, "as befits Sebald [the translations] are works of literature in their own right" (18).
4   W.G. Sebald, *Austerlitz*, trans. Anthea Bell (New York: Random House, 2001), 335. Originally published as *Austerlitz* (Munich: Hanser Verlag, 2001), 236.
5   W.G. Sebald, *The Rings of Saturn*, trans. Michael Hulse (New York: New Directions, 1998), 282. Originally published as *Die Ringe des Saturn: Eine englische Wallfahrt* (Frankfurt a.M.: Eichborn Verlag, 1995), 237.
6   Mark M. Anderson, "The Edge of Darkness: On W.G. Sebald," *October* 106 (2003): 105.
7   Ibid., 106.
8   See, for example, Stephen Clingman, *The Grammar of Identity: Transnational Fiction and the Nature of the Boundary* (Oxford: Oxford University Press, 2009), 189; Jan Ceuppens, "Das belgische Grabmal: Sebalds 19. Jahrhundert," in *W.G. Sebald: Intertextualität und Topographie*, ed. Irene Heidelberger-Leonard (Berlin: LIT Verlag, 2008), 94; Cynthia Ozick, "The Posthumous Sublime," *New Republic* (Dec. 16, 1996): 34; Gunther Pakendorf, "Als Deutscher in der Fremde: Heimat, Geschichte und Natur bei W.G. Sebald," in *W.G. Sebald: Expatriate Writing*, ed. Gerhard Fischer (Amsterdam: Rodopi, 2009), 91; here, "exterritorial"; Judith Ryan, "'Lines of Flight': History and Territory in The Rings of Saturn," in Ibid., 48–50; and Eric L. Santner, *On Creaturely Life: Rilke, Benjamin, Sebald* (Chicago: University of Chicago Press, 2006), 132, n. 47. None of these critics pursue the subject at length. By

This leads us to the broader stakes of our essay. Sebald is a major presence in a critical discourse centering on questions of cultural translation and the limits of nationalism. Michael Dirda captures this growing consensus when he says Sebald "exemplified the best kind of cosmopolitan literary intelligence."[9] A recent work describes Sebald's narratives as undoing the presumed connection between the "geographies, cultures, and languages that [would] allow us to place his novels within specific national traditions."[10] Such insights are accurate, but we still cannot locate Sebald's writings wholly beyond the nation-state. Extraterritoriality comes to English and German from juridical Latin and although it is commonly described as involving the abrogation of national authority, it is just as often used to expand the power of the nation-state. Take, for example, the period between June 2002 and January 2006 when José Padilla was declared an "enemy combatant" and held without the right to a habeas corpus hearing on the Naval Consolidated Brig in Charleston, South Carolina. Despite being a US citizen, imprisoned on a US ship in US waters, Padilla was, as a matter of law, marooned within an extraterritorial zone in which, by virtue of his identification as an "enemy combatant," he lay beyond US jurisdiction.

Such fissures within national territory don't necessarily imply the weakening of the state; in the case of Padilla, they were instruments of a strongly nationalist governing executive. Moreover, the Padilla case points toward a politics that depends, Agamben has argued, on the logic of the inclusive exclusion, in which pieces of territory are "placed outside the normal juridical order" but do not constitute "an external place." Agamben explains that the very places (and people) that are so excluded are "*captured outside,* that is, included by virtue of [their] very exclusion."[11] "*Being-outside, and yet belonging*": this is the paradoxical logic of the extraterritorial.[12]

As Keller Easterling has shown, the contemporary world is full of less spectacular extraterritorial sites, from ports and business parks to the *zones d'attente* that dot the margins of our societies.[13] Sebald critics have already

---

"poetics" we do not mean that Sebald has a fully developed theory of literary extraterritoriality, simply that this concept has significance across the range of his interests.
9   Michael Dirda, "Campo Santo." *Washington Post Book World* (Mar. 13, 2005): BW15.
10 Rebecca Walkowitz, *Cosmopolitan Style: Modernism Beyond the Nation* (New York: Columbia University Press, 2006), 160.
11 Giorgio Agamben, *Means Without End: Notes on Politics,* trans. Vincenzo Binetti and Cesare Casarino (Minneapolis: University of Minnesota Press, 2000), 40.
12 Id., *State of Exception,* trans. Kevin Attell (Chicago: University of Chicago Press, 2003), 35.
13 Keller Easterling, *Enduring Innocence: Global Architecture and its Political Masquerades* (Cambridge: MIT Press, 2005), 3.

noticed that his narratives are full of such spaces. For instance, Michael Niehaus has explored how we might locate the alienation of Sebald's emigrants on the "topological level."[14] In thinking through Sebald's topology of exile, Niehaus adapts Marc Augé's distinction between "anthropological places" (such as homes, which are overlaid with "the concrete and symbolic") and "non-places" (uniform and transitory locations such as airports, in which the social and historical richness of spatial experience is abolished).[15] It is not only that Sebald's prose is rich with non-places, but also that "the characters in Sebald's narratives [...] transform the places they cross into non-places."[16] In its focus on space and exile, Niehaus's essay has something in common with ours. We believe, however, that the concept of extraterritoriality is both more useful and more suitable—that is, more Sebaldian—than that of the non-space. This is partly because extraterritorial is Sebald's own word, partly because historically encrusted sites such as Theresienstadt are not easily described as super-modern non-places. Extraterritorial spaces possess a political weight that speaks directly to Sebald's signature themes, from the difference between forts and camps to the relation between languages and homelands. Together they figuratively shatter the ideological relation between sovereignty, territory, and population—an isomorphism that was crucial to the development of modern nationalism and is now waning even as we witness the growth "of the sovereign state to increase forces of centralization."[17] This is the paradoxical logic of an "extrastatecraft," to use Easterling's term, which is predicated on the interruption of national territory ("Petrodollars"). This paradox is, among other things, what explains Sebald's interest, not just in the racial laws of Nazi Germany, but also in Britain's imperialism in China, when a combination of gunboat diplomacy and extraterritorial law spread the bastard gospel of "free trade, which was held to be precondition of all civilized progress."[18]

Reading Sebald this way brings some political and historical clarity to his famously circuitous writings. For all their melancholy, Sebald's narratives never totalize state power: even a Holocaust narrative such as *Austerlitz*

---

14 Michael Niehaus, "No Foothold: Institutions and Buildings in W.G. Sebald's Prose," in *W.G. Sebald: History, Memory, Trauma*, ed. Denham & McCulloh, 322.
15 Marc Augé, *Non-Places: Introduction to an Anthropology of Supermodernity*, trans. John Howe (London: Verso, 1995), 51.
16 Niehaus, "No Foothold," 327.
17 Robert P. Marzec, "Militariality," *The Global South* 3, no. 1 (2009): 142.
18 Sebald, *The Rings of Saturn*, 141–2 [178].

demonstrates the presence of islands of maneuver within the landscape of sovereignty. Thus, Sebald's extraterritorial sovereignty is not a universal or inescapable force. It does not amount to a metaphysical defeatism. Our perspective therefore runs parallel to J.J. Long's compelling analysis of Sebald as an ambivalent critic of a biopolitical modernity that intrudes "into the very fabric" of works that otherwise resist it.[19]

Extraterritorial reading has a double payoff: it helps us understand Sebald's literary politics with greater clarity and complicates influential theories, such as Agamben's, that assert the singular and indivisible nature of political sovereignty. As we shall show, when one generalizes from Sebaldian extraterritoriality, one begins to understand that islands of exception can, in Eyal Weizman's words, also be "fissures and lacunae [...] beyond the reach of the mechanisms of state power."[20] When deployed by resistant narrators in difficult texts—texts that cross borders and genres as a matter of course—extraterritoriality comes to signify something different than it does for a Commander in Chief. It expresses the fraught relation between the undeniable power and the obvious limits of the nation-state as a cultural or linguistic container, political community, and psychic home.

Although our argument has interdisciplinary implications, it is not an essay in political theory. Our analyses are based in literary close reading and the critical discourse of psychogeography, which Guy Debord defined as the study of how space influences human psychology. Recent theorists have modified Debord's approach by noting the reverse movement, from psychology to geography; and, indeed, Sebald's extraterritorial poetics work in both directions: an empty coastline may be mapped onto a narrator's psychology, for example, but the narrator's sense of himself also becomes part of the landscape.[21] Finally, we suggest that there is an analogical relation between the logic of extraterritoriality and certain formal patterns within Sebald's prose, especially his vertiginous oscillation between macroscopic and microscopic points-of-view. Because of the over-determined qualities of Sebald's extraterritorial poetics, we have structured this essay around close readings of what we call Sebaldian topoi. As its root from the Greek *topos* (place) suggests,

---

19 J. J. Long, *W.G. Sebald: Image, Archive, Modernity* (New York: Columbia University Press, 2007), 20.
20 Anselm Franke, Eyal Weizman, and Ines Weizman, "'Islands': The Geography of Extraterritoriality," *this volume*, 120.
21 For a psychogeographic interpretation of Sebald, see Christopher C. Gregory-Guider, "The 'Sixth Emigrant': Traveling Places in the Works of W. G. Sebald." *Contemporary Literature* 46, no. 3 (2005): 422–49.

these topoi are both spatial and thematic. Through repeated motifs like the country house and the camp, Sebald imagines a world stuck somewhere between the desire to get lost and the inability to ever break from home. We begin, therefore, with the dilemma of the unhomely home.[22]

UNHEIMLICHE HEIMAT

Relatively few literary scholars have explored the poetics of extraterritoriality. In "Our Homeland, the Text," George Steiner makes a case for the inherent textuality of exilic Judaism, in which the "transcendent mobility" of the Torah exists in dialectical relation with the "territorial mystery of the native ground."[23] The real Zion, Steiner argues, is the text itself, which, in its constant interpretive migrations, is as much an exile as the Jew.[24] In "Englishness and Extraterritoriality," Bryan Cheyette also considers the relation between homeland and diaspora in Jewish letters. For Cheyette, English Jews remain perpetually extraterritorial because it is impossible to absorb "the Jewish past into a territorial Englishness."[25] As a result, a literature has developed that, despite the "Americanization of the diaspora and the nationalization of history in Israel," remains "neither English nor Jewish."[26] For both critics, extraterritoriality signifies an irrevocable breach within what Steiner calls "the natural bonds which unite a human person to his ancestors and their places of burial."[27]

Sebald also deals in such breaches. The difference is that, like the fragments of rock and ice that orbit Saturn, Sebald's extraterritorial condition never escapes a certain gravitational pull. This distinction can be clarified by reference to Steiner's book, *Extraterritorial*, which begins by invoking a language ideology in which great poets incarnate "the genius, *Geist*, [or] quiddity

---

[22] For this theme, see esp. John Zilcosky, "Lost and Found: Disorientation, Nostalgia, and Holocaust Melodrama in Sebald's *Austerlitz*," *Modern Language Notes* 121, no. 3 (2006): 679–98; also, J.J. Long, "Intercultural Identities in W.G. Sebald's The Emigrants and Norbert Gstrein's *Die englischen Jahre*," *Journal of Multilingual and Multicultural Development* 25, no. 5–6 (2004): 512–28, esp. 514–15; J.J. Long and Anne Whitehead, "Introduction," in *W.G. Sebald: A Critical Companion*, ed. Long & Whitehead, 7; Michael Niehaus, "No Foothold," 315; Gunther Pakendorf, "Als Deutscher in der Fremde," 91–6.
[23] George Steiner, "Our Homeland, the Text," *Salmagundi* 66 (1985): 5.
[24] Ibid., 8.
[25] Brian Cheyette, "Englishness and Extraterritoriality: British-Jewish Writing and Diaspora Culture," in *Literary Strategies: Jewish Texts and Contexts*, ed. Ezra Mendelson (Oxford: Oxford University Press, 1996), 22.
[26] Ibid., 37.
[27] George Steiner, *Extraterritorial: Papers on Literature and the Language Revolution* (New York: Athenaeum, 1971), 5.

of [their] native speech." This Herderian current of thought grew so influential, Steiner claims, that the very "idea of a writer linguistically 'unhoused'" came to seem inherently odd.[28] Steiner writes to bury this cultural-nationalist orthodoxy. His true poets of the twentieth century are "new 'esperantists'" and his extraterritorial aesthetic reaches its apotheosis in the "translations, re-translations, pastiches, [and] cross-linguistic imitations" of Vladimir Nabokov.[29] Steiner connects the "polylinguistic matrix" of Nabokov's art to the violence that made him a refugee from both his country and language.[30] This combination of linguistic playfulness and subjection to national chauvinism lends Nabokov a totemic status: "A great writer driven from language to language by social upheaval and war is an apt symbol for the age of the refugee. [...] Nabokov remains, by virtue of his extraterritoriality, profoundly of our time, and one of its spokesmen."[31]

This homage seems, at first sight, to accord with Sebald's own tribute to Nabokov in which the "young emigrants of [Nabokov's] early novels" are described as "living a quasi-extraterritorial, somehow unlawful afterlife in rented rooms and boardinghouses."[32] Most importantly, there is Nabokov's role as a leitmotif in *The Emigrants*, where, as the unnamed "butterfly man," the story of his life runs like a gossamer thread strung through the book — a figure who speaks, with hardly a word, about memories of home and the impossibility of ever going back.[33] For all this, Steiner ultimately celebrates the accomplishment of the wanderer across countries and languages: "no exile is more radical, no feat of adaptation is more demanding."[34] Sebald, however, never offers a similarly affirmative vision. Sebaldian exile is incomplete and comes at a terrible price, and if one objects that Sebald also never shows the

---

28 Ibid., 3.
29 Ibid., 5–6.
30 Ibid., 7.
31 Ibid., 11.
32 W.G. Sebald, *Campo Santo*, trans. Anthea Bell (New York: Random House, 2005), 143. Originally published as *Campo Santo* (Munich: Hanser Verlag, 2003), 186. Sebald's remarks create an unmistakable echo of Steiner. However, the Sebald Archive at the Deutsches Literaturarchiv Marbach contains no record that Sebald possessed a copy of Steiner's *Extraterritorial*.
33 Because this topic has been discussed at length, we do not discuss it here. See, for example, Jan Ceuppens, "Seeing Things: Spectres and Angels in W.G. Sebald's Prose Fiction," in *W.G. Sebald: A Critical Companion*, ed. Long & Whitehead, 192–5; Russell Kilbourn, "Kafka, Nabokov [...] Sebald: Intertextuality and Narratives of Redemption in Vertigo and The Emigrants," in *W.G. Sebald: History, Memory, Trauma*, ed. Denham & McCulloh, 53–63; Martin Klebes, "Infinite Journey: From Kafka to Sebald," in *W.G. Sebald: A Critical Companion*, ed. Long & Whitehead, 135–6; W.G. Sebald, "Ghost Hunter (Interview with Eleanor Wachtel)," in *The Emergence of Memory: Conversations with W.G. Sebald*, ed. Lynne Sharon Schwartz (New York: Seven Stories Press, 2007).
34 Steiner, *Extraterritorial*, 11.

opposite—that is, a happily rooted citizen—then this only verifies the consistently melancholic tenor of his *Weltanschauung*.

This melancholy is most evident in the realm of language, a major subject of Sebald's essay on Jean Améry.[35] Like Max Ferber, Améry becomes conscious of "the crumbling away and dwindling of his mother tongue."[36] These thoughts lead Sebald to a satisfying aphorism: "For those whose business is language, it is only in language that the unhappiness of exile can be overcome."[37] The terrible irony, however, is that in Sebald's stories, the attempt to reterritorialize language from within is both irresistible and inadequate. For instance, Ferber is neither without German, nor happily stationed at the crossroads between two tongues; he is rather haunted by the "echo" of a "muted and incomprehensible" language, which persists as the symptom of a trauma he can neither face nor wholly repress.[38] Just as he never wholly escapes the specter of his *Muttersprache*, so does he never achieve an unalienated relation to his adopted language. Linguistically speaking, Ferber is like a refugee always one step away from gaining papers of naturalization: English is the only language he speaks fluently and yet he speaks in a simulacrum of "turn of the century stage English," a synthetic dialect as obsolete as the music halls in which it was once heard.[39]

To adapt his remark about Améry, Sebald describes what it's like to feel "mal de pays" when one "wants nothing to do with [a] particular pays."[40] This is the condition that defines the quasi-autobiographical narrator of "Il ritorno in patria," irresistibly drawn to a childhood home that is nothing more than rented accommodation in an inn.[41] Such passages underwrite John Zilcosky's argument that, "instead of providing accounts of nomadism, Sebald's

---

35 Although "Against the Irreversible: On Jean Améry," is collected in *On the Natural History of Destruction*, the German original was collected in the 2003 Hanser *Campo Santo*. Page references reflect this anomaly.
36 Sebald, "Against the Irreversible" 162 [165].
37 Ibid., 161 [164–5].
38 W.G. Sebald, *The Emigrants*, trans. Michael Hulse (New York: New Directions, 1996), 182. Originally publishe as *Die Ausgewanderten: vier lange Erzählungen* (Frankfurt am Main: Eichborn Verlag, 1992), 271.
39 Sebald, *The Emigrants*, 190 [284].
40 W.G. Sebald, *On the Natural History of Destruction*, trans. Anthea Bell (New York: Random House, 2003), 164. Sebald explained his continued identification with "my country" in terms of ethical obligation: "I have inherited that backpack and I have to carry it whether I like it or not" ("Sebald, Ghost Hunter (Interview with Eleanor Wachtel)," 51. On Sebald's Germanness and expatriatism, see Pakendorf, "Als Deutscher in der Fremde."
41 W.G. Sebald, *Vertigo*, trans. Michael Hulse (New York: New Directions, 1999), 192. Originally published as *Schwindel. Gefühle* (Frankfurt a.M.: Eichborn Verlag, 1990), 218.

stories [present] subjects who could *never become sufficiently uprooted.*"[42] Sebald's home is a hotel, it is also a place to which he returns. Zilcosky finds the germ of this paradox in the title of Sebald's book, *Unheimliche Heimat* (1995), which "discusses writers [...] who all find it impossible to escape their Austrian *Heimat.*"[43]

For Steiner, this interstitial state is the great creative boon of otherwise terrible violence. In Long's account, however, Sebald's wanderers experience their "intercultural identity" not as a gift but "as crisis."[44] We agree. It is precisely this problem that, in our view, characterizes Sebald's use of extraterritoriality as a metaphor for the relation between belonging and exile: it names a condition in which individuals both choose and are compelled to adapt themselves to new places and languages but in which these choices and compulsions are never total, and never occur without loss. What's more, because it is a political limit concept—predicated on sovereign decision but signifying the fracturing or divisibility of sovereignty itself—extraterritoriality is also uniquely attuned to the paradoxes that shape that aspect of Sebald's oeuvre. To build on this claim, we now turn more directly to politics and law.

THE PALACE OF JUSTICE

When Steiner uses the word extraterritorial, he describes how literature moves between places and languages—a process that might begin with the violence of governments and armies but which, for him, finally transcends the political. As we have already suggested, this is a one-sided approach. In places like Theresienstadt, extraterritoriality does not signify the individual's transcendence of nationality or state power. In this section, we read one Sebaldian topos—the Palace of Justice in *Austerlitz*—as an allegory for an extraterritorial state of exception. But we also show how the allegory inverts itself, how the Palace of Justice is riddled with fissures that allow limited room for creative adaptation and tactical maneuver. In this way, extraterritorial sovereignty is inescapable but hardly complete.

---

42 John Zilcosky, "Lost and Found: Disorientation, Nostalgia, and Holocaust Melodrama in Sebald's *Austerlitz,*" *Modern Language Notes* 121, no. 3 (2006): 680–681.
43 Ibid., 681. Sebald alludes to Sigmund Freud's "The Uncanny" (1919) in which the etymology of *unheimlich* is excavated to show how the logic of repression binds together the language of the frightening and the familiar (*heimisch*).
44 Long, "Intercultural Identities," 517.

Weizman captures the paradoxical nature of extraterritoriality when he describes it as "rooted in the concept of sovereignty, although it is usually considered as its violation."[45] As Weizman explains, in creating such "archipelagoes of exception" from the normative operation of the law, states do not seek to violate their own sovereignty but "expand" it. This insight is one that Sebald clearly shared, as we see in the following passage from *Austerlitz*, describing the Palace of Justice in Brussels:

> The building of this singular architectural monstrosity [...] began in the 1880s at the urging of the bourgeoisie of Brussels, over-hastily and before the details of the grandiose scheme submitted by a certain Josĕph Poelaert had been properly worked out, as a result of which, said *Austerlitz*, this huge pile of over seven hundred thousand cubic meters contains corridors and stairways leading nowhere, and doorless rooms and halls where no one would ever set foot, empty spaces surrounded by walls and representing the innermost secret of all sanctioned authority.[46]

The key image comes at the end. Here is a space both vacant and impenetrable: an absurd but potent zone of law at the center of the administrative heart of the new Europe.[47] Oddly enough, the authority of this space does not stem from its public visibility, but from its occulted emptiness. As Eric Santner notes, it is an image that practically begs to be read in terms of Agamben's political theory.[48] The blind rooms in the Palace of Justice are not literally extraterritorial, not consular offices or International Zones. Still, their doorless vacancy speaks to the way that Sebald appears to locate the secret of political power in "a zone of indifference, where inside and outside do not exclude each other but rather blur with each other."[49] For Agamben, the paradigmatic instantiation of exceptional power is not the courthouse but the concentration camp; but if the state of exception is perfected at places like Auschwitz, its juridical logic is symbolized by Sebald's impenetrable chambers of law.

---

45 Franke, Weizman & Weizman, "'Islands,'" 120.
46 Sebald, *Austerlitz*, 29 [43].
47 Ceuppens refers to a radio interview in which Sebald described all Belgium as peculiarly extraterritorial (Ceuppens, "Das belgische Grabmal," 93–94). For Ceuppens, this quality explains Belgium's centrality to texts like *Austerlitz* and *Rings*.
48 Santner, *On Creaturely Life*, 132. Santner also connects Sebald's description of spaces like Theresienstadt as extraterritorial to Agamben's political theory (132). In making this argument, he also refers to the Palace of Justice passage.
49 Agamben, *State of Exception*, 23.

The German text appears to confirm this feeling with its use of *sanktionierten Gewalt* rather than *Authorität*—a wording that avoids the near tautology of "sanctioned authority" and embroiders the language of legality with that of coercion.[50] In the Palace of Justice, the unity of law, territory, and citizenry gives way to a political topology in which sovereignty fills in "empty spaces surrounded by walls."

This reading does not, however, exhaust the meanings of the Palace of Justice. As Weizman notes, extraterritoriality is also at stake "when a state fails to exercise its sovereignty over all its territory." He calls this "the ambiguity of exception" and it occurs when loopholes within the geography of power take on "aspects of self-governing enclaves." Oddly enough, we see this same ambiguity in the Palace of Justice story, which in fact contains two antithetical elements. There is no doubt that the Palace's secret chambers symbolize the dark side of the legal order; but Sebald also characterizes the law as involving a compromise between an occulted sovereignty and the mix of good intentions and proud incompetence that is bourgeois civil society. Thus, in the Palace of Justice, the dislocating localization of the law also creates hidden alleys of human movement amid the dark cells of bare life. The Palace is full of "creaking wooden stairs which gave the impression of being temporary structures," of obscure corners and empty rooms that the entrepreneurial citizens of Brussels have converted from public halls into spaces of private enterprise: "tobacconists, a bookie's, a bar, and [...] a gentleman's lavatory."[51] Its jury-rigged and semiprivatized hallways are not just spaces of exceptional power but also islands of tactical resistance. For if the space of exception exists in the sphere of extraterritoriality, so does the space of tactical maneuver. "A tactic is a calculated action," writes Michel de Certeau, "determined by the absence of a proper locus. [...] The space of a tactic is the space of the other. Thus it must play on and with a terrain imposed on it and organized by the law of a foreign power."[52] Subject to the law, yet never wholly determined by it, the political geography of *Austerlitz* is epitomized by these "dark cul-de-sacs," dead end corridors piled with unwanted furniture, "as if someone had been obliged to hold out there in a state of siege."[53] Why was someone so obliged? Did he manage to hold out? We aren't told. Rather than provid-

50 Sebald, *Austerlitz*, 29 [43].
51 Ibid., 30 [44–5].
52 Michel De Certeau, *The Practice of Everyday Life*, trans. Stephen Rendall (Berkeley: University of California Press, 1984), 36–7.
53 Sebald, *Austerlitz*, 30 [44].

ing us with a clear image of unlikely liberty or predictable subjection, Sebald maintains the ironic tension between these poles.

TRAINS AND WAITING ROOMS

For Sebald, travel is a distinctly extraterritorial experience. Travel can take us out of ourselves; but no journey is long enough, quick enough, or mazy enough, to outrun the catastrophe that is modernity. Train travel is peculiarly important to Sebald. Trains belong neither to the city from which they depart nor to the city to which they travel, while stations are transitional spaces where travelers are neither home nor away. In the Ladies' Waiting Room in Liverpool Street Station, *Austerlitz* hallucinates an image of himself as a child with his Welsh foster parents, seeing reflected on the walls "memories behind and within which many things further back in the past seemed to lie, all interlocking like the labyrinthine vaults [...] all the hours of [his] past life, all the suppressed and extinguished fears and wishes [he] had ever entertained."[54] The walls of the station's waiting room are also the spaces of *Austerlitz*'s mind: fragments of memories "interlocking" in an enigmatic labyrinth. Because he has spent so much of his life waiting — waiting to remember, waiting to belong, waiting to return to a place that is gone — the waiting room captures "all the hours" of his past.

In the first travelogue section of *Rings*, landscape, train, and passengers prove mutually constitutive. During the narrator's train journey to Somerleyton, the passengers sit "as far away from each other as they could be, and so silent, that not a word might have passed their lips in the whole of their lives."[55] The landscape is similarly isolated: "save for the odd solitary cottage there is nothing to be seen but the grass and the rippling reeds."[56] When the narrator arrives, he finds that "there was no station at the stop."[57] This example indicates the psychogeographic relationship among spaces, modes of transport, and people, all of whom are figured here as isolated or uninhabitable. The osmosis between space and inhabitants in Sebald's work means that train stations almost always evoke memories of displacement. When the narrator of *Austerlitz* first meets the title character in a waiting room, the room

54 Ibid., 136 [193].
55 Sebald, *The Rings of Saturn*, 29 [41].
56 Ibid., 30 [42].
57 Ibid., 31 [43].

is cast in twilight (an extraterritorial time, if there is one, between night and day), making its inhabitants seem like "the last members of a diminutive race which had perished or had been expelled from its homeland."[58] In *Austerlitz*, the reference to a race of people "expelled from its homeland" inevitably evokes the displacement of Jews in World War II; for, as Peter Fritzsche writes, the railways of the Third Reich "connect[ed] people to the camps and to the front, and the point of arrival and departure for thousands. [...] The German Reichsbahn hauled over three million Jews to their deaths. Trains represented the point of departure from the familiar to the unknown."[59]

For Austerlitz in particular, trains and train stations reproduce the progression from "the familiar to the unknown." In the Wilsonova train station, Austerlitz notes that the hall is "crowded with throngs of people who had spent the night there among piles of luggage, huddled together in groups of various sizes, most of them still asleep."[60] The groups of people evoke the scenes of Jewish displacement—including that of Austerlitz's own mother, whose journey from Prague to Theresienstadt represents the culmination of the process through which she is reduced from a Czech citizen to a racial object with no country. Train stations are also central to Austerlitz's own displacement: in 1939, he was exiled to England via Kindertransport, leaving behind his parents and shattering his knowledge of home. Austerlitz remains caught in these in-between spaces, as if he spent his life aboard the train that displaced him from one home without providing another, or wholly severing his connection to his homeland. His attraction to trains, then, is twofold: trains represent the moment of exile he endeavors to recover; and Austerlitz, like the train, is perpetually traveling.

THE PEDESTRIAN AND THE BOMBER

Sebald's characters and narrators also travel on foot, where freedom and mobility are inextricable from vulnerability to fatigue, exposure, and the nightly search for shelter. In *Rings*, walking provides a loose narrative scaffolding for Sebald's multigenre mélange. But walking also allows Sebald to explore the reciprocity between movement and feeling. Returning to his childhood

---

58 Sebald, *Austerlitz*, 7 [10].
59 Peter Fritzsche, *Life and Death in the Third Reich* (Cambridge: Harvard University Press, 2008), 227.
60 Sebald, *Austerlitz*, 217–18 [310].

neighborhood in Prague, for instance, Austerlitz is haunted by his lost memories, which manifest themselves as a spectral presence:

> At some time in the past, I thought, I must have made a mistake and now I am living the wrong life. Later, on a walk through the deserted town and up to the fountain colonnade, I kept feeling as if someone else were walking beside me, or as if something had brushed against me. Every new view that opened out before us as we turned a corner, every façade, every flight or steps looked to me both familiar and utterly alien. I felt that the decrepit state of these once magnificent buildings [...] precisely reflected my own state of mind.[61]

Austerlitz is lost in two senses: psychologically, he is "living the wrong life" and geographically, he is without direction. His walk through the "deserted town" amplifies his feeling of being adrift, with the desertion of the streets echoing his loneliness. His feelings of recognition and misrecognition — epitomized by the way everything looks "both familiar and utterly alien" — are the emotional mark of the *unheimliche Heimat*.[62] In such an extraterritorial state, walking reinforces what is familiar while at the same time revealing the familiar as utterly alien. Put simply, Austerlitz is not disoriented simply because he is lost; he is disoriented because of loss. Geography and emotion here create and invert one another, so that Austerlitz experiences the outer territories of Prague as the inner territory of his emotional life.

Never wholly bound by territorial or imaginative homelands, Sebald's characters are nevertheless tied to the earth by their inability to recover from loss. Their peripatetic movements are not, however, only mournful. Merlin Coverley explains that the aimless walker is subversive precisely because he "challenge[s] the official representation of the city by cutting across established routes and exploring those marginal and forgotten areas often overlooked by the city's inhabitants." [63] In their wanderings, Sebald's characters frequently find themselves in abandoned or marginal spaces with political resonances. When the narrator of *Rings* explores destroyed ghettos, or Aus-

---

61 Ibid., 212 [302].
62 On the relation between pedestrian wandering and the problem of the German *Heimat*, see Long, *W.G. Sebald*, 6.
63 Merlin Coverley, *Psychogeography* (Harpenden: Pocket Essentials, 2006), 12. For an interpretation of walking in *Rings* as resistance to a modernity that prizes ends over means, see Long, *W.G. Sebald*, 137.

terlitz ponders the mass graves underneath a "warren of putrid streets and houses" [64] in London, Sebald assaults the tendency to marginalize (geographically and literarily) the memory of history's victims. In his essay "Air War and Literature," he laments the inadequacy of historical representation, calling one record of an air raid a mere "gesture sketched to banish memory [...] to cover up and neutralize experiences beyond our ability to comprehend." [65] Sebald condemns these records as incomplete because they refuse to recognize their own incompleteness.

This psychogeographic view from the street seems to explain the disoriented-but-never-entirely-lost condition of Sebald's exilic walker. But, as other critics have noted, this narrative point of view frequently alternates with a quasi-cartographic perspective, so that the view from the ground alternates with the view from the air, in which (as Sebald writes of Thomas Browne) the capaciousness of the narrator's vision means that "the reader is overcome by a sense of levitation."[66] The irony of Sebald's style is that these points of view often overlap. Thus, to continue Sebald's reflection on Browne, the experience of reading his work comes to feel like "looking through a reversed opera glass and through a microscope at the same time." Initially, the airborne view seems to be the necessary complement to the up-close perspective; as he says of Browne, "the greater the distance, the clearer the view." [67] Yet the idea that the view from above could substitute for the view from the ground is exploded in the very first line of "Air War and Literature," where Sebald writes: "Today it is hard to form an even partly adequate idea of the extent of the devastation suffered by the cities of Germany." [68] In that essay, Sebald

---

64 Sebald, *Austerlitz*. 130 [190].
65 Sebald, "Air War and Literature," 25 [34]. Citations for "Air War and Literature" refer, first, to *On the Natural History of Destruction* and, second, to the German volume in which it was first collected, *Luftkrieg und Literatur*.
66 See, for example, Anderson, "The Edge of Darkness," 116 and Simon Ward, "Ruins and Poetics in the Works of W.G. Sebald," in *W.G. Sebald: A Critical Companion*, ed. Long & Whitehead, 59.
67 Sebald, *The Rings of Saturn*, 19 [28].
68 Sebald, "Air War and Literature," 3 [11]. Sebald often returns to the impossible task of describing destruction, calling the attempt to "take an objective view of the totally unreal kind of reality" a "remarkable" but futile task (*Campo Santo*, 67 [71]). Beck links this problem to the way Sebald's texts adopt an "imaginary position some distance above the earth" (The Rings of Saturn, 83 [103]) that they simultaneously criticize (John Beck, "Reading Room: Erosion and Sedimentation in Sebald's Suffolk," in *W.G. Sebald: A Critical Companion*, ed. Long & Whitehead, 87–8). Presner likewise argues that "Air War and Literature" "enacts an extraordinarily realistic 'view'" that "upon close inspection" is "impossible" (Todd Samuel Presner, "'What a Synoptic and Artificial View Reveals': Extreme History and the Modernism of W.G. Sebald's Realism," *Criticism* 46, no. 3 (2004): 345). For analysis of how Sebald's representations of destruction are formed by a tension between "a realist mode" and an "aesthetics of transience," see Julia Hell, "The Angel's Enigmatic Eyes, or The Gothic Beauty of Catastrophic History in W.G. Sebald's 'Air War and Literature,'" *Criticism* 46 no. 3 (2004): esp. 367–8, 374.

exposes the complementary inadequacy of both perspectives, even for those who think that the view from on high grants the insight of "some superior viewpoint."[69] Describing a BBC report of a raid on Berlin, he quotes the pilot's staccato descriptions: "a wall of searchlights, in hundreds, in cones and clusters [...] over that pool myriads of flares hanging in the sky. That's the city itself!" and then the words of "a third voice" saying "Look at that fire! Oh boy!"[70] Even while the airborne spectator can better see the extent of destruction, his reference to the burning city as "a fiery speck" reduces the conflagration to a distant generality.

We suggest, then, that Sebald's formal oscillation between large and small points of view reflects his sense that an artistic response to violence should also be poised—necessarily, if impossibly—between collective responsibility and the ineffability of individual experience. We suggest further that this formal balancing act ought to be understood through analogy with Sebald's extraterritorial thematics. The analogy is surely inexact. All analogies are. It becomes clearer, however, when we consider Sebald's representations of maps. Although they offer an apparently objective perspective on a territory, the map is an imaginative construction not so different from the walker's experience on the ground.[71] David Darby notes that, while Sebald's geographical representations might appear "topographically transparent," they are finally not "traceable on a map, and certainly not on the poorly reproduced and utterly unhelpful" maps Sebald includes in his works.[72] Instead, maps provide a symbolic link between many aspects of Sebald's oeuvre, connecting slum clearances in England to the expansion of the railways to the "total and exhaustive knowledge of bodies in space"[73] that is writ large on *Austerlitz*'s reproduced map of Theresienstadt. In the period of the World Wars, moreover, the map of Europe was hardly stable. In these circumstances, even a recent map could quickly become a fiction from the past.

These themes come together in *Rings* when William Hazel, gardener at the English country house Somerleyton, tells the narrator:

---

69 Sebald, "Air War and Literature," 20 [29].
70 Ibid., 21–2 [30–1].
71 Sebald makes this point explicit when he recalls his fascination with a map of Germany in which he saw Stuttgart and thought: "compared with the other German cities it was not too far from us. But I could not imagine a journey to it" (Sebald, *Campo Santo*, 198–9 [241–2]).
72 David Darby, "Landscape and Memory: Sebald's Redemption of History," in *W.G. Sebald: History, Memory, Trauma*, ed. Denham & McCulloh, 270. For maps as a form of power/knowledge in Sebald, see Long, *W.G. Sebald*, 75–83.
73 Long, *W.G. Sebald*, 81.

> [Lord Somerleyton] brought me a big relief map of Germany. All the place names I had heard on the news were marked in strange letters alongside symbolic pictures of the towns. [...] Those tiny images of towns, about the size of postage stamps, looked like romantic castles, and I pictured the German Reich as a medieval and vastly enigmatic land. [...] I got to know the whole country by heart; you might even say it was burnt into me. [74]

Sebald's dark humor ("burnt into me") exposes the inadequacy of the bird's-eye view, which merely transforms the multifarious cities into "enigmatic" symbols. This map sutures a "romantic" picture of the nation to the rationalized space-time of modernity. Neither register can capture the war's violence, as Hazel appears to acknowledge soon after, when he says that his quest to learn about the bombings proves "fruitless."[75]

Thus, the walker, needing a map to make sense of his surroundings, feels lost; the pilot or cartographer, feeling the absence of news from the ground, finds his view to be inadequate and distorting. In this way, the formal structure of Sebald's narratives stands in analogical relation to the political implications of his extraterritorial poetics.

THE COUNTRY HOUSE, ADRIFT

Mark Girouard has described the decline of English country house living in the early twentieth century due to a fall in the value of rural real estate and the social prestige of owning a "permanent stake in the country."[76] In this context, the ideological "mystique of the land had been exploded" and yet country living limped on for another few decades: "Nothing, it might seem, had changed," writes Girouard, "[b]ut in fact a great deal had changed."[77] In Sebald's representations of country houses, the conditions of being out of time and out of place are reciprocal. Isolated and "forgotten" parts of the English and Irish countryside are comparable to "undiscovered" lands outside of sovereignty. Their extra-temporality operates as the vertical axis of Sebald's horizontal representation of extraterritorial space.

---

74 Sebald, *The Rings of Saturn*, 39 [53].
75 Ibid., 39 [54].
76 Mark Girouard, *Life in the English Country House: A Social and Architectural History* (New Haven: Yale University Press, 1994), 300.
77 Ibid.

Consider, for example, the episode in *Austerlitz* about Iver Grove. Although this house appears intact, Austerlitz learns from the owner that it "had been requisitioned for use as a convalescent home during the war years [and] the expense of putting it back into any kind of order, however makeshift, had been far beyond his means."[78] Iver Grove's distance from blitzes and blitzkriegs affords it no sanctuary; instead, it deteriorates—so much so that when Austerlitz visits, its great hall is being used as a potato barn. This dilapidation is made only more obvious once Austerlitz discovers a walled-off zone of nurseries and billiards rooms, shuttered so long that it "seemed like a self-contained universe. It was as if time, which usually runs so irrevocably away, had stood still here, as if the years behind us were still to come."[79] The rooms appear to be somehow "outside" the catastrophe of modernity, a precious zone of intimacy and play. Austerlitz himself comments that "it is still possible to be outside time, a state of affairs which until recently was almost as common in backward and forgotten areas of our own country as it used to be in the undiscovered continents overseas."[80] And yet even these rooms do not foster some sense of living in a wholly alternative modernity; rather, their very isolation reminds us that they participate in a similar extraterritorial space-time as the Palace of Justice. Austerlitz's experience at Iver Grove sparks his recognition of "the years behind" him[81]—the unacknowledged past of the Judeocide, around which his entire narrative circulates.

The extraterritorial quality of Sebald's houses is amplified by his frequent recourse to metaphors of the sea, a literary strategy with good legal precedents. The United Nations Convention on the Law on the Sea limits the territorial authority states have over the oceans to the twelve miles beyond their shores.[82] The sea is thus the largest extraterritorial space on earth. In *Rings*, the narrator describes Somerleyton as producing a feeling of psychogeographic disorientation, akin to the experience of pelagic wandering, "when one is not quite sure whether one is in a country house in Suffolk or some kind of no-man's-land, on the shores of the Arctic Ocean or in the heart of the dark continent."[83] (The German original for "no-man's-land" is even more

78 Sebald, *Austerlitz*, 104 [152].
79 Ibid., 108 [156].
80 Ibid., 101 [147]. For Sebald's use of atemporality, see McCulloh, "Destruction and Transcendence," 400–4.
81 Ibid., 108 [156].
82 James C.F. Wang, *Handbook on Ocean Politics and Law* (Westport: Greenwood Press, 1992), 97.
83 Sebald, *The Rings of Saturn*, 36 [49].

explicit: "quasi-extraterritorialen Ort.") This experience has a counterpart in *Austerlitz*. To reach the Grande Bibliothèque in Paris, Austerlitz complains that "you have to travel through a desolate no-man's-land [Niemandsland] in one of those robot-driven Metro trains steered by a ghostly voice, or alternatively you have to [...] walk along the wind-swept riverbank."[84] The library's position beside the water creates the illusion of being aboard a ship, where visiting, you might think

> that by some mistake you had found your way to the deck of the Berengaria or one of the other oceangoing giants, and you would be not in the least surprised if, to the sound of a wailing foghorn, the horizon of the city of Paris suddenly began rising and falling against the gauge of the towers as the great steamer pounded onwards through mountainous waves, or if one of the tiny figures, having unwisely ventured on deck, were swept over the rail by a gust of wind and carried far out into the wastes of the Atlantic waters.[85]

The extraterritorial quality of this description is reinforced by Sebald's allusion to the RMS *Berengaria*, a transatlantic liner built in Hamburg in 1912 as the SS *Imperator*, seized by the US Navy in 1919 in order to repatriate American troops, and finally given to the British Cunard Line company as a reparation for the German sinking of the RMS *Lusitania*—the very incident often credited with bringing America into the war. With a history that moves between rival sovereignties, but never escapes their machinations, the *Berengaria* is a potent allegory for the ironies of Sebaldian extraterritoriality.

These political and psychogeographic implications come together in *Rings*, where the narrator visits another country house. The Anglo-Irish Ashburys, whom the narrator describes as "like refugees who have come through dreadful ordeals and do not now dare to settle in the place where they have ended up,"[86] live in one of the few estates that survived the arson attacks of the Irish civil wars. The Ashburys are nomadic even at home, camping out amid their scant belongings, transferring their sense of psychic displacement onto their house and environs. The son and heir spends his time "working

---

84 Sebald, *Austerlitz*, 275 [388].
85 Ibid., 277 [288].
86 Sebald, *The Rings of Saturn*, 210 [262].

on a fat-bellied boat"[87] that will never see the water. Mrs. Ashbury describes her first nights in the house as feeling "adrift on a sea of quicksilver"[88] and later describes the inhabitants of a burned mansion as "paralysed with horror like shipwrecked survivors on a raft."[89] Refugees in their own country, adrift on land they own but cannot settle on, caught between sovereignties and eras, the Ashburys are extraterritoriality incarnate. Sebald's narrator comes dangerously close to dissolving himself in their vagaries: he remarks that the house makes his "consciousness [...] dissolve at the edges, so that at times [he] could hardly have said how [he] had got there or indeed where [he] was," while the walls of his room remind him "of one of those maps of the far north on which next to nothing is marked."[90] The arctic, of course, is frozen ocean, conjured by the cold into a deadly facsimile of land: no-man's-land, changing with every thaw, every freeze.

THE FORTRESS AND THE CAMP

Founded in 1780, the walled town of Theresienstadt was initially a fortress and later operated as a jail for the prisoners of the Hapsburg Empire. It became a concentration camp in 1941 on the orders of Reinhard Heydrich, Stellvertretender Reichsprotektor of the Protectorate of Bohemia and Moravia — the Nazi-dominated statelet that had replaced independent Czechoslovakia. This protectorate had an unusual political character, for although it retained "attributes of sovereignty" it had to exercise power "in conformity with the political, military and economic rights of the Reich."[91] One symptom of this combination of autonomy and dependence was the emergence of a multitiered system of citizenship law, in which Czechs of German ethnicity could appeal to the "parallel extraterritorial jurisdiction"[92] of German law, whereas ethnic Slavs could make no such claim, and Jews were nakedly exposed to the Nazi reign of terror. Theresienstadt was the materialization, in brick and iron, of this racist jurisprudence, which enshrined the Reich's extraterritorial jurisdiction over the German *Volksgemeinschaft* (people's community) even as it stripped Jews of the most basic protections of citizenship.

---

87   Ibid., 211 [263].
88   Ibid., 214 [267].
89   Ibid., 216 [269].
90   Ibid., 210 [261–2].
91   Mark Mazower, *Hitler's Empire: How the Nazis Ruled Europe* (New York: Penguin, 2008), 59.
92   Ibid.

For Agamben, as we have stated, the concentration camp exemplifies the extraterritorial logic of exception in which camp inmates can be "killed without the commission of homicide" because they have been forced into "an extraterritorial threshold in which the human body is separated from its normal political status."[93] Still, Theresienstadt was never an extermination camp. Although death was a permanent fact of life, Theresienstadt operated primarily as a settlement and assembly camp in which Jews were interned before transportation to Auschwitz.[94] But Theresienstadt also had a third function: "to camouflage the ongoing annihilation process before the eyes of the free world."[95] In this sham tertiary role, the camp was variously described as an "old-age Ghetto,"[96] a "closed Jewish settlement under Jewish management," a "model ghetto" for artists and intellectuals, and even a "Judenstaat."[97] Such labels were designed to obscure Theresienstadt's function as "the stable that supplied the slaughterhouse."[98] Still, they also point to unique features such as its internal government under a Jewish Council of Elders, local currency, and postage stamps, and Jewish militia.[99] The chimera of a Jewish enclave in Nazi Europe adds another dimension to Sebald's description of Theresienstadt as "that extraterritorial place."[100]

Austerlitz has no illusions, describing Theresienstadt as directed "solely at the extinction of life."[101] This phrase comes in a sentence packed with information from H. G. Adler's *Theresienstadt, 1941–1945*, a sentence which goes on for an astonishing nine pages and is all the more terrifying for being perfectly hypotactic—as if, by the rigorous subordination of clauses, Austerlitz can somehow control his growing feelings of anger and grief. The sentence begins with an admission of the unpardonable guilt he feels for having neglected his mother's history; it ends with the story of a film, shot during a Red Cross visit to this "Potemkin village," in which he vainly hopes to catch

---

93 Agamben, *Homo Sacer*, 159.
94 Barkai calculates that over 84,500 prisoners were processed through Theresienstadt on the way to Auschwitz, while "some 33,500 died in the camp itself" (Avraham Barkai and Paul Mendes-Flohr, *German–Jewish History in Modern Times*, vol. 4: *Renewal and Destruction, 1918–1945*, ed. Michael A. Meyer [New York: Columbia University Press, 1998], 371–2).
95 Livia Rothkirchen, *The Jews of Bohemia and Moravia: Facing the Holocaust* (Lincoln: University of Nebraska Press, 2005), 233. See also Barkai & Mendes-Flohr, *German–Jewish History in Modern Times*, 370–8; Fritzsche, *Life and Death in the Third Reich*, 207–08; Mazower, *Hitler's Empire*, 388–9.
96 Barkai & Mendes-Flohr, *German–Jewish History in Modern Times*, 365.
97 Rothkirchen, *The Jews of Bohemia and Moravia*, 234.
98 Fritzsche, *Life and Death in the Third Reich*, 208.
99 Barkai & Mendes-Flohr, *German–Jewish History in Modern Times*, 373–4; Rothkirchen, *The Jews of Bohemia and Moravia*, 236–9.
100 Sebald, *Austerlitz*, 236 [335].
101 Ibid., 241 [341].

a glimpse of her face.[102] Austerlitz's appalling litany of facts and plans finally gives way to the admission that he cannot "cast [his] mind back to the ghetto and picture [his] mother."[103]

Why Theresienstadt? It is the most likely destination for a socially prominent Czech Jew like Agáta following her detention in 1942. However, there is also the curious fact that, unlike the death camps carved out of the Polish forests, it is an architectural relic of Austro-Hungary connected to a long history of military violence. Neither a rawly industrial killing zone, nor an abandoned ruin from an abstractly catastrophic past, Theresienstadt points to the ambivalence within Sebald's attitude toward the events of the war, which he depicts as singular in their brutality but connected through a complex web of causes and symbolic relations to a history of violence and exploitation almost geological in its persistence and depth.[104]

In *Austerlitz*, Sebald forges a sustained analogy between the *topoi* of the fortress and the camp. His description of Theresienstadt, for instance, is preceded by a map of the city taken from Adler.[105] The star shaped architecture of the walls creates an unmistakable echo of the early section in which Austerlitz's remarks about military architecture are accompanied by a similar illustration of the fortress at Saarlouis.[106] Austerlitz meditates on the way forts epitomize an opposition between movement and stasis and he concludes that "it is often our mightiest [architectural] projects that most obviously betray the degree of our insecurity."[107] When it comes to the forts of Belgium he tells a story of futile obsolescence: "the largest fortifications will naturally attract the largest enemy forces, and that the more you entrench yourself the more you must remain on the defensive, so that in the end you might find yourself in a place fortified in every possible way, watching helplessly while the enemy troops, moving on to their own choice of terrain elsewhere, simply ignored their adversaries' fortresses."[108] This insight seems most palpable

---

102 Ibid., 243 [344].
103 Ibid., 244 [346]. For the history of this film, see Brad Prager, "On the Liberation of Perpetrator Photographs in Holocaust Narratives," in *Visualizing the Holocaust: Documents, Aesthetics, Memory*, ed. David Bathrick, Brad Prager, and Michael D. Richardson, Rochester: Camden House, 2008), 27–9. Austerlitz desires to "gain comfort through imagined entry" into the film (30). He later fastens on an image, "both strange and familiar," of a woman who might be his mother (Sebald, *Austerlitz*, 251 [355]).
104 See Fritzsche, "W.G. Sebald's Twentieth Century Histories," in *W.G. Sebald: History, Memory, Trauma*, ed. Denham & McCulloh, 292.
105 Sebald, *Austerlitz*, 234–5 [332–3].
106 Ibid., 15 [22].
107 Ibid., 14 [21].
108 Ibid., 16 [24].

in the fortress at Breendonk, which the narrator visits shortly afterward: "a fort completed just before the outbreak of the First World War" that "proved completely useless."[109] For Austerlitz, the urge to build ever stronger defenses is betrayed by the realization that "everything [is] decided in movement."[110] His meditation therefore returns to the dialectic between the monumental force of state violence and the irresistible momentum of human movement, within which the poetics of extraterritoriality operates. Yet, as before, this opposition is never finally resolved. Austerlitz does not get the last word on Breendonk; for whereas he ends his story with its 1914 surrender, the narrator later tells us how, after a second defeat in 1940, the Nazis turned this "useless" fort into the notorious penal camp in which, among others, Jean Améry was tortured before transportation to Auschwitz.[111] At this point in its narrative, *Austerlitz* owns a historical perspective denied to its protagonist, who has yet to learn the story of his mother's internment and so assumes that the fort's obsolescence is an established fact, immanent within the limitations of their architectural form.

And so it goes on. In *Rings*, the narrator walks to Orford Castle, for centuries "the foremost bastion against [a] constant threat of invasion."[112] The castle only lost that status with the construction of new defenses during the Napoleonic wars, although they were never used and soon became "homes for the owls that make their soundless flights at dusk."[113] Finally, the narrator shifts perspective to the real subject of this episode, an abandoned military installation on the Orfordness promontory:

> The inhabitants of Orford [...] could only speculate about what went on at the Orfordness site, which, though perfectly visible from the town, was effectively no easier to reach than the Nevada desert or an atoll in the South Seas. For my part, I well recall standing down by the harbour when I first visited Orford in 1972 and looking across to what the locals simply called "the island," which resembled a penal colony in the Far East. I had been studying the curious coastal formations at Orford on the map, and was interested in the promontory of Orfordness, which seemed to have an extraterritorial quality about it. Stone by stone, over a period of

---

109 Ibid., 18 [27].
110 Ibid., 16 [24].
111 Ibid., 19–26 [28–38].
112 Sebald, *The Rings of Saturn*, 229–30 [286].
113 Ibid., 230 [287].

millennia, it had shifted down from the north across the mouth of the River Alde, in such a way that the tidal lower reaches, known as the Ore, run from some twelve miles just inside the present coastline before flowing into the sea. When I was first in Orford, it was forbidden to approach "the island," but now there was no longer any obstacle to going there, since, some years before, the Ministry of Defence had abandoned secret research at that site.[114]

At Orfordness, the juridical extraterritoriality of the camp overlaps most fully with the thematic tension between belonging and exile. The people of Orford are separated from the base by a river, kept ignorant by a doctrine of official secrets, and kept out by fences and guards—even while their country's most urgent business goes on behind its gates. Sebald compares the base, moreover, to spaces that couldn't be more different from the sceptered isle of English memory: the Nevada desert, a Pacific atoll (sites rendered uninhabitable by nuclear testing), and an Asian penal colony. Here is another island of extraterritorial exception in which the power of the nation-state is enhanced by pockets of alien space. What this reading obscures, however, is that Sebald does not apply the word extraterritorial to the base's legal or political character but to its natural geography. In the passage quoted above, extraterritorial rather describes the peninsula's unusual geology. And the adjective is just: the Orfordness peninsula is formed out of shale deposits that flow from the north, so that its shifting stones are both of the territory and apart from it, very much there but geologically allochthonous.

Whether we read extraterritorial as modifying geology or state power, its meanings for the narrator are much the same. He asks a "ferryman" to take him across the river to the promontory, with the implication that, like a passenger of Charon, he is crossing the border between worlds.[115] In this "undiscovered country," he feels "utterly liberated and deeply despondent."[116] Stuck somewhere between headlong movement and the backward glance, the nar-

---

114 Ibid., 233 [289–90].
115 Ibid., 234 [291].
116 Ibid. Shakespeare's metaphor of death as an "undiscover'd country" provides Sebald with the title of his essay on the death motif in Kafka's *The Castle*, which he reads as poised between a "yearning for peace which in K.'s world only death itself can provide, and the fear of being unable to die [...], the fear of a perpetual habitation in the no-man's land between man and thing" (W.G. Sebald, "The Undiscover'd Country: The Death Motif in Kafka's Castle," *Journal of European Studies* 2, no. 22 [1972]: 34). Rings here develops an implicit comparison between its narrator and Kafka, with the difference that the no man's land of Orfordness is both the (extra)territory of death and a place from which he can return.

rator begins to feel out of time and place, describing himself as a witness to "some future catastrophe."[117] Again, the extraterritorial functions as a gateway for the extratemporal, so that, as his memories shift from his experiences on the peninsula to his decision to return to the mainland, the narrator reflects: "Where and in what time I truly was that day at Orfordness I cannot say."[118]

It is at Orfordness that the parts of this essay finally come together. Here, the opposition between stasis and movement, native and foreign, is embodied in the paradox of an "island" connected to the mainland by a constantly shifting ribbon of shale from upstream. Here, on a shore once threatened by German invasion, the narrator is suspended somewhere between the land and the sea, between an England that is never home and a lost homeland he can never leave. Here, sovereign violence is rendered petty by wind and waves; but here, the "inclusive exclusion" of the camp persists in a timeless present.

The incredibly rich combination of extraterritorial *topoi* in this section of *Rings* demonstrates the flexibility and sophistication of this aspect of Sebald's poetics. Reading Sebald as the poet of the extraterritorial attunes us to the breadth of his engagement with the paradoxes of culture and history in the twentieth century; it also gives us a critical vocabulary both rich and specific enough to explain those paradoxes. In the Orfordness passage's final mediation on the question of home, questions of national belonging wholly merge with a landscape that is at once political and psychic, timeless and contingent. The narrator sits on the breakwater, waiting for his Charon, watching the eternal movements of the tide and sun. He sees the rooftops of Orford almost close enough to touch: "There, I thought, I was once at home."[119] In its apparent nostalgia for home, this is one of the most surprising statements in *Rings*. But the hint of grief contained in the phrase "was once" soon bursts to the surface of the narrator's consciousness, as his sense of ecstatic connection to the mainland—his dream of a fully *heimlich* identity, beyond the state of exception and the loneliness of exile—is revealed to be nothing more (or less) than a ghost: "And then, through the growing dazzle of the light in my eyes, I suddenly saw, amidst the darkening colours, the sails of the long-vanished windmills, turning heavily in the wind."[120] If there is no going home, there is no escape from it either. Such is the extraterritorial condition.

117 Sebald, *The Rings of Saturn*, 237 [294].
118 Ibid., 237 [295].
119 Ibid.
120 Ibid.

THE WORLD AND THE HOME

Homi K. Bhabha

In the House of Fiction you can hear, today, the deep stirring of the "unhomely." You must permit me this awkward word—the unhomely—because it captures something of the estranging sense of the relocation of the home and the world in an unhallowed place. To be unhomed is not to be homeless, nor can the "unhomely" be easily accommodated in that familiar division of social life into private and the public spheres. The unhomely moment creeps up on you stealthily as your own shadow and suddenly you find yourself with Henry James's Isabel Archer "taking the measure of your dwelling" in a state of "incredulous terror."[1] And it is at this point that the world first shrinks for Isabel and then expands enormously. As she struggles to survive the fathomless waters, the rushing torrents, James introduces us to the "unhomeliness" inherent in that rite of "extra-territorial" initiation—the relations between the innocent American, the deep, dissembling European, the masked emigré—that a generation of critics have named his "international theme." In a feverish stillness, the intimate recesses of the domestic space become sites for history's most intricate invasions. In that displacement the border between home and world becomes confused; and, uncannily, the private and the public become part of each other, forcing upon us a vision that is as divided as it is disorienting.

In the stirrings of the unhomely, another world becomes visible. It has less to do with forcible eviction and more to do with the uncanny literary and social effects of enforced social accommodation, or historical migrations and cultural relocations. The home does not remain the domain of domestic life, nor does the world simply become its social or historical counterpart. The

---

Originally published as Homi K. Bhabha: "The World and the Home," *Social Text* 31/32: Third World Post Colonial Issues (1992): 141–53. Reprinted with permission of Duke University Press.

1   Henry James, *The Portrait of a Lady* (New York: Norton, 1975), 360.

unhomely is the shock of recognition of the world-in-the-home, the home-in-the-world. In a song called "Whose House is This?" Toni Morrison gives this problem of "unhomely" dwelling a lyric clarity:

> Whose house is this? Whose night keeps out the light in here? Say who owns this house? It is not mine. I had another sweeter.... The House is strange. Its shadows lie. Say, tell me, why does its lock fit my key?[2]

My earliest sense of the unhomely occurred in a prosaic house in Oxford, in a narrow street reserved for college servants and research fellows. It was a noisy red-brick terraced house haunted by the hydraulic regurgitations of the Victorian plumbing system, yet strangely appropriate to the task at hand, a thesis on V.S. Naipaul. I was writing about a small-time Trinidadian journalist, the son of an Indian indentured laborer, a devotee of Samuel Smiles and Charles Dickens, who was afflicted with the most noisy and public bouts of nervous dyspepsia. As I contemplated his tragic-comic failure to create a dwelling place, to ever find *A House for Mr. Biswas*, I wrestled with the wisdom of Iris Murdoch's laudable pronouncement, "A novel must be a house for free people to live in." Must the novel be a house? What kind of narrative can house unfree people? Is the novel also a house where the unhomely can live? I was straining nervously at the edges of Iris Murdoch's combination of liberalism and "catholic" existentialism, while Mr. Biswas's gastric juices ran amok. The cistern churned and burped, and I thought of some of the great homes of English Literature — Mansfield Park, Thrushcross Grange, Gardencourt, Brideshead, Howard's End, Fawlty Towers. Suddenly, I knew I had found, in the ruins of the Biswas bungalows and their unlikely, unsettled lives, my small corner of the world of letters — a postcolonial place.

Working on *A House for Mr. Biswas*, I found that I couldn't fit the political, cultural or chronological experience of that text into the traditions of Anglo-American liberal novel criticism. The sovereignty of the concept of character, grounded as it is in the aesthetic discourse of cultural authenticity and the practical ethics of individual freedom, bore little resemblance to the overdetermined, unaccommodated postcolonial figure of Mr. Biswas. The image of the house has always been used to talk about the expansive,

---

2   Toni Morrison, "Honey and Rue," from a song-cycle for Kathleen Battle, Carnegie Hall Stagebill (January 1992), 12c.

mimetic nature of the novel; but in *Biswas* you have a form of realism that is unable to contain the anguish of cultural displacement and diasporic movement. Although the "unhomely" is a paradigmatic post-colonial experience, it has a resonance that can be heard distinctly, if erratically, in fictions that negotiate the powers of cultural difference in a range of historical conditions and social contradictions.

You can hear the shrill alarm of the unhomely at the moment when Isabel Archer, in *The Portrait of A Lady*, realizes that her world has been reduced to one, high mean window, as her house of fiction becomes "the house of darkness, the house of dumbness, the house of suffocation."[3] If you hear it thus at the Palazzo Roccanera in the late-1870s, then a little earlier in 1873 on the outskirts of Cincinnati, in mumbling houses like 124 Bluestone Road you hear the undecipherable language of the black and angry dead; the voice of Toni Morrison's *Beloved*, "the thoughts of the women of 124, unspeakable thoughts, unspoken."[4] More than a quarter century later, in 1905, Bengal is ablaze with the Swadeshi or Home Rule movement when "home-made Bimala, the product of the confined space," as Tagore describes her in *The Home and the World*, is aroused by "a running undertone of melody, low down in the bass... the true manly note, the note of power."[5] Bimala is possessed and drawn forever from the zenana, the secluded women's quarters, as she crosses that fated verandah into the world of public affairs... "over to another shore and the ferry had ceased to ply."[6] Much closer to our own times in contemporary South Africa, Nadine Gordimer's latest heroine, Aila, emanates a stilling atmosphere as she makes her diminished domesticity into the perfect cover for gun-running: suddenly the home turns into another world, and the narrator notices that "it was as if everyone found that he had unnoticingly entered a strange house, *and it was hers*."[7]

Gordimer's awkward sentence, with its rapid shift of genders and subjects—everyone, he, hers—provides the estranging syntax of the unhomely experience. Gordimer's sign of the woman's sense of possession and self-possession ("it was hers"), her ethical or historical transformation of the world, emerges retroactively, belatedly, *at the end of the sentence, towards the end of the book*. The historical or fictional subject is conscious of the "meaning" or in-

3   Henry James, *The Portrait of a Lady*, 360.
4   Toni Morrison, *Beloved* (New York: Alfred A. Knopf, 1987), 198–9.
5   Rabindranath Tagore, *The Home and the World* (London: Penguin, 1985).
6   Ibid., 70–71.
7   Nadine Gordimer, *My Son's Story* (London: Bloomsbury, 1990).

tention of the act; but its transformation into a "public" symbolic or ethical realm demands a *narrative* agency that emerges after the event, often alienating "intent," and disturbing "causal" determinism. In *The Human Condition*, Hannah Arendt meditates on just such a perplexity in signifying the social sphere as a narrative process. "In any series of events that together form a story with a unique meaning," she writes, "we can at best isolate the agent who set the whole process into motion; and although this agent frequently remains the subject, the hero of the story, we can *never point unequivocally to [the agent] as the author of the outcome*."[8]

In order to appear as material or empirical reality, the historical or social process must pass through an "aesthetic" alienation, or "privatization" of its public visibility. The discourse of "the social" then finds its means of representation in a kind of *unconsciousness* that obscures the immediacy of meaning, darkens the public event with an "unhomely" glow. There is, I want to hazard, an incommunicability that shapes the public moment; a psychic obscurity that is formative for public memory. Then the house of fiction speaks in tongues; in those undecipherable mumbling enunciations that emanate from *Beloved*'s "124," or the strange still silence that surrounds Nadine Gordimer's Aila whether she inhabits a house in the colored ghetto of Benoni (son of sorrow), or in a "grey area" of the Cape. And suddenly, literature asks questions at the very borders of its historical and disciplinary being: Can historical time be thought outside fictional space, or do they lie uncannily beside each other? Does the passage of power turn the agent of history into a stranger, a double-agent living between the lines?

The process of the aesthetic that I am proposing for the grounds of historical "re-cognition," and as a reckoning with the historical event, must be clarified. The aesthetic as the "obscuring" of the historical event that refigures it through a temporal distancing or "lag," as I've described it, must be distinguished from two familiar genealogies of the aesthetic. It must not be confused with the Kantian aesthetic, which is a mediatory process that brings existence to its fullest being in a revelation of self-reflection. Nor do I subscribe to that tradition of a materialist aesthetic that sees art as the displaced or overdetermined symptom of social reification—a fetishism of phenomenal forms that conceals "real" ideological contradictions. Both these approaches to the aesthetic involve transcendent schemes of thought

---

8   Hannah Arendt, *The Human Condition* (Chicago: University of Chicago Press, 1958), 185.

and art where the progressive movement of the dialectic at once poses the problem of difference, alienation, negation—at the ontological or epistemological level—and sublates or disavows it in the process of representation. For instance, although Louis Althusser is fully aware of the differential sites of the social formation, and the displaced or overdetermined nature of ideology more generally, the "subject" of cultural discourse is caught within the relatively homogenous, totalizing confines of the Lacanian Imaginary.

In contrast to this homogenous or transcendent temporality of the "aesthetic," I want to suggest that the aesthetic process introduces into our reading of social reality not another reified form of mediation—the art object—but another temporality in which to signify the "event" of history. I take my lead from what Walter Benjamin describes as the "constructive principle" of materialist historiography, where the "historical materialist cannot do without the present which is not a transition, but in which time stands still and has to come to a stop. For this notion defines the present in which he himself is writing history."[9] I locate the aesthetic in this time of inscription whose stillness is not stasis but a shock that Benjamin goes on to describe as "blasting a specific era out of the homogeneous course of history."[10] The present that informs the aesthetic process is not a transcendental passage but a moment of "transit," a form of temporality that is open to disjunction and discontinuity and sees the process of history engaged, rather like art, in a negotiation of the framing and naming of social reality—not what lies inside or outside reality, but where to draw (or inscribe) the "meaningful" line between them.

The unhomely moment relates the traumatic ambivalences of a personal, psychic history to the wider disjunctions of political existence. Beloved, the child murdered by her own mother, Sethe, is a daemonic, belated repetition of the violent history of black infant deaths, during slavery, in many parts of the South, less than a decade after the haunting of 124 Bluestone Road. (Between 1882 and 1895 from one-third to one-half of the annual black mortality rate was accounted for by children under five.) But the memory of Sethe's act of infanticide emerges through "the holes—the things the fugitives did not say; the questions they did not ask [...] the unnamed, the unmentioned."[11] As we reconstruct the narrative of child murder through Sethe, the slave

9   Walter Benjamin, *Illuminations* (New York: Shocken Books, 1969), 262.
10 Ibid.
11 Morrison, *Beloved*, 92.

mother, who is herself the victim of social death, the very historical basis of our ethical judgments undergoes a radical revision.

In the denouement of her novel Gordimer provides another example of the complexity of the "unhomely" when she describes what she calls "the freak displacement" that has afflicted the world of her characters:

> The biological drive of Sonny's life which belonged to his wife was diverted to his white lover [Hannah].... He and Hannah had begot no child.... The revolutionary movement was to be their survivor.... But Aila, his wife, was the revolutionary now.[12]

In the freak displacements of these novels, the profound divisions of an enslaved or apartheid society—negrification, denigration, classification, violence, incarceration—are relocated in the midst of the ambivalence of psychic identification—that space where love and hate can be projected or inverted; where the relation of "object" to identity is always split and doubled.

Such forms of social and psychic existence can best be represented in that tenuous survival of literary language itself which allows memory to speak:

> while knowing Speech can (be) at best, a shadow echoing
> the silent light, bear witness
> To the truth, it is not....

Auden wrote those lines on the powers of *poesis*, in *The Cave of Making*, aspiring to be as he put it "a minor Atlantic Goethe." And it is to an intriguing suggestion in Goethe's final "Note on World Literature" (1830) that I now turn to find a comparative method that would speak to the "unhomely" condition of the modern world. Goethe suggests that the possibility of a world literature arises from the cultural confusion wrought by terrible wars and mutual conflicts. Nations "could not return to their settled and independent life again without noticing that they had learned many foreign ideas and ways, which they had unconsciously adopted, and come to feel here and there previously unrecognized spiritual and intellectual needs."[13] Goethe's immediate reference is, of course, to the Napoleonic wars and his concept of

---

12   Gordimer, *My Son's Story*, 241–2.
13   J.E. Spingarn (ed.), *Goethe's Literary Essays* (New York: Harcourt, Brace, 1921), 98–9.

"the feeling of neighborly relations"[14] is profoundly Eurocentric, extending as far as England and France. However, as an Orientalist who read Shakuntala at seventeen, and who writes in his autobiography of the "unformed and overformed"[15] monkey God Hanuman, Goethe's speculations are open to another line of thought.

What of the more complex cultural situation where "previously unrecognized spiritual and intellectual needs" emerge from the imposition of "foreign" ideas, cultural representations, and structures of power? Goethe suggests that the "inner nature of the whole nation as well as the individual man works all "unconsciously." When this is placed alongside his idea that the cultural life of the nation is "unconsciously" lived, then there may be a sense in which world literature could be an emergent, prefigurative category that is concerned with a form of cultural dissensus and alterity, where non-consensual terms of affiliation and articulation may be established on the grounds of historical trauma. The study of world literature might be the study of the way in which cultures recognize themselves through their projections of "otherness." Where the transmission of "national" traditions was once the major theme of a world literature, perhaps we can now suggest that transnational histories of migrants, the colonized, or political refugees—these border and frontier conditions—may be the terrains of World Literature. The center of such a study would neither be the "sovereignty" of national cultures, nor the "universalism" of human culture, but a focus on those "freak displacements"—such as Morrison and Gordimer display—that have been caused within cultural lives of postcolonial societies. If these were considered the paradigm cases of a world literature based on the trauma of history and the conflict of nations, then Walter Benjamin's homeless modern novelist would be the representative figure of an "unhomely" world literature. For he "carries the incommensurable to extremes in the representation of human life and in the midst of life's fullness, gives evidence of the perplexity of living."[16] Which leads us to ask: Can the perplexity of the unhomely, intrapersonal world lead to an international theme?

Gordimer places this very question at the center of literary narrative: "Love, love/hate are the most common and universal of experiences. But no two are alike, each is a fingerprint of life. That's the miracle that makes litera-

---

14 Ibid.
15 John Oxenford (ed.), *The Autobiography of Goethe* (London: Henry G.Bohn, 1948), 467.
16 Benjamin, *Illuminations*, 86.

ture and links it with creation in the biological sense."[17] To put Gordimer's point another way: the fingerprint of literature — its imagistic impulse, its tropic topos, its metaphoric medium, its allegorical voice — these forms of narrative created from contingency and indeterminacy — may provide historical discourse with its powers of narrative "beginning." For it was Michel de Certeau who suggested, in *The Writing of History*, that "beginnings" require an "originary non-place," something "unspoken" which then produces a chronology of events.[18] Beginnings can, in this sense, be the narrative limits of the knowable, the margins of the meaningful. In what she calls her "in medias res" openings, Morrison stages such a narrative "non-space" and turns it into the performative time of the experience of slavery — no native informant, she writes, "the reader snatched as the slaves were from one place to another...without preparation or defense."[19] Her opening sign — "124 was spiteful" — offers no respite, no immediate meaning, because the house of slave-memory is not a resting place, not a Wordsworthian "spot of time." "124" is the unhomely, haunted site of the circulation of an event not as fact or fiction but as an "enunciation," a discourse of "unspeakable thoughts unspoken" — a phrase that circulates in the work and comes closest to defining its mode of utterance, the uncanny voice of memory.

To "un"-speak is both to release from erasure and repression, and to reconstruct, reinscribe the elements of the known. "In this case too," we may say with Freud, "the *unheimlich* is what was once *heimisch*, home-like, familiar; the pre-fix 'un' is the token of repression."[20] Morrison turns her narrative to just such an "affect" of distancing, obscuring the "referent," repeating and revising the "un-spoken" in order to make the act of narration an ethical act.

> A few words have to be read before it is clear that 124 refers to a house... a few more..., to discover why it is spiteful.... *By then it is clear that something is beyond control, but it is not beyond understanding since it is not beyond accommodation by both the women and the children....* The fully realized haunting... is a sleight of hand. One of its purposes is to keep the reader preoccupied

---

17 Gordimer, *My Son's Story*, 275.
18 Michel de Certeau, *The Writing of History* (New York: Columbia University Press, 1988), 90–1.
19 Morrison, "Unspeakable Thoughts Unspoken," *Michigan Quarterly Review* (Fall 1990), 32.
20 [Sigmund Freud, "The 'Uncanny'," in *The Standard Edition of the Complete Psychological Works of Sigmund Freud*, vol. 17 (1917–1919): *On Infantile Neurosis and Other Works* (London: The Hogarth Press and the Institute of Psycho-Analysis, 1955), 245 — Ed.]

with the nature of the incredible spirit world while being supplied a controlled diet of the incredible political world.[21]

If we are seeking a "worlding" of literature, then perhaps it lies in a critical act that attempts to grasp the sleight of hand with which literature conjures with historical specificity, using the medium of *psychic uncertainty, aesthetic distancing, or the obscure signs of the spirit-world, the sublime and the subliminal*. As literary creatures and political animals we ought to concern ourselves with the understanding of human action and the social world as a moment when *something is beyond control, but it is not beyond accommodation*. This act of writing the world, of taking the measure of its dwelling, is magically caught in Morrison's description of her house of fiction—art as "the fully realized presence of a haunting"[22] of history. Read as an image that describes the relation of art to social reality, my translation of Morrison's phrase becomes a statement on the political responsibility of the critic. For the critic must attempt to fully realize, and take responsibility for, the un-spoken, unrepresented pasts that haunt the historical present.

Our task remains, however, to show how historical understanding is transformed through the signifying process, represented in a language that is *somehow beyond control*. This is in keeping with Hannah Arendt's suggestion that the author of social action may be the initiator of its unique meaning, but as agent he or she cannot control its outcome.

It is not simply what the house of fiction contains or "controls" as *content*. What is just as important is the metaphoricity of the houses of racial memory that both Morrison and Gordimer construct, those subjects of the narrative that mutter or mumble like 124, or keep a still silence in a "grey" Cape Town suburb. Each of the houses in Gordimer's *My Son's Story* is invested with a specific secret or a conspiracy, an unhomely stirring. The house in the ghetto is the house of "colored" collusion; the lying house is the house of Sonny's adultery; then there is the silent house of Aila's revolutionary camouflage; there is also the nocturnal house of Will's, the narrator's, writing of the narrative that charts the phoenix rising in his home, while the words must turn to ashes in his mouth. But each house marks a deeper historical displacement. And that is the condition of being colored in South Africa, or

21   Morrison, "Unspeakable Thoughts Unspoken," 32.
22   Toni Morrison, "Honey and Rue," 12c.

as Will describes it, "halfway between... being not defined—and it was this lack of definition in itself that was never to be questioned, but observed like a taboo, something which no-one, while following, could ever admit to."[23]

This half-way house of racial and cultural origins bridges the "in-between" diasporic origins of the colored South African and turns it into the symbol for the disjunctive, displaced everyday life of the liberation struggle: "like so many others of this kind, whose families are fragmented in the diaspora of exile, code names, underground activity, people for whom a real home and attachments are something for others who will come after." Private and public, past and present, the psyche and the social develop an interstial intimacy. It is an intimacy that questions binary divisions through which such spheres of social experience are often spatially opposed. These spheres of life are linked through an "in-between" temporality that takes the measure of dwelling at home, while producing an image of the world of history. This is the moment of aesthetic distance that provides the narrative with a double-edge which like the colored South-African subject represents a hybridity, a difference "within," a subject that inhabits the rim of an "in-between" reality. And the inscription of this border existence inhabits a stillness of time and a strangeness of framing that creates the discursive "image" at the crossroads of history and literature, bridging the home and the world.

Such a strange stillness is visible in the portrait of Aila. Her husband Sonny, now past his political prime, his affair with his white "revolutionary lover" in abeyance, makes his first prison visit to see his wife. The wardress stands back, the policeman fades, and Aila emerges as an un-homely presence, on the opposite side from her husband and son:

> but through the familiar beauty there was a vivid strangeness ....It was as if some chosen experience had seen in her, as a painter will in his subject, what she was, what was there to be discovered. In Lusaka, in secret, in prison—who knows where?—she had sat for her hidden face. *They had to recognise her.*[24]

Through this painterly distance a vivid strangeness emerges; a partial or double "self'" is framed in a climactic political moment that is also a contingent

---

23 Gordimer, *My Son's Story*, 21–2.
24 Ibid., 230.

historical event—"some chosen experience... who knows where?... or *what* there was to be discovered."²⁵ They had to recognize her, but what do they recognize in her?

The history of Aila's hidden face emerges at the moment of her framing. She begins to speak, "like someone telling a story," but soon we find it "difficult to follow.... You leave so much out." In her inability to articulate her intention, to demonstrate a clear causality of commitment, or even a rational, responsible political ideology we are confronted with the novel's poignant and ambivalent interrogation of agency: "*Aila, Aila a revolutionary responsible for her acts.*"²⁶ There is no giddy suggestion that Aila's revolution is instinctive, part of her gendered "jouissance"; nor that it is the displaced symptom of her domestic oppression; or some fatal return of the repressed knowledge of Sonny's adultery. The political lesson Aila has to teach speaks through her narrative refusal to "name" her choice. With a certain obduracy and greater obscurity, she herself becomes the "image" of historical agency that the narrative is trying to wrench from her as an intention for her actions, an origin for her events, a "cause" for her consciousness. Literature, through its "distancing" act, frames this stillness, this enigmatic historical event.

> The necessity for what I've done—She placed the outer edge of each hand, fingers extended and close together, as a frame on either sides of the sheets of testimony in front of her. And she placed herself before him, to be judged by him.²⁷

Words will not speak and the silence freezes into the images of apartheid: identity cards, police frame-ups, prison mugshots, the grainy press pictures of terrorists. Of course, Aila is not judged, nor is she judgmental. Her revenge is much wiser and more complete. In her silence she becomes the un-spoken "totem" of the taboo of the colored South African. She displays the unhomely world, "the halfway between, not defined" world of the colored as the "distorted place and time in which they—all of them—Sonny, Aila, Hannah—lived."²⁸ The silence that doggedly follows Aila's dwelling now turns

25 Ibid.
26 Ibid., 239.
27 Ibid., 241.
28 Ibid.

into an image of the "interstices," the in-between hybridity of the history of sexuality and race.

Aila's hidden face, the outer edge of each hand, these small gestures through which she speaks describe another dimension of "dwelling" in the social world. Aila, as colored woman, defines a boundary that is at once inside and outside, the insiders-outsideness. The stillness that surrounds her, the gaps in her story, her hesitation and passion that speak between the self and its acts—these are moments where the private and public touch in contingency. They do not simply transform the content of political ideas; the very "place" from which the political is spoken—the "public sphere" itself, becomes an experience of liminality which questions, in Sonny's words, what it means to speak "from the center of life."

The central political preoccupation of the novel—till Aila's emergence—focuses on the "loss of absolutes," the meltdown of the cold war, the fear "that if we can't offer the old socialist paradise in exchange for the capitalist hell here, we'll have turned traitor to our brothers."[29] The lesson Aila teaches, requires a movement away from a world conceived in binary terms, away from a notion of the peoples' aspirations sketched in simple black and white. It also requires a shift of attention from the political as a theory to politics as the activity of everyday life. Aila leads us to the homely world where, Gordimer writes, the banalities are enacted—"the fuss over births, marriages, family affairs with their survival rituals of food and clothing."[30] But it is precisely in these banalities that the unhomely stirs, as the violence of a racialized society falls most enduringly on the details of life: where you can sit, or not; how you can live, or not; what you can learn, or not; who you can love, or not. Between the banal act of freedom and its historic denial rises the silence:

> Aila emanated a stilling atmosphere; the parting jabber stopped. It was as if everyone found he had unnoticingly entered a strange house, and it was hers; she stood there.

In Aila's stillness, its obscure necessity, we have glimpsed what Emmanuel Levinas has magically described as the twilight existence of the aesthetic

---

29 Ibid., 214.
30 Ibid., 243.

image—art's image as "the very event of obscuring, a descent into night, an invasion of the shadow."[31] The "completion" of the aesthetic, the distancing of the world in the "image," is precisely not a transcendental activity. The image—or the metaphoric, "fictional" activity of language—makes visible "an interruption of time by a movement going on the hither side of time, in its interstices."[32] The complexity of this statement will become clearer when I remind you of the "stillness" of time through which Aila surreptitiously and subversively interrupts the ongoing presence of political activity, using her interstitial role in the domestic world to both "obscure" her political role and to articulate it the better.

The continual eruption of "undecipherable languages" of slave-memory in *Beloved* obscures the historical narrative of infanticide only to articulate the "unspoken"—that ghostly discourse which enters the world of 124 "from the outside" in order to reveal the profound temporal liminality of the transitional world of the aftermath of slavery in the 1870s—its private and public faces, its historical past and its narrative present. The aesthetic image discloses an ethical time of narration because, Levinas writes, "the real world appears in the image as it were between parenthesis."[33] Like the outer edges of Aila's hands holding her enigmatic testimony; like 124, which is a fully realized presence haunted by undecipherable languages, Levinas's parenthetical perspective is also an ethical view. It effects an "externality of the inward" as the very enunciative position of the historical and narrative subject, "introducing into the heart of subjectivity a radical and an-archical reference to the other which in fact constitutes the inwardness of the subject."[34] Is it not uncanny that Levinas's metaphors for this unique "obscurity" of the image should come from those unhomely places in Dickens—those dusty boarding schools, the pale light of London offices, the dark, dank second-hand clothes shops?

For Levinas the "art-magic" of the contemporary novel lies in its way of "seeing inwardness from the outside,"[35] and for us, it is this ethical-aesthetic positioning that returns us, finally, to the community of the unhomely:

---

31 Emmanuel Levinas, "Reality and Its Shadow," in *Collected Philosophical Papers* (Dordrecht: Martinus Nijhoff, 1987), 1–13.
32 Ibid.
33 Ibid.
34 Robert Bernasconi, "Levinas's Ethical Discourse, Between Individuation and Universality," in *Re-Reading Levinas*, ed. Bernasconi and Critchley (Bloomington: Indiana University Press, 1991), 90.
35 Ibid.

> 124 was spiteful [...]. The house on the veld was silent.
> The women in the house knew it and so did the children.

Why, in particular, the women? Carole Pateman argues that the continual "forgetting" of domestic life in the definition of the private/public distinction introduces a negation at the very center of social contract theory.[36] Domestic life becomes, by virtue of its disavowal, a problematic boundary of civil society. It can be reoccupied by those who have taken up the position of the "inwardness from the outside." Which has indeed happened in the work of black American theorists like Patricia Hill Collins, who names the experience "the outsider-within status,"[37] and Patricia Williams, who sees the possibility of deploying this status to describe an ambivalent, transgressive, fluid positioning—of herself and her work—"that moves back and forth across a boundary which acknowledges that I can be black and good and black and bad and that I can also be black and white...."[38]

It is Toni Morrison, however, who takes this ethical and aesthetic project of "seeing inwardness from the outside" furthest or deepest—right into Beloved's naming of her desire for identity: "I want you to touch me on my inside part and call me my name."[39] There is an obvious reason why a ghost should want to be so realized. What is more obscure—and to the point—is how such an inward and intimate desire would provide an "inscape" of the memory of slavery. For Morrison, it is precisely the historical and discursive boundaries of slavery that are the issue. Racial violence is invoked by historical dates—1876, for instance—but Morrison is just a little hasty with the events in themselves: "the true meaning of the Fugitive Bill, the Settlement Fee, God's Ways, anti-slavery, manumission, skin voting [...]." What has to be endured is the knowledge of doubt that comes from Sethe's eighteen years of disapproval and a solitary life in the unhomely world of 124 Bluestone Road. What finally causes the thoughts of the women of 124, "unspeakable thoughts to be unspoken,"[40] is the understanding that the victims of violence are themselves "signified upon": they are the victims of projected fears, anxie-

---

36 [Carole Pateman, *The Disorder of Women: Democracy, Feminism, and Political Theory* (Stanford: Stanford University Press, 1989), 132—Ed.]
37 [Patricia Hill Collins, "Learning from the Outsider Within: The Sociological Significance of Black Feminist Thought, *Social Problems* 33, no. 6 (1986): S14–S32—Ed.]
38 [Patricia J. Williams, *The Alchemy of Race and Rights* (Cambridge, MA: Harvard University Press, 1991), 130—Ed.]
39 Morrison, *Beloved*, 116.
40 Ibid., 199.

ties and dominations that do not originate within the oppressed and will not fix them in the circle of pain. The stirring of emancipation comes with the knowledge that the belief "that under every dark skin there was a jungle"[41] was a belief that grew, spread, touched every perpetrator of the racist myth, and was then expelled from 124.

With this knowledge comes a kind of self-love that is also the love of the "other." Eros and Agape together. This knowledge is visible in those intriguing "interstitial" chapters which lay over each other, where Sethe, Beloved and Denver perform a ceremony of claiming and naming: "Beloved, she my daughter"; "Beloved is my sister"; "I am beloved and she is mine."[42] The women speak in tongues, from a space "in-between each other" which is a communal space. They explore an "inter-personal" reality: a social reality that appears within the poetic image as if it were in parenthesis. It is difficult to convey the rhythm and the improvisation of those chapters, but it is impossible not to see in them, the healing of history, a community reclaimed in the making of a name:

Who is Beloved?

Now we understand: She is the daughter that returns to Sethe so that her mind will be homeless no more.

Who is Beloved?

Now we may say: She is the sister that returns to Denver, and brings hope of her father's return, the fugitive who died in his escape.

Who is Beloved?

Now we know: She is the daughter made of murderous love who returns to love and hate and free herself. Her words are broken, like the lynched people with broken necks; disembodied, like the dead children who lost their ribbons. But there is no mistaking what her live words say as they rise from the dead despite their lost syntax and their fragmented presence.

> my face is coming   I have to have it   I am looking for the join   I am loving my face so much   my dark face is close to me   I want to join.[43]

My subject today has been the nest of the phoenix, not its pyre. I have attempted to show you the world forcibly entering the house of fiction in or-

---

41 Ibid., 198.
42 Ibid., 200, 205, 210.
43 Ibid., 213.

der to invade, alarm, divide, dispossess. But I have also tried to show how literature haunts history's more public face, forcing it to reflect on itself in the displacing, even distorting image of Art. When the publicity of the "event," or the certainty of "intention" encounters the silence of the Word or the stillness of art, it may lose control and coherence, but it provides a profound understanding of what constitutes human necessity and agency. I have focused this argument on the woman framed—Gordimer's Aila; and the woman, renamed—Morrison's Beloved. In both their houses great world events erupted—Apartheid and Slavery—and their coming was turned into that particular obscurity of Art. In that unhomely second coming, both Aila and Beloved embody the "freak displacements" of their times. It could be said of these moments that they are of the world but not fully in it; that they represent the outsideness of the inside that is too painful to remember. "This is not a story to pass on,"[44] Morrison insistently repeats at the end of *Beloved* in order to engrave the event in the deepest resources of our amnesia, of our unconsciousness. When historical visibility has faded, when the present tense of testimony loses its power to arrest, then the distortions of memory offer us the image of our solidarity and survival. This is a story to pass on; to pass through the world of literature on its thither side and discover those who live in the unhomely house of Fiction. In the House of Fiction, there is a stirring of the unspoken, of the unhomely... today.

---

44   Ibid., 275.

There are   **HOMELESS IMAGES: KRACAUER'S**
always holes   **EXTRATERRITORIALITY,**
in the wall for us to   **DERRIDA'S MONO-**
escape and the improb-
able to slip in.   **LINGUALISM OF**
—Siegfried Kracauer, *History*   **THE OTHER**

From this shore, yes, from this shore or this   Gerhard
common drift, all expatriation remains singular.   Richter
    —Jacques Derrida, *Monolingualism of the Other*

If it has a home at all, the proper home of the image, and even the thought-image or *Denkbild*, is homelessness. Never fully itself, the image remains at odds both with itself and with the referential burden that it is expected to carry. In its iterability, the image, which threatens to be divorced from referential functions such as time and space, tells of distance, absence, and loss, of exile and diasporic dispersal. It tells, in other words, of the states that make the image what it is and that relates it to all other images. The demand that an image can be *of* something and that it faithfully and reliably represent that something, on the one hand, and the inevitably unpredictable ways in which an image fails to comply with that demand, on the other hand, sponsor a melancholia that is shared by all images, even as it cannot travel through the structural and historical specificity of a *singular* image. The image records a historical moment at the same time that it interrupts history, perpetuating the very thinkability of history even as it breaks with the logic of historical unfolding. As the site of multiple displacements, the image is historical when it tells us of its own departure from history, capturing time most fully when it removes itself from time, the way in which, for instance, a snapshot memorializes time by stepping outside the temporal flow. Because an image can never fully represent, that is, present once again in exactly the same way, the vast network of traces and meanings that it first sets out to arrest, it performs an *Aufhebung* that simultaneously

---

Originally published as Gerhard Richter, "Homeless Images: Kracauer's Extraterritoriality, Derrida's Monolingualism of the Other," in *Thought-Images: Frankfurt School Writers Reflections from Damaged Life* (Stanford: Stanford University Press, 2007), 107–46. Reprinted with permission of Stanford University Press.

preserves and cancels the event that was once its subject. In this double gesture, the image both forestalls and commemorates loss by recording a moment, documenting its constitutive inevitability, and making it visible as the loss that it always already was. That is to say, the image reveals the ways in which an assumed presence already was a fiction at the time when it was believed to be present. We even could say that rather than simply representing its subject, the image retroactively makes visible the absence that already lay at the core of the event it set out to record.

It is the traces of these multiple displacements that connect the image with philosophical thinking—the nomadic search for a space of belonging and a sense of community where no community remains to be experienced, in short, a means of dwelling within homelessness itself—that images and philosophical thoughts share. Our task then becomes to articulate the state of homeless dwelling that occurs when the syntactical relations among building, dwelling, and thinking are caught in a perpetual *Aufbau* and *Abbau*, building and unbuilding, that shakes them to their very foundations, a fundamental ontological experience whose story Martin Heidegger narrates.[1] From this perspective, "philosophy," the Romantic Novalis tells us, "is actually homesickness, the desire to be at home everywhere." Georg Lukács cites Novalis's lines in 1920 in order to set the stage for his own well-known formulation of modernity's "transcendental homelessness [*transzendentalen Obdachlosigkeit*]," which he sees as the principal driving force of the novel since Romanticism and which, in turn, gives rise to a Marxian attempt at easing the suffering of this transcendental homelessness.[2] But what Novalis also gives us to think is the idea that when homelessness in and of philosophical thought manifests itself as the desire to be at home everywhere (*überall zu Hause zu sein*), it paradoxically enforces and undoes the idea of dwelling at home. After all, if one's home is everywhere, then it can be nowhere. This is to say that philosophical thought, not unlike the image, posits and dismantles its home, dismantling it by positing it and positing it only by dismantling it. But to say that, if one's home is everywhere, then it can be nowhere, does not erase traces of longing that motivates philosophy and the making and read-

---

[1] See Martin Heidegger's reading of the existential nature of building, dwelling, and thinking in his essay "Bauen Wohen Denken" and his discussion of Hölderlin's poetic mode of dwelling, "... dichterisch wohnet der Mensch...," Both in *Vorträge und Aufsätze* (Stuttgart: Neske, 1954), 139–56 and 181–98, respectively.

[2] Georg Lukács, *Die Theorie des Romans: Ein geschichtsphilosophischer Versuch über die Formen der großen Epik* (Darmstadt: Luchterhand, 1971), 21–32.

ing of images. Because "nowhere" also is the name of u-topia, the non-place, a "no-where" that may at any time enter, not into presence, but perhaps into legibility as the "now-here." Thus, the shared homelessness that binds the image to philosophical thought in a common hope that will not relinquish the idea that an absence, rather than being absolute, could remain thinkable as a distant and fractured presence—of and with a community that never can be thought or experienced *now* but always remains yet to come, in and as an infinite promise of unpredictable proportions and incalculable responsibilities.

Perhaps few modern writers are as sensitive to this imbrication of the image and of philosophical thinking in homelessness as Siegfried Kracauer and Jacques Derrida. If in these pages I place Kracauer's reflections on homelessness and its images into conceptual dialogue with those of Derrida, I wish to suggest a subterranean affinity that often is neglected. Kracauer and Derrida—one a displaced German Jew persecuted by Hitler, the other an Algerian Jew uneasily acculturated to "Frenchness"—for all their differences and singularities share a common set of concerns. Among many other things, they both are significant interpreters of Walter Benjamin, Franz Kafka, Marcel Proust, and Franz Rosenzweig; and both share a sustained theoretical interest in themes such as waiting, writing, media technology, photography, the self-portrait, ghosts, architecture (and the philosophy of friendship). Both Kracauer and Derrida also are inclined at times to write in languages not their "own," and to reflect on the relation between homelessness and language, cultural identity and displacement, community and dispersal, the politics of inclusion and exclusion and a writing of, from, and in the margins. For Kracauer, the "homeless image" names a central aspect common to the projects of both philosophers, a spectral aspect that manifests itself in the cracks and fissures of officially sanctioned cultural discourses. From both a theoretical and a personal perspective, these ghostly homeless images sometimes are given the difficult name "extraterritoriality" (Kracauer), and other times the name "monolingualism of the other" (Derrida).

HOMELESS IMAGES, ARCADES, AND THE TERROR OF TERRITORY

In a sense, the entire corpus of Kracauer's work, from the Weimar essays to his philosophy of history, speaks, implicitly or explicitly, to the problematics of homelessness, exile, and the image. That he would be so receptive to Lukács's figure of transcendental homelessness is not surprising, given the fact that his work as a whole is saturated with reflections on space, spatial relations, territoriality, and topography. Having first completed a doctorate in architecture, he discusses space, spatial relations, city streets, and other geo-topographical issues in many of his Weimar writings, including the novels *Ginster* and *Georg* and his essays in cultural criticism. Indeed, his very language is often constructed around an intricate geometry of space-specific metaphors.[3] Many of these spatial performances are microcosmically condensed in Kracauer's 1930 "Farewell to the Linden Arcade [*Abschied von der Lindenpassage*]," one of the *Denkbilder* from the 1920s and 30s that he later included in the book *Streets in Berlin and Elsewhere* [*Straßen in Berlin und anderswo*]. There, Kracauer speaks of the land—and cityscapes that concern him as "homeless images [*obdachlose Bilder*]." As Kracauer puts it, what he observes all around him are "homeless images, illustrations of passage-like movements, that, here and there, shimmer through the cracks of the fence that surround us."[4] Echoing Lukács's language of ten years prior, Kracauer inscribes himself into a genealogy of homelessness by aligning his gaze with that of the homeless image.[5]

Like the photographic image, which assumes spectral dimensions in his reflections on photography, and like the workers who seek "Asylum for the Homeless [*Asyl für Obdachlose*]," a chapter title in his 1930 book *The Salaried Masses* (*Die Angestellten*)[6]—the images that circulate through the streets of Kracauer's Weimar Germany are fleeting and elusive signifiers, divorced from any proper origin, inhabiting no permanent space. These homeless images radicalize the meaning that Gilles Deleuze and Félix Guattari later give to the concept of nomadism. Although this theoretical conceptualization of

---

3   I am grateful to Dirk Oschmann for reminding me of this point.
4   When in 1963 Kracauer selected thirty-three of his Weimar thought-images, which had originally appeared in the 1920s and 1930s in the *Frankfurter Zeitung*, for a collection with the title *Straßen in Berlin und anderswo* (Streets in Berlin and Elsewhere), he divided them into four sections: "Straßen" (Streets), "Lokale" (Sites), "Dinge" (Things), and "Leute" (People). The thought-image "Farewell to the Linden Arcade" appears in the first section and also was chosen by Kracauer to be included in a 1963 collection of longer essays of his Weimar period (1920–31), *Das Ornament der Masse* (*The Mass Ornament*). I cite Kracauer's texts from his collected works, whose three-book volume 5 contains many of his essays, albeit in strictly chronological order, an order that disrupts Kracauer's own constellation of texts and thought-images. I quote the English translation of Kracauer's thought-image from the English version of *Das Ornament der Masse*. Siegfried Kracauer, "Farewell to the Linden Arcade," in *The Mass Ornament: Weimar Essays*, ed. and trans. Thomas Y. Levin (Cambridge, MA: Harvard University Press, 1995), 337–42, at 340–41; "Abschied von der Lindenpassage," in *Schriften*, vol. 5 book 2, ed. Inka Mülder-Bach (Frankfurt a.M.: Suhrkamp, 1990), 260–5, at 263.
5   For a general discussion of Kracauer's reception of Lukács, see Dirk Oschmann, *Auszug aus der Innerlichkeit: Das literarische Werk Siegfried Kracauers* (Heidelberg: Winter, 1999), 81–9.
6   A title that Adorno takes verbatim from Kracauer's thought-images for his own in *Minima Moralia*.

homelessness is shared by fellow members of the Frankfurt School, such as Adorno, Benjamin, and Horkheimer, Kracauer's work deepens this conceptualization with a force that mitigates against the reduction of his work to any single paradigm, even as it exhibits elective affinities with several.[7]

The image of homelessness that permeates Kracauer's thinking bespeaks a displacement that is shared by every image which one may wish to read, including Kracauer's own self-portrait, which encodes homelessness without which, the signature that signs his sentences would hardly be legible. This homelessness, felt even at home, haunted Kracauer's empirical life from the beginning: born in 1889 to a middle-class Jewish family, his childhood was marred by a pronounced speech impediment that marked his mother tongue, German, as "other," even within the German context. Kracauer spoke his proper native language only as something improper and alien. Living in the schism between a disabling stutter and the refined ear that made him one of the most gifted stylists of the German language during the Weimar period, between the worlds of Jewish and non-Jewish Germans in Frankfurt, Berlin, and beyond, between what was perceived by his contemporaries as a bizarre personal appearance and the highly developed aesthetic and philosophical sense that propelled him to study architecture, philosophy, and sociology, prompted Kracauer to describe his life as "extraterritorial." The Frankfurt School's historian, Martin Jay, reminds us that although "marginality, alienation, outsiderness have been among the stock obsessions of intellectuals ever since the time of Rousseau," Kracauer's insistence on launching his thoughts and sentences from a position of extraterritoriality makes a singular demand of his readers. "Kracauer's sense of marginality," Jay continues,

> must have begun almost at birth. Physically, he was set apart from his peers by two characteristics. The first was a speech defect, a stammer which would preclude, among other things, a teaching career at any time in his life. The second was his physiognomy, whose peculiarity struck all

[7] That the trope of homelessness, in its Lukácsian inflection and beyond, was privileged among Kracauer and his friends is confirmed in the reflections of another Frankfurt School colleague, Leo Löwenthal. As he recalls, Kracauer "called himself homeless in a way. In October 1923 [...] on the occasion of my wedding to my first wife, I received a letter of congratulations in an envelope decorated by Kracauer and with the return address: 'General Headquarters of the Welfare Bureau for the Transcendentally Homeless'; and below, again in Teddie's [Wiesengrund Adorno's] handwriting: 'Kracauer and Wiesengrund. Agents of the Transcendentally Homeless. General Management in Frankfurt Oberrat.' That, of course, was an allusion to Lukács's *Theory of the Novel*. But 'transcendentally homeless' is the true category for Siegfried Kracauer." Leo Löwenthal, "As I Remember Friedel," *New German Critique* 54 (Fall 1991): 5–17, at 12–13.

who knew him. To Adorno, who actually used the word "extraterritorial" in describing his face, he looked as if he were from the Far East. Asja Lacis, the Latvian Marxist director who met him in the late 1900s, said that he looked like an "African." To Hans Mayer, the Marxist literary critic, he was a "Japanese painted by an Expressionist." And Rudolf Arnheim, the aesthetic theoretician, remembers him as having a squashed nose that made his face "almost grotesque, but somehow beautiful."[8]

We might add that other contemporaries were more drastic and even meanspirited. For instance, Joseph Roth spoke in a letter of Kracauer's "un-European face" and of the alleged "patience" required "to wait for half an hour before he finally stutters up his wisdom," while Harry Graf Kessler evoked a "Kracauer, to whose monstrous ugliness that I cannot get accustomed."[9] For Kracauer, the marginality imposed by this extraterritoriality is not to be read as a postlapsarian state, as a fall from an original wholeness and a primordial stability of meaning from which his trajectory unfortunately has deviated. On the contrary, his otherness, inscribed by his extraterritoriality, is the very condition of possibility that makes him who he is: the one who is extraterritorial, the one who belongs to what does not belong, the one who is conjoined only by what is out of joint. For Kracauer, as for his friend Benjamin, the *Ursprung* is not merely an origin or a home, but also, always, an *Ur-sprung*, a primal leap or crack.

This homeless image portrays the nomadic extraterritoriality that traverses all of his *Denkbilder*, and, in fact, every one of his sentences.[10] Kracauer

8   Martin Jay, "The Extraterritorial Life of Siegfried Kracauer," *this volume*, 277.
9   These remarks by Roth and Kessler, respectively made in letters and diaries, are cited in Momme Brodersen, *Siegfried Kracauer* (Reinbek bei Hamburg: Rowohlt, 2001), 150. Further reflections on Kracauer's status as cultural outsider and his meditations on the dislocations of identity can be found in Ingrid Beike, "Identitätsprobleme Siegfried Kracauers (1889–1966)," in *Deutsch-Jüdisches Exil: Das Ende der Assimilation? Identitätsprobleme deutscher Juden in der Emigration*, ed. Wolfgang Benz and Marion Neiss (Berlin: Metropol, 1994), 45–65. Finally, for an analysis of how Kracauer's status as an outsider inflected his practice of philosophical journalism of the Weimar period, see Helmut Stalder, *Siegfried Kracauer: Das journalistische Werk in der "Frankfurter Zeitung," 1921–1933* (Würzburg: Königshausen und Neumann, 2003).
10 The overall sense that Kracauer's prose snapshots and philosophical miniatures from his Weimar years are best understood as belonging to the genre of the *Denkbild*, the form of the philosophically charged literary thought-image that also plays such a central role in the writings of his friends and colleagues Adorno, Benjamin, Bloch, Horkheimer, and others, is generally shared by Kracauer's readers. Several commentators suggest the term *Denkbild* for Kracauer's Weimar texts Heinz Schlaffer, "Denkbilder: Eine kleine Prosaform zwischen Dichtung und Gesellschaftstheorie," in *Poesie und Politik: Zur Situation der Literatur in Deutschland*, ed. Wolfgang Kuttenkeuler (Stuttgart: Kohlhammer, 1973), 137–54; Inka Mülder, *Siegfried Kracauer: Grenzgänger zwischen Theorie und Literatur; Sein frühen Schriften, 1913–1933* (Stuttgart: Metzler, 1985), 103–6; Gerwin Zohlen "Notizen zur Ausgabe und zum Autor," in Siegfried Kracauer, *Straßen in Berlin und anderswo*, with

refers, directly or indirectly, to his (and others') extraterritoriality as early as his Weimar *Denkbilder,* and the reference continues through his last work, on the theory of history. Even his wife, Lili Kracauer, records in a letter her husband's preoccupation with extraterritoriality as a word and as a concept.[11] For Kracauer, the fact that home is not a home derives not from the state of exile from his native Germany, but from the sense that its legibility as a home is fundamentally predicated upon its internal division and self-differentiation, the internal otherness that reenacts, refracts, and multiplies its external otherness to the point at which the very binarism of the internal and external dissolves. Writing in October 1958 to his similarly displaced Frankfurt School friend, Leo Löwenthal in Berkeley, Kracauer registers the trauma of returning to his "home" from an extended European trip. "When we," Kracauer writes, "after a smooth flight returned to our apartment, I had a fit of claustrophobia. It is really unnatural to have a permanent residence, a so-called home; the existence as a vagabond is the only true thing. The following day I was reconciled with my life here. It is good for working and I here feel, as if it were, extraterritorial."[12] The only reconciliation, for Kracauer, is the absence of reconciliation that the condition of extraterritoriality furnishes. Like Adorno, for whom *erpreßte Versöhnung,* or forced reconciliation, named the worst instincts, Kracauer can imagine reconciliation only as what refuses to be reconciled, a refusal that carries the name and signature of the extraterritorial.

Extraterritoriality: the condition of existing in a territory beyond territory, belonging to a territory while at the same time, being "extra" or superfluous to it, being outside or other to one's own or to another's territory. For someone or something to exist in a state of extraterritoriality means to depart from territory as a space and as an idea while still remaining deeply attached to it, that is, attached to it precisely in the act of departing from it. Extraterritoriality names the experience of radical insecurity in which the self

---

an essay by Gerwin Zohlen (Berlin: Das Arsenal, 1987), 120–28; Helmut Stalder, "Hieroglyphen-Entzifferung und Traumdeutung der Großstadt: Zur Darstellungsmethode in den 'Städtebildern' Siegfried Kracauers," in *Siegfried Kracauer: Zum Werk des Romanciers; Feuilletonisten, Architekten, Filmwissenschaftlers und Soziologen,* ed. Andreas Volk (Zurich: Seismo, 1996), 131–55; and Tom Levin, introduction to Kracauer's *The Mass Ornament,* 1–30.

11 Lili Kracauer's unpublished letter to Leo Löwenthal, in which she speaks of Kracauer's "extraterritoriality of chronological time," is cited in Dagmar Barnouw's *Critical Realism: History Photography, and the Work of Siegfried Kracauer* (Baltimore: Johns Hopkins University Press, 1994), 323, n 45.

12 Kracauer's letter to Löwenthal dated October 27, 1958 is now available in *In steter Freundschaft: Leo Löwenthal–Siegfried Kracauer, Briefwechsel, 1921–1966,* ed. Peter-Erwin Jansen and Christian Schmidt (Springe: zu Klampen, 2003), 211–13, at 212.

encounters itself as another. But precisely this encounter of the self with itself as another also names the promise of possibility. As Deleuze reminds us, "The Other, as structure, is *the expression of a possible world*: it is the expressed, grasped as not yet existing outside of that which expresses it."[13] Kracauer's extraterritoriality becomes readable not simply as the trace of displacement, but also as the anticipatory expression of a possible world that is still to come and to be thought of as that which is not yet, as that whose territory, if it is anywhere, is always elsewhere.

Kracauer's emphasis on this experience of territoriality as extraterritoriality returns us to the very core of "territory." A territory designates that which is settled, circumscribed, defined, articulated, and distinguished—whether in geographical, political, disciplinary, juridical, national, ethno-ontological, or even anatomical terms. Territory is what underwrites the very idea of having something settled, of having established something for good. It can even carry the connotation of property and propriety, of ownership, of possessing and living in one's territory—in short, a way of being at home.

But while territory signifies a certain settlement, and the ex-perience (literally, the moving through) of that settlement, a strange tension haunts the ground of territory that suggests that the settlement of the territory also is deeply unsettling and unsettled. Indeed, the very etymology of the word territory is unsettling. While territory, as the *Oxford English Dictionary* tells us, derives from the Latin formation *territorium*, that is, "the land around a town, a domain, district," the derivation of that formation in turn is "unsettled":

> Etymology unsettled: usually taken as a deriv. of *terra* earth, land (to which it was certainly referred in popular L. when altered to *terratorium*); but the original form has suggested derivation from *terrere* to frighten, whence *territor frightener, *territorium*? "a place from which people are warned off" (Roby *Lat. Gr.* §943). So F. *territoire* (1278 in Godef. Compl.): see also TERROIR.

Etymology unsettled: the history of territory also is the history of terror and fright. What is settled as territory is unsettled, that is, settled only as the dissimulation of what is unsettled, *heimlich* and *unheimlich* all at once. In this

---

13   Gilles Deleuze, "A Theory of the Other," in *The Deleuze Reader*, ed. Constantin V. Boundas (New York: Columbia University Press, 1993), 59–68, at 60.

unsettling trajectory, that which delimits a domain or a space also de-limits it, circumscribing its limits while simultaneously abolishing them. What shelters is also what expels ("people are warned off"), and what settles is also what terrorizes. The home that the territory provides cannot be thought apart from terror itself, the terror sponsored by the threat of expulsion is much as the terror of remaining, unsettled, in the settlement. As an unsettled settlement, territory is not entirely distinguishable from what could be called a "terror-tory." What makes one feel at home also frightens one, frightens one when one feels at home and makes one feel at home only, perhaps, when one is frightened. That the homey comforts of territory cannot be distinguished from the terror that resides within it names the condition of a certain *Unheimlichkeit* that remains unsettling in any settlement.

Kracauer's emphasis on extraterritoriality now can be read as a form of experience that not only conscious of the unsettlingly indecisive imbrications of territory and terror, but that also enacts this undecidability in the form of a meta-commentary. If territory, and the condition of territoriality that corresponds to it, work to erase any clearly delimited borders between territory and terror-tory, settlement and unsettlement, then extraterritoriality, in its "extra"-ness, its beyondness or otherness to territoriality, enacts the very distance that resists territoriality, as a word and as a concept, collapsing competing and contradictory forces that traverse it and that will not allow it to come into its own as a legible self-identity. Extraterritoriality, then, is the condition or experience that allows for articulation and mobilization of the ways in which territoriality is at odds with itself, a liberation of the terror that always already was hauntingly at work in territoriality, if only as a form of dissimulation. In other words, territoriality itself cannot exist without the extraterritoriality that is at work when settling and unsettling; territory and terror can no longer be distinguished reliably. Both as a condition and as a form of experience, extraterritoriality constitutes a displaced proper name for its alleged other, territoriality—but a potentially nonblinded experience that no longer takes readability of itself and its others simply for granted. On the contrary, it invites this unreadability as a promise to be fulfilled through textual encounters—cultural, national, personal, or otherwise—whose outcome cannot be scripted in advance.

It is hardly an accident, then, that in "Farewell to the Linden Arcade," the *Denkbild* that mobilizes the trope of the "homeless image," Kracauer focuses on the haunted passageways (*Passagen*) of a Berlin arcade (*Passage*), placing himself into dialogue with "my friend Walter Benjamin, whose work has been focused for years on the arcades of Paris" and to whose "book *One-Way Street*," the collection of *Denkbilder* published two years prior, Kracauer's own *Denkbilder* respond.[14] Like Benjamin's *Denkbilder* of *One-Way Street* and like the fragments of his *Arcades Project*, Kracauer's *Denkbild* is obsessed with the arcades as a ghostly space that creates the feeling of dwelling inside and outside at the same time, a constellation in which nothing is what it appears to be:

> In the arcades, and precisely because they were arcades, the most recently created things separated themselves from living beings earlier than elsewhere, and died still warm (that is why Castan's panopticon was located in the arcade). What we had inherited and unhesitatingly called our own lay on display in the passageways as if in a morgue, exposing its extinguished grimace. In this arcade, we ourselves encountered ourselves as deceased. But we also wrested from it what belongs to us today and forever, that which glimmered there unrecognized and distorted.
>
> Now, under a new glass roof and adorned in marble, the former arcade recalls the vestibule of a department store. To be sure, the shops are still there, but its postcards are mass-produced commodities, its World Panorama has been superseded by a cinema, and its Anatomical Museum has long ceased to cause a sensation. All things have been struck dumb [*Alle Gegenstände sind mit Stummheit geschlagen*]. They huddle timidly behind the empty architecture, which, for the time being, acts completely neutral, and will later on breed who knows what — perhaps fascism, perhaps nothing at all. What would be the point of an arcade [*Passage*] in a society that is itself only a passageway? [*Was sollte noch eine Passage in einer Gesellschaft, die selber nur eine Passage ist?*][15]

In Kracauer's reading, the passageways of the arcades delimit a space in which extraterritoriality is experienced, a no-man's-land in which trajectories of history criss-cross and distort one another, and objects become unreliable traces because the signs of the object world have ceased to speak — "alle Gegenstände sind mit Stummheit geschlagen." In fact, it is here, in the passageways of the arcades, that we encounter ourselves as another — a dead

14 Kracauer, "Farewell," 342 [263].
15 Ibid., 342 [264–5].

other. In this way, the arcade becomes an extraterritorial site of our encounter with ourselves as the finite other, that is, with finitude itself. But the arcade, with its homeless images, remains a hauntingly unreadable extraterritorial site. Because of the impossibility of reducing its conflicting significations in advance to this or that political program—it retreats as an illegible text—the arcades may or may not become a pretext for fascism, may or may not authorize a sociopolitical program. As a form of undecidability, its meaning is always yet to come. Coming to terms with this undecidability by facing its threat in light of the requirements that a properly political stance would demand: these are the ethical stakes of Kracauer's extraterritoriality and the homeless images in which it manifests itself. It is hardly an accident that in a 1930 review Benjamin describes Kracauer as a relentless outsider, a marginal yet revolutionary ragpicker of history, a designation of which Kracauer always remained proud. "And if we wish to gain a clear picture of him in the isolation of his trade," Benjamin writes there,

> what we will see is a ragpicker, at daybreak, picking up rags of speech and verbal scraps with his stick and tossing them, grumbling and growling, a little drunk, into his cart, not without letting one or another of those faded cotton remnants—"humanity," "inwardness," or "absorption"—flutter derisively in the wind. A ragpicker, early on—at the dawn of the day of the revolution."[16]

The spatial dimension of Kracauer's extraterritoriality, as it figures in the language of the ghostly arcades passageways, is extended by a temporal component. In two 1963 letters to Adorno—missives that Kracauer, according to the literary critic Inka Mülder-Bach, privately designated as "Letters on Extraterritoriality"—Kracauer expresses his desire for "chronological anonymity": "My mode of existence literally would be put on the line if dates were roused and assaulted me from the outside." As Kracauer emphasizes, it "is not as if I were trying to appear young or younger; it is solely my fear of losing chronological anonymity by the fixation of dates and the unavoidable con-

---

16 Walter Benjamin, "An Outsider Makes His Mark," trans. Rodney Livingstone, *Selected Writings: Volume 2, 1927–1934*, ed. Michael W. Jennings, Howard Eiland, and Gary Smith (Cambridge, MA: Harvard University Press, 1999), 305–10, at 310; "Ein Außenseiter macht sich bemerkbar: Zu S. Kracauer, 'Die Angestellten,'" in *Gesammelte Schriften*, vol. 3, ed. Hella Tiedemann-Bartes (Frankfurt a.M.: Suhrkamp, 1972), 219–25, at 225.

notations of such a fixation."[17] What precisely would chronological anonymity mean, and just what might the "unavoidable connotations of such a fixation" be? It certainly is reasonable to suggest, with Jay, that Kracauer, on the one hand, is reflecting on his own finitude and, on the other, wishes to reject the easy compartmentalization of his work as that of yet another "Weimar intellectual," a periodization that, like all periodizations, seeks to program in advance all subsequent readings and thus to police the meanings that can be liberated from a text that ultimately will refuse to be arrested for good.[18]

But more is at stake here. Kracauer's insistence on chronological anonymity stages his own theoretical conviction that historical phenomena cannot be assimilated, without the mediation that language itself demands, to an allegedly stable and unchangeable historical context. This does not mean that Kracauer opposes the historical contextualization of phenomena—on the contrary, his preoccupation with, for instance, the historicity of everyday objects and quotidian life in the cultural text of Weimar Germany (collected in the *Denkbilder* of *The Mass Ornament*), his interest in the psychosocial dimension of German film (developed in his 1947 *From Caligari to Hitler*), and, indeed, his major posthumous work on the theory of history (*History: The Last Things before the Last*), all speak to his attention to genealogical issues in the reading of concepts and phenomena. But these historical contexts, for Kracauer, are never simply given or self-identical—as con-texts, they are also *textual* events whose elusiveness and ever-changing modes of resisting the historian demand to be read on their own terms.[19]

From this perspective, Kracauer shares a textual model of the historical with Benjamin. Kracauer insists on destabilizing the notion that, as he puts it in *History*, "people actually 'belong' to their period. This must not be so. Vico is an outstanding example of chronological exterritoriality; and it would be extremely difficult to derive Burckhardt's complex and ambivalent physiognomy as a historian from the conditions under which he lived and worked."

---

17   Kracauer's two "Briefe zur Extraterritorialität" to Adorno, dated October 25 and November 8, 1963, are located among his papers at the Deutsches Literaturarchiv in Marbach. They are quoted in Mülder-Bach, "History as Autobiography: The Last Things before the Last," trans. Gail Finney, *New German Critique* 54 (Fall 1991): 139–57, at 154–5.
18   Jay, "The Extraterritorial Life of Siegfried Kracauer," 276. It is doubtful, however, that Kracauer's extraterritorial investment can be reduced to a "heightened expression for escape," as Mülder-Bach suggests. "History as Autobiography," 155.
19   As Gertrud Koch puts it, emphasizing the figural character of all of Kracauer's texts: "His philosophical treatises, just as much as his essays and short feuilletons, are connected by a literary style that turns them into an infinite simultaneous texture," even into a "rhetoric of metaphors." *Kracauer zur Einführung* (Hamburg: Junius, 1996), 8.

Kracauer continues by arguing that like "great artists or thinkers, great historians are biological freaks: they father the time that has fathered them."[20] Here, he implicitly convenes with Benjamin, who explains in his early essay "*Trauerspiel* and Tragedy": "The time of history is infinite in every direction and unfulfilled at every moment. This means that no single empirical event is thinkable that would stand in a necessary relationship to the particular historical situation in which it was produced." Benjamin therefore argues that "the determining force of historical time cannot be fully grasped by, or wholly concentrated in, any empirical process."[21] For Benjamin, as for Kracauer, the promise of historical thinking finally is lodged in our willingness to begin to read the ways in which a historical phenomenon registers the elements of its Foucauldian episteme while at the same time breaking with that episteme. The genuinely historical event both confirms and undoes its time, confirms it by undoing it and undoes it by confirming it, in a gesture that demands our thinking of the event's singularity and materiality. Viewed in this light, Kracauer's insistence on chronological anonymity also can be read as a desire to avoid the "unavoidable connotations" of a historical "fixation" that seeks once and for all to foreclose the reading of history. From this perspective, then, the temporality of Kracauer's life, while empirical, to be sure, is empirical only *among other things* and, as such, remains open to the plurality of what always will have been other, and more, than one.

EUROPEAN, AMONG OTHER THINGS

Kracauer's concern with extraterritoriality and all that it implies, both as a mode of being and as a concept, is shared by Derrida in his meditations on the relations among language, cultural particularity, and national identity. In his *Le monolinguisme de l'autre: Ou la prothèse d'origine* (1996), translated as

---

20 Siegfried Kracauer, *History: The Last Things before the Last*, ed. Paul Kris-teller (Princeton: Wiener, 1995), 68–9. For a discussion of this passage in the context of Kracauer's effort to transform the self into an other by "disappearing" into his own texts, see Mülder-Bach, "History as Autobiography," 155–6. Given the subterranean affinity between Kracauer's project and Derrida's, it is perhaps no accident that Geoffrey Bennington makes a similar point regarding Derrida when he writes that "we have absorbed Derrida, his singularity and his signature, the event we were so keen to tell you about, into a textuality in which he may well have quite simply disappeared." Geoffrey Bennington, "Derridabase," in *Jacques Derrida*, trans. Geoffrey Bennington (Chicago: University of Chicago Press, 1993), 316.

21 Walter Benjamin, "Trauerspiel and Tragedy," trans. Rodney Livingstone, in *Selected Writings*, vol. 1, 1913–1926, ed. Marcus Bullock and Michael W. Jennings (Cambridge, MA: Harvard University Press, 1996), 55–8, here 55; in German: "Trauerspiel und Tragödie," in *Gesammelte Schriften*, vol. 2., ed. Rolf Tiedemann and Hermann Schweppenhäuser (Frankfurt a.M.: Suhrkamp, 1974), 134.

Monolingualism of the Other; or, The Prosthesis of Origin, Derrida's reflections on the readability of linguistic, cultural, and national identity are inseparable from the many specters, conceptual and personal, that traverse his far-ranging oeuvre from the 1960s to the present—from such early texts as *Writing and Difference*, *Of Grammatology*, and *Margins of Philosophy*, via his "middle" phase and such works as *The Post Card*, *Glas*, and *Psyché*, to the later, more overtly ethico-political works of the 1990s and the new millennium, such as *Specters of Marx*, *On the Name*, *The Other Heading*, *The Politics of Friendship*, and *Cosmopolitanism*. His reflections in *Monolingualism of the Other* are prefigured and supplemented by earlier passages in which he, as a Jew born in El Biar, near Algiers, the capital of French-occupied Algeria, meditates on the ways in which his experience as a non-European European Jew inflects his philosophical trajectory. In a passage that echoes Kracauer's notion of "extraterritoriality," Derrida emphasizes the "exteriority" of his experience. In "There Is No One Narcissism (Autobiophotographies)," a conversation in which Derrida reflects on aspects of his Judaism, his relation to the French language and France, and his life growing up in the language of the "other" that also is that of the self (French) along the war-torn southern Mediterranean coast, we read:

> There is certainly (and here I am describing naively a naive experience) a feeling of exteriority with regard to European, French, German, Greek culture. But when, as you know I do, I close myself up with it because I teach and write all the time about things that are German, Greek, French, even then it is true that I have the feeling I am doing it from another place that I do not know: an exteriority based on a place that I do not inhabit in a certain way, or that I do not identify. That is why I hesitate to call it Judaic. There is an exteriority! Some might say to me: But it's always like that, even when a German philosopher writes about the German tradition, the fact that he is questioning, writing, interrogating inscribes him in a certain outside. One always has to have a certain exteriority in order to interrogate, question, write. But perhaps beyond this exteriority, which is common to all those who philosophize and write, ask questions

[...] beyond this exterioriry there is perhaps something else, the feeling of *another* exteriority.[22]

What Derrida names his exteriority travels through a number of interlaced discourses: that of canonical "Western" thought (one thinks of his extensive writings and teachings on a vast number of central European writers, from Plato via Hegel to Husserl and Heidegger, from Kant and Rousseau to Kafka and Celan, from St. Augustine to Joyce and Benjamin, among so many others); that of a Judaism that is not quite Judaic, or rather, that brings to light the ways in which there never has been a single Judaism alone, in a gesture that opens up Judaism, along with the very question of "religiosity" itself, to the ways in which it differs from and with itself; and that of the critical writer who joins the community of exteriority of all those who think, write, and call into question. If, at the same time, Derrida speaks of *another* exteriority, an exteriority that is not encompassed by a prior exteriority, we can infer that this "other" exteriority is another, perhaps, not only to the rhetoric of any interiority, but also to the very notion of exteriority as a function or even an invention of the binary code of the internal and the external. This more radical exteriority cannot be reduced to the logic of interiority and exteriority—it remains exterior to that logic. The exteriority of this "other" exteriority manifests itself, if it manifests itself at all, as the exteriority that has no interior or exterior other: it is an exteriority without and beyond exteriority. We thus could say that beyond exteriority lies exteriority, but it could only be an exteriority that already has been altered by its beyondness. It is this elusive movement of alteration of which the thought of exteriority will not cease to think.

Such a thinking of the "beyond" of exteriority is performed not for its own sake, but always in the name of something else, a something else that remains exterior and, in its radical exteriority, still to come. This is its spectral desire and its haunted promise. Derrida, in *Monolingualism of the Other*, implicitly reformulates the logic of exteriority and the desires and promises that its thinking presupposes. He imagines a desire and a promise that would unfold beyond "memory and time lost," a desire and promise inseparable from the questions that lie, in multiple formulations, at the intersection of

---

22 Jacques Derrida, "There Is No One Narcissism (Autobiophotographies)," in *Points... Interviews, 1974–1994*, ed. Elisabeth Weber, trans. Peggy Kamuf et al. (Stanford: Stanford University Press, 1995), 196–215, at 206.

all his work—a desire and promise, in short, that struggles to come to terms with the ethical, political, and personal implications of engaging the vexed moment in which an unveiling becomes indistinguishable from a veiling, in which every encounter with a self becomes infinitely conditioned by the specters of a non-self, another that is another both to the self and to itself, to itself as other, and that makes the self visible, in the other, as the other that it always already was. As Derrida writes:

> This desire and promise let all my specters loose. A desire without horizon, for that is its luck or its condition. And a promise that no longer expects what it waits for: there where, striving for what is given to come, I finally know how not to have to distinguish any longer between promise and terror.[23]

Derrida gestures toward a desire that acknowledges it is horizonless, that is, without a delimiting force of expectation that could condition in advance the telos and the unfolding of the desire and that could, by the same token, be employed as a measurement of the extent to which this or that expression of a desire has led to its fulfillment in a particular form. That this desire does not possess the comforts of a delimited space, telos, and horizon (not even, presumably, that of a Gadamerian interpretive *Erwartungshorizont*, or horizon of expectation) and that its fulfillment not only cannot be guaranteed, but also would threaten to remain unreadable even if it were to materialize—this, for Derrida, names both its "condition" (which is to say, philosophically, the condition of its possibility, but also, more negatively, the difficult condition it is in, as though it had a medical condition of sorts) and simultaneously its "luck," the accident and fortunate coincidence that bestow upon it its desirable features. Likewise, Derrida's promise is a promise that will not content itself with expecting simply what it expects; it has given up waiting for what it expects without having given up the task of expecting. This is an expectation without expectation, an expecting without expecting, in which expecting can survive only as an intransitive verb, that is, as something that takes no object and that perpetuates itself as a promise precisely in its refusal or inability to take an object, even if it can hardly be thought outside of a logic

---

23 Jacques Derrida, *Monolingualism of the Other, or, The Prosthesis of Origin*, trans. Patrick Mensah (Stanford: Stanford University Press, 1998), 73.

in which, if the very movement of expecting is not to be erased, one expects to expect *something* rather than nothing. This desire and this promise name the very possibility of a thinking of what is to come, of what as yet has no name but imposes itself in and as an expectation—"what is given to come." What this desire and promise occasion is itself a desire and a promise: to have learned, even as that having-learned is always in the process of being forgotten, in a formulation that echoes the imbrication of territory and terror in Kracauer, "not to have to distinguish any longer between promise and terror." It is worth noting that Derrida's desire is directed not at a learning that does "not distinguish any longer," but at one that does not "have to distinguish any longer." This gesture implies an envisioned liberation from a power of agency that would pass judgment upon, enforce, and administer matters of distinguishing and questions of distinction. Thus, what Derrida envisions is the formulation of a more radical promise, one that, rather than merely departing from the model of distinguishing once and for all between this and that, or even from the act of distinguishing itself, actually departs from the very *logic*—tied to narrowly conceived notions of reason and self contained identity—of a system of thinking that seeks to police the horizon and the space in which the activities of distinguishing, and even the distinguishing among various distinctions, first can be performed.

These multiple movements away from the moment of distinguishing are not to be thought as a call for the abandonment of a thinking that is invested in making distinctions or of the notion of distinction itself. On the contrary, Derrida would seem to call for a new form of distinguishing, a distinguishing that distinguishes among various forms and unspoken assumptions that underlie the very idea of making distinctions and the ethico-political consequences of such acts. What his writing moves toward is the thinking of an ethics that cannot be considered in isolation from the ways in which it finds itself on unstable ground. The blind triumphalism that believes itself to have performed once and for all a stable, binding, and normative distinction between promise and terror, good and evil—and thus to be protected from it, ideologically and epistemologically—is the greatest danger of all. Derrida's writing suggests that only when we open ourselves up to the possible reversal of the one into the other, to the threat of opposing and contradictory meanings emerging within the "same" phenomenon, to the haunting prospect that a concept or phenomenon may carry its own opposite within itself, to the unsettling possibility of having to build one's house on a defective cornerstone: it is only in these aporetic moments that the promise of an ethical impulse is first articulated, because it is only here that the making of distinctions becomes an aporetic—and therefore rigorously *ethical*—experience.

That there can be no theory of this ethical mode that does not attend to its own blind spots and internal alterities also means that any ethical response to this mode must be equal to its abyssal aberrations, to the ways in which selves perpetually are made and unmade in language, even the language of the other. Derrida's imagined position, in which he "finally know [s] how not to have to distinguish any longer between promise and terror," exhibits illuminating intertextual relays to Paul de Man's project. Attempting to articulate the stakes of a certain "resistance" to theory, de Man writes:

> Nothing can overcome the resistance to theory since theory is itself this resistance. The loftier the aims and the better the methods of literary theory, the less possible it becomes. Yet literary theory is not in danger of going under; it cannot help but flourish, and the more it is resisted, the more it flourishes, since the language it speaks is the language of self-resistance. What remains impossible to decide is whether this flourishing is a triumph or a fall.[24]

Just as presumably nothing could permanently stabilize the difference between promise and terror in Derrida, so nothing could overcome the resistance to theory in de Man: theory's very condition of possibility cannot be occasioned without that which, within it, works both with and against it, enabling it and resisting it at the same time. The resistance to theory therefore would be a resistance only to resistance itself, a movement of resistance to resistance that would not work to resist resistance at all but rather to expand and to solidify it as resistance. If it remains impossible to decide whether this "flourishing" that the resistance to theory as resistance occasions is to be applauded or mourned, invited or resisted, then that impossibility itself cannot be separated from any promise it may contain. Indeed, our ability to decide once and for all between a triumph and a fall would at the same time foreclose the promise that any mode of resistance may still harbor. As in Derrida's desire and promise to learn not to have to distinguish between

---

24 Paul de Man, "The Resistance to Theory," in *The Resistance to Theory* (Minneapolis: University of Minnesota Press, 1986), 3–20, at 19–20.

promise and terror in a gesture of finality, de Man's diagnosis of the impossibility of distinguishing a triumph from a fall is not the end of ethico-political thought, but rather, in its encounter with the aporia of decision, an opening up to and radicalization of such thought.

This inability to distinguish with final certainty between a triumph and a fall, between promise and terror, bespeaks certain homelessness, even extraterritoriality, of thought in which the systematic and reliability of thought itself cannot be fully secured. Here, thought is exposed to its homelessness. The homelessness evoked in Kracauer's homeless image is staged in Derrida's discussion of the "defective cornerstone" in de Man's reading of the Hegelian system. Problematizing Heidegger's concept of *Versammlung*, or gathering, a notion that could be understood as promoting the dangerous illusion of being at home as well as the paranoid nationalism such an illusion could inspire, Derrida elaborates upon the notion of a defective cornerstone as encrypting a home without a home, the idea of a home that conceals within itself the permanent threat of its opposite. Here, "the very condition of a deconstruction may be at work, in the work, *within* the system to be deconstructed; it may *already* be located there, already at work, not at the center but in an eccentric center, in a corner whose eccentricity assures the solid concentration of the system, participating in the construction of what it at the same time threatens to deconstruct."[25] Rather than being administered from the outside, as an external intervention, the deconstruction of the system or home occurs from within, having already occurred at the moment in which its occurrence enters into legibility. Such a defective cornerstone threatens the very foundation upon which its house rests, even while remaining a necessary and integral feature of the structure without which there would be no house in the first place. The homelessness effected by this defective cornerstone produces a being at odds with oneself, the experience of an otherness in which the dependence of the self on the voices and traces of the always already defective—but nevertheless constitutive—other become visible. Placing Kracauer and Derrida into syntactical relation through de Man, we

---

25 Jacques Derrida, *Memoirs: For Paul de Man*, revised ed., trans. Cecil Lindsay, Jonathan Culler, Eduardo Cadava, and Peggy Kamuf (New York: Columbia University Press, 1989), 73. For a general discussion of the relation between deconstruction and the very question of "foundations," see Rodolphe Gasché, "Deconstructive Methodology," in *The Tain of the Mirror: Derrida and the Philosophy of Reflection* (Cambridge, MA: Harvard University Press, 1986), 121–76, and Nicholas Royle, "Philosophy and the Ruins of Deconstruction," in *After Derrida* (Manchester: Manchester University Press, 1995), 124–42.

could conceive of the defective cornerstone as a homeless image and an image of homelessness. The one who dwells in the house experiences himself as other or, more precisely, experiences himself as other and as an otherness precisely when he can no longer reliably differentiate between the cornerstone as an architectural necessity for maintaining the structure of the house and the cornerstone as the potential precipitant of the house's collapse.[26]

To emphasize the sustained and threatening logic of the defective cornerstone in Derrida's thinking also is to return it to the homelessness of his own experience, an experience that connects this logic to aspects of Kracauer's extraterritoriality within, and beyond, the Germany of his time. Born in Algeria in 1930 as a Francophone Algerian Jew, Derrida's ancestors had emigrated from Spain in the nineteenth century.[27] At the time of his move to France at age nineteen to continue the studies he had begun in Algeria, a form of identity imposed itself on him even more forcefully than before, one that was European and non-European, Jewish and non-Jewish, French and non-French, all at the same time.[28] Derrida writes of a hybridity that is at odds with itself:

---

26 It is no accident that the German writer Reinhard Lettau reminds us, in his allegorical tale "Schwierigkeiten beim Häuserbauen," a story that, like E.T.A. Hoffmann's romantic tale "Rat Krespl," revolves around the very concept of building a house, that "the difficulties in building a house are enormous [*die Schwierigkeiten beim Häuserbauen sind gewaltig*]." "Schwierigkeiten beim Häuser-bauen," in *Schwierigkeiten beim Häuserbauen* (Munich: Hanser, 1962), 89–95, at 94. By the same token, Kafka's tale "The Burrow" ("Der Bau") stages a self that obsessively constructs a home in the face of an imaginary other who never appears. Franz Kafka, *Das Ehepaar und andere Schriften aus dem Nachlaß*, Gesammelte Werke, vol. 8, ed. Hans-Gerd Koch (Frankfurt a.M.: Fischer, 1994), 165–208.

27 For an autobiographically inflected meditation on his aporetic Jewish heritage, a Jewish heritage without a Jewish heritage, see Derrida's "Circumfession," a rhetorico-conceptual conflation of "confession" and "circumcision" that in turn unfolds in the margins, or circumference, of Geoffrey Bennington's attempt at presenting some major trajectories of Derrida's life and work. In the bottom margin of this "circumfession" Derrida comments on, modifies, challenges, and elaborates what is said "up" on the "official" page. "Circumfession," trans. Geoffrey Bennington, in Geoffrey Bennington and Jacques Derrida, *Jacques Derrida* (Chicago: University of Chicago Press, 1993).

28 The complex "Jewishness" of Derrida's thought and experience is insightfully discussed in John D. Caputo, *The Prayers and Tears of Jacques Derrida: Religion without Religion* (Bloomington, IN: Indiana University Press, 1997). Compare further Joseph G. Kronick, "Edmond Jabès and the Question of the Jewish Unhappy Consciousness: Reflections on Deconstruction," in *Derrida and the Future of Literature* (Albany: SUNY Press, 1999), 69–99. From the perspective of a lifelong friend who shares Derrida's experience of being a French Jew in Algeria, Hélène Cixous investigates their mutual belonging and non-belonging in *Portrait of Jacques Derrida as a Young Jewish Saint*, trans. Beverly Bie Brahic (New York: Columbia University Press, 2004). Some of the multiple relays between Derridis philosophy and the tradition and politics of "Frenchness" are explored by the essays collected in *The French Connections of Jacques Derrida*, ed. Julian Wolfreys, John Brannigan, and Ruth Robbins (Albany: State University of New York Press, 1999). The ways in which deconstruction transforms the very concepts of tradition, legacy, and inheritance are subtly analyzed in Michael Naas, *Taking on the Tradition: Jacques Derrida and the Legacies of Deconstruction* (Stanford: Stanford University Press, 2003). Finally, it would be necessary to supplement the current discussion with Derrida's recent meditations on traveling and "traveling with" as they are inflected by concepts of identity, topographical location, and spacing; see Catherine Malabou and Jacques Derrida, *Counterpath:*

I am European, I am no doubt a European intellectual, and I like to recall this, I like to recall this to myself, and why would I deny it? In the name of what? But I am not, nor do I feel, European *in every part*, that is, European through and through. By which I mean, by which I wish to say, or *must say*: I do not want to be and must not be European through and through, European *in every part*. Being a part, belonging as "fully a part," should be incompatible with belonging "in every part." My cultural identity, that in the name of which I speak, is not only European, it is not identical to itself, and I am not "cultural" through and through, "cultural" in every part.

If, to conclude, I declared that I feel European *among other things*, would this be, in this declaration, to be more or less European? Both, no doubt. Let the consequences be drawn from this. It is up to others, in any case, and up to me *among them*, to decide.[29]

Far from undoing the concept of cultural identity, Derrida brings to the fore the ways in which this identity is at odds with itself, is clustered around not a core of stable meaning, but a network of differences. Thus, to lay claim to a cultural identity such as Europeanness means to invite the ways in which the self is *plus d'un*, more than one: more than itself and no longer simply itself. Cultural identity thus becomes visible as a fractured concept in which one claims allegiance to this or that culture only among other things, that is, in and as a part of many possible and competing identities. If any one aspect of the self's cultural identity is not self-identical, we also could say that the specific ways in which that aspect is non-self-identical point to its moment of identity: the self becomes readable as the one whose identity is fractured and multiple in this or that *particular* way. Here, even the very notion of being or having something "cultural"—such as a "cultural" identity—opens up to its internal differentiations, for it is only among other things that one is or has something "cultural." Thus, not only does the self merely "possess" this or that cultural identity among others—that is, among other things and among *other* others—but even the notion of its readability as something having culture or being cultural is only one among many others, in a way that does not fetishize the ideology of culture itself, even a culture of multiplicity

---

Traveling with Jacques Derrida, trans. David Wills (Stanford: Stanford University Press, 2004), esp. ch. 5, "Of Algeria," 75–92.

29 Jacques Derrida, *The Other Heading: Reflections on Today's Europe*, trans. Pascale-Anne Brault and Michael E. Naas (Bloomington: Indiana University Press, 1992), 82–3.

and difference. We could say that such guardedness with respect to the idea of the cultural corresponds to Adorno's dictum that "the greatest fetish of cultural criticism is the concept of culture as such. For no authentic work of art and no true philosophy, according to their very meaning, has ever exhausted itself in itself alone, in its being-in-itself [*An-sich-Sein*]. They have always stood in relation to the actual life-process of society from which they separated themselves [*von dem sie sich schieden*]."[30] To do justice to the ways in which the cultural departs from itself and its culture, even when it stands in relation to the culture that produced it, means to invite the specters of otherness as something constitutive of—rather than merely threatening to—any cultural identity.

This perspective is confirmed and elaborated in "A 'Madness' Must Watch Over Thinking," in which Derrida is asked by his interlocutor, "Do you mean to say that you do not want to have any identity?" To which Derrida replies: "On the contrary, I do, like everyone else. But by turning around this impossible thing, and which no doubt I also resist, the 'I' constitutes the very form of resistance." "Each time," he continues, "this identity announces itself, each time a belonging circumscribes me, if I may put it this way, someone or something cries: Look out for the trap, you're caught. Take off, get free, disengage yourself. Your engagement is elsewhere."[31] In the moment in which identity, as a form of desire, appears to manifest itself and to tighten its grip on the self, there is also a moment that resists that formation of identity. This resistance is not simply a refusal to play along, the narcissistic declining of a welcome invitation, but rather signals a commitment to what within identity remains nonidentical, to what eludes identity even in the name of identity—with an eye to the incalculable and resistant future of non-self-identical subject positions.

The promise of, and desire for, the incalculable and resistant future is intertwined with the trajectory of Derrida's "own" experience, an experience of otherness that makes him singular and at the same time connects him to so many other singularities. The Algerian war, one in a series of conflicts in his native region, impressed upon the young Derrida, as we learn in "Unsealing ('The Old Language')," the "animal fashion" in which one can be displaced even within what one considers one's "most natural habitat." "Even for a

---

30 Theodor W. Adorno, "Cultural Criticism and Society," in *Prisms*, trans. Samuel and Shierry Weber (Cambridge, MA: MIT Press, 1981), 17–34, at 23; "Kulturkritik und Gesellschaft," in *Gesammelte Schriften*, vol. 10, book 1, ed. Rolf Tiedemann (Frankfurt a.M.: Suhrkamp, 1997), 11–30, at 16.
31 Derrida, "A 'Madness' Must Watch Over Thinking," in *Points... Interviews*, 339–64, at 340.

child," he explains, "who was unable to analyze things, it was clear that it would all end in fire and blood. No one could escape that violence and that fear." Derrida "knew from experience that the daggers could be bared at any moment, as one left school, in the football stadium, in the midst of the racist taunts that spared no one: the Arab, the Jew, the Spaniard, the Maltese, the Italian, the Corsican. [...] Then, in 1940, the singular experience of the Algerian Jews. The persecutions, which were unlike those of Europe, were all the same unleashed in the absence of any German occupier." As Derrida elaborates:

> It is an experience that leaves nothing intact, an atmosphere where one goes on breathing forever. Jewish children are expelled from school. The principal's office: You are going to go home, your parents will explain. Then the Allies landed, it was the period of the so-called two-headed government (de Gaulle–Giraud): racial laws maintained for almost six months, under a "free" French government. Friends, who no longer knew you, insult the Jewish high school with its expelled teachers and never whisper protest from their colleagues. I was enrolled there but I cut school for a year. [...] From that moment, I felt — how to put it? - just as out-of-place in a closed Jewish community as I did on the other side (we called them "the Catholics"). In France, the suffering subsided. At nineteen, I naively thought that anti-Semitism had disappeared, at least there where I was living at the time. [...] Paradoxical effect, perhaps, of this brutalization: a desire for integration in the non-Jewish community, a fascinated but painful and suspicious desire, nervously vigilant, an exhausting aptitude to detect signs of racism, in its most discreet configurations or its noisiest disavowals. Symmetrically, sometimes, an impatient distance with regard to the Jewish communities, whenever I have the impression that they are closing themselves off by posing themselves as such. Whence a feeling of non-belonging I have no doubt transposed.[32]

Being homeless in one's own home, being at odds with oneself, or even being known as the one who is at odds with himself: these images of homelessness and homeless images haunt a philosophical stance or attitude that centers on cracks and fissures, on that which, within the overarching system — be it a cultural identity, a set of social codes, a geo-topographical space, or a com-

---

32 Jacques Derrida, "Unsealing (The Old New Language')," in *Points... Interviews*, 115–31, at 120–1.

munity within a community—is extraterritorial. Here, these unpredictable shifts and displacements of identity, in which belonging can be felt only in terms of particular forms of non-belonging, are transposed onto theoretical thought itself. They, too, work to render such thought homeless, even at home.

EUROPEAN HEADINGS

It is this displaced and fractured relation to the concept of cultural identity that conditions, for all their differences and singularities, both Derrida's and Kracauer's thinking and experience. Just as Derrida, an Algerian-born Francophone Jew, is fully European without being fully European, French only among so many other things, Kracauer, as a German-born Jew, was German only among other things, Jewish only among other things, and in later life, like Derrida, perhaps partially American. Writing for a prestigious German paper, the *Frankfurter Zeitung*, Kracauer experienced increasing anti-Semitism from the early 1930s on, a reduction in his salary, and, when his decidedly critical tone with regard to the overtly nationalistic films produced by the German UFA company continued, the organism of his German newspaper expelled him as though he were a foreign body. On February 28, 1933, the day after the Reichstag Fire, Kracauer and his wife escaped Germany for France and attempted to establish themselves in Paris. At age forty-four, Kracauer, whose ear has made him a distinguished stylist of German prose, was forced to live, uncomfortably and clumsily, without an ear, as it were, in the French language. His increasingly difficult Parisian exile was marked by, among other things, several internments when French authorities imprisoned Kracauer, Benjamin, and so many other people of German descent living in France, without regard to political background. After being interned and released several times, Kracauer escaped again, this time to the French port of Marseille, where by chance he reunited with his friend Benjamin, who was also attempting to flee after the Nazi invasion of France.[33] While Benjamin, in the

33 For a discussion of the friendship between Benjamin and Kracauer, especially as it centers on their common experiences as exiles in Marseilles, see Klaus Michael, "Vor dem Café: Walter Benjamin and Siegfried Kracauer in Marseille," in "*Aber ein Sturm weht vom Paradise her*": *Texte zu Walter Benjamin*, ed. Michael Opitz and Erdmut Wizisla (Leipzig: Reclam, 1992), 203–21. Elements of their complex personal and philosophical friendship become readable in what survives of their correspondence: Walter Benjamin, *Briefe an Siegfried Kracauer: Mit vier Briefen von Siegfried Kracauer an Walter Benjamin* (Marbach: Deutsches Literaturarchiv and Theodor W. Adorno-Archiv, 1987). For a reflection on Kracauer's general theory of friendship, see Gerhard Richter, "Siegfried Kracauer and the Folds of Friendship," *German Quarterly* 70, no. 3 (Summer 1997): 233–46.

face of severe difficulties, committed suicide at the Franco-Spanish border, Kracauer managed to leave France, traversed Portugal, and reached New York City in 1941. At age fifty-two, Kracauer learned yet another language, English—growing yet another ear, as it were—and a few years later published his first major book in English, *From Caligari to Hitler,* with Princeton University Press (1947). The last two decades of Kracauer's life were spent suspended between Europe and the United States, between languages, and even between cultural identities. Unlike his friends and colleagues such as Adorno and Horkheimer, Kracauer did not receive a call to return permanently to Germany after the war, even though, as Adorno writes in Kracauer's obituary, "he who was armored against ideologies could have done an infinite amount of good" in the cold-war world of Germany and Europe.[34] But what would it have meant for Kracauer to "return" to Europe? To whom or what would such a "return" have responded? What would his heading toward "Europe" have signified in the face of his own extraterritoriality, his desire for chronological anonymity, and the homelessness of his image(s)?

These questions, raised by the homeless image of Kracauer's extraterritoriality, especially their ethical and political dimensions, are cast into sharp relief in Derrida's elaborations of cultural identity and "Europeanness," issues that form the core of such texts as *The Other Heading: Reflections on Today's Europe* and *Monolingualism of the Other,* in which he, the Algerian Jew who, rather than being almost European, is not quite not European, reflects on the politics of having only one language, yet that language not being one's own.[35] Derrida wishes to conceptualize Europe in a post-essentialist way by rethinking facile programs of identity politics, including those of Eurocentrism as well as anti-Eurocentrism, in terms of what they simultaneously presuppose and marginalize.[36] Based on a radical respect for and openness toward the

---

34 Theodor W. Adorno, "Nach Kracauers Tod," in *Gesammelte Schriften,* vol. 20, book 1, 195.
35 I borrow the paragraphs on Derrida in this section from an earlier essay of mine in which I address the concepts of universalism and Eurocentrism in the work of Slavoj Žižek, Benjamin, and Derrida: "Sites of Indeterminacy and the Specters of Eurocentrism," *Culture, Theory and Critique* 43, no. 1 (2002): 51–65. These sentences appear here in revised form.
36 The politics of the *arrivant* should also be put into conversation with other names for the political in Derrida. For attempts to elaborate some of these other names, see, among others, Richard Beardsworth, *Derrida and the Political* (London: Routledge, 1996), and Geoffrey Bennington, "Derrida and Politics," in *Jacques Derrida and the Humanities: A Critical Reader,* ed. Tom Cohen (Cambridge: Cambridge University Press, 2001), 193–212. Derrida's engagement with Marxian politics in particular, as it emerges in his *Specters of Marx,* has occasioned a collection of responses, collected in *Ghostly Demarcations: A Symposium on Jacques Derrida's Specters of Marx,* ed. Michael Sprinker (London: Verso, 1999). This volume also includes an illuminating response by Derrida to his political respondents, "Marx & Sons," trans. G. M. Goshgarian, 213–69.

other, to the one who has as yet no name and who has not yet been subjected to a set ideological standard of evaluation—and even the self that is legible only in the other—Derrida hopes to cast into relief the spectral contours of a European democracy, a still unrealized democratic potential to come. Although this democratic promise draws on the Enlightenment's universalist principles, values of justice, and striving toward a liberal democracy, it also breaks with a certain thinking that always already will have defined—and thereby, in effect, foreclosed—what such principles in their full complexity otherwise might signify. Therefore, Derrida asks, "Is there then a completely new 'today' of Europe beyond all the exhausted programs of *Eurocentrism* and *anti-Eurocentrism*, these exhausting yet unforgettable programs? (We cannot and must not forget them since they do not forget us.)"[37] This thinking neither follows the established political and intellectual programs of the Eurocentric tradition nor blindly denounces them. Rather, what is at stake is a thinking through of the ways in which what made these programs possible is refracted and folded back onto itself in movements of thought that threaten to fail at a difficult task. This task is simultaneously to think the liberating potential of that tradition and of its violent regression, which are so often interlaced. Attending to these concerns is vital because, after all, whether one acknowledges it or not, they continue to speak through us.

This double structure of the Eurocentric tradition speaks to the ways in which "we *today* no longer want either Eurocentrism or anti-Eurocentrism. [...] Beyond these all too well-known programs, for what 'cultural identity' must we be responsible? And responsible before whom? Before what memory? For what promise? And is 'cultural identity' a good word for 'today'?"[38] The crux of Derrida's reflections on Europe could be condensed in the complex question of whether it is possible and desirable to be faithful to a certain Eurocentrism without Eurocentrism. That is to ask, what will it have meant to have remained loyal to a tradition of thinking by breaking with it and to reinscribe oneself in it precisely by breaking with it? And is this reinscription, predicated upon a break or radical "ex-scription," again to be subsumed under the programmatic impulse of the tradition itself, or does it instead make visible some of the internal breaks and fissures from which this tradition always has benefited and under which it always has suffered, the

37 Derrida, *The Other Heading*, 12–13.
38 Ibid., 13.

tradition upon which it has drawn and whose internal tensions it continues to foreclose?

To make possible the thinking through of such questions within the concrete borders of today, Derrida's writing revolves around the political question of the other who arrives at one's intellectual, geographic, or immediately personal border. We could think of this other, with both Derrida and Levinas, not simply as an "other," but as the "wholly other" (*tout autre*).[39] The other, by virtue of its counterdistinction from the self, is to a certain degree still comprehensible, calculable, and predictable—to the extent that it can be negatively assimilated into the available and comforting binary structure of self and other. The wholly other, by contrast, cannot be assimilated into that binarism. In its radical incomprehensibility, inscribed only in faintly legible traces but never encountered as a stable presence, it remains another to the very structure of self and other, irreducible to any prescribed system of classification. As a triple structure or triple event, this wholly other is another to the self, another to the other, and another to the self-other. Only in encountering this wholly other can certain political and ethical questions that link our response with our responsibility be posed.

By way of attempting to do justice to this structure of the wholly other, and to the responsibilities that it entails, Derrida revisits such an other in *Aporias: Dying-Awaiting (One Another at) "the Limits of Truth."* This text helps us to theorize the possibility of doing justice to the arriving other, the other that unexpectedly presents itself to us at our doorstep, at our border, the European border for example. Derrida casts this problem in the language of the *arrivant*, a term that signifies "arrival," "newcomer," or "arriving." The *arrivant* is the arriving other as such-another, however, that

> does not cross a threshold separating two identifiable places, the proper and the foreign, the proper of the one and the proper of the other, as one would say that the citizen of a given identifiable country crosses the border of another country as a traveler, an emigre or a political exile, a refugee or someone who has been deported, an immigrant worker, a student or a researcher, a diplomat or a tourist. Those are all, of course, *arrivants*,

---

39 This notion of the *tout autre*, inspired in part by Levinas, traverses much of Derrida's work of the last two decades. For a recent discussion of the *tout autre*, see further J. Hillis Miller, *Black Holes* (Stanford: Stanford University Press, 1999), 157–69.

but in a country that is already defined and in which the inhabitants know or think they are at home.[40]

Beyond his or its concrete manifestations, the figure of the *arrivant* names the political and ethical predicaments that emerge in the context of geopolitical spaces, Europe for example. The *arrivant* stands in as a figure for the series of displacements that its movement both triggers and describes. As Derrida explains,

> [t]he absolute *arrivant* is not even a guest. He surprises the host [...] enough to call into question, to the point of annihilating or rendering indeterminate, all the distinctive signs of a prior identity, beginning with the very border that delineated a legitimate home and assured lineage, names and language, nations, families and genealogies. The absolute *arrivant* does not yet have a name or an identity. It is not an invader or an occupier, nor is it a colonizer, even if it can also become one. This is why the *arrivant* [is] not someone or something that arrives, a subject, a person, an individual, or a living thing, even less one of the migrants. [...] It is not even a foreigner identified as a member of a foreign, determined community.

Being someone or something before or in excess of stable identity, this *arrivant* also transforms the site or space that it enters. Something happens during its scene of arrival to the site in which this arriving occurs. As Derrida's passage continues:

> Since the *arrivant* does not have any identity yet, its place of arrival is also de-identified: one does not yet know or one no longer knows which is the country, the place, the nation, the family, the language, and the home in general that welcomes the absolute *arrivant*. This absolute *arrivant* as such is, however, not an intruder, an invader, or a colonizer, because invasion proposes some self-identity for the aggressor and for the victim. Nor is the *arrivant* a legislator or the discoverer of a promised land. As disarmed as a newly born child, it no more commands than is commanded by the memory of some originary event where the archaic is bound

---

40 Jacques Derrida, *Aporias: Dying—Awaiting (One Another at) the "Limits of Truth,"* trans. Thomas Dutoit (Stanford: Stanford University Press, 1993), 34.

with the final extremity, with the finality par excellence of the *telos* or the *eskhaton*. It even exceeds the order of any determinable promise. Now the border that is ultimately most difficult to delineate, because it is always already crossed, lies in the fact that the absolute *arrivant* makes possible everything to which [...] it cannot be reduced, starting with the humanity of man, which some would be inclined to recognize in all that erases, in the *arrivant*, the characteristic of (cultural, social, or national) belonging and even metaphysical determination (ego, person, subject, consciousness, etc.). [...] This border will always keep one from discriminating among the figures of the *arrivant*, the dead, or the revenant (the ghost, he, she, or that which returns).[41]

From the perspective of thinking of the geopolitical and theoretical notion of Europe and of a future politics that would do justice to the homeless images that traverse it, we learn in this account how the movement of the *arrivant* allows for the identification—as a stable subject or identity—of neither the *arrivant* nor the site of arrival, Europe for example. The relation between what arrives and what is arrived at always is as much in flux as are the internal shifts and movements at play within each concept or site. This means that one's relation to who or what arrives always is as much a function of one's hospitality to what is radically other as it is a function of one's critical reflection on one's own situatedness, prejudices, and evaluation of the claims to authority from which the arrival could be judged. Such critical reflection, prompted by the arrival of the *arrivant*, also extends to the power relations that are inscribed in any scene of hospitality—that of Europe, for example, in which, in order to share or to invite, one must remain the master of one's own space and its boundaries, installing oneself in a superior position in relation to the one who, or that which, arrives in the moment of having to respond to the event of his or her arrival. The full thinking of the scene of the *arrivant* is a thinking of a multitude of different relations between certain geopolitical spaces and the hope that might still be found in them. The *arrivant* helps us name what propels us to be open to the other, to invite it, to be hospitable to it, while respecting its potential withdrawal from meaning, that is, its irreducible otherness. Neither the languages of discrimination and nationalism nor even the rhetoric of well-meaning universalism appear

41 Ibid., 33–6.

adequate any longer to negotiate the transformations unfolding with and as the temporary borders between the highly differentiated site of arrival and another who is always yet to come—even in the guise of a democracy. That the fiction of self-identity and unmediated transparency grows ever more difficult to maintain in the face of the *arrivant*'s transgressiveness also means that questions of Eurocentrism and a new or reinvigorated sense of the political are opened up to their own self-differentiation, to the complexity that cannot be thought in isolation from their political urgency.

This opening up—which could be understood as a liberation or a making visible of what always already was the case, with a Freudian *Nachträglichkeit* that unfolds on the far side of this or that external intervention or application—this opening up also activates what already is excessive or supplemental in any French, German, or "European" cultural identity. In this sense, it could be claimed that the concept of cultural identity activates its political promise when it is transformed from within, rather than abandoned. This radical transformation from within remains necessary, not because of any desire to implement its individual dogmas, rather because it shares an irreducible elective affinity with concepts that remain undeconstructable, such as democracy and even justice itself. Thus, to remain faithful to undeconstructable concepts is also to break with them; one remains close to them by not following them. Just as nothing could be more enlightened than to criticize the Enlightenment—that is, remaining faithful to its belief in critique by radicalizing that critique and turning it against the very structure of thought and relations from which it emerged—so too no gesture of cultural identity could be more faithful than the gesture that perpetually undoes the notion of a cultural identity in a move that, rather than abandoning it, ceaselessly ushers its internal differences to the fore.

HOMELESS PHOTOGRAPHS

For Derrida, as for Kracauer, questions that speak to the aporetic nature of cultural identity cannot be thought of in isolation from a consideration of the technologies of visual representation. Derrida explores these concerns in a meditation on televisual images as well as in extensive analyses of painted images and photographs,[42] while Kracauer addresses them in his theoretical works on film, in his Weimar essay "On Photography," in *Theory of Film*, and in *History*. Photography, for Kracauer, in important respects belongs to the domain of those homeless images that allow us to consider "modes of being which still lack a name."[43]

To consider the homeless image that manifests itself in Kracauer's meditations on photography is to attempt to return to that to which one can never properly return because one never can have left it fully behind: extraterritoriality. Kracauer himself theorizes the imbrication of extraterritoriality and the homeless image of photography when, in *History*, he locates them both within the "image-space" that Benjamin calls a *Bildraum*. The inability of photography to coincide with itself, its particular way of never being able fully to capture what it attempts to present, is elaborated in his Weimar essay on photography. As a spectral medium, then, photography is the name for a particular disjunction that simultaneously inscribes itself in and removes itself from history. "Ghosts," Kracauer writes, "are simultaneously comical and terrifying. [...] Now the image wanders ghost-like through the present, like the lady of a haunted castle. Spooky apparitions occur only in places where a horrible deed has been committed. The photograph becomes a ghost."[44] This haunted image of the photograph from Kracauer's Weimar essay reappears several decades later, in his discussion of the photograph in *Theory of Film* (1960), as well as in his final work, *History*. In both instances, it is the appearance of his grandmother's image that causes Marcel, the protagonist of Proust's *In Search of Lost Time*, to encounter the figure of finitude itself. There,

---

42 Jacques Derrida and Bernard Stiegler, *Echographies de la télévision: Entretiens filmés* (Paris: Editions Galilée, 1996). Compare further, among other texts on the problem of the image, Derrida's reflections on Barthes's study of photography in "The Deaths of Roland Barthes," trans. Pascale-Anne Brault and Michael Naas, *Philosophy and Non-Philosophy since Merleau-Ponty*, ed. Hugh Silverman (New York: Routledge, 1989), 259–96; his conversation on the photographic image in "Die Photographic als Kopie, Archiv und Signatur: Im Gespräch mit Hubertus v. Amelunxen und Michael Wetzel," *Theorie der Fotografie*, vol. 4, 1980–1995, ed. Hubertus v. Amelunxen (Munich: Schirmer/Mosel, 2000), 280–96; his extended reading of the images by Belgian photographer Marie-Françoise Plissart in *Right of Inspection*, trans. David Willis (New York: Monacelli, 1998); his meditations on painted self-portraits in *Memoirs of the Blind*, trans. Pascale-Anne Brault and Michael Naas (Chicago: University of Chicago Press, 1993); and his investigations of drawings and paintings, including Valerio Adami's drawing "Ritratto di Walter Benjamin," in *The Truth in Painting*, trans. Geoffrey Bennington and Ian McLeod (Chicago: University of Chicago Press, 1987). Finally, a general meditation on the relation, in Derrida's texts, between the image of the artwork and questions of mourning can be found in David Farrell Krell, *The Purest of Bastards: Works of Mourning, Art, and Affirmation in the Thought of Jacques Derrida* (University Park: Pennsylvania State University Press, 2000).
43 Kracauer, *History*, 4.
44 Siegfried Kracauer, "On Photography," in *The Mass Ornament*, 47–63, at 56; "Die Photographie," in *Schriften*, vol. 5 book 2, 83–98, at 91.

the image of the grandmother is the homeless image of the one who, in a temporal disjunction, is both dead and going to die. In *Theory of Film*, Kracauer cites the following passage from Proust:

> I was in the room, or rather I was not yet in the room since she was not aware of my presence of myself [...] there was present only the witness, the observer with a hat and traveling coat, the stranger who does not belong to the house, the photographer who has called to take a photograph of places which one will never see again. The process that mechanically occurred in my eyes when I caught sight of my grandmother was indeed a photograph. We never see the people who are dear to us save in the animated system, the perpetual motion of our incessant love for them. [...] How, since into the forehead, the cheeks of my grandmother I had been accustomed to read all the most delicate, the most permanent qualities of her mind; how, since every casual glance is an act of necromancy, each face that we love is a mirror of the past, how could I have failed to overlook what in her had become dulled and changed. [...] I, for whom my grandmother was still myself, I who had never seen her save in my own soul [...] saw, sitting on the sofa, beneath the lamp, red-faced, heavy and common, sick, lost in thought, following the lines of a book with eyes that seemed hardly sane, a dejected old woman whom I did not know.[45]

Proust's Marcel encounters his grandmother as though she were a photograph—as though she had always already been a photograph. This photograph, lodged in the character's mind, reveals the writing of death, the thanatography that is inseparable from the medium of photography. (Like Proust's recollections of the photograph of his grandmother, mobilized in Kracauer's theory of photography, Roland Barthes's reflections on photography, written about a century after Proust, pivot on a mourning of his mother, and her absent presence through a photograph that, while never shown in the text, nevertheless lies at its core.)[46] This recognition of the relation between the

---

45 Marcel Proust, *Remembrance of Things Past*, vol. 1, trans. C. K. Scott Moncrieff (New York: Boni, 1930), 814–15. Kracauer quotes this passage in *Theory of Film: The Redemption of Physical Reality*, introd. Miriam Hansen (Princeton, NJ: Princeton University Press, 1997), 14.

46 It will be necessary to read Kracauer's theory of photography more rigorously in the comparative contexts of the history of such theories, and specifically in relation to Roland Barthes, whose theory of photography exhibits many similarities with Kracauer's. Writing several decades later, he does not seem to have been aware of Kracauer's reflections. For a useful beginning of an investigation of the relation between Kracauer and Barthes, see Heide Schlupmann, "Stellung zur

grandmother and death, the relation in which Proust understands that "my grandmother was still myself," also exposes him to himself as the one who is more than one, the one who exists, as a palimpsest, in the multiple and faintly visible traces of the many texts that intersect within him in order to make him who he is, even as he never can simply be "himself." Kracauer takes up this trope again in *History*: "No sooner does Marcel enter his grandmother's room," he writes there, "than his mind becomes a palimpsest, with the stranger's observations being superimposed upon the lover's temporarily effaced inscription." Continuing his spectral meditation in relation to the Proustian photograph, Kracauer writes, as if of himself, in a gesture that recalls the term "auto-biophotography" from the title of one of Derrida's conversations:

> Sometimes, life itself produces such palimpsests. I am thinking of the exile who as an adult person has been forced to leave his country or has left it of his own free will. As he settles elsewhere, all those loyalties, expectations, and aspirations that comprise so large a part of his being are automatically cut off from their roots. His life history is disrupted, his "natural" self relegated to the background of his mind. To be sure, his inevitable efforts to meet the challenges of an alien environment will affect his outlook, his whole mental make-up. But since the self he was continues to smolder beneath the person he is about to become, his identity is bound to be in a state of flux; and the odds are that he will never fully belong to the community to which he now in a way belongs. (Nor will its members readily think of him as one of theirs.) In fact, he has ceased to "belong." Where then does he live? Near the vacuum of extra-territoriality, the very no-man's land which Marcel entered when he first caught sight of his grandmother. The exile's true mode of existence is that of a stranger. So he may look at his previous existence with the eyes of one "who does not belong to the house." And he is just as free to step outside the culture which was his own, he is sufficiently uncommitted to get inside the minds of the foreign people in whose midst he is living. There are great historians who owe much of their greatness to the fact that they were expatriates. [...]

Massenkultur: Barthes' 'Bemerkung zur Fotografie' mit Kracauer gelesen," in *Ein Detektiv des Kinos: Studien zu Siegfried Kracauers Filmtheorie* (Basel: Stromfeld, 1998), 55–65.

Fig. 1. Siegfried Kracauer. Photographic print of the surviving shards from the original glass plate (1930). Courtesy of the Kracauer Estate, Deutsches Literaturarchiv, Marbach am Neckar, Germany.

> It is only in this state of self-effacement, or homelessness, that the historian can commune with the material of his concern. [...] The most promising way of acquiring such knowledge is presumably for him to heed Schopenhauer's advice to the art student. Anybody looking at a picture, Schopenhauer claims, should behave as if he were in the presence of a prince and respectfully wait for what the picture may or may not wish to tell him; for were he to talk first he would only be talking to himself. Waiting in this sense amounts to a sort of active passivity on the historian's part.[47]

Among so many other things, this passage suggests how the spectrality of the photograph intersects with the homeless image that Kracauer evokes in his *Denkbild* "Farewell to the Linden Arcade." Here, the image of homelessness, as a homeless image, constitutes an instantiation of the state of extraterritoriality, that is, the multiple displacements of the self that are inextricably intertwined with the ways in which that self struggles to make sense of itself in relation to what it is not: the other culture, the other cultural identities, the other modes of belonging, along with all the other others who already are at work in the palimpsest we call the self. This "state of self-effacement, or homelessness" not only echoes the trope of the homeless image within the space of the photograph, it also shows that the extraterritorial inscriptions of such a homeless image can serve a critical function. Evoking Schopenhauer, Kracauer argues that rather than merely finding again and again in every image the confirmation of our previously held assumptions, we may learn to read by allowing the enigmatic image to speak to us, by allowing it to reveal and conceal its multiple secrets in its singular way. It is here, in each encounter with a never-before-seen image, that we must allow the visual text to reinvent us, assumptions, methods, and all. In this perpetual making and undoing, the photograph itself can be read as a homeless image of extraterritoriality.

In order to visualize some of the implications of the relations among extraterritoriality, photography, and homelessness, we may turn to a photographic image of Kracauer himself—a photograph that enacts his fractured self as a homeless image (fig. 1).[48] Placing this photograph into syntactical

---

47 Kracauer, *History*, 83–4.
48 For a discussion of Kracauer's image in the context of Benjamin's theory of photography, see Hubertus von Amelunxen, "Ein Eindruck der Vergängnis. Vorläufige Bemerkungen zu Walter Benja-

relation with Kracauer's historical and philosophical concerns, we witness Benjamin's observation that "history [*Geschichte*] breaks down into images, not into stories [*Geschichten*]," while heeding Kracauer's methodological admonition that "the vast knowledge we possess should challenge us not to indulge in inadequate syntheses but to concentrate on close-ups and from them casually to range over the whole, assessing it in the form of aperçus. The whole may yield to such light-weight skirmishes more easily than to heavy frontal attack."[49] We could say that Kracauer's emphasis on the close-up touches both the logic of his *Denkbilder* and his philosophical engagement with the photographic image. His emphasis on the close-up also touches this photograph, which he made available, in partial detail, for publication in a reference book, the *Reichshandbuch der Deutschen Gesellschaft*.[50]

This extraordinary black-and-white photograph from about 1930 — the year of Kracauer's *Denkbild* "Farewell to the Linden Arcade" and the year in which the increasing anti-Semitism of his employer, the *Frankfurter Zeitung*, forced him into an ever more decisive extraterritoriality at home — shows him sitting on his desk in half-profile, his right leg crossed over his left, wearing a shabby pinstriped suit, a light-colored shirt, and a bow tie, his melancholy gaze directed to the right. The top button of his jacket is illuminated, presumably by the photographer's flash, while the lower button appears dark, a play with light that demarcates a peculiar asymmetry along Kracauer's midline. Although we faintly perceive the black fountain pen that his left hand holds, his right hand is almost completely obscured by the shadow that hovers over the dark surface of his desk, a surface that is punctured only by

min," *Fotogeschichte* 9 (1989): 3–10.
49 Walter Benjamin, *The Arcades Project*, trans. Howard Eiland and Kevin McLaughlin (Cambridge, MA: Harvard University Press, 1999), 476; *Das Passagen-Werk*, vol. 5 of *Gesammelte Schriften*, ed. Rolf Tiedemann (Fankfurt a.M.: Suhrkamp, 1982), 596; Kracauer, *History*, 149.
50 By focusing on the "surface-level" quality of the photograph, we enact with respect to Kracauer's texts the stance that he wishes to apply to the reading of entire historical paradigms. As he writes in "The Mass Ornament," three years before this picture was taken: "The position that an epoch occupies in the historical process can be determined more strikingly from an analysis of its inconspicuous surface-level expressions than from that epoch's judgments about itself [...] The surface-level expressions [...] by virtue of their unconscious nature, provide unmediated access to the fundamental substance of the state of things. Conversely, knowledge of this state of things depends on the interpretation of these surface-level expressions. The fundamental substance of an epoch and its unheeded impulses illuminate each other reciprocally." Kracauer, "The Mass Ornament," in *The Mass Ornament*, 75–86, at 75; in German: "Das Ornament der Masse," in *Schriften* 5.2, 57–67, at 57. For discussions of Kracauer's engagement with the surface structure of modern culture, see Miriam Hansen, "Mass Culture as Hieroglyphic Writing: Adorno, Derrida, Kracauer," *New German Critique* 56 (Spring–Summer 1992): 43–73, as well as Inka Mülder-Bach, "Der Umschlag der Negativität: Zur Verschränkung von Phänomenologie, Geschichtsphilosophie und Filmästhetik in Siegfried Kracauers Metaphorik der Oberfläche," *Deutsche Vierteljahrsschrift* 61, no. 2 (1987): 359–73.

the whiteness of what appears to be a slightly crumpled piece of paper in Kracauer's right hand. The windows above his head have a hauntingly distant quality about them: their white frames, which parallel the white paper on his desk, enclose dark panes that neither permit a glimpse of what lies behind them nor reflect what stands before them. These are windows that appear to belong to a no-man's-land, the paradoxical visual instantiations, perhaps, of the interior of Leibniz's windowless monad. The dark, framelike space that borders the photograph at the bottom and on the right contributes to this hauntingly claustrophobic effect.

The spectrality of Kracauer's photograph is augmented by the material fact that it was printed from the cracked glass plate that survived as part of his *Nachlaß*. Like the empirical Kracauer, the surviving image, a homeless image that, following a homeless life, survives the homeless one, is fractured and multiple, shattered and dispersed. Missing entire pieces, the fissured glass plate corresponds to the ruins and debris left behind by the sweep of history. The fault lines in the image effectively present Kracauer as a marionette, tied to, and manipulable by, the "strings" to which he seems to be attached. Significantly, one of these "strings" cuts through his left eye, disfiguring the face of the one whom the photograph commemorates. Here, we recall that for Kracauer it "is only in this state of self-effacement, or homelessness, that the historian can commune with the material of his concern." Indeed, the photograph was disfigured by history. It works to enact this state of self-effacement and homelessness, staging its history and the history of the one whom it presents as a history of ruins and shards. As a homeless image, the photograph unwittingly stages something of Kracauer's extraterritoriality, reminiscent of Benjamin's allegory of his friend as a philosophical ragpicker who lives among the shards—the shards of the homeless image and the shards of history.

The transcendental homelessness of this homeless image, finally, also is enacted by the triangular void immediately above Kracauer's head. As if to literalize the German word for homelessness, *Obdachlosigkeit*, or rooflessness, a roof-shaped segment is missing at the top of the photograph. Is it an absent, triangular roof out of which one almost can imagine smoke rising from a chimney on the left-hand side? In the ruined image, an image shattered by the effects of time, war, displacement, and extraterritoriality, Kracauer emerges as the one who possesses no roof, only the thought of a roof, a roof that remains absent—absent either as a radical absence or as a distant presence that cannot be reached or read but that remains inscribed in his image. Its absence makes itself felt by leaving a trace—the contours of a void and the outlines of a ruined whole.

In 1927, a few years before this photograph was taken, Kracauer insisted that photography "represents what is utterly past, and yet this debris was once the present." As if commenting on the double future of his own image, Kracauer spoke to the fact that this photograph had yet to be taken and that it would survive after his death, explaining that the photograph's "ghost-like reality is *unredeemed*" and "consists of elements in space whose configuration is so far from necessary that one could just as well imagine a different organization of these elements. Those things once clung to us like our skin, and this is how our property still clings to us today. Nothing of these contains us, and the photograph gathers fragments around a nothing."[51] What the ruins of this image of photography both contain and disperse is the fragmented nature of what they record in and as history. Like the glass shards of Kracauer's melancholic image and the montage of broken fragments that once seemed to relate incontrovertibly to his skin, the photograph records the aleatory and contingent quality of any attempt to arrest the presentation of an object for good and to secure that presentation in a mimetic model of historical and subjective transparency.

HOMELESS LANGUAGE: ONLY ONE, NOT OURS

For Derrida, the roofless homelessness that Kracauer's sentences and images mobilize, cannot be thought in isolation from an aporetic experience of language that opens up "the relationship among birth, language, culture, nationality, and citizenship."[52] While Kracauer engages this *Obdachlosigkeit* in the figures of multiple extraterritorialities, Derrida's nonautobiographical autobiographical reflections in *Monolingualism of the Other*, in concert with his more general concerns regarding the very possibility of autobiographical writing throughout his work,[53] consider this aporetic experience as it emerges in the tension that results from having only one language (French) without fully possessing it, from living in one's own language without being able

---

51 Kracauer, "On Photography," 56 [91–2].
52 Derrida, *Monolingualism of the Other*, 13.
53 The most extensive treatment of this general aspect of Derrida's work is Robert Smith, *Derrida and Autobiography* (Cambridge: Cambridge University Press, 1995).

to claim it as one's own, from speaking, reading, and writing a language that is neither native nor foreign, but both at once. Derrida offers the figure of a self in language, a self that seeks the homey comforts of speaking a language in a "severely idiomatic way, without, however, ever being at home in it."[54] The self here dwells, if it dwells at all, in a "language that fails, lastingly [*à demeure*], to reach home."[55] Taking as a point of departure his own experience of living in the French language as a non-French other, a Francophone Algerian Jew, who, along with other members of his community was stripped of French citizenship only to have it reinstated later, and who was subjected to colonialist policies—policies that marginalized "indigenous" languages such as Arabic and Berber in Algerian schools—Derrida reflects on fantasies of linguistic purity (including his own) and the ways in which one's multiply fractured relation to one's language modulates both the experience of cultural identity and its loss not simply as a lack, but also as something constitutive. In the belonging and non-belonging that language occasions, in its affiliations and exclusions, language raises questions about its own capacity to be possessed, in the double meaning of the word:

> But who exactly possesses it? And whom does it possess? Is language in possession, ever a possessing or possessed possession? Possessed or possessing in exclusive possession, like a piece of personal property? What of this being-at-home [*être-chez-soi*] in language toward which we never cease returning?[56]

The openness of the question of linguistic possession also names a perpetual deferral of possessing a roof, the *Dach* of the *Obdach*.

The *Obdachlosigkeit* around which language turns cannot be thought without considering the distinction between identity and identification. As Derrida reminds us,

> an identity is never given, received, or attained; only the interminable and indefinitely phantasmatic process of identification endures. Whatever the story of a return to oneself or to one's home [*chez-soi*], into the "hut" ["case"] of one's home (*chez* is the *casa*), no matter what an odyssey

---

54 Derrida, *Monolingualism of the Other*, 57.
55 Ibid., 69.
56 Ibid., 17.

or bildungsroman it might be, in whatever manner one invents the story of a construction of the *self*, the *autos*, or the *ipse*, it is always *imagined* that the one who writes should know how to say *I*.[57]

To the extent that identity has no a priori status but, rather, is invented and reinvented with every process of identification, the identity that a self possesses is subject to perpetual revision in the variegated events of identification. Indeed, the self that speaks of its cultural or linguistic identity evokes a process of identification with a particular modulation that temporarily makes it what it is. But because this self can enter legibility only in a series of identifications *with* something or someone, we may conceptualize its being, not in terms of its identity nor even in terms of its identifications, but rather in terms of its *identifications-with*. This "with-ness" of its identifications exposes the self to its dependence on the other, the one with whom or that with which it first can enter the process of identifying-with. This identifying-with—not unlike Heidegger's *Mit-Sein*, or being-with, but also not identical to it because of its refusal of all communal. *Versammlung* or a gathering-like convocation—tells the self that it emerges, if it emerges at all, only in and through another, and that it will always have been affected by that encounter in as yet unforeseeable ways. As such, self and other become affirmative witnesses of each other, even of each other's aleatory nature, through the logic that links with-ness and the wit-ness.

This other can be language itself, even if that language it not fully and simply itself. What Derrida calls the "monolingualism of the other" is a form of experience and cognition that is not limited to the other inasmuch as that other is also at odds with itself and even constitutively traverses the self. The monolingualism of the other, then, which also is a monolingualism of the self, of the self in its relation to the other, marks the fact "that in any case we speak only one language—and that we do not *own* it. We only ever speak one language—and, since it returns to the other, it exists asymmetrically, always *for the other*, from the other, kept by the other. Coming from the other, remaining with the other, and returning to the other." In Derrida's own situation, "once access was barred to the language and writing of another—in this case Arabic or Berber—and to all the culture which is inseparable from

57   Ibid., 28.

it as well, the inscription of this limit could not leave traces."⁵⁸ The traces of this monolingualism inscribe the movement by which one speaks a language, such as French, of which one also is strangely deprived, a language that one calls one's own without owning it. Monolingualism "conditions the address to the other, it gives its word, or rather it gives the possibility of giving its word, it gives the given word in the ordeal of a threatening and threatened promise: monolingualism and tautology, the absolute impossibility of metalanguage."⁵⁹ With the absolute impossibility of metalanguage—the *meta* of with, the among, and the after—with this impossibility of the *meta*, the monolingual self, who may in fact speak more than one empirical language, is deprived of an originary identification with (a) language, an originary identification that could be called his own origin in language. To the monolingual self, there are thus only prostheses of origins, never origins "as such" or that are intact. The monolingual possesses an originary self without origin. As Derrida suggests:

> The monolingual of whom I speak speaks a language of which he is *deprived.* The French language is not his. Because he is therefore deprived of *all* language, and no longer has any other recourse—neither Arabic, nor Berber, nor Hebrew, not any languages his ancestors would have spoken-because this monolingual is in a way *aphasic* (perhaps he writes because he is an aphasic), he is thrown into absolute translation, a translation without pole of reference, without an originary language, and without a source language [*langue de départ*]. For him, there are only target languages [*langues d'arrive*], if you will, the remarkable experience being, however, that these languages just cannot manage to reach themselves because they no longer know where they are coming from, what they are speaking from and what the sense of their journey is. Languages without an itinerary and, above all, without any superhighway of goodness knows what information.⁶⁰

Derrida continues, taking up the language of arrivals, arriving, and the arriving that traverses his earlier reflections in *Aporias*:

---

58 Ibid., 40.
59 Ibid., 22.
60 Ibid., 60-1.

As if there were only arrivals [*arrivées*], and therefore only events without arrival. From these sole "arrivals," and from these arrivals alone, desire springs forth; since desire is borne by the arrival itself, it springs forth even before the ipseity of an *I–me* that would bear it in advance; it springs forth, and even sets itself up as a desire to reconstruct, to restore, but it is really a desire to invent a *first language* that would be, rather, a *prior-to-the-first* language destined to translate that memory. But to translate the memory of what, precisely, did not take place, of what, having been (the) forbidden, ought, nevertheless, to have left a trace, a specter, the phantomic body, the phantom-member—palpable, painful, but hardly legible—of traces, marks, and scars. As if it were a matter of producing the truth of what never took place by avowing it.[61]

Hence, the experience and the event of the monolingual, understood either as an other or as a self, or as the traversal of each of these in the other, situates both the sense of homelessness that accompanies the insight into one's prosthetic—rather than originary—relation to language, native or foreign, acquired by birth or by choice, and, at the same time, the desire for an imagined dwelling, not only in an "imagined community" of others, as Benedict Anderson suggests, or in a gesture of "dissemiNation" that would mark the "liminality" of cultural identity, as Homi Bhabha imagines it, but also for an imagined dwelling in language prior to language, a first language before the first.[62] To read the self as an effect of the prosthetic status of origin—such as the original language, one's native home, one's cultural community, among many other things—is to identify the ways in which it engages in multiple *acts* of identification. These acts articulate an ever-renewed, ever-transformed self, a self that "itself" is the event of an arriving without arrival, the promise of an arrival or absolute translation to come. Here, the homeless self is itself a prosthesis. Just like the photograph of Kracauer's "spooky" lady of the haunted castle, and just like the haunted extraterritoriality encoded in the homeless image of Kracauer's own photograph, Derrida's experience of the monolingual, and all that it implies, hardly can be understood without the

---

61 Ibid., 61.
62 See Benedict Anderson, *Imagined Communities: Reflections on the Origin and Spread of Nationalism* (London: Verso, 1983), and Homi K. Bhabha, "DissemiNation: Time, Narrative, and the Margins of the Modern Nation," in *The Location of Culture* (London: Roudedge, 1994), 139–70. For a book-length treatment of the question of "origin," compare further John Pizer, *Toward a Theory of Radical Origin: Essays on Modern German Thought* (Lincoln: University of Nebraska Press, 1995).

"spectrality of the phenomenon," which is to say, "the phantom, the double, or the ghost."[63] Phantoms and ghosts—it is these homeless images that both Kracauer and Derrida leave behind for us to learn to read.

CULTURES: TRANSITIONS

The learning to read that Kracauer and Derrida ask of us is a sort of learning that transforms the very notion of cultural identity and the very thinkability of belonging, through language, birth, or blood, to this or that cultural realm. The call for this kind of learning to read connects these two thinkers to a whole constellation of other modern philosophers and writers who have meditated on these issues. To recall only those proper names that Derrida himself mentions in *Monolingualism of the Other*: Adorno, Hannah Arendt, Paul Celan, Franz Kafka, the Moroccan Abdel-kebir Khatibi, Emmanuel Levinas, Franz Rosenzweig, and Gershom Scholem. While Derrida refers to Adorno's 1965 essay "On the Question: 'What Is German?" only in passing, Adorno's argument is well worth recalling here, not only because of his significance as a conceptual link between Kracauer and Derrida, but also because his "non-identical" thinking convenes with that of Kracauer and Derrida in a way that will prove fruitful in our engagement with the issues of language and cultural identity that dwell in the homeless images we have considered so far.

In "On the Question: 'What Is German?'" Adorno stages a careful transgression of the essentializing quest for "Germanness" and the ideology of a stable German identity. Having transgressed the ideology of a German essence, Adorno writes that it "is in the loyalty to the idea that the current state of affairs ought not to be the last—rather than in hopeless attempts to establish once and for all what is German—that the meaning this concept still may claim can be suspected to reside: in the transition to humanity [*In der Treue zur Idee, daß, wie es ist, nicht das letzte sein solle—nicht in hoffnungslosen Versuchen, festzustellen, was das Deutsche nun einmal sei, ist der Sinn zu vermuten, den dieser Begriff noch behaupten mag: im Übergang zur Menschheit*]."[64] Adorno wishes to remain faithful to the idea ("Treue zur Idee") that the last word has

---

63 Derrida, *Monolingualism of the Other*, 25.
64 Theodor W. Adorno, "On the Question: 'What Is German?,'" trans. Thomas Y. Levin, *New German Critique* 36 (Fall 1985): 131; "Auf die Frage: Was ist deutsch," in *Gesammelte Schriften*, vol. 10, book 2, 691–701.

not yet been spoken, that the definitive reading has not been given, that there will be an other that is yet to arrive—an other that is an other primarily to any ontologizing notion of what is German. By extension, the infinitely mediated complexity of the concept of Germanness should not be exhausted and closed off because of a delusional chase after its elusive essence in a single dominant interpretation. Such a violent positing would foreclose any faithfulness to what is to come. Adorno's transgression here consists in a double movement that opens up the concept of Germanness to difference and otherness without, however, abandoning the thinkability of that concept altogether. That is to say, he violates the concept even while remaining faithful to it. The double movement of this transgression enables him to suggest that what is German should not be posited in terms of an essential presence or a positive set of verifiable features, but rather should be sought in its fluid movement, its transition toward humanity (*im Übergang zur Menschheit*). Adorno does not advocate a transparent, communicative model of substitution, an exchange of one predetermined program for another; such a model would claim, perhaps too easily, to elevate a culture from a blemished Nazi past, for instance, to a new, higher, and Nazi-proof humanity. For Adorno, it simply would be delusional to assume that one could arrive once and for all at a stable concept or state of "humanity," a program that one easily could follow. Here, humanity, like its vital dimensions of ethics, justice, and democracy, always is still to come. In order to remain effective as the promise of a future—indeed, as the promise that there will be a future at all—these concepts never can be assumed simply to be present. Instead, Adorno locates the prospect of a future, a future Germanness, in the moment of transition itself. This new concept—if it is one—would suggest that what properly is German is its movement toward something else, rather than the programmed arrival at a secure new destination. It is most properly itself when it is on its way toward something else. This perpetual transition (*Übergang*) names the political stakes of Adorno's double reading—it is an *Übergang* that is still to be thought.

Adorno's *Übergang* helps us to imagine a subject of culture, even a cultural "self," whose identity no longer is measured by its allegiance to this or that nation-state, originary realm, or cultural space that could endow it with a determinate meaning. Rather, the cultural "self," to the extent that it becomes readable at all, migrates between cultures, the interstices of multiple cultural identifications. *Übergang* thus also names the state of being "between" cultures in a space that, on the far side of the mechanisms of assimilation that encroach upon any act of cultural recognition of otherness within a given hegemonic state or culture, first makes the gesture of recognizing cultural otherness possible.[65] This *Übergang* leads not to the promised land of cultural identity, but to the realm of extraterritoriality itself, where selves can be recognized as the ones that are gathered and dispersed in language.

Adorno's *Übergang*, his undoing of any fixed cultural identity in terms of what it is not yet and in terms of what it promises, can be thought of as setting the stage for the kind of work that Kracauer's and Derrida's texts will have asked of us. After all, what Kracauer's *Denkbild* of extraterritoriality and Derrida's monolingualism of the other will have asked us to consider, among so many other things, is the question of thinking and living in culture, of thinking and living culturally, even multiculturally, as a question of a certain homelessness: homeless images, homeless selves, and even homeless cultures. Both Kracauer and Derrida, each in "his" idiom and in "his" experience of expatriation, an experience that is singular at the same time that it is shared by many, invite us to expose cultural identity, even multiculturalism, to the plurality that these terms both name and exceed. That is to say, because of the internal tensions and heterogeneities in both thinkers' elaborations of the homeless—the tensions and heterogeneities that make it possible for us to speak of the promise and suffering of homelessness in the first place—these elaborations are exposed to their own multiplicities and non-self-identities. As Werner Hamacher puts it in his discussion of multiculturalism, "If the historical and structural *a priori* of every culture is its multiplication, then one multiculturalism cannot be enough, and there needs to be *many* multiculturalisms. There must be more than one, there must be more than many, and thus, across cultures, there must be the possibility of more than that which today we still call cultures: this is the imperative of the *ac*culturation, alterculturations." For this, he continues, there "must be something other than culture and its mere multiplicity. It is the imperative of autonomization. This imperative must count, and must count many, but it cannot do so unless it exposes the countable cultures, in and beyond counting, to what cannot be counted."[66]

---

65 This significance of the "between" in acts of cultural recognition is made vivid by Alexander García Düttmann, *Zwischen den Kulturen: Spannungen im Kampf um Anerkennung* (Frankfurt a.M.: Suhrkamp, 1997).

66 Werner Hamacher, "One 2 Many Multiculturalisms," trans. Dana Hollander, in *Violence, Identity and Self-Determination*, ed. Hent de Vries and Samuel Weber (Stanford: Stanford University Press,

Without this exposure to its own alterities, even multiculturalism can be used as a concept that masks certain monocultural ideologies and colonizing gestures. If we open up Kracauer's extraterritoriality to its own internal extraterritorialities and Derrida's spectral monolingualism of the other to the plurality of monolingualisms that traverse it, there must be many extraterritorialities and many monolingualisms. Just as the autonomy that is promised by multuculturalization in order to deserve the politically charged promise of autonomy at all "cannot be only one autonomy, there would have to be many, innumerably many, and there is only one that would be too many, which would be one and only one," so there would have to be many extraterritorialities and many monolingualisms; in short, there would have to be innumerably many homeless images.[67] But such a multiple and perpetually fractures homeless image always is yet to come — is cannot simply be assumed to be present, lest it be mistaken for having a proper home, the false home that would be present in our stable hermeneutic decoding of that image, its reduction to one meaning and "the one" of meaning.

The homeless images that Kracauer's *Denkbilder* and Derrida's meditations offer us posit a cultural identity beyond cultural identity, a cultural practice in which one no longer is simply oneself and no longer simply one, the one who is present. Because the reality of this imagined cultural identity cannot be reduced to this or that form of presence — its desires, genealogies, contexts, overdeterminations, hidden filiations, promises, commitments, secrets, and debts always are *elsewhere*, invested differently, and not always fully visible — we must look for its homeless images *in the future*. But this future cannot be executed in advance, even by a program that would attempt to install a system of reading such homeless images with an eye to their futurity and with the best of intentions. Homeless images, if they do anything, challenges us to consider the ways in which they, and we in and with them, always are still to come, even as an other or as others. Homeless images, along with the extraterritorialities and monolingualism's that they perform, are homeless precisely because they still remain to be invented, thought, and read, again and again. *Read*: always already and always as if for the very first time.

1997), 284–325, at 298.
67   Ibid., 325.

Language is no longer linked to the knowing of things, but to men's freedom.

—Michel Foucault[1]

THE OUTER WORLD AND INNER SPEECH: BAKHTIN, VYGOTSKY, AND THE INTERNALIZATION OF LANGUAGE

Caryl Emerson

In this statement from *The Order of Things*, Michel Foucault speaks of the nineteenth-century revolution in linguistics that, in effect, rediscovered language and made it the object of systematic study in its own right. Language, no longer seen as a transparent medium, was granted "its own particular density [...] and laws of its own." Yet it is not self-evident how we are made more free by understanding that words are not just a repository of knowledge. The density of language is a troublesome postulate. That postulate, according to Foucault, raises difficult epistemological problems and presents theorists with a choice:

> The critical elevation of language, which was a compensation for its subsidence within the object, implied that it had been brought nearer both to an act of knowing, pure of all words, and to the unconscious element in our discourse. It had to be either made transparent to the forms of knowledge, or thrust down into the contents of the unconscious.[2]

The debate on the status of language has been enormous and subtle, but it would seem that these two poles described by Foucault remain constantly in effect. Language is, on the one hand, a transparent medium from which to deduce a metalanguage and on which to build statistical and mechanical models, or language is, on the other hand, a product of the individual psy-

---

Originally published as Caryl Emerson, "The Outer Word and Inner Speech: Bakhtin, Vygotsky, and the Internalization of Language," *Critical Inquiry* 10, no. 2 (1983), 245–64. Reprinted with permission of University of Chicago Press.

1   Michel Foucault, *The Order of Things: An Archaeology of the Human Sciences* (New York: Vintage Books, 1973), 296.
2   Ibid., 299.

che and ultimately subject to psychic transformation, to what Foucault calls "dim mechanisms, faceless determinations, a whole landscape of shadow."[3]

In the twentieth century, these two poles were reevaluated in the light of Ferdinand de Saussure's celebrated binary oppositions: synchrony/diachrony, syntagmatic/paradigmatic, *langue/parole*. Language had moved from the realm of naming to the realm of relationships—a truly revolutionary shift. But as is so often the case with intellectual revolutions, success tended to institutionalize and finalize the new terminology. One of the most productive (and most quickly canonized) distinctions was that between *langue* and *parole*, between the social-collective institution of language (the code) and the individual act of combination and actualization (the message). Not surprisingly, such an unbridged opposition was not congenial to Marxist dialecticians, and in the Soviet Union of the 1920s Saussure's dichotomy stimulated vigorous debate. Literary scholars, philosophers of language, and developmental psychologists all questioned that opposition in their separate disciplines and were concerned to explain the integration of individual with society in a more benevolent way. It became a central issue in clinical psychology, especially in the branch dealing with language acquisition. And it was a lifelong preoccupation for those members of the Bakhtin circle who were especially interested in language: Mikhail Bakhtin, Valentin Vološinov, and Pavel Medvedev. These various groups, it should be emphasized, worked in and with the terminological frameworks of their time, including an experimental and open-ended Marxism that stressed process, change, and the interaction between organism and environment. Among the most eloquent contributions to the debate were two books that appeared under Vološinov's name: *Freudianism: A Marxist Critique* (1927) and *Marxism and the Philosophy of Language* (1929).[4] Each in its own way reassessed the two Saussurian poles and attempted a synthesis. The nature of that synthesis, and the light it casts on the interplay between language and consciousness, is the focal point of this essay.

---

3   Ibid., 326.
4   See Valentin Nikolaevich Vološinov, *Freudianism: A Marxist Critique*, ed. in collaboration with Neal H. Bruss, trans. I. R. Titunik (New York: Academic Press, 1976). The title has been translated in an unnecessarily misleading way; the Russian is simply *Frejdizm: kritičeskij očerk* (*Freudianism: A Critical Sketch*). And see Vološinov, *Marxism and the Philosophy of Language*, trans. Ladislav Matejka and Titunik (New York: Seminar Press, 1973). Vološinov's authorship of these two texts is disputed: there is evidence that Mikhail Bakhtin wrote them both, or substantial portions of both. The collaboration between the two men was, at any rate, very close. In the text of this article, I refer to Bakhtin as the author of both works.

Members of the Bakhtin circle objected in particular to one fundamental aspect of the *langue/parole* schema, namely, its opposition of the social to the individual. Instead of opposition, they spoke of inter-action—and warned the while against understanding this interaction in a mechanical and narrowly rational (by which they meant formulaic) way. As Bakhtin defined the problem:

> The idea of the *conventionality, the arbitrariness of language*, is a typical one for rationalism as a whole, and no less typical is the *comparison of language to the system of mathematical signs*. What interests the mathematically minded rationalists is not the relationship of the sign to the actual reality it reflects nor to the individual who is its originator, but the *relationship of sign to sign within a closed system* already accepted and authorized. In other words, they are interested only in the *inner logic of the system of signs itself*, taken, as in algebra, completely independently of the ideological meanings that give the signs their content.[5]

This insensitivity to "ideological meanings," Bakhtin suggests, is the ultimate danger behind the fascination with the arbitrary nature of the sign. The corrective, in his view, is a proper understanding of the concept of *ideologija*. Its English cognate "ideology" is in some respects unfortunate, for our word suggests something inflexible and propagandistic, something politically unfree. For Bakhtin and his colleagues, it meant simply an "idea system" determined socially, something that *means*. In this sense of the term, all sign systems are ideological, and all ideologies possess semiotic value.[6] But in contrast to Saussure's claim that a verbal sign is ultimately a mental construct—that the acoustic image and the concept are both contained in an arbitrary closed system—the members of the Bakhtin circle posited four social factors that make the understanding of speech and writing possible.

First, they assumed that the sign and its effects occur in outer experience. "[In the] chain of ideological creativity and understanding [...] nowhere is there a break in the chain, nowhere does the chain plunge into inner being, nonmaterial in nature and unembodied in signs."[7] Each ideological product is meaningful not in the soul but in the objectively accessible ideological material.

---

5 Vološinov, *Marxism and the Philosophy of Language*, 57–8.
6 Ibid., 9–10.
7 Ibid., 11.

Second, this outer experience, if it is to register significance, must in some way be organized socially. Signs "can arise only on *interindividual territory.*" But this territory "cannot be called 'natural' in the direct sense of the word: signs do not arise between any two members of the species *Homo sapiens.* It is essential that the two individuals [...] compose a group (a social unit); only then can the medium of signs take shape between them."[8] A social unit is therefore an indispensable aspect of semiotic activity—and for this reason the study of ideologies cannot be grounded in individual psychology. Far from positing a Saussurian tension between society and the individual, Bakhtin posits an individual who actively creates the society in which his discourse occurs. The whole tradition opposing individual to society is misguided: an individual person is simply one biological specimen in a group.[9]

Third, the ideologies that are generated by the material reality of language must be studied *inter*-systemically, not as independent and isolated phenomena. That is, ideology always exists as a relation between (or among) speakers and listeners and, by extension, between or among social groups. According to Bakhtin, each social group—each class, profession, generation, religion, region—has its own characteristic way of speaking, its own dialect. Each dialect reflects and embodies a set of values and a sense of shared experience. Because no two individuals ever entirely coincide in their experience or belong to precisely the same set of social groups, every act of understanding involves an act of translation and a negotiation of values. It is essentially a phenomenon of interrelation and interaction.[10]

Fourth and last, Bakhtin profoundly redefined the Word itself and attempted to infuse it with its original Greek sense of *logos* ("discourse"). For

---

8 Ibid., 12.
9 Ibid., 34.
10 For a clear and provocative discussion of this aspect of Bakhtin's work, see Gary Saul Morson, "The Heresiarch of Meta," *Poetics and Theory of Literature* 3 (1978): 407–27. In a note written near the end of his life, Bakhtin emphasized the necessity of difference in any act of understanding: "Understanding cannot be understood as emotional empathy, or as the placing of oneself in another's place (the loss of one's own place). This is required only for the peripheral aspects of understanding. Understanding cannot be understood as translation from someone else's language into one's own language" ("Iz zapisei 1970–1971 godov," *Éstetika slovesnogo tvorčestva* (Moscow: 1979), 346; my translation). Even understanding, itself, is a threshold phenomenon.
The Tartu school of Soviet semioticians has been very creative with Bakhtinian concepts, which it recognizes as complementary to its own work. For an extension of Bakhtin's insights into the micro-dynamics of the psyche, see Iu. M. Lotman, "On the Reduction and Unfolding of Sign Systems (The Problem of 'Freudianism and Semiotic Culturology')," in *Semiotics and Structuralism: Readings from the Soviet Union*, ed. Henryk Baran (White Plains, NY: International Arts and Sciences Press, 1976), 301–9. For an extension of Bakhtin's insights into the macro-dynamics of history, see B.A. Uspenskii, "Historia sub Specie Semioticae," in *Semiotics and Structuralism*, 64–75.

Bakhtin, words cannot be conceived apart from the voices who speak them; thus, every word raises the question of authority. Fully half of *Marxism and the Philosophy of Language* is devoted to an investigation of "indirect" and "quasi-direct" discourse, multileveled speech acts in which more than one voice participates. For Bakhtin, words come not out of dictionaries but out of concrete dialogic situations. He saw the distinction between dialogic words—that is, utterances—and dictionary words as one between *theme* and *meaning*:

> Theme is the *upper, actual limit of linguistic significance*; in essence, only theme means something definite. Meaning is the *lower limit* of linguistic significance. Meaning, in essence, means nothing; it only possesses potentiality—the possibility of having a meaning within a concrete theme.[11]

Words in discourse always recall earlier contexts of usage, otherwise they could not mean at all. It follows that *every* utterance, covertly or overtly, is an act of indirect discourse.

These, then, are the amendments the Bakhtin circle would attach to Saussure: the sign is external, organized socially, concretely historical, and, as the Word, inseparably linked with voice and authority. These four dialectical alterations work a great change in the original distinction between *langue* and *parole*. Bakhtin deals with this dichotomy (in somewhat expanded form) in his discussion of the twin sins of "abstract objectivism" and "individualistic subjectivism."[12] Abstract objectivism can be seen as the Cartesian extreme, language taken as a code independent of its interpreters. This is an excess to which the Neogrammarians were prone, the myth that language makes poets. Individualistic subjectivism, on the other hand, is the Humboldtian extreme, embodied for Bakhtin in the Vosslerites. They are faulted for grounding the message too exclusively in the individual psyche—thus giving rise to the myth that poets make language. Bakhtin himself does not deny the two poles. But he would synthesize them, and he claims that their opposition in real life, at any given moment, is a fiction. In the Bakhtinian model, every individual engages in two perpendicular activities. He forms lateral ("horizontal") relationships with other individuals in specific speech acts, and he simultaneously forms internal ("vertical") relationships between the outer

---

11 Vološinov, *Marxism and the Philosophy of Language*, 101.
12 Ibid., 47–63.

world and his own psyche. These double activities are constant, and their interactions in fact *constitute* the psyche. The psyche is thus not an internal but a boundary phenomenon. Or to use Bakhtin's political metaphor, the psyche "enjoys extraterritorial status [...] [as] a social entity that penetrates inside the organism of the individual person."[13]

This concept of the psyche is indeed radical. The assumption that the psyche is, at its base, a "social entity," a space to be filled with ideological signs, sets the Bakhtinian concept of consciousness at odds with much of Western thinking since Freud on the subject. In his remarkable descriptions of the transitions from "social intercourse" to "outer speech," and from "outer speech" to "inner speech" and to consciousness, Bakhtin fundamentally rethinks both the relation of consciousness to the world around it and the relation of the self to others. We read that a poet's style "is engendered from the style of his inner speech, which does not lend itself to control, and his inner speech is itself the product of his entire social life."[14] And in *Marxism and the Philosophy of Language* we read:

> Although the reality of the word, as is true of any sign, resides between individuals, a word, at the same time, is produced by the individual organism's own means without recourse to any equipment or any other kind of extracorporeal material. This has determined the role of [the] word as *the semiotic material of inner life — of consciousness* (inner speech).[15]

When so firmly tied to outer experience, this tripartite equation of inner life = inner speech = consciousness is quite audacious. "People do not 'accept' their native language," Bakhtin insists, "it is in their native language that they first reach awareness."[16] Individuation of the personality is the process of a consciousness working over the "ideological themes" that penetrate it "and there take on the semblance of individual accents."[17] Indeed, a clear distinction between inner and outer speech is impossible, because the very act of introspection is modeled on external social discourse: it is self-observation,

---

13 Ibid., 39.
14 Vološinov, "Discourse in Life and Discourse in Art (Concerning Sociological Poetics)," appendix 1, in *Freudianism: A Marxist Critique*, ed. in collaboration with Neal H. Bruss, trans. I. R. Titunik (New York: Academic Press, 1976), 114.
15 Vološinov, *Marxism and the Philosophy of Language*, 14.
16 Ibid., 81.
17 Ibid., 22.

communion with the self, "the understanding of one's own inner sign."[18] Thus, the problem of origins in personality is in fact no problem at all, and there is likewise no problem of self-expression:

> *Not only can experience be outwardly expressed through the agency of the sign* [...] *but also, aside from this outward expression (for others), experience exists even for the person undergoing it only in the material of signs.* Outside that material there is no experience as such. In this sense *any experience* is expressible, i.e., is potential expression....
>
> Thus there is no leap involved between inner experience and its expression, no crossing over from one qualitative realm of reality to another.[19]

Individual consciousness is a socio-ideological fact. If you cannot talk about an experience, at least to yourself, you did not have it.

A person's experiences exist "encoded in his inner speech."[20] Thus the word, Bakhtin affirms, "constitutes the foundation, the skeleton of inner life. Were it to be deprived of the word, the psyche would shrink to an extreme degree."[21] Purely private, speechless, isolated experience—the realm of the mystic, the visionary—is essentially impossible *as experience*. It can only be viewed as erratic, as something bordering on the pathological. Experience that "lacks a socially grounded and stable audience" cannot "take firm root and will not receive differentiated and full-fledged expression."[22]

Bakhtin would say, therefore, that we evolve the mechanisms to express that which our environment makes available for us to experience. At any given time the fit between self and society may not be perfect, indeed cannot be perfect, but the mechanisms are always present to engage self and society in dialogue. In such a model of reality, there is no room for — and perhaps no conceptual possibility of — an independent unconscious.

Bakhtin develops this argument in his polemical work *Freudianism: A Marxist Critique*. For Bakhtin, the teachings of Freud represent a debasing of that already discredited extreme, individualistic subjectivism. As Western culture declines and its social fabric disintegrates, Freud's star rises. Bakhtin

18 Ibid., 36.
19 Ibid., 28.
20 Ibid., 118.
21 Ibid., 29.
22 Ibid., 92.

opens his "critical sketch"[23] on this comment, and it is no accident: Freudianism is analyzed here not as a viable scientific theory but as a social symptom. Psychoanalysis saves bourgeois man by taking him out of history, by explaining him to himself not as a concrete social entity but as an "abstract biological organism." According to Bakhtin, Freud would have us everywhere seek the answers within; we forget the social crisis and "take refuge in the organic warmth of the animal side of life."[24] The "ideological motif of Freudianism" is an emphasis on sex and age, common motifs, Bakhtin claims, in eras of crisis and decline, when nature (especially "human nature," in the form of biological drives) is seen as all-powerful and history is seen as impotent.[25]

It need hardly be pointed out that Bakhtin is very selective in his reading of Freud. Nowhere does he engage Freud's most provocative works, the great sociopsychological essays of the war years and the 1920s. In those works Bakhtin would have found a more complex opponent and, at times, an uncomfortable ally. But it was precisely the early clinical Freud, and his pioneering assumptions and methods of psychoanalysis, that posed a challenge to the Bakhtinian model for perceiving and assimilating reality. Those assumptions and methods had to be confronted. In Bakhtin's model, phenomena originate in the external material world, as do the means to express them. The "unconscious," that is, the part of ourselves that is outside our control and awareness, is best comprehended as merely that portion of the conscious not yet articulate — an "unofficial conscious," if you will, or perhaps a struggle among various motives and voices within the conscious.[26] According to Bakhtin, Freud's projection of autonomous drives and nonnegotiable demands is mere "psychologization of the somatic."[27] It follows that the forces of id and ego that emerge so colorfully during psychoanalysis are not repressed inner realities in the process of discharge but reflections of overt social dynamics, including those between doctor and patient.[28] For Bakhtin, in short, the unconscious in the Freudian sense is a myth — and it functions in society as Roland Barthes has claimed all contemporary myths function: "Semiology has taught us that myth has the task of giving an historical inten-

23 Vološinov, *Freudianism: A Marxist Critique*, 261, n. 2.
24 Ibid., 11.
25 Ibid.
26 Ibid., 76, 85.
27 Ibid., 71.
28 Ibid., 79.

tion a natural justification, and making contingency appear eternal."[29] This evasion of history and the social process is the real sin of the "mythical" unconscious. Eliminate time and society, and a structure cannot be modified. It can only be satisfied or repressed.

Bakhtin's model had to account for the phenomena Freud had observed but do it differently. An alternative system of explanation would have to provide, through experimental work and clinical documentation, specific answers to the key psychological question: How precisely does environment impress a personality, how do outer words become inner speech? One remarkable scholar committed to this project was Bakhtin's contemporary Lev Vygotsky — a man comparable to Bakhtin in productivity and interdisciplinary brilliance. Vygotsky's final work, *Thought and Language* (1934),[30] supplemented by his essays of the 1930s, can be read as an important predecessor and perhaps even as clinical underpinning to Bakhtin's philosophy of language. Soviet scholars such as Vyacheslav Ivanov have made this connection explicitly in discussions of Bakhtin's contribution to semiotics.[31]

It must be said at the outset that this interaction between Bakhtin and Vygotsky is somewhat hypothetical, although none the less intriguing for that. There is no direct evidence that Bakhtin and Vygotsky ever met, and Vygotsky makes no reference to Bakhtin in his work.[32] Interest in dialogic rela-

---

29 Roland Barthes, "Myth Today," in *Mythologies*, trans. Annette Lavers (New York: Hill and Wang, 1972), 142.
30 Lev Semyonovich Vygotsky, *Thought and Language*, ed. and trans. Eugenia Hanfmann and Gertrude Vakar (Cambridge, MA: MIT Press, 1962). A more precise translation of the work's title, *Myšlenie i reč*, would be "Thinking and Speech": the thinking is specifically a process and not a product, and the language is *uttered*. An edited selection of Vygotsky's essays has been published in English, with two excellent explanatory essays, as Vygotsky, *Mind in Society: The Development of Higher Psychological Processes*, ed. Michael Cole, et al. (Cambridge, MA: Harvard University Press, 1978).
31 Vyacheslav Vsevolodovich Ivanov, "The Significance of M.M. Bakhtin's Ideas on Sign, Utterance, and Dialogue for Modern Semiotics (1)," in *Semiotics and Structuralism*, 310–67. I should point out, however, that Ivanov makes very wide claims for Bakhtin's influence; in certain of his cases, parallel development would be a more reasonable hypothesis.
32 For this information I am grateful to James V. Wertsch of Chicago's Center for Psychosocial Studies, who read this manuscript and made a number of very astute and helpful suggestions. It is his conviction that Vygotsky's ideas about dialogue are less influenced by Bakhtin than by the formalist linguist Lev Yakubinsky, whose 1923 essay "On Dialogic Speech" Vygotsky does cite (see L.P. Iakubinskij [Lev Yakubinsky], "O dialogičeskoi reči," in *Russkaja reč*," ed. L. V. Ščerba [Petrograd: 1923]). In this essay, Yakubinsky advises those who study "practical language" to investigate first the seminal distinction between monologic and dialogic speech (or, better, dialogic processes). Dialogue, he claims, is the prior and more natural form, while monologue requires an artificial structure. Yakubinsky also argues (as Bakhtin does) that dialogue does not depend solely on words: shared context, intonation, visual stimuli are all also powerful carriers of a message. There are certainly areas of overlap in the thinking of Bakhtin, Yakubinsky, and Vygotsky on the question of dialogic speech. But Yakubinsky's treatment remains rather naive. For a comprehensive discussion of the Vygotsky–Yakubinsky connection, see chapter 4, "The Semiotic Mediation of Human Activity," from Wertsch's forthcoming study, *Cognitive Developmental Theory: A Vygotskian*

tions and the social context of speech was, of course, rather widespread in the 1920s; both men doubtless pulled upon and were pulled by many of the same social and scholarly currents. Where Bakhtin and Vygotsky intersect is not on the plane of their actual texts, that is, not in the reality of a cross-reference, but in the ultimate implications of their thought. It is this projected intersection that I will now discuss.

Vygotsky's initial inquiry was very similar to that of the Bakhtin circle. Could not the unsatisfactory stalemate between individualistic subjectivism and abstract objectivism — or, as Vygotsky casts the opposition, between idealist and behaviorist psychology — be resolved with a dynamic synthesis focusing on the concrete speech act itself? At both those extremes, the loser had been time: "Whether inclining toward pure naturalism or extreme idealism, all these theories have one trait in common — their antihistorical bias."[33] Time, Vygotsky argues, had long been misunderstood and misapplied in the psychological sciences. The development of the child had once been described in terms of botanical models (maturation, "kindergarten") and then in terms of zoological models (the performance of animals under laboratory conditions), but in Vygotsky's view it is precisely what can*not* be learned from plants and lower animals, namely, the uniquely human assimilation and production of language, that psychologists should examine.[34] Language is man's greatest tool; and so it should be seen precisely as a tool, that is, as a means for communicating with and extracting from the outside world. So viewed, language offers special problems to the psychologist. For if language is always a means of interaction with the world, it is perilous to study it in isolated environments or in traditional controlled experiments. Vygotsky replaced those conventional locales of science with much looser "task situations," which involved putting subjects in confrontation with real problems in a real social setting.[35] Vygotsky's distrust of the classic psychological experiment (what he derisively called the "stimulus-response framework") should in fact recall Bakhtin's distrust of the classic linguistic model, with its ideal speaker and ideal (or nonexistent) listener. Both were suspicious of modeling, for both insisted that only the concrete historical event could validate a human communication or lead to an act of learning.

Approach. I thank its author for generously sharing with me a draft of this chapter. [It appears this study was never published under above title — Ed.]
33 Vygotsky, *Thought and Language*, 153.
34 Vygotsky, "Tool and Symbol in Child Development," in *Mind in Society*, 19–20.
35 Vygotsky, "Problems of Method," in *Mind in Society*, 58–69.

Vygotsky created for himself a powerful clinical tool out of two convictions: that psychological events must be studied in history and that external society is the starting point of consciousness. The two are closely allied, for whatever we can perceive in outer reality, we can change, or try to change, through time. In ingenious experiments, Vygotsky extended (and then modified or rejected) the language-learning maps offered by Jean Piaget, William Stern, and Freud. His primary target was Piaget's "egocentric thought," a stage Piaget claimed is intermediate between autistic play and directed (that is, reality-oriented) thought. Piaget had assumed that a child's thought was originally autistic and became realistic only under social pressure; visible here is the direct impress of Freud's pleasure principle and reality principle. Vygotsky was unsympathetic to the idea that an individual is reluctant to adjust to its environment, that reality, work, and social intercourse are somehow not "pleasurable." In order to test the opposite assumption, Vygotsky conducted the experiments described in *Thought and Language*—and created his own scenario for language acquisition.

According to this scenario, the child's first efforts at perception result in an isolation of word meanings—but "meanings" only in the sense of verbal stimuli, functioning in context as signals rather than as proper signs.[36] A child cannot translate much of the speech he hears into his rudimentary "signal systems," because the ability to generalize comes slowly. Until the age of two years, language serves the human child much as a thirty-two-"word"

36 "Signals" and "signal systems" are basic concepts in the Russian school of psychology. The school traces its fundamental assumptions and terminology to Ivan Pavlov and, in particular, to two physiological laws which were worked out for lower animals and then extended to man. The first law provides that all learning is conditional (*uslovnyj*, usually mistranslated into English as "conditioned," as in the phrase "uslovnyj refleks"). In a human context, this means that learning is basically not intuitive but environmental. The second law posits a "second signal system," a derivation and extension of classical conditioning. According to Pavlov, speech introduces a new principle into nervous activity: the ability to abstract and generalize signals from the environment. Whereas animals develop at most a "primary signal system" that links concrete stimuli and visual relationships, speech provides man with a second level of links, by which we inhibit direct impulses and project ourselves in time and space. Through language, man knows time. We can control the strength of stimuli on our senses and thereby modify the rule of force by which all organisms are bound. Thus man assumes conscious control over his behavior when the word becomes, in Pavlov's terms, a "signal of signals." For a helpful discussion, see Alexander R. Luria, *The Role of Speech in the Regulation of Normal and Abnormal Behavior*, ed. J. Tizard (New York: Pergamon Press, 1961), 20–42. See also Stephen Toulmin's summary in his excellent review of Vygotsky's work: "The Mozart of Psychology," *New York Review of Books* (Sept. 28, 1978): 51–7. The distinction between sign and signal is not, of course, exclusively Pavlovian. Vygotsky also incorporated the Husserlian distinction between *meaning* and *objective reference* (the latter term Vygotsky rendered as "the indicatory function of speech"). Although these categories are similar to Charles Sanders Peirce's symbolic sign and indexical sign, there is no evidence that Vygotsky got them from Peirce. I am grateful to James Wertsch for bringing the above to my attention.

vocabulary serves the chimpanzee throughout its life: words—or, better, vocalizations—are purely emotional; they coincide with gestures but exclude any simultaneous intellectual activity. The child passes out of this chimpanzoid stage when he begins to ask for the names of objects, and at this point one of the critical moments in human maturation occurs: "Thought becomes verbal and speech [becomes] rational."[37] Vygotsky could not define the precise mechanism linking overt to inner speech, but he assumed—and this, of course, is the crucial point—that this process followed the same course and obeyed the same laws as did other operations involving signs. External experiments could be devised to monitor and refine the seepage between levels.

To this end, Vygotsky isolated four stages of "internalization": the natural or pre-intellectual stage, the stage of naive psychology, the stage of egocentric speech, and the so-called ingrowth stage. The third stage, egocentric speech, was the most conducive to analysis in task situations. Uncomfortable with Piaget's conclusion that this speech is fantasy-talk and generated asocially, Vygotsky ran a series of experiments designed to socialize and complicate the child's environment at precisely the age when the child "talked to himself." He demonstrated that a child talks twice as much when presented with obstacles[38] and that this externalized "conversation with oneself," commenting on and predicting the results of an action, is in fact the natural dynamic of problem solving.[39] Furthermore, this talk turned out to be extremely sensitive to social factors. Piaget had observed similar phenomena: that egocentric speech occurs only in a social context, that the child assumes he is being understood by others, and that such speech is not whispered or abbreviated but spoken as an utterance, that is, as public speech in a specific environment. Vygotsky accepted this data but then devised experiments to detach it from Piaget's conclusions.

When Vygotsky varied the social factors—by isolating the child, placing him with deaf-mutes, putting him to play in a room filled with deafening music—it was found that egocentric speech dropped drastically, to one-fifth its previous rate.[40] Vygotsky concluded that egocentric speech was not, as

37 Vygotsky, *Thought and Language*, 44.
38 Ibid., 16–17.
39 Vygotsky, "Tool and Symbol in Child Development," 24–6. Vygotsky proceeds to enumerate the advantages of the speaking child over the ape in the area of problem solving: the speaking child is more independent of his immediate field of vision, more capable of planning, and has greater control over his actions. Speaking children "acquire the capacity to be both the subjects and objects of their own behavior" (Vygotsky, "Tool and Symbol in Child Development," 26).
40 Vygotsky, *Thought and Language*, 136–7.

Piaget had suggested, a compromise between primary autism and reluctant socialization but rather the direct outgrowth (or, better, ingrowth) of speech which had been from the start socially and environmentally oriented. Piaget was correct when he observed that private and socialized speech did indeed intersect at this stage. Development, however, was proceeding not along the lines of Piaget's scenario but in the opposite direction. The child was not externalizing his internal thoughts but internalizing his external verbal interactions. That was why egocentric speech is relatively accessible in three-year-olds but quite inscrutable in seven-year-olds: the older the child, the more thoroughly has his thought become inner speech.[41] "Development in thinking," Vygotsky concludes, "is not from the individual to the socialized, but from the social to the individual."[42]

Like Bakhtin, Vygotsky offers us a restructuring of the Saussurian dichotomy. In Vygotsky's model of language acquisition, a child's first speech is social; words evoke specific responses and must be reinforced by adults. Only gradually does language assume the role of a "second signal system," that is, become for the child an indirect way of affecting his environment. When it does, his speech differentiates into two separate though interlocking systems: one continues to adjust to the external world and emerges as adult social speech; the other system begins to "internalize" and becomes by degrees a personal language, greatly abbreviated and predicative.[43] In this inner speech, the *sense* of a word — a "dynamic, fluid, complex whole" — takes predominance over a word's *meaning*.[44]

When internalization begins, egocentric speech drops off. The child becomes, as it were, his own best interlocutor. Crucial to this process, however, is the presence of a challenging verbal and physical environment. The descriptive "monologue" of which egocentric speech is composed can be internalized creatively only if questioned and challenged by outside voices. In this way

---

41 Ibid., 134.
42 Ibid., 20.
43 Vygotsky, "Tool and Symbol in Child Development," 27–28.
44 Vygotsky, *Thought and Language*, 146. Vygotsky further states: "The sense of a word [...] is the sum of all the psychological events aroused in our consciousness by the word. [...] Meaning is only one of the zones of sense, the most stable and precise zone. A word acquires its sense from the context in which it appears; in different contexts, it changes its sense. Meaning remains stable throughout the changes of sense. The dictionary meaning of a word is no more than a stone in the edifice of sense, no more than a potentiality that finds diversified realization in speech. (Ibid.) Vygotsky's distinction here between meaning and sense has a nice parallel in Bakhtin's distinction between meaning and theme cited earlier in this essay (see p. 427). Again, I thank James Wertsch, for pointing out this parallel.

alone is intelligence possible, "intelligence" defined not as an "accumulation of already mastered skills" but as a "dialogue with one's own future and an address to the external world." It should come as no surprise that Vygotsky was unsympathetic to the standard intelligence test, which measured (in a competitive and isolated context) prior achievement and punished children for "cheating." A true test of intelligence, Vygotsky argued, was one that posited problems beyond the capacity of the child to solve and then made help available. How a child seeks help, how he utilizes his environment, how he asks questions of others—all these constitute the child's "zone of proximal development," where all true learning occurs.[45] Intelligence is a *social* category.[46]

Speech and behavior interact dynamically in a child's development. First, speech accompanies action, then precedes it, finally displaces it—that is, speech assumes the planning function so essential for the higher mental processes.[47] Just as children outgrow the need to count on their fingers or memorize by means of mnemonic devices, so do they outgrow the need to vocalize their activities. This final stage of speech development, the ingrowth stage, coincides with the appearance of logical memory, hypothesis-formation, and other mature mental processes.

Vygotsky does not, however, claim a one-to-one fit between thought and speech. There is speech without thought, as in chimpanzees and infants; there is also thought without speech. The two areas overlap in "verbal thought," and this is coincident with language.[48] Since we can share only what we articulate and communicate, it is this linguistic dimension alone that has historical validity. In this respect, Vygotsky seems somewhat more modest than Bakhtin, who suggests more strongly that experience can be given absolute expression—inwardly to oneself, outwardly to others—through the word.

For Vygotsky, the Word is a powerful amalgam: part sign, part tool, it is the significant humanizing event.[49] One makes a self through the words

---

45 Vygotsky, *Thought and Language*, 103.
46 See Vygotsky, "Interaction between Learning and Development," *Mind in Society*, 84–6. The American educator John Holt seems to have something similar in mind when he writes, with wonderful simplicity: "The true test of intelligence is not how much we know how to do, but how we behave when we don't know what to do" (*How Children Fail* [New York: Dell Publishing Company, 1964], 205).
47 Vygotsky, "Tool and Symbol in Child Development," 27–28.
48 Vygotsky, *Thought and Language*, 47–8.
49 Vygotsky's distinction between tool and symbol has a parallel in the bifurcating functions of speech. Both tool and symbol involve mediated activity, but tools are externally oriented, aids to mastering nature, whereas signs are internally oriented, ultimately aids to mastering oneself. See his "Internalization of Higher Psychological Functions," in *Mind in Society*, 55.

one has learned, fashions one's own voice and inner speech by a selective appropriation of the voices of others. It would obviously be of great interest to know how this process of self-fashioning takes place. Here we can turn to Bakhtin, to an essay from the 1930s and thus contemporary with Vygotsky's last writings.[50] In this essay Bakhtin mentions two ways of assimilating the words of others. Each plays its own part in shaping the process of inner speech, and each has a ready analogue in the way schoolchildren are asked to learn texts. One may "recite by heart" or "retell it in one's own words." In reciting, the language of others is authoritative: it is distanced, taboo, and there can be no play with the framing context. One cannot even entertain the possibility of doubting it; so one cannot enter into dialogue with it. To change a word in a recitation is to make a mistake. The power of this kind of language, however, has its corresponding cost: once discredited, it becomes a relic, a dead thing. Retelling in one's own words, on the other hand, is a more flexible and responsive process. It is the only way we can *originate* anything verbally. In retelling, Bakhtin argues, one arrives at "internally persuasive" discourse—which, in his view, is as close as anything can come to being totally our own. The struggle within us between these two modes of discourse, the authoritative and the internally persuasive, is what we recognize as intellectual and moral growth.

Both Bakhtin and Vygotsky, as we have seen, responded directly or indirectly to the challenge of Freud. Both attempted to account for their data without resorting to postulating an unconscious in the Freudian sense. By way of contrast, it is instructive here to recall Jacques Lacan—who, among others, has been a beneficiary of Bakhtin's "semiotic reinterpretation" of Freud.[51] Lacan's case is intriguing, for he retains the unconscious while at the same time submitting Freudian psychoanalysis to rigorous criticism along the lines of Bakhtin. By focusing attention on the dialogic word, he encourages a rereading of Freud in which the social element (the dynamics between doctor and patient) is crucial. As Lacan opens his essay "The Empty Word and the Full Word":

---

50 See Mikhail Bakhtin, "Discourse in the Novel," in *The Dialogic Imagination: Four Essays*, ed. Michael Holquist, trans. Caryl Emerson and Holquist (Austin: University of Texas Press, 1981), 259–422, esp. 341–2.
51 See Vyacheslav Vsevolodovich Ivanov, "The Significance of M.M. Bakhtin's Ideas," 314.

> Whether it sees itself as an instrument of healing, of formation, or of exploration in depth, psychoanalysis has only a single intermediary: the patient's Word. [...] And every word calls for a reply.
>
> I shall show that there is no word without a reply, even if it meets no more than silence, provided that it has an auditor: this is the heart of its function in psychoanalysis.[52]

The word is conceived as a tool not only of the external world but also of an autonomous internal world as well. And what emerges, it would seem, is a reinterpretation of the role of dialogue in the painful maturational processes of the child. For Vygotsky, the child's realization of his separateness from society is not a crisis; after all, his environment provides both the form and the content of his personality. From the start, dialogue reinforces the child's grasp on reality, as evidenced by the predominantly social and extraverted nature of his earliest egocentric speech. For Lacan, on the contrary, dialogue seems to function as *the* alienating experience, the *stade du miroir* phase of a child's development. The unconscious becomes the seat of all those problems that Bakhtin had externalized: the origin of personality, the possibilities of self-expression. The *je–moi* opposition in the mirror gives rise to that permanent hunger for "a locus where there is constituted the *je* which speaks as well as he who has it speak."[53] And consequently, the Word takes on an entirely different coloration: it is no longer merely an ideological sign but a potent tool for repressing knowledge of that gap, the face in the mirror, the Other. Lacan's celebrated inversion of Saussure's algorithm, with the line between signifier and signified representing repression, created a powerful but ominous new role for language. The child is released from his alienating image only through discovering himself as Subject, which occurs with language; but this language will inevitably come to him from the Other. Thus speech is based on the idea of lack, and dialogue, on the idea of difference.

Here the contrast with the Bakhtin circle is especially fruitful, for dialogue between inner and outer speech is central to both approaches. In each case, the gap between inner and outer can be a cause of pain: in Lacan it is the

---

[52] Jacques Lacan, "The Empty Word and the Full Word," in *Speech and Language in Psychoanalysis*, ed. and trans. Anthony Wilden (Baltimore: Johns Hopkins University Press, 1981), 9.
[53] Lacan, from "La chose freudienne" (1955), quoted in Anthony Wilden, "Lacan and the Discourse of the Other," in *Speech and Language in Psychoanalysis*, 266.

pain of desire, in Bakhtin, the pain of inarticulateness.[54] But Bakhtin defines "the *strife*, the *chaos*, the *adversity* of our psychical life" as conflicts of motives *within* the conscious sphere (albeit an expanded conscious sphere) and thus retains for the Word an objective role in a historically concrete context.[55] He does not deny the reality of internal conflicts, but he does socialize them, thus exposing their mechanisms to the light of day. If enough individuals experience the same gap, it is re-socialized: there develops a political underground, and the potential for revolution.[56]

Thus we see that alienation, if it is to survive at all, must be externalized—at which point it can become the basis for collective rebellion, or for a new dynamic community. One can never, it seems, be existentially alone. In fact, the very concept of solitude is a fiction—or, rather, it is a paradox. When in 1961 Bakhtin returned to his 1929 study of Dostoevsky (then scheduled for republication), he jotted down an eloquent series of thoughts on this question of solitude:

> No Nirvana is possible for a *single* consciousness. A single consciousness is a contradiction in terms. Consciousness is essentially multiple.
>
> I am conscious of myself and become myself only while revealing myself for another, through another, and with the help of another. [...]
>
> Separation, dissociation, and enclosure within the self as the main reason for the loss of one's self. Not that which takes place within, but that which takes place on the *boundary* between one's own and someone else's consciousness, on the *threshold*. [...] Thus does Dostoevsky confront all decadent and idealistic (individualistic) culture, the culture of essential and inescapable solitude. He asserts the impossibility of solitude, the illusory nature of solitude. The very being of man (both external and internal) is the *deepest communion*. *To be* means *to communicate*. [...] To be means to be for another, and through the other, for oneself.[57]

---

54 On this, see Vološinov, *Freudianism*, 89: "The wider and deeper the breach between the official and the unofficial conscious, the more difficult it becomes for motives of inner speech to turn into outward speech."
55 Vološinov, *Freudianism*, 75.
56 Ibid., 89–90.
57 Bakhtin, "K pererabotke knigi o Dostoevskom" [Toward a reworking of the Dostoevsky book], in *Éstetika slovesnogo tvorčestva*, 313, 311–12 (my translation). The complete text of Bakhtin's 1961 notes for the Dostoevsky book is included as an appendix in my forthcoming translation of Bakhtin, *Problems of Dostoevsky's Poetics* (Minneapolis: University of Minnesota Press, 1984). [This book was in fact published in 1993 —Ed.]

This passage is in part the product of that deep meditation on Christianity that occupied Bakhtin all his life.[58] But it is also an integral part of his philosophy of language. In a world beset with the existential image of no exit, this insistence on community, on true socialism, gives the Bakhtin circle an aura of almost old-fashioned coziness in an insecure age.[59]

In the Russian model, inner speech is thus a benevolent quantity, a "unique form of collaboration with oneself."[60] Lacan, as we have seen, also depends on the Word to discharge the negative potential of the gap between self and society. But as part of the Freudian model, this word is only with great difficulty available for "collaboration." It is potentially neurotic, the proof of that permanent gap between objectification and identification. It can be mediated only through that structure whose presumed presence makes it possible to pose (and solve) the problem at all: the unconscious. In Lacan, language is a means of expressing the inexpressible. For Bakhtin and Vygotsky, there is, in essence, no inexpressible. In Lacan's world, therefore, the Word is a tool of psychoanalysis. For Bakhtin and Vygotsky, it is a tool of pedagogy.

✣

The gap between self and society has been, of course, a theme not only of modern linguistics but also of the modern study of literary genres. We may recall that Georg Lukács defines the epic as a genre embodying the absence of such a gap, as the product of "integrated civilisations" where there "is not yet any interiority, for there is not yet any exterior, any 'otherness' for the soul."[61]

---

58 In Leningrad of the 1920s, Bakhtin was well known as a *cerkovnik*, a devout Orthodox Christian; it was for his connections with the underground church that he was arrested in 1929. During these years he wrote a huge metaphysical work—only portions of which survive—on the meaning of Christian "responsibility," on "the Word become flesh," and on the implications of the Biblical injunction "In the Beginning was the Word." On this and other points of biography and doctrine, I am indebted to Katerina Clark and Michael Holquist, who have generously shared draft chapters of their forthcoming *Mikhail Bakhtin* [published in 1986 by Harvard University Press—Ed.]. Until that definitive volume appears, see Michael Holquist, "The Politics of Representation," in *Allegory and Representation*, ed. Stephen J. Greenblatt, (Baltimore: Johns Hopkins University Press, 1981), 163–83.

59 For an American echo of the voices of Bakhtin and Vygotsky, see Stephen Toulmin, "The Inwardness of Mental Life," *Critical Inquiry* 6 (Autumn 1979): 1–16. Very much in their spirit, Toulmin argues that "inner" and "outer" are not on either side of a great divide but that "the moral and emotional ambiguities of our inner lives are simply the moral and emotional ambiguities of our open lives internalized" (9).

60 Vygotsky, quoted in Ivanov, "The Significance of M.M. Bakhtin's Ideas" 326.

61 Georg Lukács, *The Theory of the Novel*, trans. Anna Bostock (Cambridge, MA: 1971), 29–30.

Invoking a rather primitive Marxism, Lukács also defines the novel as the opposite extreme: for him, the novel is the product of a fragmented world, a world in which the interior not only exists but is also maximally at odds with the exterior. It would appear that Lukács needed to posit a time when there was no gap between self and society, so that he might better describe by contrast the world in which, he thought, we now live.

Two decades after Lukács, Bakhtin addressed the issue of epic and novel in an essay that borrowed some of Lukács's terminology but reversed almost entirely its ethical charge.[62] For Bakhtin, the healthy individual *in life* is the one who can surmount—not deny—the gap, who can break down the barriers between inner and outer; likewise, the healthy *artistic genre* is the one that guarantees a *non*-coincidence between hero and environment. The gap so lamented by Lukács is seen, in Bakhtin's "Epic and Novel," as the beginning of dialogue, of temporal development, and of consciousness. The fullest realization of all three is the novel. For Bakhtin, then, the novel-epic distinction, though historically instantiated, is really trans-historical, a relationship between different *perceived qualities of time*—or, as he would say, "chronotopes"—whenever in history they might occur. When he describes the epic narrative as taking place in an "absolute past" and novel time as truly novel, he is really drawing an ontological distinction. He is speaking of temporal types that are always potential: whenever we talk about a world that does not know time, we are "epicking."

And whenever we talk about a world that fully experiences time, we are "noveling." The novel is alienated from epic wholeness. What results in Bakhtin's construct, however, is not loneliness but freedom. Specifically, characters in novels experience the freedom to be more than their roles in given stories. The epic hero, by contrast, is inseparable from his plot; there is only one way his life could be lived.

Neither an epic nor a tragic hero could ever step out in his own character during a pause in the plot or during an intermission: he has no face for

---

62 Bakhtin, "Epic and Novel: Toward a Methodology for the Study of the Novel" (1941), in *The Dialogic Imagination: Four Essays*, ed. Michael Holquist, trans. Caryl Emerson and Holquist (Austin: University of Texas Press, 1981), 3–40. In this essay, Bakhtin posits three generic characteristics of the novel that free it from the strictures of epic: the novel is stylistically multi-languaged ("heteroglot"); it uses time in a way maximally open to the future; and it creates a new zone for structuring images, a zone maximally close to the present. As a result, novelistic heroes are never exhausted by their plots; there is always some other way they might have acted and some other way of understanding their actions. Epics can prophesy; novels only predict.

it, no gesture, no language. In this is his strength and his limitation. The epic and tragic hero is the hero who, by his very nature, must perish.[63]

Novelistic heroes, on the other hand, are like medieval fools on stage: their roles are temporary, their masks are not their selves. "These are heroes of free improvisation and not heroes of tradition, heroes of a life process that is imperishable and forever renewing itself, forever contemporary—these are not heroes of an absolute past."[64] A novelistic hero always has a "surplus of humanness" that is not embodied in his biography: thus "there always remains in him unrealized potential and unrealized demands. [...] There always remains a need for the future, and a place for this future must be found. All existing clothes are always too tight, and thus comical, on a man."[65] When we think away his roles, there is something left: that remainder, that non-coincidence of self and social categories, that capacity to change into different clothes, is freedom.

Novelists rejoice in subjects that are homeless, that is, free to develop. Novels also grant freedom for the *author* to develop, which is to say, freedom for the author to play with his own image on the plane of his own work. The reader (or, for that matter, the creator) of the *Iliad* cannot imagine himself chatting with Hector on the walls of Troy; epic heroes need neither audience nor author. But the writer of novels has an implicated voice. He can enter and manipulate, fuse or distribute his voice among characters. Or he can—and this requires an extra measure of commitment to freedom—grant autonomy to his characters; he can create not just objects but full-fledged *subjects*. This was the "Copernican revolution" that Bakhtin had, in 1929, attributed to Dostoevsky. In Dostoevsky's novels, the author is no longer the creator around whom characters are forced to revolve but is, so to speak, himself but a planet among planets. By the end of his life, Bakhtin had come to see this freedom as characteristic of all true novels. Or to put the point another way, he had come to see the force of "novelness" as the guarantee of freedom.

✖

---

63 Ibid., 36.
64 Ibid.
65 Ibid., 37.

These, then, are the ways an awareness of the gap between inner and outer might function in both life and literature: as an index of individual consciousness, as a measure of our escape from fixed plots and roles, as a prerequisite for discourse itself. What now remains is for us to return to Foucault's statement that language, de-privileged, is an instrument of man's freedom. In light of this discussion, we can understand this freedom two ways, both valid and both linked to the persistent dichotomy between *langue* and *parole*, between the code and the message.

One way of understanding this freedom can be found in a passage from *The Order of Things* which argues that literature as such could emerge only when language was deprived of privilege and thus made self-conscious.[66] This being so, the purpose of literature could be seen as the preserving, and perhaps even the widening, of this self-consciousness. Through the artistic word we learn who we are. And that knowledge could be harnessed to utilitarian purposes, including, for example, the purpose Freud in "The Relation of the Poet to Day-Dreaming" attributes to literature. In that essay, Freud discusses poetry as a sort of fantasy-play for adults and suggests that our appetite for art has at its base the desire to discharge guilt for such indulgence in play: "The true enjoyment of literature proceeds from the release of tensions in our minds."[67] Literature thus serves as a psychic safety valve, much as, in the Aristotelian view, catharsis serves as a social safety valve. In his role as psychoanalyst, Lacan would probably agree with Freud. If the acoustic image is defined as the repressor of the concept, then human neuroses can be released through, and only through, their identification in the Word. Words have a purpose and a function: they are a code, they can pin down. Definition implies release, and therefore freedom.

In contrast, we might consider Freud's essay as Vygotsky treats it in "Art and Psychoanalysis," a chapter from his early work *The Psychology of Art*. In opposing what he considers a reduction of art, Vygotsky argues that Freud left largely unexplained the effects of the artwork on the audience. Moreover, Vygotsky contends, "such an interpretation of art reduces its social role; art begins to appear as an antidote whose task it is to save mankind from vice, but which has no positive tasks or purposes for man's psyche."[68] Vygotsky be-

---

66   Foucault, *The Order of Things*, 299–300.
67   Sigmund Freud, "The Relation of the Poet to Day-Dreaming," trans. I. F. Grant Duff, *On Creativity and the Unconscious: Papers on the Psychology of Art, Literature, Love, Religion*, comp. Benjamin Nelson (New York: Harper, 1958), 54.
68   Lev Vygotsky, *The Psychology of Art* (Cambridge, MA: MIT Press, 1971), 79.

gan his career as a teacher of literature. The affinities among language, literature, and psychology were never far from his mind, and in studying all three he raised the same question: How might man be kept from closing in on his self? One answer he gives is that we learn, through the word, who we are *not*, who we might yet become. It is precisely this positive task—not identification but liberation—that is taken up by Foucault and by such philosophers of language as Paul de Man. In the modern era, Foucault writes in *The Order of Things*,

> the name ceases to be the reward of language; it becomes instead its enigmatic raw material.
>
> This proper being of language is what the nineteenth century was to call the Word (*le Verbe*), as opposed to the Classical "verb", whose function is to pin language, discreetly but continuously, to the being of representation. And the discourse that contains this being and frees it for its own sake is literature.[69]

The same sentiments are echoed by de Man:

> Here, [...] consciousness does not result from the absence of something, but consists of the presence of a nothingness. Poetic language names this void with ever-renewed understanding and [...] it never tires of naming it again. This persistent naming is what we call literature.[70]

The eternal and inevitable inadequacy of all names permits new meanings to happen and new messages to be created. This permission—or intermission—is Bakhtin's novelistic gap, which not even the author can (nor should wish to) bridge. And it is the lack, the absence at the center, that keeps the outer word and our inner speech in permanent dialogue, out of that danger Bakhtin saw of collapse into single consciousness, which would be non-existence. Inside that gap, it is always worthwhile to try naming it again.

---

69 Foucault, *The Order of Things*, 118, 119.
70 Paul de Man, "Criticism and Crisis," in *Blindness and Insight: Essays in the Rhetoric of Contemporary Criticism* (New York: Oxford University Press, 1971), 18.

EXTRATERRITORIAL
OBJECTS

Valéry Proust Museum

Theodor W. Adorno

The German word, *museal* ("museum-like"), has unpleasant overtones. It describes objects to which the observer no longer has a vital relationship and which are in the process of dying. They owe their preservation more to historical respect, than to the needs of the present. Museum and mausoleum are connected by more than phonetic association. Museums are like family sepulchers of works of art. They testify to the neutralization of culture. Art treasures are hoarded in them, and their market value leaves no room for pleasure of looking at them. Nevertheless, that pleasure is dependent on the existence of museums. Anyone who does not have his own collection (and the great private collections are becoming rare) can, for the most part, become familiar with painting and sculpture only in museums. When discontent with museums is strong enough to provoke the attempt to exhibit paintings in their original surroundings or in ones similar, in baroque or rococo castles, for instance, the result is even more distressing than when the works are wrenched from their original surroundings, and then brought together. Sensibility wrecks even more havoc with art than does the hodgepodge of collections. With music, the situation is analogous. The programs of large concert societies, generally retrospective in orientation, have continually more in common with museums, while Mozart performed by candlelight is degraded to a costume piece. In efforts to retrieve music from remoteness of the performance and to put it to immediate context of life there is not only something ineffectual but also a tinge of industriously regressive spite. When some well-intentioned persons advised Mahler to darken the hall during the concert for the sake of the mood, the composer rightly replied that a performance at which one didn't forget about the surroundings was

Originally published as Theodor W. Adorno, "Valéry Proust Museum," trans. Shierry Weber Nicholsen and Samuel Weber, in *Prisms* (Cambridge, MA: MIT Press), 173–86. © 1982 Massachusetts Institute of Technology. Reprinted with permission of the MIT Press.

worthless. Such problems reveal something about the fatal situation of what is called "the cultural tradition." Once tradition is no longer animated by a comprehensive substantial force, but has to be conjured up by means of citations, because "It's important to have tradition," then whatever happens to be left of it is dissolved into a means to an end. An exhibition of applied art only makes a mockery of what it pretends to conserve. Anyone who thinks that art can be reproduced in its original form through an act of will is trapped in hopeless romanticism. Modernizing the past does it much violence and little good. But, to renounce radically the possibility of experiencing the tradition would be to capitulate to barbarism out of devotion to culture. That the world is out of joint is shown everywhere, in the fact that however a problem is solved, the solution is false.

One cannot be content, however, with the general recognition of a negative situation. An intellectual dispute, like the one on museums, must be fought out with specific arguments. Here two extraordinary documents are available, for the two authentic French poets of the last generation have expressed themselves on the question of the museum. Their positions are diametrically opposed, but the statements are not directed polemically against each other, nor in fact does either betray any acquaintance of the other. In contribution to a volume of essays dedicated to Proust, Valéry emphasized that he was not very familiar with Proust's novels. Valery's remarks on museums are entitled "Le problème des musées" and appear in the volume of essays, *Pièces sur l'art.* The passage from Proust occurs in the third volume of *A l'ombre des jeunes filles en fleurs.*

Valéry's appeal is obviously directed against the confusing over abundance of the Louvre. He is not, he writes overly fond of museums. The more marvelous the treasures which are preserved in them, the more do all delight disappear. The word Valéry uses, "délices," is one of those which are utterly untranslatable. "Delicacies" sounds too journalistic, "joys," too heavy and Wagnerian. "Delights" is perhaps closest to what is intended, but, none of these words express the faint reminiscence of feudal pleasure that has been associated with *l'art pour l'art* since Villiers de l'Isle Adam. The only echo of it in German is the "deliziös" ("delicious") of the *Rosenkavalier.* In any case, in the Louvre, the seignorial Valéry feels himself constrained from the first by authoritarian gesture that takes away his cane and by the "No Smoking" sign. Cold confusion, he says reigns among the sculptures, a tumult of frozen creatures, each of which demands non-existence of the others, disorder strangely organized. Standing among the pictures offered for contemplation, Valéry mockingly observes that one is seized by a sacred awe: conversation is louder than in the church, softer than in real life. One does not know why one has come — in search of culture or enjoyment, in fulfillment of an obligation, in obedience to a convention. Fatigue and barbarism converge. Neither a hedonistic nor a rationalistic civilization could have constructed a house of such disparities. Dead visions are entombed there.

The ear, Valéry argues, which is further removed from music than the eye is from painting, can therefore harbour illusions, is better off — no one can ask it to listen to ten orchestras at once. Furthermore, the mind is certainly not capable of performing all possible operations simultaneously. Only the mobile eye is forced to apprehend in the same moment a portrait and a seascape, a kitchen and a triumphal march, or, worst of all, styles of paintings completely incompatible with one another. The more beautiful a picture is, the more it is distinct from all others: it becomes a rare object, unique. This picture, one sometimes says, kills the ones around it. If this is forgotten, Valéry warns that the heritage of art will be destroyed. Just as man loses his abilities through excess of technical aids, so an excess of riches can impoverish him.

Valéry's argumentation bears the stamp of cultural conservatism. He certainly did not concern himself with the critique of political economy. It is therefore all the more astounding that the aesthetic nerves which register false wealth should react so precisely to the fact of over-accumulation. When he speaks of accumulation of excessive and therefore unusable capital, Valéry uses metaphorically an expression literally valid for the economy. Whether artists produce or rich people die, whatever happens is good for the museums. Like casinos, they cannot lose, and that is their curse.

For people become hopelessly lost in the galleries, isolated in the midst of so much art. The only other possible reaction to this situation is the one which Valéry sees as the general, ominous result of any and all progress in domination of material — increasing superficiality. Art becomes a matter of education and information: Venus becomes a document. Education defeats art. Nietzsche argues along very similar lines in his *Untimely Meditation*, "On the Use and Abuse of History for Life." The shock of the museum brings Valéry to historical-philosophical insight into the perishing of art works: there he says, we put the art of the past to death.

Even afterwards, in the street, Valéry cannot free himself from the magnificent chaos of the museum (a metaphor, one could say, for the anarchical production of commodities in fully developed bourgeois society), and he searches for the basis of his malaise. Painting and sculptures, the demon of knowledge tells him, are like abandoned children. "Their mother is dead, their mother, architecture. While she lived, she gave them their place, their definition. The freedom to wander was forbidden them. They had their place, their clearly defined lighting, their materials. Proper relations prevailed between them. While she was alive, they knew what they wanted. Farewell, the thought says to me, I will go no further." With this romantic gesture, Valéry's reflection ceases. By breaking it off, he avoids the otherwise inevitable conclusion of the radical cultural conservative: the renunciation of culture out of loyalty to it.

Proust's view of the museum is woven most skillfully into the fabric of the *Recherche du temps perdu*. Only there can its meaning can be interpreted. Proust's reflections, which represent a return to the techniques of the pre-Flaubertian novel, are never mere observations on the material represented. They are bound up with it through subterranean associations and hence fall like the narrative itself, within the great aesthetic continuum of his inner dialogue. In speaking of his trip to the sea resort Balbec, Proust remarks on the caesura which voyages make in the course of life, by "leading us from one name to another name." The caesuras are particularly manifested in railway stations, "these utterly peculiar places [...] which, so to speak, are not a part of the town and yet contain the essence of its personality as clearly as they bear its name on their signs." Like everything surveyed by Proust's memory, which seems to drain the intention out of its objects, the stations have become historical archetypes and, as the archetypes of departure, tragic ones. Of the glass dome of the Gare St.-Lazare he writes: "Over a sprawling city it stretched its wide, wasted heaven full of ominous dramas. Certain skies of Mantegna or Veronese are as modern, almost Parisian—under such a vaulting sky only terrible and solemn things can happen, the departure of a train or the raising of the cross."

The associative transition to the museum is left implicit in the novel: it is the picture of that station painted by Claude Monet, whom Proust loved passionately, which now hangs in the collection of the *Jeu de Paume*. Briefly, Proust compares the station to a museum. Both stand outside the framework of conventional pragmatic activity, and, one might add, both are bearers of a death symbolism. In case of the station, it is the ancient symbolism of the voyage: in that of the museum, the symbolism associated with the work of art—"l'univers nouveau est périssable," the new and fragile cosmos the artist has created. Like Valéry, Proust returns again and again to the mortality of artifacts. What seems eternal, he says at another point, contains within itself the impulse of its own destruction. The decisive lines on the museum are contained in Proust's physiognomy of the station.

> But in all areas our age is obsessed with the desire to bring things before our eyes in their natural surroundings and thus to suppress what is essential, the mental event that raised them out of those surroundings. Today, one "shows" a picture amidst furniture, small art objects, and curtains "of the epoch," in a trivial decorative display produced by the hitherto ignorant lady of the house after having spent her days in archives and libraries. But the masterpiece observed during dinner no longer produces in us an exhilarating happiness that can be had only in a museum, where the rooms, in their sober abstinence from all decorative detail, symbolizes the inner spaces into which the artist withdraws to create the work.

It is possible to compare Proust's thesis with Valéry's because they share the presupposition that works of art should be enjoyed. Valéry speaks of "délices," Proust of "joie enivrante," exhilarating joy. Nothing is more characteristic than the presupposition of the distance which not merely is present between the present generation and the previous one, but also between the German and the French attitudes towards art. As early as the writing of *A l'ombre des jeunes filles en fleurs*, the expression *Kunstgenuß* ("aesthetic pleasure") must have sounded as touchingly philistine in German as a Wilhelm Busch rhyme. This aesthetic pleasure, furthermore, in which Valéry and Proust have as much faith as in a revered mother, has always been a questionable matter. For anyone who is close to the works of art, they are no more objects of delight than is his own breathing. Rather, he lives among them like a modern inhabitant of a medieval town who replies with a peremptory "yes, yes," when a visitor remarks on the beauty of the buildings, but who knows every corner and portal. But it is only when the distance necessary for enjoyment to be possible is established between the observer and works of art that the question of their continuing vitality can arise. It would probably never occur to anyone who was at home with art and not a mere visitor. But since they both continually reflect upon their own work as well as produce it, Valéry and Proust are certain of the pleasure which their works provide those on the outside. They agree even to the point of recognizing something of the mortal enmity which exists among works and which accompanies the pleasure of competition. Far from recoiling before it, however, Proust affirms this enmity, as though he were as German as Charlus affects to be. For him, competition among works is the test of truth. Schools, he writes at one point in *Sodom and Gomorrah*, devour each other like microorganisms and ensures through their struggle the survival of life. This dialectical attitude, which transcends fixation on the individual as such, brings Proust into conflict with Valéry, the *artiste*. It makes his perverse tolerance of museums possible, whereas for Valéry, the duration of the individual work is the crucial problem.

The criterion of duration is the here and now, the present moment. For Valéry, art is lost when it has relinquished its place in the immediacy of life, in its functional context: for him, the ultimate question is that of the possible use of the work of art. The craftsman in him fashions poems with the precision of contour which embodies attention to the surroundings, has become infinitely sensitive to the place of the work of art, including its intellectual setting, as though the painter's feelings for perspective were intensified in him to a feeling for the perspective of reality, in which it becomes possible for the work to have depth. His artistic standpoint is that of immediacy, but is driven to the most audacious consequences. He follows the principle of art for art's sake to the verge of its negation. He makes the pure work of art the object of absolute, unwavering contemplation, but he scrutinizes it so long, and so intensely that he comes to see that the object of such pure contemplation must wither and degenerate to commercialized decoration, robbed of the dignity in which both its *raison d'être* and Valéry's consist. The pure work is threatened by reification and neutralization. This is the recognition that overwhelms him in the museum. He discovers that the only pure works, the only works that can sustain serious observation, are the impure ones, which do not exhaust themselves in that observation but point beyond, towards a social context. And since, with the incorruptibility of the great rationalist, Valéry must recognize that this stage of art is irrevocably past, there is nothing left for the anti-rationalist and Bergonian in him but to mourn for works, as they turn into relics.

Proust, the novelist, virtually begins where Valéry, the poet, stopped —with the afterlife of works of art. For Proust's primary relationship to art is the precise opposite of that of the expert and producer. He if first of all an admiring consumer, an amateur, inclined to that effusive and for artists highly suspect awe before works that characterizes only those separated from them as though by an abyss. One could almost say that his genius consisted not least of all in assuming this attitude (which is also that of the man who conducts himself as a spectator even in life) so completely and accurately that it became a new type of productivity, and the power of inner and outer contemplation, thus intensified, turned into recollection, involuntary memory. The amateur is incomparably more comfortable in the museum than is the expert. Valéry feels himself at home in the studio: Proust strolls through an exhibition. There is something exterritorial about his relation to art, and many of his false judgments, as in questions of music, displays traces of dilettante to the end (what, for instance, has the conciliatory kitsch of his friend, Reynaldo Hahn, to do with Proust's novel, where each sentence puts an established attitude out of business with remorseless gentleness). But he moulded this weakness into an instrument of strength, as only Kafka could. However naïve his enthusiastic judgments of individual works of art, especially those of the Italian Renaissance, may sound, in comparison to Valéry's, he was far less naïve in his relation to art as such. To speak of naïveté in an artist like Valéry, in whom the process of artistic production is so indissolubly merged with reflection upon the process, may sound like a provocation. But he was in fact naïve in having no doubts about the category of the work of art as such. He took it for granted, and the force of his thought, his historical-philosophical energy, increased as a result. The category becomes the criterion in terms of which Valéry can see changes in the internal structure of works of art and in the way they are experienced. Proust, however, is entirely free of unconditional fetishism of the artist who makes things himself. For him works of art are from the outset something more than their specific aesthetic qualities. They are a part of the life of the person who observes them: they become an element of his consciousness. He thus perceives a level in them very different from that of the formal laws of the work. It is a level set free only by the historical development of the work, a level which has as its premise death of the living intention of work. Proust's naïveté is a second naïveté. At every stage of consciousness a new and broader immediacy arises. Whereas, Valéry's conservative belief in culture as a pure thing in itself affords incisive criticism of a culture which tends by its very historical nature to destroy everything self-subsistent, Proust's most characteristic mode of perception, his extraordinary sensitivity to changes in the modes of experience, has as its paradoxical result the ability to perceive history as a landscape. He adores museums as though they were God's true creations, which in Proust's metaphysics is never complete but always occurring anew in each concrete experience, each original artistic intuition. In his marveling eye he has preserved something out of his childhood: Valéry, by contrast, speaks of art like an adult. If Valéry understands something of the power of history over the production and apperception of art, Proust knows that even within the works of art themselves history rules like a process of disintegration. "Ce qu'on appelle la postérité, c'est la postérité de l'œuvre" might well be translated as, "What is called posterity is the afterlife of the work." In the artifact's capacity for disintegration Proust sees its similarity to natural beauty. He recognizes the physiognomy of decomposing things as that of their second life. Because nothing has substance for him but what has already been mediated by memory, his love dwells on the second life, the one which is already over, rather than on the first. For Proust's aestheticism the question of aesthetic quality is of secondary concern. In a famous passage he glorified inferior music for the sake of the listener's memories, which are preserved with far more fidelity and force in an old popular song than in self-sufficiency of a work by Beethoven. The saturnine gaze of memory penetrates the veil of culture. Once they are no longer isolated as domains of the objective mind, but are drawn into the stream of subjectivity, distinctions between the levels of culture lose their pathetic quality that Valéry's heresies constantly accord them. Valéry takes offense at the chaotic aspect of the museum, because it distorts the works' expressive realization: for Proust this chaos assumes tragic character. For him it is only the death of the work of art in the museum which brings it to life. When severed from the living order in which it functioned, according to him, its true spontaneity is released—it's uniqueness, its "name," that which makes the great works of culture more than culture. Proust's attitude preserves, in adventurously sophisticated form, the saying from Ottilie's journal in Goethe's *Elective Affinities*: "Everything perfect of its kind must go beyond its kind," a highly un-classical thought, which does art the honor of relativizing it.

Yet anyone who is not satisfied with intellectual history alone must face the question: Who is right, the critic of the museum or its defender? For Valéry the museum is a place of barbarism. His conviction of sanctity of culture (which he shares with Mallarmé) underlies this judgment. Since this religion of spleen provokes so much opposition, including objections with a simplistic social orientation, it is important to affirm its moment of truth. Only what exists for its own sake, without regard to those to whom it is supposed to please, can fulfill its human end. Few things have contributed so greatly to dehumanization as has the universal human belief that products of the mind are justified, only in so far as they exist for men-the belief itself bears witness to the dominance of manipulative rationality. Valéry was able to show the objective character, the immanent coherence of the work in contrast to the contingency of the subject with such incomparable authority, because he gained his insight through subjective experience of the discipline of the artist's work. In this he was unquestionably superior to Proust: incorruptible, he had greater resistance. In contrast, the primacy that Proust assigns to the flux of experience and his refusal to tolerate anything fixed and determinate have a sinister aspect—conformity, the ready adjustment to changing situations which he shares with Bergson. Proust's work contains passages on art which approach in unbridled subjectivism, the philistine attitude that turns the work into a battery of projective tests. In contrast, Valéry occasionally complains—and hardly without irony—that there are no tests which can determine the quality of a poem. Proust says in the second volume of *Le temps retrouvé*, that the work is a kind of optical instrument offered to the reader, in order that he makes self-discoveries perhaps not otherwise possible. Proust's arguments in favor of museums also have as their point of reference not the thing itself, but the observing subject. It is not coincidental that it is something subjective, the abrupt act of production in which the work becomes something different from reality, that Proust considers to be preserved in the work's afterlife in the museum. For him, the moment of production is reflected in the same isolation of the work that Valéry considers its stigma. Proust, in his unfettered subjectivism, is untrue to objectifications of the spirit, but it is only this subjectivism that enables him to break through the immanence of culture.

In the litigation implicitly pending between them, neither Proust nor Valéry is right, nor could a middle-of-the-road reconciliation be arranged. The conflict between them points up in the most penetrating way a conflict in the matter itself, and each takes the part of one moment in the truth which lies in the unfolding of contradiction. The fetishism of the object and the subject's infatuation with itself finds their correctives in each other. Each position passes over into the other. Valéry becomes aware of the intrinsic being of the work through unremitting self-reflection, and, inversely, Proust's subjectivism looks to art for the ideal, the salvation of the living. In opposition to culture and through culture, he represents negativity, criticism, the spontaneous act that is not content with mere existence. Thus he does justice to the works of art, which can be called art only by virtue of the fact that they embody the quintessence of this spontaneity. Proust holds on to the culture for the sake of objective happiness, whereas, Valéry's loyalty to the objective demands of the work forces him to give up culture for lost. Just as they both represent contradictory moments of truth, so both, the two most knowledgeable men to have written about art in recent times, have their limits, without which, in fact, their knowledge would not have been possible. Quite obviously Valéry agrees with his teacher, Mallarmé in finding, as he wrote in his essay "The Triumph of Manet," that existence and things are here only to be devoured by art, that the world exists to produce a beautiful book and finds its fulfillment in an absolute poem. He also saw clearly the escape to which *poésie pure* aspired. "Nothing leads so surely to complete barbarism," another of his essays begins, "as complete absorption in what is purely spiritual." And his own attitude, the elevation of art to idolatry, did in fact contribute to the process of reification and dilapidation, which, according to Valéry's accusation, art undergoes in museums. For it is only in the museum, where paintings are offered for contemplation as ends in themselves, that they become as absolute as Valéry desired, and he shrinks back in terror from realization of his dream. Proust knows the cure for this. In a sense works of art return home when they become elements of the observer's subjective stream of consciousness. Thus, they renounce their cultic prerogative and are freed of the usurpatory aspect which characterized them in heroic aesthetics of Impressionism. But, by the same token Proust overestimates the act of freedom in art, as would an amateur. Often, almost in the manner of a psychiatrist, he understands the work all too much as a reproduction of the internal life of the person who had the good fortune and the misfortune to produce it or enjoy it. He fails to take full account of the fact that even in the very moment of its conception the work confronts its author and its audience as something objective, something which makes demands in terms of its own inner structure and its own logic. Like artists' lives, their works appear "free" only when seen from the outside. The work is neither a reflection of the soul, nor embodiment of a Platonic Idea. It is not pure being, but rather a "force field" between the subject and the object. The objective necessity of which Valéry speaks is realized only through an act of subjective spontaneity, which Proust makes the sole repository of all meaning and happiness.

It is not merely because protestations of culture against barbarism go unheard that Valéry's campaign against museums has a quixotic aspect—hopeless protests are nevertheless necessary. But Valéry is a bit too ingenuous in his suspicion that museums alone are responsible for what is done to paintings. Even if they hung in their old places in the castles of the aristocrats (with whom Proust is in any case more concerned than is Valéry), they would be museum pieces without museums. What eats away at the life of the art work is also its own life. If Valéry's coquettish allegory compares paintings and sculptures to children who have lost their mothers, one must remember that in myth the heroes, who represent emancipation of the humans from fate, always lost to their mothers. Works of art can fully embody the *promesse du Bonheur,* only when they have been uprooted from their native soil and have set out along the path to their own destruction. Proust recognized this. The procedure which today relegates every work of art to the museum, even Picasso's most recent sculpture, is irreversible. It is not solely reprehensible, however, for it presages a situation in which art, having completed its estrangement from human ends, returns, in Novalis's words, to life. One senses something of this in Proust's novel, where physiognomies of paintings and people glide into one another almost without a break and memory traces of experiences fuse with those of musical passages. In one of the most explicit passages of the work, the description of falling asleep on the first page of *Du côté de chez Swann,* the narrator says, "It seemed to me that I was the thing the book was about: a church, a quartet, the rivalry between Francis the First and Charles the Fifth." This is the reconciliation of that split which Valéry so irreconcilably laments. The chaos of cultural goods fades into bliss of the child, whose body feels itself at once with the nimbus of distance.

The museums will not be shut, nor would it even be desirable to shut them. The natural-history collections of the spirit have actually transformed works of art into hieroglyphics of history, and brought them a new content, while the old one shriveled up. No conception of pure art, borrowed from the past and yet inadequate to it, can be offered to offset this fact. No one knew this better than Valéry, who broke off his reflections because of it. Yet, museums certainly emphatically demanded something of the observer, just as every work of art does. For the *flaneur,* in whose shadow Proust walked, is also a thing of the past, and it is no longer possible to stroll through museums, letting oneself be delighted here and there. The only relation to art that can be sanctioned in reality that stands under the constant threat of catastrophe is one that treats the works of art with the same deadly seriousness that characterizes the world today. The evil Valéry diagnoses can be avoided only by the one who leaves his naïveté outside, along with his cane and his umbrella, who knows exactly what he wants, picks out two or three paintings, and concentrates on them as fixedly, as if they really were idols. Some museums are helpful in this respect. In addition to light and air they have adopted the principle of selection that Valéry declared to be guiding one of his schools and that he missed in museums. In the *Jeu de Paume*, where the Gare St.-Lazare now hangs, Proust's Elstir and Valéry's Degas live peacefully near each other in discrete separation.

SUBSPATIAL AND SUBTEMPORAL

Graham Harman

Perhaps the most famous debate about space and time in the entire history of philosophy occurred in the Leibniz–Clarke correspondence of 1715–1716.[1] The English clergyman Samuel Clarke, acting as a surrogate for his friend Isaac Newton, made the case for space and time as absolute, empty containers in which objects reside and events unfold. The great German philosopher and polymath Leibniz countered that it is meaningless to ask whether the universe could have been created ten minutes earlier than it was, or forty meters further to the west than it was; there is no external spatial or temporal measuring stick that would allow us to claim that everything has been moved as a whole. Instead, space and time for Leibniz emerge from the relations between entities, thus paving the way for Einstein's breakthrough nearly two centuries later.

It seems to me that the views of both Leibniz and Clarke are wrong, even if I feel much closer to Leibniz. Space cannot be relational, for the simple reason that it is both relational and non-relational. If space is where things meet, it is also where they stand at a distance from each other. At this moment we are obviously in relation with Cairo and Tokyo by standing at a certain measurable distance from them, yet we are also not in relation with them insofar as they currently exceed our grasp. It takes work to travel to Egypt or Japan, and even once we arrive we will not have exhausted their many secrets. Insofar as relation means contact, space is the zone of both contact and non-contact. If objects engage in spatial relations, then at the same time they also withdraw from these relations into a private inner life that might be described as *subspatial* rather than outside space in the manner of God. With time it is different: here a relational approach is more successful,

---

This text was first presented at an Exterritory Project Symposium, May 8, 2012, Jaffa, Israel.
[1] G.W. Leibniz and Samuel Clarke, *Correspondence*, ed. R. Ariew (Indianapolis: Hackett, 2000).

though it must be a different sort of relational approach than Leibniz had in mind. To explain both of these claims, it is first necessary to give a brief account of object-oriented philosophy.

1. TWO KINDS OF OBJECTS

For Edmund Husserl, phenomenology was a way to root philosophy in unshakeable immediate evidence. The natural sciences may have greater social prestige in our time than philosophy, but the sciences give us mediated theories rather than direct evidence of their subject matter. For example, physics demonstrates that a mailbox like all physical things is made up of quarks and electrons, or perhaps of tiny vibrating ten-dimensional strings. Yet none of us have ever seen such minuscule particles. However solid the evidence for their existence may be, for Husserl such evidence must ultimately be grounded in phenomenological experience, the only source of direct insight we have. Instead of reducing the mailbox downward to the unseen corpuscles of which it is built, we can instead describe our experience of the mailbox in intimate detail, finding ever-subtler perceptual layers and increasingly shadowy dimensions in our experience of it. Philosophy suspends or "brackets" all consideration of a real material world, and becomes instead a painstaking description of the phenomenal. The price Husserl pays for this maneuver is a deeply idealist conception of philosophy, in which nothing exists except as the actual or potential target of some observing consciousness. Even if the mind is always already outside itself, pointing at objects, these objects are still just phenomena in consciousness, not real autonomous entities that lead an independent life outside of being recognized or perceived by us.

But Husserl is not a typical idealist. When reading Husserl (just as when reading Maurice Merleau-Ponty), he so often *feels* like a realist. Husserl *feels* like he is discussing the autonomous existence of mailboxes, blackbirds, and battles of centaurs, even though for phenomenology these objects exist only as correlates of our consciousness. The reason for this is that despite being an idealist, Husserl is almost certainly the first *object-oriented* idealist in the history of philosophy. His teacher Franz Brentano paved the way for phenomenology by reviving the medieval concept of "intentionality."[2] The

---

2   Franz Brentano, *Psychology From an Empirical Standpoint*, trans. A.C. Rancurello, D.B. Terrell, and L. McAlister (London: Routledge, 1995).

difference between mental acts and physical events, says Brentano, is that mental acts always aim at some object. To hear is to hear something; to wish is to wish for something; to judge is to judge about something; to hate is to hate something or someone. This is sometimes misinterpreted to mean that consciousness always points at some object in the *outside* world, and that has led in later years to misunderstandings about the meaning of the term "intentionality." Yet Brentano is quite clear that intentionality means *immanent* objectivity. Conscious acts are aimed at objects *inside*, not outside, the mind. This is already obvious if we consider that it is possible to perceive hallucinations, wish for non-existent things, make judgments about the powers of non-existent monsters, or fall in love with charlatans and frauds.

Brentano's philosophical psychology was focused on what is immanent in the mind. But that left open the question of how this immanent sphere related to any outside world. A clean and candid solution to this problem was attempted by Brentano's exceptional Polish student Kazimierz Twardowski, who doubled up the world into an *object* outside the mind and a content inside the mind.[3] Also among Brentano's students at the time was the older but greener ex-mathematician Edmund Husserl. Husserl never liked Twardowski's approach, since it seemed to make our knowledge a mere phenomenal knowledge of content, unable to grasp the object itself. In Husserl's famous example, the Berlin of which I speak is the same Berlin that exists in the real world; there are not two Berlins. Yet what is often overlooked is that Husserl did not simply eliminate Twardowski's distinction between object and content. Instead, he preserved both terms while *collapsing* them into the phenomenal realm of consciousness. Phenomenology does not consider the phenomenal world to be made up solely of content. Instead, experience shows a constant tension between object and content *within* the phenomenal universe. This is surely Husserl's greatest philosophical insight, and we can explain what it means by contrasting it with what empiricism says about objects.

David Hume famously claimed that there is no such thing as unified "objects" in experience. What we call a grapefruit, for instance, is really just a "bundle of qualities." We experience such qualities as spherical, soft, spongy, pulpy, sour, yellow or pink, and internally sectioned. Our only immediate experience is of these discrete qualities. From seeing these qualities go together

---

3   Kasimir Twardowski, *On the Content and Object of Presentations: A Psychological Investigation*, trans. R. Grossmann (Dordrecht: Springer, 1977).

regularly, we form the habit of thinking that there are things called grapefruit in the world, when in fact we only have evidence of qualities. This empiricist dogma is often subtly adopted even by those who are not otherwise followers of Hume. We still find traces of it in Brentano and Twardowski, especially the latter when he describes experience as made up of "content," which really means the same thing as "qualities." Husserl's most remarkable gesture was to treat the whole intentional object as prior to its parts. What we experience is not a "bundle of qualities," but simply a *grapefruit*, and the grapefruit dominates those qualities as if they were its servants or satellites or mindless drones. The grapefruit can be rotated in my hand, showing different qualities at different moments, yet I never cease to think of it as the same grapefruit. I can view the fruit from behind, from a greater or lesser distance, first in full sunlight and later in shadow. In all these cases the grapefruit shows different aspects, and is therefore a different "bundle of qualities," yet it does not cease to be the same grapefruit. In fact, this is the very meaning of what Husserl calls "eidetic reduction." By varying our perceptions of an object, either experientially or more often through imagination, we strip away the *inessential* qualities and arrive at those absolutely necessary qualities that the grapefruit cannot lose without ceasing to be this very grapefruit that it is. The fruit is not a bundle of qualities, but a nucleus that can support many variations in qualities—many *Abschattungen* or "adumbrations," as Husserl puts it.

And yet, the essential and inessential qualities of the grapefruit turn out to be of two vastly different kinds. First, there are the phenomenal qualities of the grapefruit: the exact pinkish or yellow hue of its interior; the precise sponginess of the spherical fruit as I squeeze it in my hand; the soft deadness of sound as I snap it repeatedly with a fingernail; the wise and somber appearance of the fruit as it sits in the bowl of a still life painter. Since all of these qualities belong to the immanent phenomenal realm, we might call them intentional qualities. But for various reasons, I prefer to call them *sensual* qualities. These sensual qualities are the accidental chaff that shifts atop the surface of any object, whirling like a kaleidoscope without changing the underlying object. Husserl speaks for example of "my friend Hans," who can be encountered in just about any physical posture and suit of clothing without changing the identity of Hans himself.[4] These are sensual qualities. The sen-

---

4   Edmund Husserl, *Logical Investigations*, vol. 1, trans. J.N. Findlay, (London: Routledge & Kegan Paul, 1970), 380.

sual object is not "hidden" behind them, since we always have direct contact with Hans or a grapefruit simply through the fact of acknowledging their presence. Instead, these sensual qualities are encrusted on the surface of the sensual object like feathers and rhinestones on a carnival samba dancer, who always remains the same dancer despite the wildest gyrations.

But the truly pivotal qualities of a sensual object are not like this. Husserl admits that they cannot be perceived through the senses at all, but only through an intellectual or categorial act. It is not as if we perceived one million qualities on a level playing field and then chose three or four of them as the most important. Instead, *all* of the sensual qualities of a sensual object turn out to be inessential. The essential or eidetic qualities of an object are buried at a sub-sensual level, graspable only by the intellect. Oddly enough, this entails that the sensual object does not just have sensual qualities, but also has real qualities as well. This turns out to be rather paradoxical once we have taken a look at Heidegger, as we are now about to do.

Heidegger is famous for asking the question of the meaning of being, which is nowhere near as obscure as it sounds. His own innovations are aimed against the *idealism* of Husserl's view that reality is based in phenomenal presence to the conscious mind. Beginning in his first lecture course at the age of twenty-nine, Heidegger explains that for the most part, our way of dealing with things *is not* explicitly conscious of them.[5] My minimal conscious activity in any given moment is rooted in a gigantic empire of items taken for granted: the oxygen I breathe, the ground that is currently free of earthquakes, the heart and lungs and kidneys that keep me alive, the English grammar I have now mastered and no longer struggle with—all of these things tend to vanish unnoticed into the background as long as they are functioning efficiently. This, of course, is the famous tool-analysis, first published in 1927 in *Being and Time*.[6] The hammer and the bus route tend to remain invisible unless they malfunction. This is not just true of widely recognized hand tools such as screwdrivers, wrenches, and axes. Instead, all objects are caught up in a reversal between silent functionality and explicit visibility.

This is generally taken to mean that for Heidegger all conscious theory is grounded in unconscious praxis. But this interpretation is superficial, since there is a deeper sense in which theory and praxis are the same. In Hei-

---

[5] Martin Heidegger, *Towards the Definition of Philosophy*, trans. T. Sadler (London: Continuum, 2008).
[6] Heidegger, *Being and Time*, trans. J. Macquarrie and E. Robinson (San Francisco: Harper & Row, 1962).

degger's account, what happens when we hold a hammer and stare at it is that we have oversimplified the hammer. That is to say, we have reduced it to a tiny selection of its vast qualitative reality; the hammer has been turned into a caricature, a distortion, or at least a translation. But notice that exactly the same thing happens when we simply use a hammer rather than staring at it. To touch the hammer unconsciously does not exhaust its reality any more than staring at it does. The hand is just as finite as the eye. Dogs and mosquitoes notice fleeting nuances of smell in the hammer that I myself will never detect. In other words, the supposedly mighty theory/praxis distinction isn't much of a distinction at all, at least not when it comes to ontology. Both conscious and unconscious human activity are equally guilty of failing to exhaust the reality of whatever they confront. The reality of objects is something deeper than either theoretical or practical human contact.

But this can be pushed one step further to demonstrate that inanimate objects caricature, translate, and distort *each other* as well. The inability to touch the full depths of any given thing is not just some poignant feature of human finitude. Instead, objects fail to grasp each other just as much as we fail to grasp them. Fire burns a cotton ball without ever having made contact with the color or smell of this cotton, stupidly limited as it is to the cotton's flammable features. Once we realize this, the philosophy of the human subject is in deeper peril than ever before. But since this theme is a digression from the topic of space and time, it can be left for another occasion.

Heidegger dislikes like the term "object," which he uses negatively for things reduced to appearances in human consciousness. Nor does he always think that the world is made up of a *plurality* of things, since he generally treats the world of tool-beings as a global relational system in which each thing gains reality from its reference to other things, and thus all things turn into a gigantic relational whole. But we don't need to follow him in either of these claims. The fact that individual entities can break for Heidegger means that they must have some private surplus deeper than the system of equipment. And there is no reason not to call them "objects" simply because Heidegger happens not to like that word; it has a long and admirable tradition, and was central to early phenomenology.

In Husserl's case we spoke of sensual objects. These are always directly before us rather than hidden or withdrawn; they are simply encrusted with superfluous information that must be stripped away to reach the truly essential features of the thing. If I perceive a mailbox, the sensual mailbox is directly there in front of me as soon as I acknowledge it, not "hidden" behind all the confusing details on its surface. But there is also the real mailbox, deeper than any access to it, and the sensual mailbox is merely a translation of it. This real object is withdrawn from relation, deeper than any contact that animate or inanimate objects might have with it. And since real objects are a surplus beyond any relation they might have with other entities, it remains a mystery how they can make contact at all. Causation and influence more generally can only be indirect, never direct, and this is why I have called for a theory of "vicarious causation."[7] But once again, this theme is peripheral to the main topic of the lecture and can be left to another occasion.

Earlier, we saw that Husserl's sensual objects were in tension with two different kinds of qualities: the sensual, accidental qualities that shift and swirl from one moment to the next without affecting the object to which they belong, and the real qualities that the object can never lose without falling out of existence. The same dual set of qualities can be found in Heidegger's *real* objects. Consider any entity insofar as it is exists outside its relations, purely in its own right. Hammers, volcanoes, cargo ships, and birds cannot simply generate their individual qualities for the first time as soon as they come into contact with something else. The reason our encounters with each of these things is so different is because they all have their own qualities from the start. If each of them did not have its own qualities, then they would all be completely indistinguishable; all would be featureless perceptual lumps. For this reason, real objects must have real qualities. But at the same time, real objects can also announce their presence through *sensual* qualities, as happens for instance in the case of Heidegger's broken tool. The hammer that breaks is never directly before us. What we have instead are a specific shape, a grainy wooden texture, a partially damaged steel head—all of them sensual qualities in tension with an absent real hammer-object.

We now come to the goal of all these discussions of Husserl and Heidegger. Namely, there are two kinds of objects: not just autonomous things outside consciousness, but also durable units that sustain many changes *inside* consciousness. Stated more simply, there are real objects and sensual objects. There are also two kinds of qualities: the sensual qualities that we experience directly, and the real qualities that can never be sensed, but only hinted at by some of intellectual, categorical act that (in my view if not Hus-

---

[7] Graham Harman, "On Vicarious Causation," *Collapse* 2 (2007), 171–205.

serl's) can never make these real qualities directly accessible to the mind. These considerations lead us to see that there is a fourfold structure of real objects, real qualities, sensual objects, and sensual qualities. And though four terms can usually be paired up in six different ways, if we consider only those cases in which objects are in tension with their qualities, then we also have just four possible pairings to consider here: real objects with real or sensual qualities, and sensual objects with real or sensual qualities. The reason this is relevant to us here is because these four tensions can be redescribed as time, space, essence, and eidos, as can be clarified easily enough. When we speak of a real thing in relation to its real qualities, the traditional name for this is *essence*, and there is no reason not to preserve this term (though it is has long been under assault for reasons that do not concern us here). And as for *eidos*, this is the term Husserl used for the relation a sensual object has with its real qualities, accessible only to the intellect.

That leaves us with *sensual* qualities and the relations they have to the two kinds of objects. And I hold that these relations are the metaphysical root of space and time. What leads us, for instance, to feel the passing flow of time? Whatever the neurological reason might be, the phenomenological reason is a sense of change within stability. The world does not seem to be reinvented anew at each instant. Instead, candles flicker and trees sway in the wind; dogs walk and trains rush past. If objects were really just bundles of qualities that changed completely in each instant, there would be no continuity from one moment to the next. But the sense that time is passing is connected with the relative durability of units that support shifting perceptual configurations—the flame that remains the same flame for us amidst all its contortions in the wind; the dog that remains the same dog no matter the angle or distance from which we view him. This is time. Time is not an independent cosmic force driving things through some sort of flux or "becoming" irreducible to individual states. Instead, time is more like a distracting noise emitted by individual states which serves to mask the fact that quite often nothing is really happening. If the tension between real objects and their real qualities is called essence, that between sensual objects and their sensual qualities is the purely *inessential*, or the *accidental*. Time, in the sense of our experience of the flow of time, is thus the kingdom of the inessential, the site where nothing has happened yet. Turn an apple in your hand and toss it into the air; view it from five meters rather than three; polish the apple a bit more. It hardly matters. An object is not a bundle of qualities, and therefore an object is not affected by any of the trivial fluctuations on the surface of that bundle.

But what about space? We said earlier that, contra Leibniz, space is not the site of relation, but of both relation *and* non-relation. Real objects cannot relate directly, since they withdraw behind all possibility of direct contact. But *indirect* content is inevitable, since objects do evidently affect each other. Sensual qualities are the ambassadors or emissaries of real objects that never meet in person. Consider once again our experience of a broken hammer. Its various damaged qualities lie directly before us, subject to our inspection. Yet the hammer itself is not here. It is, or was, something over and above these qualities—a formerly operative unit deeper than all its qualities. The hammer is not present in consciousness but belongs to a different place, even though it still makes contact with us through the medium of its sensual qualities. If space is the tension between distance and nearness, then there is no better exemplar of this than an object that withdraws from direct contact even while leaving its qualities behind to confront us directly. In terms of object-oriented philosophy, space and time are the two tensions concerned with sensual qualities, just as essence and eidos pertain to real qualities. Let's see if this can tell us anything about the subtemporal and subspatial character of objects.

2. SPACE AND TIME

Treating space and time as different dimensions of reality seems to run counter to twentieth-century physics. Four-dimensional space-time was implicit in Einstein's special relativity and openly proclamied by Hermann Minkowski in 1907, and has enjoyed an illustrious career in physics ever since.[8] But we cannot tether philosophical speculation to the state of the sciences at any given moment; science must be an inspiration for philosophy rather than a straitjacket. Consider the views of Lee Smolin, who in *The Life of the Cosmos* laments the days when philosophers actually challenged the sciences, and in *The Trouble with Physics* shares his hunch that space and time might need to be de-coupled again for further progress in physics to occur. Philosophy must be free to speculate about space and time on the basis of its own internal con-

---

8   Hermann Minkowski, "Space and Time," in *The Principle of Relativity*, ed. Albert Einstein et al. (Mineola: Dover, 1952), 73–91.

cerns. Who is to say what the physics of a half-century from now will look like, and whether it will continue to function so independently of metaphysics as it has for the past fifty years.

From mapping the two kinds of objects and two kinds of qualities, it turned out that they yield the four tensions of time, space, essence, and eidos. What time and space have in common is their link with sensual rather than real qualities. And what is most characteristic of *sensual* qualities is their purely *accidental* nature. For Husserl, since the mailbox or the blackbird is not a bundle of qualities, these sensual objects do not need any particular configuration of qualities in order to be what they are. We can watch the blackbird fly from any number of angles and distances and under any imaginable lighting conditions (twilight, sunrise, under strobe lights or illumined with lasers) and we look straight through these variations at the blackbird as an underlying unit of our experience. And for Heidegger, since real objects such as hammers are deeper than any of their sensual manifestations, the hammer cannot be identified either with the specific details of its shattering, its precise obtrusive heaviness, the exact arbitrary color of its handle, or other such features. The hammer announces itself through breaking and calling attention to various qualities that announce it, but the hammer is never built out of these visible qualities. Instead, it withdraws into subterranean shadows that no gaze can even partially penetrate. It is quite different with *real* qualities, such as the essence of a concealed hammer or the eidos of an apple or pear experienced by consciousness. In both cases these qualities are essential to the objects in question, and hence there is no room for maneuver. Change the real qualities of a real or sensual object and you have quite simply destroyed that object and turned it into something else. But space and time are concerned only with the *inessential*, and paradoxically, this gives them a tremendous degree of power. Insofar as the sensual qualities of a real or sensual object shift wildly within a wide range of variation, these sensual qualities are the sole emissaries of change in the world.

It is a deeply classical principle, in the *good* sense of classical, that nothing can change its essence but everything can change its accidents. Insofar as we want to discover how change occurs in the world, or what prevents the world from becoming a static garden of unmoving statues, we need to look at the sensual or the inessential. A related principle has been familiar in sociology since the early 1970s — the so-called "strength of weak ties."[9] From our family and closest associates we are often rewarded with loyalty, emotional support, the safekeeping of secrets, and supportive ears for complaints of mistreatment. Yet there is also something static and repetitive about such relations, which in a sense are already all that they can ever be. Rewarding though such relationships are, in some respects they are resistant to change. It is different with casual acquaintanceships, which may lack much in terms of trust, loyalty, and intimacy, but which provide numerous avenues into possible new opportunities or perhaps entirely new worlds. It is such a good analogy that we might even borrow the phrase "the strength of weak ties" to describe the weak ties that any object has with its sensual qualities as opposed to the strong and intimate bond of loyalty it enjoys with its real ones. Indeed, weakness may always be the genuine agent of change in the world. Somewhere, Levinas describes violence as the attempt to control what is strong in someone through what is weak in them. But this turns out to be true of causal links in general, not just the ones we call violent.

Although space and time both have connections with sensual qualities, there is a basic asymmetry between them. Qualities never exist in a vacuum, but are always the servants or lackeys of some object. Merleau-Ponty is perhaps even stronger than Husserl at showing that a quality such as green is not an isolated, objective wavelength of light, but that the exact same wavelength of green appears differently depending on whether it is the green of grass, ink, a shirt, or the fluorescent lights on a mosque.[10] In each of these cases, the character of the object infects the quality itself. Sensual qualities always belong to objects, but the objects to which they belong are *sensual* objects, not real ones. There is no bundle of qualities, but a primordial *bond* between sensual objects and their sensual qualities. Initially, we encounter them as belonging together. Our instinctive, commonsense approach to sensual objects is to view them lazily as bundles of qualities. I turn an object in my hand, and after seeing it from all sides I am quietly satisfied that I have exhausted the thing by experiencing the sum total of its qualities.

But now and then, we do experience a separation or fission between the sensual object and its qualities. In these cases we suddenly grasp that the sensual object is not a bundle of sensual qualities, but an autonomous source

---

9   Mark S. Granovetter, "The Strength of Weak Ties," *American Journal of Sociology* 78, no. 6 (May 1973), 1360–80.
10 Maurice Merleau-Ponty, *Phenomenology of Perception*, trans. C. Smith (London: Routledge, 2002).

capable of generating new qualities under different conditions. This often occurs with delightfully variable objects such as kaleidoscopes and holograms, or with electronic toys that utter different random phrases whenever a button is pushed. But in a non-technological context we know such cases through simple, natural experiences such as watching the light fade over rural landscapes, observing the changing colors of the Taj Mahal every few minutes at dawn, or following the shifting adventures of a fictional character. A good general name for all of these phenomena would be *simulation*. Although this word is increasingly associated with computer models, the phenomenon is much more general. We have a simulation whenever we isolate a basic underlying principle in any given situation and try to generate the results of this principle in counterfactual situations. What might Baudelaire have written if he were a San Francisco beat poet instead of a post-Romantic Frenchman? How would German philosophy have differed if, instead of eliminating Kant's thing-in-itself as the German idealists did, it had eliminated Kant's fixation on the human–world pair and extended the phenomenal–noumenal split to inanimate nature? How might World War III in Europe have played out in 1985? (I once read such a study, commissioned by NATO.) What if we reversed the nationalities of Henri Bergson and William James—how would this have affected their philosophies? What if I had accepted job Z rather than job X? Or on a humbler level: how would this pear look if I viewed it from the other side of the kitchen? We have simulation anytime we break the usual bond between a sensual object and its customary range of qualities, so that the object is grasped as an underlying unit capable of moving into different contexts and yielding different results about which one can speculate. Sensual objects and sensual qualities are united when they arrive on the scene, and it is our job to split them apart. In doing so, we come to see that the sensual object is *subtemporal*, not to be identified with the shifting on its surface that gives a sense of dynamic temporal flow, since we have seen that these shifts are irrelevant to the sensual object.

One implication of calling objects subtemporal is that we must embrace what in the philosophy of time is sometimes called "presentism." The *élan vital* so beloved by Bergson, the primordial "becoming" of Deleuze and Guattari, looks from our new standpoint like sheer qualitative noise. Most becoming leads nowhere; most flux is a surface effect without exit. Sensual objects are relatively durable units that change or perish infrequently. The river of Heraclitus is still there, but there are stones in the river, and those stones are not altered or destroyed automatically every time a bit of water passes. The becoming of the stones is a very special case that requires work, not a preordained entitlement for everything that exists. Becoming must be earned. But if sensual objects are subtemporal, we cannot even call them subspatial, since they have nothing to do with space at all. Insofar as objects are sensual, we are in direct contact with all of them. Even distant towers, forests, and mountains are in immediate contact with them insofar as we recognize them. As John Locke already knew, distance is inferred rather than seen; babies must *learn* that they cannot grab everything within eyesight, and cannot touch the moon with their hands simply because they touch it with their eyes.

The situation between real objects and sensual qualities is completely different. Here, there is no pre-existent bond between the two. If we notice the qualities of a hammer, we link these qualities with a sensual object directly before us. Normally, we do not link them with some withdrawn, subterranean hammer-thing hiding in the dusk of the world. True, there is always a link insofar as some real object must *generate* the sensual qualities of a broken hammer. But the real object with which we link those qualities need not be the same one that generates the qualities. For example, if I suddenly find the hammer too heavy, this might not be the result of the hammer itself, but of a strange degenerative disease by which I am gradually weakened. Or I may be unusually ignorant of tools, so that I blame the broken hammer for what is actually the effect of a broken mallet. Or I may be delusional, and curse the broken hammer when what I actually hold in my hand is a plastic toy. If these examples seem outlandish and contrived in the context of hammers, there are more credible examples—mistaken inferences in scientific work, false conspiracy theories that miss the true conspiracy, or shoddy historical work that weighs cause and effect incorrectly.

The point of these examples is simply to note that the link between sensual qualities and real objects does not just flow from the objects to the qualities (as when Kant says that there must be noumena to generate the phenomena). It also flows in reverse, from qualities to objects. When the hammer breaks, to use Heidegger's most famous example, there is a transfer of qualities to a new and unseen object. Previously we saw the sensual qualities of the hammer in a bond or union with the sensual *object* hammer. But now those qualities are reassigned to an object entirely outside our grasp. The malfunction of the hammer does not make the hammer present, but calls our attention to its absence. The real hammer is not made up of the obtrusive qualities that announce its breakdown, but lies at a layer much deeper than those qualities or any other qualities. The broken hammer does not give us any more knowledge of hammers than a reliably functional hammer does, but at least it strips hammer-qualities away from a sensual object and assigns them to an absent real one.

There is something unsettling about this experience, something lacking in the playful and addictive expectancy of simulation. It is unnerving to be alerted to an object that cannot be pinned down to any qualities at all, but merely shatters all accessible qualities. This is not a matter of simulation like the previous case. In simulation we have a fairly good tacit grasp of what the sensual object is, and simply apply it to numerous additional counterfactual cases. In the new case just described, of real objects lying behind sensual qualities, we barely have a grasp of the object at all. We can do nothing more than *allude* to the object, and for this reason I have often spoken of the related noun *allure*. There is allure whenever we sense a *real* object in impossible fusion with sensual qualities. Only here do we get a sense of space, because only here is there any distance; this space need not be physical, but encompasses every form of distance.

The showcase example of allure would be artworks, which cannot in any sense be paraphrased. A prose summary of visual art or literature cannot replace the work itself unless that work is of the most negligible quality, or unless such replacement is meant as a conceptual artwork in its own right. An especially beautiful landscape or jewel gives the sense of a disembodied force even deeper than the already startling qualities it displays. In cases of extreme courage, we encounter a force of character deeper than the venal calculations normally required by the relations between people and things. In cases of disappointment, the same thing happens for the opposite reason: a feeble underlying thing or human character now seems to have generated deceptive accidental qualities of which it was never truly worthy. If space is the interplay of distance and nearness, then real objects are *subspatial*, because they never approach us in nearness, but withdraw beyond any attempt to grasp them directly via qualities. As for time, we cannot even call real objects subtemporal, because they are not immersed in the stream of time at all, but erupt into the flow of time as if from another world—not a Platonic otherworld of eternal, perfect things, but a secular otherworld of fragile, destructible, and imperfect but beautiful things.

One frequent critique of recent civilization is that it turns everything into a simulation, so that the reality principle is thereby lost. Baudrillard is condemned for turning the Gulf War and 9/11 from cases of genuine human suffering into hypnotic media events. Police and even insurance companies are criticized for predicting future behavior or future liability on the basis of statistical models. Pre-emptive war causes outrage, since it responds not to actual events, but to possible scenarios of aggression by the enemy that must be cut off in advance. Videogames are blamed for the inability of two full generations to distinguish illusion from reality. In terms of our fourfold model, simulation can be viewed as a de-temporalization, since it no longer lets sensual objects run their course in the normal flow of shifting qualities, but turns them into an extra-temporal source of variation that can be mastered in immaterial form. By contrast, allure cannot be viewed as a kind of de-spatialization, since it is the only experience that produces space at all: without allure there is no space, but only withdrawn objects cut off from one another, just as in the occasionalist theologies of past centuries. If the era of simulation is accused of stripping reality from the contemporary world, allure cannot possibly be accused of this, since it is the source of an unparalleled *heightening* of reality. The destruction of time would be countered not by a reconstruction of time, but by a production of space. Instead of the Heideggerian cliché of citing Hölderlin's "where the danger is, there too lies the saving power," we would claim instead that simulation is the danger and allure is the saving power, and that the two have nothing to do with each other except for their common link in sensual qualities. Andy Warhol's age of simulation would give way to an era of allure, and the extraterritorial would serve as the reality principle—objects not localizable in any given place because they punch holes in every place they touch.

About the Contributors

Theodor W. Adorno (1903–1969) was a sociologist, a philosopher, and a key figure in the Frankfurt School of critical theory. His influential writings include *Dialectic of Enlightenment* (with Max Horkenheimer, 1947), *The Authoritarian Personality* (1950), *Minima Moralia* (1951), *Negative Dialectics* (1966), and *Aesthetic Theory* (1970).

Giorgio Agamben is a philosopher. He is Baruch Spinoza Chair at the European Graduate School (EGS) and a Professor of Aesthetics at the University of Verona. He also teaches philosophy at the Collège International de Philosophie in Paris. His many publications include *The Coming Community* (1993), *Means Without End* (1996), *Homo Sacer: Sovereign Power and Bare Life* (1998), and *Remnants of Auschwitz: The Witness and the Archive* (1999), *Language and Death: The Place of Negativity* (2006), *The Sacrament of Language: An Archaeology of the Oath* (2010), and *Opus Dei: An Archaeology of Duty* (2013).

Zygmunt Bauman is Professor Emeritus of Sociology at the University of Leeds. He is the author of many books, including *Memories of Class: The Pre-History and After-Life of Class* (1982), *Legislators and Interpreters: On Modernity, Post-Modernity and Intellectuals* (1987), *Modernity and the Holocaust* (1989), *Liquid Modernity* (2000), *Liquid Life* (2005), *Collateral Damage: Social Inequalities in a Global Age* (2011), *Does the Richness of the Few Benefit us All* (2013), and *Strangers at Our Door* (2016).

Victoria Bernal is Professor of Anthropology at the University of California, Irvine. Among her books are *Cultivating Workers: Peasants and Capitalism in a*

Sudanese Village (1991), and *Nation as Network: Diaspora, Cyberspace, and Citizenship* (2014).

Robert Bernasconi is Edwin Erle Sparks Professor of Philosophy at Pennsylvania State University. His books include *Heidegger in Question: The Art of Existing* (1993), and *How to Read Sartre* (2014). He is a co-editor of the journal *Critical Philosophy of Race*.

Homi K. Bhabha is the Anne F. Rothenberg Professor of English and American Literature and Language and the Director of the Humanities Center at Harvard University. His many publications include *The Location of Culture* (1994), *Front Lines, Border Posts* (1997), and *Nation and Narration* (2013).

Angus Cameron is Senior Lecturer in Spatial Organization at the University of Leicester. He is co-author of *Placing the Social Economy* (with Ash Amin and Ray Hudson, 2003) and *The Imagined Economies of Globalization* (with Ronen Palan, 2004) and co-editor of *Body/State* (with Jen Dickinson and Nicola Jo-Anne Smith, 2013), among other publications.

Stuart Elden is Professor of Political Theory and Geography at the University of Warwick. Among his books: *Mapping the Present: Heidegger, Foucault and the Project of a Spatial History* (2002), *Understanding Henri Lefebvre* (2004), *Terror and Territory: The Spatial Extent of Sovereignty* (2009), *The Birth of Territory* (2013), and *Foucault's Last Decade* (2016).

Caryl Emerson is A. Watson Armour III University Professor of Slavic Languages and Literatures at Princeton University. She has published extensively, with books including *Boris Godunov: Transpositions of a Russian Theme* (1986), *The Life of Mussorgsky* (1999), *The First Hundred Years of Mikhail Bakhtin* (2000), and *The Cambridge Introduction to Russian Literature* (2008).

Anselm Franke is a curator and writer based in Berlin, where he is Head of Visual Art and Film at the Haus der Kulturen der Welt. In 2012 he curated the Taipei Biennial, *Modern Monsters / Death and Life of Fiction*. His project *Animism* has been presented in Antwerp, Bern, Vienna, Berlin, New York, Shenzhen, Seoul, and Beirut since 2010.

ABOUT THE CONTRIBUTORS

Steven Galt Crowell is a philosopher who has taught at Rice University since 1983 and is Chair of its Department of Philosophy. Among his publications: *Husserl, Heidegger, and the Space of Meaning: Paths Toward Transcendental Phenomenology* (2002), *Transcendental Heidegger* (2007), and *Normativity and Phenomenology in Husserl and Heidegger* (2013).

Graham Harman is Professor of Philosophy at the American University in Cairo. His numerous books include *Tool-Being: Heidegger and the Metaphysics of Objects* (2002), *Guerrilla Metaphysics: Phenomenology and the Carpentry of Things* (2005), *Prince of Networks: Bruno Latour and Metaphysics* (2009), and *Bruno Latour: Reassembling the Political* (2014).

Matthew Hart is Assistant Professor of English and Comparative Literature at Columbia University. He is Associate Editor of *Contemporary Literature*, Founding Co-Editor of the Columbia University Press book series Literature Now, and Vice President of the Association for the Study of the Arts of the Present. He is the author of *Nations of Nothing But Poetry: Modernism, Transnationalism, and Synthetic Vernacular Writing* (2010). He is the co-editor of ASAP / Journal, Site Specificity Without Borders (with David J. Alworth).

Mireille Hildebrandt is Professor of Smart Environments, Data Protection and the Rule of Law at the Institute for Computing and Information Sciences (ICIS) at Radboud University, Nijmegen, and Research Professor of Technology and Law at the Research Group on Law, Science, Technology and Society (LSTS) at Vrije University, Brussels. Her publications include *Profiling the European Citizen* (with Serge Gutwirth, 2008) and *Smart Technologies and the End(s) of Law: Novel Entanglements of Law and Technology* (2015).

Martin Jay is the Sidney Hellman Ehrman Professor of History at the University of California, Berkeley. He has published many books, including *Marxism and Totality: The Adventures of a Concept from Lukács to Habermas* (1984), *Downcast Eyes: The Denigration of Vision in Twentieth-Century French Thought* (1993), *Essays from the Edge: Parerga and Paralipomena* (2011), and *Refractions of Violence* (2013).

Emmanuel Levinas (1906–1995) was a philosopher and Talmudic commentator based in France. Among his works: *Difficile liberté* (1963), *Existence* *and Existents* (1978), *Totality and Infinity: An Essay on Exteriority* (1979), *Otherwise Than Being, or Beyond Essence* (1981) and *Entre Nous: Thinking-of-the-other* (1998).

Tania Lown-Hecht completed her PhD in English at the University of Illinois at Urbana–Champaign, where she studied space and twentieth century literature. She is currently the Communications Director for a nonprofit based in Washington DC.

Ed Morgan, formerly Professor of International Law at the University of Toronto, was appointed as a trial judge of the Ontario Superior Court of Justice in 2012. His publications include *International Law and the Canadian Courts: Sovereign Immunity, Criminal Jurisdiction, Aliens' Rights, and Taxation Powers* (1990) and *The Aesthetics of International Law* (2007).

Gerhard Richter is a Professor of German Studies, Professor of Comparative Literature, and Chair of German Studies at Brown University. Among his books are *Walter Benjamin and the Corpus of Autobiography* (2000), *Thought-Images: Frankfurt School Writers' Reflections from Damaged Life* (2007), *Afterness: Figures of Following in Modern Thought and Aesthetics* (2011), and *Inheriting Walter Benjamin* (2016).

Cedric Ryngaert is Professor of Public International Law at the Utrecht University School of Law, where he heads the Master's Program in Public International Law. Since November 2013 he has headed two research projects on jurisdiction subsidized by NWO (VIDI) and the European Research Council (ERC Starting Grant). His books include *Jurisdiction in International Law* (2015) and *Unilateral Jurisdiction and Global Values* (2015).

Julien Seroussi is a member of the French International Crime Unit investigating crimes against humanity, genocide and war crimes, and formerly an analyst for the Trial Division at the International Criminal Court (ICC) in the Hague. He is author of *The Cause of Universal Jurisdiction: The Rise and Fall of an International Mobilization* (2012) and published articles in a number of peer-reviewed journals on the topic of universal jurisdiction.

Eyal Weizman is an architect, Professor of Visual Cultures, and Director of the Centre for Research Architecture at Goldsmiths, University of London. Since 2011 he also directs the Forensic Architecture—a research agency undertaking counter forensics directed at police and state violence. His books include *A Civilian Occupation* (2003), *Hollow Land* (2007), *The Least of All Possible Evils: Humanitarian Violence from Arendt to Gaza* (2012), *Mengele's Skull* (with Thomas Keenan, 2012), and *The Conflict Shoreline: Colonization as Climate Change in the Negev Desert* (with Fazal Sheikh, 2016).

Ines Weizman was trained as an architect and teaches at the Bauhaus-Universität Weimar. Together with Prof. Dr. Max Welch Guerra, she is Co-Director of the Bauhaus-Institut für Geschichte und Theorie der Architektur und Planung. She is the editor of *Architecture and the Paradox of Dissidence* (2014), and her articles have appeared in various journals and anthologies.

Maayan Amir and **Ruti Sela** are artists whose works have been presented in exhibitions such as the Biennale of Sydney, the Istanbul Biennial, the Berlin Biennial, Manifesta, the New Museum Triennial, and at venues such as the Tate Modern, Centre Pompidou, Jeu de Paume, Stedelijk Museum, Ludwig Museum, the Fondazione Sandretto Rebaudengo, and HKW in Berlin, among many others. In 2011, they received the Young Artists award from UNESCO for their work on the *Exterritory Project*, initiated in 2009. The have contributed essays to books by Sternberg Press and Multitudes, as well as various journals.

www.ingramcontent.com/pod-product-compliance
Lightning Source LLC
Chambersburg PA
CBHW031323230426
43670CB00006B/217